Economics from a global perspective
Second Edition

A TEXT BOOK FOR USE WITH THE INTERNATIONAL BACCALAUREATE
ECONOMICS PROGRAMME

Alan Glanville

For Dexter Memphis

Published by:	Glanville Books Ltd, 33 Five Mile Drive, Oxford, OX2 8HT, United Kingdom
Sales:	Glanville Books Ltd
Telephone:	+44 (0)1865 557736
Mobile:	+44 (0)7961 010857
e-mail:	alan@glanville.demon.co.uk
Fax:	+44 (0)1865 557736
Website:	www.glanvillebooks.com
Proof-reading:	Chris Taylor
Graphics:	David Harrison
Layout:	David Harrison
Cover Design:	Steve Fleming, Kate Glanville
Printed and bound by:	The Alden Group, Oxford, UK

© Alan Glanville 2003

ISBN 0 952 4746 5 4

Contents

Section 5: Development Economics

Section 6: Study Methods

BOXED ARTICLES

Section 3

Section 4

Section 5

PREFACE

Economics From A Global Perspective is an independently produced textbook, specifically written and designed for the International Baccalaureate course in Economics at both Higher and Standard Levels. The first edition, published in 1997 met a long-established need of IB students and teachers. The perspective is global. Other economics texts focus on specific national examination requirements, and are therefore of limited relevance to students of the International Baccalaureate.

The first edition was structured to the IB Economics syllabus introduced in 1997. The second edition is organised to the syllabus introduced in September 2003 valid through to the final examinations in May and November 2011. Like the IB syllabus, this book has a strong international emphasis through all the topics. In addition it has a wide coverage of international economics. Uniquely for a pre-university text, there is a major treatment of poverty and development.

Section 3 of the book embodies the latest consensus in macroeconomics, which was a difficult and controversial area for many years. *Economics From A Global Perspective* thus adopts the consensus which emerged from the old Keynesian/Monetarist arguments. The second edition, following the new syllabus, omits the Keynsian 45° and Keynsian X models and retains the multiplier and the multiplier-accelerator models.

The IB course requires all students to study core topics with Higher Level students studying additional 'extension' topics. The second edition of *Economics From A Global Perspective* has retained the colour coding of these 'Higher Level Extensions' for ease of recognition and use. This colour separation is simple to follow and directly addresses a problem for IB teachers and students. Thus Standard Level students are required to study the core pages only (white pages), omitting all of the Higher Level Extensions (blue pages). Higher Level students need to study everything in the text.

Unlike texts written for non-IB students, there is little here that is not in the IB syllabus. Students and teachers therefore do not have the problem of sorting out what to include and what to omit. Nor do they have to guess the depth of study required of a particular topic. Everything that is required is in this text. That is not true of other texts. An earlier book, *Introduction to Development Economics*, proved to be a popular supplement for the most glaring deficiency of national textbooks, and was well received by IB schools. That book, restructured to the syllabus, was embodied as Section 5 of *Economics from a Global Perspective*. Thus this text is complete and sufficient. Only one book is required for the whole course.

The colour marking of the Higher Level Extensions is useful to teachers who have to instruct Higher and Standard students together in one class. One approach is to teach the whole of the Core Course to all students, and then to make a second pass through the syllabus studying the Higher Level extensions, after students have been divided in their second year. Alternatively if extra Higher Level classes are taught in each week throughout the two years, the core is taught to the joint classes, and the Extension sections are taught the Higher Level only classes.

The book is structured almost exactly to the syllabus and almost in the same order, but not completely. In a few instances, *eg* in Section 3, some topics are sequenced differently for clearer learning. In some other cases there is no gain in reordering material imported from the first edition. The second edition, follows the lead of the 2003 IB syllabus in bringing forward the topic of growth and development. Thus Section 3, *Macroeconomics*, now contains two major sub-sections on development *ie* 'Introduction to development' and 'Measuring economic development'. 'Distribution of income' is segregated into its own sub-section in the syllabus. In the textbook the topic is integrated into the Sections on *Macroeconomics* and *Development economics*. The five sections of the book are renamed and reorganised to the new 2003–11 syllabus. For example a great deal of Section 1 now appears in Section 2. This consolidates market theory with the theory of the firm under the heading of *Microeconomics*. Section 1 is now an *Introduction to economics*.

Topics new to the syllabus are introduced in the relevant place *eg* 'Collusive oligopoly' and 'The theory of contestable markets' are to be found in Section 2; 'The Harrod–Domar growth model' in Section 5. Economic planning has been downgraded in the 2003 syllabus. However I have maintained a fuller treatment of this on the grounds of its importance, not least to the many IB students from formerly planned economies, and also its general absence from other books at this level. A brief study of planning gives insights into market operation, and the problems of transition are likely to be very relevant for a long time. There have been a number of changes to the boundaries between Higher and Standard Level. These are delineated clearly in the book. One of these boundary changes has been to exclude the introductory treatment of market structures from the SL syllabus. Personally I recommend that SL students read the first four pages of 'Theory of the firm – market structure'. This is a general nonanalytical treatment of competition and monopoly, and will be helpful to SL students even though they do not cover the detailed analysis.

Case studies are used throughout the book to add depth and realism to many of the topics. Many new case studies have been added to those of the first edition. Some of these studies include questions to test comprehension and reinforce learning together with answer guidelines. Country profiles have been added for Bangladesh, China, Nigeria, South Korea and Venezuela. These aim to add interest and realism to the study of development. Another new feature is a list of relevant web sites.

Economics from a Global Perspective is pitched at exactly the level and international background of IB students. This includes a sharp awareness that many students are working in a second language and that all Diploma students have many demands upon their academic time.

Each sub-section of the five main sections concludes with multiple choice questions. This enables students to test their understanding. Multiple choice questions remain an integral part of the book, even though they will not be used as an examination mode from September 2005. They remain a quick method of self assessment by the student during the learning process. Answers to many of the case studies and all of the multiple choice questions are printed at the back of the book. Some questions require a discursive answer however and are better left to the teacher. Further questions and answers are available in the course companion workbooks: *Multiple Choice Questions for Economics* and *Data Response Questions for Economics*. Details at the back of this book.

Section 6 is dedicated to improving and practising study and examination skills. This is specifically directed at the type of questions set by examiners. Advice is offered on essay, short answer and data response questions, as well as Internal Assessment and Extended Essays in Economics. The advice offered is personal, based on a long experience as a teacher and examiner. However for official IB advice teachers are strongly recommended to consult the relevant publications of the IB.

The book is written and produced for a small, dispersed, but dedicated market. The First Edition succeeded because it is what IB teachers and students asked for. The author welcomes and encourages further suggestions and comments to improve the text in order that it should be the most useful classroom tool possible. Please do e-mail with suggestions for further improvement.

ACKNOWLEDGEMENTS

First Edition

Mark Stump was the main ally and support in producing computer diagrams and electronic layout for *Introduction to Development Economics*, published in 1994. Most of this was rearranged to form Section 5 of the First Edition of *Economics from a Global Perspective*. In turn much of the First Edition of *Economics from a Global Perspective* has been embodied into this Second Edition. Therefore I should like to acknowledge again the support I received back in those early years. The First Edition would not have been possible without the help and expertise of a number of friends, family and colleagues. Emma Coles was responsible for the initial typed layout and Steven Scott adapted that script for publication. Others who helped were Bob Anderson, Jacob Glanville, Kate Glanville, Roni Hameiri, Chris Leftley, John Palmer, Steven Scott, Toni Tattersall and Barbara Young. My wife, Judith, was indirectly of enormous help in allowing me the luxury of the time to produce the book. Rob Bowman made the corrections and alterations to subsequent reprints and in particular to the Revised Edition in 1999.

Second Edition

This Second Edition has been completely overhauled in layout, and is technically superior to the first edition. I hope the appearance of the new book will enhance the quality and enjoyment of those studying IB economics. The credit for that is down to David Harrison whose knowledge and expertise I have relied upon entirely. To him goes a massive vote of thanks. He fully shared those inevitable dreadful moments en route to publication when things go wrong. Steve Fleming has again been responsible for adapting the original cover. Chris Taylor of St Peters College, Adelaide has carefully proof read all I could send him as the process unfolded. He was the obvious choice to ask to do this as he had politely queried and suggested for several years as a teacher-user of the first edition. To him a very big thank you also. Finally I should like to thank the staff of the Alden Group, my printers, for their advice and collaboration.

Source material

The publisher would like to thank the following specifically, for permission to reproduce statistical and copyright material: Philip Allan Publishers Ltd, *Can we measure economic development*. BBC: *Structural adjustment in Ghana*. Daily Information: *Who will type your extended essay?* Economist: *Problems of transition – Russia*; *Poorest people*; *Valuing natural resources*; *Developing countries growth*; *How to help Africa, Policies for sustained development*. Financial Times: *A Chinese multiplier*. Guardian: *Fished out*. Sue Hepper and Dorothy Foster: *Nigeria's kerosene cookers*. IMF: *Real non-oil commodity terms of trade*. Independent on Sunday: *Population policy in Pakistan*. Institute of Development Studies, University of Sussex: *IDS Reprint by Dudley Seers*; *The New International Economic Order*. International Fund for Agricultural Development: *Poverty and Gender, Poverty and Age*. John Hopkins University Press: *Of cowboys and spacemen*. Lloyds TSB: *Imperfection in the market for houses*. Longman: *Quotation from Todaro defining development*. Macmillan: *Keynes, the Classicists and the Great Depression*. Newspaper Publishing PLC: *Too small a world*; *The state of world rural poverty*; *Coffee price soars after Brazilian frost damage*. Nick Lee, St. Clares, Oxford: advice on writing extended essays. Norman McRae: *Purchasing power parity*. W.W. Norton & Co: *Population and family planning in China*. Open University: *Ram Prasad and Somi*; *Kerala – a model for development?* Oxford University Press: *World Bank, World Development Reports*; *Development in a Javanese village*; *The poor of three continents*; *Development and the environment*; *Family planning and vasectomy festivals in Thailand*; *The East Asian miracle*; *The Human Development Report*; many statistical tables in Section 5. World Resources Institute: *Index of per capita food production in Africa*. Penguin: *Dwarfs and giants*. Phoenix House: *Vikram Seth, A suitable boy*. Population Reference Bureau: *Population statistics*. Prentice Hall: *John Sloman, Personal profiles of JM Keynes and Milton Friedman*. Times Newspapers: *The Human suffering index*; *To smoke or not to smoke? That is the question*. United Nations: *The end of central planning in Eastern Europe*; *UN international development goals*; *Development statistics*. UNCTAD: *Structure of world merchandise trade*. US Bureau of Labor: *US Consumer Price Index*. Washington Post: *Tickets for U2*. Martin Weinelt of kk+w digital cartography who wrote the OMC mapping software package (country profiles) www.aquarius.geomar.de World Trade Organization: *Case for open trade*; *NAFTA and free trade*.

Every effort has been made to locate the copyright owners of material used in this book. Any omissions brought to the notice of the publisher are regretted and will be credited in subsequent printings.

THE AUTHOR

Alan Glanville has a Bachelors Degree in Economics and a Masters Degree in Development Studies from the University of East Anglia. He has been fully involved with the IB Economics programme for 32 years from 1971, teaching IB Economics full-time for 26 of those years, as Head of Department at the UWC of the Atlantic, Wales; Lester B Pearson UWC of the Pacific, Canada; Sigtunaskolan Humanistiska Laroverket, Sweden; and St. Clares, England. Alan was an IB Examiner from 1981 to 1996, Acting Chief Examiner for one year and a Deputy Chief Examiner for five years. During those years he was involved in all stages of exam setting, marking and moderating and ran IB teacher workshops all over the world. Since 1994 as an independent author and publisher he has produced resource materials for the use of students and teachers, ie *Introduction to Development Economics*, *Economics from a Global Perspective*, *Multiple Choice Questions for Economics*, and *Data Response Questions for Economics*.

Section 1

Introduction to Economics

1.1   INTRODUCTION TO ECONOMICS

Economics is about *scarcity*. Scarcity means there is not enough of something. The opposite of scarcity is *abundance*. The air in your classroom is abundant – you can have as much as you want. Economics concerns itself only with those things which are scarce. All things that are scarce are known as *economic* goods. Those things which are abundant are known as *free* goods. Although economics does not concern itself with free goods, free goods transform into economic goods if they become scarce. Air is an economic good to sub-aqua divers and operators of passenger air-lines. At this time fresh air is becoming increasingly scarce in traffic-filled cities. Many environmental issues are of growing importance to economists because they were formerly abundant (free) and are now becoming scarce (economic) *eg* whales, tropical forests, traffic-free city centres.

> 'Free' Air
>
> In Mexico City there are oxygen booths in parks and malls to counter very bad air pollution. Private firms sell the air ($1.60 a minute in 1992). In Los Angeles air pollution abatement costs about $1,200 a year for every resident of the metropolitan area.

Where there is scarcity there has to be choice. Your time is scarce. You have to choose how to spend your time, today, this evening, this weekend. Machines, water, and land are all scarce. Choice must be made as to what they should produce. The money that you own is scarce. How will you choose to spend it?

Thus the basic economic problem is *scarcity*. It follows that because there is scarcity there is choice. This question of choice can then be sub-divided into three basic types of choice question:

▎ *What* to produce?
▎ *How* to produce?
▎ *For whom* to produce?

These questions are faced by every society, by every individual, family, business, and government. *What* to produce, the first of these three questions addresses the problem of scarce resources. Should an IB student use his time to study history or economics? Should a peasant farmer grow maize or wheat? Should a government build more schools or more military weapons?

How to produce tackles the method of production – the technology. Should electricity be produced by burning coal or gas or oil, or by atomic, hydro or solar means? Should dishes in a restaurant be washed by hand or by machine? Should manufactures be produced by many workers and few machines, or by few workers and many machines?

Should cattle and poultry roam freely over farm land feeding themselves or be confined to pens with their food brought to them. Should Higher and Standard Level economics students be taught together in the first year of the IB or time-tabled separately?

For whom is the problem of distributing economic goods and services. Should those who earn most or inherit most have most goods and services? Should schools and universities be for everyone or only those who can afford to pay? Should resources be taken from the richest and re-distributed to the poor, the sick, the unemployed, the unlucky? Is it just that a small percentage of the world's population enjoys most of the economic goods and services produced whilst the majority of the world's population enjoys very little – little health care, little education, little shelter, little security? Should men earn more than women?

UTILITY

People buy things for the satisfaction that they expect to receive from owning and using them. Just about everything that people have, they get more satisfaction the more of it they have. Economists call this satisfaction 'utility'. It is not possible to measure utility as the idea is highly subjective. However all goods that are desired have this property of utility. The amount of utility that people obtain from goods and services depends upon their taste and preferences. If an individual buys more of good x than of good y (when both are equally priced) we observe that the individual gains more utility from good x than from good y. The amount of utility obtained from the many different goods and services available will determine how any individual allocates his or her scarce income. The individual will choose to spend his income on those items from which he derives most utility.

INFINITE WANTS

Will scarcity ever disappear? Can there be a Utopia, a land of plenty? This seems highly unlikely because human wants appear to be unlimited.

The problem of scarcity is obvious when life itself is threatened. Consider the drama of a scuba diver tangled in a net and her air supply running low. Again scarcity is evident in many countries of the southern hemisphere – food, clothing, housing, and safety are all visibly lacking compared to the rich countries of the north.

How though can there be scarcity in the richest districts of Los Angeles, London or Tokyo? Well, even the richest people want more and better health care, entertainment, houses, vacations, designer labels and education for their children. Meanwhile manufacturers in rich countries work hard to create new and improved products to create even more wants.

OPPORTUNITY COST

As scarcity in society leads to people having to choose, then choice means that something is given up. When the 'best' alternative is chosen from a range of alternatives the second best choice is known as the *opportunity cost*.

When you made the decision to study the IB at your present school what did you give up (or forgo)? Was it to study for the IB at a different school? Was it to continue a different programme in your previous school? Was it to go to Art College? Take a full time job? Whichever was the second best choice is the opportunity cost of what you are presently doing. Notice the difference in how the economist thinks from the accountant. To an accountant the cost of studying the IB is '*x* thousand dollars', to the economist the cost is 'not doing the next best thing'. Let's say your parents made a decision to buy a house in the country for $200,000 rather than an apartment in the city. The opportunity cost of the house is not $200,000, but the apartment in the city. The opportunity cost of a government decision to increase defence spending is what has to be sacrificed *eg* it might be fewer hospitals or reduced road building.

ECONOMIC RESOURCES

The scarce resources which are used to produce economic goods are called the *factors of production*. Factors of production are needed to produce any economic good. For example in order to produce rice: seeds, water, fields, workers and tools are required. To produce fish: boats, engines, nets and fishermen are a few of the many factors of production needed; to produce economics lessons books, blackboards, classrooms and teachers. In practice many hundreds of things (factors) are required to produce a finished product.

Now economists simplify all of these hundreds of things into just a few basic factors of production. They all fit into one of four categories. They are *land*, *capital*, *labour*, and *enterprise*: two non-human and two human factors.

Students often confuse land and capital, so pay particular attention to these two definitions in particular.

⎮ Land is any factor of production that is *provided by nature*. Land is not man-made.
⎮ Capital is any factor of production which is *man-made*.

Notice that common to both is the fact they are factors of production, that is, they are used to produce something else. Thus a computer in your house used solely for playing games is not a factor of production. The same model of computer used in a bank or an in an office is a factor of production.

Land includes all natural factors which are used to produce something else. Clearly the intrinsic quality of the soil itself is 'land' when used to grow wheat or to build a factory upon it. The sea is a natural factor of production to the fishing industry – *ie* the factor 'land'. The payment for land is 'rent'.

To the summer tourist industry sea, sand, beach, and sunshine are all essential factors – and they are all 'land'. A downhill skiing holiday requires slopes, snow, scenery and sunshine – and these are usually natural *ie* land. Minerals like gold, silver, iron, tin, coal, and oil are also 'land'.

Capital is 'man-made'. Thus machines, lorries, ships, office blocks, factories, farm buildings, roads, computers and telephones are all capital. Remind yourself however that a man-made thing is only capital if it is used to produce something else. If your family car is used only for social and private use it is not a capital good (it is a consumption good). If your parents use the car to run their business, then the car is a capital good. If the car is used as a taxi it is a capital good. If the car is used for business and pleasure then it is capital only when it is being used for business. The payment for capital is 'interest'.

Labour is the human input into production, the muscle and the brain which combines with capital and land to produce. Coal miners, bus-drivers, actors, doctors, cooks and engineers are all forms of the factor labour. The payment for labour is 'wages'.

Enterprise or entrepreneurship is also a human factor and is that activity which organises the other three factors. It is characterised as the factor which takes risks by combining land, labour, and capital to produce goods. Sometimes this function is combined with labour *eg* independent farmers, builders and shopkeepers. Sometimes it is specialised and separate, taking all the work-time of the entrepreneur. One way of distinguishing enterprise is by the payment received. In a money economy labour is paid a wage or salary, but entrepreneurs gain only profit. Profit is what is left over after selling a product and deducting all of the costs – payments for land, labour and capital. The entrepreneur takes risks because the profit could be negative – that is a loss.

Adam Smith, The First Economist
(1723–1790)

Economics has been a subject for study for thousands of years. The first person we would call an economist, however, was Adam Smith. His book An enquiry into the Nature and Causes of the Wealth of Nations published in 1776 was one of the most important economic books ever written. He argued that with few exceptions the state should not interfere with the functioning of the economy. It should adopt a laissez-faire or hands-off policy. There should be free enterprise for firms and free trade between countries. His ideas are still alive and still powerful today, 230 years on.

He was born in 1723 in Kirkaldy, a small Scottish sea-side town near Edinburgh. His father died when Adam was young and he lived, unmarried, for most of his life with his mother. He graduated from Glasgow University at age 17 and then became a fellow of Balliol College, Oxford, before returning to Glasgow at age 29 as Professor of Moral Philosophy. At age 40 he spent three years touring the continent where he met many influential economists and philosophers. Many of these ideas he synthesised into the Wealth of Nations, especially the thinking of the French economists known as the Physiocrats.

The central theme of his book is that the pursuit of self-interest by people in a market actually serves society well. Markets guide consumption and production like an invisible hand. For example he writes:

'Man has almost constant occasion for the help of his brethren and it is in vain for him to expect it from their benevolence only. He will be more likely to prevail if he can interest their self-love in his favour, and show them that it is for their own advantage to do for him what he requires of them. Whoever offers to another a bargain of any kind, proposes to do this. Give me what I want, and you shall have this which you want, is the meaning of every such offer; and it is in this manner that we obtain from one another the far greater part of those good offices which we stand in need of. It is not from the benevolence of the butcher, the brewer or the baker that we expect our dinner, but from their regard to their own interest. We address ourselves, not to their humanity but to their self-love, and never talk to them of our necessities, but of their advantages.'

And in another passage:

'Every individual is continually exerting himself to find out the most advantageous employment of whatever capital he can command. It is to his own advantage, indeed, and not that of society, which he has in view. But the study of his own advantage naturally, or rather necessarily, leads him to prefer that employment which is most advantageous to the society…he intends only his own gain, and he is in this, as in many other cases, led by an invisible hand to promote an end which was no part his intention. Nor is it always the worse for the society that it was no part of it. By pursuing his own interest he frequently promotes that of society more effectually than when he really intends to promote it.'

ECONOMIC SYSTEMS

The way is which a society organises itself to address the problem of scarcity, the way in which it decides *what*, *how*, and *for whom* to produce is known as an economic system. Thus we can speak about the economic systems of Australia, Chile or Namibia.

There are three fundamental methods of resource allocation which go to make up an economic system. These are:

| Tradition
| Market
| Planning

All real world economic systems are a combination of these three. No actual economy is purely of one type although it is likely to be characterised as traditional, market or planned where one system dominates.

Traditional resource allocation employs methods which have been handed down through the generations, rarely changing. Such systems are widespread amongst rural dwellers in the poorest countries of the world – and are thus important for a large number of the world's population. Here one finds traditional crops, traditional seeds, traditional production techniques and a traditional division of labour.

In many parts of the globe the way of life is little different than it was hundreds of years ago. Farmers grow the same crops with the same primitive methods and the same simple tools. Boys learn the tasks of the father and girls the tasks of the mother. Change is very slow.

In the modern sector of poor countries, and in all industrialised countries, change is continuous and has been rapid since the Industrial Revolution, that is over the last 100–200 years.[1] Here the choice of resource allocation is between the use of markets and plans. The two methods have advantages and disadvantages. Deciding which is better pervades almost all the economic topics you are about to study. Should the ownership of land and capital be private or public? Should education and health be provided in the market sector or in the planned sector? Should foreign trade be free or controlled? What about exchange rates? Should governments plan to achieve full employment of labour or leave it to the market? The ideology between these two systems was the major divisive force between the centrally planned Communist countries of Eastern Europe and China, and the market based democratic countries of Western Europe and North America during the 45 years following World War II. After 1945 there was a massive increase in the use of planning in Eastern Europe, China, India, Africa, and indeed most of the world, with huge industries being nationalised and welfare state systems set up. In the 1980s and 1990s much of this has been dismantled and the shift has moved dramatically towards markets. However as there are advantages and disadvantages to both methods of resource allocation, the issue will not go away. You, reader, are likely throughout your lifetime to continue to choose where the boundary between markets and planning should fall in each of the many areas which will affect your life. Some areas will not be controversial. There is a very strong economic case for the defence of the country and its police force to be planned. There is a strong case for the restaurant industry and shoe manufacturing to be run by the market. However what about inner-city transport, primary school education, and health care? The case is less clear cut, the balance of advantages and disadvantages is more equal. These industries may be planned in one time period and market organised in another in one particular country, or be different in different countries during the same time period.

A country using only planning techniques would be called a *centrally planned economy*, or a *command economy*. A country with only market organisation, a *free market* or *laissez-faire economy*. Classifying particular countries into these economic systems we would see that none was purely one thing or the other.

In Figure 1.1 a spectrum has been drawn between the two pure forms of resource allocation, central planning and free markets with mixtures of the two forms in between. Traditionally based economies, like many of those in Africa, can also be classified like this according to how their modern sectors are organised.

Figure 1.1 – Economic Systems

The diagram illustrates a selection of countries loosely categorised according to its mix of planning and market economic decision making. The upper spectrum shows an approximate position of these countries in the early 1980s. The lower spectrum illustrates the marked shift towards more market based decisions which occurred over the next 20 years.

As economies all have both planned sectors and private sectors – economies in the middle of the spectrum are often known as mixed economies. China and the USSR were planned economies in 1975 and North Korea and Cuba would still be considered such today. Hong-Kong is a market economy. However, there is no really definitive agreement on the countries between. Thus, the USA could justifiably be called a market or capitalist economy. On the other hand, it could be referred to as a mixed economy. Many of the countries which were formerly centrally planned and with resources public owned are now restructuring their economies towards a much greater use of markets and private ownership. These economies in transition are referred to as 'transitional economies'.

In conclusion, the important point to realise is that all economies have a mix of all three methods of resource allocation.

OWNERSHIP OF RESOURCES

Economic systems can also be classified by ownership – private or public. Because market systems tend to be found with extensive private ownership and planned systems with public ownership, adjectives of ownership, capitalist (private ownership of capital and land) and public (public ownership of capital and land) are often used interchangeably with market systems and planned systems. Public ownership includes ownership by the state, by co-operatives, by communes, and by villages – where ownership resides in a group of people rather than in an individual.

However, this division is not absolute. The Nazi government of Germany used extensive planning with private ownership as did the former Yugoslavia with its blend of market socialism. The gigantic privately owned multinational companies of the world use planning techniques and decisions very extensively within their own capitalist organisations.

METHODOLOGY IN ECONOMICS

Economics is a social science, a study of people in society. Economists attempt to understand the real world and to predict events. To do this they use the same methods as a scientist.

Scientific Method

Scientific Method has five steps:

1 Recognising the problem or issue
2 Cutting away unnecessary detail by making assumptions
3 Developing a model, or story of the problem or issue
4 Making predictions
5 Testing the model
   The test of a model is how well it predicts events. Good models explain or predict well. Poor models do not.

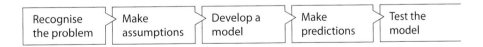

Building Models

The world is very complex. To understand how it works we simplify it by using a model. A midwife teaching mothers-to-be how to bath a baby might use a doll – a model of the baby. A navigation class for sailors might use a table with toy boats, buoys and lighthouses to teach 'the rules of the road at sea' – a model of the real ocean. Student pilots may begin their flying lessons in 'virtual-reality' – an electronic model. Models are extensively used in learning to help focus upon the important factors and to isolate other less important factors which complicate the issue.

Economics is complicated, so economists build models, simplifying reality to focus upon a particular aspect. The insight gained from the model then enables a better understanding of the more complex reality. In both your text book and in your classroom you will use many models – word models, picture models, and simple mathematical models. Professional economists build more complicated computerised models expressed as algebraic equations.

In this chapter you will meet the production possibility frontier model. Then in the following chapter you will meet the most commonly used model in economics – the supply and demand model.

Ceteris Paribus – other things equal!

In building and using economic models we often want to see the effect on one thing, of something else changing. Something that can change is known as a variable. Thus we want to see the effect on one variable of a second variable changing. We may, for example want to see the effect on sales of mobile phones if the price of mobile phones falls. We may want to see what happens to inflation money supply increases?

When laboratory scientists want to see the effect on one variable of a second variable changing they ensure that they hold all other variables constant. If a biologist wishes to check the effect of sunlight upon plant growth, she will set up an experiment with many plants, vary the quantity of sunlight each receives and record the result. However, the scientist will have been painstakingly careful to hold all the other factors which affect plant growth constant. Thus the plants will be of the same size and type. In each plant pot the soil, and the nutrients in the soil will be of the same quality and quantity. The temperature, the pot size, the amount of water each receives, all will be identical for each plant.

It is not possible to do such controlled experiments with people. However, in learning economics, or discussing economics we *assume* that all variables are constant other than the one variable that we are changing. This assumption is known as *'ceteris paribus'* or *'other things equal'.*

In practical work economists try hard to minimise the effects of more than one variable changing by selecting data as carefully as possible. However, it is usually the case that several variables are changing at the same time. This is a major reason for the lack of certainty in economics.

Defining Terms

It is very important to define all terms that you use in economics. Words have very specific meanings. Many disagreements between people occur because they are not actually discussing the same thing. It may well explain why a government minister who claims crime figures are falling is directly contradicted by an opposition politician who says the crime figures are rising. Are they both referring to all crime, only to certain categories of crime, only to crimes that are reported, only to crimes committed in a certain time period?

In this book we have already defined some economic terms *eg* free, capital and land. Notice that these words have everyday usage in the English language. You must learn to use them precisely in economics. Of the two statements

1 I have some capital in the bank

2 Machines are capital goods

only the second is correct in economics. You will learn later that money in the bank is called savings.

It is a good idea to highlight all new definitions as you come across them in your course and/or keep a separate list of them at the back of your book. You will find the important ones used in this book listed as an appendix at the back.

Normative and Positive Statements

In becoming an economist you need to be aware that the statements you make or read can be split into two kinds – normative and positive. Normative statements are characterized by being subjective or political, a matter of opinion. 'Women should be paid the same as men'. 'Pensions should be increased'. 'Defence spending ought to be cut'. These are all normative statements, a matter of opinion; they cannot be proven right or wrong. These statements can often be recognized by having the words 'should' or 'ought' in them. Positive statements on the other hand can be tested and are either right or wrong. 'Women are paid less than men'. 'Spending on defence is greater than spending on education'. 'The moon is made of green cheese'. 'These are all positive statements, they are all testable, and all are either right or wrong.

It is important to be aware of this distinction. It is quite common for normative statements to be passed off as though they are positive statements by people trying to influence others.

Economists do try to make positive statements in their work. However it is impossible to avoid being normative. For example the decision to emphasize the topic of economic development in the IB syllabus was a normative one. Do be aware of the difference from now on when reading or listening and do look out for examples of each type.[2]

Micro and Macro

Economics is commonly divided into microeconomics and macroeconomics for convenience of study. Micro means small and macro large. Microeconomics is the study of a section of an economy, macroeconomics is the study of the whole economy. Microeconomics is concerned with the behaviour of households and firms and how the prices of goods and services are determined. Macroeconomics looks at economy-wide issues like unemployment, inflation and economic growth.

PRODUCTION POSSIBILITY FRONTIER

Each country or economy has a finite amount of each of the factors of production, land, capital, labour and enterprise. Therefore, what it can produce is limited, and choices must be made. In our production possibility frontier (PPF) model we assume that the country can produce only two products. We could call these industrial goods and agricultural goods, or alternatively military goods and civilian goods. Any two products could be put into this model. We use *guns* and *food*, a simplification of military goods and civilian goods.

Figure 1.2 – A Production Possibility Curve

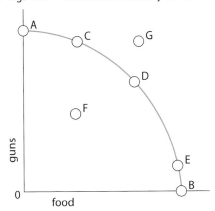

On the graph (Figure 1.2) one product is marked on each axis. If the country were to use all of its resources (all of its land, capital, labour, and enterprise) to produce guns it would produce at A a large amount of guns but no food at all. If it put all its resources into food it would produce at B, lots of food but no guns. Of course there are other less extreme possibilities. Thus combinations of guns and food are possible at C, D and E, indeed at any point on the line joining A and B. This model can be used to highlight a number of things. For example, if you want more guns, food production has to be sacrificed. Thus there is an opportunity cost to having more food. There is alternatively an opportunity cost to having more guns.

Notice that point F is also a possible combination of guns and food. However from this point one can obtain both more guns and more food by moving to D at no opportunity cost. F is not on the production possibility frontier, but inside it. All resources are not being used at F, that is, there is unemployment at F. The model illustrates a common situation in many countries – a situation of unemployment. It would benefit such a society to reorganise its economy to move close to the frontier. It can thereby gain more goods and services, more health care, more education, more cars, etc – or in a limited model more guns and more food.

PPF, Economic Growth and Development

Point G is also an interesting point. This is outside the PPF. It is impossible to produce at this point with the fixed resources. However if over time a country can increase its resources (land, labour, capital and enterprise) or increase the productivity of these resources (through for example better education or better technology) it could shift its PPF outwards as in Figure 1.3. The model is now illustrating economic growth – an increase in national output.

Figure 1.3 – Economic Growth

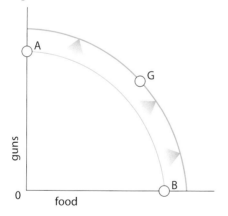

Economic growth is an increase in a country's output. The increased output could in turn raise the living standard or 'development' of the country. This is of the utmost importance for the Less Developed Countries. Thus, if a poor country can cause its economy to grow, it will enable higher levels of consumption. If this increase in goods and services reduces poverty, by for example improving nutrition, health care and literacy, then development will have occurred as well as economic growth. However poverty may not be reduced, as growth and development are not the same thing. The increased growth may be in the increased output of military goods or the increased output of 'luxury'

goods used only by the rich. Production possibility curves below show economic growth in every case but development only in the third one.

Figure 1.4 – Sustainable Development

The term sustainable is used by environmentalists to highlight the balance between economic growth on the one hand and the preservation of the environment on the other. Sustainable development is about meeting the needs of the present generation without compromising the needs of future generations. Economists would say that development is sustainable only if a country's capital and land assets remain constant or increase over time. These assets include the environment, the quality of air, water and land. Thus over-fishing, deforestation and air pollution may give economic growth but are not sustainable. Sustainable economic development is one of the greatest global challenges of the twenty first century

PPF and Trade

A country restricted to producing within its PPF, like that bounded by AB in Figure 1.3, can still consume beyond it however (at G for example). It could do this by specializing its production and trading some of it for other products from other countries. The gain from trade between individuals, communities and countries, is a major explanation for the high living standards enjoyed by most of those who live in the developed countries. How countries can make consumption gains through trade is studied in Section 4 of the IB syllabus.

MULTIPLE CHOICE QUESTIONS – INTRODUCTION TO ECONOMICS

1 Positive statements differ from normative statements because

	Positive Statements	Normative Statements
A	involve a value judgement.	do not involve a value judgement.
B	can be tested empirically.	cannot be tested empirically.
C	predict the future.	explain the past.
D	are correct.	are incorrect.

2 There is an 'opportunity cost' when

I   resources are scarce and have alternative uses.

II   society's wants exceed its ability to satisfy those wants.

III there is too much money.

A I only   B I and II   C II and III   D I, II and III

3 If a country has scarcity then

A the country is poor.

B there is no saving.

C choices must be made.

D there are no free goods.

4 'Pop stars should not be paid more than nurses.' This statement can best be described as

A normative   B free-market   C empirical   D positive

5 In economics a 'free good' is defined as one which

A has a zero price to the consumer.

B is provided free by the government.

C does not use scarce resources in its production.

D is provided by nature.

Chart A	Chart B	Chart C	Chart D

P

M

T

M T

P T

P M

M

T

P

Key   M = Manufacturing Sector   T = Tertiary Sector   P = Primary Sector

6   Charts A, B, C and D represent four countries, each with a different economic structure.
    Which one is likely to represent one of the world's poorest countries?

A   Chart A   B   Chart B   C   Chart C   D   Chart D

7   It is generally the case that water, which is essential to life is cheap, and diamonds which
    are not are expensive. This is best explained by
    A   the power of the diamond industry.
    B   the irrationality of consumers.
    C   heavy advertising for diamonds.
    D   the relative scarcity of water and diamonds.

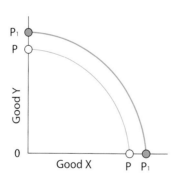

8   In the diagram above the shift of the production possibility frontier from PP to P_1P_1 is best
    explained by
    A   a fall in the level of unemployment.
    B   a lowering of sales tax on Good X and Good Y.
    C   an increase in imports of Good X and Good Y.
    D   an improvement in technology.

9   In a pure market economy

   A   resource allocation is determined by demand and supply.

   B   prices remain stable.

   C   there is no scarcity.

   D   income is distributed evenly.

10   An economy produces at point X on its production possibility frontier, illustrated in the diagram below.

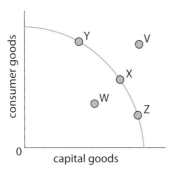

How can the economy move production to point V?

   A   Move to point W   B   Move to point Y   C   Move to point Z   D   Use idle resources

11   The four factors of production

   I   are scarce relative to potential demand.

   II   become cheaper in price, the more plentiful their supply.

   III   can often be substituted for each other within a given productive process.

   A   I only   B   I and II   C   II and III   D   I, II and III

12   Bus drivers are paid A\$400 for working a 45 hour week. The company offers to increase wages by 10% or alternatively to increase the wage to A\$405 and reduce the working week to 40 hours. What is the opportunity cost of the bus drivers choosing the shorter working week?

   A   5 hours   B   45 hours   C   A\$35   D   A\$40

13 A student paid NZ$700 for a PC two years ago. He would like a new PC priced at NZ$900 and could get NZ$550 by selling the old PC. The opportunity cost of owning the old PC is?

A $150   B $200   C $550   D $900

14 Which of the following statements is normative?
   A Planners decide what is produced in a market economy.
   B More consumer goods are produced in a command economy than in a market economy.
   C Command economies have higher unemployment than market economies.
   D A command economy is a more desirable form of economic system than a market economy.

15 Which of the following is a free good?
   A Sunshine.
   B A full scholarship.
   C An expenses-paid business trip.
   D A gift.

16 A straight-line production possibility curve illustrates
   A a constant rate of opportunity cost in the production of two goods.
   B a decreasing rate of opportunity cost in the production of two goods.
   C an increasing rate of opportunity cost in the production of two goods.
   D a decreasing rate of opportunity cost in the production of one of the goods and an increasing rate of opportunity cost in the production of the other.

Notes

1   Industrialisation has taken place at different times in different countries. The first Industrial Revolution began in the United Kingdom around about 1760.

2   If you use the 'Data Response Workbook for Economics' by Alan Glanville you might now work the first exercise which contains examples of both types of statement.

Section 2

Microeconomics

2.1 MARKETS

A market is a meeting of buyers and sellers. They do not have to physically meet – buying and selling shares in the stock market could be done over the phone or by e-mail for example. However there must be both buyers *and* sellers. The absence of one or the other prevents a market forming.

Thus at this time there is a demand to remain young, but there are no sellers, for it is not possible to stop the ageing process. Of course there is a vast market for products that may delay or disguise the symptoms of ageing – face creams, hair dyes, styled clothes, and cosmetic surgery. However, as yet there is no market for stopping time! Similarly a seller of sand in the Sahara Desert is unlikely to find the buyers required to form a market for sand.

Markets may be local, national or international. The markets for childcare and gardening services are likely to be local. The markets for daily newspapers and train services are likely to be national and the markets for cars and computers global.

Alternative Market Structures

Economists characterise markets by their competitive structure. The degree of competition in turn depends upon the number of buyers and sellers of the product, the type of product and whether there are high or low barriers to a firm setting up in that industry (or market). It is the degree of competition which determines the degree of control a firm has over the price of its product. There are four major models of market structure: perfect competition, monopolistic competition, oligopoly and monopoly. Higher level students will analyse these in detail. Here just a brief description is offered. There is a slightly fuller account, designed for Standard Level students, at the beginning of *Section 2.3 Theory of the Firm*.

Perfect competition and monopoly are the theoretical extremes of competition. In perfect competition there are very many firms competing and there is freedom of entry to new firms. Firms produce identical (homogenous) products. Each firm is so small compared to the whole industry that it cannot affect the price. It is a price taker. Agricultural markets *eg* for vegetables and fruit approximate to perfect competition, assuming that governments do not intervene (which they often do).

At the other extreme is monopoly, with a single firm in the industry, and hence no competition at all. The freedom of entry is very restricted or completely blocked and the product is unique.

In the middle of these two extremes monopolistic competition has a lot of firms competing and a freedom for new firms to enter the industry. The firms produce differentiated products and thus have some control over their prices. Examples might include house builders and restaurants. Finally, also between the extremes, there is oligopoly, where there are a few firms and entry of new firms into the industry is restricted. The markets for cars and TV sets are currently oligopolistic.

Market Prices as signals and incentives

We are about to study how market prices are formed by the meeting of buyers and sellers. These prices are extraordinarily important. It is prices which allocate resources in a market economy. It is the price system or market system which Adam Smith in 1776 called *the invisible hand*. It is the invisible hand that determines resource allocation in a market system. By contrast in a centrally planned economy, as in the old Soviet Union, the hand was very visible. It was the hand of government and planning committees which decided answers to the economic questions of what, how and for whom. In a market system prices act as signals and as incentives. A price move is a signal to give consumers and producers the incentive to change their behaviour. For example if the price of a good, say coffee, falls there is an incentive for consumers to buy more coffee and less of other drinks like tea. At the same time the incentive for growers to produce coffee falls. This in turn will reduce the demand for those factors of production which produce coffee and they will tend to move out of coffee production. Meanwhile the market price of tea is affected. This changes the behaviour of buyers and sellers in that market. The repercussions spread through many markets and cause adjustments to be made right across the economy.

DEMAND AND SUPPLY

The forces of demand and supply are the two forces or actions in a market. Buyers *demand* things and sellers *supply* things.

Demand is the amount of a good or service that is bought at a particular price over a particular time period. Thus we could say 'the demand for Coca Cola in the school shop on Fridays is 150 cans at 60¢, or the demand is 700 cans at 60¢ in a week', or '30,000 cans at 60¢ in a year'. It makes no sense to say 'the demand for Coca Cola is 560 cans' – as price and time are unspecified – unless of course price and time are implied as given.

Do notice that demand is the amount bought. Demand is not the same thing as wish, desire or need. It is the action of buying, the ability and willingness to buy.

Supply often differs from demand in that most supply decisions have to be made ahead of the market transaction. Suppliers have to guess what will be demanded. They might well get it wrong and supply either too little or too much.

Supply then is defined as the quantity of a good or service which a seller is willing to provide at a particular price over a particular time period.

Demand and supply will now be dealt with in more detail separately. Much of what you learn about demand is very similar to what you need to learn about supply, so having learnt the important points of one, the other is relatively simple.

The Demand Function

A function expresses a relationship between two or more variables. You will meet many functions whilst studying economics. The demand function is the first.

We need to understand what demand depends upon. What determines the quantity demanded of a good over a particular time period? Certainly the *price* of the product itself is important and is included in the definition of demand. Thus we can show the quantity demanded of a good x as a function of its own price, the price of x:

$$Q_{Dx} = f_{Px}$$

Any study of buying behaviour shows that the price of a product is one of the most important determinants of how much will be bought. However it is not the only determinant, the *prices of close substitutes* to x and the *prices of complements* to x are also important. Thus the price of beef is not the only determinant of demand for beef. The price of substitute meats like lamb, pork, poultry and fish are also important. The price of petrol (gasoline) is important to the demand for motor cars because cars and petrol are complementary goods, that is, goods which are demanded together. The demand function is thus extended to include the prices of close substitutes and complements:

$$Q_{Dx} = f_{Px} \; ; \; P_s \; ; \; P_c$$

Household income is another important determinant of demand. Usually when households have more income they demand more goods. This is also true of a country as a whole. As the total income – the National Income – of Australia has increased over the last 50 years so has the demand for most goods and services in Australia. If you compare poor households and rich households in your own country you will see that demand is strongly related to the ability to buy *ie* household income. If you compare rich and poor countries it goes a long way to explain why the demand for goods and services in Japan or Germany is very much higher than the demand for goods and services in Namibia or Ethiopia. In economics it is standard practice to use the letter Y for income (the letter I is reserved for Investment) – thus our function becomes:

$$Q_{Dx} = f_{Px} \; ; \; P_s \; ; \; P_c \; ; \; Y$$

Before looking at the next determinant of demand, it is worth pausing on income a little longer. When income changes, demand for a good usually changes in the same direction *ie* it is positively correlated. Thus if income increases, demand for the good increases. If income decreases demand for the good decreases. Such goods have a specific name in economics. They are known as *normal* goods. There are goods however, which are inversely related to income. Thus when income increases demand for these goods falls. Conversely when income falls demand increases. These are known as *inferior* goods – another specialised economic term. It does not mean there is anything wrong with the goods. Inferior goods may differ in different societies and at different times. Usually there is a normal substitute. Thus in the UK over the last 25 years the motor car has been a normal good and buses and trains have been inferior goods. In fast growing Pacific Rim countries the diet of rice is likely giving way to more expensive substitutes *eg* fish, meat, and fresh vegetables, making rice an inferior good as incomes rise. If household incomes fall, families may be forced to give up meat and resort to rice, showing the income/demand relationship working in the other direction. That is, as incomes fall, demand for rice rises.

In Western Europe 30 years ago the sale of bicycles would suggest that they were an inferior good, for as households earned more, they gave up cycling and travelled by car. However, with a heightened interest in exercise for health and increased traffic congestion in cities there has been a resurgence of interest (and spending) on bicycles. This increased spending on bikes, enhanced by innovations such as the mountain bike, is positively correlated with income. Bikes appear to be normal goods again.

There are a number of other factors which affect the demand for a product which are important but harder to quantify.

For example, household demand for coffee depends on whether members of the household like coffee, personal demand for beef is related to whether or not one is a vegetarian; demand for cigarettes on whether or not members of the household smoke. The current boom in sports equipment sales in many countries is highly related to the current concern to be fit and healthy. All of these psychological factors which affect demand the economist classifies as *taste*. Thus taste goes into the demand function.

Returning to the demand function you may recall that one reason for the demand for goods and services being higher in Japan than in Namibia is due to Japan's higher income. However you might think of another reason to explain higher Japanese demand. There are more Japanese than Namibians! Thus the size of the population is an important determinant of demand. The demand for eggs is greater in France than it is in the city of Paris alone. The demand for shoes is greater in India than in Sri Lanka.

There are other variables which may also be important in determining demand for a product. If you were to research the demand for a product for your extended essay you would need to look hard for all the possible factors which are important. Thus if you were looking at the demand for ice cream or the demand for umbrellas – the weather is obviously important to include in your demand function. Advertising is very important to a number of consumer industries and might be included. However, we have already identified the most common important variables for the majority of demand functions.

Thus we could write 'the demand for a product is a function of its own price, the price of substitutes, the price of complements, income, taste, population, advertising etc.'. Alternatively the demand function could be written as an equation:

$$Q_{Dx} = f_{Px} \; ; \; P_s \; ; \; P_c \; ; \; Y \; ; \; taste \; ; \; population \; ; \; advertising \; ; \; etc.$$

CETERIS PARIBUS – OTHER THINGS EQUAL!

The next stage in understanding demand requires that you have understood 'ceteris paribus' (other things equal) a most important study method used in economics. As we want to see the effect of changing one variable upon the quantity demanded we need to prevent the other variables from changing. But we cannot. It is usually the case that several variables are changing at the same time.

Thus in looking at the effect of price changes upon demand, we assume that 'other things are equal'. That is, we pretend that we can hold constant the prices of all complementary and substitute goods and prevent them changing, as well as income, taste, population, and anything else which could affect demand.

A DEMAND SCHEDULE

We can now look at a demand schedule. That is we can show how quantity demanded for a good x will change against its own price, 'other things equal': ie $Q_{Dx} = f_{Px}$ whilst all other variables $P_s; P_c; Y; taste; population; advertising; etc.$ are assumed equal or constant when Px changes. When price and quantity are set out as a table, the table is known as a demand schedule. A demand schedule is shown in Figure 2.1.

Figure 2.1 – A Demand Schedule

Price of x ($)	Quantity demanded of x (units per week)
1.00	100
1.10	95
1.20	90
1.30	85
1.40	80
1.50	75

The direction of change of the quantity demanded as price changes is critical. All observation and experiment shows that if the price of a product changes the quantity demanded changes in the opposite direction. That is, there is an *inverse relationship*. If the price of a product increases (all other things held equal) the quantity demanded will fall. If the price falls then, other things equal, the quantity demanded will rise. This relationship is so strong that it is often known as *the law of demand*. Whilst laws are common in physics they are rare in the more uncertain world of human behaviour – as in economics. If the law appears to be broken, that is, if quantity demanded increases when price increases then the explanation is most likely to be that something else is changing *ie* other things are not equal.

HYPOTHESIS, THEORY, AND LAW

A *hypothesis* is a word picture of a possible relationship between two or more variables *eg* 'making movies about violent crime cause more crime to be committed on the streets'. However, as yet this is not been convincingly shown by testing. Thus it is an equally valid hypothesis that increased violent crime on the streets causes film makers to make more films about violent crime in order to reflect reality.

If an hypothesis is tested and every time it is tested it shows the same result, and if in addition it can be used to predict future events, then it is known as a *theory*.

Where a theory is so strong that is has never shown any exception it may be called *a law*. For example, Newton's Law of Gravity. If I let go of my pen it will fall down, never up.

> ### An Economist's Joke!
> A chemist, an engineer and an economist were cast away on a desert island with no food or water. However a crate of canned food washed up on the beach. Their delight was dampened when they realised that they had no can-opener. They decided each should use his expertise to find a solution to opening the cans. The chemist searched and found certain minerals that, when mixed and heated, would burn through the metal. The engineer calculated heights and weights to drop rocks from a palm tree to break them open, then collected the rocks and found a suitable tree. The economist sat on the beach, looked at the sea, and pondered, 'Assuming we had a can opener...'

A DEMAND CURVE

If the relationship between price and quantity demanded is plotted on a graph' the demand curve will always slope downwards from left to right (Figure 2.2). Notice that when price is high quantity demanded is low, when price is low quantity demanded is high.

 Figure 2.2 – A Demand Curve

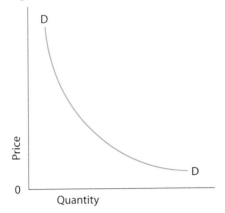

Figure 2.2 illustrates the law of demand: price and quantity are inversely related. When price falls quantity demanded rises. When price rises quantity falls.

If price changes, say from p_1 to p_2 in Figure 2.3, then quantity demanded changes from q_1 to q_2. There is a correct way of expressing this and care is needed here to note it. Thus if price changes we say the quantity demanded changes. Alternatively using a diagram we can say there has been a movement along the curve – from *A* to *B* in Figure 2.3.

 Figure 2.3

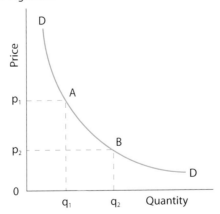

Figure 2.3 illustrates a change in the quantity demanded. When price changes there is a movement along the demand curve.

A CHANGE IN DEMAND

A demand schedule and a demand curve show the relationship between price and quantity demanded when everything else is held constant *ie 'other things equal'.* If some other variable in a demand function changes *eg* income, this demand data becomes invalid. A new schedule and a new demand curve must be plotted to show the new situation.

Figure 2.4

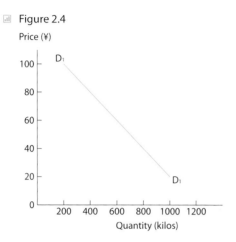

Price of x (¥)	Quantity demand of x (kilos)
20	1000
40	800
60	600
80	400
100	200

If the original demand schedule and demand curve were as in Figure 2.4 and then incomes increased, the demand data would change. The most likely effect would be a higher demand at each price as shown in the new schedule, and curve in Figure 2.5. Both Figure 2.4 and Figure 2.5 show the quantity demanded against price for the same product in identical conditions – except one. Income is higher in the second case and this has caused demand to increase at every price.

Figure 2.5

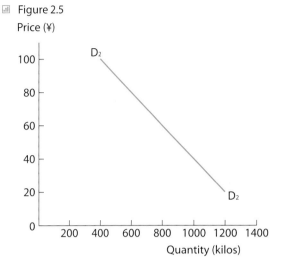

Price (¥)

Price of x (¥)	Quantity demand of x (kilos)
20	1200
40	1000
60	800
80	600
100	400

Again the terminology of what has happened is important. There has been a *change in demand* because income has changed and the demand curve has *shifted* to the right.

Compare this to what happened in Figure 2.3 when price changed. When price changes there is a *change in quantity demanded* and a *movement along a demand curve*.

When any other variable changes (other than price that is – the one that is graphed) there is a *change in demand*, a *shift of the curve*. This can be made even more clear if both demand curves are plotted on the same graph instead of two separate ones – Figure 2.6. The curves are labelled D_1 and D_2 to indicate the direction of the shift.

Figure 2.6

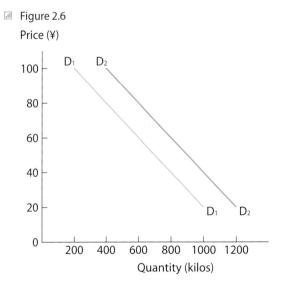

Price (¥)

To Smoke or Not to Smoke? That is the Question

The health risk posed by smoking cigarettes has caused governments around the world to respond in different ways.

Poland has the world's lowest prices and one of the world's highest levels of consumption, roughly 40% more per person than in America.

USA cigarette prices increased by 65% in the early 1980s. One estimate calculated that 2 million gave up smoking and over half a million teenagers did not begin to smoke.

UK tax rates are higher on those cigarettes with a high tar and nicotine content than on less harmful cigarettes.

Spain and **Germany** have laws which prohibit smoking in many public areas *eg* on buses and trains, offices and restaurants.

Sudan has banned cigarette advertising .

Sweden has strict rules on advertising.

Source: Adapted from the Times newspaper, June 1996

Questions

1) Use your knowledge of a demand function to explain how different methods used in each country might affect the demand for cigarettes
2) Why not use price increases alone?

A demand curve will shift if any variable other than its own price changes. It will shift to the right if the change increases demand and to the left if the change reduces demand. Thus a rightward shift of the demand curve, from D_1 to D_2 in Figure 2.7 would occur if: taste moved in favour of the product; population increased; the price of a substitute good increased; the price of a complementary good fell; or, a successful advertising campaign was run. In almost all cases *ie* if the good is a normal good, the curve would also shift to the right if income rose.

Figure 2.7 – Rightward Shift of a Demand Curve

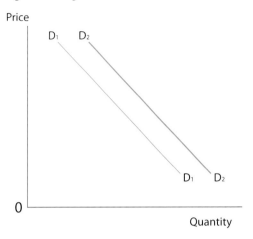

The demand curve would shift to the left (Figure 2.8) if taste moved away from the product, or population fell, or price of substitutes fell, or price of complements rose, or (in most cases) incomes fell.

Figure 2.8 – Leftward Shift of a Demand Curve

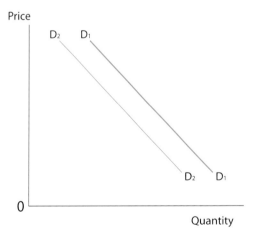

Because it is easy to confuse movements along a curve with shifts of a curve it is well worth developing a systematic step by step reasoning process.

THE SHAPE OF THE DEMAND CURVE

There are two main reasons why demand curves slope downwards. They are known as the *substitution effect* and the *income effect*.

THE SUBSTITUTION EFFECT

Consumers are presumed to be *rational*[2] which means that they will purchase a basket of goods and services so as to gain the highest total satisfaction from their income. If the price of one good rises, whilst other prices and income remain constant, consumers will be inclined to switch away from the more expensive good to the now relatively cheaper substitutes. Thus quantity demanded will fall when price rises. If there is a very close substitute to the good there will be a large fall in demand *eg* if the price of one type of potato rises whilst other types do not. On the other hand if there are few substitutes, as for example to water, there may be only a small fall in demand. There will be a fall in demand, however, as one possible substitute always is to use less of a good.

The substitution effect will work in reverse. If the price of a good falls consumers will switch towards it from its now relatively higher priced substitutes.

THE INCOME EFFECT

Income is the amount people earn over a particular time period. However, *real income* is as much a function of prices as income. If income remains constant and prices rise then real income falls.

Returning to the demand curve, if the price of a good rises then a consumer's real income falls. The consumer can buy less of all goods and services. This is the second reason why demand curves slope down from left to right. If price rises, real income falls and quantity demanded falls. Conversely if price falls real income rises and quantity demanded rises.

In a modern industrial country with consumption spread over hundreds and hundreds of goods the income effect of a change in most prices is hard to identify. Even so if the price change is for a good on which a large proportion of income is spent – houses or oil for example, it is likely to be noticed. In a poor country, families on low income and with few purchases, could feel income effects severely. For example a common cause of famine is an increase in food prices without a corresponding increase in income.

So substitution and income effects change demand in the same direction. Together they explain why price and quantity demanded are inversely related. In other words this explains inverse relationship which is the law of demand[3].

POSSIBLE EXCEPTIONS TO THE LAW OF DEMAND

GIFFEN GOODS

In the case of inferior goods income and substitution effects alter demand in opposite directions to each other. In most cases (perhaps all cases) the substitution effect of a single price change is likely to be greater than its income effect. However it is theoretically possible that the income effect of a price change in an inferior good is greater than the substitution effect. The product would have to be one that formed a large part of total expenditure. A nineteenth century economist by the name of *Giffen* claimed that such a case was to be observed in England at that time (many economists dispute this claim, however).

Bread formed the basis of the diet at that time. Many people were so poor that a very large proportion of their expenditure was upon food *ie* upon bread.

When the price of a Giffen good rises, the substitution effect will of course reduce the quantity demanded as consumers switch away from it. The income effect of a rise in the price of such a good is so great, however, that the reduction in real income dominates the substitution effect. For example, the rise in English bread prices reduced real income so much that consumers bought more bread (bread being an 'inferior' good). In this case the demand curve slopes backwards *ie* an increase in price actually increases demand.

If you can think of an example where quantity demanded increases when price increases, take care to check that the true explanation is not that some other variable has in fact changed as well. For example there may well be an improvement in the quality of the good.

VEBLEN GOODS

Another hypothesis suggesting that demand curves can slope the other way was put forward by an economist named *Veblen* to explain consumers' behaviour toward ostentatious goods. The argument is that some goods are bought as a display of wealth, for ostentatious or snobbery reasons. The argument is that if the price rises some people may buy them *because* they are more expensive, and buy less if they are cheaper. There is again no evidence for this in practice. Even if some individual people behave in this way, and that is plausible, the whole market demand is neverless likely to change like that for any other good.

If fur coats, diamonds and Rolls Royce motor cars became cheaper it is possible that some people for whom public displays of wealth are important may indeed switch away from them. You can be certain, however, that consumers as a whole would buy more of them.

THE ROLE OF EXPECTATIONS

A third claim that price and quantity demanded may be positively related is to do with people's expectations. It is observed that a price increase could cause consumers to buy more of a good if they are expecting prices to rise even further in the future. Alternatively a price decrease will cause people to buy less if they expect that there will be further price falls to follow. They will delay their purchases. This argument however confuses a change in a price 'other things equal' with a situation of two variables changing, price and expectations. It is the change in expectations which causes the demand to change in this case.

Nigeria's Kerosene Cookers

Could kerosene be considered a Giffen good in Nigeria? The poor in this populous West African State cook on simple cookers fuelled by kerosene, a derivative of oil refining. The price of oil and hence kerosene is now rising markedly as world oil prices soar and heavy Nigerian subsidies are cut back. (See Reading in the Data Response Workbook). It is claimed that the price increase is causing more kerosene to be bought rather than less. The reasoning goes like this: as incomes rise the poor replace their simple stoves with cookers connected up to the electricity and gas main supplies. The stoves and hence their complement kerosene are inferior goods. As kerosene prices rise there is of course a negative substitution effect. However it is possible that the positive income effect outweighs this. The poor have very low incomes and cooking fuel forms a large part of their cash expenditure. As fuel prices soar poor households have lower real income to spend. They turn to more basic foods which require more cooking and hence more fuel is bought. There is a positively sloped demand curve over a certain price range *ie* the rise in price of kerosene leads to greater demand for kerosene, not less. So is kerosene a Giffen good in Nigeria, or could there be a different explanation?

Source: IB teachers Sue Hepper and Dorothy Foster. (April 2001)

SUPPLY

The Supply Function

The supply of a good is a function of its own price. Other things equal, the higher the price of a product the more sellers will supply. There is a positive relationship between price and quantity supplied. This is the *law of supply*.

Thus, with other things equal, the supply schedule of a good *x* will look like the one in Figure 2.9 and a supply curve like the one in Figure 2.10.

 Figure 2.9

Price of x (euros)	Quantity supplied (units of x)
1	0
2	5
3	10
4	15
5	20
6	25

A supply schedule – The law of supply is that price and quantity are positively related. When price rises quantity supplied rises. When price falls quantity supplied falls.

Figure 2.10

A *movement along the curve* will occur when the price of the good changes. We say there has been a *change in quantity supplied*.

A *shift of the curve* or a *change in supply* will occur if a variable other than price changes. Let us now examine the other major determinants of the supply of a good.

Firstly, the *prices of substitute producer goods* (not to be confused with consumer substitute goods). These are alternative goods the seller might supply. If the owner of a herd of goats supplies goats' milk to the market, then a rise in the price of goats' cheese might cause her to supply less milk. A fisherman supplying crabs to the market is likely to supply less if the price of lobsters rises and he can switch his efforts to catching more lobsters. If the price of beef falls farmers who can switch to sheep or pigs will do so, and the supply of lamb and pork will rise.

The *prices of factors of production* will affect the supply of a product. Less newspapers will be supplied at each price if the price of newsprint rises. More newspapers will be supplied if journalists cost less to employ.

Similarly, *government action* can affect the quantity supplied. One common action is to apply *indirect taxes* to goods thus increasing sellers' costs. Another is to offer *subsidies* to producers thus reducing their costs. These actions will shift the supply curve to the left, Figure 2.11, and to the right, Figure 2.12, respectively.

Figure 2.11

The supply curve of good x shifts to the left when a tax is imposed on good x.

Figure 2.12

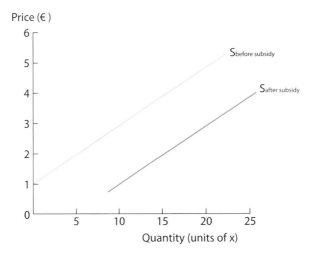

The suppy curve of good x shifts to the right when good x is subsidised.

In Italy, train travel is subsidised, so more train services are supplied at any given price. In Sweden alcohol is taxed highly, and thus less is supplied at each price.

Improvements in *technology* will cause supply to increase *ie* the supply curve shifts to the right. New applications of electronic technology are currently increasing the supply of many goods and services *eg* mobile telephones and car navigation systems.

The *weather* is a very important determinant in the supply of most agricultural products. Good summer weather may increase grain harvests dramatically. A severe frost may wipe out a large part of coffee and citrus fruit crops.

In summary the supply function can be written as:

$$Q_{Sx} = fP_x\,;\,P_s\,;\,P_f\,;\,G\,;\,\text{technology; weather; etc.}$$

Where P_x is own price; P_s other product substitute prices; P_f factor prices and G government policy.

INTERACTION OF SUPPLY AND DEMAND TO FORM EQUILIBRIUM PRICE AND QUANTITY

Having initially defined a market we have since studied demand and supply separately. Now we bring demand and supply together again. If we plot both demand and supply schedules next to each other as in Figure 2.13 and then plot them on the same graph as in Figure 2.14, we can plot the unique equilibrium price and equilibrium quantity.

Figure 2.13

P_x	Qd_x (kilos)	Qs_x (kilos)		Effect on price
6	50	110	Excess supply	↓
5	60	100	Excess supply	↓
4	70	90	Excess supply	↓
3	80	80	Equilibrium	–
2	90	70	Excess demand	↑
1	100	60	Excess demand	↑

Figure 2.14

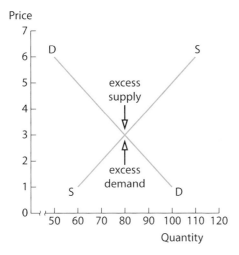

In both schedules and diagrams it can be clearly seen that quantity demanded and quantity supplied are equal at a price of $3: at this price 80 kilos are demanded and 80 kilos are supplied. The *market clears*. This is known as the *equilibrium* point with $3 being the *equilibrium price* and 80 kilos being the *equilibrium quantity*. The market is at equilibrium, in balance. There is no upward or downward pressure on this price.

Who Will Type Your Extended Essay?

The following advertisements appear in today's *Daily Information*, a broadsheet which is posted in Oxford (England) each week.

Word processing, including from tapes. Tel. Cathy 779031	**Desk-top publishing.** Quality leaflets, posters, brochures etc. Samples available. Tel. Aaron 510462 (eves) 310011 (day)	**Self-service word processing,** disk transfers, printing, laminating, 7 days a week. PCs and Macs. D.I. Computers, 31 Warnborough Rd Oxford

Questions

1) What have these advertisements to do with the theory of the market?
2) If you want your extended essay typed professionally, what further piece of information will you need to know by telephoning the advertisers?
3) Cathy agrees to type your essay at a rate of £5 per thousand words. How would your request for her to do this be classified in market terms?

At any other point there is *disequilibrium*. There is either an excess of demand, that is a shortage; or there is an excess of supply, a glut. At any price lower then $3 there is excess demand. For example, at a price of $1 the quantity demanded is 100 kilos whilst supply is only 60 kilos. This shortage in the market will tend to force the price up towards equilibrium.

Willing buyers who cannot obtain the good will offer a higher price. Sellers realising they can obtain more than $1 and still sell all their goods will raise the price. An auction house is a very good place to see excess demand acting quickly to raise prices.

At any price above $3 there is excess supply in the market. A glut forms. With a surplus in the market, traders cut prices to get rid of the excess. For example clothes shops and shoe shops have frequent sales to get rid of unsold stock by cutting their prices.

The concept of equilibrium in a market is very, very important. A great deal of economic debate centres around whether particular markets do clear in practice. There are often big players in individual markets who can prevent the free interplay of supply or demand by exercising some monopoly power. These include government, large companies and labour unions. Thus the European Union sets farm prices higher than a market would, in order to help farmers. They do this by using the force of law. The Sierra Leone and Zambian governments set food prices lower than the market price to help consumers, again using the power of the law. Centrally planned economies like the former USSR overruled the majority of their markets and set their own planned prices. The vast majority of producers of manufactured goods and services in market economies exert some power over the market to prevent their prices fluctuating and to keep them higher than they would otherwise be.

Labour Unions too are in the business of exerting power. In this case collective power, to keep the price of labour higher than it otherwise would be.

However, the forces of demand and supply are themselves very powerful and are a force to be reckoned with, even if the big players do try to control them. This will be highlighted in the following section on price controls.

Oil Prices and the War in the Gulf

In July 1990 the price of oil fell to $13 a barrel. Iraq badly needed more revenue from its oil exports and repeatedly asked its smaller Gulf neighbour Kuwait to produce less oil. Kuwait refused. Iraq's army invaded Kuwait and closed down the Kuwaiti oil field. A group of countries led by the United States attacked Iraq, effectively closing down its oil production and exports as well. With the oil fields of both Kuwait and Iraq out of action the world supply of oil fell by 4 million barrels a day. Oil prices rose over the next few weeks to over $40 a barrel.

PRICE CONTROLS

Price controls are prices which are imposed upon a market so that the control price prevails and not the equilibrium price. *Maximum prices* or *ceiling prices* are imposed below the equilibrium price, designed to help the consumer by making prices cheaper than they would otherwise be. *Minimum prices* or *floor prices* are imposed above market equilibrium, designed to help producers by making prices higher than they would otherwise be. Simple economic analysis will show us what consequences should be expected from imposing controlled prices.

Maximum (Ceiling) Price

Figure 2.15 shows a market where the equilibrium price is at $0p_1$ and the equilibrium quantity is at $0q_1$. A maximum price is imposed at $0p_2$. Thus sellers are not allowed to sell the product for more than $0p_2$. (Note that a maximum price will always be below equilibrium – there is no point at all in legislating for a maximum price above its market price). The maximum price forms an upper limit or 'ceiling' just as a ceiling forms an upper boundary to a room. Imposing a maximum price is usually designed to benefit poorer consumers.

Figure 2.15 – Price Controls: Maximum Price

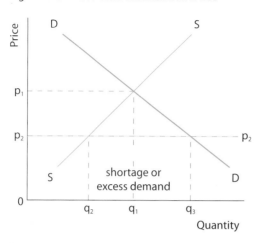

Notice, however, that because price is now lower than equilibrium, fewer people enjoy the product. Quantity supplied is now at $0q_2$, as producers reduce their quantity supplied, whilst quantity demanded increases to $0q_3$.

There is a situation of excess demand or shortage. The action to reduce the price has benefited those consumers who are able to buy the product, but many cannot because demand is now greater than supply.

If a government, or other agency, prevents a market from allocating resources according to supply and demand, then it must substitute some other non-market or planning mechanism to allocate resources instead. One mechanism commonly used is *queuing (forming lines)*, consumers may physically stand in line or do it indirectly by entering their names onto a waiting list.

Another mechanism is *rationing*, where the relatively small amount of production is shared in some way amongst the numerous customers. In addition the government could reduce the shortage problem by *subsidising* the product. This will shift the supply curve to the right and reduce excess demand. This, however, will mean that taxpayers are then subsidising the consumers of the good.

The existence of excess demand may lead to the development of a *parallel market* (parallel markets were formerly known as *black markets*). The government will need police or inspectors to stop this happening – but of course this incurs costs, compared to a free market which does not require such enforcement. The parallel market exists because at price $0p_2$ there is excess demand. Consumers represented by q_2q_3 in Figure 2.15 cannot obtain a product that they want. Moreover they are all willing to pay much more than $0p_2$ to enjoy the product. (The demand curve is, everywhere above the line p_2p_2, showing how much would be demanded if price could move.) Some of these consumers, those who would be willing to pay the highest prices, will be willing to offer more than Op_2 to those consumers, Oq_2, who did receive the good. Some of the consumers who don't value the good so highly may be tempted to sell at a price higher than Op_2. In addition there is likely to be a third group of people who will enter the business of parallel markets (black marketeering), acting as buyers and sellers of the good to make a profit from the trading itself.

Wherever you live in the world you will probably be able to find examples of this. Find out if there are maximum price controls on any product. In former (and present-day) communist countries low planned prices for most products were normal. Housing, food, clothes, and cars could not be obtained at market prices. Queuing for consumer goods was common – it was said that under communism a Moscow housewife would spend on average 3 hours a day standing in line. Shops were often completely sold out due to excess demand. *Consumer durables* like cars were obtained by joining a waiting list, and housing obtained by rationing and waiting lists. In Poland it took 7 years to move through the waiting list for cars.

During war time, supply is often restricted, leading to price increases. In order to keep prices low, rationing is introduced to keep public morale up. This was very common in Western Europe during World War II and in the many localised wars since that time. Parallel markets flourish during wars.

Many countries set a low price on their currency or foreign exchange. By setting a low price (exchange rate) the government intends that the country's exports are cheap to buy, and imports expensive to buy. This has been a common ploy of those poor countries which wish to encourage the growth of exports and to protect their home industries by discouraging imports. Exchange controls are substituted for a freely floating market exchange rate. Exchange controls involve rationing, bureaucracy and queuing. Parallel markets and corruption grow as a result.

Price controls are commonly observed at unique sporting events, like football finals, world championship boxing matches, tennis championships and so on. Popular rock concerts are also often organised like this. With a unique event, a price is set by the organisers. To make absolutely certain the stadium will be full, and to ensure younger, poorer fans can attend, the price is often set relatively low. Look out for such an event in your region of the world and you are likely to see excess demand, queuing, waiting-lists, rationing and parallel market techniques of resource allocation.

Rent Controls – New York and Moscow

In a market, the price of hiring accommodation (renting) is determined by demand and supply. Demand will depend on incomes, taste, prices of other goods and expectations. Some people will prefer to spend a lot of their income on where they live while others will prefer to spend more on other goods, like cars, clothes, eating-out, travel or investing in their business. Some will prefer better accommodation but are limited by their income. All of the factors will be reflected in the demand curve, see Figure 2.16. More rented accommodation will be demanded the lower is the rent. The figure also shows the supply curve. If rents are high there is a strong incentive for builders to build more rental units, for home owners to rent out their houses or even rent out spare rooms in their houses. The market rent is established at point A where demand and supply intersect.

📊 Figure 2.16

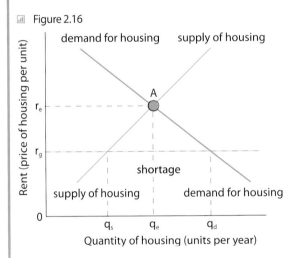

Some people who would like housing at rent r_g do not get it. All of those people represented by the demand curve to the right of point A would like to have rented accommodation but are not able or willing to pay for it. They will remain at home with parents, share accommodation, rent cheaper rooms or live in cheaper neighbourhoods. Very few will be homeless, yet all would *wish* that housing were cheaper. The people who are getting housing, above point A on the demand curve, would also like cheaper housing. They would then have more money to spend on other things.

continued on next page...

Governments are often persuaded by their citizens that housing *ought* to be more affordable and that rent controls are therefore desirable. Many governments and city councils do in fact intervene and impose a price ceiling on rents. New York is one such city. However elementary economics should enable you to predict the outcome. Quantity demanded will increase. At the same time quantity supplied will decrease. It will no longer be profitable to build to rent. Existing rentals will be taken off the rental market and sold. It will no longer be worthwhile for homeowners to rent out rooms to pay for the inconvenience of having someone else in the house. A shortage will develop (q_s-q_d). Property will deteriorate as the maintenance will be less worth while. As price cannot now allocate this scarce resource, new methods develop. When a house comes onto the market people will race to be the first to get it. They will try to be the first to buy the evening paper and be ready to rush instantly to a house in response to a new advertisement. People will have to join long waiting lists. Bribes will be offered to agents or landlords who control apartments. In New York some people in rent controlled apartments 'sell' their tenancy when they leave. Well off people are just as likely to benefit from the rent controls as the poor. Many celebrities in New York have rent controlled apartments. In Moscow under the communists house rentals were very, very low; $10 a month for an apartment. It was difficult for President Yeltsin to raise rents due to the expected political backlash.

Question

Why should Moscow City Council have wished to raise rents? What would your knowledge of markets have led you to expect to find in the Moscow housing market?

Tickets for U2 – USA

The following is extracted from a story in the Washington Post. Four students slept in a car for four nights to maintain their position of first in line at the ticket office at the JFK Stadium. It was predicted that the ticket office, due to open at 8am, would run out of tickets within an hour, due to the popularity of the group U2. The students plan to sell their $28.50 tickets for several hundred dollars to other individuals. The buyers have jobs and therefore cannot afford the time to wait in line, but are willing to pay the students several hundred dollars for a ticket. When the band played in Los Angeles some profiteers were selling tickets at $1200 each. In Washington, brokers had stationed students and unemployed people in line several days before tickets went on sale, in order to snap up hundreds of the best seats.

Source: Washington Post April 25, 1992

Questions

1) What is the equilibrium price for tickets for the U2 concert in Washington?

2) What is the method of resource allocation employed?

3) What is the opportunity cost of time to the four students compared to those they sell their tickets to?

Minimum (or Floor) Prices

A minimum price is a downward limit or a 'floor' under which price must not fall. In this case the authority will be aiming to protect the supplier. In Figure 2.17 the equilibrium price $0p_1$ and quantity $0q_2$ are shown. A floor price is set at $0p_2$. This is the minimum price that this product may now be sold for. It is clear that at this relatively high price less of the product is demanded, $0q_2$ in fact, and that more is supplied *ie* $0q_3$. The amount q_2q_3 is an excess supply. There is a surplus or glut of this product. The price controlling authority now has the problem of getting rid of the surplus. It cannot be sold on this market – otherwise price would fall and defeat the initial object of raising the price. A price support scheme is needed to replace the market system which has been overruled.

Figure 2.17 – Price Controls: Minimum Price

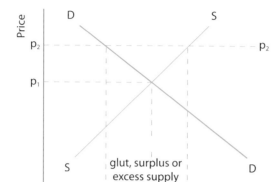

Many examples of setting prices higher than equilibrium are to be found in farm produce markets in the industrialised countries. The United States, Japan and the European
Union have all tried to protect farmers incomes by holding farm prices high. Planning
measures have had to be taken to deal with the excess supplies generated. One of these
schemes is called *set-aside* whereby farmers are paid not to produce, to leave their fields
fallow in order to reduce supplies. Another scheme uses *buffer stocks* whereby an agency
is given funds to buy and stockpile the product when there is a surplus, and to release it
onto the market when there is a shortage. With price set above equilibrium this is
doomed to produce surpluses in most years – and 'sugar mountains', 'wine lakes', and
'butter mountains' grow. The agency is then faced with getting rid of the surpluses. All of
the agricultural price support schemes incur an opportunity cost of course. Firstly they
produce high prices for consumers and higher burdens on tax payers. Set-aside means
people are being paid not to work. Surpluses in buffer stock schemes lead to embarrassing opportunity costs in disposing of the excess.

Good food may be buried, tipped into the sea or otherwise destroyed. It is sometimes
adulterated by the addition of colour dyes to make it suitable only for animal feed or fertiliser. In the days of the cold-war, European high cost food was sometimes sold to Eastern
European countries like the USSR. As this was 'outside' the normal market it didn't risk
bringing the price down and in addition some money was recovered towards the cost of
the scheme. However, it was still embarrassing that Europeans were producing high cost
food and selling it cheaply to their military enemies! Dumping it free or cheaply in poor
countries was not a costless solution either. It made the recipients aid dependent, and
worse, it harmed the farmers in LDCs. The conclusion to draw is that market forces are
very powerful, and interfering with markets should only be done if the benefits outweigh

the inevitable costs.

Another area of the economy in which minimum prices are often found is in the market for labour. Governments may pass legislation that requires minimum wages to be paid. These are usually to protect vulnerable groups of unskilled workers – females, young people or immigrants, for example. Paying a reasonable wage to those who work can be justified on humanitarian grounds. However, your ability to analyse price controls should enable you to see the opportunity cost of such an intervention in the labour market.

A minimum wage will be sought only if the market wage is considered too low. A minimum wage must therefore lie above equilibrium (Figure 2.18). W_{min} is the minimum wage in a labour market which would normally clear at a wage of we with Oe employment. The minimum wage will reduce the quanity demanded for labour to e_d as employers economise upon the use of labour, by substituting labour with machines, for example. The higher wage will attract a greater quantity supplied of labour – e_s in Figure 2.18. Thus excess supply of labour develops, $e_s - e_d$ in the diagram. This is known as *unemployment*. (There are however likely to be dynamic effects to a minimum wage. Our analysis is essentially static. Thus a minimum wage will increase spending in the economy which in turn will create more demand for output and employment).

📊 Figure 2.18

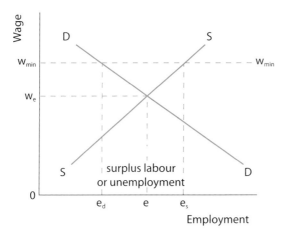

A minimum wage imposed in a labour market. Note that the words on the axes, wage and employment, are just specialized words for price and quantity.

Taxpayers Milked Instead of the Cows – USA

A year after deciding to pay farmers not to grow crops, President Reagan authorised payments to dairy farmers not to produce milk. The government agreed to pay farmers $10 for every 12.5 gallons cut from their normal production, up to 30% of total production. The law also agrees that the government should continue to prop up dairy prices by buying up surplus milk, cheese and butter that farmers cannot sell. The cost of buying and storing surplus milk had soared to $2.7 billion in the preceding year with surpluses remaining as large as ever. The Congressional Budget Office had concluded that paying farmers not to produce milk would save $1.7 billion over the next four years.

Question

Use a supply and demand diagram and analysis to explain why the US government has decided that taxpayers should pay dairy farmers not to produce.

Commodity Agreements

Commodities are a collective name for primary products like wheat or tin. The prices of commodities fluctuate much more than manufactures and services, partly due to wide supply changes.[4] Many commodities are produced in developed countries like the USA, Canada and Australia. However commodities are signally important to most of the poorest countries in the world. The LDCs (less developed countries) are predominantly primary producers. There have been many schemes which have attempted either to stabilize commodity prices or to raise them. Raising prices is of course popular with producers whilst consumers tend to prefer either price stabilization or free market prices. Attempts to raise prices involve restricting supply of the product by operating a producers' cartel[5] and issuing production quotas to members. Opec, an oil cartel, has been the most successful international cartel for a commodity. *Commodity agreements* to stabilize prices operate a *buffer stock.* They buy into, or sell from, this stock to reduce price movements. Sugar, tin, coffee and rubber have all been subject to international commodity agreements at some time. However the forces of the market undermine these schemes and few last very long. They are further discussed in Section 5 of the course.

MULTIPLE CHOICE QUESTIONS – MARKETS

1   In a market economy, a change in which of the following would lead to a change in the pattern of demand?

I   The population ages.

II   Income is redistributed more evenly.

III Advertising budgets increase.

A   I only   B   I and II   C   II and III   D   I, II and III

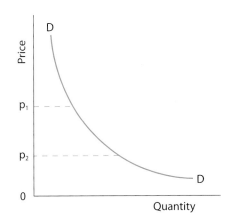

2   The diagram above illustrates the demand curve for cameras. If p_1 is the original equilibrium price, a fall in price to p_2 could have been caused by a fall in

A   real incomes.

B   raw material prices.

C   the price of film.

D   advertising expenditure on cameras.

Price ($)	Quantity demanded per month	Quantity supplied per month
200	10000	0
400	5000	0
600	1000	0
800	0	0
1000	0	500
1200	0	600
1400	0	700

3   The table above gives the demand and supply schedules for a new type of video phone. Which of the following is correct?

A   The equilibrium quantity lies between 1000 and 500 units per month.

B   The equilibrium price is $800.

C   There is excess supply at $200.

D   There is no market for the product.

4   Which of the following statements is incorrect? The demand curve for a good will be shifted to the left by

A   a rise in the price of complements.

B   a fall in the price of substitutes.

C   a successful advertising campaign.

D   a redistribution of income away from people consuming the good.

5   A good has a downward sloping demand curve and an upward sloping supply curve. Which of the following would result in a rise in both the price and the quantity demanded?

A   An increase in production costs.

B   More efficient production techniques.

C   A rise in incomes.

D   A fall in the price of a substitute.

6   The government imposes a tax on newspapers. This will cause

A   an increase in the supply of newspapers and an extension of demand.

B   a decrease in the supply of newspapers and a contraction of demand.

C   a decrease in demand for newspapers and a contraction of supply.

D   an increase in demand for newspapers and an extension of supply.

7 An LDC government reduces the subsidy on tractors. What effect will this have on the market for tractors?

A A shift in the demand curve and a decrease in price.

B A shift in the demand curve and an increase in price.

C A shift in the supply curve and an increase in price.

D A shift in the supply curve and a decrease in price.

8 The government intervenes in the market for rice. Which of the following would tend to raise the price of rice?

I   A tax on rice production.

II Intervention purchasing of rice.

III Rationing the consumption of rice.

A I only   B I and II   C II and III   D I, II and III

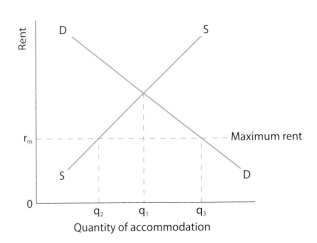

9 To help low income families a government imposes a maximum rent that landlords can charge for accommodation. In the diagram above this is shown as r_m. The effect of this action will be to

A raise the accommodation available from q_2 to q_3.

B raise the accommodation available from q_1 to q_3.

C lower the accommodation available from q_1 to q_2.

D lower the accommodation available from q_3 to q_1.

10 Supply and demand curves for videos are shown in the figure below.

A movement from A to B could be caused by

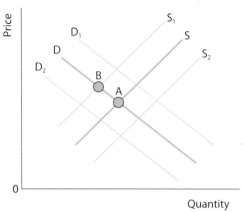

A   an increase in wages in the video industry.

B   an increase in incomes.

C   an increase in the availability of inputs used to produce videos.

D   a removal of tariff barriers on videos.

11 The supply curve for eating fish in Canada is graphed below.

Which of the following would not cause a movement from X to Y?

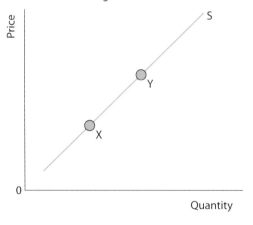

A   Publication of evidence proving that eating fish improves health.

B   An increase in subsidies to fishermen.

C   An increase in the price of meat.

D   An increase in the population of Canada.

12 If a maximum price is imposed on the price of tickets for the 2006 World Cup soccer final which of the following is (are) likely to occur?

I The development of a parallel market for tickets.

II Excess demand for tickets.

III Rationing of tickets.

A I only   B I and II   C II and III   D I, II and III

13 If a demand curve for good Y is drawn which of the following is not assumed to be constant?

A The price of good Y.

B The price of substitute goods.

C The price of complementary goods.

D Household's real income.

14 The demand curve for a normal good shifts to the right when

A the price of the good itself falls.

B the price of a complement falls.

C the price of a substitute falls.

D an indirect tax is imposed on the good.

HL ONLY

15 The demand curve for lamb slopes downwards because if the price of lamb falls
   A   more lamb will be for sale.
   B   the price of other meats will rise.
   C   consumers will buy less of other meats.
   D   lamb will be seen as an inferior good.

16 A Giffen good is a good whose
   A   demand rises with income.
   B   demand rises with a rise in its price.
   C   demand rises with a rise in the price of a substitute.
   D   income and substitution effects work in the same direction.

17 The relationship between Giffen goods and inferior goods is best described by which of the following statements?
   A   All Giffen goods are inferior goods, but not all inferior goods are Giffen goods.
   B   All inferior goods are Giffen goods, but not all Giffen goods are inferior goods.
   C   Giffen goods are the same thing as inferior goods.
   D   Giffen goods are never inferior goods.

2.2   ELASTICITIES

Elasticity is the measure of responsiveness in one variable when another variable changes. We use the analogy of elastic – because elastic, as it's made of rubber, stretches when pulled. Thus when the price of a good changes we can observe the degree to which quantity demanded changes (or stretches). It is possible to discuss the elasticity of any variable with respect to a change in any other. In the IB courses we examine four of the most important: *price elasticity of demand*, *price elasticity of supply*, *income elasticity of demand*, and *cross price elasticity of demand*.

PRICE ELASTICITY OF DEMAND

The law of demand states that quantity demanded changes inversely in relation to price. In this section, we learn to measure the *degree* of change with relation to a change in price and apply the concept – that is, the price elasticity of demand to real economic situations.

Price elasticity of demand is measured as follows:

$$\text{Price Elasticity of Demand} = \frac{\text{percentage change in quantity demanded}}{\text{percentage change in price}}$$

Using letters this can be shortened to:

$$PED = \frac{\%\Delta Qd}{\%\Delta P}$$

Thus, if the price of a product increases by 5% and the quantity demanded fell by 10%, the price elasticity of demand is:

$$PED = \frac{\%\Delta Qd}{\%\Delta P} = \frac{-10\%}{+5\%} = -2$$

If price falls by 2% and quantity increases by 1%, then:

$$PED = \frac{\%\Delta Qd}{\%\Delta P} = \frac{+1\%}{-2\%} = -0.5$$

NOTES ON THE MEASUREMENT OF ELASTICITY

Elasticity is always expressed as a decimal figure. It is expressed as a pure number: there are no units, it is not -2 *something*, it is just -2.

Price elasticity of demand is always negative (see below). Due to this the minus sign is sometimes omitted. Thus, in the examples above it would be acceptable to say that elasticity is 2, and elasticity is 0.5. PED must always be negative because of the inverse relationship of the law of demand. If price increases (+) then quantity demand falls (–); if price falls (–) then quantity demanded increases (+). This is clear if these signs are put into the formula:

$$PED = \frac{\%\Delta Qd}{\%\Delta P} \frac{-}{+} = -\text{ and } \frac{+}{-} = -$$

AN ALTERNATIVE FORMULA FOR PRICE ELASTICITY OF DEMAND

If the price and quantity figures are expressed in a price schedule, rather than as percentages, it is easier to calculate elasticity by using a modification of the formula above, rather than converting each one separately to a percentage. Thus

$$\text{Price Elasticity of Demand} = \frac{\text{percentage change in quantity demanded}}{\text{percentage change in price}}$$

can be rewritten as:

$$\frac{\dfrac{\Delta Q}{Q} \times \dfrac{100}{1}}{\dfrac{\Delta P}{P} \times \dfrac{100}{1}}$$

This is merely showing how a change in quantity ΔQ can be expressed as a percentage of quantity, Q, or how a change in price ΔP can be expressed as a percentage of price, P. 100/1 appears above and below the line and cancls out leaving the expression:

$$\frac{\dfrac{\Delta Q}{Q}}{\dfrac{\Delta P}{P}}$$

This in turn is rearranged to:

$$\frac{\Delta Q}{Q} \times \frac{P}{\Delta P}$$

In an introductory economics course like this, it is satisfactory to use the first price and the first quantity method in calculating elasticity. As an example, if the price of a cup of coffee increases from *50¢* to *60¢* whilst the quantity demanded falls from *100* cups per day to *90* cups per day – the price P_1 is *50¢* and the quantity Q_1 is *100*. Thus:

$$\frac{\Delta Q}{Q_1} \times \frac{P_1}{\Delta P} = \frac{-10}{100} \times \frac{50}{10} = -0.5$$

ADDITIONAL FORMULAE FOR MEASUREMENT OF ELASTICITY

Using the first price and first quantity when measuring price elasticity of demand is not strictly correct, *ie*

$$\frac{\Delta Q}{Q_1} \times \frac{P_1}{\Delta P}$$

Elasticity should really be measured over the whole range of the change *ie* between Q_1 and Q_2, and between P_1 and P_2. Thus it would be neither better nor worse to use P_2 and Q_2 in the formula *ie*

$$\frac{\Delta Q}{Q_2} \times \frac{P_2}{\Delta P}$$

An improvement over using P_1 and Q_2, however, is to take the average of P_1 and P_2, and the average of Q_1 and Q_2, *ie*

$$\frac{P_1 + P_2}{2} \quad \text{and} \quad \frac{Q_1 + Q_2}{2}$$

We are then measuring elasticity at the mid-point of the arc of change, an improvement over taking either end of the arc. The formula is therefore:

$$\frac{\Delta Q}{\frac{Q_1 + Q_2}{2}} \times \frac{\frac{P_1 + P_2}{2}}{\Delta P}$$

In the previous example of coffee prices increasing from 50¢ to 60¢, and the quantity demanded falling from 100 cups to 90 cups, the three formulae give different results:

$$\frac{\Delta Q}{Q_1} \times \frac{P_1}{\Delta P} = \frac{-10}{100} \times \frac{50}{10} = -0.5$$

$$\frac{\Delta Q}{Q_2} \times \frac{P_2}{\Delta P} = \frac{-10}{90} \times \frac{60}{10} = -0.66$$

$$\frac{\Delta Q}{\frac{Q_1 + Q_2}{2}} \times \frac{\frac{P_1 + P_2}{2}}{\Delta P} = \frac{-10}{95} \times \frac{55}{10} = -0.58$$

Elasticity can be different at every point along the arc of change. Thus, continuing with our coffee example, if we graph the demand curve for coffee as in Figure 2.19, it can be seen that price elasticity of demand is different at each of the three points: *a*, where first price and quantity are used; *b*, where second price and quantity are used; and *c*, where the mid-point is used.

In fact, elasticity is different at every point, so the greater the arc on the demand curve, the greater the change of price, and the wider is the disparity between the three methods. There is a mathematical technique in *calculus* for measuring the degree of change at a specific point. It is known as *differentiation*, and you are likely to meet it if you are studying Higher or Standard Level mathematics. Students are not expected to be able to calculate elasticity, other than by the simplest formula, but it is useful to be aware of the limitations of doing this, and to be aware of the existence of more accurate methods.

Figure 2.19 – Price Elasticity of Demand

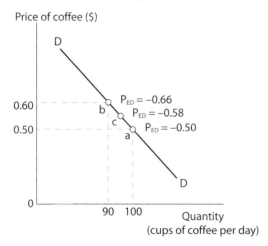

Price elasticity of demand is different at every point on a straight line demand curve.

For many purposes in economics a precise figure of elasticity may not be required. The concept of 'relative' elasticity may be used instead. In this case elasticity is related to one.

An elasticity of one is known as *unit elasticity*. An elasticity greater than one is known as *elastic*. An elasticity of less than one is known as *inelastic*. See Figure 2.20. Thus it might be useful to describe cigarettes and alcohol as being *price inelastic in demand*; or movie tickets or foreign vacations as being *price elastic in demand*. Note that it is incorrect to say foreign vacations are elastic, only one thing is elastic and that is the product elastic itself! Foreign vacations are more correctly described as *price elastic in demand*.

⊞ Figure 2.20 – Price Elasticity

Price elasticity	>1	elastic
Price elasticity	=1	unit elastic
Price elasticity	<1	inelastic

Price elasticity is related to one (1).

PRICE ELASTICITY OF DEMAND AND SLOPE

Care must be taken not to confuse elasticity with *slope*. It is tempting to conclude that a steep curve is inelastic and a flat curve is elastic. However any curve can be made to have a steep slope or a gentle slope merely by altering the scale of the axis. Figure 2.21 and Figure 2.21 illustrate this.

It is however possible to compare the demand elasticity for two products by graphing them on the same diagram. Thus in Figure 2.23, $D_1 D_1$ is *less* elastic than $D_2 D_2$, or put another way, $D_2 D_2$ is more elastic than $D_1 D_1$ at any price. This is a relative statement, however. We cannot tell the actual elasticity of either without measuring them.

⊞ Figures 2.21 and 2.22 – Elasticity should not be confused with Slope

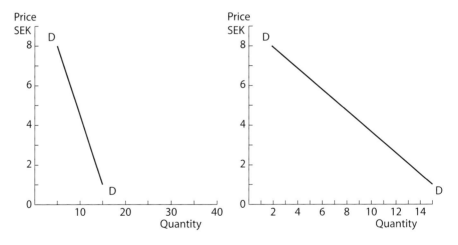

The price change in Swedish Krona (SEK) has exactly the same response in both graphs. The demand curve in Figure 2.22 only appears to be more elastic than the demand curve in Figure 2.21, because the quantity scale has been drawn larger.

Figure 2.23 – Slope and Elasticity

Two demand curves on the same diagram can be compared for elasticity. D_2D_2 is more elastic than D_1D_1, although the actual elasticity of neither curve is known.

That elasticity and slope are not the same thing can be shown by calculating price elasticity of demand for each price change shown in the demand schedule, and demand diagram, shown in Figure 2.24. Using the formula:

$$\frac{\Delta Q}{Q_1} \times \frac{P_1}{\Delta P}$$

the elasticity is calculated for each price change: (1) from \$0 to \$1; (2) from \$1 to \$2, and so on. This gives price elasticities as follows:

1 $\quad \frac{\Delta Q}{Q_1} \times \frac{P_1}{\Delta P} = \frac{1}{5} \times \frac{0}{1} = 0$

2 $\quad \frac{\Delta Q}{Q_1} \times \frac{P_1}{\Delta P} = \frac{1}{4} \times \frac{1}{1} = \frac{1}{4} = 0.25$

3 $\quad \frac{\Delta Q}{Q_1} \times \frac{P_1}{\Delta P} = \frac{1}{3} \times \frac{2}{1} = \frac{2}{3} = 0.67$

4 $\quad \frac{\Delta Q}{Q_1} \times \frac{P_1}{\Delta P} = \frac{1}{2} \times \frac{3}{1} = \frac{3}{2} = 1.5$

5 $\quad \frac{\Delta Q}{Q_1} \times \frac{P_1}{\Delta P} = \frac{1}{1} \times \frac{4}{1} = \frac{4}{1} = 4$

6 $$\frac{\Delta Q}{Q_1} \times \frac{P_1}{\Delta P} = \frac{1}{0} \times \frac{5}{1} = \frac{5}{0} = \infty$$

This shows that, although the slope of a straight line is clearly constant, the price elasticity of demand is different at every point.

Figure 2.24 – Slope and Elasticity

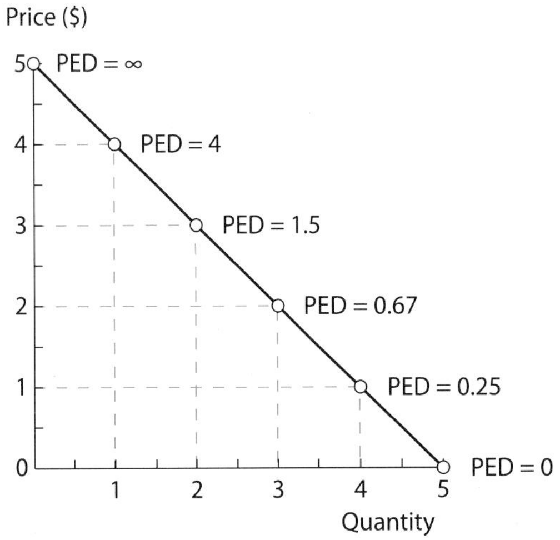

Price ($)	Quantity demanded (litres)
0	5
1	4
2	3
3	2
4	1
5	0

A demand schedule and demand diagram illustrate that price elasticity and the slope of a curve are not the same. The slope is constant but the elasticity is different at every point.

There are, however, three exceptions to this. There are three diagrams where the slope of the demand curve has the same elasticity at any point, and where the elasticity can be known just by looking at the diagram. These are where the demand curves are vertical, horizontal, or the slope of a rectangular hyperbole. See Figures 2.25, 2.26, and 2.27.

In Figure 2.25, the vertical curve illustrates one limit of elasticity, perfect inelasticity or zero elasticity. This means the same quantity, q, will be bought at *any* price.

In Figure 2.26, the horizontal curve illustrates the other limit of elasticity, perfect elasticity or infinite elasticity. At price P_1 an infinite amount will be demanded. At any other price, *eg* 1¢ more or 1¢ less, nothing at all will be bought. There is an infinite change in quantity demanded for any change in price:

$$PED = \frac{\%\ \Delta Qd}{\%\ \Delta P} = \frac{\infty}{\Delta P} = \infty$$

In Figure 2.27, the properties of the curve are such that any percentage change on one axis, x%, is offset by an exactly opposite change on the other axis *ie* also x%. In other words $P \times Q$ is constant. Thus:

$$PED \ = \ \frac{\% \ \Delta Qd}{\% \ \Delta P} \ = \ \frac{x\%}{x\%} \ = \ 1$$

📊 Figure 2.25, 2.26 and 2.27 – Slope and elasticity

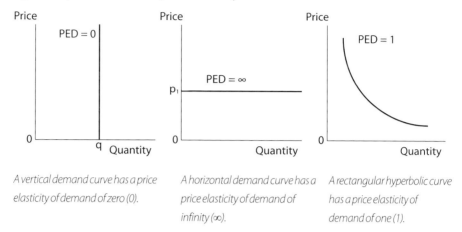

A vertical demand curve has a price elasticity of demand of zero (0).

A horizontal demand curve has a price elasticity of demand of infinity (∞).

A rectangular hyperbolic curve has a price elasticity of demand of one (1).

Although these elasticities are unlikely ever to represent real goods or services, they do nevertheless have practical applications in economics. By understanding the properties at extremes of elasticity, we can get a good approximation of what happens to real products with relatively price elastic or relatively price inelastic properties.

PRICE ELASTICITY AND TOTAL REVENUE

The total revenue *(TR)* of a business is the income that it receives from selling its product. This is arrived at by multiplying the price of the product by the quantity it sells, *ie* $TR = P \times Q$

If the price of the product changes up and down, how the total revenue will change depends upon how the quantity purchased responds to the price change. This is precisely what we have been measuring with price elasticity of demand. If the product price changes one way, and quantity demanded changes by an equal percentage in the opposite direction, total revenue will remain constant. That is to say, if price elasticity of demand is unity, total revenue will remain constant when price changes.

If a product is price elastic in demand then a change in price will lead to a bigger percentage quantity response. Thus if price falls, quantity increases by more, and total revenue will rise. If price rises, quantity will fall by a bigger percentage, and the total revenue will fall.

If a product is price inelastic, then a change in price is met by a relatively small change in quantity. Thus if price rises total revenue will rise. If price falls total revenue will fall. This is summarised in the table in Figure 2.28, and illustrated in the Figures 2.29, 2.30, and 2.31. Rectangles are highlighted to show *TR* gained and *TR* lost.

Figure 2.28 - Price Elasticity of Demand and Total Revenue

	Price Increase	Price Decrease
P_{ED} 1	Quantity falls more than proportionally. TR falls.	Quantity rises more than proportionally. TR rises.
$P_{ED} = 1$	Quantity falls proportionally. TR is constant.	Quantity rises proportionally. TR is constant.
P_{ED} 1	Quantity falls less than proportionally. TR rises.	Quantity rises less than proportionally. TR falls.

Figure 2.29 – Price Elastic Demand

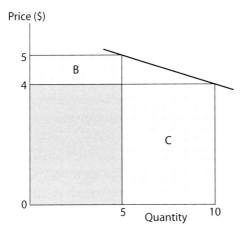

1 **P rises**, *Q falls proportionately more; therefore TR falls.*
        (Rectangle B is gained; rectangle C is lost).
2 **P falls**, *Q rises proportionately more; therefore TR rises.*
        (Rectangle B is lost; rectangle C is gained).

📊 Figure 2.30 – Price Inelastic Demand

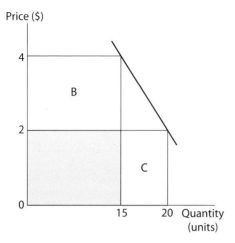

1 **P rises**, *Q falls proportionately less; therefore TR rises.*
          (Rectangle B is gained, rectangle C is lost).
2 **P falls**, *Q rises proportionately less, TR falls.*
          (Rectangle B is lost, rectangle C is gained).

📊 Figure 2.31 – Unit Elastic Demand

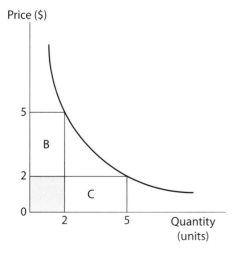

1 **Price rises**, *Q falls proportionately; TR remains constant.*
          (Rectangle B is equal in area to rectangle C).
2 **Price falls**, *Q rises proportionally; TR remains constant*
          (Rectangle B is equal in area to rectangle C).

It is therefore important for a business to know the price elasticity of demand of its products when it comes to setting or changing prices.

INCOME ELASTICITY OF DEMAND

In a demand function, income is a major determinant of demand; household income impacts on the household demand for goods and services; and, national income impacts on the national demand for goods and services

$$Qdx \; = \; fPx; \; Ps; \; Pc; \; Y; \; taste; \; population; \; etc$$

We have already noted in Section 2.1 that when income changes, the quantity demanded of most goods and services changes in the same direction. These are *'normal'* goods. The quantity demanded of some other goods, known as *'inferior'* goods, changes in the opposite direction. The responsiveness of quantity demanded to changes in income can be measured in the same way as responsiveness to price. This concept, unsurprisingly, is known as *income elasticity of demand*, and is measured as follows:

$$\text{Income Elasticity of Demand} = \frac{\text{percentage change in quantity demanded}}{\text{percentage change in income}}$$

and in letters:

$$YED_x = \frac{\%\Delta Qd_x}{\%\Delta Y}$$

The alternative way of expressing this is:

$$YED_x = \frac{\Delta Q_x}{Q_1} \times \frac{Y_1}{\Delta Y}$$

The terms for describing elasticity are the same. Goods with an elasticity equal to one are known as *unit income elastic*; greater than one as *income elastic*; and less than one as *income inelastic*.

The sign of elasticity, however, may be positive *or* negative and is very significant. With *normal goods* when income increases quantity demanded increases so income elasticity is positive:

$$YED \; = \; \frac{+}{+} \; = \; +$$

Similarly when income falls quantity demanded falls. Again income elasticity is positive:

$$YED \ = \ \frac{-}{-} \ = \ +$$

So all normal goods have positive income elasticity. They may, in fact, be defined in that way.

Similarly, inferior goods have negative elasticity, and may also be defined in that way. Thus when income rises the quantity demanded of an inferior good falls:

$$YED \ = \ \frac{-}{+} \ = \ -$$

When income falls quantity demanded rises:

$$YED \ = \ \frac{+}{-} \ = \ -$$

CROSS PRICE ELASTICITY OF DEMAND

The responsiveness or sensitivity of the quantity demanded of a good may also be measured against the price of other goods. This is known as *cross price elasticity*. It is important for a business to know how sensitive demand for its own products is to the prices of complementary and substitute goods. The method of measurement of cross price elasticity is very similar to price and income elasticities. Note that as with the income elasticity of demand, the sign is very significant.

$$\text{Cross Price Elasticity of Demand}_{x,y} \ = \ \frac{\text{percentage change in quantity demanded of good}_x}{\text{percentage change in price of good}_y}$$

$$\text{or } Cross \ PED_{x,y} \ = \frac{\% \Delta Qd_x}{\% \Delta P_y}$$

$$\text{alternatively } Cross \ PED_{x,y} \ = \frac{\Delta Q_x}{Q_{1_x}} \times \frac{P_{1_y}}{\Delta P_y}$$

COMPLEMENTARY GOODS

If the two goods x and y are complements to each other *eg* compact discs and compact disc players, then an increase in the price of one will lead to a fall in the quantity demanded of the other. The cross price elasticity of demand will be negative.

$$Cross \ PED_{x,y} \ = \frac{\% \Delta Qd_x}{\% \Delta P_y} \ = \ \frac{-}{+} \ or \ \frac{+}{-} \ = \ -$$

Goods with negative cross price elasticity may be defined as *complementary goods.*

SUBSTITUTE GOODS

Substitute goods have positive cross price elasticity. Thus if Coca-Cola raise their prices, the quantity demanded of Pepsi Cola rises:

$$Cross\ PED_{x,y} = \frac{\%\Delta Qd_x}{\%\Delta P_y} = \frac{+}{+}\ or\ \frac{-}{-} = +$$

A definition of substitute goods is those that have positive cross price elasticity.

ELASTICITY OF SUPPLY

Elasticity of supply is the measure of responsiveness of the quantity supplied to a change in price. It is measured as follows:

$$Price\ Elasticity\ of\ Supply = \frac{percentage\ change\ in\ quantity\ supplied}{percentage\ change\ in\ price}$$

$$or\ PES_x = \frac{\%\Delta Q_{Sx}}{\%\Delta P_x}$$

The alternative formula is $PES_x = \frac{\Delta Q_{Sx}}{Q_1} \times \frac{P_1}{\Delta P_x}$

As the quantity supplied of a product changes positively with its price, the sign is always positive. So if the price of x increases, the quantity supplied increases; if the price of x falls, the quantity supplied falls.

$$PES = \frac{+}{+}\ or\ \frac{-}{-} = +$$

The slope of a supply curve is not the same as elasticity (see the discussion of demand elasticity, above). The price elasticity of supply of a product is likely to be different at every price *ie* different at all points along the supply curve. The exceptions to this are again threefold.

1 Where the supply curve is vertical the price elasticity of supply is zero.

$$PES_x = \frac{\Delta Q_{S_x}}{P_x} \times \frac{0}{\Delta P} = 0$$

The same quantity is supplied whatever the price (Figure 2.32).

Figure 2.32 – Price Elasticity of Supply and Slope

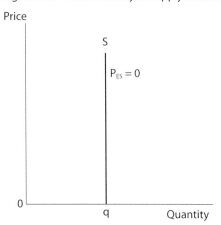

A vertical supply curve has an elasticity of zero.

2   Where the supply curve is horizontal the price elasticity of supply is infinitely elastic. An unlimited amount will be supplied at the price where the supply curve meets the vertical axis (Figure 2.33).

$$PES_x = \frac{\Delta Q_{S_x}}{P_x} \times \frac{\infty}{\Delta P} = \infty$$

Figure 2.33 – Price Elasticity of Supply and Slope

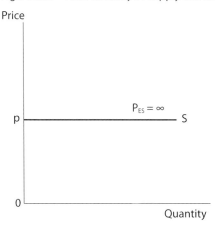

A horizontal supply curve has an elasticity of infinity.

3   Any straight line supply curve passing through the origin must have an elasticity of one. The percentage change on each axis will always be proportional (Figure 2.34).

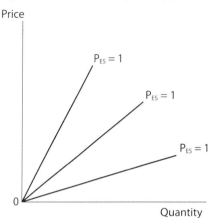

⤓ Figure 2.34 – Price Elasticity of Supply and Slope

A straight line supply curve from the origin has an elasticity of one.

DETERMINATION OF PRICE ELASTICITY OF DEMAND

Suppose you were to consider a range of goods and services. How would you know whether to expect whether they would be price elastic or price inelastic in demand? There are certain general characteristics of goods and services which can help you to decide.

1 The number and closeness of substitute goods

If the price of a product changes and there are many close substitutes, it is very easy for consumers to switch to, or away from, the product. If there are few substitutes, or the substitutes are not close substitutes, it is more difficult to change behaviour. For example, if the price of a particular brand of training shoe increases, say Nike, then there are many other brand possibilities to switch to. The products of the many other companies *eg* Reebok and Adidas are very close substitutes. If the price of all footwear rises, then the quantity of footwear demanded will be very price inelastic, because there is little to substitute for all footwear.

The example above follows a principle that the broader a product is defined, the fewer substitutes there will be. Thus the product sequence: footwear, sports footwear, trainers, Nike trainers, Nike Air trainers, white Nike Air trainers: would be a sequence from inelastic to very elastic, as the number of substitutes increases.

2   The passage of time

When price elasticity of demand is measured, the degree of elasticity will depend upon the time gap between the price changing and the recording of the new quantity figures. The longer the passage of time, the more elastic will be the quantity response. This is because consumers have a longer period of time in which to change their demand for the product.

For example, if train fares increase the demand for train travel will fall. However, the demand fall will be slight over the first days after the price increase as many people will need time to make alternative arrangements to travel by bus, bicycle, plane or car. As the days extend to weeks, weeks to months, and months to years the quantity demanded will change even more. Alternative modes of travel may appear, patterns of commuting to work may change.

3   Addiction

Certain goods are addictive. Alcohol and tobacco are examples. The price of an addictive good therefore may be relatively unimportant compared to the addictive determinant in the demand function. The price inelasticity of 'hard' drugs like heroin is very marked. If prohibition is strictly enforced, the parallel market price of a hard drug can rise to extraordinarily high levels. The helplessness of addicts to reduce demand is a significant factor behind burglary and theft as they attempt to raise money to pay drug dealers.

4   Proportion of income spent on the good

If a small proportion of income is spent on a good, *eg* on pencils or matches, a change in price has such a low income effect, the quantity demanded may be quite unresponsive. However, for goods which form a large part of spending, like housing or electricity in cold climate countries, the income effect is likely to be significant. A price increase may well force consumers to consider economising in that product.

5   Branding and Advertising

Businesses which produce products which have close substitutes try to reduce the number and closeness of those substitutes by branding their products and advertising. They will use the real or psychological differences of their particular brand and advertise these heavily. This is designed to increase consumer loyalty to that brand and thereby reduce the importance of the price element in the demand function. Entertainers and pop singers do much the same when selling their services. By dressing bizarrely or behaving extrovertly, they may instil consumer loyalty to their particular brand of entertainment, and in doing so, reduce the competition from substitute performers.

DETERMINATION OF PRICE ELASTICITY OF SUPPLY

We can also look at the factors which made supply more or less responsive to price changes *ie* the determination of price elasticity of supply.

1 The closeness of producer substitutes

A word of caution is required before proceeding. Producer substitutes are the different products a business can produce. These are not the same as consumer substitutes. All students are consumers and tend to understand consumer substitutes easily whereas few students are yet producers. Hence the caution not to confuse the two.

A close producer substitute to milk might be butter or cheese. A close producer substitute to glass windows might be mirrors or glass shelves (notice that these would *not* be regarded as consumer substitutes).

If a producer can produce several products, the quantity supplied of any one product will be quite price elastic. For example, a printer can print menus, wedding invitations, business cards, calendars, advertising sheets and much more. A change in price up or down of any one product will see an easy shift to, or from, another product.

If the producer cannot produce more than one product, then the supply will be very inelastic. The owners of copper mines are committed to producing copper, and continue to produce with little change in quantity when the price of copper changes.

2 The passage of time

When a price change occurs, the price elasticity will be greater the longer is the time that elapses between the price changing and measuring the quantity response. From the momentary time period to the very long run, the price elasticity of supply will increase.

As an example, consider the supply of salt-water fish in a local fish market for inshore fishing. Boats land their catch in the early hours of the morning. Now suppose that for some reason fish prices are particularly high. The momentary supply of fish is perfectly inelastic. The supply cannot increase that day, as it takes time to refuel boats, return to sea and catch more fish.

Over the week the supply might become a little more responsive as boats stay at sea for longer hours, as boat skippers delay refitting or repainting, and are less put off by bad weather.

If prices remain high over a period of months, the fish supply might increase further as new boats move to the area, and more labour is recruited and trained.

In the long run, new boats can be built, new nets and equipment purchased, harbours and fish loading facilities improved.

In the very long run new technology may be developed. Better boats, better fish finders, more powerful engines, and the development of fish farming are all possibilities.

Figure 2.35 illustrates how the passage of time is likely to increase the elasticity of supply of a product, in this case fresh fish.

Figure 2.35

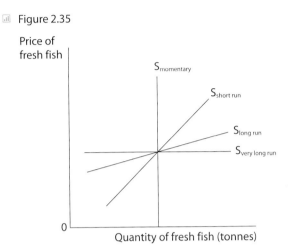

Price of
fresh fish

$S_{momentary}$

$S_{short\ run}$

$S_{long\ run}$

$S_{very\ long\ run}$

0

Quantity of fresh fish (tonnes)

The price elasticity of supply is likely to increase with the passage of time

3 Unused capacity and costs of inputs

If an industry is operating to full capacity, with all factors of production fully employed, it would be difficult to produce more in the short run. Supply would be inelastic to price increases. If, however, there was considerable spare capacity in the industry, then a price increase could produce a very elastic response as idle machines and unemployed workers were swiftly brought into production.

From the point of view of a business which is considering expansion, the relative availability of factors of production affects the costs of inputs. The factors of production which are at, or close to, full employment will enjoy a high price rise if the firms that use them expand supply. If there is unused capacity, however, more can be employed without significantly raising the price or cost of those inputs.

APPLICATIONS OF CONCEPTS OF ELASTICITY

We have already looked at the significance of price elasticity of demand to businesses when they set the prices of new products, or alter the prices of existing products. The price elasticity of demand has a direct effect upon the total revenue of the firm, and is therefore of great importance.

The income elasticity of demand for a product is also of great significance to businesses. If the long term trend of income is one of growth in a country, then normal goods will see increased sales, and inferior goods will suffer a drop in sales, other things being equal.

The degree of price elasticity is also important to businesses producing normal goods. In a situation of longer term economic growth the industries which will expand will be those which are most income elastic. Many of the world's fastest growing industries at this time are in the service sector. Health care, education, holidays, entertainment and foreign travel are all income elastic. By and large, businesses in these industries might expect long term growth.

Income elasticity has a particular significance for economic growth and development. The long run trend of world income is one of growth. As incomes rise households demand more of all normal goods. The more income elastic the goods and services the more they are demanded. The less income elastic they are, the lower is the increased demand. Most primary goods are income inelastic in demand so the primary sectors of economies are often poor compared to the secondary (manufacturing) and tertiary (service) sectors. A major characteristic of the Less Developed Countries is that they are heavily reliant upon primary production – forestry, farming, fishing and mining. Developed country production by contrast is dominated by manufacturing and service production. As world income grows there is increasing demand for the products of the rich countries and fairly static demand for the products of the poor.[6] The income gap widens.

However for any business the responsiveness of its products to income is important. National income or output is subject to booms and slumps (known as the business cycle or trade cycle). Products with high income elasticity of demand will be subject to much greater swings in demand, both up and down, than products which are income inelastic. Sales of furniture and cameras, for example, are much more sensitive to income swings than sales of food or alcohol. The latter industries will have much more stable sales figures than the former. See Figure 2.36.

Figure 2.36 – Elasticity, Businesses And Income

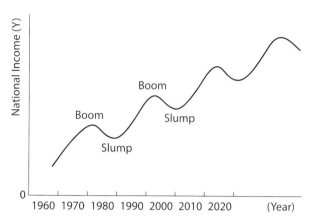

The world economy as a whole is growing. It is however subject to booms and slumps, the so called trade cycle, or business cycle. The sales of income-elastic products are strong as income increases. However these same products are the most vulnerable to a fall in short-term income.

It is also important for businesses to be aware of the responsiveness of their products to changes in the prices of substitutes and complements to their products. In Europe, the pricing of the channel tunnel link and the substitute cross channel ferries are intimately linked. The producers of steel and aluminium; or of coffee and tea will be well aware of the importance of cross price responsiveness. It helps to explain why businesses may buy up rival businesses which produce substitutes (one airline buying up a rival). Complementary goods like computers and computer software; leisure centres and sports clothing or hotels and air flights are very price sensitive to each other, so some businesses will take over or collaborate with producers of complements (air charters and holiday hotels; tennis racquets and tennis clothing).

We have already noted that the ease with which a firm can react to changes in market conditions is another way of expressing price elasticity of supply. The factors which determine the price elasticity of supply (availability of producer substitutes, time, spare capacity, *etc*) are the factors which determine the flexibility of a business towards changed market prices.

Price elasticities

Price elasticities are an important consideration when governments impose indirect taxes and subsidies on goods and services. The government may be aiming to raise revenue by imposing an indirect tax (sales tax) or it may be trying to alter behaviour away from a good *eg* to use less fossil fuels or cigarettes. How successful the government is in these aims depends critically upon elasticities. If a good is price inelastic in demand a tax on the good will raise its price but not reduce sales very much. This would be an excellent feature if the aim is to raise government revenue, but no good at all in altering behaviour. If the good is price elastic in demand sales will fall significantly after a tax is imposed. This is therefore effective in changing behaviour but ineffective in raising revenue.

INCIDENCE OF INDIRECT TAXES AND SUBSIDIES

The concept of elasticity is highly relevant in determining who actually pays (consumers or producers), when an indirect tax is put on a good or service. Similarly it determines whether consumers or producers benefit if a good or service is subsidised. This division of the indirect tax or subsidy between buyers and sellers is known as the *incidence of a tax*.

It is also possible to see how much *revenue* a tax will raise for a government, or how much a subsidy will cost. Finally it is possible to discover the extent to which economic behaviour is altered by a tax or subsidy. Any change in behaviour is described as a change in *resource allocation*. To summarise, this section will examine the imposition of indirect taxes and subsidies with respect to:

1   Incidence,
2   Revenue, and
3   Resource allocation.

Before we look at the impact of indirect taxes and subsidies, however, we should first note that there are two major types of taxes, *direct taxes* and *indirect taxes*; and that indirect taxes can be imposed in one of two ways – as a *specific* flat rate tax, or as a percentage or *ad valorem* tax.

A *subsidy* is effectively a *negative tax*. Subsidies on goods and services are therefore analysed and treated in the same way as indirect taxes.

A direct tax is a tax upon income. It directly taxes wages, rent, interest and profit. Most people tend to think of this type of tax when taxation is discussed. The other type of tax is an indirect tax. This is an expenditure or sales tax upon goods and services. It is indirect as it is not directly taken from the consumer or producer's income, but is taken indirectly when spending occurs.

A specific or flat rate indirect tax is when a specific amount is imposed upon a good, *eg* 1 Swiss franc on a bottle of whiskey. An ad valorem tax is expressed as a percentage of the selling price, *eg* 15% on sales. Ad valorem taxes are the most commonly applied indirect taxes. VAT in the European Union is an example. When the price of a good changes the amount of tax collected changes automatically. This is especially relevant during times of inflation. If only flat rate taxes were applied, inflationary price rises would lead to governments receiving a smaller percentage of spending as tax.

Indirect taxes are collected by sellers and passed to the government – although as we shall see, some or all of the tax may well be passed on to the consumer in the form of rising prices.

To understand what happens when a tax is imposed it is useful to review your understanding of a demand and supply schedule using Figure 2.37, columns 1, 2 and 3.

Over a range of prices the demand schedule records the quantity demanded of whiskey per week. The supply schedule similarly records the quantity that sellers are willing to supply at each price. Equilibrium is 4 million litres of whiskey per week at 7 Swiss francs (Swf) per bottle. Now if a specific tax of 1 Swf is charged on each litre bottle it means that when the price of a bottle of whiskey is for example 10 Swf, the seller must hand over 1 Swf. to the government tax collector, leaving 9 Swf for itself. So when the price is 10 Swf the seller actually receives 9 Swf. The supply schedule tells us that when sellers get 9 Swf they will produce 6 million litres.

These figures can be fitted into an 'after tax' supply schedule as in Figure 2.37, column four.

The effect of putting a tax on the good has been to shift the supply schedule by 1 Swf. The supply curve also shifts up, to the left, up by the amount of the tax. However, the price has not gone up by the amount of the tax. If it had, the new equilibrium price would be 8 Swf but it is not. Equilibrium is between 7 Swf and 8 Swf.

If these schedules are graphed as in Figure 2.38 we can see how the tax causes the supply curve to shift upwards by the amount of the tax. We can also see that because the demand curve is sloping, not vertical, that the price rises less than the tax. In fact, it is shown to increase by 50¢, or half of the tax. Quantity bought has fallen from 4 million litres per week to 3.5 million litres per week.

Three economic observations can be made about the effect of imposing the tax.

1 *Incidence* – the incidence of the tax, who actually pays, is shared equally between buyers and sellers. This is because both buyers and sellers previously exchanged at the equilibrium price. Buyers paid 7 Swf for the good. Sellers received 7 Swf for the good. After the tax is imposed buyers pay 7.50 Swf *ie* they are paying 50¢ more because of the tax. Sellers must hand over 1 Swf from the 7.5 Swf to the tax collector. They are left with 6.50 Swf, 50¢ less than they previously received.

2 *Government revenue* – the government will receive the amount of the tax, 1 Swf per unit multiplied by the quantity sold. Thus it will receive 1 Swf × 3.5 million per week = 3.5 million Swf per week in tax. Notice that the tax has reduced demand from the original 4 million per week demanded.

3 *Resource Allocation* – it is of interest in itself that the quantity demanded and produced of this good has fallen and by how much. In this case quantity has fallen from 4 million litres of whiskey to 3.5 million litres of whiskey produced and consumed. Thus resource allocation has been changed by the tax. It could be the cause of some regret to the consumers and producers of the good. On the other hand, if the good or service is

deliberately restricted by government because of some perceived harm it causes (a de-merit good) *eg* alcohol consumption causing traffic accidents, or cigarette smoking causing poor health, then a fall in sales might be welcomed by society.

Figure 2.37 – Imposition of an Indirect Tax on Whiskey

(1) P_{swf}	(2) Q_D	(3) Q_S	(4) Q_S after tax
(millions of litres per week)			
10	1	7	6
9	2	6	5
8	3	5	4
7	4	4	3
6	5	3	2
5	6	2	-

When an indirect flat rate tax of 1 Swf is imposed on a litre of whiskey, the supply schedule shifts up by 1 Swf ~ the amount of the tax.

Figure 2.38 – the Effect of Imposing a Flat Rate Tax of 1 Swf on a Litre of Whiskey

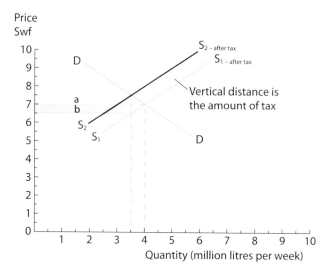

The supply curve shifts up by the amount of the tax. Rectangle a represents the total incidence of the tax on buyers, rectangle b on sellers.

TAXATION AND ELASTICITY

It is the price elasticity of demand and the price elasticity of supply together which determine:

1 the incidence of an indirect tax
2 the revenue a government receives from a particular indirect tax
3 the effect of an indirect tax upon resource allocation

To illustrate this we can make use of those extremes of price elasticity that we met earlier. In Figure 2.39 to Figure 2.42 market demand and supply curves are plotted. In Figure 2.39 the demand curve is perfectly inelastic; in Figure 2.40 demand is perfectly elastic; in Figure 2.41 supply is perfectly inelastic; and in Figure 2.42 supply is perfectly elastic.

Fig. 2.39 PED = 0 Perfectly inelastic demand   Fig. 2.40 PED = ∞ Perfectly elastic demand

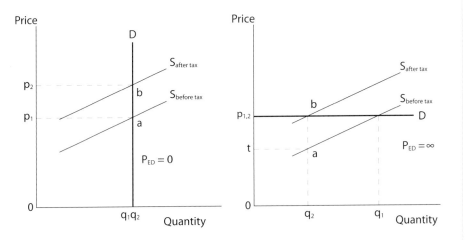

Figure 2.39

When the supply curve shifts up by the amount of the tax the price rises from p_1 to p_2 which is also the amount of the tax. So regarding the three effects of the tax, it can be seen that:

1 *Incidence* – the incidence of the tax falls wholly upon the consumers. The price they pay has risen by the same amount as the tax. Producers get the same as before.
2 *Government revenue* – the area p_1abp_2
   is large, as there has been no fall in the quantity bought at all.
3 *Resource allocation* is unaffected. The same quantity is being bought and produced.

Figure 2.40

When a tax is imposed the supply curve doesn't move, the price remains at p_1 whilst the quantity falls from q_1 to q_2.

1 *Incidence* – the incidence of the tax falls wholly upon the sellers. The price has not changed, $p_1 t$ has to be deducted from the original price.

2 *Government revenue* – the area $tabp_1$ is relatively small as there has been a very large fall in demand as a result of imposing the tax.

3 *Resource allocation* is significantly affected. There has been a major decline in trading with the fall in production from q_1 to q_2.

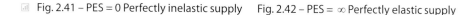 Fig. 2.41 – PES = 0 Perfectly inelastic supply   Fig. 2.42 – PES = ∞ Perfectly elastic supply

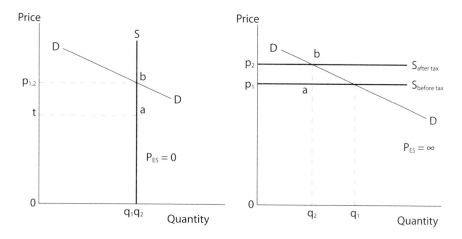

Figure 2.41

There is only one equilibrium possible here. The supply curve cannot move up – after all a zero elasticity means that the same quantity will be supplied at any price. When a tax is imposed it must all be taken from the price $p_1 p_2$.

1 *Incidence* – this falls wholly upon producers. Consumers pay the same price as before. Producers receive the price minus the whole amount of the tax.

2 *Government revenue* – this will be relatively large (area $tabp_1$) as there is no fall in quantity.

3 *Resource allocation* – there is no change in resource allocation, quantity sold remains unchanged.

Figure 2.42
The supply curve shifts up by the amount of the tax. Price rises from p_1 to p_2 and quantity
falls from q_1 to q_2.

1 *Incidence* – the incidence falls wholly upon consumers as price increases by the amount
   of tax p_1p_2, the vertical distance between the two supply curves.
2 *Government revenue* – government revenue is relatively small for any given elasticity of
   demand – area p_1abp_2.
3 *Resource allocation* – this is likely to change considerably.

CONCLUSION

Using these four extremes of elasticity it is now possible to consolidate the effects of putting a tax on any particular product with regard to incidence, government revenue and resource allocation.

1 *Incidence* – the more inelastic is demand and the more elastic is supply the higher is the
   incidence of a tax on consumers. The more elastic is demand and the more inelastic the
   supply the higher is the incidence of a tax on producers.
2 *Government revenue* – government revenue will be greater the lower the elasticity of
   demand and the lower the elasticity of supply.
3 *Resource allocation* – resource allocation will be most changed the higher is the elasticity of demand and the higher is the elasticity of supply.

AD VALOREM OR PERCENTAGE TAXES

When a tax is applied as a percentage of the selling price the supply schedule and curve
will move up proportionately at each price. This means that the amount of tax collected
will be higher at higher prices. The supply curve after tax will diverge from the original
supply curve as in Figure 2.43. In all other respects the analysis is the same as with a specific or flat rate tax. In practice most indirect taxes are of this type. This ensures that government revenue increases automatically with inflation.

Figure 2.43 – an Ad Valorem or Percentage Tax

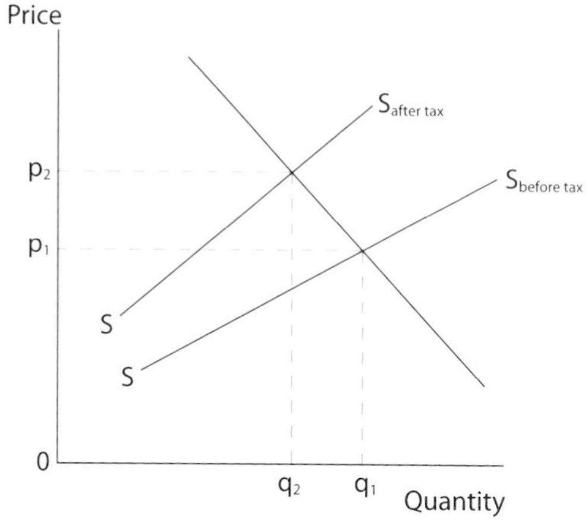

The supply curve shifts up proportionately at each price.

SUBSIDIES ON GOODS AND SERVICES

Subsidies may be regarded as negative indirect taxes. Whereas the government takes money from the sale of products with indirect taxes, it gives money when it subsidises products. The analysis is very similar to that for indirect taxes. A subsidy shifts a supply schedule and a supply curve by the amount of the subsidy, downwards, to the right in a diagram.

This is shown in a schedule and a diagram, Figure 2.44, for a flat rate subsidy of mealie-meal. Before receiving a subsidy, producers will supply 4 thousand kilos at a price of Z$1. They will supply 5 thousand kilos at a price of Z$2. If, however, at a market price of Z$1 they also receive a subsidy of Z$1 from the government – making Z$2 in total – they will supply 5 thousand kilos. At a market price of Z$2 they will receive Z$3 in total – they will supply 6 thousand kilos, and so on. The supply schedule and curve shifts up by Z$1, the amount of the subsidy.

Figure 2.44 – the Effect of Placing a Z$1 Subsidy on Mealie Meal (Price in Zambian Dollars)

Price (Z$)	Q_D	Q_S	Q_S after subsidy
		(millions of tons per week)	
1	10	4	5
2	9	5	6
3	8	6	7
4	7	7	8
5	6	8	9
6	5	9	–

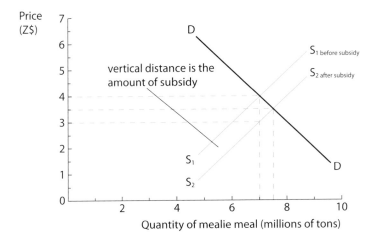

1 *Incidence* – the incidence of the subsidy is 50¢ to the producer, 50¢ to the consumer.
2 *Government revenue* – it costs the government Z$1 × 7.5 million = Z$7.5 million per week.
3 *Resource allocation* – resource allocation has changed. An extra 0.5 million tons of mealie meal is produced & consumed per week

The three issues we looked at with indirect taxes can again be addressed here.

1 *Incidence* – who benefits from the subsidy, producers or consumers?
2 *Government expenditure* – what is the total cost to the government?
3 *Resource allocation* – how is the consumption and production of mealie-meal affected?

The answer to these questions will depend upon demand and supply elasticities just as they did with indirect taxes.

MULTIPLE CHOICE QUESTIONS – ELASTICITIES

1   The demand curve for a normal good will shift out to the right if there is a fall in

A   the price of the good.

B   levels of direct taxation.

C   the price of a substitute good.

D   the cost of factors of production.

2   Question 2 refers to the diagram below.

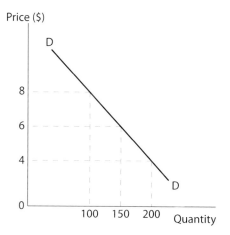

For which of the following price changes below is demand the most elastic?

A $8 to $6   B $6 to $4   C $6 to $8   D $4 to $6

3   The elasticity of supply of a good will tend to be greater when

A   average costs of production are constant as output changes.

B   there are many substitutes for the good.

C   the good has many uses.

D   the good is an intermediate good.

4　The cross elasticity of demand of good X with respect to good Y is negative. The cross elasticity of demand of good Y with respect to good Z is positive. It follows that

I　X and Y are complements.

II　Y and Z are substitutes.

III　X and Z are neither complements nor substitutes.

A　I only　　　　　B　I and II　　　　　C　II and III　　　　　D　I, II and III

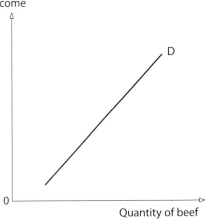

Income

0

Quantity of beef

5　The diagram above graphs the demand for beef against a rising income. From this it can be concluded that

A　the income elasticity for beef is negative.

B　beef is a normal good.

C　there are few substitutes for beef.

D　as income rises, income elasticity of demand for beef falls.

6　The supply of a product is less elastic the

I　shorter the time period.

II　smaller are reserve stocks.

III　less mobile are factors of production.

A　I only　　　　　B　I and II　　　　　C　II and III　　　　　D　I, II and III

Price (€)	Quantity Supplied (thousands)
15	9
20	10
25	12
30	15

7 A supply schedule for a good X is tabled above. The elasticity of supply when price rises from €20 to €25 is

   A 0.5   B 0.8   C 1.0   D 1.25

8 The price of apples falls from 40 cents per kilo to 30 cents per kilo, as a result the quantity of plums demanded falls from 100 kilos a day to 50 kilos a day. The cross elasticity of demand between apples and plums is

   A -2   B -0.5   C +0.5   D +2

9 Which of the following groups is most likely to have the lowest price elasticity of demand for rail travel?

   A Holiday makers
   B Old people
   C Children
   D Businessmen

10 A shopkeeper sells 2000 bottles of cola when the price is 20 cents a bottle. The price elasticity of demand of cola is -1. If she lowers the price to 18 cents a bottle her expected sales would be

   A 1800 bottles   B 2000 bottles   C 2200 bottles   D 2400 bottles

11 Cross price elasticity of demand would be of interest to a company when considering

   I   the response of a rival to a potential price change.
   II how the introduction of a new brand might affect the sales of existing brands of the company's product.
   III how a change in the price of a product might affect the demand for that product.

   A I only   B I and II   C II and III   D I, II and III

HL EXTENSION

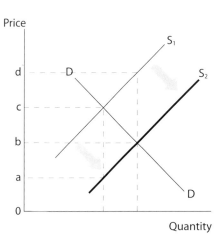

12 The diagram shows the demand and supply for bus travel in city X both before and after the government subsidises bus travel. The revenue per journey to the city bus company following the subsidy is

A 0a   B 0b   C 0c   D 0d

Questions 13 and 14 refer to the following diagram

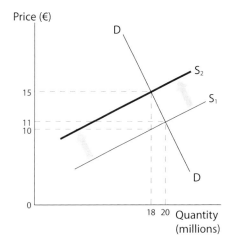

13 The diagram above shows the market equilibrium for aviation fuel in Europe. It also shows the effect of an indirect tax placed on aviation fuel by the EU. The incidence of the tax falls

A mainly on the consumer.

B mainly on the producer.

C mainly on the government.

D equally on the consumer, producer and government.

14 The daily revenue the EU collects from the aviation fuel tax is

A €72 million   B €90 million   C €220 million   D €270 million

15 A good has a negative income elasticity of demand. The quantity demanded will rise as

A the price of the good rises.

B real income falls.

C the price of the good falls.

D real income rises.

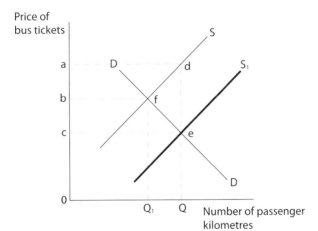

16 The diagram above shows the demand and supply for bus travel both before and after a government decision to subsidise bus tickets. Which area represents the total cost of the subsidy to the government?

A cade   B bfec   C $0bfQ_1$ D $0ceQ$

2.3i   THEORY OF THE FIRM – COSTS

INTRODUCTION

Firms (*companies* or *businesses*) are legal units of production. A firm may consist of one, several or very many factories, farms, shops or offices. A firm may consist of one person or employ a workforce of thousands. A firm which produces in more than one country is known as *a trans-national corporation (TNC)* or a *multi-national corporation (MNC)*. An *industry* consists of all the companies which produce a particular product. Thus *Coca-Cola* belongs to the soft drinks industry, *Honda* to the motor industry, and *de Beers* to the diamond-mining industry.

Firms that are privately owned will be motivated to some large extent by profit. Profit is itself the difference between the firm's total revenue and its total costs. Thus

Total Profit = Total Revenue minus Total Cost
Total Profit = TR – TC

Total Revenue is the total income of a firm. It is obtained by multiplying the price of the product by the amount it produces (P × Q). Total Cost is obtained by adding together all the firm's costs.

Higher level students now need to make a detailed study of a firm's costs, its revenue and its profits. However in order to understand costs the production function needs first to be introduced.

PRODUCTION FUNCTION

A production function expresses output (or production) as a function of the inputs required to make it. Thus the output of steel requires inputs of raw materials; iron ore, coal, and limestone; inputs of capital, such as furnaces and rolling mills; and inputs of labour, such as furnace-men, drivers and chemists. These are required in certain proportions. Simplifying, we might note that to produce 100 tons of steel it requires 200 tons of raw material, 500 units of capital and 50 units of labour. Simplifying further, we could write down the production function as:

100 output = 200 land + 500 capital + 50 labour.

Generalising, all output can be expressed as a function of the broadest categories of inputs that we use: land, labour, capital, and enterprise. This can be expressed in a simple diagram Figure 2.45. The box labelled 'Production Process' represents the transformation of inputs into output. It would represent what goes on inside a factory, a farm, a bank, an office, or a film studio for example. The pattern of a firm's costs will depend upon how input costs change when output increases. To do this we first need to pay regard to the concept of 'time'.

Figure 2.45 – a Production Function

Land

Labour

Capital

Production process

Output

Enterprise

Output is a function of inputs. In its simplest form output is a function of land, labour, capital and enterprise.

SHORT RUN AND LONG RUN COSTS

A study of a firm's costs requires that time be first sub-divided into two periods: the *short run* and the *long run*.

The short run is defined as that time period where at least one factor of production is fixed. Thus if a firm wishes to increase or reduce its output it cannot alter at least one of its inputs. For example a factory might be able to increase its raw material and unskilled labour inputs but not be able to increase its floor space or machinery. A rice farmer might be able to increase her labour hours but not her area of land.

The long run is that time period when all inputs can be changed. There are no fixed factors at all. Thus if a firm expands there are no restrictions to increasing any of its inputs.

Short and long run are precisely defined according to whether there are fixed factors or not. The time periods are not defined by the clock or calendar. In practice the long run might be a matter of years to nuclear energy producers and yet only a matter of days to street vendors.

SHORT RUN OUTPUT – THE LAW OF DIMINISHING RETURNS OR THE LAW OF VARIABLE PROPORTIONS

A firm in the short run, by definition, has at least one factor fixed and at least one factor variable. If the firm changes its output it follows that the proportion of the factors used must change one to the other. If the firm expands output then each unit of the variable factor has less and less of the fixed factor to work with. If, for example, the owner of a paddy field wants to increase the output of rice, and can increase the amount of fertiliser used but not the area of land, the proportion of fertiliser to land changes. If a TV studio wants to increase its broadcasting output, and hires more staff but cannot increase the studio floor space, the factors of production are changing in proportion to each other.

When some factors are changed and one or more of the others remain fixed, the output of the firm changes in a strictly predictable pattern. This relationship is known as the *Law of Variable Proportions* because of what happens to the input proportions. It is also known, more commonly, as the *Law of Diminishing Returns* because of what happens to the output.

The law states that *'if some inputs are increased whilst at least one other input remains fixed, then, whilst the extra output produced by each extra unit of input may at first increase it will reach a point where it will diminish'.* This point is known as the point of diminishing returns. This law expresses a physical relationship between input and output. Diminishing returns will occur because each additional unit of input has less and less of the fixed input to combine with. Let us illustrate this with an example of a rice farmer with one paddy field and no chance of increasing the land, but with an abundant labour supply available. If no labour is used, nothing will be produced. If one worker works on the land, output is positive. If a second worker joins the first worker it is possible that the total output could more than double. The extra or *'marginal'* worker may well cause the *'average output'* to increase. Because the two workers can now specialise and divide the various tasks between them the total output may more than double. It is possible that output may continue to rise more than proportionately with the addition of further extra (or marginal) workers. There will come a point, however, when the extra output from the last extra worker is lower than the one before. Put another way, there will come a point when marginal output begins to decline. This is the *point of diminishing marginal returns*. The marginal output of each extra worker will continue to be less than the one before. This is because each worker has less and less land to work with effectively.

The Law of Diminishing Returns can be seen in action in all activities where there are fixed and variable factors combining. Try to identify some in your own experience. For example if you were to clear the dinner table of dishes after a big family meal, wash them, dry them and put them away you might measure your output to be the length of time that it takes you. If a second family member offers to help, the time taken may be reduced by significantly more than half. By dividing the task into the specialised functions of clearing and stacking dishes, and washing up for example, time is saved from continually 'downing tools' and changing jobs (and becoming more efficient in your speciality)! It is possible that the addition of a third person may speed up the process even further. Unfortunately you are then likely to be approaching the point of diminishing returns. Some factors, such as the sink and workspace are fixed, so the extra labour will find it increasingly difficult to help in reducing the average overall time.

We will return now to the example of land and labour for growing rice. This example has particular significance. Firstly, it was the example used by David Ricardo in the early nineteenth century when he first developed the concept of Diminishing Returns. His contribution was particularly apt in post industrial revolution England, with rapid popu-lation growth and a fixed supply of the most important factor of production at that time, land. Secondly, the situation of many of the poorest people on earth is also one of fixed small plots of land and rapid population growth. The Law of Diminishing Returns helps to explain rural poverty in many poor countries. Figure 2.46 and Figure 2.47 show hypo-thetical input and output figures for a rice farm. The addition of up to three workers to farm the land allows total output to go up by an increasing amount. The fourth worker further increases output but by less than the third worker – diminishing returns have set in. On the graph the curve gets steeper with the first three workers (increasing returns to labour) but flattens after the third worker with the onset of diminishing returns. The addition of the eighth worker actually lowers total output. On the graph the total output curve declines. However, take care not to confuse this with diminishing returns, which takes place whilst total output is increasing.

📊 Figure 2.46 – the Law of Diminishing Returns

Quantity of variable factors: Number of workers	Total Output of rice per year
0	0
1	1
2	5
3	12
4	18
5	20
6	21
7	21
8	20

📊 Figure 2.47 – the Law of Diminishing Returns

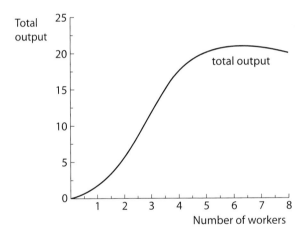

Rice production on a hypothetical farm.

Average Output And Marginal Output

Diminishing returns to a variable factor can also be shown by looking at what happens to average output and marginal output. Average output is the average amount produced by the variable factor – the average per worker in this case Figure 2.48. It is calculated as:

$$\frac{total\ output}{number\ of\ workers} = average\ output\ per\ worker$$

It can be seen in Figure 2.48 that average output at first increases as there are increasing returns to labour, but after a peak of 4.5 tonnes per year the average falls. This point with average output at 4.5 tonnes per year and 4 workers is the point of average diminishing returns. Average output is graphed as a curve in Figure 2.49.

Figure 2.48 – Average Output and Marginal Output

Quantity of the variable factor (number of workers)	Total output (tonnes of rice per year)	Average output* (tonnes per year)	Marginal output** (tonnes per year)
0	0	-	
1	1	1.0	1
2	5	2.5	4
3	12	4.0	7
4	18	4.5	6
5	20	4.0	2
6	21	3.5	1
7	21	3.0	0
8	20	2.5	-1

$$* \quad = \quad \frac{total\ output}{number\ of\ workers}$$

$$** \quad = \quad \Delta\ output$$

Figure 2.49 – Average Output and Marginal Output

Average output and
marginal output

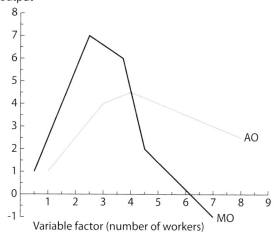

Variable factor (number of workers)

Marginal output peaks between 2 and 3 workers. This is the point of diminishing marginal returns.

It is the marginal output, the extra output produced by the last worker which determines the average. Thus when marginal output is rising it is 'pulling up' the average. Even after marginal output begins to fall it still pulls up the average if it is higher than the average; up to the fourth worker in the example. When marginal output is less than the average output it must be pulling down the average. (See the boxed reading on the relationship between average and marginal). When the marginal output is exactly the same as the average, the average will not change. This point must be at the top of the average output curve where the output is neither rising nor falling, and where it is cut by the marginal output curve.[10]

The law of diminishing returns is an important feature of all economic production. It does, therefore, have an important role in determining the costs of a firm in the short run. Notice that it applies only in the short run and not the long run. Only in the short run are there fixed and variable factors. In the long run, no factors of production are fixed.

The Relationship between Marginal and Average

In studying the Law of Diminishing Returns we came across the concepts of *marginal output and average output. The idea of the margin is one of the most important concepts in the whole subject of economics. In studying the theory of the firm we will come across the idea of the margin several more times, and in particular its relationship to the average. There are three simple rules which govern the relationship between margin and average. If the margin equals the average, the average will not change. If the margin is above the average, the average will rise. If the margin is below the average, the average will fall.*

Imagine a room of 10 students with an average age of 20 years. Another 20 year old enters. The average age remains at 20 years. The teacher, aged 44, enters the room. The average age of the people in the room rises, not to 44 of course, but to 22. This figure is obtained by adding the 12 ages (=264 years) and dividing by 12 (=22 years). If an 18 year old student now enters this will pull the average down to below 22 years.

Question

A basketball player scores the following number of points in the first five games of the season:

Game	1	2	3	4	5
Points	2	0	20	10	0
Total Points					
Average Points					

Using the marginal number of points from each additional game, calculate teh total and average points after each game. Show how the average and marginal number of points illustrate the rules above.

SHORT RUN COSTS

A firm's costs in the short run are determined by the fact that certain factors are fixed, whilst others are variable. The law of variable proportions will ensure that costs follow a fairly predictable pattern.

FIXED COSTS AND VARIABLE COSTS

The presence of fixed and variable factors of production results in costs being similarly divided between those that are fixed and those that are variable. Total costs of the firm are the sum of fixed costs and variable costs:

$$TC = FC + VC$$

Fixed costs are those costs which have to be paid regardless of the firm's level of production. In other words, fixed costs do not change with output. Rental of a factory or farm, bank interest charges on a loan, fixed rental payments for access to a telephone line, wage payments to staff on fixed contracts are some common examples. Fixed costs are also known as *indirect costs* or *overheads* to business people. Figure 2.50 graphs fixed costs against output, showing how costs do not change as output varies.

Figure 2.50 – Fixed Costs

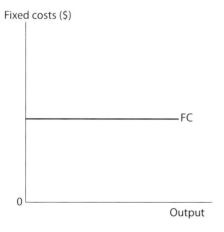

Variable costs, on the other hand, are directly related to output. They are often called *direct costs*. If a firm produces nothing it pays no variable costs. Its variable costs rise as output rises. Figure 2.51 illustrates this. The curved shape of the line is explained later – it is the result of the law of diminishing returns. Raw materials, energy and hourly paid labour are likely to fall into the variable cost category. Some of a firm's bills may have a fixed element and a variable element. Thus there are often fixed charges for water, electricity, gas and telephone, to cover equipment supply and connection, with additional direct charges according to the amount used.

Figure 2.51 – Variable Costs

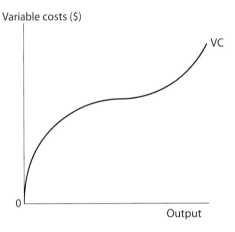

Variable costs ($)

Total cost, the sum of fixed costs and variable costs, is shown in Figure 2.52.

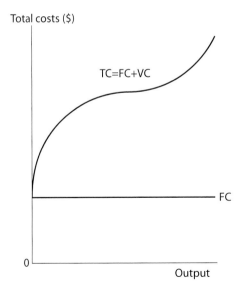

Total costs ($)

Figure 2.52 – Total Costs
Total Costs = Fixed Costs + Variable Costs

AVERAGE COSTS AND MARGINAL COSTS

If each of the short run cost measures – fixed cost; variable cost; and total cost – are divided by the number of units of output that the firm is producing, average cost measures can be calculated *ie* average fixed cost, average variable cost and average total cost.

$$AFC = \frac{FC}{Output}$$

$$AVC = \frac{VC}{Output}$$

$$ATC = \frac{TC}{Output}$$

Average total cost is equal to average fixed cost plus average variable cost.

$$ATC = AFC + AVC$$

Marginal cost is the cost of producing the 'last', or marginal unit. It can be measured as the total cost of *n* units minus the total cost of *n-1* units, where *n* represents any number.

$$MC = TC_n - TC_{n-1}$$

Average fixed cost is shown diagrammatically in Figure 2.53. The average fixed cost is initially high because the whole of the fixed costs are being averaged over a small number of units. They descend steeply, however, and continue to fall as they are spread over more and more units. All businesses are concerned to 'spread their overhead costs' by producing a sufficient output. At small levels of output fixed costs are of particular concern to businesses. This concern decreases as more and more output reduces the average fixed costs, only to be replaced by a different source of worry: average variable costs. Understanding how average variable costs behave is the most critical part of understanding short run costs as a whole. The Law of Diminishing Returns is the key to this understanding. You are advised to revise this concept before attempting the next section.

 Figure 2.53 – Average Fixed Costs

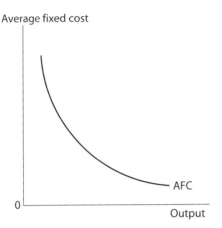

Average fixed cost

AFC

0

Output

Average variable cost and marginal cost are shown diagramatically in Figure 2.54. Because of its shape, the *AVC* curve is described as a 'U' shaped curve. The reason for its 'U' shape, that is, why average variable costs at first fall and then rise, is explained by the law of diminishing returns. Average output and marginal output curves, showing diminishing returns, are graphed beneath the *AVC* curve as Figure 2.55.

Figure 2.55 shows how marginal output and average output behave when increasing quantities of a variable factor are added to a fixed factor, for example, more and more labourers are put to work on a fixed area of land. Marginal output at first increases and then decreases. Consequently average output increases, and then falls.

Figure 2.54 – the 'U'-shaped AVC and MC Curves

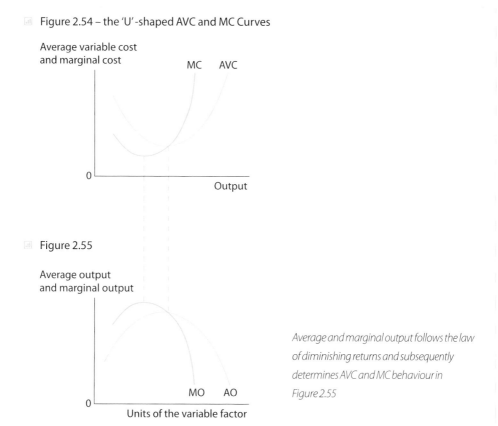

The variable cost is the cost of the variable factor – in this case the wages of workers. Variable costs rise steadily as workers are hired. Thus variable cost with one worker is $1 \times$ the wage; two workers $2 \times$ the wage; 10 workers $10 \times$ the wage and so on. The variable cost increases regularly as more workers are hired. However, output does not rise regularly as we have noted – because of the *Law of Diminishing Returns*. Marginal output at first increases *ie* output increases more than proportionately compared to the increased cost (variable cost). Thus the *marginal cost* of producing the first units of output declines. This will continue as long as marginal output is increasing right up to the point where marginal output peaks, as firm begins to experience marginal diminishing returns. As marginal output declines, so the marginal cost of producing extra units of output will increase.

The behaviour of marginal cost, itself determined by marginal output, determines the average costs of the firm. As long as marginal costs are lower than average costs they will be lowering the firm's average costs. Average costs will be constant at the point where marginal costs are equal to average costs, that is at the bottom of the *AC* curve where average costs are neither falling nor rising. Average costs will then rise as marginal cost is higher than average cost.

Another way of looking at the behaviour of average costs is to observe that the *AC* curve mirrors the behaviour of the *AO* curve. If the addition of variable factors (*eg* labour) causes average output to rise then average cost must be falling. If the addition of variable factors cause the average output to fall then the average cost must be rising.

AVERAGE TOTAL COST

Average total cost *ATC* (sometimes known simply as average cost or *AC*) is the sum of average fixed cost and average variable cost at each level of output.

$$ATC = AFC + AVC$$

If average fixed costs are added to average variable costs and plotted as a curve of average total costs it will appear as in Figure 2.56.

Figure 2.56 – Average Total Costs

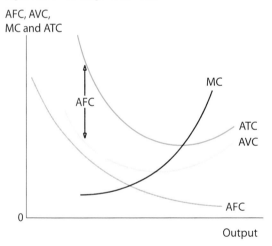

Average Total Costs are the sum of Average Fixed Costs and Average Variable Costs.

As average fixed costs *(AFC)* are large at low output and get smaller and smaller with increased output the 'gap' between the *ATC* curve and the *AVC* curve also gets smaller.

The shape of the *ATC* curve is determined by the shape of its constituent *AFC* and *AVC* curves. Both average fixed and average variable costs fall over the initial range of output, so *ATC* also falls. *AVC* will reach a turning point, however, as diminishing returns become effective. Average fixed costs continue to fall. This makes the *ATC* curve less steep than the *AVC* curve, and they converge as *AFC* continue to decline. However, the *ATC* curve is also markedly 'U' shaped.

As more output is produced by the firm, its costs are increasingly dominated by expanding average variable costs, whilst average fixed costs become less and less significant.

As the firm expands its fixed costs remain constant, so all of its marginal costs are due to increased variable costs. It is therefore the marginal cost curve which most powerfully shapes the firm's average total costs. As long as marginal costs are lower than average costs, producing more will lower the firm's average costs. If marginal costs are higher than average costs then producing more will raise average costs. When marginal costs are equal to average costs so that average costs are neither rising nor falling, the *MC* curve must cut the *ATC* curve at its lowest point at the bottom of the 'U'.

Firm's Short Run Costs ($)

Output in units	Total fixed cost	Total variable cost	Total cost	Average fixed cost	Average variable cost	Average cost	Marginal cost
0	40						
1		6					
2		11					
3		15					
4			60				
5			66				

Question
Complete the table.

Revenue

A firm's revenue is the product of two variables:

1 the price of the good or service it sells – p, and
2 the quantity of goods or services it sells – q.

So the firm's total revenue *(TR)* is equal to price times quantity.

$$TR = p \times q$$

Total revenue can be represented by the area under a demand curve as in Figure 2.57. Refer back to the section on elasticity and total revenue to review the relationship between area under a curve and elasticity.

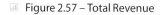 Figure 2.57 – Total Revenue

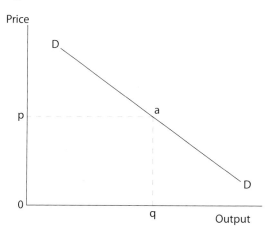

Total revenue is equal to p × q or the area 0qap.

Total revenue can be graphed against output. If the firm sells its output at a constant price the total revenue curve will appear as a straight line through the origin as in Figure 2.58.

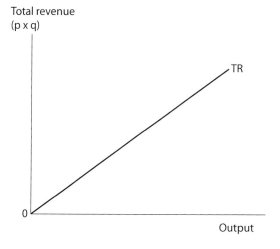 Figure 2.58 – Total Revenue for a Firm

The price of the product is assumed to be constant, so the TR curve is a straight line. The total revenue of the firm rises steadily with quantity sold.

PROFIT

Profit has already been defined as the total revenue of the firm minus the total cost. Economists however have their own special meaning of the word profit. This is known as *economic profit* to distinguish it from the more usual meaning of the word, which is known to economists as *accounting profit*. Accounting profit is shown in Figure 2.59 as the total revenue minus the total accounting costs. Accounting costs are the costs which have a money value like raw materials, energy, rent, interest and wages. Economic costs include any further opportunity costs to the firm in addition to the accounting costs. The most important of these is the opportunity cost of capital employed in production. If a firm had $100,000 tied up in the company, that $100,000 cannot be used for anything else. Nevertheless, tying it into the company has an opportunity cost, because that money could have been used in an alternative business. Even if it had been left in the safest form of saving it could have earned a rate of interest. That rate of interest is part of the opportunity cost of using it in the business. Using it in this way is not as safe as saving it in the bank however, so a risk premium must be added to the bank rate. The total rate of interest that the $100,000 could earn in another firm with the same degree of risk is its opportunity cost. After all, if the firm decided not to operate, the $100,000 could be lent to another such firm and earn interest. This interest rate is the true cost of using the capital. Its use is not free. It must be costed as if used in its next best alternative use.

Figure 2.59

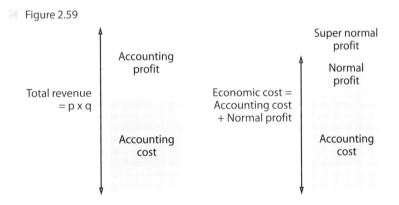

This 'cost' is known in economics as 'normal profit'. That is the amount of profit that *must* be earned by a firm to cover its opportunity cost. It is defined as that level of profit which will just keep the firm in the industry. Any lower amount of profit is not worthwhile. A profit seeking firm will close down and lend out its money to earn higher interest than it earns by staying in business. Of course firms will strive to earn more than 'normal' profit. Any extra profit is known as *'super normal' profit* or *'abnormal' profit* to economists.

PROFIT MAXIMISING EQUILIBRIUM

In any study of people or social organisations one of the most important things to establish in explaining behaviour is *motivation*. Firms could be motivated by a number of different objectives. However, privately owned firms are all likely to have the pursuit of profit as one of their main objectives. In a first course in economics such as this we made the assumption that firms will behave so as to reach the maximum possible profit. We assume that they are *'profit maximisers'.* Everything that follows in Section 2 of this book is based upon that assumption. If a firm does not conform closely to the theories which follow the most likely reason is that the firm is not a profit maximizer. In the real world there are indeed many such firms. A fuller examination of those firms must await a deeper study in a subsequent, second level, course.

A profit maximising firm will by definition produce at the point where it will make the biggest possible profit. This point can be identified as the level of output which leaves the largest positive gap between total cost and total revenue. This is shown in Figure 2.60.

Figure 2.60

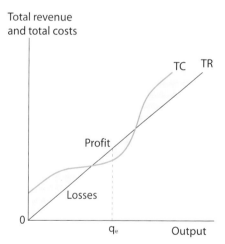

Maximum profit is earned at q_e where total revenue exceeds total cost by the biggest amount.

A second way of identifying that output which gives the firm maximum profit is to look at marginal revenue and marginal cost. In other words, the firm looks at the cost and revenue of producing the last unit. If the marginal cost is greater than the marginal revenue the firm should not produce that unit. It is making a loss on that unit and it would be more profitable not to produce it. The firm should reduce its output if $MC > MR$.

If on the other hand the last unit yields more revenue than it costs to produce that unit, *ie MR > MC* then the firm will gain extra profit from that unit. (As marginal costs include normal profit the firm will be making supernormal profit on this item.) The firm should expand. Marginal cost will rise as the firm expands (Law of Diminishing Returns), the firm should keep expanding as long as *MR > MC*. The point it should increase production to, its equilibrium point, is where *MR = MC*. This is shown in Figure 2.61.

Figure 2.61

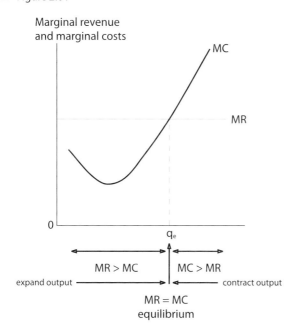

Maximum profit is earned at q_e where *MR = MC*. At any other point more profit can be made by expanding or contracting output towards this point.

Long Run Output – Returns to Scale

In the long run all factors of production can change freely. Thus it is possible for a firm to change all of its inputs proportionately if it wishes. There is no fixed factor to cause diminishing returns. The firm can change its scale of production *ie* it can make the firm bigger or smaller in proportion.

There are three potentially different outcomes when inputs are increased. If the inputs are increased output can increase proportionately, less than proportionately, or more than proportionately. Whatever happens to output is due to the scale of the firm changing, and thus we speak of *returns to scale*. If inputs are increased and output increases proportionately then the firm is experiencing *constant returns to scale*. If output increases more than proportionately the firm experiences *increasing returns to scale*. If output increases less than proportionately the firm experiences *decreasing returns to scale*. This is summarised below:

	Inputs	Outputs	Returns to Scale
1	increase	increases more than proportionately	increasing returns to scale
2	increase	increases proportionately	constant returns to scale
3	increase	increases less than proportionately	decreasing returns to scale

The increased output per unit of input that is gained where there are economies of scale is one important motivation for businesses to grow. It is also a major reason why output and consumption have increased so much in the developed world since the industrial revolution. It is therefore worth looking at some of the reasons why increasing returns to scale can exist.

Sources of Increasing Returns to Scale

The sources of increasing output per unit of input when a firm grows include technical, managerial, purchasing, marketing and financial economies. We will look at each of these in turn.

Technical Economies

Some factors of production are indivisible, so that to make full use of them a large output is required. If a small firm buys a computer and uses it for only a few hours a week there is a relatively high input for a relatively small output. If a larger firm buys the same computer and can keep it in use for most of each day the output to input ratio improves significantly. A small IB school may employ specialists in minority languages. If they have very small classes the input to output ratio is high. A much larger school could gain returns to scale by being able to run fuller classes. A bigger school would similarly make fuller use of capital which is indivisible, *eg* a gymnasium, swimming pool or science laboratory. Another technical economy arises from the scale of capital where volume is important. Aeroplanes, ships, and lorries all increase their volume and carrying capacity by approximately three times when their surface area, and thus their construction costs, double. The labour to operate the larger transport units does not increase proportionately with size. Thus the average cost of carrying cargo, or of carrying passengers falls with size.

Managerial Economies

In a small company one person may have to undertake all functions *eg* telephone operator, receptionist, accountant, production manager, salesman and so on. A bigger company can employ specialist staff and gain greater output from the division of labour and specialisation.

Purchasing Economies

Bigger firms can often obtain lower prices for their raw materials by ordering large quantities. For example the printing costs of a textbook come down very markedly with the size of the print run placed by the publisher. Food supermarkets can offer much lower prices to their customers than small corner stores largely because they order such huge quantities from their suppliers.

Marketing Economies

Marketing a product can become very much cheaper the more units of the product are sold. The creative work behind a magazine advertisement or television advertisement is much the same whether it is for sales of 10 thousand units or 20 million units. Clearly the unit cost (average cost) of advertising the bigger output is much lower. Similarly, the payment to the publishers of a magazine or the owner of a TV station to run an advertisement is the same whether the company sells a few units or millions of units of the product. The unit costs of marketing are much cheaper the higher the number of products sold.

Pins and Chips

In 1776 Adam Smith observed the huge increases in output being obtained at the beginning of the Industrial Revolution. He set out to explain the source of this wealth in the world's first economics book *An Enquiry into the Nature and Causes of the Wealth of Nations*. The most important factor in this incredible increase in output was, he observed, the *division of labour*. *Free trade* was a second necessary condition. Free trade allowed markets to be large enough to utilise the vastly increased outputs that the division of labour and the use of machinery brought. The most quoted example of all time to illustrate the division of labour, comes in the first few pages of his book. It describes the production process in a pin factory.

One man draws out the wire, another straightens it, a third cuts it, a fourth points it, a fifth grinds it at the top for receiving the head; to make the head requires two or three distinct operations; to put it on is a peculiar business; to whiten the pins is another; it is even a trade by itself to put them in the paper. Making pins in this way ten workers without very much skill made 48,000 pins of a middling size in a day. One worker, toiling alone, could have made perhaps twenty pins in a day; therefore, ten workers could have produced two hundred. The division of labour allowed for an increase in daily output of the pin factory from 200 to 48,000! This specialisation became even more productive when applied to creating new technologies. Scientists and engineers trained in narrow fields, became specialists at inventing. The machines invented as a result of the division of labour made production faster and more accurate.

Now take a look at a modern day example of a pin factory, a chip factory. Memory chips give your computer its instant-recall ability, logic chips provide its number-crunching power, and customized chips take the complexity out of using your camera. The computer chip is an example of the productivity to be obtained in the division of labour. Designers, using computers made from microchips, create the chip's intricate circuits. Machines print the circuit design onto paper and photograph it onto glass plates called masks that work like stencils. Workers prepare silicon wafers onto which these circuits are printed. Some slice the wafers, others polish them, others bake them, and yet others coat them with a light-sensitive chemical. Technicians put masks and wafers into a machine that shines light through the mask, imprinting the copy of the circuit onto the wafer. Chemicals eat the unexposed portion of the wafer. A further series of passes through a gas-filled oven deposits atoms that act as transistors. Aluminium is deposited onto the wafer to connect the transistors. Finally a diamond saw or laser separates the hundreds of chips that are on the wafer.

Financial Economies

Larger firms with larger resources often present a lower risk to banks and other financial institutions when they wish to borrow money, and can therefore usually borrow money at lower rates of interest. The unit cost of borrowing falls with increased scale of production.

A Note on Decreasing Returns to Scale

Decreasing returns to scale are thought to be caused by the increasing difficulty of managing very large companies. It is difficult to find clear examples of decreasing returns to scale in practice.

LONG RUN COSTS

The long run has already been defined as that period of time when no factors of production are restricted or fixed. All inputs are variable. Therefore there are no fixed costs, only variable costs. It has also been noted that when inputs are increased in the long run, the output may:

1   rise more than proportionately, *ie* there are *increasing returns to scale*
2   rise proportionately, *ie* there are *constant returns to scale*, or
3   rise less than proportionately, *ie* there are *decreasing returns to scale*.

If output rises more than proportionately to inputs the average cost of producing that output will fall. The firm's costs, its inputs bill, will rise less than the output of goods. There are said to be *'economies of scale'* and this is shown as section *a* in Figure 2.62. If inputs and outputs change proportionately there is said to be *'constant returns to scale,'* as the average cost of products will remain constant. This is shown as *b* in Figure 2.62. If inputs are producing less and less output proportionately as they are increased there are *'diseconomies of scale.'* This is shown as section *c* in Figure 2.62.

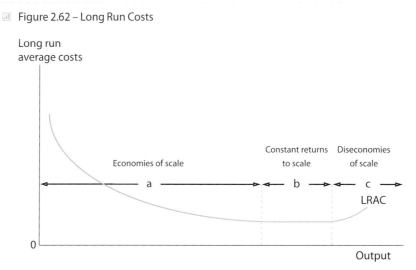

Figure 2.62 – Long Run Costs

As the firm's output expands, average costs at first fall (economies of scale), then remain constant (constant returns to scale), and finally rise (diseconomies of scale).

At any moment in time a firm is always in a short run situation. The long run consists of all the short run periods as a firm expands. The *LRAC* curve is therefore the track of all the *SRAC* curves as the firm grows. This is shown in Figure 2.63. The average costs of the firm at its smallest are shown as $SRAC_1$ (short run average costs 1). As the firm expands, its average costs fall to the bottom of the U shaped curve, and then begin to climb as a result of diminishing returns. The firm then removes the fixed constraint of production by expanding its scale of production. It moves into another short-run situation shown by $SRAC_2$. However, as there have been economies of scale, average costs have fallen. In Figure 2.63 $SRAC_2$ is lower than $SRAC_1$. Economies of scale are gained with each further expansion up to $SRAC_{12}$. Thereafter there are constant returns to scale up to $SRAC_{14}$, after which diseconomies of scale arise. The production path of the firm in the long run is shown by the smoothed black line tangent to the *SRAC* curves. This is the origin of the smoothed and simplified *LRAC* curve in Figure 2.62.

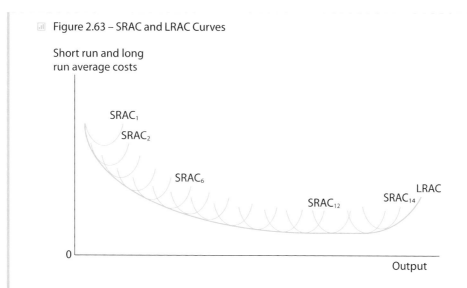

Figure 2.63 – SRAC and LRAC Curves

2.3ii THEORY OF THE FIRM – MARKET STRUCTURE

The introductory pages here are designed as a broad introduction and as such might be helpful to Standard Level students even though the theory of the firm is not a part of the SL course.

MARKET POWER

The way a firm behaves, that is, how much output it decides to produce and the price it sells its products at, depends upon the structure of the market for that product. The major characteristic of *market structure* is the degree of competition in the market. Structures in the real world range from monopolistic competition through oligopoly to monopoly. Further it should be stressed that these models of market structures are not pure and exclusive. In practice there is a continuum of competition.

MONOPOLISTIC COMPETITION

Monopolistic competition is the name given to markets that are very price competitive. There will typically be a large number of firms each producing a relatively small percentage of the total output. There are very low barriers to entering and leaving the industry, so that high profits are quickly eroded by new entrants. Due to the fierce competition sellers have little control over their prices. Customers can buy elsewhere if one seller raises his price. With there being a very large number of firms it is not practically possible for firms to collude to fix prices. To a large extent they have to accept the price that the market determines. In response to this, however, firms frequently attempt to differentiate their products. Product differentiation is where small differences in products are strongly emphasised, usually through branding and advertising. This is to try to make demand for that product more dependent upon taste than upon price, that is, to make demand less price elastic. The producer gains more control over the price than if the goods were homogenous *ie* identical. The availability of close substitutes to the brand, still means however, that price control is very limited.

At first sight there would seem to be many products which are monopolistically competitive. If you are in a classroom situation at this moment look around you. The pens your fellow students are writing with are likely to be differentiated, even though they are very close substitutes. Jeans, trainers, spectacles, shampoos, soap, toothpaste, many processed foods in the supermarket indeed a large number of products we use are differentiated close substitutes. If you investigate further, however, you will discover that very many competing products are in fact produced by the same few firms! For example, in the USA four companies between them produce all of the huge variety of breakfast cereals and just three firms produce all the cameras and film. A similar pattern is found with cigarettes, soft drinks, toothpaste and razor blades. The markets for many of these products are better explained by a model of *oligopoly*, where just a few firms exist in an industry.

Some of the best examples of monopolistic competition are to be found in retailing. Different shops selling very similar products compete fiercely with each other. They emphasise small differences that a customer might like, such as unsociable trading hours, personal service, home delivery, temporary credit, convenience and so on. Restaurants too offer differentiated menus and differentiated decor yet have to remain fairly price competitive with each other. City centre fruit markets sell very similar products yet emphasise display of their goods and the charisma of their sellers to attract consumer loyalty. Pop singers use distinct appearance and behaviour in order to differentiate their own product in a very competitive market. It is true that in many cases of monopolistic competition the geographical range of the consumer limits competition to less producers then the theory suggests. However these industries are so easy to enter and leave that new producers will move in where prices are abnormally high.

OLIGOPOLY

Oligopoly is a market structure that is characterised by a *few* firms. 'Few' is an imprecise word – it can mean anything from two firms, up to a fairly large number of firms, say one hundred. In the latter case, however, the market is still likely to be dominated by a smaller number of large sellers. An oligopoly always has high barriers to entry, to prevent other firms from easily entering the market, which would increase supply and reduce prices. Barriers might be technological: like the high research and development costs of the pharmaceutical drugs market; the high tooling up and production costs of the automobile and aeroplane markets; or the high marketing costs associated with perfume, chocolate and soft drinks. The important defining characteristic is that the small number of competitors leads to *interdependent behaviour*. The firms see themselves as rivals, and consider the reactions of other firms when making their own decisions on output and price.

The theories of how such firms behave come from *game theory*. Game theory explains situations where there are interdependent rivals. An example is given in the box *'The Prisoner's Dilemma'*. Another branch of society which uses game theory is the military. The actions and reactions of soldiers, sailors and fighter pilots are very dependent on those of their rivals. Competition between firms in oligopoly is so similar to this that the language of warfare is often used *ie* strategy, campaign, corporate attack, price war and so on.

The Prisoner's Dilemma

Oligopolists face a dilemma between co-operating and competing. This is known as the prisoner's dilemma after the following game:

Juan and Maria are arrested by the police for jointly committing a crime and are questioned seperately. They know that if neither confesses to the crime they will each get a light prison sentence. Each is told, however, that if either claims to be innocent while the other confesses guilt, the one who claims to be innocent will get a severe sentence whilst the one who pleads guilty will go free. If they both confess they get a medium sentence. These possibilities can be set out as a matrix:

		Maria's plea			
		Innocent		Guilty	
Juan's plea	**Innocent**	Maria	light sentence	Maria	go free
		Juan	light sentence	Juan	severe sentence
	Guilty	Maria	severe sentence	Maria	medium sentence
		Juan	go free	Juan	medium sentence

Juan reasons as follows: "Maria has to plead guilty or innocent. First, assume she pleads innocent. I get a light sentence if I also plead innocent but no sentence at all if I plead guilty, so guilty's my better plea. Second assume she pleads guilty. I get a severe sentence if I plead innocent and a medium sentence if I plead guilty. So once again it is better to plead guilty."

Maria reasons in the same way and, as a result, they both plead guilty and get a medium sentence, wheras if they had been able to communicate they could both have agreed to plead innocent and get off with a light sentence.

Exercise

Two firms, A and B, are making sealed bids for a government contract to build a road bridge across a river. Only two bids are possible, either at a low price bid or a high price bid. The high price bid will lead to a profit of $20 million, whereas the low price bid will lead to a profit of $14 million. If the firms bid at the same price, they will be asked to share the job and each will earn half the profits. if they submit different bids, the firm offering to build at the lower price will get the job and all the profits. Draw up a matrix (as in the Prisoner's Dilemma) to show the possible outcomes under competing and co-operative behaviour.

In practice the interdependence of firms helps to explain why many product markets exhibit long periods of *price stability*. It also helps to explain why price competition is replaced by *non-price competition*. If two giant companies have a *price war* they know that one likely outcome is that they both end up worse off. Like two super powers armed with missiles it may be better to have a less harmful propaganda fight. These firms may compete very fiercely by *branding and advertising* their products and stressing their *product differentiation* rather than price. An oligopolistic airline may stress its superior seat space, in-flight movies, departure-lounges, friendly cabin staff – but not a lower price. Offering free gifts and competition prizes are common ways firms compete one with another without altering their product price.

Alcohol, Branding and Competition – UK

British "pubs" or public houses are strongly characteristic of that country's social life. In these pubs there is a bewildering variety of brands of alcohol on sale. Amongst the beers available are: Ansells Bitter, Tetleys Bitter, John Bull Bitter, Burton Ale and Double Diamond. Major brands of lager, which is a close beer substitute, include: Lowenbrau, Castlemaine XXXX, Skol and Oranjeboom. Amongst the competition from cider is Gaymer's Old English and Whiteways. Major brands of whiskey available include: Teacher's, Ballantine's, Grant's, Glenfiddich, Hiram Walker, Irish Mist and Laphroaig. Other major alcoholic drinks include: Courvoisier brandy, Lamb's Navy rum, Tia Maria and Kahlua liqueurs, Harvey's sherry, Cockburn's port, VP and Rougemont wine. Would it then surprise you to know that all of these brands belong to one company, Allied-Domecq PLC? Alcohol is only one of many industries that Allied operates in. It has huge interests in foods, and amongst its restaurants are the American Baskin Robbins and Dunkin' Donuts chains.

Allied does have competition in alcohol however. Another very large multi-brand firm is Guinness. Guinness owns: Bell's, Black and White, Booths, Canadian LTD, Cardhu, Cossack Vodka, Dewar's, Glenkinchie, Glen Elgin, Glen Ord, Gordons, Guinness, Haig, Harp, Hennesey, Hine, IW Harper, Johnnie Walker, Lagavulin, Mercier, Moët & Chandon, Oban, Old Parr, Pimms, Rebel Yell, Tanqueray, Talisker, Ushers, VAT 69 and White Horse.

Question

Why should a single firm wish to produce a large number of brands in competition with other products of their own?

MONOPOLY

Monopoly, at least *pure monopoly*, is a situation with a *single seller*. This might be an industry with only one large company. Alternatively there could be a sole selling agreement between several companies known as a *cartel agreement*. There will have to be very high barriers to entry to prevent other firms from entering the market and breaking the monopoly. Legal barriers granted by government lead to a situation closest to pure monopoly, often with state control over the industry.

In practice a high degree of control over market supply (as against total control) is usually sufficient to justify the term 'monopoly'. A *concentration ratio* is one way of measuring the degree of monopoly in an industry. A concentration ration measures the percentage of total output that is produced by the three, or five, largest firms in that industry. The three biggest firms might produce say 60% or 90% of the total in which case the industry is said to be highly monopolistic. If however the three biggest firms produce only 1% or 2% of the total then the industry is clearly very competitive.

There are a number of reasons why a monopoly might be positively beneficial to society. If, for example, there are large *economies of scale* to be gained in an industry, a monopoly might lead to greater output and lower prices than if a government insisted on keeping several firms competing in the industry. It is possible that only a monopoly would be financially able, or willing, because of its sole beneficiary status, to undertake *research and development* and to introduce new products. In certain situations monopoly may even give consumers *more product choice* than competition (see the box on Competition, Monopoly and Consumer Choice).

Competition, Monopoly And Consumer Choice

Which will give consumers a greater choice and variety of product, an industry that is monopolised by a single seller or an industry with many competing firms? An economist named Hotelling showed that choice might in fact be greater with monopoly.

As a model, consider the locational behaviour of ice cream sellers on a beach. All factors other than their location are the same, the ice cream quality is identical, bathers are spread absolutely evenly across the sand, the beach can be entered and exited at any point *ie there is no one place where people must all pass. A single ice cream seller would locate at the very centre of the beach. This would minimize the distance walked by customers on the beach, the opportunity cost of ice cream being its price, plus travel time to the ice cream seller. The location is shown as A in Figure 1.*

Figure 1   [**A**   ]

If a rival ice cream seller, B, sets up a stall in competition, where should the stall be placed to maximize sales? Right bang up against A is the best place, Figure 2. He then stands to get 50% of the sales.

Figure 2   [**BA**   ]

It can be shown that at any other point seller A will have more than 50% of sales and B will have a smaller amount. For example if B locates half way across the stretch of beach between A and the end of the beach to the left, Figure 3, the seller will get only 3/8 of the customers. He/she will gain all of those to the left and half of those to the right, those closest to B. A will get the other half of these, plus all of those to the right of A, a total of 5/8.

Figure 3   [**B**   **A**   ]

The best place is right in the centre. However this is not best for consumer choice. They are faced with two ice cream sellers side by side in the centre of the beach. If, on the other hand, ice cream sales were controlled by a monopolist, so that positioning was no longer rivalrous, where would the ice cream sellers be placed? Figure 4 shows the optimal locations, those which minimize the walking time for all consumers. They are better off with monopoly, (at least for location, they may of course be worse off on price, without the stimulus of competition).

Figure 4   [**B**   **A**   ]

Questions

When I first visited the United States in 1980 I was surprised at the lack of variety of television programmes compared to the UK. The US had a very large number of competing channels, perhaps 60, whereas in the UK there were only three, two of which were controlled by the BBC. Hotelling's theory helps to explain this.

Assume that during the peak viewing times the following proportion of viewers wish to watch these types of programme:

1 Soaps 55%   2 Movies 24%   3 Sport 16%   4 Documentaries 5%

1 If there were four competing TV stations what would they broadcast to gain most viewers?
2 How many companies would there have to be before Documentaries were screened?
3 How would a monopolist owning the four stations behave?

However, there are major reasons why the public should remain suspicious of monopoly. It can be shown that *very often monopolists charge higher prices and produce lower outputs* than under competition. The absence of competition can also lead to the firm operating *inefficiently*. Governments, therefore, maintain laws and courts to examine monopoly power and to rule whether or not it is in the public interest to allow monopoly to exist in a particular industry.

It is a common fallacy that monopolies have total market power, *ie* they can set whatever price and output they choose. They cannot. They cannot because although they control supply, *they do not control demand*. Therefore if a monopolist sets a particular price for a product, the quantity sold is determined by the demand curve. Similarly, controlling supply leads to a certain price being determined by its interaction with the demand curve. Nevertheless, of all the market structures monopoly is the one where the greatest power over price or output lies with the producer, the situation with the greatest *producer sovereignty. Consumer sovereignty*, literally where consumers are king, is found where markets are very competitive. The more choice that consumers have between sellers, the more power they have over price and output. The greater the restrictions in the market, that is, the greater the degree of monopoly, the more power resides with producers.

If there is just one buyer of a product a situation known as a *monopsony*, or just a few large buyers, then the consumer can be extra-ordinarily powerful compared to the sellers if they are many. In some cases the government may be the only buyer. This might be the case with military weapons or with the services of teachers or policemen. Many primary products are produced by a large number of sellers *in less developed countries,* all competing hard against each other. The buyers of the product on the other hand, may be a small number of large multi-national companies (MNCs) located in the more developed countries. Tea, coffee, cocoa and bananas are examples of such products. It is well known that major exporters of oil used the monopoly power of the *cartel* OPEC (Organization of the Petroleum Exporting Countries) to restrict oil output in the 1970s and raise the price of oil to extremely high levels. Before that time, however, a small number of giant oil companies based in the USA and Europe used their combined power to expand output and keep oil prices very low.

As the monopoly power of big business or big unions may distort the efficient operation of the market system, governments often intervene. The existence of monopoly is a major form of *'market failure'.*

A more detailed analysis of market structure now follows.

PERFECT COMPETITION

Perfect competition is the name given to a market structure where competition between firms is perfect or absolute, that is the degree of competition is total. Whilst the extreme conditions which are required for this to occur are not found in the real world, it is nevertheless a useful model to understand. Firstly, some markets do approximate to the model by displaying a very high degree of competitive behaviour. Some of the closest are found in agricultural markets. For example, the market for fresh vegetables. Secondly, by comparing perfect competition to pure monopoly (also very unlikely to exist in practice) conclusions can be drawn about what to expect when a real industry becomes a little more competitive or a little less competitive. The extreme models act as reference points for real world situations.

THE ASSUMPTIONS OF THE PERFECT COMPETITION MODEL

There is only one single *necessary and sufficient condition* for perfect competition to exist. That is that the firm has no control whatsoever over the price of the product. The firm is a *'price taker'.*

There are, however, a number of conditions which are likely requirements for a firm to end up as a price taker. These are that:

1 there are many sellers
2 there are many buyers
3 the products are homogenous *ie* identical
4 there are no barriers to entry into or exit from the industry
5 there is perfect knowledge. Firms and buyers are completely informed about the product prices of each firm in the industry
6 the factors of production are completely mobile

Because there are very many sellers, the product of every firm is identical, buyers know all prices and new firms can enter the industry easily, the sellers have no control whatsoever over the price of their product. As a result, they face a *perfectly elastic demand curve*. This means they can sell as much of their product as they want at one price, but nothing at any other price. Figure 2.64 illustrates the demand curve for any one of the many firms. *The price itself is determined in the market place by demand and supply.* The firm has to sell at this market price. The conditions above ensure that no one will buy at any higher price (perfect knowledge, homogenous product *etc*) and it would be irrational for a profit maximising firm to sell at a lower price. It can sell all it wants at the market price.

📊 Figure 2.64 – Perfect Competition

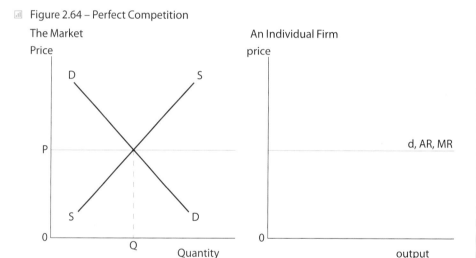

Price is determined in the market. Each individual firm 'takes' this price from the market. Because of market conditions they cannot sell at a higher price. Because they are profit maximizsers it is irrational to sell at a lower price. They will not sell more. They can sell as much as they like at the market price.

OUTPUT UNDER ASSUMPTIONS OF PERFECT COMPETITION

A profit maximising firm will produce where profit is at its highest. To determine profit we need to examine the firm's revenue and costs.

The firm's total revenue TR is obtained by multiplying price times output. In perfect competition, price is constant, therefore average revenue AR must be equal to price:

$$TR = p \times q$$

$$AR = \frac{TR}{q} = \frac{p \times q}{q} = p$$

Every extra or marginal unit of output is also sold at the constant price. Therefore marginal revenue also equals price. MR = AR = p. These are shown on Figure 2.64.

The firm's short run costs will be 'U' shaped, (as shown previously), both average costs and marginal costs. These are shown superimposed upon the firm's revenue curves as in Figure 2.65.

Figure 2.65 – The Short Run Equilibrium, or Firm's Equilibrium

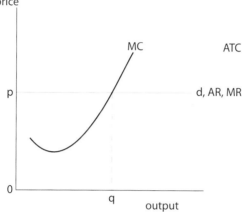

The firm will produce where MR = MC as this is where profit is maximised. At any output other than 0q, either MR>MC, or MC<MR. In either case more profit will be made by moving to 0q.

The firm will produce *0q* units of output. This is where marginal revenue is equal to marginal cost. The firm cannot do better than this. If it were to produce one unit less it would lose a little of the profit to be made on that unit. As with other units to the left of *q*, marginal revenue from selling the unit is greater than the marginal cost of producing that unit.

If the firm were to produce one more unit than *q* the marginal cost of producing that unit would be greater than the marginal revenue from selling it. The firm would make a loss on that unit which would reduce its total profit. It could make more profit by not producing that unit.

A profit maximising firm will always produce where MR = MC. This is known as the *'firm's equilibrium position'* or the *'short run equilibrium position'*. However, this needs to be distinguished from the *'industry equilibrium'* or *'long run equilibrium'*.

Figure 2.66 is a reproduction of Figure 2.65. *0qap* is the total revenue of the firm. *0qbc* is the total cost, obtained by multiplying the quantity produced by the average cost – ATC. Recalling our earlier study on profit, we noted that 'normal' profit is included in the definition of economic cost. Therefore the difference between total revenue and total cost, the area *cbap* is *'supernormal profit'*. So the firm shown in Figure 2.66 is in equilibrium because MR = MC, but it is also earning supernormal profit. This is now shown to be a short run equilibrium. The industry is not in equilibrium, and the firm is not at its long run equilibrium profit. This is because of these supernormal profits, profits over and above the amount that is required to keep firms in the industry.

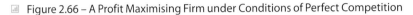 Figure 2.66 – A Profit Maximising Firm under Conditions of Perfect Competition

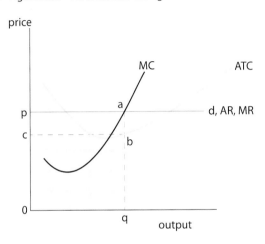

The firm is in short-run equilibrium at 0q where MR=MC and is earning 'supernormal' profit of cbap.

Recall that under an assumption of *perfect knowledge*, it is not secret that there are high profits to be earned in this industry. There are *no barriers to entry*. Other firms attracted by the higher than normal profit are attracted into the industry. As other firms move in, the supply of the product expands and the price falls. This is shown in Figure 2.67. The supply curve slides out to the right. As it does so, price falls. As price is the firm's MR curve it will contract production down its MC curve as MR falls, always producing where MR = MC. Price p_2 output q_2 is just one intermediate point. It is still a short run equilibrium because at p_2 the total revenue of the firm is greater than the total cost. Supernormal profit is still being made. Other firms continue to be attracted. Supply expands. Price falls. Firms contract and so on. The process will stop only when supernormal profit no longer exists: that point where only normal profit is made. As 'normal' profit is included in economic cost, the expansion of the industry and the contraction of output of each individual firm continues until the firm's total revenue equals the firm's total cost. This occurs at the bottom of the ATC curve where MR = MC = ATC. The area $0q_3 \times 0p_3$ is both total cost and total revenue. As firms are earning only normal profit, new firms are not attracted in. *Individual firms are in long run equilibrium. The industry is in equilibrium.*

Figure 2.67 – The Market   An Individual Firm

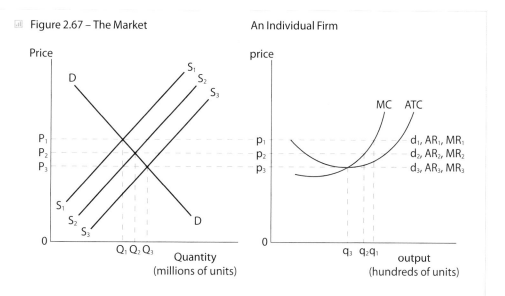

Competition in the Video Rental Market (United States)

Reliable electronic video recorders became available for the first time in the early 1980s. In 1980 less than 1% of American families owned a videocassette recorder (VCR). By 1990 over 70% of families owned one. This growth led to a huge demand for movie rentals on videotape.

The owners of the first video rental outlets benefited from this increase in demand. A tape would rent for five dollars a night and paid for itself after a few rentals. There were however no significant barriers to entry into the rental industry. It was easy for new entrants to rent space, hire low-skilled labour, and buy shelving and tapes. Between 1982 and 1987 the number of outlets expanded by 400%. Gas stations and grocery stores also rented tapes. By 1990 tape rental rates had fallen to $1.50 a night and entry into the industry had ceased. Profits had fallen to normal and firms were in long-run equilibrium.

With the present growth of satellite and cable TV and growth of pay-per-view movie rental the video rental industry may contract as quickly as it grew.

Exercise

Using your knowledge of the perfect competition model, draw diagrams to illustrate changes in the video rental market.

Imperfections in the market for houses (UK)

There are four main factors that go against the housing market being regarded as a 'perfect market' in the UK. First, there are large transactions costs incurred in both buying and selling houses. Second, information asymmetries abound between buyers and sellers, both about individual properties and about the state of the market. Third, expectations about future house prices and future interest rates can be more important than their current levels. And fourth, markets are highly localized, which can result in severe excess demand and excess supply in different areas, and in different price brackets, at the same time.

Source: Economic Bulletin, Lloyds TSB, 27 July 1999

Avoiding Lemons

Imperfect information in a market can lead to only low quality goods being traded due to the presence of 'lemons'. A 'lemon' is a poor quality good. For example, in the market for used cars the seller is likely to know the deficiencies of the car being sold. The buyer is not. If used cars are divided into two groups, good cars and 'lemons' the market price for any particular type of car is an average of the two. However owners of good used cars will be unwilling to sell at this price whilst owners of 'lemons' will be keen to sell. Lemons thus dominate the market as good quality cars are withdrawn.

Of course buyers can try to get around the problem of spotting lemons by acquiring more expertise. They can for example hire an independent expert to check out a car. Sellers of good cars also devise ways to reassure potential buyers. For example, traders will offer warranties with their cars.

Question

Now consider the transfer market for professional football players. Can you explain why players on transfer lists are more likely to suffer fitness problems than players who have their contracts renewed?

THE FIRM'S SUPPLY CURVE

If market price should rise again, the firm will expand output up its MC curve, always moving to keep $MR = MC$. The firms MC curve is in fact its supply curve. However, this needs to be qualified because the firm will also produce below the ATC curve in the short run, but never below the AVC curve. To summarise, the firm's supply curve is in fact 'the MC curve above the AVC curve'.[14] The firm will close down and stop producing when $MR = MC = AVC$. We need to show why this is so.

If the market price of the product should fall below the long run equilibrium point, that point where firms are just earning normal profit, then firms will make a loss. This is a situation which cannot be sustained. If price does not rise again firms will move out (recall that they need to earn 'normal' profit just to keep them in the industry). In the short-run, however, they can justify producing at a loss as long as they cover their *direct* or *variable costs* of producing. Figure 2.68 illustrates just such a situation: at price *p* the firm will produce *Oq* where *MR = MC*. It is making a loss because its total revenue *Oqap* is less than its total cost *Oqbc*. The firm is making losses of *pabc*, which it cannot sustain in the long term. However, in the short-run it is better for a profit maximizer to produce something, that is *Oq* rather than close down and produce nothing. If the firm produces nothing it will have no variable costs but it will have to meet its fixed costs. Fixed costs have to be paid even if the firm produces nothing. At output *Oq* in the diagram the firm's total variable costs are its average variable costs times quantity – area *Oqed*. All of the variable costs are covered by the revenue *Oqap* and the surplus *deap* helps to offset the fixed costs of *debc*. The firm makes a smaller loss than if it closed down. As the firm is a profit maximise it is logical that it is a loss minimise. After all, a loss can be defined as negative profit.

Figure 2.68 – Profit Maximising Firm under Conditions of Perfect Competition in Short Run Equilibrium

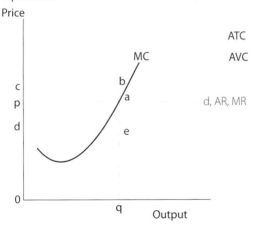

The firm is making losses of pabc. However the revenue 0qap is greater than the total variable cost 0qed. The firm makes deap to set against the fixed costs of debc. The fixed costs have to be paid even if the firm closes down. It makes the least loss possible where MR=MC, as long as MR=MC is greater than AVC.

At any price below the *ATC* curve and above the *AVC* curve the firm will minimise its losses by continuing to produce. At the bottom of the *AVC* curve the firm will close down. This point is defined as *MR = MC = AVC* and is known as the firm's shut-down point, or close-down point – Figure 2.69. At any price below the *AVC* curve the firm will not even cover its variable costs and so would lose more by producing than closing down. At prices between *AVC* and *ATC* the firm will produce, but only in the short run. Firms cannot sustain making losses and will move out. As they move out the market supply curve will shift to the left, raising price up to the long run equilibrium position where *MR* = *MC* = *ATC*.

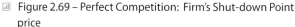

Figure 2.69 – Perfect Competition: Firm's Shut-down Point

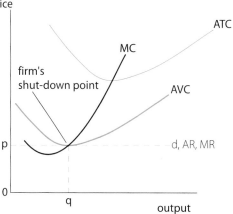

At prices lower than Op firms will not cover their variable costs. They will make a loss on variable costs as well as having to pay fixed costs. The firm makes a smaller loss by closing down and paying only fixed costs. MR=MC=AVC is the firm's shut-down point.

Shut-downs in the real world occur most frequently in primary industries. If the price of tin falls, tin mines temporarily stop producing. If the price of gold fails to cover the direct costs of mining it, gold mines close. If the price of fish is insufficient to cover the variable costs, the boats stay tied up in the harbour. Farmers will plough crops back into the ground if the price falls below the variable costs of harvesting and transport to market. This temporary shut-down can also be observed in manufacturing. Shipyards close if there are no orders (ie if no orders can be obtained with a price greater than the variable costs of building ships).

A firm's supply curve, in the short run, is its *MC* curve above the *AVC* curve, Figure 2.70. The firm's supply curve is entirely related to its costs. This explains why a firm's supply curve is upward sloping against price, it explains the Law of Supply. The supply for the whole industry is merely the supply of all firms added together at each price Figure 2.71. The supply curve of the industry is also upward sloping, and it also represents the marginal cost of production in the industry, as it is derived from the upward sloping marginal cost curves of firms.

Figure 2.70

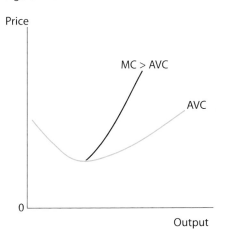

A firm's supply curve under conditions of perfect competition is its MC curve above the AVC curve, (MCAVC=S)

Figure 2.71

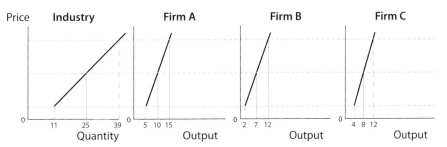

The market supply or industry supply is the sum of the supplies from each firm at each price. In an industry with 3 firms, A,B and C, the market supply at any price is the sum of supply from firm A, supply from firm B, and supply from firm C. For example at price P_2 the industry supply is $10 + 7 + 8 = 25$.

Jaguar Shuts Down

Ford Motors, the owners of Jaguar, has announced that it will be closing down the production lines for Jaguar cars for 5 weeks. This follows an earlier announcement that Jaguar has been making heavy losses during the current recession in the car market.

Questions

1 How will the costs of Jaguar be affected by this decision?
2 What is the economic reasoning behind the decision to halt production for 5 weeks?

EFFICIENCY AND OPTIMAL ALLOCATION

A pure market system is likely to be both *technically efficient* and *allocatively efficient*. *Technical efficiency* occurs when output is produced with the minimum amount of resources. There is no waste. This will occur under perfect competition because firms continually seek to cut costs in order to survive in a competitive market. Profits can be increased by either raising prices or lowering costs. As firms are price takers they cannot raise their prices. They must continuously seek to lower their costs.

Allocative efficiency occurs where suppliers are producing the optimal mix of goods and services required by consumers. Consumers express their preferences through demand. If one good becomes more desirable and another less desirable, demand for the former will increase, shifting the demand curve to the right and raising its price. Demand for the other good will shift to the left and its price will fall. Under conditions of perfect competition producers have to react to these changes of demand. As price rises in one industry, firms expand along their MC curves. As price contracts in the other industry supply contracts back along the MC curve. Economic resources, land, labour and capital are reallocated moving out of the declining industry and into the expanding one. Expansion will continue in the first industry as long as there is supernormal profit available. Resources move out of the other industry where losses are being made. The process continues in each case until just normal profit is being earned in each industry. The suppliers react and resource owners react to produce the precise mix of goods and services which consumers wish to buy. Consumer preferences are clearly expressed by their demands, which translate into prices; and suppliers react to the prices causing the economic factors of production to move. Under perfect competition the *consumer is sovereign*. The goods and services produced are exactly in the relative quantities that consumers demand. This is the *optimal allocation of resources*. At least it is with respect to private decisions. We have already noted a very important caveat with respect to externalities, which are not taken into account by any market system.

However, externalities aside, perfect competition leads to allocative efficiency. All markets move to a position where price and marginal cost are equal. The price is the value that people are willing to pay for the good. That is they value the good at least that much relative to all other goods. The marginal cost represents the cost to society of all the scarce resources used in making the good, including the cost of risk-taking represented by normal profit. If price is greater than marginal cost, P > MC, it shows that consumers value the product more than it costs to produce it. Under perfect competition output will expand further until P = MC. We shall see in the next section that this will not happen under monopoly. It will be shown that monopoly is not allocatively efficient. Similarly if MC < P society is using more resources in producing a product than its value to consumers. The industry should contract and under perfect competition this will happen. Externalities aside, optimum allocation will occur where P = MC.

PROFIT MAXIMISATION IN A MONOPOLY

A *monopoly* is an industry with a *single seller*. The demand curve facing a monopolist is the demand curve of the whole industry. Unlike perfect competition there are no separate demand curves for the firm and the industry, they are one and the same thing. As the industry demand curve is downward sloping, the monopolist has to reduce the price to sell more of the product. The monopolist has considerable control over price by being able to vary total supply of the product – but not total control over price because consumers control demand. Unlike a firm in perfect competition the monopolist is not a '*price-taker*', passively reacting to price changes. The monopolist can change price by altering supply. The monopolist is therefore a '*price-maker*'.

MONOPOLY PRICE AND MARGINAL REVENUE

Under perfect competition firms always obtain the same price for their product, and so marginal revenue is always equal to price. Because a monopolist has to lower the price to sell more, marginal revenue will be lower than price. To understand why look at Figure 2.72. To sell one more unit the monopolist has to lower the price from p_1 to p_2. The marginal revenue is $1 \times p_2$ which is less than p_1 ie MR < P. However the price is lowered not only on the last unit sold but on every unit sold. Thus there is a loss of revenue on $0q_1$ units which previously sold at p_1. The marginal or extra revenue gained from selling one more unit is therefore 1 times p_2 minus $0q_1$ times the fall in price. In Figure 2.54 this is the area marked by a (+) sign minus the area marked by a (−) sign. Marginal revenue is clearly considerably less than price. Graphed in Figure 2.73 the *MR* curve of a monopolist will appear well below the demand curve. This fact will lead to very different production outcomes under monopoly than under perfect competition.

Figure 2.72 – Monopoly: Price and Marginal Revenue

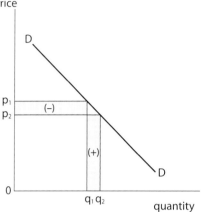

In order to sell one more unit (q_2 minus q_1) a monopolist must lower the product price from p_1 to p_2. The price of the additional unit sold p_2 is lower than the original price p_1. Therefore MR<P. However in order to sell one more unit the monopolist has to lower the price on all units sold, that is, on Oq_1, units as well as the extra unit. The marginal revenue is thus further reduced. In the diagram MR is equal to the area marked (+), minus the area marked (-). Marginal revenue is therefore well below price.

Figure 2.73 – Monopoly

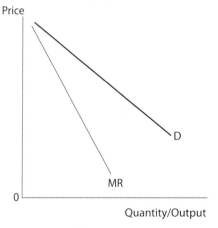

Under conditions of monopoly the marginal revenue of a firm is below the demand curve. (If the D curve is a straight line the MR curve falls twice as steeply.)

Referring to Figure 2.74, the monopolist, as a *profit maximizer*, will produce where $MR = MC$, (price = p, quantity = q).[15] Because MR is always less than price under monopoly, then MC must be less than price, *ie MC < P*. Monopoly is not optimally efficient. Consumers value the product at *p*. The product costs only *MC* to produce. Output should expand, ideally with price falling and *MC* rising until they are equal. However the industry is not competitive, there is only one seller and there are high entry barriers preventing new firms entering the industry.

Figure 2.74 – Monopoly

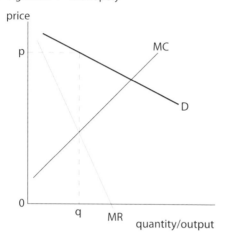

A profit maximising monopoly will produce where MR=MC. As MR is always less than price then MC must be less than price, (MC<P).

MONOPOLY AND SUPERNORMAL PROFITS

It is quite likely (though not totally certain) that monopolists will earn supernormal profits. If the *AC* curve is below the *AR* (demand) curve the monopoly can earn supernormal profit. As there are high barriers to entry, it is likely to maintain high levels of profit because they cannot be bid away. Sustained high profit levels are a common feature of monopoly. They are one way to recognize that monopoly is present in an industry. Thus if the profit figures for the industry are examined and are found to be persistently high over a period of time, then it is likely that monopoly conditions exist. In Figure 2.75 the monopolist will produce at *q* where *MR* = *MC*. The price charged however is *p*, the price which consumers are willing to pay for quantity *q*. Total Revenue is shown by the rectangle *0qap*. Total cost of quantity *q* is the average cost times the quantity – the rectangle *0qbc*. As this cost 'area' includes provision for 'normal' profit, the rectangle *cbap* represents supernormal profit. The monopoly is sustained by high barriers to entry, so this high level of profit can persist. Other firms cannot enter the market to increase supply, reduce price, and erode profit back to 'normal' levels as they would under conditions of perfect competition.

Figure 2.75 – Monopoly and Supernormal Profit

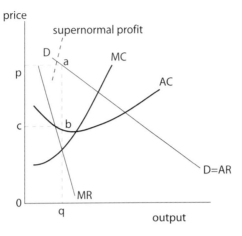

The monopolist will produce at q and sell at p earning total revenue of p x q = area 0qap. The total cost is AC x q = area 0qbc. The area bapc is supernormal profit. Because of barriers to entry other firms cannot enter and bid away this profit.

Students tend to recall the fact that monopolies often make 'supernormal' profit, and not the fact that resource allocation is non-optimal. It is the latter which is the more important for resource allocation. Governments can tax away supernormal profits.

It is possible that a monopolist makes small 'supernormal' profits – it all depends upon the position of the AC curve. Figure 2.76 shows the limit where $AC = AR$ and a monopolist makes only 'normal' profit. Figure 2.77 shows a situation where costs are so high a private monopolist would not produce at all.

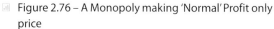
Figure 2.76 – A Monopoly making 'Normal' Profit only

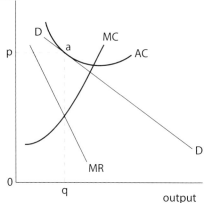

Total cost equals total revenue. The monopolist makes normal profit.

Figure 2.77 – A Situation where a Monopolist would not Produce

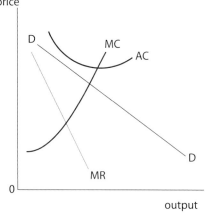

Total cost is always greater than total revenue.

In the real world it is also possible that a monopolist would expand output, lowering both price and profit more than this model predicts. If the monopolist feared that the barriers to entry were not high enough to keep out another firm attracted by very high profit, it may adopt a strategy of expanding output and reducing profit levels to discourage others contesting the monopoly. It might also fear that high profit would attract public criticism and the unwelcome attentions of government.

It is important to note the boundaries of the market when regarding monopoly. Many markets are global markets, and what appears to be a domestic monopoly may in fact be a fiercely competitive international market. Thus Fiat dominates Italian car production, yet has to compete with many foreign car companies. The motor car industry is very competitive in practice, with small profit margins.

COMPETITION VERSUS MONOPOLY

In the real world you are unlikely to find market structures which conform either to perfect competition or to pure monopoly, although very competitive markets and very monopolistic ones do exist. It is illuminating, however, to make a direct comparison of the two models to highlight what happens when an industry becomes slightly more competitive or slightly more monopolistic. The most important consideration in doing this, is whether or not there are economies of scale to be gained by firms increasing in size. We now look at an industry where (a) there are no economies of scale to be gained, and another (b) where there are large economies of scale to be gained. We will conclude that if long-run costs do not fall as in (a), then competition is likely to be superior to monopoly. If long-run average costs fall as the scale of the firm increases, then it is possible that monopoly is superior to competition.

a   Competition versus monopoly when no economies of scale are gained

Here we will assume that an industry is in perfect competition. The industry is then monopolised and run as a multi-plant monopoly, that is, although a monopolist makes the decisions, there remain the same number of 'plants' (a plant is a factory, farm or office). Figure 2.78 shows the industry operating under perfect competition. Output decisions are made at the level of the firm, each accepting the price which is determined neutrally by market supply and demand. Firms produce where $MR = MC$. P_{pc} and Q_{pc} are the price and output figures for the industry as a whole – formed where the supply and demand curves intersect.

Figure 2.78 – Industry Operating under Conditions of Perfect Competition

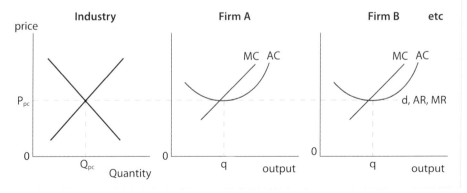

When a monopolist takes over the industry the output decisions are taken at industry level, not at the individual plant level. The monopoly firm's demand curve is the downward sloping demand curve of the whole industry, see Figure 2.79. The marginal revenue curve is therefore below the demand curve. The monopolist will produce at q_m and charge price p_m. Notice that the quantity produced by the monopolist is less than the quantity produced by the competitive industry $q_m < q_{pc}$. The price charged by the monopolist is greater than the competitive price $p_m > p_{pc}$. Finally price has moved from the allocatively efficient position $p = MC$, to the allocatively inefficient position $p > MC$. In summary, prices are higher, quantities lower and resource allocation is non-optimal.

Figure 2.79 – A Multi-Plant Monopolist

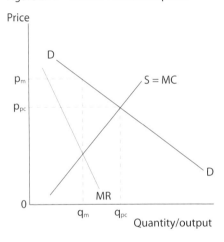

A monopolist takes over the industry and, with no economies of scale available, runs it as a multi-plant firm.

b Competition versus monopoly when economies of scale are gained

One powerful reason for a firm to grow larger is the presence of economies of scale in the industry. If economies of scale do exist then the monopoly will be equating marginal revenue with a different, and lower, marginal cost than that of perfect competition. In Figure 2.80 many small firms will have high average and marginal cost curves as shown by $SRAC_1$ and MC_1. If a monopoly develops, through one firm growing larger in order to exploit economies of scale, the firm might produce at $SRAC_2$ and MC_2. This is shown in Figure 2.81: many small competing firms would produce at $0p_{pc}$ and $0q_{pc}$. However, with economies of scale present, one firm is likely to grow to a monopoly and produce at quantity $0q_m$ and price $0p_m$. It is quite possible that the price is lower than under perfect competition and the quantity produced greater. Consumers would be better off under monopoly. Of course price is still greater than marginal cost *ie* resource allocation is non-optimal. Society values $0q_m$ at price $0p_m$ which is more than its marginal cost, oc. It would be even better if production occurred where the MC curve cut the demand curve. Of course a profit maximising monopolist will not do this. One possibility is for the government to subsidise the product to shift the MC curve further to the right. Another possibility is for the government to nationalise the industry so that it is no longer a private profit maximizer, and to order it to set the price equal to the marginal cost. A third possibility is for the government to regulate private monopoly prices. This has been a common option when privatising former nationalised industries in recent years.

Figure 2.80 – Monopoly versus Perfect Competition

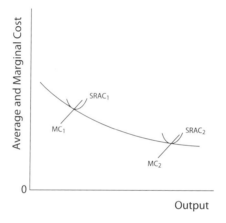

Cost curves of small competing firms compared to the cost curves of a monopolist when economies of scale are present.

Figure 2.81 – Monopoly versus Perfect Competition

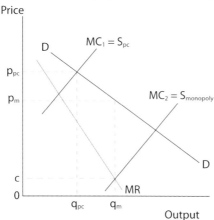

With substantial economies of scale present, the price under monopoly may well be lower than price under competition, $p_m < p_{pc}$. Quantity under monopoly may be greater than under perfect competition, $q_m > q_{pc}$. However price is still greater than marginal cost $p > MC$, resource allocation is non-optimal.

PRICE AND OUTPUT IN IMPERFECT MARKETS

Between the two extreme models of market structure, perfect competition and pure monopoly there is a whole range of intermediate possibilities. These are known collectively as *imperfect competition*. Two models within the range serve to highlight the behaviour of firms; in uncompetitive markets, *oligopoly* and in very competitive markets, *monopolistic competition*.

OLIGOPOLY

Oligopoly is a form of market structure commonly found in the real world. A few large firms dominate the market, and high barriers to entry allow them to maintain their dominance. The characteristic behaviour of oligopolists is determined by their *interdependence*. Because there are just a few giant companies the behaviour of any one company affects and is affected by the behaviour of the others and each is aware of this. Oligopolies are therefore pulled in two opposing directions. The first is to *collude* and act together as a monopoly to maximise the profits of the group. The other is not to collude and compete fiercely as *rivals* in order to gain a bigger share of the industry. The two policies are incompatible. If firms compete they will drive down the price and profits of the industry. Non price competition through advertising will raise the costs of the industry and reduce profits. Competition law often bans collusion. However oligopolists sometimes do collude and sometimes not. We first look at *collusive oligopoly* and then at *non collusive oligopoly*.

Collusive Oligopoly

A formal collusive agreement is called a *cartel*. Firms make an agreement on price, market share, advertising *etc.* to reduce the uncertainty in the industry and the losses that would come about if they competed with each other. They would therefore behave much like a single monopoly seller, see Figure 2.82. Profits are maximised at output q and price p. Having agreed on the price and total output the cartel members could then engage in non-price competition to gain a bigger market share of the fixed total, although this will raise their costs. Alternatively they agree on *quotas* for each of the members. The sum of the quotas must equal 0q in Figure 2.82. The most common way of determining the size of quotas in practice is based upon the existing percentage share of the market.

Figure 2.82 – Collusive Oligopoly

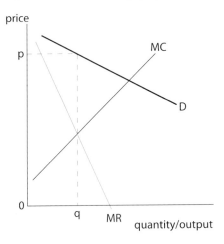

A collusive oligopoly will behave like a monopoly, ie it will produce where MR=MC. The Industry MC curve is the sum of each firm's marginal costs at each price.

As cartels are often illegal on the grounds that they are against the public interest firms may break the law and risk being fined or they may collude tacitly. One form of *tacit collusion* is where firms set the same prices as the dominant firm. This is known as *dominant firm price leadership*.

Non-collusive Oligopoly

Cartels keep prices higher than they would be if the firms were in competition. There is of course a temptation to cheat by any single firm. If the others don't react the firm could sell more at the high price by not sticking to its quota. Of course other firms are not likely to allow one member to do this. Open competition will break out and the cartel will collapse. In many industries the conditions for a successful cartel do not exist in the first place. We need to look therefore at behaviour in a non collusive oligopoly.

The first thing to note is that there is no analytical technique for determining a unique output and price as there is under conditions of perfect competition and monopoly. However, it was noted earlier in this book that a study of *'Game Theory'* throws some light on the observed behaviour of giant firms as they battle in the market place.

Although economic theory cannot show where an oligopolist will produce, and at what price, it can help to explain the observed characteristics of price and output in oligopolistic markets. Even when there is no collusion, prices of goods in these markets remain stable for long periods of time. There is little movement of price up or down *ie* there is *price stability*. The firms rarely compete with each other on price. When they do it is a wonder to behold. A *price war* is dramatic. Prices are slashed competitively, often to a fraction of the usual price. In such a situation it is likely the firms involved will all end up losers, whilst consumers gain at their expense. This helps to explain the observed price stability or rigidity, even without collusion. Firms are afraid of starting a price war because they are likely to end up losing. Thus in oligopoly inter-firm competition is based upon anything but price. Common features are the branding of goods, advertising, free offers, competitions, an emphasis upon quality or service, in fact the stressing of anything but price. Of course profits are affected by the increased marketing costs.

KINKED DEMAND CURVE

One theory which gives a reasoned analysis of price rigidity and non-price competition is known as the *kinked demand curve theory*. In Figure 2.83 price and output is graphed for a firm operating under conditions of oligopoly. The price and output are taken as the starting point for analysing subsequent behaviour. Where an oligopolist will produce cannot be determined.

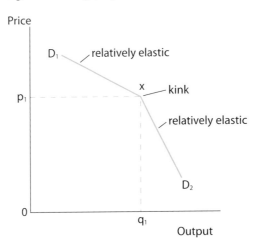

Figure 2.83 – Oligopoly: the Kinked Demand Curve

From point p_1q_1 the firm assumes that a price increase will not be matched by other firms. Demand above this point will be very elastic. They also assume that if they decrease the price rival firms will follow and cut their prices. Demand below p_1q_1 is therefore inelastic.

From price p_1 and quantity q_1: point x, the oligopolist firm has three options with respect to its pricing policy (i) raise prices (ii) lower prices (iii) leave prices unchanged. The kinked demand curve theory reasons why (iii) is the most likely option, why price is not likely to change and why the firm is most likely to engage only in non-price competition.

From price p_1 company A considers raising its price. What it expects its rivals to do is of the greatest importance. If company A raises its prices and the other companies follow suit, also raising their prices, then all will lose some customers. This is the basic law of demand. However, their relative prices will remain unchanged, they will not lose customers to each other, they will retain market share. If, however, the other companies do not raise their prices company A will lose a lot of customers, as they now switch to the products of rival companies. This alarming scenario is likely to cause company A to view the price elasticity of demand for its product as very high if it should raise its price. This is shown in Figure 2.84 as a 'flattish' demand curve above point x. This is labelled D_1.

If company A considers lowering its product price and other firms do not cut their prices, company A will not only gain because quantity demanded increases at lower prices, but will gain a lot of extra demand from customers switching from other companies. Company A is likely to reason that other companies will not let this happen and will also cut their prices. If all companies cut prices they will all gain a little, because quantity demanded increases at lower prices. However, individual company demand would not increase much because each would retain its market share. Company *A* therefore assumes that its demand curve below point *x* will be inelastic. This is drawn as demand curve *D₂*. Company *A* is likely to neither raise nor lower prices but to attempt non-price competition.

 Figure 2.84 – Oligopoly: Kinked Demand Curve

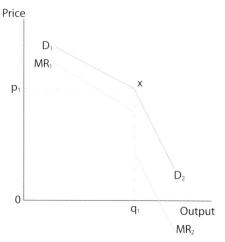

Because the demand curve is kinked there are two separate marginal revenue curves. Below point x there is a 'gap' in the marginal revenue curve.

Thus oligopolists may face not one, but two demand curves each of differing elasticity, the elasticity depending upon whether prices are raised or lowered. The demand curve appears to be 'kinked' at the current price, hence the name *'kinked demand curve'*. The marginal revenue curve for *D₁* stops immediately below point *x*. The marginal revenue curve for curve *D₂* begins directly below point *x*. The 'kink' or break in the demand curve causes a 'gap' to exist between the marginal revenue curves. A whole range of cost curves between *MC₁* and *MC₂* will give the same price and output solutions to a profit maximising oligopolist – see Figure 2.85. That is, even quite large shifts in costs will cause prices to remain fixed.

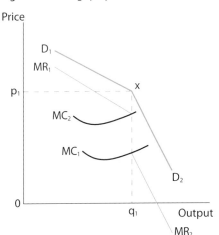

Figure 2.85 – Oligopoly: Kinked Demand Curve

A whole range of costs between MC_1 and MC_2 will lead a profit maximising oligopolist to produce at price p_1 and quantity q_1.

THEORY OF CONTESTABLE MARKETS

A theory which has gained a great deal of support in recent years because of the realism it has brought to the theory of the firm is that of contestable markets. *'The theory of contestable markets'* argues that it is the *threat* of competition rather than *actual* competition which determines a firm's price and output. Thus a firm with a market monopoly would modify its pricing policy if there was a threat that another firm could enter and take over its market.

The extreme case would be a market which is *perfectly contestable*. Here the costs of entry and exit are zero. Other firm's could enter very rapidly if there was any possibility of earning supernormal profits. The threat of this happening keeps the prices of the monopoly firm low and its production efficient. The threat also ensures that it would take advantage of any economies of scale and technology improvements. Thus by keeping costs as low as possible it remains unattractive to potential rivals.

In Figure 2.86 it is assumed that a single monopolist with high exit and entry costs will maximise profit at q_1, with a price of p_1 and supernormal profit shown by the shaded rectangle. If entry and exit costs were low however the threat of other firms entering would cause the monopoly to lower prices and increase the quantity. In the extreme case of a perfectly contestable market the monopoly would increase production to q_2 at a price of $p_2 = AC_2$ where profit is normal.

Figure 2.86 – A contestable monopoly

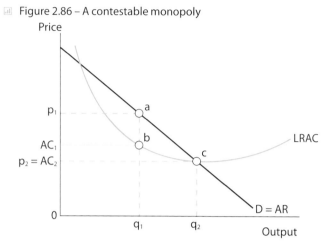

A perfectly contestable monopoly will produce at q_2 rather than q_1.

The firm in Figure 2.86 is a natural monopoly as there is a downward sloping LRAC curve. If two or more firms are in the market they will produce at a higher cost than a single firm. Thus a single monopoly seller will survive. Another firm will enter only if it believes it can knock out the first firm and take over the whole market itself. It will not be able to do this if the existing monopolist keeps its prices low, doesn't make supernormal profit and is efficient with respect to costs and technology. Thus in this case, even though there is a monopoly, the firm behaves very competitively, benefiting consumers, and this is due to of the *threat* of competition rather than the *actual* competition.

The importance of exit costs

The costs of leaving an industry, the exit costs, are very important in determining how contestable a market is. A firm will incur fixed set up costs in entering a new industry. If these are competitive with the existing firm then it might win and take over the market. However it must contemplate the possibility that it might lose and have to withdraw from the market. In this case its exit costs are crucial. If these fixed costs are *sunk costs ie* they cannot be moved from the industry and will be lost (*eg* building a steel mill), then the new entrant is less likely to attempt to take over that market and the incumbent is more likely to be able to make monopoly profit. If, however, the fixed costs can be easily transferred to another industry then the market is likely to be much more contestable. For example if an airline tries to break into a particular route monopolised by another airline and fails, its exit costs would be low if its planes and staff could be easily transferred to another route.

In so far as industries are monopolies and perfectly contestable the public may gain the advantages of both worlds. Consumers will gain from the low costs of economies of scale and gain from low prices and high outputs due to high contestability. Government monopoly or anti-trust policy focuses upon the contestability of an industry *ie* the size of the entry and exit barriers which determine the threat of competition.

MONOPOLISTIC COMPETITION

Monopolistic competition is the name given to highly competitive markets with the following characteristics: many sellers, many buyers, low barriers to entry, differentiated products with a proliferation of brand names and product advertising. Firms have a 'monopoly' over their own brand and thus some price control. There are many close substitutes, however, and brand loyalty gives only limited price control. The demand curve facing the company is downward sloping (*ie* there is some price control) but demand is *highly* elastic (*ie* there is little price control). As demand is downward sloping then the *MR* curve is below the *D* curve – just as it is under conditions of monopoly – see Figure 2.87.

Figure 2.87 – Monopolistic Competition

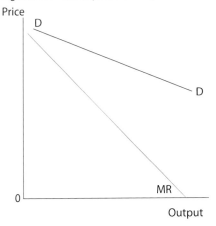

The firm's demand curve is downward sloping. Demand is highly elastic as there are many close substitutes to the product. The MR curve is, however, below the D curve.

If cost curves are superimposed upon the demand and marginal revenue curves the figure will appear as in Figure 2.88. The firm will profit maximise where *MR* = *MC*. This will give a quantity output of *q* at price *p*. Total revenue, *0qbp*, is greater than total cost, *0qac*, and a supernormal profit of *cabp* is earned. This point, where *MR* = *MC*, is the short run equilibrium point or firm's equilibrium point. Because entry barriers are very low in the industry, other firms will enter the market, producing similar, but differentiated products. As the total supply of the product increases, the demand for the products of any one firm will fall. From the situation in Figure 2.88 the demand curve will begin to shift to the left. The firm will produce back along its *MC* curve as *MR* also moves to the left. New firms will enter and supply will increase to the point where firms are earning only 'normal' profit. This is shown in Figure 2.89 where the demand curve is tangent to the *ATC* curve. At this point, total revenue *0qap* is just equal to total cost also *0qap*. As *TR=TC* only 'normal' profit is being earned.

Prices under monopolistic competition are higher than under perfect competition, and quantities are lower. Price is greater than marginal cost. These are the arguments against monopoly. The difference with monopolistic competition however, is one of degree. In this market structure, producers face very elastic demand curves. Their control over price is not high. The degree of inefficiency from optimal resource allocation is small. Further it may be argued that the opportunity cost of inefficiency is worth paying in return for the gain in the variety of goods available to consumers. Consumers enjoy differences in products and maybe this is sufficient compensation for the small economic inefficiency.

Figure 2.88 – Monopolistic Competition

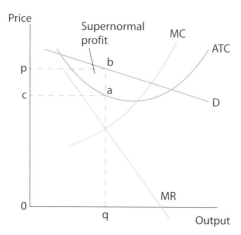

The firm's equilibrium, or short run industry equilibrium is where MR=MC. At this point supernormal profit of cabp is earned and attracts new entrants to the industry.

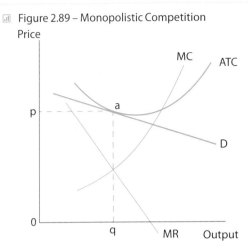

⬛ Figure 2.89 – Monopolistic Competition

The firm's long run equilibrium, or the industry equilibrium, is where MR=MC, p=ATC, and TR=TC. Normal profit is being earned in this situation.

PRICE DISCRIMINATION

Price discrimination occurs when units of a product which cost the same to produce are sold at different prices to different customers. An example of this would be the selling of train tickets at a lower price to students than to non-students. An alternative type of price discrimination is when a product with different costs of production is sold at the same price. For example it is price discrimination if the New Zealand postal service charges the same amount to post a letter from an address in Auckland to another address in Auckland as is charged to post a letter from Auckland to a remote address in the Southern Alps.

Price *'discrimination'* must not be confused with price *'differentiation'*. Price differentiation is where different prices are charged because there are different costs of production. A cup of coffee has a higher price in the lounge of a five star hotel than it does in a roadside transport cafe. The high costs of the luxury surroundings at the hotel are reflected in its prices. However, if the hotel runs a disco club for young people charging an entry fee for males but not females, we are back to price discrimination – pricing according to who is buying rather the than costs of production.

REASONS FOR PRICE DISCRIMINATION

Different people put different values on the same product. That means that different people are willing to pay different prices for a product. A downward sloping demand curve reflects this. Only a few people are willing to pay a high price for a product, whereas many are prepared to demand it at a low price. Most products have a single price irrespective of who is buying. Figure 2.90 shows the single profit maximising price of a product. This is the optimal price – if the product is sold at one price. If, however, the seller could sell the product to different consumers at different prices the firm might make even more profit.

All of those consumers whose demand is represented by the portion of the demand curve above x are willing to pay more for the product than price p. The difference between what they would be willing to pay and the price they have to pay is called 'consumer surplus'. If you want to fly home at the end of this school year how much would you be willing to pay? If that amount is less than the ticket price you will not buy a ticket. If your upper limit is $500 and the airfare is $300 you will pay $300 and fly. Your consumer surplus is $200. In everyday life your consumer surplus is most obvious when it is the greatest, *ie* on those occasions when you feel you have 'got a bargain'.

Figure 2.90 – Single Price Monopolist

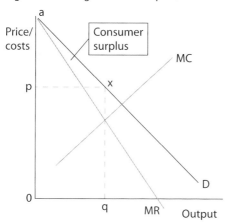

The demand curve above point x represents consumers who are willing to pay more than price p for the product. Area pxa represents total consumer surplus.

Now if the firm can capture some of this consumer surplus, transferring it to the company, it can make greater profit than it can by selling at a single price. The firm may be able to do this by selling the product at different prices to different consumers.[17]

NECESSARY CONDITIONS FOR PRICE DISCRIMINATION

There are three market conditions which must exist for price discrimination to be possible.

1 The supplier must have some monopoly power, *ie* the supplier must be a price maker. Thus price discrimination can occur in any market structure except perfect competition. Under perfect competition the firm is a 'price-taker' and has no power over price at all. The greater the monopoly power the easier it is to price discriminate. In many countries there is extensive price discrimination in the national monopolies that supply gas, electricity, telephone services, and rail travel. However price discrimination is found in monopolistic competition with small price controls. For example your college drama society could charge teachers and students different entry prices for tickets to a play.

2 There must be groups of buyers with different elasticities of demand for the product, ie different consumers must be willing to pay different prices. For example, it is likely that women as a group are willing to pay more to have their hair cut and styled than men are. That is, the price elasticity of demand for hairdressing is lower for women than men. If so, then this condition for price discrimination is present. Business people are likely to have a lower price elasticity of demand for air travel than tourists. Part of the consumer surplus of business people could be appropriated by airlines, by charging a higher price for business travellers than they do for tourists.

3 The third condition is that these different groups can be identified and separated. Price discrimination cannot work if one group can buy and resell to the other group. If children could buy newspapers at half price few parents would ever buy them, they would send their children along to the newsagent instead. This is a reason why it is more common to price discriminate in service industries than in goods industries. Identification may mean carrying an ID card *eg* to identify a student, or a retired person. You may well have encountered the ID problem of age discrimination if you have ever tried to get a child's fare on the bus, en route to a bar, where you need to persuade the barman that you are legally old enough to drink alcohol! A passport may be required to gain a price advantage offered only to foreigners. 'Time' may be used to separate groups. High telephone and travel charges are often found in business hours, with cheaper off-peak charges at week-ends and evenings. Have you wondered about the Saturday night 'stop-over rule' to qualify for cheaper airline fares? Business people want to be home at week-ends with their families. Holiday makers are more flexible (more price elastic). Airlines offer cheaper fares for travellers who stay away over a Saturday night. In this way consumer surplus can be removed from the price inelastic business travellers.

Figure 2.91 illustrates a situation where a firm with some control over price identifies two groups of consumers with differing demand curves. It is assumed that the firm has a way of separating these groups and preventing the re-sale of its product. It thus has two separate demand curves D_1 and D_2. By definition, the marginal cost of producing for either group is the same. The steeper demand curve, of the group with lower price elasticity, means that there is a steeper *MR* curve than with the other demand curve. The profit maximising firm will produce where *MR* = *MC* in each separate market. This gives a higher price in one group, extracting some part of their consumer surplus.

Figure 2.91 – Price Discriminating Monopolist

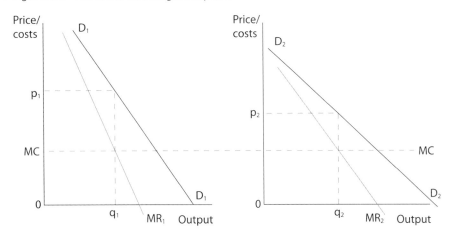

By separating consumers into two groups, and selling at MR = MC in each market, the firm can sell at a higher price to group 1, and take away some of their consumer surplus for itself. (Marginal cost has been assumed constant for simplification.)

Figure 2.92 shows how a price discriminating monopolist can extract more and more income, by finer and finer market separation. Profit would rise as long as costs remained unchanged. *Pure price discrimination* would exist if the firm could charge every single consumer a different price, extracting every single cent of consumer surplus. In practice, however, the complication of administering many prices raises costs.

Figure 2.92 – Total Revenue and Price Discrimination

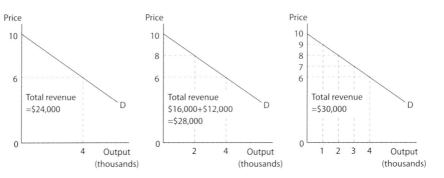

If the firm sells at a single price, total revenue (p x q) is $24,000. If the firm can successfully sell at two prices, total revenue can be increased to $28,000. By selling at four prices, TR can be increased to $30,000.

London–New York route

As I write, British Airways discriminates between different groups of travellers on the London-New York route as follows:

No restrictions – weekend travel	£728
No restrictions – weekday travel	£688
21 days notice – weekend travel	£539
21 days notice – weekday travel	£499
30 days notice – weekend travel	£449
30 days notice – weekday travel	£419

Because price discrimination may be resented by those in the higher priced group you may notice that price differentiation (different costs) is frequently involved as well. This serves to disguise the degree of price discrimination. For example on a transatlantic flight a passenger travelling first class may pay £1000 whilst one in economy class pays £300. Carrying the first class passenger does incur higher costs: more foot-room, wider seats, special departure lounge, different menu – *ie* there is price differentiation. Nevertheless the basic product, is transport from A to B. However the 'pampering' of first class passengers helps to sugar the pill of the price discrimination.

MULTIPLE CHOICE QUESTIONS – THEORY OF THE FIRM
HL ONLY

1   The companies owning diamond mines form a cartel. This arrangement would be best
    described as

    A   natural monopoly.

    B   monopolistic competition.

    C   collusive oligopoly.

    D   perfect oligopoly.

2   A supplier of soft drinks is subject to 'constant returns to scale'. This means that as the
    company expands output of soft drinks there is no increase in its

    I   average costs.

    II   total costs.

    III variable costs.

    A   I only   B   I and II   C   II and III   D   I, II and III

3   The table below shows a company's total costs as its output expands

Output	0	1	2	3	4
Total cost (US$)	15	19	22	24	26

    What is the average fixed cost of producing 3 units?

    A   US$2   B   US$5   C   US$8   D   US$15

4   The cost of producing 6 units of a good is 48 baht. The marginal cost of the seventh unit is
    15 baht. Which of the following must be true?

    A   Fixed costs are 8 baht.

    B   Fixed costs are 33 baht.

    C   The average total cost of 7 units is 9 baht.

    D   The average variable cost of 7 units is 9 baht.

5   The table below shows the average costs of a Chinese manufacturer producing different levels of output

Output (units)	Average cost (renminbi)
100	20
200	50
300	90
400	130

Over the range of output shown, the company experiences

A   diminishing returns.

B   increasing returns.

C   diminishing returns followed by increasing returns.

D   constant returns.

6   A company increases its advertising expenditure to improve its product image and increase brand loyalty. It may expect its profits to increase because

I   the firm's demand curve will be shifted to the right.

II   the barrier to entry may be increased.

III   demand will become more elastic in response to price increases.

A   I only   B   I and II   C   II and III   D   I, II and III

7   It is valid to criticise the theories of perfect competition and monopoly as being unrealistic due to their

I   assumptions of profit maximisation.

II   assumptions of knowledge of marginal cost and revenue.

III   failure to distinguish between the owners and managers of modern firms.

A   I only   B   I and II   C   II and III   D   I, II and III

8   If a company's aim was to 'satisfice' it would try to

A   maximise its profits.

B   make an adequate rate of return.

C   represent the interest of shareholders.

D   maximise its market share.

9   A profit maximizing firm in a perfectly competitive market may charge a price that is NOT necessarily equal to

A   marginal cost.

B   marginal revenue.

C   average cost.

D   average revenue.

10 The average revenue curve of a firm slopes downwards from left to right. This firm is therefore NOT operating under conditions of

A   perfect competition.

B   monopoly.

C   monopolistic competition.

D   oligopoly.

11 The kinked demand curve theory explains why

A   demand and price are inversely related

B   price discrimination can occur in monopoly markets.

C   products are differentiated in monopolistically competitive markets.

D   prices in oligopoly markets tend to be stable.

12 A characteristic of monopoly is that it

A   has barriers to entry.

B   cannot make losses in the short run.

C   makes only normal profits in the long run.

D   is very large.

13 A hairdresser charges clients prices which are directly related to the length of time taken to cut their hair. This an example of price

A   controls.

B   discrimination.

C   differentiation.

D   indexation.

14 In an industry which has no economies of scale perfect competition will allocate resources better than monopoly because

I the price would be lower.

II total output would be higher.

III price would equal marginal cost.

A I only B I and II C II and III D I, II and III

15 A monopoly will maximise total revenue when

I the coefficient of price elasticity of demand is one.

II marginal revenue is equal to zero.

III marginal cost equals marginal revenue.

A I only B I and II C II and III D I, II and III

16 Conditions for the market state of monopolistic competition to exist include

I barriers preventing the entry of competitors.

II differentiated products.

III a large number of producers.

A I only B I and II C II and III D I, II and III

17 Conditions for price discrimination to occur include

I different groups of consumers having different price elasticities of demand.

II production by a monopoly supplier.

III prices being unrelated to production costs.

A I only B I and II C II and III D I, II and III

18 The diminishing marginal returns theory states that

A as additional variable inputs are used, total output always decreases.

B marginal output may at first increase but will decline eventually.

C all factor inputs are increased in equal amounts.

D average costs will fall as output increases.

19 The table below lists cigarette companies in the United States and their share of the US market in 1997.

Firm	Percentage Market Share	Typical Brand
Philip Morris	49%	Marlboro
RJR Nabisco	24%	Winston
BAT Industries	16%	State Express
Others	11%	–

The United States cigarette market is therefore likely to be characterised by

I   normal profit.
II barriers to entry.
III product differentiation.

A I only B I and II C II and III D I, II and III

20 An IB student has a monthly demand schedule for pizza as follows

Number of pizzas in a month	Price
1	NZ$6
2	NZ$5
3	NZ$4
4	NZ$3
5	NZ$2

If the price of a pizza is NZ$4 and the consumer buys three pizzas in a month what is her consumer surplus?

A Zero B NZ$3 C NZ$4 D NZ$6

2.3iii ECONOMIC EFFICIENCY

One of the most important economic criteria is that of *efficiency*. The market mechanism, planning and tradition are ways of allocating resources. Efficiency is concerned with how well they do this, that is how well scarce resources are allocated to solve the three problems of what to produce, how to produce, and for whom production should take place.

Productive Efficiency

Productive efficiency occurs within a firm. It occurs when the firm is producing output with the minimum amount of inputs. The firm is technically efficient if it is not wasting inputs. The incentive for firms to be technically efficient is profit. Firms gain more profit by reducing costs. The price system will lead to firms being technically efficient as managers react to the relative prices of factors given to them from outside the firm. Technical efficiency must be present for economic efficiency to be achieved in a society.

Economic Efficiency

Economic efficiency occurs outside firms. It occurs when society is producing the goods and services most valued by society. (In a market system it is prices which signal the value that consumers put on different goods and services.) The society is economically efficient if it is impossible to move resources to make people better off without making others worse off.[18] If factors of production can be moved so that some people gain without others losing, then economic efficiency has not yet been reached.

Competetion and Efficiency

It was shown earlier, that with certain reservations, the situation of perfect competition will lead to *Pareto efficiency* or *economic efficiency*. Perfect competition leads to price equality with marginal cost, whilst monopoly and imperfect competition lead to situations of price being greater than marginal cost. If more resources were allocated to these latter industries prices would fall and marginal costs would rise. Society would (other things being equal) become more economically efficient.

An example may help to illustrate this. Figure 2.93 shows two markets, one for rice and one for wine. The equilibrium price of each is marked as p_1 where demand equals supply. Under perfect competition this is where $MR = MC$, marginal revenue being the value that consumers place on the last unit of the product, marginal cost being the cost to society of producing the last unit of the good.

Assume now that rice is sold in a perfectly competitive market and that wine is controlled by a monopoly. Further assume that the government interferes with the rice market by subsidising rice. They set a price above equilibrium at p_2 and subsidise rice from taxes to sell the whole output at price p_3. The price of rice is therefore below the marginal cost p_2. The product is costing more to produce than the value put on it by consumers, p_3. Resources could be moved out of rice production. As output contracted the marginal cost would fall along the supply curve, price would increase back along the demand curve to p_1, where $MC = MR = price$. This is at the optimum output of rice.

In the wine industry, because of monopoly, price p_2 is above marginal cost. Consumers are paying more for the product than it is costing to produce it $(P > MC)$. Economic efficiency would be improved by expanding this industry. The resource allocation, at production $0q_2$, does not reflect peoples' preferences. They value this product more highly at this price than it costs to produce it. The industry should expand, lowering price and raising cost until p = MC at price p_1. This is the optimum output of wine.

Thus in the above example, economic efficiency in resource allocation is improved if the economic resources of land, labour and capital move out of rice production and into wine production.

If all markets were working under conditions of perfect competition all resources would be allocated at optimal efficiency where price = marginal cost. Although that is a useful observation, unfortunately in practice it is not true because there are additional factors to consider. Two of these factors are economies of scale and externalities.

We have already shown that if economies of scale are present society may benefit from substantially increased output and lower prices. We have also shown that the market fails if there are externalities, that is if private cost or benefit differs from social cost or benefit. For example in Figure 2.94 the marginal social cost is greater than the marginal private cost due to negative externalities. The market will produce $0q_1$ at price p_1 which is privately economically efficient. However, it has ignored the costs to society. $0q_2$ at price p_2 is socially optimal.

There is a third reason why perfect competition may not be optimal. The models we look at in this course are static models, they look at resource allocation at a point in time. Dynamic economics is concerned with resource allocation over time. It could be that inefficient resource allocation in one time period could prove dynamically more efficient in a later time period – leading to a greater growth in the economy for example. Dynamic economics are beyond the scope of the IB course.

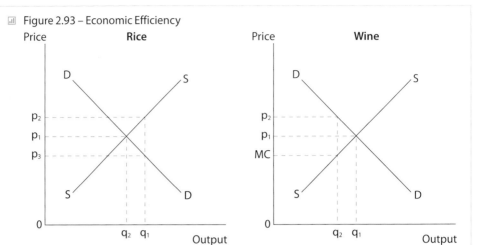

▣ Figure 2.93 – Economic Efficiency

In these diagrams the price of rice is not at equilibrium because of government activity – paying farmers a support price p₂, and selling to consumers at a subsidised price, p₃. The price of rice is below the cost of rice. The price of wine is at p₂, due to monopoly. The price of wine is above the cost of wine. If resources were moved out of rice production, and into wine production, greater economic efficiency could be obtained.

▣ Figure 2.94 – Economic Efficiency

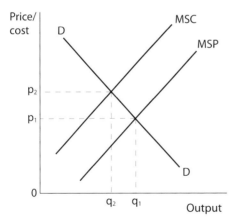

The private equilibrium is socially non-optimal due to the presence of negative externalities.

USES AND LIMITATIONS OF GOVERNMENT POLICY TO CONTROL MONOPOLY

Due to the possibility of monopoly reducing efficiency and harming consumers, most governments have legislation in place to limit monopoly power. In the United States for example, *anti-trust legislation* dates back to 1880 with the Sherman Act. This was used to break up many of the great industrial empires in the United States at the turn of the twentieth century. Modern *competition policy* is likely to be wide ranging and to include the examination of restrictive practices in any type of market structure. A referral to the law which results in action against the restrictive practice then acts as a case law to similar restrictive practices in other industries, so the effects can be more wide ranging than to the industry under investigation. Some of the possible tools at the disposal of the anti-monopoly (anti-trust) body are the imposition of taxes, subsidies, price controls, nationalisation, monopoly break-up, restrictions on mergers, and the reduction of entry barriers. Let us look at each of these in turn.

Taxation

Profits taxes can be imposed on monopolists to remove supernormal profits which may be offensive to consumers. This will not, however, address the basic problems of misallocation of resources.

Subsidies

To improve *allocative efficiency* marginal cost needs to be closer to price. By subsidising the product this can be achieved. In Figure 2.95 a subsidy on the product shifts the MC curve to the right to reduce price and increase quantity to p_2 and q_2. In addition, a tax on supernormal profit could be used to finance the subsidy.

 Figure 2.95 – Subsidising a Monopoly to Improve Resource Allocation

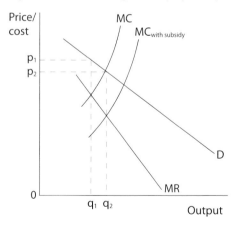

A private monopolist will produce at $p_1 q_1$. A subsidy can shift the MC curve to the right to give an optimal solution of $p_2 q_2$. A profit tax on the supernormal profit could be used to pay for the subsidy.

In practice, there are problems to this as a solution. Estimating where the MR and MC curves is one practical problem. There is also likely to be political opposition to subsidising private monopoly products.

Nationalising the Industry

This was the preferred technique used by many countries just after the Second World War, for those industries regarded as natural monopolies, *eg* postal delivery, telephones, rail travel, gas, water and electricity supply. The way that nationalisation attacks the efficiency problems of motivation is by altering that motivation. The $p = MC$ solution of private monopoly follows from the assumption of profit maximisation. The nationalised industry can be given price and output objectives which lead to price being set at, or closer to, marginal cost.

In practice however, the removal of the profit motive and competition has too often led to technical inefficiency. Therefore since the 1980s there has been a reversal of the policy and major privatisations of nationalised industries have taken place in country after country right across the globe.

Price Controls

A solution widely employed where the nationalised monopolies have been privatised is the use of price controls. The government appoints an industry 'watchdog' with power to control the prices and profits of the monopoly. Thus it sets up a countervailing power to that of the private monopoly, charged with acting in the interests of the public.

A maximum price can be imposed on the industry at the allocatively efficient level. Thus in Figure 2.96 a price p is imposed at the point where MC cuts the demand curve (not the MR curve as an unregulated monopolist would). This would give an optimum price, quantity and resource allocation where $p = MC$.

Figure 2.96 – Price Controls on Monopoly

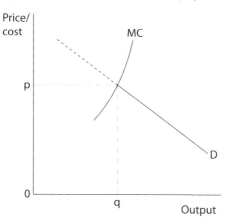

A maximum price is imposed at the point where the MC curve cuts the demand curve.

Monopoly Break-Up

If the monopoly can be cost-efficient at a smaller size, it can be broken up into competing units. This is suitable for a *multi-plant monopoly* or a *cartel agreement*. It would be inappropriate for a natural monopoly.

Restriction on Mergers

Where a proposed merger of two or more existing companies would lead to a high controlling share of the total market, the government may refuse permission for the merger to take place.

Reduction of Entry Barriers

The barriers to other firms entering the industry might be weakened or removed by government action – allowing market forces to break up the monopoly. In other words the market would become more contestable. One possible way is to remove any trade restrictions so that foreign competition erodes a domestic monopoly, *eg* in Australia, foreign banks were allowed to enter the financial markets during the 1980s.

Changing Demand and Technology

Government action is not always necessary to break monopoly power. The forces of the market are very powerful and may end the monopoly naturally and without intervention. IBM, the giant computer company, had anti-trust action against it dropped when it was realised, correctly, that fierce competition in the personal computer markets was about to end its monopoly anyway.

MULTIPLE CHOICE QUESTIONS – ECONOMIC EFFICIENCY

1   Markets under perfect competition will be efficient because

   A   incomes will be equally distributed.

   B   prices and costs will be at their lowest.

   C   producers will be able to make long run supernormal profits.

   D   consumers do not have perfect information.

2   In an industry that is 'economically efficient'

   I   prices are equal to marginal costs.

   II   marginal costs are equal to average costs.

   III   normal profit is equal to zero.

   A   I only   B   I and II   C   II and III   D   I, II and III

3   If price is higher than marginal cost

   A   the industry is not allocatively efficient.

   B   a monopolist would increase its output.

   C   firms in perfect competition would decrease their output.

   D   the industry should be subsidised.

2.4   MARKET FAILURE

Market forces are very powerful. Problems are created if they are over-ruled, as we noted with maximum and minimum price legislation. Markets do have many benefits for ensuring efficiency in resource allocation. They tend to be responsive to consumer demand and they tend to keep production costs low. There are cases, however, where markets clearly do not work at all, and others where they do not work well. These cases are collectively known as *market failure*. Where there is market failure there is a case for modifying the way the market works or substituting a planning technique for the market mechanism. The existence of externalities, inequalities in income and wealth and the abuse of monopoly are three specific types of market failure. We now look at these in order:

1   *the existence of externalities* – with a consideration of
     the lack of *public goods*
     the underprovision of *merit goods*
     the overprovision of *demerit goods*
     and *environmental degradation*

2   *inequality* in the distribution of income and wealth

3   the abuse of *monopoly* power.

1   EXTERNALITIES

A market represents the private forces of demand and supply. Consumers demand products to maximise their own utility or welfare, and producers supply them to maximise their own profit. A market diagram uses demand and supply curves to show these forces. Figure 2.97 is the diagram we have previously used but with demand and supply curves now labelled *private*. This is to show that these represent the benefits and costs to the individuals participating in the market, that is, the private benefits and the private costs. However, very many market activities affect other people – both positively and negatively. These benefits and costs are not represented in the market model, they are external to the market. They are known as *externalities – positive externalities* and *negative externalities*. If the externalities of an economic activity, producing or consuming, are very large there may be a case for altering resource allocation to reflect the externalities.

Figure 2.97

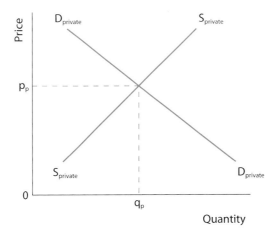

Positive externalities

Oxford, England, the city I live in – is renowned for its beautiful old university buildings. In addition the buildings benefit Oxford University members, and the University bears the cost of their upkeep.

Thousands of tourists and residents also benefit from seeing the buildings however. They are enjoying a positive externality. The academic reputation of Oxford University is very high. Other schools and colleges in the area may benefit by locating in the town and having the name 'Oxford' in the address. If a college benefits in this way it is enjoying a positive externality. If you spend money to make your garden beautiful, or to dress well, there may be positive externalities for others.

Expressing this graphically, Figure 2.97, the price p_p and the quantity q_p are at the market equilibrium for the private benefits and costs of an economic activity. They do not reflect the additional benefits or costs to others not involved in the market. Taking the case of beautiful buildings, the value of enjoying the the buildings is not represented in the market place. The demand curve in Figure 2.97 represents only the private benefits to the purchasers, not the external benefits to society. If we could measure these benefits and put a value upon them, a new demand curve could be drawn as in Figure 2.98 showing the external benefits added to the private benefits. This demand curve would be further out to the right. The new situation where externalities are added to internal private benefits shows why the market fails to allocate resources well in this industry. Society as a whole would prefer more resources allocated to the industry, and would be willing to bear the extra price to obtain the extra quantity. The market alone reflects only private benefits, so in a pure market economy we are likely to get more cheap and ugly buildings.

📊 Figure 2.98

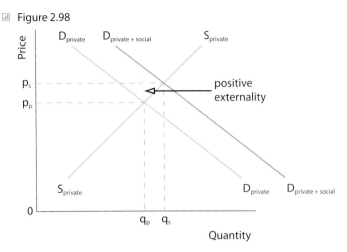

When external social benefits are added to internal private benefits, total demand can be shown to be greater than that of private market demand alone. There is a case for the activity to be expanded. Society would be willing to pay a higher price to receive a greater quantity of this product, eg beautiful buildings.

The existence of externalities is a very important consideration in economic decision making. We will now look at a few specific cases of market failure, cases where externalities are important.

The Lack of Public Goods

Public goods have such massive positive externalities compared to small private benefits they would barely be produced at all in a purely market economy.

The word *public* has many different uses in the English language. Students, especially non-mother tongue speakers, need to pay particular attention to the use of this word. Even economists use it in different ways. You can distinguish its meaning from the context in which it is used. The most common use in economics refers to ownership, 'public' meaning some form of social ownership in contrast to 'private' ownership. Thus when we speak of the public and private sectors of the economy we are talking about ownership. However there is an entirely different meaning of public and private in the context of market failure. There are two characteristics of goods which define them as public or private.[19] These characteristics are *rivalry* and *excludability*.

Rivalry – a good is rivalrous if the use of it by one person prevents the use of it by another. Thus your pen and computer are both rivalrous: if you are using them others cannot. A good is non-rivalrous if the use of it by one person does not diminish its use by others. Receiving radio and TV broadcasts in your house is non-rivalrous. Other households can enjoy the same broadcasts at the same time without diminishing your use of them. If this good was supplied to one person alone there would be huge positive externalities to others.

Excludability – the suppliers of goods and services need a mechanism for allocating their scarce goods to consumers. The price system is such a method. People are excluded from using the good unless they pay a price for it. It is difficult, however, to exclude people from using some goods and services. If people cannot be excluded, making them pay becomes a problem. Defence is a good example of this. If defence forces exist to protect a country from external aggression, then it is impossible to exclude anybody in that country from being defended. If a beam of light or a radio signal is transmitted from a lighthouse in the sea to guide certain ships safely past rocks, it is not possible to exclude other ships from this service.

Private goods are defined as both rivalrous and exclusive. Most goods and services we enjoy fall into the category of private goods. Because such goods are exclusive it is easy to identify who uses the good and who does not and therefore who is required to pay for the good and who is not. Further, as private goods are excludable the purchaser enjoys the benefits of the good and the non-purchaser does not. The benefits are wholly or largely internal with relatively few positive externalities.

Public goods are defined as both non-rivalrous and non-exclusive. If use of the good is non-rivalrous it makes it hard to identify who is using the good and who is not. As it is not possible to exclude anyone from using the good it is not possible to make them pay for it. This gives rise to the free-rider problem. Some people will be able to enjoy the benefits of the public good without paying a share of its cost. As others are effectively then paying for the free riders, they too are likely to refuse to pay.

In summary the overall problem is, that a market system will not provide public goods. However public goods are valued by society, and so there is *market failure* – the market fails to provide public goods.

The solution is to use some form of *planning technique* as an alternative resource allocation mechanism.

Defence, policing, navigation systems, flood control, broadcasting, pavements (sidewalks), and street lighting are all public goods, or have a very strong element of the characteristics of a public good *ie* non-rivalry and non-excludability. One way of making sure society enjoys the benefits of these goods is for the government to provide them directly and pay for them from the taxation system. Thus defence arguably benefits everyone, it is impossible to exclude anyone, and it is therefore universally paid for by general taxation. Policing services, such as keeping the streets safe and arresting criminals, are activities which are also very difficult to exclude anyone from. Police forces are therefore usually provided by government and paid for out of taxation. In practice, policing is often restricted to an area – the city boundaries for example – and are therefore paid for by a tax on city dwellers. Property policing on the other hand is both rivalrous and excludable. If police operate in shops to reduce stealing, or inside sports grounds to assist crowd control, their services can be charged for. Thus in most countries there is a market for these services. Security guards, transport police, body guards and bouncers at discos are all examples of private resource allocation in specific areas of policing. The benefits of these activities are largely internal to the market. Externalities are less important.

The Underprovision of Merit Goods

A *merit good* is a private good which has positive externalities. It has social benefits which are enjoyed by other people. A market will provide a private optimum level which is less than the social optimum. A government could respond to this under-provision and attempt to increase the resource allocation towards the socially optimal quantity. One method is illustrated in Figure 2.99. The government sponsors an advertising campaign to promote use of the merit good. For example the use of contraception is promoted in many countries to reduce family size and to prevent the spread of AIDS.

 Figure 2.99

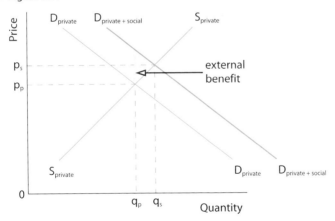

When the social benefit (private benefit plus externality) requires a higher price to increase the quantity supplied of the merit good, the government could run an advertising campaign to attempt to shift the demand curve up to the right. For example advertising is widely used to encourage the use of contraception, to reduce population growth, and the transmission of diseases like AIDS.

Used on its own, a successful advertising campaign will shift the demand curve up to the right raising the product price and increasing the quantity demanded and supplied. If the good has massive positive externalities the government might abandon the market altogether and provide the good directly. If it provided the good free and without restriction, it would supply $0q_2$ in Figure 2.100, all demand would be met at zero price to the consumer *eg* primary school education for children. If free provision was too costly or too wasteful the good could be limited by price. In Figure 2.100, a fixed price $0p_3$, below the market price, encourages greater use than a market would. In some countries medicines and dental care are sold below market price like this.

Figure 2.100

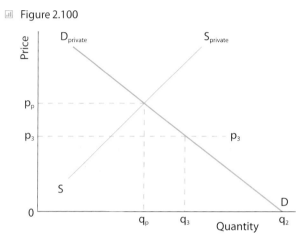

If the merit good has massive positive externalities the government may abandon the market and provide the goods directly. If it provided the good free and without restriction it would supply $0q_2$. However it could limit the good by charging a certain price, say p_3, to restrict quantity demanded to $0q_3$. Alternatively it could provide the good free and then ration it, eg medical care to children and the elderly.

A different approach is to offer the good free but to ration the supply. Medical care, for example, might be free to consumers but with supply controlled by medical professionals *ie* doctors might decide which patients can receive certain medical services.

Some goods might be rationed by age *eg* free bus transport to infants and the elderly, other goods rationed by condition *eg* health care to pregnant women. Alternatively the government might modify the supply of the merit good by offering a producer subsidy. In Figure 2.101 a subsidy shifts the supply curve to the right: lowering price and increasing quantity produced and consumed.

📊 Figure 2.101

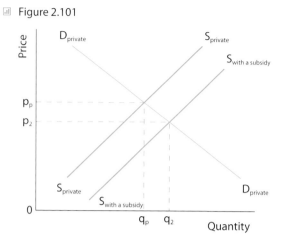

A government could leave the resource allocation decision of a merit good to a market – but modify the market. By offering a subsidy and thereby reducing producer costs, the supply curve can be shifted to the right. This gives a lower price to consumers, and increased use of the product, points $0p_2$ and $0q_2$ in the diagram.

Negative externalities

Many economic activities have *negative externalities*, *ie* costs not paid for by the producer. The users of buses, lorries, and cars pay the private costs of running their vehicles. There are external costs they do not pay, however, such as the costs of death and injury to pedestrians, the costs of blocking up the streets of towns, the costs of global warming and air pollution. These are negative externalities, costs borne by society as a whole. If a steel works releases smoke, dirt and chemicals into the atmosphere in a market system it does so at no cost. Unfortunately there are costs imposed on people that live close to the steel works in the form of dirty cars and buildings, erosion of buildings, poor health and lower quality of life generally. These are external costs, costs external to the economic decision of the market place. Negative externalities are ignored in the market place. There is therefore 'market failure' and society may look for a better solution – perhaps by modifying the market, perhaps by using a non-market mechanism. Figure 2.97 showed a market with demand and supply, reflecting only private benefits and costs. If the external costs could be measured and valued a new supply curve could be drawn to reflect this.[20] In Figure 2.102 the social costs have been added to the private costs to produce a new supply curve above and to the left of the original.

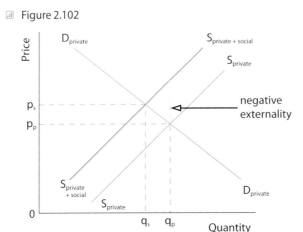

📊 Figure 2.102

A market diagram, with negative externalities added to private supply costs, giving a new supply curve above and to the left of the private supply curve. When negative externalities are included like this the resulting price is higher and the quantity traded is reduced. Including the externality corrects the market failure.

Overprovision of Demerit Goods

Demerit goods are private goods which have negative externalities and are deemed politically undesirable. They are goods which are rivalrous and exclusive, so the market will provide them. However they have net social costs which are borne by other people. For example, alcohol is usually considered to be a demerit good. The consumption of alcohol impairs judgement and alters behaviour. Some of the consequences of this may have negative effects on other people. Drunkenness can cause road traffic accidents, violence to other people and family breakdown. The market price for alcohol does not reflect these additional costs. Figure 2.102 shows that if they could be measured and included, the supply would be less at each price – reflecting the higher costs. This would result in a higher price and a lower quantity of resources allocated to alcohol than would be the case in a pure market.

Traffic Congestion in Athens

The capital city of Greece has severe car exhaust pollution problems. On hot days pollution quickly rises to unacceptable levels. The solution has been to zone the city and to restrict car and taxi access on certain days. An emergency day, typically two or three days a month, is declared when pollution levels rise to certain levels. All cars and half of all taxis are immediately banned from the inner city zone. On calendar dates with an even number, only taxis with even numbered registration plates can use the zone. On odd numbered dates only taxis with odd numbered registration plates can use the zone. In the outer zone all taxis can operate but the odd/even registration number restriction applies to cars and reduces their number to half. Cars are not allowed to have two registration plates, although people can own two cars!

One method a government might employ is negative advertising to try to diminish private demand for a demerit good – Figure 2.103. Anti-smoking, anti-drink and anti-drug campaigns are common examples of this.

 Figure 2.103

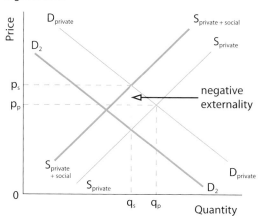

Negative advertising could be employed by a government to attempt to correct the market failure of a demerit good. If the socially optimal quantity of a demerit good was $0q_s$, an advertising campaign might try to shift the demand curve to D_2. Thus, government might finance advertising campaigns against, say, smoking or drink-driving.

The government may also choose to target supply – one method is to levy a tax on the product just sufficient to shift the supply curve up, by the same amount as the externality. In this way the government aims to reduce the quantity to the socially desirable level – Figure 2.104.

(An even better economic solution would be to pass this tax revenue to the people who suffer the externality. The cost of the externality would thereby be borne by the industry and passed to the innocent victims as compensation.)

 Figure 2.104

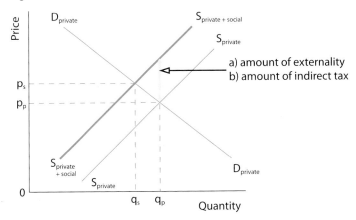

The market fails to provide the socially desirable level of a demerit good ~ providing q_p instead of q_s because it ignores the externality. A government can shift the supply curve by imposing a tax on the good to reduce its consumption.

If the negative externalities are very significant, the government might use the law rather than taxes to achieve the desired outcome. It might, for example, totally prohibit the ownership of handguns or the possession of hard drugs, because of the potentially serious external costs to others in society (Figure 2.105).

ıllı Figure 2.105

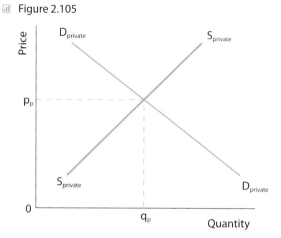

Legislation: If the demerit good is considered by society to have massive externalities eg heroine use, or gun ownership, the government could overrule the market entirely, use the law, and ban use of the good. The aim would be to reduce quantity supplied to zero. Its effectiveness would depend upon the effectiveness of the law, including the policing of the inevitable parallel market.

There are some important differences between public goods on the one hand and merit/demerit goods on the other. We have noted that because public goods are by definition non-rivalrous and non-excludable a market would not provide them at all. There is a clear and unequivocal case for a planning mechanism to do the resource allocation. All societies, whether extreme capitalist or extreme socialist, will acknowledge the completeness of market failure and the need for planning in the provision of public goods.

Merit and demerit goods on the other hand are rivalrous and excludable and will be provided by the market mechanism. The ratio between the private costs and benefits and the externalities is therefore smaller than with a public good. There is more scope for debate about the existence and importance of externalities and therefore whether government intervention is necessary. In the case of vaccination against infectious diseases, medical science is fairly conclusive and there is likely to be a strong case for government provision or subsidy. With many merit/demerit goods, however, there is a whole spectrum of opinion. People may take widely different views about whether dental health is a merit good. What about education? The majority of governments in the world do regard education as a merit good, providing primary and secondary education free. Division and debate is deeper with tertiary education. What is the balance of advantages to the private individual and to society of a university education. The argument for the existence of positive externalities in this case is more subjective, less testable, than it is for vaccination. Thus developed countries have different policies to the degree to which they subsidise university students. In LDCs where resources are more scarce the issue is even more acute.

Do you think museums, opera, and ballet should be treated as merit goods? What about the preservation of a language or culture (*eg* France and Wales subsidise films and TV programmes)? Can you reason your case in terms of private and social benefits?

There is a similar subjectivity about demerit goods. Tobacco smoking, for example, is widely believed to be a demerit good in many countries. Smokers can inflict externalities by increased litter and fire damage. It is currently argued that passive-smoking is an externality. This has not yet been totally proven, but the theory has gained widespread acceptance and some courts *eg* in California have awarded damages based on the acceptance of this externality. Smoking is definitely linked to the incidence of certain diseases in the smoker, however. If the country operates health care as a merit good, it may be argued that smoking increases the costs of the health care programme and should be taxed highly to compensate the rest of society. On the other hand, smokers die before old age and therefore put less pressure on the health service. Economists might attempt to measure the relative costs and benefits objectively. Nevertheless, there is a great deal of scope for subjective judgement to enter the valuation. The social acceptance of smoking and drinking, for example, varies widely between countries. The evaluation of most merit and demerit goods involves an element of subjectivity.

Environmental Concerns

Economic activity, whether it is production or consumption, often has damaging effects on the environment. As world economic activity grows, the danger to the environment grows. In this area there are numerous cases of market failure – and some of the most intractable problems.

Polluting activities are a particular problem because the pollutant represents an externality: the costs imposed by the pollutant are not borne by the polluter. Motorists who throw litter out of the car window and onto the highway are reducing their private cost of disposal. It takes more time and effort to keep the litter and dispose of it at the end of the journey. The cost of its unsightliness at the edge of the road is borne by other users (and there may be other costs, such as dangers to wildlife from glass bottles for example). The noise of a rowdy party, or a low flying jet imposes costs on others – costs which are not borne by the perpetrators of the noise. The purchaser of a cool drink from a refrigerator is not paying for the damage to the ozone layer caused by chlorofluorocarbons (CFCs) released at no cost into the atmosphere. The cost in terms of increased risk of skin cancer is borne by others. Burning fossil fuels to make electricity, heat houses or drive auto engines is almost certainly contributing to global warming. The long term external costs could be enormous, but because they are external and not paid for by the agents causing it, there is no economic incentive in a market system to cause it to stop.

In addition, there is a *distributional problem*. The people who are benefiting from the activities which are causing the pollution are imposing some of the costs on others. Therefore reducing pollution is one problem, but compensating the victims is another. This distributional problem is further worsened as some of the most pressing environmental problems of today are international problems *eg* ozone depletion, over-fishing, global warming, rain forest depletion and acid rain. A government's will to control polluters is reduced if the victims are foreigners!

Another particular problem of environmental issues is that of *valuing the external cost*. How do you put a value upon noise? How do you value the loss of the rain forest, the Indian tiger, the white rhino, whales? How do you put a value on health, beauty, or on life itself? How do you put a value upon the increased risk of contracting skin cancer, upon the possible, but unpredictable, consequences of global warming? If we are to address environmental problems properly, balancing the full social costs of economic activity against the benefits, we have to make estimates of values. Banning activities only makes economic sense where the costs are judged to be enormous in proportion to the benefits. Otherwise a ban, that is using the law, is too crude, as it does not allow for the benefit of the activity. Extreme 'greens' believe that the costs to the planet are so huge that they advocate zero economic growth. This stance is unacceptable to the majority of people in developed countries. The poorest countries have even more reason to reject zero growth as they urgently need growth to enable development. It is also increasingly vital that future growth and development are sustainable.

The difficult problem of placing a value on things without a market price has to be tackled. Every day law courts make compensation payments for injury, or loss of life, or loss of freedom for someone wrongfully imprisoned. There is also a whole branch of economics which is known as *social cost-benefit analysis (CBA)* which grapples with these problems. For example under CBA a new motorway scheme would put a money value on the number of lives saved by this relatively safe form of road and include it as an external benefit in the investment appraisal. It would also include a dollar value for the reduction in vehicle damage caused by traffic accidents. It would include a dollar value for the time saved by users of the motorway, and indeed the time saved by non-users too because they will be able to travel faster on the other less congested roads. It would try to cost the damage to any beautiful countryside crossed by the motorway, and the loss of value to households who will have their peace disturbed by the new motorway. There is now an increased urgency to develop this branch of economics, as we face up to vast new environmental problems.

How Do You Value Life?

Investment appraisal involves measuring the costs and benefits of a new project in order to decide whether the benefits outweigh the costs sufficiently to justify the expenditure. However many projects have costs and benefits which do not have a price. Should these costs and benefits be left out of the equation? Should they be valued? If so, how? Consider the value of human life. Many projects are designed to save lives *eg* new hospitals, roads, flood and earthquake controls, passenger safety measures and so on. Some people might respond by saying human life is priceless, a value cannot be put on it. This implies that the value is infinitely high and the project should be carried out whatever the cost, even if other benefits were zero. Another response is to say that a price cannot be put on life and therefore it should be left out of project calculations. This implies, however, that the value of life is zero. Clearly neither of these approaches is acceptable. The value of life must be somewhere between zero and infinity, the problem is deciding where.

Question

Can you suggest a method for valuing human life?

A further enormous problem with valuation is that of the *time perspective*. What value do we put upon the future? From observation it has long been known that people put lower value on the future than the present. Professor Pigou who did a lot of the initial work on *time preference* likened our attitude to the future to that of looking down the wrong end of a telescope, the future diminishes in size and importance. However, many of our most urgent pollution problems *eg* resource depletion, the ozone layer, global warming, extermination of animal and plant species, appear to have the most severe consequences for future generations. How do we value the quality of life of our children and our children's children? What value would you put on your knowing that there are wild elephants in Africa, even if you never see them? What value would you put on your grand-children one day also knowing that elephants still exist in the wild?

POSSIBLE GOVERNMENT RESPONSES TO MARKET FAILURE

There are a number of possible responses a government can make to improve resource allocation where there are significant externalities. Some of these were covered in the preceding section:

▍ The direct provision of merit goods and public goods
▍ Taxing demerit goods
▍ Subsidising merit goods
▍ Negative and positive advertising to shift demand

However some of the most intractable problems concern the global environment and are not within the powers of any one nation's government.

International Co-operation Between Governments

Where externality problems are international there is now an urgency to establish an international authority to address them. The 'Rio summit', held in Brazil in June 1992, although not very effective in practice, was important as the first international summit to address environmental issues. This was followed by the Kyoto Protocol in Japan in 2001. Significantly the USA refused to sign it.

Methods of Control

There are three main methods a government can use to reduce environmental externalities like pollution:

1 *modify the market* – tax the activity which causes the externality
2 *extend property rights* – to internalise the externality
3 *legislate* – use the law

Modify the Market – Taxing the Externality

This is the method favoured by economists, where it can be made to work. A tax is imposed on the activity to equate with the value of the externality. In Figure 2.104 the social supply curve ($S_{private\ +\ externality}$) is shown above the private supply curve ($S_{private}$).[21] The gap is equal to the value of the externality. In other words it is the true opportunity cost of the activity. The private market resource allocation decision leads to price $0p_p$ and quantity $0q_p$. There is too much of this product. Including the externality gives a socially optimal resource allocation of $0p_s$ and $0q_s$ where the benefits represented by the demand curve are equated with the true cost of the activity. The government should now impose a tax *b)* on this product to shift the supply curve by exactly the amount of the externality, *a)*, to obtain $0p_s$ and $0q_s$.

The external costs of motoring, for example, could fairly easily be tackled in this way: using a tax to bring the externality into the market decision of the motorist. Road pricing in city centres is already in existence. In Barcelona, Dallas, Lisbon, London, Oslo, Singapore and Stockholm cars are charged for the time they spend inside the city 'box', in order to increase the private cost to the motorist, and reduce the demand for bringing cars into the city. In many countries, *eg* Australia, taxes were increased on leaded petrol relative to unleaded petrol, to encourage a switch to the latter. Leaded petrol was shown to cause brain damage to children on the pavements as they breathed in fuel emissions. By lowering the price of a close substitute, lead free petrol (the price elasticities of close substitutes are very high [22]), the change from leaded to unleaded occurred quickly and smoothly without a lawyer in sight! Even so, this method does not directly address the problem of distribution. Victims of the polluting activity are not recompensed by the polluters.

Transport Policy in Singapore

Singapore has one of the densest urban traffic congestion problems of any city in the world. Despite very high licence fees for cars and excellent mass rail transit and subsidised buses the Singaporeans continue to have too much road traffic in the city centre. The response of the authorities was to make the city centre a restricted zone. To enter the area at any one of 33 points a ticket has to be bought. Police checked cars that have paid and displayed. Then a new electronic system was introduced. This saves on the high policing costs and enables a variable price to be charged according to the amount of congestion. As congestion rises so does the price of entry.

Vehicles are fitted with an in-vehicle unit (IU). Drivers feed a smart card into the IU on setting out. As they drive into the city zone overhead cameras read the IU, deduct a charge from the drivers account and photograph the licence plate. If the deduction is made satisfactorily the photograph is overwritten. If there are problems the details are relayed to a control centre, and a penalty is imposed.

Extending Property Rights

Another method of tackling pollution problems is to *internalise the externality*. Consumers and companies already have to meet the costs of damage to other peoples lives or property. If a truck hits you, your car, or your house you have a claim on the truck owner because you have property rights over all of these things. If there are goods that no-one owns then polluters can escape paying for the damage that they cause. A solution is to internalise these externalities. The government can do this by *allocating property rights* over them. Thus the polluting activity will no longer be free.

For example people can be granted the right to enjoy clean beaches, smoke-free work places, or dirt and noise free residential areas. Rights can be allocated to coastal communities so that over-fishing or spilled oil is no longer an externality. Villages in Africa can be given property rights over 'big game' animals so that they have an interest in protecting animals from poachers.

Externalities and Property Rights

Professor Ronald Coase's 1960 journal paper, *'The problem of social cost',* demonstrated that negative externalities do not require government intervention in situations where property rights are well defined and transaction costs are relatively low.

For example, if a farmer wishes to burn straw he will cause pollution. The farmer will take the air for granted and use it as a waste sink. If society, however, were able to put a value on the cost of this pollution, the farmer may be forced to revise his action. For instance, if the farmer happened to cause fire damage to a neighbour's field or house, he would have to pay some compensation to the owner of the property.

The problem that this example illustrates is that the atmosphere is usually regarded as common property. Hence, if a straw-burning farmer can pollute the air with no financial implications, he will. If, however, air could be organized in such a way that it belonged to an individual or organization, the farmer could be charged for making use of it. The essential point is that negotiations between parties become a possibility. The pollution may then stop or be reduced. Creating a market for an externality is therefore a solution, since it enables polluters to buy rights to pollute and victims to charge to the level that they feel justifies their suffering.

Tradable permits

Extending property rights is altogether more difficult where the property is 'internationally used and abused'. Who is there to grant property rights over the atmosphere, the oceans or the ozone layer? It is a problem that requires urgent address. One imaginative scheme that has been put forward is to set up an internationally recognised body, perhaps a UN agency which would have the authority to issue *'permits to pollute'*. The agency would have to calculate a permissible overall level of pollution; that level of damage to the global environment that was deemed scientifically acceptable. Licenses would then be issued to ration pollution to just that amount. Various methods of distributing the licenses have been discussed – although they would be 'tradable', that is a market would be established for licenses. One distribution method advocates licences going to the highest bidders. That means that those who would find it most expensive to stop polluting would bid the highest. Those who could most easily and cheaply stop polluting would find it more economical to do so. In this way, there could be a rapid and efficient reduction in global pollution. Another scheme would have pollution licences distributed to countries on the basis of population size. The poorest countries, with the least industry and thus pollution, could sell their pollution 'quota' to the industrialised countries who pollute the most (in 1989 50% of all the world's air pollution was caused by just six countries USA, USSR, Germany, Japan, UK and Poland) (*eg* India, one of the most polluting LDCs, with 16% of world population causes 6% of global warming. The US with only 5% of the population causes 25%). The money earned by the LDCs would be restricted to development projects which were environmentally friendly, and to transfers of the latest least-polluting technology from the developed countries. Does this sound far-fetched? Such imaginative and highly innovative methods are being discussed because of widespread recognition of the seriousness of present day environmental destruction.

Permission to Pollute (World, 1989)

Global warming, the so called *greenhouse effect*, was the subject of a report by the Institute of International Affairs in December 1989. Global warming is caused mainly by the emission of carbon dioxide when fossil fuels like coal, oil and gas are burned. They suggested the setting up of an international system of *marketable carbon permits*. Each country would be issued permits to emit carbon dioxide according to the size of its population. These permits could be traded internationally. Developed countries with most of the world's industry and cars would be unlikely to have enough permits, whilst poor countries would have a surplus. Developing countries could then sell some of their permits to rich countries. The money received would be restricted to development projects and pollution friendly programmes.

Questions

1 Why do the authors expect this system to reduce carbon dioxide emissions world-wide?
2 Why might it be difficult to implement such a programme?

Permission to Pollute (USA, 1992)

In May 1992 the Wisconsin Power and Light Corporation noted that it was emitting a lower level of pollutant into the atmosphere than was allowed under the Clean Air Act. It therefore sold the right to emit the balance of its allowable pollutants – 10,000 tonnes of sulphur dioxide. Two other power companies bought this right for an estimated 2.5 to 3 million dollars.

Within a year permits to pollute, known as 'smog futures', were being traded on the Chicago Board of Trade. The price of the right to emit 1 tonne of sulphur dioxide fluctuated between $122 and $450 US.

Legislation

Regulation is the third method used to tackle market failure; especially the various types of pollution. Examples are maximum emission levels on cars or from chimneys – maximum decibel levels on noise from aeroplanes and other machines; maximum permissible radiation levels; and, maximum impurity levels permitted in food, in sea-bathing water and so on. This method, however, takes little account of balancing benefits with costs. If the legislation is too tough the benefits of the polluting activity will be curtailed too much.

If the legislation is too slack there is little incentive for polluters to cut back to the point of social equilibrium. The ideal legislation is where marginal social cost is equal to marginal social benefit (the concept of marginal cost and marginal revenue is part of the Theory of the Firm for HL students only).

Of Cowboys and Spacemen

The closed earth of the future requires economic principles, which are somewhat different from those of the open earth of the past. For the sake of being picturesque, I am tempted to call the open economy the 'cowboy economy', the cowboy being symbolic of the illimitable plains and also associated with reckless, exploitative, romantic, and violent behaviour, which is characteristic of open societies. The closed economy of the future might similarly be called the 'spaceman' economy, in which the earth has become a single spaceship, without unlimited reservoirs of anything, either for extraction or for pollution, and in which, therefore, man must find his place in a cyclical ecological system which is capable of continuous reproduction of material form even though it cannot escape having inputs of energy...

In the cowboy economy, consumption is regarded as a good thing and production likewise, and the success of the economy is measured by the amount of the throughput from the 'factors of production', a part of which, at any rate, is extracted from the reservoirs of raw materials and non-economic objects, and another part of which is output into the reservoirs of pollution. If there are infinite reservoirs from which material can be obtained and into which effluvia can be deposited, then the throughput is at least a plausible measure of the success of the economy. The gross national product is a rough measure of this total throughput. It should be possible, however, to distinguish that part of the GNP which is derived from exhaustible and that which is derived from reproducible resources, as well as that part of consumption which represents effluvia and that which represents input into the productive system again...

By contrast, in the spaceman economy, throughput is by no means a desideratum, and is indeed to be regarded as something to be minimized rather than maximized. The essential measure of the success of the economy is not production and consumption at all, but the nature, extent, quality, and complexity of the total capital stock, including in this the state of the human bodies and minds included in the system. In the spaceman economy, what we are primarily concerned with is stock maintenance, and any technological change which results in the maintenance of a given total stock with a lessened throughput (that is, less production and consumption) is clearly a gain.

Source K E Boulding, 'The economics of the coming spaceship earth', in H. Jarrett (ed.). Environmental Quality in a Growing Economy, John Hopkins University Press, 1966.

Fished Out

World fish stocks are seriously depleted. More and more vessels are chasing fewer and fewer fish, and prices are soaring. Attempts to control over fishing and save the industry from collapse have failed for thirty years.

Canada, Newfoundland: Grand Banks, once the richest fishing grounds in the world where cod stocks were so great they were thought inexhaustable. The stock collapsed in 1992 and has never recovered. 40,000 people were put out of work.

Southern Ocean: (Falklands, South Georgia, southern tip of South America, South Africa, sea south of Australia and New Zealand) Patagonian tooth fish, known as white gold because of its high value, being fished out by pirate vessels. Expected to disappear in two years.

Iceland: (200 mile limit) Cod war fought with UK in the 1970's. Since then Iceland has managed stocks and has the most successful managed stock in the world.

African Coast: Mauritania and Senegal: EU busy setting up fishing rights to make up for missing European fish.

Mediterranean: Twenty years ago meat was twice the price of fish but now fish is a luxury. Most species are seriously depleted and those high value species that remain such as blue fin tuna are hunted by highly sophisticated boats fishing illegally.

Black Sea: Serious industrial pollution and broken sewage works in former Soviet countries, led to the extinction of 14 commercial species of fish and the laying up of fishing fleets. Some recovery is now occurring because heavy industries have shut down.

Eastern Atlantic/Ascension Island: Big-eye tuna, worth as much as £30,000 a piece, now as endangered species. Blue fin worth £600 each for the Japanese sushi market are also widely hunted by pirate boats.

North sea/Irish Sea and European coast: EU fisheries policy has been a disaster. Warnings from scientists ignored and size of fishing fleet too large. Herring stock collapsed in 1976 and only recovered after total ban on fishing. Cod wiped out in areas such as the Irish Sea and cod and haddock depleted everywhere.

Source: The Guardian, London 14th August 2000

Web Links

www.panda.org/endangeredseas – WWF endangered seas campaign
www.fao.org/fi – UN food and agriculture organisation – fisheries.
www.wwf-uk.org/orca – WWF oceans recovery campaign

2   INEQUALITY OF INCOME AND WEALTH [23]

There are two measures of the economic goods and services received by people. One is *income* and the other is *wealth*. Income is the *flow* of economic payments in the form of wages, rent, interest and profit over a period of time – a week, a month, a year. Wealth on the other hand is the *stock* of economic goods and services owned and measured at one particular point in time. The wealth of a family might consist of a house, savings in the bank, furniture and a car. Its income would be the wages and salaries of family members plus any rent, interest or profit earned.

The distribution of income and wealth amongst people in a society is not necessarily 'the best' if distribution is left to the market alone. It is possible that some families, by owning many economic resources could be very rich, whilst others are very poor. A market system allocates nothing to those who cannot pay. If people do not enjoy living in a society with extremes of rich and poor, and prefer to live in a society with a more even distribution of income and wealth, then the market may be deemed to 'fail' on this account. *Government intervention* may take place to redistribute income and wealth more evenly. This was one of the major aims of the former and present day centrally planned economies.

Dwarfs and Giants

In 1963 the Dutch economist, Jan Pen, represented the income distribution of the UK as though it were a parade of the whole population marching past an observer of average height. The whole parade takes exactly one hour to pass, and the income of each marcher is represented by his or her height. At the front of the parade are the smallest people, those on the lowest incomes, and at the end are giants, those on the highest incomes.

'...we see tiny gnomes pass by, the size of a matchstick, a cigarette... housewives who have worked for a short time for some money and so have not got anything like an annual income, schoolboys with a paper round. Suddenly we see an increase by leaps and bounds. The people passing by are still very small ones – about three feet[24] – but they are noticeably taller than their predecessors... they include some young people, especially girls who work regularly in factories, but above all people who are not in paid employment; very many old age pensioners, some divorced women, people with a physical handicap. Among them are owners of shops doing poor trade. And we see artists – they may include geniuses, but the public do not understand their work and the market does not reward their capacities.

After the average income recipients have passed by, the scene changes rather quickly. The marchers' height grows; six minutes later we see the arrival of the top ten per cent. The first to arrive are around six feet six inches, but to our surprise we see that they are still people with modest jobs.

In the last few minutes giants suddenly loom up. A lawyer, not exceptionally successful, eighteen feet tall. A colonel, also of much the same height. Engineers who work for nationalised industries. The first doctors come into sight, seven or eight yards, the first accountants. There is still one minute to go, and now we see towering fellows. University professors, nine yards, senior officers of large concerns, ten yards, a Permanent Secretary, thirteen yards tall, and an even taller High Court judge; a few accountants, eye-surgeons and surgeons of twenty yards or more.

During the last seconds the scene is dominated by colossal figures: people like tower blocks. Most of them prove to be businessmen, managers of large firms and holders of many directorships, and also film stars and a few members of the Royal Family.

The rear of the parade is brought up by a few participants who are measured in miles. Indeed they are figures whose height we cannot even estimate: their heads disappear into the clouds and probably they themselves do not even know how tall they are.'

Source: Jan Pen Income Distribution Penguin 1971

Government intervention, rather than reliance upon the market, is the major reason why most rich developed countries have more equality of income and wealth distribution than poor countries. Whilst individual governments can and do address this form of market failure there is of course no world government to address the wide inequality of income and wealth between the rich countries and the poorer countries. This international inequality is a massive problem and forms a major part of the IB syllabus – Section 5 of this text. The high degree of absolute poverty in Less Developed Countries is very highly correlated to the unequal distribution of income and wealth in those countries. The study of inequality in the context of poverty and development will also be left to Section 5, as will methods of measuring inequality.

Within any one country the major redistributive method is the taxation system. Direct taxes are usually *progressive*, that is, higher rates of tax are levied on those with higher incomes. This reduces incomes at the top end of the income spread. Negative direct taxes can be paid to the poor to increase incomes and reduce the spread at the bottom end. These are more commonly known as *transfer payments* and include unemployment benefit, sickness and disability benefits, child benefit and old age pensions. Income from taxation is also widely used to provide free or low cost *merit goods* which benefit the poor relatively more than the rich. Low cost housing, health care, education and food are goods which fall into this category, and are often subsidised. Education is of special significance as it enables the recipient to raise his/her income in the future. A market system would ensure education only goes to those who could afford to pay, thereby perpetuating income disparity into future generations.

3   THE ABUSE OF MONOPOLY POWER

The abuse of monopoly power is a major source of market failure. In a market system, producers and owners of the factors of production (which includes labour unions, as well as sellers of goods and services) strive to increase their market power – that is, raise income by reducing output and raising prices. This practice is called monopoly power and is exercised in varying degrees, with partial *monopoly power* far more common than total monopoly power in practice. When monopoly power is wielded, the economy is not at its most efficient. Government usually has *anti-trust*, or *anti-monopoly* laws, and *restrictive practices courts* to reduce the concentration of power in such markets. Courts often exist to investigate and curtail the restrictive practices of individual firms, or groups of firms, where these practices work against the interests of the public.

Adam Smith and Market Failure

Adam Smith, the champion of laissez-faire and free markets, recognised the danger of monopoly.

'A monopoly granted to an individual or a trading company has the same effect as a secret in trade or manufactures. The monopolists, by keeping the market constantly under-stocked, by never supplying the effectual demand, sell their commodities much above the natural price, and raise their emoluments, whether they consist in wages or profit, greatly above their natural rate.'

He also says of *collusion*, 'People of the same trade seldom meet together, even for merriment or diversion, but the conversation ends in a conspiracy against the public or in some contrivance to raise prices.'

Source: Adam Smith, The Wealth of Nations (1776).

MULTIPLE QUESTIONS – MARKET FAILURE

1 Because A has been vaccinated against measles B is less likely to catch them. B will therefore receive
   A an external benefit of consumption.
   B a private benefit of production.
   C a public good.
   D a free good.

2 Merit goods may be subsidised by government because
   I   externalities are not included in their prices.
   II   the market might underprovide them.
   III they benefit both users and non-users.

   A I only   B I and II   C II and III   D I, II and III

3 Primary education is regarded as a merit good. It follows that
   A it is supplied by the government.
   B it is non-excludable.
   C its benefits are felt by non-users.
   D it is paid for out of taxation.

4 Tradable permits are an economic device to deal with

   A hyperinflation.   B market failure.   C protectionism.   D barter.

5 Market failure may be due to the presence of
   I   free markets
   II   externalities
   III inflation

   A I only   B I and II   C II and III   D I, II and III

6   Tradable carbon emission permits may best be described as

   A   a type of 'green tax'.

   B   a form of direct regulation by the government.

   C   a means of shifting the cost of pollution from firms to governments.

   D   a market based solution to the problem of negative externalities.

7   Goods and services which are non-excludable and non-rivalrous are known as

   A   inferior goods.   B   merit goods.   C   public goods.   D   normal goods.

8   A free market is likely to under provide merit goods for all of the following reasons except

   A   the presence of income inequality.

   B   the existence of positive externalities.

   C   the difficulty of predicting future needs.

   D   the problem of non-excludability.

9   The diagram below shows the market for a demerit good and an attempt by the government to reduce its consumption.

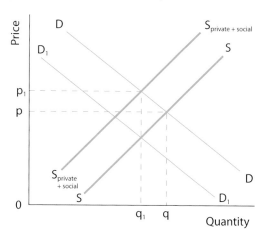

Which of the possible government actions listed below is the one most likely to have been used?

   A   Imposing an indirect tax on the demerit good.

   B   Advertising against the use of the demerit good.

   C   Rationing of the demerit good.

   D   Imposing a licence fee on users of the demerit good.

CENTRALLY PLANNED ECONOMIES

Planning is an expression of intent about future goals, and a method of achieving them. Individuals plan, families plan, companies plan, and governments plan. All of these plans involve a target or objective, and a method for attaining it. Thus many of you reading these words may have career plans *eg* to become doctors, engineers or business managers. If your target is to become a business manager in the future you are likely to have a medium term target of gaining a degree in economics or business studies. Your plan must then contain intermediate targets like gaining entry to your chosen university. Your plan will therefore have to include achieving a certain number of points on your IB Diploma. That in turn may require a certain grade in economics. Your very short term plan may be to get a good grade for an economics test on market failure this week!

The Nature of Central Planning

There is nothing particularly mysterious about planning. Even firms operating in the most extreme capitalist systems use planning techniques for allocating resources within the company, as within the company there are no markets. Governments also use planning methods in cases of market failure. Defence forces, for example, are likely to be planned in every country. Merit[25] goods, like health care and education, may well be planned rather than left to a market. Societies which use a mixture of markets and planning to allocate resources are known as *mixed economies*.

Cuba

In 1958 a revolution in Cuba brought Fidel Castro to power, and a socialist planning system to allocate economic resources. All major industries were nationalised and are now owned by the state, including the very large sugar industry. Education, health care and other social services are provided free by the state. Other essential goods and services are subsidised and rationed *eg* food, clothes and petrol. Although a poor country, Cuban redistribution policies have led to much higher real living standards than other Latin American countries with comparable GNP per capita. Parallel markets flourish however, due to widespread shortages.

The USA, hostile to the communist government from the outset, imposed an embargo on Cuban exports in the 1960s and this remains in place today (2002). The former Soviet Union plugged the trade gap by buying all of Cuba's exports at preferential prices from the 1960s to the 1980s, thus sustaining the Cuban economy.

With the collapse of the Soviet economy in the early 1990s Cuba has found it very difficult to replace the Soviet export market. Output has fallen and unemployment has risen. Previously the state had maintained completely full employment amongst the 11 million population. There are acute shortages of imports, however, because there are too few exports to pay for them. The economy is attempting to restructure, allowing the growth of small businesses and foreign tourism for example – although under restrictive rules to maintain socialist principles. Thus, small firms cannot employ anyone other than family members.

The governments of some countries have been so concerned at the inability of markets to allocate resources efficiently or fairly that they have adopted planning as the overriding method of resource allocation. These are known as *centrally planned economies*, or *CPEs*. They have been closely associated with countries which wish to grow and develop rapidly from a very poor background. They have also been closely associated with socialist/communist societies, which by definition seek social ownership of the factors of production. Many African countries, and some Asian countries *eg* India, adopted central planning after independence in the post World War II years. Leaders of these countries believed that the extent of market failure was such that the mobilisation of economic resources necessary for rapid economic growth was just not feasible. Many normally democratic, market orientated countries used planning during both World Wars to over-ride market systems. Planning, in one form or another, has therefore been employed in a wide variety of economic contexts. However, the communist led countries, such as the former USSR and present day China, have made the greatest efforts to make central planning work. The former USSR and present day China are two of the biggest. Others which are, or have been CPEs include: Albania; Bulgaria; Cuba; Czechoslovakia; East Germany; Hungary; North Korea; Poland; Romania and Vietnam.

In CPEs, the government appoints planners to allocate resources – and actively curtails the market mechanisms for resource allocation. Planners set prices to regulate demand to match the planned supply. In order to effectively control resources, land and capital ownership is transferred to *social ownership* – to government, commune, village or co-operative. Companies are usually owned and managed centrally by the state, with managers required to work to the plan. Production methods are not greatly different to those in a *nationalised* industry in a mixed economy. The extent of planning is much greater, however, usually covering all but fairly small scale economic activity, such as small workshops and professional services employing no more than a few people.

Development plans usually have the overall aim of *increasing economic growth and raising the standard of living*. The economic plan is a critical component, and involves the setting of quantitative targets for the economy to be reached over a specific time period.[26] Increasing the overall growth of the economy involves planning for each individual sector of the economy to grow; agriculture, industry, transport, energy, education and so on. The aim of the plan would be to show how this could be done. The planners also have to ensure that the plan targets are *consistent*, that is, they can be achieved and do not conflict.

Types of Planning

In a country with a heavy reliance upon the market as a resource allocator, the use of directives is restricted to *public sector plans*. Planning allocates public goods like defence, and important merit goods such as health care and education.

Planning can be more extensive, however, covering most of the private as well as the public sector. A loose overall form of planning, pioneered by France, is known as *indicative planning*. Without the degree of control that the social ownership of property brings, indicative planning is restricted to 'pointing the way' an economy should take. This type of planning is used by countries where the basic structure of the economy is taken as given. Planned changes are therefore relatively limited.

Central economic planning, pioneered by the Soviet Union and utilised by the former communist bloc countries, is a more pervasive form of planning than indicative planning. Under central planning even the basic parameters of society are likely to change, for example the ownership of resources, the mix between agriculture and industry, the prevailing technology, and so on. Amongst present day LDCs, Cuba and North Korea are centrally planned, and also parts of China, though China is rapidly changing.

Most *development planning* has, however, been in the context of a mixed economy, with private and public ownership. (India for example has produced development plans since independence in 1949, and is only since the 1990s turning to privatisation and markets). Such planning was thought to be eminently suitable for *LDCs*. They often do have a need to transform the structure of their economies as well as to use their scarce resources efficiently. In addition, the planning exercise is relatively simple compared to an indus-trialised economy, as the number of products which need planning are fewer in number.

Planning Rationale in LDCs

The main argument for using development planning is that of *market failure*. The poor structure of markets, (or their complete absence in parts of many LDCs), leads to incor-rect price signals being given, and prices are the market guide to resource allocation. Thus incorrect prices may divert resources into non-optimal uses. Capital, labour and foreign exchange, for example, are commonly used inefficiently in relation to their true opportunity cost to a low income society.

Unless guided, investment projects may allocate scarce resources to socially non-opti-mal uses. Thus planning can adjust economic decisions to take account of *externalities* such as job creation, poverty alleviation or the production of necessities. Finally, planning can act as a psychological stimulant to the development process by focusing national attention onto development problems.

Stages of Planning

A development plan consists of three stages of modelling the economy: *a macro-eco-nomic growth model*, an *inter-industry co-ordination model*, and *micro-economic project appraisals*.

Aggregate growth models focus upon the major variables for increasing national income; savings, investment and foreign exchange. They model an economy in the broadest sense. The most common aggregate growth model used in practice is the *Harrod-Domar growth model*, named after the economists who developed it. These broad models are then translated into detailed inter-industry plans.[27]

Input-output or inter-industry planning is a series of equations set out in the form of a matrix. This is designed to co-ordinate the economic activity of the economy. If the aggregate macro-plan aims to get GNP to grow by say 10%, then that has to be broken down into increases in specific industries. Each industry, however, requires inputs to pro-duce outputs. To increase agricultural and industrial output, planners must also allow for the required increase in the inputs. These inputs too are outputs of other industries. To increase these outputs requires an increase in their inputs, and so on. The problem rap-idly becomes very complex, yet the plan needs to be *consistent*, or it will fail.

Recall how this complex problem of co-ordination is solved in a market system. It is *the invisible hand* which co-ordinates it.[28] If markets do not exist, as they do not in many LDCs, or they are displaced, as in the former USSR, then planners will need to co-ordi-nate economic activity.

If, for example, the demand for steel increased under a market system, the price would rise. The quantity supplied would increase. The increased supply would have increased the demand for the factors of production: iron ore, limestone, furnaces, energy, land, labour, etc. Demand for these factors would, in turn, require more inputs – of steel, lorries, energy and labour for example. This chain of activity is brought about without any central co-ordination by the government. It occurs through prices changing which, in turn, induce owners of factors of production to act.

Planners have to try to replace this automatic mechanism with a mathematical solution. The career of *Wasily Leontieff*, the Russian inventor of input-ouput planning, illustrates the nature of the problem remarkably well. Leontieff worked upon input-output tables to try to solve the co-ordination problem in the planned USSR of the 1940s. He was 'loaned' to the newly communist China in 1950 to help co-ordinate that economy as it adopted central planning. Whilst there, however, he defected to the United States of America. His input-output technique was first put to practical use within the United States Air Force. At the height of the cold war this was politically ironic. Economically, however, it was entirely consistent. The USAF is a complex organisation *without a market mechanism* to allocate its resources.

In practice, planning techniques range from the simple, such as *material balances*, to the sophisticated – like *input-output* planning. The material balances technique is essentially the drawing up of a list of potential demands for a product, say steel, and then matching this with the potential supply. Demand and supply then have to be adjusted until they balance.

Project appraisal is a micro-economic technique used to appraise individual investment projects. Cost-benefit analysis is used to measure the costs and benefits in order to decide whether the investment should be undertaken. In a broader social CBA *externalities* can be taken into account by forming *shadow prices*. If, for example, the viability of a paper mill was being assessed, a private investor would treat labour input as a cost at the market wage rate. A planner, however, would use a wage which reflects the total opportunity cost to society, not just the private cost to the firm. In an LDC where labour is abundant this *shadow wage* is likely to be lower than the market wage. The shadow wage would reflect the external gain to society of reducing unemployment and poverty. Whereas a private investor would aim to maximise private profit, an LDC government is likely to want to maximise *net social welfare*.

FEATURES OF A CPE WHICH LEAD TO ECONOMIC PROBLEMS

In practice, planning has been most effective in simple economies or in wartime. As economies grow richer, they grow more complex. The number of goods and services produced expands rapidly, and the planning mechanism finds it difficult to cope. In the Soviet Union the central planning agency, *Gosplan*, set production targets for 70,000 items and set 200,000 prices each year. To ensure that the plans were *consistent* was extremely difficult, and the risk of making errors therefore large.

To achieve a greater equality in income distribution, the private ownership of factors of production was virtually outlawed. (Income from the ownership of land and capital accounts for a large proportion of the income disparity in capitalist countries.)

There was however a direct opportunity cost associated with the prohibition of this private capital. In the absence of private owners seeking optimal returns, scarce resources were liable to be used very wastefully. Recall that prices (wages) are used to allocate labour in a market economy. If material incentives are reduced to a sufficient extent in the pursuit of greater equality, there may be a problem of motivating people to work hard, to accept responsibility, to innovate, and to take risks. The opportunity cost of promising full employment and job security is reducing the motivation to work. CPEs did make fuller use of non-material incentives – awarding accolades such as 'worker of the month' or 'hero of the Soviet Union', for example – in an attempt to stimulate effort. However, the Soviet planners also used material incentives – wage differentials, improved access to housing, holidays and bonuses – to encourage fulfilment of the plans.

Another planning method designed to gain greater income equality is the setting of prices – low prices on basic commodities like food, housing, health care and public transport; and high prices on 'luxuries' like cars. In China, for example, rent on a two room apartment in 1996 cost about $8 per month in the city, and a visit to a doctor about 10 cents. In East Berlin, apartment rental was only one fifth of the market price of the equivalent apartment rental in West Berlin. In Moscow the price of bread remained at 15 cents a loaf for 60 years! Contrast these low prices with the prices put on cars. Whereas a car in West Germany would take 10 months salary to buy, in East Germany it would take 10 years salary.

Figure 2.106 (a repeat of the maximum price diagram Figure 2.15) illustrates one consequence of the low price policy. Demand conformed to the law of demand, low prices meant high quantity demanded. Supply, however, was constrained to what the planners decided. Basic foodstuffs and other commodities were subject to chronic shortages, as elementary market theory would predict. Empty shelves, long lines, rationing and parallel markets (black markets) were very common in Russia and China. In 1981 Poles were spending 4 hours a day waiting in line. The subsequent rationing, and continuing food shortages led to workers' strikes and political confrontation. Similarly, below equilibrium prices for apartments led to very long waiting lists. Rationing of the limited accommodation led to small living areas. (Most Russians live in cramped apartments often with shared kitchens and bathrooms). The waiting list for a motor car in East Germany was 15 years. There was a long wait to get a telephone. With such ordinary goods as jeans or soap becoming unobtainable at times, it was very hard to motivate people to work. Huge amounts of involuntary saving was generated in the Soviet Union because of the shortage of consumer goods upon which to spend it.

Figure 2.106 – Price Controls: Maximum Price

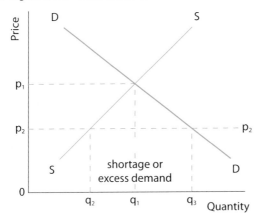

Consumer sovereignty, where producers produce what consumers wish to buy, did not exist in the CPEs. The situation was one of *producer sovereignty,* or rather – *planner sovereignty.* The consumer could only choose to spend income on those things that the planning body decided to produce. Consumer wishes were often a poor third in the plan after investment needs and defence needs were met.

Communist CPEs often proudly boasted of full employment and zero inflation. In one sense these boasts were justified – employment levels and the absence of inflation did appear to be superior features of the planning system compared to the market system. There was a promise of full employment, everyone was offered a job, indeed all were expected to work. Many people even now would see this as a great benefit.

However, having job creation as the target rather than the consequence of demand for the products that labour could produce, led to a great deal of *hidden* or *disguised unemployment.* In other words many people produced very little, their *marginal product* was very low. Inefficiency was markedly high.

Inflation was non existent because planners set and maintained all prices, including wages. Moreover, as we have already noted, low fixed prices were accompanied by serious shortages. To have stable prices but insufficient goods is not to solve the basic problem, merely to cover the problem up. Such a situation is known as *suppressed inflation.*

These problems of shortages could not easily be solved by importing goods and services. The plans did not permit industrial firms to export and import. Internal prices bore no relationship to market prices outside the CPE. The currency of the CPE bore no market-based value to other currencies. That is they had *non-convertible currencies.* To trade with other countries a currency must be convertible. The lack of convertibility meant that very little foreign trade took place. That trade which did occur, was mainly amongst CPEs themselves. The small amount of trade with market economies had to be part of a transaction *barter.* Bartering is both time consuming and cumbersome. Trading is difficult and huge benefits are lost as a result (see Section 4 on *Reasons for Trade*).

Problems of Transition from a Centrally Planned to a Market Economy

By the early 1990s, many of the former CPEs abandoned communism and central planning. They currently aim to transform their economies to mixed economies relying to a much greater extent on markets. This requires fundamental changes to major areas of the economy. These include the *reform of prices, foreign currency, banking, property ownership and institutions* like the law to support market operation.

Prices

Planned prices did not give correct market signals because they were deliberately designed to achieve the social aims of the plan rather than reflect the market. Freeing up the artificially low prices for basic goods, and the removal of subsidies, are important reforms of the transition period. Price rises provide the incentive and signal for producers to supply more. Consumers are initially shocked by high price rises, but shops fill and shortages disappear as there becomes a real incentive for people to produce. In the first week of the new Solidarity government in Poland, prices rose dramatically: bread by 40%; ham by 55%; electricity and gas by 400%; gasoline by 100%.

Currency

The banking system in a CPE also used to function as an instrument of planning. Today, in the new mixed economy, the Central Bank has to primarily ensure strict control of the money supply. If the money supply increases to accommodate price increases, inflation will result. Real prices will not rise. If real prices do not rise producers will not be induced to increase supplies. Shortages will not disappear. In Russia, for political reasons, the money supply has expanded enormously giving very high rates of inflation, known as *hyper-inflation*. The Rouble became almost worthless, and people resorted to bartering goods and using foreign currency for domestic transactions.

Banking

In addition, domestic money has to be made convertible with foreign currencies in order that foreign trade can take place. The previous artificially high exchange rates are being *devalued* (lowered).

Problems of Transition in Russia

There has been considerable market reform in Russia in the last few years. More than 14,000 large and middle sized enterprises had been privatised by the end of the first phase on 1 July 1994. One million small businesses are now privately owned. Just 2 years earlier there were only 35 private restaurants in existence in the whole of this huge country! 40 million Russians own shares. Over 70 per cent of industrial workers are now employed by private firms. Moscow spawns new shops and casinos every day and expensive foreign cars fill the streets.

Most firms and mines are, however, close to bankruptcy. When they can no longer hold out, the unemployment rate will soar. In addition, criminal activity has blackened the name of capitalism. Many of the new rich have effectively stolen former communal property or have bribed officials into obtaining licences to corner particular markets. The honest are tarnished by the activity of the dishonest and there is little trust in the market system. Tax evasion is enormous with the state collecting only a fraction of the taxes which are due. Social services are near to collapse. The military is not being paid. The transition in Russia then, is very fragile, and the market reforms have still to come to fruition.

Source: Adapted from an article in The Economist, 9 July 1994.

Property Ownership

To give an incentive for people to produce more, the privatisation of property is a major part of the transitional reforms. Land, industries and houses have to be transferred from social to private ownership. Private profit has to be reintroduced to give the new capitalists an incentive to set up companies, or to make existing ones more efficient. In some CPEs with a recent market tradition, like Poland, Hungary, and the Czech Republic, this is going ahead quite smoothly. In others, like many former republics of the USSR, there is virtually no memory of a market system after 70 years of planning, and the reforms are proceeding slowly and with difficulty.

Institutions

Institutional reform is vital, and must proceed hand in hand with the development of markets. Legal and judicial infrastructure has to be put in place to support both the ownership of private property and market transactions.

Resistance

The practical problems of the transition are compounded by a problem of resistance, as the benefits of the old planned system disappear. The resistance centres around equity, security and stability. The CPEs were founded on a significant commitment to *equity*. Income distribution was considerably more equal than in market countries. This was mainly due to two factors: 1) private ownership of land and capital was virtually non-existent, with individual income derived almost totally from individual labour; and 2) the high provision of merit goods, with subsidies and low fixed prices. Today, to gain efficiency, the private ownership of resources is leading to a wider inequality in the distribution of income and wealth. Millionaires and beggars have become commonplace. Many people resent this aspect of the reforms.

Security has also been eroded. Job security in particular has disappeared. There are no more jobs for life, and unemployment figures have increased markedly as the new privatised firms have shed labour to gain efficiency. In addition, the low prices and the subsidies have disappeared. High rates of inflation have eroded real income. State health care and pensions are also fast eroding. It is not difficult to see why many in these countries oppose the reforms.

Finally, economic freedoms necessarily give political freedoms. It was economic unrest in Poland that gave birth to Solidarity and the change of government. Whole governments and planned economies were swept away right across Eastern Europe. However, the speed and uncertainty of such political change also induced resistance. In China it was swiftly crushed in Tiananmen Square. In Russia a counter-revolution nearly succeeded.

The End of Central Planning in Eastern Europe

In the 1990s the countries of Eastern Europe switched their economic decision making from central planning towards markets. This coincided with the fall of communism and state controls. Under central planning factories were told what to produce what inputs they were allowed and who they were producing for. In the new market system they had to persuade consumers to buy. However many consumers now preferred to buy foreign products. In addition firms cut jobs as they sought to become more efficient. The buying power of unemployed workers fell. The defence industries in particular were badly affected, finding it difficult to switch their production to civilian goods. Poland, The Czech Republic and Hungary with fairly recent experience of capitalism acted decisively to privatise the ownership of state firms and made the switch relatively successfully. However most countries, like Russia, Ukraine and Bulgaria have been very slow to reform and output has fallen markedly.

National Income of five Eastern European countries, 1999 as % of 1989

Country	Percentage Change 1989–1999
Poland	122.4
Hungary	100.1
Bulgaria	71.1
Russia	54.5
Ukraine	39.0

Source: United Nations, Economic Survey of Europe

Question

Draw production possibility diagrams for a) Poland and b) Russia showing the shift in the PPF from 1989 to 1999.

MULTIPLE CHOICE QUESTIONS – CENTRALLY PLANNED ECONOMIES

1   The resource allocation of a centrally planned economy, in the process of transition to a more market based economy, is likely to give greater emphasis to the

   A   nationalisation of key industries.

   B   basic needs of the poor.

   C   requirements of the economy for merit and public goods.

   D   effective demand for goods and services

2   A characteristic of a centrally planned economy is that

   A   income distribution is very unequal.

   B   a wide variety of consumer goods are on sale.

   C   targets are set for producers.

   D   prices are set to reflect the scarcity of factors.

3   The resource allocation decisions in a centrally planned economy are made primarily by

   A   government.

   B   consumers.

   C   monopolistic producers.

   D   worker co-operatives.

4   Input-output planning addresses which planning issue?

   A   incentive to take risks.

   B   plan consistency.

   C   hidden unemployment.

   D   suppressed inflation.

5   Centrally planned economies often have shortages of consumer goods because

   A   planners cannot predict the quantity demanded at the plan price.

   B   of cheaper foreign imports.

   C   of a wide income distribution.

   D   income is insufficient to buy the goods available.

6   Which of the following is a defining characteristic of a market economy?

   A   Full employment.

   B   Stable prices.

   C   Public ownership of resources.

   D   Consumer sovereignty.

7   In a pure command economy production responds to

   A   prices.

   B   directives.

   C   the preferences of producers.

   D   the preferences of households.

Notes

1   By convention price, the independent variable, is graphed on the vertical axis.

2   An assumption that underlies the whole study of economics.

3   More developed theories of demand, such as 'Revealed Preference', 'Marginal Utility', and 'Indifference Curves' are not a requirement of the IB syllabus.

4   As I write this in 2003 coffee prices have plunged. This is due to new coffee producers supplying the world market from countries which formerly produced very little coffee *eg* Vietnam.

5   A single selling organization.

6   Made much worse by developed countries subsidising their own agriculture.

7   This links with a later Chapter on Monopoly and Competition

8   This topic is dealt with in more depth as a Higher Level Extension.

9   Marginal is a term widely used in economics. It refers to the last or extra unit, just as the margin of a page is the extra or last bit on a page.

10 When you draw the curves for yourself make sure that you always draw the MO. curve cutting the AO exactly at the top of the AO curve.

11 There may be other opportunity costs. The economist would value these in terms of their next best use, their opportunity cost, and add that amount into the economic cost. For example, if a language teacher worked only half time in order to run her own translation business in the other half of her week, she must cost her own labour. Thus if she could earn 50,000 Swiss francs in a year as a language teacher but gives up 25,000 Swiss francs by not teaching for half the week, she should cost her time as a translator at 25,000 Swiss francs. Her time should not be treated as free when calculating profit. If she uses a room in her house it has an opportunity cost. This too is part of the economic cost.

12 'Economic profit' and 'excess profit' are other names for 'super normal' profit.

13 See the Adam Smith reading 'Pins and Chips'.

14 in the short run. In the long run it is above the ATC curve.

15 We noted why MR = MC gives the greatest profit, when studying perfect competition.

16 Recall that in practice a single monopoly is uncommon. The term monopoly is also used to indicate a high degree of control by firms.

17 Price discrimination may even be beneficial to consumers. Thus when all segments of a market need serving, price discrimination allows effective cross-subsidisation. For example doctors can vary fees according to patient income, to ensure medical care is available to all.

18 This is known as a Pareto optimum after the Italian economist who first noted it.

19 This includes services also. Public 'goods' are in fact often services.

20   A valuation difficulty is that, where there is a chance of the cost of a good being borne by taxpayers, people who value the good have an incentive to understate its value to themselves. This helps to ensure that the good is publicly provided – an aspect of the free-rider problem.

21   Marginal cost is studied further in Section 2 by HL Students only

22   The topic of elasticity is covered in Section 2.

23   This second type of market failure is treated fairly briefly here, but covered more fully in Section Five in the context of less developed countries.

24   3 feet = 1 yard = 0.9144 meters.

25   Private goods with benefits to society. Covered in Section 2.4.

26   Most development plans cover a 5 year time period. This is sub-divided into annual plans. The 5 year plans then often form part of a twenty to 25 year long term or perspective plan.

27   A colourful description of the growth process in macro-economic terms was provided in the early 1960s by WW Rostow, an American economic historian. Rostow's account of economic growth uses an analogy of an aeroplane taking off. The plane standing at the end of the runway is likened to a traditional economy, *ie* stationary or moving very slowly. The second stage, 'the preconditions for take-off stage' sees the aircraft gathering speed down the runway. This is paralleled in growth terms with increased savings ratios and increased capital accumulation in a country. The critical third phase, 'the take-off', is analogous to when economies enter the 'self-sustaining growth', climbing up with increased GNP per capita. Finally 'the age of mass consumption' when development has occurred, is likened to an aircraft cruising at high altitude, having levelled off in flight.

28   The concept first fully explained by Adam Smith to show how prices act impersonally as signals to reallocate resources.

Section 3

Macroeconomics

3.1   MACROECONOMICS

Economics is usually divided into microeconomics and macroeconomics for convenience of study. So far we have studied only microeconomics. Micro, meaning small, is concerned with a section, or part, of an economy, the study of a particular market, the behaviour of households or of businesses. Even if the study is of a large industry, *eg* of the Zambian copper industry, or of the Russian steel industry, the study is microeconomics as an industry is only a part of an economy. Macro, meaning large, is concerned with the whole economy, *eg* the output of all industries, the total unemployment of a whole country, the economic growth of a nation and so on.

Macroeconomic policy objectives

Governments have policies concerning the five major macroeconomic issues. These are:

I economic growth,
I economic development,
I full employment,
I price stability, and
I external equilibrium.

Economic growth policy is concerned with the overall increase in goods and services: the increase in national output. Growth of national output is a major factor enabling improvements in the standard of living. Economic growth is a prized objective of all countries, but is arguably most necessary in the poorest countries, where living standards are very low compared to industrial countries.

Economic development is a much broader concept than economic growth. It is when the standard of living of all, or most, of the population of a country improves. It may well occur when economic growth occurs, but the two are not the same, and growth may occur without development. Economic development is introduced as a major topic in this Section and concludes the course as Section 5. The issue of Development contains some new theory but is mainly *applied economics.* Almost all the other topics in the syllabus can be applied to the study of development. It is central to the IB course.

External equilibrium is concerned with the balance of payments of a country, that is, payments to and from abroad. Sales of goods and services to foreigners, and purchases from foreigners, known respectively as exports and imports, make up part of these foreign-related flows. International movements of bank deposits, and the selling and buying of foreign investments are also part of the overall external balance. These are studied in Section 4 of the course – International Trade Theory. Also in Section 4 is a treatment of exchange rate determination, the market for currencies which enables trade to take place between countries. So do keep in mind that external equilibrium is one of the four macroeconomic policy objectives of government. For ease of study it is, however, treated initially as a separate topic.

Employment and *price stability* are the other two macroeconomic issues and are covered fully in this section, Section 3 of the course. Employment centres around the policy objective of trying to reach a situation of full employment. Price stability is concerned with limiting rises in the overall price level, *ie* controlling inflation. It may also be concerned with preventing price levels from falling *ie* deflation.

Macroeconomics, then, is about five major issues, and government macroeconomic policy focuses upon these five issues. You should make a note to recall these five issues as a group, even though for convenience of treatment they are divided into the two short-term domestic issues – unemployment and inflation; the external issue – balance of payments and exchange rates; and the long-term issues – economic growth, and development.

For several decades short run macroeconomics has been relatively difficult to study because there were, and still are, large areas of uncertain knowledge, and controversy has been common. However, by the same token it is a most interesting area of study exactly because of that controversy. This section begins with a study of the most important measure used in macroeconomics, National Income.

3.2 MEASURING NATIONAL INCOME

THE CIRCULAR FLOW OF INCOME

'National Income is the sum total of all final goods and services produced in a year and measured in money terms'. Because it is measured over time, national income is a 'flow'. A 'stock' is a measure at a point in time whereas a 'flow' is a measure over a period of time. If you count the number of students who are in your classroom at the moment, you are measuring a stock; if you count the number of students who use your classroom during the day, the week, or the year, you are measuring a flow. It is common to confuse the concept of 'wealth' with income. Wealth is a *stock* concept: it is the sum total of all things of an economic value *at a point* in time. The wealth of a family from an industrialised country might consist of a house, a car, furniture, bank savings, and a claim on a pension fund. The money value of these things added together is the family wealth at a particular time, *eg* on 1 January 2004. Family income is derived from adding together the flow of income from wages, rent, interest and profit over a period of time: a week, a month or a year. Wealth and income are distinct measures. There are connections, however. Families who earn high incomes tend to spend some of that income accumulating wealth by buying houses, paintings, books, shares in companies, bank deposits and pension funds. Families who own considerable wealth often hold some of that wealth in forms that give income streams, *eg* shares in companies, savings accounts, and property. What is true of the microeconomic unit, the family, is likely to be true of the macroeconomic unit, the country. A country which creates high national income will invest part of it in wealth creation: factories, hotels, roads, schools and hospitals. This wealth can then help to create higher future incomes.

As national income is a flow it can be expressed as a flow diagram. This is known as a 'circular flow of income diagram', or a 'circular flow diagram'. A circular flow diagram is a model of the macroeconomy. It is a simple model but it is the basis of more complex, and more realistic models. At its simplest, the model assumes only two sectors in the economy – households and firms (businesses). The model assumes that there is no government, and there is no foreign trade. Figure 3.1 shows the resource flows between these two sectors. Firms produce goods and services for households. Households own and provide the factors of production which are hired to firms. During the morning and evening 'rush-hours', you can see much of the labour and enterprise physically moving to and from work. You cannot see capital and land moving, but the services of capital and land are nevertheless rented daily to companies by landowners and shareholders. You can, of course, see goods and services changing hands in any high street shopping centre.

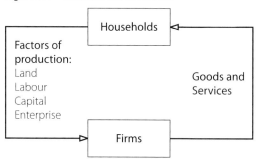

Figure 3.1 – Circular Flow of Income

Each of these resource flows has a financial counter-flow. Figure 3.2 shows the payments for goods and services running from households to firms (consumer expenditure). It also shows payments for factors of production running from firms to households (wages, rent, interest, and profit).

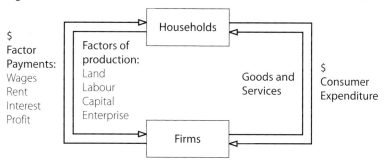

Figure 3.2 – Circular Flow of Income

INJECTIONS AND LEAKAGES

The two sector circular flow model (Figure 3.2) is so simplistic as to be of very limited use. In reality, all income earned by households is not passed back to firms. Some part of income leaks out of the circular flow. There are three main leakages which are: saving, taxes, and spending on imports. Thus, households spend only a part of their incomes on the goods and services of domestic firms. The government taxes their incomes directly (*eg* income tax, profits tax) and indirectly (*eg* sales tax, value added tax). Households save some part of their income (*eg* into bank accounts and pension funds). Some part of their spending finds its way abroad to foreign firms to pay for imported goods and services (Figure 3.3).

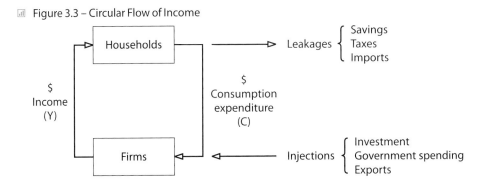

⊞ Figure 3.3 – Circular Flow of Income

However, even though firms do not get back all the income they pay out to households in the form of consumption spending, they do receive spending flows from other economic agents, namely other firms, the government and foreigners. Other firms buy investment goods or capital goods (*eg* machines, factories, office blocks). Governments buy goods (*eg* fire engines, computers) and services (*eg* the time of judges, policemen, soldiers). Foreigners buy exports.

MAJOR CONCEPTS IN NATIONAL INCOME ACCOUNTING

National Income, National Expenditure, National Output

If the flow of goods and services is summed over a period of one year, the total would be National Output. Care would have to be taken only to add all *final* goods and services, so as to avoid counting *intermediate* goods twice. Thus, the output of steel should not be added if its value is already included in the output of cars and refrigerators. The value of cars which are used as taxis should not be included: their value is included in the value of 'taxi rides'. Refrigerators used in restaurant kitchens are not final output either. In Figure 3.2 one might imagine putting a meter[1] in the flow line of goods and services from firms to households. If the meter was read at midnight on December 31st, and again one year later, it would record the flow of all final goods and services passing through it. The meter could of course only add them together if they were expressed in common units, *ie* money.

As these goods and services are transferred to households an exact money equivalent flows back the other way. This is the arrowed flow 'consumption expenditure'. If a meter were inserted in this line, to record all expenditure over the same calendar year *ie* National Expenditure, this would be equal in value to total output in a year *ie* National Output. Thus National Expenditure must equal National Output.

A meter inserted in the 'factor incomes flow' could total all wages, rent, interest and profit in a year to arrive at National Income. It can be shown that National Income must also be equal to National Output. This is because all output generates factor payments. Payments for all goods and services can be broken down into wages, rent, interest and profit elements. National Income must also be equal to National Expenditure as one person's expenditure is another person's income. Thus National Income ≡ National Output ≡ National Expenditure.

The three measures are not only equal, they *must* be equal, by the way they are defined. Yet in practice there are many errors and omissions in attempting to measure National Income. However all three measures must be equal by definition, and so a figure for error is included by statisticians to make them appear equal.

The term National Income has both a specific meaning (Income as against Expenditure or Output), and a generic or family meaning (as the overall term for all three measures). Thus it can be used in two ways, just as, for example, the word 'man' can be used specifically, *eg* 'my teacher is a man' (as against a woman) or generically, *eg* 'man has been on earth for x million years' (both men and women).

SOME DISTINCTIONS IN NATIONAL INCOME ACCOUNTING

'Gross' National Income and 'Net' National Income

The difference between a 'gross' measure of income and a 'net' measure is 'depreciation'. Depreciation is the wearing out of capital goods. This may also be called 'capital consumption'. A country's 'gross' output includes all investment, irrespective of whether the investment adds new capital stock or replaces capital which is worn out. If all investment goods are included in National Income, the total is Gross National Income. If depreciation is subtracted so that only net investment (new, additional investment) is included, the aggregate figure is Net National Income.

For most working purposes it is preferable to have the net figure, *ie* to subtract from total output capital which has had to be replaced during the year. However in practice it is very difficult to measure depreciation, and so it is common to find gross figures in use.

Gross 'National' Income and Gross 'Domestic' Income

All the aggregates discussed so far are national aggregates, yet in practice one often finds the term 'domestic' used, *eg* Gross Domestic Product, Net Domestic Product. The difference between national and domestic is 'net property income to abroad'.

Domestic income is the sum of all economic activity within the geographical boundaries of a country. This therefore includes the output and incomes generated by foreign firms operating there. To arrive at National Income there has to be an adjustment for the income accruing to foreign owners of property. A foreign company will send interest, rent and profit payments back to its shareholders. These income payments have been earned by citizens of another nation – not the domestic one in question. By the same token, property income earned abroad has to be added to domestic income. So whilst domestic statistics are geographical measures, national statistics are measures of ownership.

An example might be helpful here. An American soft drinks company owns factories in Australia. An Australian communications company owns newspapers and TV channels in the USA. The Australian Domestic Product includes all the incomes created by the drinks company in Australia, and none of the incomes created by the communications company in the USA. The Australian National Product however would include the income flows from the USA to Australian owners of the communications company. It would exclude the property income going abroad, to the American owners of the drinks company.

If the focus of interest was the economic welfare of Australians, then national income would be the better measure to use. On the other hand if the focus was upon employment and unemployment in Australia, then domestic income would be the more relevant measure.

National Income at 'Factor Cost' and National Income at 'Market Prices'

National Income figures are expressed in money terms. Wristwatches cannot be added to newspapers. However the value of wristwatches can be added to the value of newspapers. Market price is the best available measure of the value of most economic goods. At least, it would be if the government did not distort market prices by adding indirect taxes to some, and deducting subsidies from others. Thus, if final goods and services are valued at *market* prices, the values will not be giving a true measure of the incomes generated in their creation. A true measure of value of a good or service is obtained by looking at its factor cost, that is the cost of all the factors of production used to make it, before any adjustment for taxes and subsidies. National output at factor cost is therefore equal to national output at market prices, minus indirect taxes plus subsidies.

If it costs $1 to produce a litre of beer which sells at $2.20 after the addition of a sales tax, then $2.20 is the value to include for measuring National Income at market prices, but $1 is the value to include in measuring National Income at factor cost. If it costs $1 to produce a litre of milk, but due to a subsidy the milk sells for 60¢, then 60¢ is the value to include when measuring National Income at market prices, and $1 when measuring National Income at factor cost. Taxes and subsidies distort the true value of output and the incomes generated. National Income at Factor Cost is the more useful statistic.

'Nominal' National Income and 'Real' National Income

We have already noted that money is used as the measure of output. Money is not, however, a stable measure. Its own value can change as prices change. If prices rise, a process known as *inflation*, then the value of money falls. If prices fall then the value of money rises. The latter is less common, but it can and does happen, *eg* Japan at this time, 2003.

When National Income is measured, the prices of the current year are the ones normally used. If prices change over time then it is not possible to compare National Income in different years. For example, in a country with inflation, the National Income will rise because prices are rising. The object of most comparisons however, is to measure the change in output (real output). The National Income measured in current prices is sometimes called just that – 'N.I. at current prices' – or 'Nominal National Income'. If the N.I. is adjusted for the price changes, which is, in effect, like measuring the quantity of output in each year with the prices of one specific year, the N.I. is said to be at 'constant prices'. It is also known as 'real' National Income. For example, if a country has 10% inflation, that is, if prices on average are rising by 10%, then National Income in year one is treated as a base line measure and N.I. in year two is 'deflated' by 10% to make it a real N.I. figure. There are some interesting problems caused by doing this. These are treated under the topic 'Inflation' further on in this section of the book.

Total and Per Capita

National Income figures have many uses, and are very widely used statistics. One useful variation is to divide a country's National Income by its population to arrive at National Income per capita. That is, the National Income per head. Some Less Developed Countries which have a high National Income *eg* China, India and Egypt also have very large populations, and National Income per head is in fact relatively small. Some relatively small but More Developed Economies *eg* Denmark and New Zealand have very high *GNP* per capita, due to a small population. *GNP* per capita is in fact the most widely used single statistic for comparing the standard of living between countries. We will look closely at the validity of doing such comparisons in Section 5 of the course.

THE CALCULATION OF NATIONAL INCOME

Simplified accounts are shown for the UK for 1988. The component of the three basic measures are shown in turn. Note that National Expenditure totals are the same as National Income and National Output. The initial figures shown are Gross and Domestic. These are converted to Net and then to National figures. Expenditure figures, which are initially measured at Market Prices, are then adjusted to Factor Cost so that they equal the incomes generated and totalled under the Income method. Total figures are divided by population to show per capita figures. Finally nominal amounts are adjusted to real amounts.

GROSS DOMESTIC PRODUCT – BY THE EXPENDITURE METHOD

Figure 3.4 – Gross Domestic Product at Market Prices – by the Expenditure Method

		1988 (£m)
Consumer expenditure	(C)	293,569
Government consumption	(G)	91,847
Fixed investment	(I)	88,751
Change in stocks and work in progress	(I)	4,371
Exports	(X)	108,533
minus imports	(M)	-125,194
Gross domestic product at market prices		461,877
minus expenditure taxes		-75,029
plus subsidies		5,883
Gross domestic product at factor cost (measured)		392,731
Statistical error		2,056
Gross domestic product at factor cost (corrected)		394,787

Figure 3.4 shows the components of Gross Domestic Product *GDP* by the expenditure method. The components are the figures for the four economic groups which spend in an economy: consumers *(C)*, government *(G)*, investors *(I)* and foreigners *(X)*. All four groups spend some part of the total on imports *(M)*, so this amount is deducted. Thus, *GDP* by the expenditure method (or *GDE* as it is sometimes called) = $C + G + I + X - M$.

As these spending figures are valued at market prices, expenditure taxes have been deducted, and subsidies added back in, to give the true cost, or factor cost of *GDP*.

The figures for expenditure are collected from industrial sources and household surveys.

Statistical Error

In theory all the methods of measuring national income must be equal because of the way they are defined. In practice it is extremely difficult to measure them accurately. Therefore a figure is included for statistical error.

Consumer Expenditure (C)

There are three categories of consumer spending added together here: durable consumer goods, non-durable consumer goods, and services. Durable goods are defined as those which last for more than one year (approximately), *eg* cars, furniture, and TVs.

Non-durable goods are all the other goods, *eg* food, clothing, and fuel. Services are intangible products such as banking services, health care, mobile phone calls and haircuts.

Government Consumption *(G)*

Central, regional and local governments buy final goods and services, *eg* fire-engines and police services. Many of these goods and services are provided free to consumers by the government, so there is no market price to use as a measure of value, *eg* there are no prices for defence and police services. In practice the costs of these services are included in the accounts as a proxy for their prices.

Investment *(I)*

Investment is made up of Fixed Investment, plus Change in Stocks and Work in Progress. Fixed investment is the expenditure on capital goods such as factories, machines, roads and bridges. Businesses hold stocks of raw materials and finished products. (These are also known collectively as 'circulating capital'). In National Income accounting a 'change in stocks' is a measure of the amount that these stocks have increased or fallen during the year. In addition some forms of output take more than one year to build, *eg* some civil engineering projects, tunnels, bridges and roads. In this case only the 'work in progress', the work of the accounting year is included in the current year's National Income.

Exports Minus Imports

A part of domestic product is bought by foreigners. This is export expenditure, or exports. Domestic spending by consumers, government, and investors includes imports. These are the intermediate and final goods and services, bought from firms in other countries. These imports are part of another country's *GDP*. Import expenditure must therefore be deducted from export expenditure to arrive at 'net exports' or 'exports minus imports'.

Market Prices to Factor Cost

The sum total of spending $C + G + I + X - M$ is Gross Domestic Product at Market Prices. These prices include indirect taxes which are now deducted. Similarly, subsidies are added back in. The result is the Gross Domestic Product at Factor Cost.

GROSS DOMESTIC PRODUCT – BY THE INCOME METHOD

Figure 3.5 shows the components of *GDP* measured by summarising the incomes which are generated in production. The key point to remember is that there are only four ways to earn income, corresponding to the four factors of production – labour, land, capital and enterprise. There are therefore only four types of payment – wages, rent, interest and profit The table in Figure 3.5 is a sum of all the incomes in an economy. In practice measures are not quite as straightforward, but in most cases you are likely to be able to identify the four types of income from the description given.

Figure 3.5 – Gross Domestic Product – by the Income Method

	1988 (£m)
Income from employment (wages)	249,755
Income from self-employment (wages+profit)	42,617
Private sector company profits (profit)	70,242
Public sector company profits (profit)	7,216
Rent	27,464
Imputed charge for consumption on non-trading capital (interest)	3,408
minus stock appreciation	-6,116
Gross domestic product (measured)	394,606
Statistical error	181
Gross domestic product (corrected)	394,787

Employment income is straight-forward, as is rent. Income from self-employment – the income of small farmers, shopkeepers and taxi operators for example includes elements of both wages and profit. Other profit has been subdivided according to whether it comes from the privately owned or the publicly owned sector of the economy.

Stock appreciation is deducted. Recall that in the expenditure method of measuring that changes in stocks are regarded as changes in investment spending. However stocks can change in two ways: (1) by a physical amount and (2) by value due to price inflation. To be consistent we need to measure just the physical change in stocks in a year. If the value of stocks increases arbitrarily due to inflation, the price increase or 'appreciation' of stock has to be deducted.

Most of the income information is obtained from income tax collection statistics.

GROSS DOMESTIC PRODUCT – BY THE OUTPUT METHOD

Figure 3.6 shows output generated, classified by broad industrial groupings. The figures are collected from census returns provided by industry, plus income related figures. The figures for each group represent 'final' output only. Intermediate input has been deducted so as to avoid double counting.

Figure 3.6 – Gross Domestic Product At Factor Cost – by the Output Method

	1988 (£m)
Agriculture, forestry and fishing	5,625
Energy and water supply	21,845
Manufacturing	93,433
Construction	25,745
Distribution, hotel, catering, repairs	55,131
Transport and communications	28,657
Banking, finance, insurance	76,922
Ownership of dwellings	21,407
Public administration and defence	27,023
Education and health service	35,237
Other services	25,785
Adjusted for financial services	-22,204
Gross domestic product	394,606
Statistical error	181
Gross domestic product (corrected)	394,787

The final output figure is identical to the income figure because all output generates rewards to the factor inputs – land, labour and capital. The reward to risk, profit, always balances the equation. Any income left over after paying wages, rent and interest is profit (or loss if negative).

CALCULATING GROSS NATIONAL PRODUCT *(GNP)* FROM GROSS DOMESTIC PRODUCT *(GDP)*

Figure 3.7 records the property income earned by nationals of one country in another country. It also records the property income that is paid abroad to nationals of other countries. If one is taken from the other 'net property income from (to) abroad' is calculated. This could be positive or negative. In the example it is positive £5,619 million.

Figure 3.7

	1988 (£m)
Property income from abroad	55,526
Property income paid abroad	49,907
Net property income from abroad	5,916

The net figure is added to (or subtracted from) the Gross Domestic Product to calculate Gross National Product, see Figure 3.8.

📊 Figure 3.8 – Calculating Gross National Product (GNP) From Gross Domestic Product (GDP)

	1988 (£m)
Gross domestic product	394,787
Net property income from abroad	5,619
Gross national product	400,406

CALCULATING NET NATIONAL PRODUCT *(NNP)* FROM GROSS NATIONAL PRODUCT *(GNP)*

Figure 3.9 shows depreciation, or capital consumption, deducted from Gross National Product to leave Net National Product.

📊 Figure 3.9 – Calculating Net National Product (NNP), from Gross National Product (GNP)

	1988 (£m)
Gross national product	400,406
Less depreciation	-54,769
Net national product	345,637

CALCULATING GNP PER CAPITA FROM TOTAL GNP

The total *GNP* figure, £400,406 million, is divided by the population of the country, 56 million, to give the average *GNP* for each person – Figure 3.10. This is a widely used indicator for comparing living standards over time and between countries.

📊 Figure 3.10 – Calculating GNP Per Capita from Total GNP

GNP ÷ population = GNP per capita

$$\frac{400,406 \ (£ \ \text{million})}{56 \ (\text{million})} = £7,150 : 10 \ (1988 \ \text{figures})$$

CALCULATING REAL *GDP* FROM NOMINAL *GDP*

The *GDP* of the UK in 1993 was £627,000 million, an increase in *GDP* of 56% over the 1988 figures. However, over the five year period prices also rose, and thus part of the increase in *GDP* is a nominal increase, not a real increase in the output of goods and services. The nominal figure has to be *deflated* by the price increase to attain the real increase in output. The price increase over the five years, *ie* the rate of inflation is used as a *deflator*.

If prices had risen by 20% over the period £627,000 million would be reduced by 20% to give real *GDP*:

$$£627,000 \text{ million} \times \frac{100}{120} = £522,500 \text{ million}$$

If prices had risen by 50% the real *GDP* would be:

$$£627,000 \text{ million} \times \frac{100}{150} = £418,000 \text{ million}$$

Figure 3.11 graphs the *GDP* of the UK from 1968 to 1993. The upper line shows the *GDP* measured in current prices, (nominal *GDP)*, an increase of more than fourteen times between 1968 and 1993. However, when the inflation element is taken out, by remeasuring each year using 1968 prices, real *GDP* growth is shown to be very much less. Real *GDP* actually fell in 1974, 1975, 1979 and 1980. In Section 3.4 you will learn to measure inflation.

Figure 3.11 – Gross Domestic Product, 1968 – 1993, UK

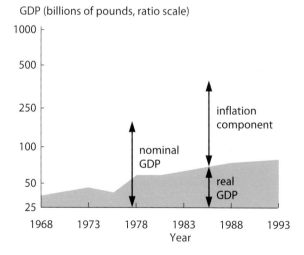

Source: CSO (UK) Economic Trends 1994.

CONSIDERATION OF USES & LIMITATIONS OF NATIONAL INCOME ACCOUNTS

National income statistics have many uses:

⏐ They are used by governments, firms and economists to forecast changes in the economy. The forecasts are then used to plan for the future.

⏐ They provide the data to test hypotheses about how the economy works. This furthers our understanding of economic behaviour.

⏐ They are used to make comparisons of economic performance, both over time and between countries. Thus the GNP of Japan in 2004 could be compared with that of Japan in 1997, or it could be compared with the GNP of China in 2004.

National Income per capita is used to make judgements about economic welfare. Growth of national income is broadly equated with a rise in living standards.

Although national income statistics are some of the most useful and widely used figures available to economists, problems arise in their measurement and which lead to major deficiencies in the end figure. (One such problem, that of unrecorded economic activity, is illustrated here in the reading *'The Parallel Economy in the USA'*) All students must be aware of these shortcomings before using N.I. tables as a measure of total final economic output. In addition, particular care must be taken when comparing different things. The economic structure of a single country may change over time. The economic structure of different countries may be widely different, making international comparisons unreliable.

The Parallel Economy in the USA

Data from the US Department of Labor enabled the University of Michigan to make estimates of the size of unofficial, parallel market activity in different industries in the USA in 1993.

Activity	Estimate of the percentage of services provided by the parallel market
Lawn maintenance	90
Domestic help	83
Child care	49
Home repair	34
Laundry/sewing	25
Appliance repair	17
Car repair	13
Haircutting/beauty treatment	8
Catering	8

Questions

Why do small scale service industries figure so highly in the underground economy?

What effect does the parallel economy have on GNP figures?

GNP per capita is the most commonly used single indicator of the standard of living within a country, and for purposes of comparison, between countries. For example, Less Developed Countries (LDCs) and More Developed Countries (MDCs) are defined by their level of GNP per capita. However, the problems and shortcomings of using GNP per capita as though it were the same thing as standard of living are enormous. Students must exercise even greater caution in coming to conclusions concerning the standard of living. Some of the major problems of using GNP per capita are covered in Section 5, in the context of economic development.

To gain an insight into the problems, however, Figure 3.12 and Figure 3.13 are included here. They both highlight the fact that GNP per capita is an *average* figure. The *distribution of income* is not reflected in GNP per capita. Figure 3.12 shows the percentage of national income which goes to the richest ten per cent of the population in a selection of countries. In Sweden and Austria, for example, the richest 10% receive about 20% of total national income. In poorer countries the share of the richest 10% may rise to 40–50%. There is not one standard of living in a country. Thus in Brazil a few extremely rich people share a country with masses of desperately poor people. The GNP per capita is a very poor measure of the standard of living in Brazil. Figure 3.13 illustrates uneven income distribution within the United States of America. 'Poverty', as officially measured, can be seen to be unevenly distributed among different ethnic groups of Americans and family structures. The GNP per capita of the United States of America is among the highest in the world. It masks, however, a wide disparity in the living standards of Americans.

Figure 3.12 – Income Distribution

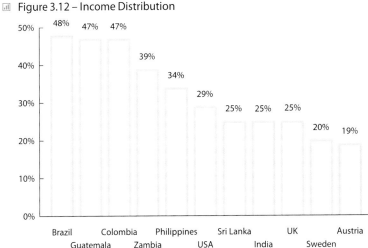

The figure shows the percentage of national income which is received by the richest 10% of the population (mid 1990s). Inequality tends to diminish as a country develops. In poor, developing nations the richest tenth of the population typically receives 30-50 percent of all the income. In developed countries the richest tenth get 20-25 percent of total income.

Figure 3.13 – USA: Percentage of Persons in Poverty by Demographic Group, 1993

Group	Official Measure	Adjusted for transfers in kind (food, housing, medical benefit)
All	15.1	11.7
White	12.2	9.4
Black	33.1	26.6
Hispanic	30.6	22.8
Female households ~ no husband present	35.6	N/A

Source: Statistical Abstract of the United States, 1994

Despite all these problems, GNP does remain a very useful measure of marketed national output. However its use as a comparator of living standards across a wide range of countries, which are then ranked like teams in a football league, is perhaps demanding too much of this statistic. Nevertheless, GNP per capita does correlate reasonably well with more complex definitions of what is meant by 'standard of living'. It represents the best single indicator that we have. This only serves to highlight the absence of, and need for, a better measure of the standard of living. Section 3.3 looks more closely at this problem as an introduction to Section 5 where the problem of world poverty is studied.

MULTIPLE CHOICE QUESTIONS – MEASURING NATIONAL INCOME

1 GDP at factor cost is equal to GDP at market prices minus

A indirect (sales) taxes plus subsidies.

B net income flows from foreign capital.

C depreciation (capital consumption).

D direct (income) taxes and transfer payments.

2 Simplified national income accounts for a country are shown below.

	US$ million
Consumers' expenditure	20,000
General government final consumption	7,000
Gross Domestic Investment	5,000
Exports of goods and services	4,000
Imports of goods and services	4,500
Capital consumption	3,000

The GDP is

A US$28,500   B US$29,000   C US$31,500   D US$32,000

3 Which of the following is the best indicator of a country's standard of living?

A National income

B Net national product at factor cost

C Real income per head

D Personal disposable income

4 GNP per capita is commonly used as an indicator of economic development because

I it generally includes most goods and services in a country.

II most countries attempt to measure it in similar ways.

III it gives a precise measure of the standard of living.

A I only   B I and II   C II and III   D I, II and III

5   The table lists items from a country's national income accounts.

	€ (billion)
Wages and salaries	60
Profit interest and rent	6
Net income from abroad	6
Capital depreciation	4

What is the value of this country's GNP?

A   € 68 billion   B   €70 billion   C   €72 billion   D   €80 billion

6   Which of the following is not a macroeconomic policy objective?

A   Economic growth

B   Full employment

C   Price stability

D   Monopoly restriction

3.3   INTRODUCTION TO DEVELOPMENT

DISTINCTION BETWEEN ECONOMIC GROWTH AND ECONOMIC DEVELOPMENT

Economic growth is the increase in a country's output over time, that is an increase in its national income. Growth is a macroeconomic variable and can be measured in a fairly straight forward fashion. Development is a much broader concept involving non-economic and often quite intangible improvements to the standard of living. This may involve trying to measure improvements in variables like freedom of speech, freedom from oppression, health care, education and employment.

Economic growth is not the same thing as development. It is very desirable to have growth to create the extra resources to allow development but it is essential to recognise that development is a much broader concept than economic growth. It is, for example, possible to have growth without development. In the 1950s and 1960s Less Developed Country (LDC) governments pursued growth as their over-riding objective. It was widely believed that if rapid growth of a could be achieved, usually an urban/industrial sector, then the expansion of GNP would 'trickle down' to the rest of the economy in time. Despite considerable success with growth, 'trickle-down' has spectacularly failed to happen. Nevertheless, growth is an important target, as it enables development. Economic growth creates resources which can be used to reduce poverty. For example development would occur if the increased output improved the provision of health care, housing, education, jobs and achieved a more even income distribution.

ECONOMIC GROWTH

Economic growth then, is an increase in national income. However national income can increase in two ways. A Production Possibility Frontier graph is a useful tool in understanding this. In Figure 3.14 a hypothetical country is modelled which can produce either manufactures or agricultural goods, or combinations of both. In the diagram, point A is attainable but inefficient. There is unemployment and under-utilised capital. More of either product, or both, can be obtained at no opportunity cost by moving outwards towards the curve or frontier. Points B to E are on the production possibility frontier (PPF). They are not only attainable but efficient. All resources are being used. There is no unemployment. To produce more of one product here, say more manufactures, moving from point D to point C, involves an opportunity cost in agricultural goods. Finally point F is unattainable. This country cannot produce this combination of goods.

 Figure 3.14 – Actual Growth

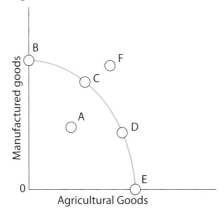

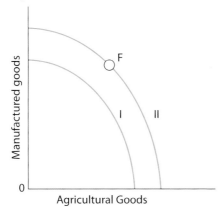 Figure 3.15 – Potential Growth

Note that the movement of production from A to C in Figure 3.14 would increase output. This is described as an increase in actual output. When the whole PPF moves out the growth is described as an increase in potential output. Whilst it is an important objective of policy makers to attempt to steer the economy out towards the PPF i.e. to reduce unemployment and produce the maximum possible, this is qualitatively different from an increase in the potential to produce, shown as a shift of the curve, as in Figure 3.15. The two need to be distinguished from each other. The problems of understanding and increasing actual growth are dealt with in Section 3.4, *Macroeconomic models*. In this section we concentrate our understanding on improving potential growth. In practice however it is difficult to separate an increase in GNP into the two component parts.

REAL GNP AND GNP PER CAPITA

As GNP may also increase due to price inflation, the money GNP figure is adjusted to give real GNP. An example is shown below:

Year 1 GNP   Year 2 GNP

$100m $110m $= \dfrac{\$110m}{\$100m} \times \dfrac{100}{1} =$ 10% growth

However, if inflation was at 7.5% during this year then three quarters of the increased GNP is due to price increases. Therefore only 2.5% is due to growth of real output (10%–7.5% = 2.5%).

It is common to define economic growth more narrowly than 'an increase in total output' by relating it to growth of population to show the 'increased output per capita'. This is especially significant in many of the world's poorest countries as population is growing fastest there.

If, in the previous example, the population is also growing, say at 2%, then the increase in output per capita is: 2.5%–2% = 0.5%

For many purposes therefore, economic growth is defined as the increase in real GNP per capita, over a certain time period, usually one year.

GNP Per Capita

1. In 1998 Bolivia had a GNP per capita of $1000. The population was 8 million. What was the GNP in 1998?

2. In 1998 Papua New Guinea had a GNP of $4.1 billion and a population of 5 million people. Calculate the GNP per capita of PNG in 1998.

THE SIGNIFICANCE OF THE GROWTH RATE

An arithmetical relationship worth remembering is that of "Doubling-time". If any variable grows at a rate of 1% per annum, then it will double in size in 72 years approximately. If it grows at 2% it will double in 72 years divided by 2 and so on, see Figure 3.16.

Figure 3.16 – Growth Rates and Doubling Time

growth rate (%)	doubling time (years)
1	72
2	36
3	24
4	18
5	14.4
10	7.2
etc	etc

This is a useful yardstick when judging the significance of growth rates. For example China currently has a GNP growth rate of approximately 7% (2003). China's GNP will double in 72/7 = 10.3 years, if this rate continues. Mexico's growth rate of 1.4% means that GNP will take 72/1.4 = 51.4 years to double.

The two growth rates which combine to form the GNP per capita growth rate, that is GNP growth and population growth, are therefore of major importance.

Returning to the distinction between growth and development, point F is attainable in Figure 3.15 because economic growth has caused the PPF to move outwards. Thus, if an LDC can cause its economy to grow, it enables higher levels of production and consumption. If the increase in goods and services is such that it reduces poverty by improving nutrition, health care or literacy for example, then development has occurred as well as growth.

Figure 3.17 shows economic growth with development and Figure 3.18 economic growth without development. The benefits of growth have all accrued to the rich. As unequal income distribution is a major characteristic of many poor countries the situation in Figure 3.18 is entirely possible. After all, demand is determined by income or purchasing power. If that is largely concentrated amongst a rich elite sector then their purchases will effectively determine a large proportion of the production mix. Economic growth could mainly consist of an increased output of grand houses, swimming pools, luxury cars and restaurant meals. In Figure 3.17 on the other hand, growth has gone towards producing goods and services used by the poor, such as food, simple clothing, basic housing, elementary schools, transistor radios and bicycles.

Figure 3.17

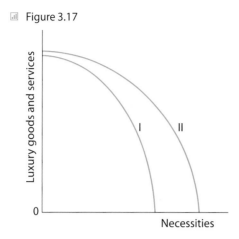

Figure 3.18

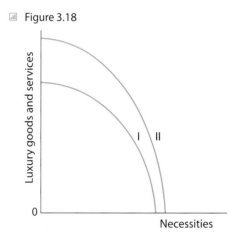

The Poor of Three Continents

A Poor Subsistence Farmer's Household in Ghana

In Ghana's Savannah region a typical family of seven lives in three one-room huts made from mud bricks, with earthen floors. They have little furniture and no toilet, electricity, or running water. Water is obtained from a stream a fifteen-minute walk away. The family has few possessions, apart from three acres of unirrigated land and one cow, and virtually no savings.

The family raises sorghum, vegetables and groundnuts on its land. The work is seasonal and physically demanding. At peak periods of tilling, sowing and harvesting, all family members are involved, including the husband's parents, who are sixty and seventy years old. The soil is very low in quality, but the family lacks access to fertiliser and other modern inputs. Moreover, the region is susceptible to drought; the rains fail two years out of every five. In addition to her farm work, the wife has to fetch water, collect firewood, and feed the family. The market town where the husband sells their meagre cash crops and buys essentials is five miles away and is reached by dirt tracks and an unsealed road that is washed away every time the rains come.

None of the older family members ever attended school, but the eight year old son is now in the first grade. The family hopes that he will be able to stay in school, although there is pressure to keep him at home to help with the farm in busy periods. He and his two younger sisters have never had any vaccinations and have never seen a doctor.

A Poor Urban Household in Peru

In a shantytown on the outskirts of Lima a shack made of scraps of wood, iron, and cardboard houses a family of six. Inside there is a bench, a table, a radio, and two chairs. The kitchen consists of a small kerosene stove and some tins in one corner. There is no toilet or electricity. The shantytown is provided with some public services, but these tend to be intermittent. Garbage is collected twice a week. Water is delivered to those who have a cement tank, but this family has been unable to save enough for the cement. In the meantime, the mother and eldest daughter fill buckets at the public standpipe 500 yards away.

Husband and wife are Indians from the same mountain village in the Sierra. Neither completed primary school. They came to Lima with two children almost four years ago, hoping to find work and schools. Although they have jobs, the economic recession of the past few years has hit them hard. Better-off neighbours who arrived in Lima three to six years before they did say that it was easier to get ahead then. Still, husband and wife are hopeful they will soon be able to rebuild their house with bricks and cement and, in time, install electricity, running water, and a toilet like their neighbours. They now have four children, after losing one infant, and the two eldest attend the local community school, recently built with funds and assistance from a non governmental organisation (NGO). All the children were given polio and diptheria-pertussis-tetanus (DPT) inoculations when a mobile clinic came to the shantytown. Community solidarity is strong, and a community centre is active in the shantytown. The father works in construction as a casual labourer. The work is uncertain, and there are periods when he must take any odd jobs he can find. When he is hired on a construction site, however, it is frequently for a month or so. His wife worries that he will be injured on the job like some of his fellow workers, who can no longer work and yet receive no compensation. She earns some income doing laundry at a wealthy person's house twice a week. To get there she must take a long bus ride, but the job does enable her to look after her one- and three-year old children. She is also in charge of all domestic chores at home. When she is away from the house for long periods, the two oldest children take morning and afternoon turns at school so as not to leave the house unattended. There have been many burglaries in the neighbourhood recently, and although the family has few possessions, radios and kerosene stoves are much in demand. The family lives on rice, bread and vegetable oil (all subsidised by the government), supplemented with vegetables and, occasionally, some fish.

A Poor Landless Labourer's Household in Bangladesh

In a rural community in a drought-prone region of Bangladesh a landless labourer and his family attempt to get through another lean season.

Their house consists of a packed mud floor and a straw roof held up by bamboo poles from which dry palm leaves are tied to serve as walls. Inside there is straw to sleep on and burlap bags for warmth. The labourer, his wife, three children and niece do not own the land on which the shack is built. They are lucky, however, to have a kindly neighbour who has indefinitely lent them the plot and a little extra on which they are able to grow turmeric and ginger and on which they have planted a jackfruit tree.

The father is an agricultural day labourer and tends to be underemployed most of the year. During slow agricultural periods in the past he could sometimes find non-agricultural wage labor – for example, in construction in a nearby town – but he lost the strength to do much strenuous work after a bout of paratyphoid. He therefore undertakes petty services around the village for very low pay.

His wife typically spends her day cooking, caring for the children, husking rice, and fetching water from the well. She is helped in these tasks by her thirteen year old niece whose parents died in a cholera epidemic some years ago. The woman and her niece are always on the lookout for ways to earn a little extra. Such work as husking rice, weeding fields, and chopping wood is sometimes available from better off neighbours. The nine year old son attends school a few mornings a week in a town an hour's walk away. The rest of the day he and his seven year old sister gather fuel and edible roots and weeds. The sister also looks after the baby when her mother and cousin cannot.

The household spends about 85% of its meagre income on food – predominantly rice.

Family members are used to having only two meals a day. They hope to struggle through to the rice harvest without having to cut down and sell their jackfruit tree or the bamboo poles supporting their roof.

Source: The World Bank, World Development Report, 1990

LDC Characteristic	Ghana	Peru	Bangladesh
1 A low standard of living			
a Low GNP per capita			
b poor health			
c poor housing			
d high illiteracy			
e absolute poverty			
2 High population growth			
3 Primary production			
4 Low productivity and high unemployment			
5 Unequal power distribution			

Question

1   How many of the characteristics of LDCs can you identify from each of the three readings? Tick the appropriate country column if the characteristic is present, or seems likely to be present.

2   Using World Bank statistics from the tables in the World Bank's World Development Report, compare the characteristics noted in 1a to 1e, 2 and 3 above with those for Japan and Australia.

DEVELOPMENT

Compared to growth, development is not an easy concept to define, as 'to develop' necessarily involves normative or value judgements being made. Dictionary synonyms are 'to improve' or 'to progress'. Views will differ as to whether certain activities improve life or not. A new city airport is a welcome improvement to a busy executive but is a reduction in the quality of life to a local resident who suffers increased noise pollution and traffic congestion. Television broadcasting, private car ownership and increased foreign travel have a balance of advantages and disadvantages.

Fortunately there is little need for the student of development to grapple with these issues and concepts initially, for there is wide consensus of opinion about overwhelmingly obvious basic problems. So, whilst there may be disagreement about, say, the restriction of motor car use in the cities of Germany, Canada or Japan, there is almost universal agreement on certain fundamental conditions for life to be lived satisfactorily. Sufficient food for the family is a requirement as much to a Peruvian as it is to an American. The survival of her babies is as desirable to an Afghan as it is to an Australian. The desirability of freedom from servitude and freedom from aggression would find little opposition from any family on any continent. Self-respect and dignity are universally prized.

Yet billions of the world's people suffer from insufficient basic requirements; food, clothing, shelter and health care; from the lack of a job; and from indignity and fear. Poverty and employment are of course related to income, and levels of income. Therefore the growth of income forms an important element of any study of development. Whilst economic growth is immensely helpful in aiding development, however, growth alone is not sufficient. Development is a broader, multi-dimensional process.

It is quite possible to have economic growth without development. There are countries today which illustrate that. Thus economic growth might benefit only a small rich sector of the society, or increase the country's military preparedness, without there being any improvement in the situation of the poor. Yet until recently development was regarded as almost synonymous with economic growth, the effort to increase GNP per capita.

The increased prosperity of the country was expected to 'trickle down' from the rich to the poor, raising the overall standard of living. Using the process of development of the now rich industrial countries as a model, many poor countries concentrated their efforts on narrow economic criteria: on the growth of savings, investment and GNP. However, several decades of such 'development' has left the problem of poverty largely unaffected or worse than before. This has happened even where GNP per capita has increased significantly. The deterioration has been of an absolute magnitude, as the populations of the less developed countries increase rapidly. It has also been a relative deterioration – for as the rich grow richer the gap between rich and poor widens. The rich include the elite within the Third World as well as the populations of the industrialised countries, the so-called First World.

As an example of the difference between growth and development consider the economic experiences of Libya with South Korea since the 1960s. In Libya the increase in national income is almost totally attributable to a single product, oil. The oil has largely been extracted by foreign technicians for sale to foreigners. The local population have had little involvement other than as recipients of oil receipts. In South Korea there has been broad industrialisation, accompanied by urbanisation. There has been wide involvement of the population with a marked improvement in living standards, education and health.

One leading academic economist, Professor Dudley Seers[3] defines development as "the reduction and elimination of poverty, inequality and unemployment within a growing economy". Thus he writes:

"The questions to ask about a country's development are therefore: What has been happening to poverty? What has been happening to unemployment? What has been happening to inequality? If all three of these have become less severe, then beyond doubt this has been a period of development for the country concerned. If one or two of these central problems have been growing worse, especially if all three have, it would be strange to call the result 'development', even if per capita income had soared. This of course applies to the future too. A 'plan' which conveys no targets for reducing poverty, unemployment and inequality can hardly be considered a 'development plan'. Of course the true fulfilment of human potential requires much that cannot be specified in these terms. They include adequate educational levels (especially literacy), participation in government and belonging to a nation that is truly independent, both economically and politically, in the sense that the views of other governments do not largely predetermine one's own government's decisions. As undernourishment, unemployment and inequality dwindle, these educational and political aims become increasingly important objectives of development. Later still, freedom from repressive sexual codes, from noise and pollution, become major aims".

Another prominent academic, Professor Michael Todaro,[4] concludes that "development in all societies must have at least the following three objectives:

1 to increase the availability and widen the distribution of basic life-sustaining goods such as food, shelter, health and protection to all members of society;

2 to raise levels of living, including, in addition to higher incomes, the provision of more jobs, better education and more attention to cultural and humanistic values. These all serve not only to enhance material well-being but also to generate greater individual and national self-esteem; and

3 to expand the range of economic and social choice to individuals and nations by freeing them from servitude and dependence, not only in relation to other people and nation-states but also to the forces of ignorance and human misery."

Development in a Javanese Village

The story of Balearjo, an east Javanese village of 4,000 people, shows what declining poverty means to individuals. The village is about eight kilometres from the town of Gongdanglegi and is connected to the outside world by bumpy but passable dirt roads. Although Balearjo is still somewhat poorer than its neighbours, research conducted in 1953 and 1985 shows that the lives of its inhabitants improved greatly in the intervening years. Rice yields increased dramatically, from 2 tons to 6 tons of paddy per hectare for the wet season crop, and the wage for a day's work increased from 2 kilograms of rice in 1953 to nearly 4 kilograms in 1985. In 1953 the village would have been considered poor by most definitions. Rice was available for only four months; the diet for the rest of the year consisted of corn and, when that ran out, cassava. Clothes were worn until they were in tatters, and few people had shoes. A typical house was made of thatch and bamboo, with an earthen floor. Furnishings were sparse and uncomfortable. Few villagers could read, and few had travelled any distance from the village. A daily paper brought from a nearby town supplied the only outside news.

By 1985 things had changed. Clothing was much better, and shoes were commonplace. Most villagers had radios and some even had television sets. More than 90% of the houses were made of colourful painted brick and stucco, with partial cement floors. Furnishings were more extensive and included chairs and tables bought from stores. Literacy had improved dramatically thanks to two primary schools, one financed by the village and the other by the central government. Travel outside the village was common, and knowledge of national events, provided through hourly radio broadcasts, was widespread. In 1953 villagers relied on home made kerosene lamps that provided little illumination, but by 1982 electric power lines had reached Balearjo, and by 1985 many households had electric light. Such burdensome activities as rice pounding and shoulder transport had disappeared, relieving women of some of their most exhausting tasks. Higher incomes had led to demands for new products and services and hence to more productive work, such as construction, trade, and small manufacturing. Growing specialisation was also evident. Houses in 1953 were constructed by the owners with the help of neighbours, but by 1985 most of the work was done (and done better) by full-time carpenters.

Source World Bank, World Development Report 1990.

Question

1   Why were the villagers of Balearjo considered poor in 1953?
2   What development had taken place by 1985? To what extent does your answer meet the three development objectives of Todaro?

Problems of Measuring Development

The problems of measuring development by GNP per capita and alternative use of indicators of development are returned to in the last part of Section 3 of the textbook.

United Nations International Development Goals

1 Halve the proportion of people living in extreme poverty between 1990 and 2015.

2 Enrol all children in primary school by 2015.

3 Empower women by eliminating gender disparities in primary and secondary education by 2005.

4 Reduce infant and child mortality rates by two thirds between 1990 and 2015.

5 Reduce maternal mortality rates by three quarters between 1990 and 2015.

6 Provide access to all who need reproductive health services by 2015.

7 Implement national strategies for sustainable development by 2005 so as to reverse the loss of environmental resources by 2015.

CHARACTERISTICS OF ECONOMIC GROWTH

VARIATION IN LONG RUN GROWTH RATES

Economic growth can vary enormously over time and between countries. Figure 3.19 illustrates this variation between a selection of countries, showing the growth rate for 1998–1999. These range from minus 7.3% for Ecuador to plus 7.1% for China.

Figure 3.19 –Economic Growth Rates

Country	Growth of GNP % 1998–1999	Country	Growth of GNP % 1998–1999
Ecuador	-7.3	Papua New Guinea	3.2
Argentina	-3.2	Russian Federation	3.2
Niger	-0.6	USA	3.6
Indonesia	0.3	Guatemala	3.6
Saudi Arabia	0.4	Pakistan	4.0
Brazil	0.8	Australia	4.4
Nigeria	1.0	Malaysia	5.8
Germany	1.5	India	6.5
Namibia	3.1	China	7.1

Source: World Development Indicators. World bank 2001

Bearing in mind that total GNP will double in seven years with a growth rate of 10%, differences in growth rates can open up wide differences in income and wealth between economies. Two notes of caution however: i) it is statistically easier to achieve a high growth rate in a poor economy than a rich one. Even a massive increase in absolute output in the USA would represent only a small percentage of a large base figure, the GNP of that country. A modest increase in absolute income in an economy with a small GNP will represent a large percentage increase. ii) Increases in economic growth need to be weighed against population increase for most purposes. Thus growth of GNP divided by population growth is more significant in considering most issues concerning development. As many poor countries have fast rates of population growth their GNP per capita figures tend to be much more modest than raw output figures and many become negative. A selection of countries in Figure 3.20 illustrate this.

Figure 3.20 – Growth of GNP per capita

Country	Growth of GNP % per capita 1998–1999	Country	Growth of GNP % per capita 1998–1999
Ecuador	-9.0	Papua New Guinea	0.9
Argentina	-4.4	Russian Federation	3.6
Niger	-3.9	USA	2.4
Indonesia	-1.3	Guatemala	0.9
Saudi Arabia	-2.1	Pakistan	1.5
Brazil	0.5	Australia	3.2
Nigeria	-1.5	Malaysia	3.3
Germany	1.4	India	4.6
Namibia	0.7	China	6.1

Source: World Development Indicators. World bank 2001

CHANGES GENERALLY ASSOCIATED WITH ECONOMIC GROWTH

Changes in Economic Structure

There is a clear relationship between the level of a country's income and the structure of its production. Poor countries tend to have a high proportion of production in the primary sector. As a country's income rises, production shifts to the secondary or manufacturing sector, and then into the tertiary or services sector with further associated income increases. Figure 3.21 illustrates this characteristic in low, middle and high income countries.

Figure 3.21 – Structure of Production (1990)

	Per capita GNP	Agriculture % of GNP
Ethiopia	100	52
Tanzania	260	45
Laos	290	53
Somalia	320	44
Uganda	320	44
Ghana	400	36
Albania	930	53
Iran	1810	21
Thailand	2010	10
Peru	2130	7
Argentina	7550	5
Australia	20950	3
Netherlands	25140	3
Japan	32030	2

Source: The World Bank, World Bank Atlas 2001

Productivity on the land is very low however, as many more people are working and living in the rural sector than the GNP distribution percentage suggests (see Figure 5.5). Overall, 66% of all people in LDCs live in the rural sector as against 27% in more developed countries (MDCs).

Primary products also form the basis of exports from LDCs. Excluding those few countries with abundant oil and minerals, foodstuffs and raw materials account for most exports. In sub-Saharan Africa they account for over 80% of all exports. These primary exports form the major source of foreign exchange earnings.

As the world economy grows, however, the percentage share of primary products in total world merchandise trade falls; 33% of the total in 1950, down to 25% currently. In other words, primary products are income-inelastic.

When we study supply-side economics we will note that for output to grow factor inputs must increase in quantity or in quality, or both. Whilst this is helpful, it still does not determine that a poor country will actually grow. The willingness to grow, which by definition requires a willingness to change, depends upon human attitudes and human institutions. Attitudes are critical, but are notoriously difficult to quantify.

As an analogy, consider what is required to study economics successfully; study time, books, teacher, literacy, numeracy, food, health and so on. However, even with all these measurable factors present a student may learn little. On the other hand, a student who is well motivated may achieve success under otherwise poor conditions.

Characteristics of the Growth Process in the Already Developed Countries

Historical evidence may help to identify the requirements necessary for the process of growth. In a major study on the causes of economic growth, Professor Simon Kuznets identified characteristics which were found in each of the present day developed countries during their own periods of change. These were:

- GNP growth
- GNP per capita growth
- population growth
- productivity growth
- structural transformation
- international trade
- social and ideological change

Since the start of the industrial revolution, developed countries have averaged rates of growth of 3% of GNP, 1% of population, and 2% of GNP per capita. These are large increases on the rates of all earlier periods. Most of the huge gains in output are accounted for by increases in productivity; itself brought about by technological change, including improved human skills.

These changes have been accompanied by a shift in the structure of production. In particular the economic emphasis has shifted from primary to secondary, and finally to tertiary output. Small family production units have given way to large impersonal companies. At the same time families have moved from the countryside to swell the towns and cities.

International trade grew markedly during the growth process. Industrialising countries scoured the globe for raw materials and for markets. In many instances this trade was established and maintained by force and by colonisation. Growth itself, spread less widely however, affecting only about a third of the world's population in total.

Finally, there have been changes in beliefs, ideologies and institutions. 'Traditional' ideas were replaced by modern ideas, where modern is characterised by being 'rational', 'scientific', 'ordered' and 'change-oriented'.

All of these characteristics are inter-dependent and self-reinforcing. For example:

- rapid growth arising from increased productivity encourages further research and further technological change, which in turn leads to further growth. Figure 3.22 (diagram 1);
- growth in productivity raises incomes, which raises demand, which stimulates markets to grow and innovate further. Figure 3.22 (diagram 2); and

as incomes rise, demand for income-elastic industrial products grows faster than demand for inelastic agricultural products and therefore moves production from the farm to the factory. This move in turn encourages urbanisation as people move from rural living to urban living. This further breaks up the traditional values and practices which restrict growth. Figure 3.22 (diagram 3).

Figure 3.22

diagram 1

Growth

Research and
development

diagram 2

Growth

Breakdown of
traditional values

Demand for industrial
goods rather than
agricultural

Industrialisation
and urbanisation

diagram 3

Growth

Stimulates markets

Raises income

Raises demand

MULTIPLE CHOICE QUESTIONS – INTRODUCTION TO DEVELOPMENT

1 Growth is not the same as development because:

A growth always results in higher standards of living but development may not.

B development is a qualitative concept, growth is a quantitative concept.

C growth is never negative whereas development can be negative.

D development involves economic planning, growth does not.

2 The table below shows the growth in population and the growth in real output in countries A,B,C and D over a period of four years.

Country	Growth in Population	Growth in Output
A	12%	14%
B	5%	10%
C	9%	12%
D	5%	5%

Other things equal, which country is likely to have the greatest improvement in its standard of living?

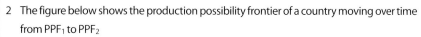

2 The figure below shows the production possibility frontier of a country moving over time from PPF$_1$ to PPF$_2$

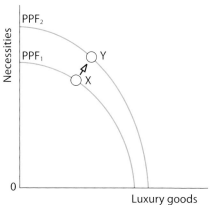

The country's actual production mix moves from point X to point Y. This movement does not show

A   economic development.

B   economic growth.

C   falling unemployment.

D   increased aggregate supply.

4 Which of the following characteristically accompany development?

I   Demand for food rising more slowly than income.

II   A shift in demand towards services.

III The per capita consumption of energy falls.

A I only   B I and II   C II and III   D I, II and III

5 Which of the following tends to accompany economic development in the high income industrial countries?

A   An increase in the workforce relative to the total population.

B   An absolute rise in primary sector employment and an absolute fall in tertiary sector employment.

C   A tendency for the proportion of personal income spent on food to increase.

D   An absolute rise in tertiary sector employment.

6 The unemployment caused by the shrinking shipbuilding industry in country X is largely absorbed by the leisure industry. This represents a shift in employment sectors from

A tertiary to secondary.

B primary to secondary.

C secondary to tertiary.

D secondary to primary.

3.4 MACROECONOMIC MODELS

The macroeconomy, or whole economy, is far too complex to understand in its entirety. It is therefore essential to build a model of the economy: a simplification of reality. We have already encountered one simple model – the circular flow of income model. Here we develop the 'Aggregate Demand – Aggregate Supply model', abbreviated to 'AD/AS model.'

The *AD/AS* model seems at first glance to be very similar to the microeconomic demand/supply model. There are, however, very important differences, and you need to be certain that you understand these differences when studying this model. Aggregate demand is the *sum total* of all goods and services demanded in an economy. In the model aggregate demand is related to the price level. Note that this is the price level and not price. There is no such thing as a single price for all goods and services, as there is for a single good in a microeconomic market model. Here we are dealing with an average of all prices, measured by using an index of prices,[5] and known as the 'price level.'

Derivation of the Aggregate demand curve

The aggregate demand curve is the sum of all demands for all the goods and services in all final markets. We have already noted that this figure is known as National Income and is measured in three separate ways. This expression of aggregate demand as used in the model corresponds with the expenditure method of measuring national income. That is, *AD* is the sum of the planned spending of consumers, the government and net exports. This may be written as:

$$AD = C + I + G + X - M.$$

As we are relating the total output of goods and services to changes in the price level we use *real* national income. Further as a primary concern will be to explain employment and unemployment we use *GDP* rather than *GNP*.

An Aggregate Demand Schedule and an Aggregate Demand Curve are shown in Figure 3.23. All of the factors which affect *AD* are assumed to be held constant except the price level. The *AD* curve is shown sloping downward against the price level. A change in the price level results in a movement along the *AD* curve. Later we examine why a change in any other variable results in a shift of the *AD* curve.

📊 Figure 3.23 – the Aggregate Demand Schedule and Aggregate Demand Curve
Price level (GDP deflator, 2004 = 100)

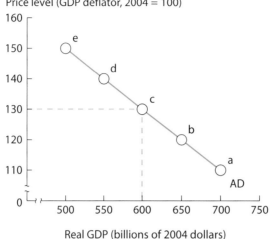

Real GDP (billions of 2004 dollars)

	Price level (GDP deflator)	Real GDP (billions of 2004 dollars)
a	110	700
b	120	650
c	130	600
d	140	550
e	150	500

The aggregate demand curve (AD) traces the quantity of real GDP demanded as the price level varies, everything else remaining the same. The aggregate demand curve is derived from the schedule in the table. Each point a to e on the curve corresponds to the row in the table identified by the same letter. Thus when price level is 130, the quantity of real GDP demanded is $600 billion, point c.

Why does the Aggregate Demand Curve slope downwards?

Aggregate demand is the total planned spending of consumers, investors, government and foreigners. The amount they spend will depend upon their *real incomes.* Real income in turn has two component parts: money incomes and prices. For any given *money* income the higher are prices, the lower is *real* income and the less people can spend. In other words, if there is a given level of money income in an economy and the price level rises, aggregate demand will fall. If money income is fixed and the price level falls, real income rises and aggregate demand will rise. Thus aggregate demand and the price level are inversely related. The *AD* curve slopes down. This is known the *income effect.* However, there is also a *substitution effect.*

A *microeconomic* demand curve slopes downwards against price largely because of the availability of substitutes. If the price of Nissan motor cars rise people can switch to substitutes like Hondas, Fords and Fiats. Even if the prices of all motor cars rise people can switch to other forms of transport, or switch from travelling to increased purchases of other goods. If all prices rise, however, what are the substitutes for all goods and services? If the price level falls, what do people switch *from* to buy more goods and services?

There are three macroeconomic substitution possibilities, and these are known as:

▎ The net export effect
▎ The real balance effect, and
▎ The interest rate effect

1) The Net Export Effect

If the price level in a country is increasing, *ie* there is inflation, domestic prices will be increasing relative to foreign prices. This will encourage import spending and discourage export spending. Recall that Aggregate Demand is made up of $C + I + G + X - M$. The increase in M and the fall in X will reduce AD. That is, a rise in the price level (inflation) reduces aggregate demand through a fall in net exports $(X - M)$.

Conversely a fall in the price level (deflation) increases aggregate demand through a rise in net exports.

2) The Real Balance Effect

When prices rise the value of bank balances fall. In order to maintain the purchasing power of these balances people might react by cutting back on their spending on goods and services. Thus, when the price level rises, people may act to maintain their real money balances. If they do, AD falls.

Conversely when the price level falls, if people act to maintain their real money balances then AD will rise.

3) The Interest Rate Effect

It has just been argued that people may maintain their real bank balances by cutting their spending on goods and services. They may, alternatively, attempt to prevent cutting their spending by increasing their borrowing. With a given money supply, an increase in borrowing will raise interest rates. If interest rates rise, there will be a reduction in interest-sensitive spending. Consumer spending on durable goods, (where credit buying is important), is likely to fall. Investment spending is also likely to fall. Thus, if people try to offset an increasing price level by borrowing, this is likely to raise interest rates and affect consumer and investment spending negatively.

Conversely if people offset a falling price level by borrowing less, this is likely to lower interest rates which will then increase spending on consumer durables and investment.

Derivation of the Aggregate Supply Curve

Aggregate supply is the sum total of all final goods and services which firms plan to produce. In order to study this we need to distinguish two time periods: the macroeconomic short run, and the macroeconomic long run. The *macroeconomic short run* is that time period when the prices of final goods and services change, but factor prices do not, *ie* there is a time lag. So final prices are in equilibrium but factor prices are not.

The *macroeconomic long run* is that time period when factor prices do adjust to final price. Aggregate demand and aggregate supply are equal in all markets in the long run, *ie* final markets and factor markets are in equilibrium. Note that factor markets includes the factor labour. Thus by this definition, the demand for and the supply of labour are in equilibrium in the macroeconomic long run. There is therefore full employment in the long run. Any unemployment which still exists at the 'full employment' level is called the *natural rate of unemployment.* In fact, the natural rate of unemployment is defined as that level of unemployment which still exists when the labour market clears. (Note that unemployment is never at zero per cent.) In this text, short run aggregate supply *(SRAS)* is studied first, and then long run aggregate supply *(LRAS).*

Short run aggregate supply

Short run aggregate supply is the relationship between the aggregate supply of final goods and services and the price level, holding everything else constant. Figure 3.24(a) shows a *SRAS* schedule and the corresponding *SRAS* curve, Figure 3.24(b). A second diagram, Figure 3.24(c), focuses upon the range of *SRAS* where an economy would normally operate. The points *a* to *e* show the real level of output *(GDP)* at each price level.

Figure 3.24(a)

	Price level (GDP deflator)	Real GDP (billions of 2004 dollars)
a	120	500
b	125	550
c	130	600
d	135	650
e	140	700

Figure 3.24(b) – the short run aggregate supply curve (SRAS)

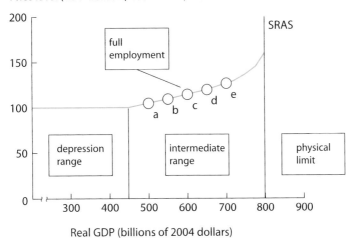

Figure 3.24(c) – Intermediate range of SRAS curve and LRAS curve

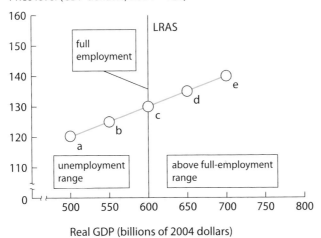

The short run aggregate supply curve (*SRAS*), traces the quantity of real *GDP* supplied as the price level varies, holding everything else constant. The short run aggregate supply curve in this figure is derived from the schedule in Figure 3.24(a). Figure 3.24(b) shows the SRAS curve over its entire range and Figure 3.24(c) zooms in on the intermediate range.

In a depression, see Figure 3.24(b), firms are willing to increase the quantity sold with no increase in price and the *SRAS* curve is horizontal. At its physical limit, the economy can squeeze out no more production and the *SRAS* curve becomes vertical. Normally the economy operates in the upward-sloping intermediate range. In that range, full employment occurs at point c where real *GDP* is $600 billion.

The long run aggregate supply curve (*LRAS*) shows the relationship between full-employment real *GDP* and the price level. The level of real *GDP* is independent of the price level, so the *LRAS* is vertical as shown in Figure 3.24(c). At levels of real *GDP* below the long run level, unemployment is above the natural rate, and at levels of real *GDP* above the long run level, unemployment is below the natural rate.

Figure 3.24(b) shows three sections of the full *SRAS* curve, *ie* horizontal, upward sloping, and vertical sections. The horizontal section shows output changing without price level changes. It corresponds to a situation of economic depression. That is, there is mass unemployment of factors of production. Firms are able and willing to produce more at existing prices, so the incentive of higher prices is not needed to make them produce more.

The sloping section is where an economy would normally operate. As the price level rises, real *GDP* rises. Higher prices induce firms to supply more. Remember that in the short run, by definition, final prices rise without factor prices rising. If factor prices did rise, it would cancel out the price incentive for firms to produce more. The *SRAS* is upward sloping however, and not horizontal. There are two reasons for this:

‖ the law of diminishing returns, and
‖ the existence of resource bottlenecks.

Taking these two reasons in turn (i) the law of diminishing returns – as firms produce more, some of their inputs may be increased readily but other inputs may remain fixed. Thus the law of diminishing returns will apply and as in microeconomics, the macroeconomic *SRAS* curve slopes upwards; (ii) resource bottlenecks – as the economy moves further and further towards full employment, even some variable resources may become short in supply. For example certain types of labour-force skills, or certain raw materials may become scarce. These are known as supply side bottlenecks. Just as the neck of a bottle slows the flow of liquid through it, so bottlenecks in the economy slow the supply of output. In summary, for both reasons (i) and (ii) the costs of suppliers are raised. Therefore while output can increase in the intermediate range of the *SRAS* curve, firms need the incentive of an increased price level to compensate for their rising costs.

The vertical section of the *SRAS* curve corresponds to the physical limit to the output that an economy is able to produce. In Figure 3.24(b), this occurs at $800 billion. This is the point where further increases in the price level can no longer induce further output.

Machines are running flat-out, labour is both fully employed and at the physical limit of overtime it is willing to work. The *SRAS* curve becomes perfectly inelastic to the price level, *ie* vertical.

Long run aggregate supply

Long run aggregate supply is the relationship between real output and the price level at full employment. Recall that long run macroeconomic supply is defined as that period of time when all markets are in equilibrium, including the labour market. At this point unemployment is described as being at its 'natural rate'. The LRAS curve is vertical at point c in Figure 3.24(c). An increased price level will not induce more output in the long run, because factor prices adjust upwards to final prices. That is, firms' costs adjust to price increases. There is no longer any price incentive to produce more as there was in the short run.

Note that the long run aggregate supply curve is below the physical limit of production. Real output can be increased above the full employment level only by driving unemployment below its natural rate. When this happens the shortage of labour drives up wages faster than prices, and output falls back to its long run level. In Figure 3.24(b) this would occur to the right of point *c*, the full employment level of output. Conversely if real *GDP* falls below point *c* then unemployment will rise above the natural rate.

Shifts in Aggregate Demand

The *AD* curve shows the relationship of aggregate demand to the price level, when other things are constant. However aggregate demand frequently changes, *ie* the *AD* curve shifts, see Figure 3.25(a) and Figure 3.25(b). The main factors which cause the aggregate demand curve to shift are:

- Fiscal policy
- Monetary policy
- Foreign income changes
- Expectations
- External shocks

 Figure 3.25(a) – Shifts in Aggregate Demand

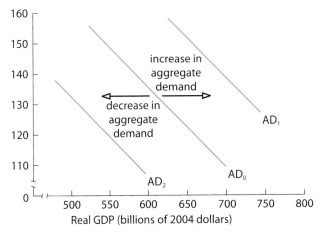

 Figure 3.25(b) – Aggregate Demand

Aggregate Demand Decreases if	Aggregate Demand Increases if
Fiscal policy decreases government spending or increases taxes	Fiscal policy increases government spending or decreases taxes
Monetary policy decreases the money supply, or increases interest rates	Monetary policy increases the money supply or decreases interest rates
Foreign income decreases or the exchange rate increases	Foreign income increases or the exchange rate decreases
Expected inflation, expected income or expected profits decrease	Expected inflation, expected income or expected profits increase

Fiscal Policy

Government, both central and local, affects aggregate demand in several ways. It increases *AD* by spending directly on goods and services. It taxes firms and consumers, causing them to spend less. It also makes transfer payments between people which changes aggregate demand. When government changes these amounts with the intention of changing the macroeconomy, the action is known as *fiscal policy*. For example, if international tension increases, government is likely to want to increase its defence spending. If crime increases, spending on police and prisons may increase. A high birth rate may cause government education spending to increase. If people live longer, and medical science improves, then government health care spending may increase. Conversely if a government spends less, without reducing taxes, then aggregate demand will fall.

If government reduces taxes or increases transfer payments (pensions, unemployment benefit, child benefit etc.) without reducing its own spending, then aggregate demand will increase. Both reduced taxes and increased benefits increase consumers' *disposable* income. The greater the disposable income, the greater the aggregate demand. Conversely both increased taxes and reduced benefits reduce consumers' *disposable income* and lower aggregate demand.

Monetary Policy

Changes to the money supply and the rate of interest affect aggregate demand. These are made by the government and/or the Central Bank. Where these are deliberately changed to affect the economy, the action is known as *monetary policy*.

Money Supply

The money supply is determined by the Central Bank. The greater the quantity of money supplied, the greater will be aggregate demand. An increase in the quantity of money leads to people spending some of the increase on more goods and services. An increase in the quantity of money has a secondary effect on spending through the interest rate. As the supply of money increases, its price (the interest rate) falls. A lower interest rate will increase the consumption of consumer durables and increase investment spending. Conversely the lower the quantity of money supplied, the lower will be aggregate demand.

Interest Rates

Interest rates affect spending on consumer durables, investment spending, and saving. If the Central Bank raises interest rates, consumer durable spending will fall, and investment spending will fall, because borrowing is more expensive. Consumption generally will fall as saving becomes more attractive. Conversely if the Central Bank lowers interest rates, consumer durable spending and investment will rise, as it becomes cheaper to borrow. Consumption generally will rise as saving becomes less attractive.

Therefore changes in the money supply and the interest rate have a direct influence on aggregate demand.

Foreign Income Changes

Aggregate demand can increase because exports increase. The major determinant of export demand is the income of foreigners. The demand for the exports of Korea and Australia depend not upon the incomes of Koreans and Australians, but upon the incomes of Japanese, Americans and Europeans. Thus the rising national income of one country will cause it to spend more on imports. Imports are the exports of another country and so the aggregate demand is increased in the exporting country. Conversely aggregate demand will fall if exports fall.

Exchange Rate

The exchange rate is another international factor which can alter aggregate demand. The exports of a country become more attractive the cheaper is its currency, that is, the lower is its exchange rate. Conversely the higher is its exchange rate, the lower is the international purchasing power of foreigners, the lower is the demand for imports, and the lower the aggregate demand in the exporting country.

Expectations

A change in the *expected* rate of inflation will change aggregate demand. If inflation is expected to rise in the future, consumers and businesses may increase present purchases. If inflation is expected to fall, then expenditure may be delayed.

Business expectations also affect investment decisions. If business people feel optimistic about future sales, they will be encouraged to increase investment. If they are pessimistic about future sales, investment will fall and aggregate demand will fall.

If consumers expect future incomes are to grow, they are likely to increase their spending. If the expectation is that future incomes are likely to fall then consumption expenditure and aggregate demand are also likely to fall.

External Shocks

Aggregate demand may increase temporarily and then fall back to its previous level. Such an increase is known as *external*, or *demand side, shock*. National or international political, social or natural events can affect the mood and attitudes of firms, governments and consumers, and thus affect aggregate demand.

Shifts in aggregate demand will shift the *AD* curve as illustrated in Figure 3.25(a).

Shifts in Aggregate Supply[6]

The aggregate supply curve can also shift. Factors which could cause such a shift are:

▌ changes in the quantity and quality of capital investment
▌ changes in the quantity and quality of labour
▌ changes in supply side policies
▌ changes in legislation

All of these factors affect aggregate supply in both the short run and in the long run. There are, however, two other factors which affects the short run curve alone *ie* the long run supply is unaffected. These two factors are a change in factor prices and, a change in the weather.

A Change in Factor Prices

The *SRAS* curve plots the levels of output which will be supplied at each price level. It is, however, plotted on the assumption that 'everything else is constant', including factor prices. If these factor prices change, *eg* if wages change or if raw material prices change, then the whole supply curve will shift. Figure 3.26 shows the effect of an increase in a factor price. At each price level firms will supply less output, *ie* the supply curve shifts to the left.

Figure 3.26 – A Decrease in Short Run Aggregate Supply. The Supply Curve Shifts to the Left

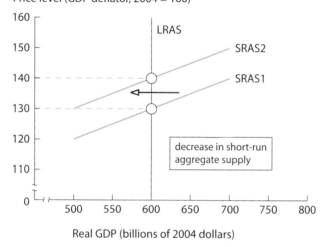

The long run aggregate supply will not be affected in such a situation. The reason is that in the long run all prices change equally, that is, changes in factor prices are matched by changes in product prices. As all prices have changed proportionately there is no incentive for firms to change their output.

A Change in the Weather

A change of weather is likely to have an effect upon the agricultural sector, increasing aggregate supply with a good harvest and reducing it with a bad one. This clearly shifts the *SRAS* curve. However these are temporary changes of supply and leave the *LRAS* curve unaffected.

Other than changes in factor prices and the weather, supply side changes will shift both the *SRAS* curve and the *LRAS* curve. Figure 3.27 shows both *SRAS* and *LRAS* curves shifting to the right in response to supply side changes.

Figure 3.27 – An Increase in Short Run and Long Run Aggregate Supply

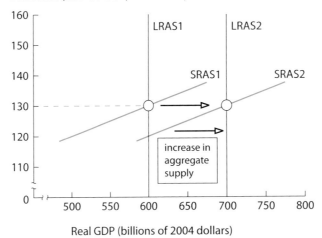

Real GDP (billions of 2004 dollars)

Aggregate supply increases in the long run if:

▌ *The labour force increases*

▌ *The capital stock increases*

▌ *Technological change increases the productivity of labour and capital*

▌ *Incentives are strengthened*

Both the long run and short run aggregate supply curves shift to the right by the same amount. The aggregate supply curves will shift to the left if the labour force decreases, capital stock decreases or incentives are weakened.

A Change in Quantity and Quality of Capital Investment

An increase in the stock of capital will increase the productivity of the labour force and the output it produces. Improvements in technology, *ie* new and better ways of producing, are a major source of increased aggregate supply. Much new technology is actually embodied in capital goods, *ie* to acquire the new technology the firm invests in the latest capital.

A Change in Quantity and Quality of Labour

The larger the labour force the larger the output, other things being equal. An increased labour force may come from population growth, or migration, or an internal change. The biggest increase to the labour force in most industrialised countries in the last fifty years has come about through an internal change: the increased participation of women in the labour market.

An improved quality of labour, *ie* a more skilled labour force, is an important source of increased output. Improvements in education, training, and health lead to increased productivity.

A Change in Supply Side Policies

Supply side policies are government policies aimed at increasing aggregate supply. The deliberate action to increase the quantity and quality of capital or the quantity and quality of labour are supply side policies. Many such policies focus upon incentives. Taxes and allowances might be adjusted to encourage work, encourage risk-taking or encourage investment. For example, reducing income tax raises the opportunity cost of not working. Reducing unemployment benefit also raises the opportunity cost of not working. Offering tax allowances may induce firms to invest in new plant and machinery. These are all government supply side policies designed to increase the incentive to produce more, *ie* to increase aggregate supply.

A Change in Legislation

The law might be changed to affect aggregate supply. For example, laws on the school leaving age or retirement affect the supply of labour.

Macroeconomic equilibrium

Macroeconomic equilibrium occurs at the price level where aggregate demand equals aggregate supply. In Figure 3.28, this occurs where the *AD* curve intersects the *SRAS* curve. The equilibrium level of real *GDP* is $600 billion, in this case at a price level of *130*. At any other price level the economy is in disequilibrium. At a price level of *140* for example, there is a surplus of goods and services over the demand for them. Firms will cut prices to get rid of the surplus. At a price level of *120* excess demand will encourage firms to raise prices.

⊞ Figure 3.28 – Macroeconomic Equilibrium

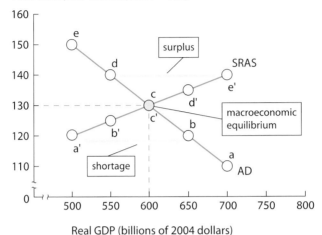

Macroeconomic Equilibrium and Full Employment

Macroeconomic equilibrium occurs where *SRAS* equals *AD*. However, this may not coincide with the full employment level of output. The economy is at full employment when it is on its *LRAS* curve. Aggregate demand and aggregate supply may be equal where real *GDP* is smaller or larger than full employment real *GDP*. In Figure 3.29(a) the actual real *GDP* is seen fluctuating around the long run real *GDP* level over a period of years. In year two, for example, actual real *GDP* is *$500* billion, $100 billion below Full Employment real *GDP* level. The gap between actual output and full employment output is known a 'recessionary gap'. This gap is shown also in Figure 3.29(b) as an 'unemployment equilibrium'. Full employment equilibrium is shown in Figure 3.29(c). In year four, actual real *GDP* has increased to $700 billion, $100 billion greater than full employment *GDP*. The difference is known as an 'inflationary gap', and is shown on the *AD/AS* diagram Figure 3.29(d) as an 'above full employment' equilibrium. As aggregate demand and aggregate supply fluctuate, macroeconomic equilibrium fluctuates through three different states: unemployment, full employment and above full employment. Using the model we can examine how these fluctuations occur.

Figure 3.29(a) Fluctuations In Real GDP

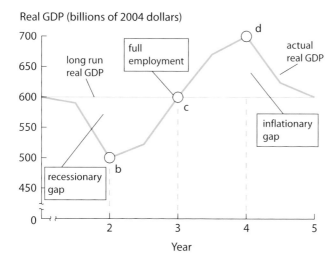

Real GDP (billions of 2004 dollars)

Figure 3.29(b) Unemployment Equilibrium

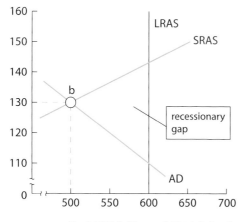

Price level (GDP deflator, 2004 = 100)

📊 Figure 3.29(c) Full Employment Equilibrium

Price level (GDP deflator, 2004 = 100)

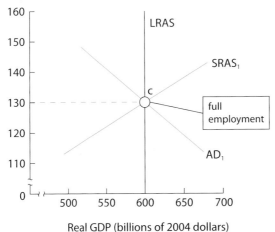

Real GDP (billions of 2004 dollars)

📊 Figure 3.29(d) Above Full Employment Equilibrium

Price level (GDP deflator, 2004 = 100)

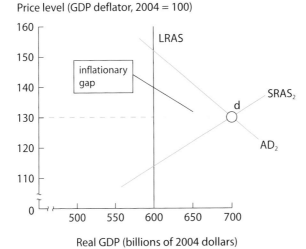

Real GDP (billions of 2004 dollars)

In Figure 3.29(a) real GDP fluctuates around its long run level. When actual real GDP is below long run real GDP, there is a recessionary gap (as in year 2). When actual real GDP is above long run real GDP, there is an inflationary gap (as in year 4). When actual real GDP is equal to long run real GDP, there is full employment (as in year 3). In year 2 there is an unemployment equilibrium, as illustrated in Figure 3.29(b). In year 3 there is a full employment equilibrium, as illustrated in Figure 3.29(c). In year 4 there is an above full employment equilibrium, as illustrated in Figure 3.29(d).

Macroeconomic Equilibrium And Shifts In Aggregate Demand

Figure 3.30 shows an initial situation of short run macroeconomic equilibrium at full employment. The AD_1 curve and the $SRAS_1$ curve intersect at *$600 billion* on the *LRAS* curve. Then aggregate demand increases from AD_1 to AD_2. This could be for any of the reasons listed earlier: fiscal, monetary, foreign income changes, etc. The new aggregate demand, curve AD_2, intersects the $SRAS_1$ curve at an increased real output of *$650 billion*, and at a higher price level of *135*. There is now an inflationary gap, real *GDP* is above the full employment level. The increased aggregate demand has increased real output, but raised the price level. Prices of goods and services have risen to cover the increased production costs of firms. However this short run equilibrium cannot remain above full employment. As the owners of factors of production find that their rewards have been effectively reduced, by final prices rising, they will demand higher factor prices. Thus, for example, the real wage of labour will have reduced, due to the increased price level, and labour will demand a wage rate rise to restore the situation. As factor prices like wages rise, the *SRAS* curve shifts upwards to the left. As the *SRAS* curve shifts, real output falls, and the price level rises. This process will continue as long as the macroeconomic equilibrium level is greater than the full employment level of real output. The process will halt only when $SRAS2$ cuts the *AD* curve at the *LRAS* curve. Real output will have fallen back to the full employment level of real output, at *$600* billion. So in the long run there will have been no increase in real output. Further, the price level is higher – at *145* in Figure 3.30. Unemployment is again at the natural rate. The initial rise in aggregate demand caused a temporary rise in real output, but with rising costs firms cut back their output until they were producing the same amount but at higher prices and with higher costs. The ratio of costs to final prices will be the same as it was at the beginning of the process.

📊 Figure 3.30 – The Effects of an Increase in Aggregate Demand

Price level (GDP deflator, 2004 = 100)

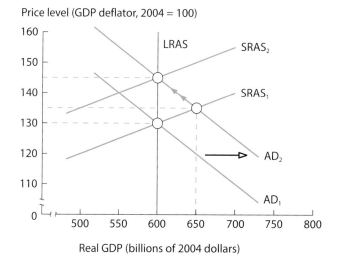

Real GDP (billions of 2004 dollars)

An increase in aggregate demand shifts the aggregate demand curve from AD₁ to AD₂. Real GDP increases from $600 billion to $650 billion and the price level from 130 to 135. There is an inflationary gap. A higher price level induces higher wage rates, which in turn causes short run aggregate supply curve to shift to the left. As the SRAS curve shifts to the left from SRAS₁ to SRAS₂ it intersects the aggregate demand curve AD₂ at higher price levels and lower real GDP levels. Eventually, the price level increases to 145 and real GDP falls back to $600 billion, its full employment level.

A decrease in aggregate demand causes similar but opposite effects. When *AD* falls, real *GDP* falls below the full employment level and unemployment increases above its natural rate. There is a recessionary gap. The price level falls and this increases the purchasing power of factor prices like wages. Firms with lower goods prices but maintained input costs will renegotiate input costs to lower them. As costs fall the *SRAS* curve falls down to the right. As it moves, real output increases and the price level falls. This will continue as long as a recessionary gap exists. It will only halt when the *SRAS* curve cuts the *AD* curve at full employment real *GDP*. Real output will be restored but at a lower price level. Unemployment will once more be at the natural rate.

Figure 3.31(a) – The Effects of an Increase in the Price of Oil in the Short Run…

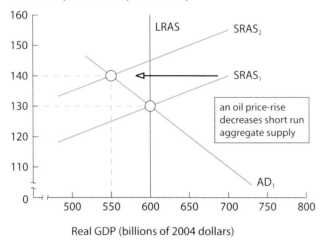

Figure 3.31(b) – …and in the Long Run

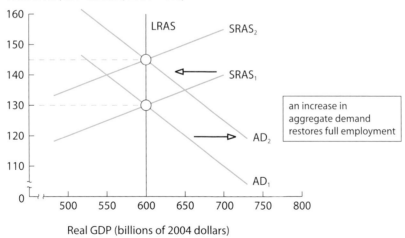

An increase in the price of oil decreases short run aggregate supply and shifts the short run aggregate supply curve to the left from SRAS₁ to SRAS₂, as shown in Figure 3.31(a). Real GDP decreases from $600 billion to $550 billion and the price level increases from 130 to 140. The economy experiences both recession and inflation at the same time ie stagflation. To counteract this, the government undertakes fiscal and monetary policy to stimulate aggregate demand and shifts the aggregate demand curve to the right from AD₁ to AD₂, as shown in Figure 3.31(b). Real GDP returns to its original level but the price level rises still further from 140 to 145.

Macroeconomic Equilibrium And Shifts In Aggregate Supply

Let us now examine the effect of a change in aggregate supply. Figure 3.31(a) shows an equilibrium position, with AD_1 cutting $SRAS_1$, and with the $LRAS$ curve at the full employment level of real GDP. Suppose, as an example, that there is an increase in oil prices, such as occurred in 1973. This increases firms' costs and the $SRAS$ curve shifts up to $SRAS_2$. The new equilibrium is at a lower real GDP ($550 billion). This is an unemployment equilibrium, unemployment is above the natural rate. In other words there is a recessionary gap. The price level, however, has also risen – to *140*, *ie* there is inflation. There is both recession and inflation at the same time. This combined situation is known as *stagflation*.If the government tries to counteract the stagflation by expanding aggregate demand, which it can do by using fiscal and monetary policy, real GDP will increase again to its original level. It will, however, be at a higher price level again.

Controversy over the shape of the AS curve

We have examined the effect of shifts of aggregate demand and aggregate supply upon the price level and real output. In practice, however, the acceptance of the shape of the $SRAS$ curve is controversial and is at the very centre of present macroeconomic debate. Thus the following questions might be asked. Does an increase in aggregate demand increase real output but not inflation? Does an increase in aggregate demand increase inflation without affecting real output? Does an increase in aggregate demand increase both output and inflation? The answer to these questions lies in the shape of the aggregate supply curve. We will return to this after an in-depth study of unemployment and inflation.

THE KEYNESIAN EXPENDITURE MULTIPLIER

It has been established that macroeconomic equilibrium is where aggregate demand is equal to aggregate supply. We have examined factors which cause the aggregate demand curve to shift. Here we look more closely at what happens to macroeconomic equilibrium when aggregate demand shifts.

One of the great insights of the Keynsian macroeconomic model was that an increase or decrease in aggregate demand would cause an even greater change in national income. This is known as *the multiplier effect*. Real *GDP* changes by the amount of the initial autonomous expenditure change, plus a further amount of expenditure which is income-dependent. The autonomous expenditure change could be a change in government spending, a change in investment spending, a change in export spending or a change in the proportion of income that consumers spend. For example if the government were to increase spending with a new road building programme. The construction firms and construction workers would have increased incomes. They will spend some of this increased income. The firms that receive this spending will themselves spend some of the extra income. The firms that receive this extra spending will spend some of it and so on and so on. At each stage of the cycle the amount of extra spending will become less and less as some of the income leaks out into extra saving, extra taxes and spending on imports. However the initial increase in spending has led to further spending and thus a bigger increase in national income. It is this effect which is known as the multiplier. The size of the multiplier depends upon how much income gets passed on at each stage. If the whole amount were withdrawn into extra taxes, saving, and import spending, nothing at all would be passed on and the multiplier would be zero. However if most of it were passed on in extra domestic spending then the multiplier would be large.

The size of the multiplier

The size of the multiplier then depends upon how much of an increase (or decrease) in autonomous expenditure is spent on domestic goods and services. As an example and referring to Figure 3.32, let the increased autonomous expenditure of $120 billion be an increase in planned investment, (itself due to say the introduction of a new computer-based technology). The investment spending will reduce inventories of new computer equipment, and computer firms will expand output to restore their own planned investment levels. This increased output generates factor incomes, wages, rent, interest and profit of *$120 billion*. Households are taxed, they save and they import. Lets say that *60% or 0.6 of* income leaks out of the circular flow in this way. That is *40% or 0.4 of this income is spent* on domestic goods and services *ie 0.4 × $120 billion = $48 billion.* Firms, finding inventories of consumer goods falling, expand output, which in turn increases household factor incomes by *$48 billion*. After further leakages into taxes, savings and imports, *0.4 of what remains is spent on domestic goods and services ie 0.4 × $48 billion = $19.2 billion*. Firms expand output again by *$19.2 billion*. After leakages *0.4* of this is spent domestically *ie 0.4 × $19.2 billion = $7.68 billion*, ad infinitum. Real *GDP* has been increased by *$120 billion + $48 billion + $19.2 billion + $7.68 billion + … + … etc*. If this series was completed, the total increase in real *GDP* would actually total *$200 billion*. The multiplier process is shown diagrammatically in Figure 3.32. (However, as you will now see, the new real *GDP* level can be calculated directly, by multiplying the autonomous increase in spending by the multiplier. In this case new equilibrium real *GDP = 1.67 × $120 billion = $200 billion*.)

Figure 3.32 – The Size of the Multiplier

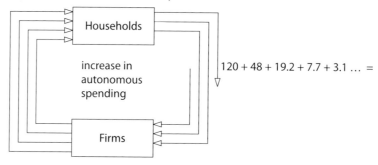

Increased autonomous expenditure of $120 billion causes firms to expand output to restore their depleted inventory levels. This increased output generates factor incomes of $120 billion. 0.4 of this increased income is spent on domestic goods and services ie 0.4 x $120 billion = $48 billion. Firms, finding inventories of consumer goods falling, expand output again, which increases household income by $48 billion. 0.4 of this extra income is spent on domestic goods and services ie 0.4 x $48 billion = $19.2 billion. Firms expand output again by $19.2 billion. 0.4 of this is spent domestically ie 0.4 x $19.2 billion = $7.68 billion, and so on, ad infinitum. Real GDP has been increased by $120 billion + $48 billion + $19.2 billion + $7.7 billion + $3.1 billion + … +… etc. If this series was completed the total increase in real GDP would sum to $200 billion.

The size of the multiplier depends upon how much of an increase in autonomous spending is passed on as increased purchases of domestic goods and services. The increase in consumption arising from an increase in income is known as the *marginal propensity to consume* (*MPC*). However some of this consumption spending is upon imports so we need to reduce this to *the marginal propensity to consume domestic goods and services* (*MPC*$_{domestic}$). The more spending that is passed on, that is, the higher the *MPC*$_{domestic}$, then the higher the multiplier will be. The multiplier is calculated as

1/1–MPC$_{domestic}$. For example if the *MPC$_{domestic}$* had been *0.5* instead of *0.4* the multiplier would have been *1/1–0.5 = 1/0.5 = 2*. The higher the propensity to consume domestic goods and services the higher the multiplier and the higher the increase in real *GDP* from an increase in autonomous spending. Say the *MPC$_{domestic}$* had been even higher at 0.6 of income. Then an increase of autonomous expenditure of *$120 billion* would increase real *GDP* by:

Δ real GDP = the multiplier × Δ in autonomous expenditure...
= 1 / 1 − MPC$_{domestic}$ × $120 billion
= 1 / 1 − 0.6 × $120 billion
= 1 / 0.4 × $120 billion
= 2.5 × $120 billion
= $300 billion

The multiplier will always be greater than 1 because any increase in autonomous expenditure will cause further income-dependent expenditure. Thus any increase in autonomous expenditure will cause a bigger change in real *GDP, ie* the shifts of the *AD* curve are amplified by the multiplier. This works downwards as well as upwards, that is a fall in autonomous expenditure is also amplified by the multiplier. Real *GDP* will fall more than the initial fall in spending. The higher the propensity to consume domestic goods and services, the higher the multiplier, and the greater the fall in real *GDP* from a fall in autonomous spending.

The multiplier acts upon any change in autonomous expenditure. This includes changes to government taxation and spending. However the original Keynsian model was based upon the existence of severe unemployment. In a fully employed economy real output cannot increase and an increase in autonomous spending results in increasing prices. In other words the effectiveness of the multiplier depends upon the shape of the *AS* curve. If this were flat, *ie* there were massive unemployed resources, the multiplier would cause output and real income to change. If the *AS* curve were vertical *ie* there was full employment there would be price increases, real *GDP* would not change. If the *AS* curve slopes upwards the multiplier will cause some increased output and some inflation.

A Chinese Multiplier

According to a report in the *London Financial Times* on November 7 1994, the Anglo/Dutch multinational Unilever is experiencing one of the fastest growth rates of any foreign company in China. The company produces a wide range of consumer goods including soaps (Lux), detergents (Omo) and beauty products (Ponds). As the Chinese economy grows, and incomes grow, so does the demand for Unilever products. In 1984 Unilever had a tiny operation in China employing only a handful of people. By 1992 this had grown to 700 employees. Now (in 1994) they employ 2,500 of whom only 80 are ex-patriots. The locals work at all levels from production workers to management. These include 80 recent graduates undertaking management training at home and abroad. Unilever expects its sales to rise from the current $200 million a year to $1.5 billion by 1999.

Question

How does the story illustrate the multiplier effects in the Chinese economy?

THE MULTIPLIER-ACCELERATOR MODEL

This model distinguishes the consequences of a change in investment spending from the causes of a change in investment spending. The focus then is on how changes in income can *cause* accelerated changes in investment spending.

The accelerator model of investment assumes that firms' profit expectations in the future are determined by extrapolating[7] the growth of output from the past. That is future output depends upon changes in past output. Thus the demand for capital goods to produce the future output also depends upon changes in past output. Constant growth of output leads to a constant level of investment and a constant rate of growth of the capital stock. For there to be an increase in the planned level of investment there needs to be *accelerating* output growth.

A simple version of the multiplier-accelerator model is developed here. In so far as it is valid it can help to explain business cycle fluctuations. In Figure 3.33 it is assumed that the value of the multiplier is two. Each unit of investment increases output by 2 units. It is also assumed that current investment responds to the growth in output in the last period. For every two units of increased output in the last period it is assumed that firms increase investment by one unit.

📊 Figure 3.33 – The Multiplier-Accelerator Model of the Business Cycle

Time Period t	Change in last period's output $(Y_{t-1}-Y_{t-2})$	Investment I_t	Output Y_t
t = 1	0	10	100
t = 2	0	10	120
t = 3	20	20	140
t = 4	20	20	140
t = 5	0	10	120
t = 6	−20	0	100
t = 7	−20	0	100
t = 8	0	10	120
t = 9	20	20	140

The economy begins in equilibrium with output in time period t equal to 100, *ie* Y_t = 100. As in equilibrium output is constant, the change in last period's output is zero. Investment (I_t) is 10. This is replacement investment only, to maintain the capital stock at 100.

Suppose that in time period 2 aggregate demand increases by 20 units, causing output to rise from 100 to 120.

The increased output of 20 units induces extra investment of 10 units in period 3. (total investment is 20, replacement investment is 10, increased investment is 10) The multiplier acts on the increase in investment to increase output by: *the multiplier* $\times \Delta I = 2$ x 10 = 20. Output increases from 120 to 140.

In period 4 investment remains at 20, consisting of 10 units for replacement investment, and 10 units for investment induced by the extra 20 unit increase in output. Output remains at 140.

As there was no *increase* in output in period 4, in period 5 investment falls to its original level. The fall of 10 units in investment is acted upon by the multiplier to cause output to fall by 20, from 140 to 120, in period 5.

In turn this fall in output causes a further fall in investment in period 6, and thus a further fall in output. However, as the output change is not accelerating, investment in period 7 remains the same as in period 6. Hence output is stabilized at the level of 100 in period 7.

With no output change in the previous period, investment in period 8 returns to the replacement investment, that is 10 units again. The multiplier acts on this to increase output by 20 units. In period 9 the 20 unit increase in output induces investment to increase from 10 to 20. The cycle begins all over again.

It is not clear just how important the accelerator is in determining investment. For example the accelerator will not induce increased investment when there is spare capacity in the economy. That is, the accelerator will not work when there is unemployment. An increase in output can be met with existing capital in this circumstance. However the multiplier-accelerator model may have some role in explaining the swings of the trade cycle.

FISCAL POLICY AND THE MULTIPLIER

Changes in private sector spending are amplified in their effect upon aggregate expenditure by the multiplier. Any change in autonomous expenditure will result in a multiplied increase in real *GDP*. However the variable most susceptible to frequent change in industrialised countries is investment. Changes to investment times the multiplier largely explain the fluctuations in real *GDP* which are experienced in industrialised countries. In Less Developed Countries it is changes to export revenues times the multiplier which are of most concern. As you will see in Section 5, export revenues may fluctuate considerably as a result of fluctuations in the prices of primary exports.

These private sector expenditure changes cause aggregate expenditure, and therefore real *GDP*, to fluctuate. The government could attempt to smooth out these fluctuations by varying its own expenditure and taxes to act in the opposite direction. Such government attempts to smooth macroeconomic fluctuations, by varying taxes and government spending, is called fiscal policy. Thus if the government were able to anticipate a fall in private sector autonomous expenditure, it could increase public sector purchases of goods and services to compensate. It would of course need to take account of the multiplier effects of such actions. Alternatively, the government could increase autonomous consumption spending by reducing taxes on consumers and increasing transfer payments to them. Again there would be multiplier effects to consider.

MULTIPLE CHOICE QUESTIONS – MACROECONOMIC MODELS

1   Employment is likely to increase with a rise in aggregate demand when

   I   there is excess capacity in the economy.

   II   the aggregate supply curve is vertical.

   III   the increased demand is for imports.

   A   I only   B   I and II   C   II and III   D   I, II and III

2   The diagram below shows a country's aggregate demand and aggregate supply curves

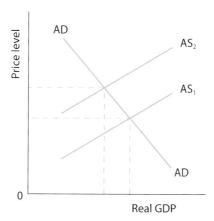

The shift of the AS curve from AS_1 to AS_2 is most likely to have been caused by a rise in

A   a rise in the money supply.

B   a rise in money wage rates.

C   a fall in the price level.

D   a fall in investment.

3   Of every euro of income, a community spends 10 cents on imports, saves 10 cents, and pays taxes of 20 cents. What is the value of the multiplier?

   A   0.4   B   1.6   C   2.5   D   4.0

4 Which one of the following would cause a rise in a country's multiplier, other things equal?

A A rise in the marginal propensity to save.

B A rise in the marginal rate of income tax.

C A fall in the marginal propensity to consume.

D A fall in the marginal propensity to import.

5 The accelerator model states that

A the level of investment depends on the level of national income.

B the level of investment depends on the rate of inflation.

C the level of investment depends on the rate of change of national income.

D the rate of change of investment is equal to the rate of change of national income.

3.5   UNEMPLOYMENT

DEFINITION OF UNEMPLOYMENT

Unemployment is present in an economy when there are workers who are able and willing to work but who do not have jobs. The total number of people who do have jobs, plus those who are unemployed, is known as the *labour force*. A country's *unemployment rate* is the number of unemployed expressed as a percentage of the labour force. For example, a country with a population of one hundred million people might have a labour force of sixty million people. The other forty million would consist of children, students, full-time mothers, retired people and others not wanting to work. If there were six million people without jobs and fifty-four million working the unemployment rate would be:

$$\frac{\text{number of unemployed}}{\text{number of unemployed} + \text{employed}} \times \frac{100}{1} = \frac{6\text{ million}}{6\text{ million} + 54\text{ million}} \times \frac{100}{1} = 10\%$$

Problems of Measuring Unemployment

Unemployment is a '*stock*' concept. That is, unemployment is a measure at a point in time. The stock changes as people enter unemployment and as others leave unemployment. The difference between the number entering and the number leaving will determine whether unemployment rises or falls. Official government statistics for unemployment are very sensitive politically, the rate of unemployment generally being considered one of the most important measures of how healthy an economy is. The official government figures for unemployment may differ considerably from the broad definition of unemployment given above. Great care should be exercised in using the figures and in comparing unemployment rates between countries, because different measures may be used in different countries. Only unemployed people who are registered as unemployed will appear in national statistics. The incentive to register is the availability of unemployment benefits. If benefit is not available, as in many developing countries, official unemployment figures may be virtually meaningless. In countries offering benefit, groups of people excluded from receiving benefit will not appear in the figures, thus underestimating unemployment. On the other hand some people may claim to be unemployed, when they are not, in order to gain benefit. The unemployment figure in this case will be an over-estimate.

Unemployed people who may not qualify for benefit might include school-leavers, people getting near to retirement, mothers returning to the work force after raising children, part-time workers, or people temporarily unemployed. *Underemployment* and *disguised unemployment* may further reduce the value of the statistic. A job seeker may accept a part-time job if a full-time job is not available. The person is not unemployed but is certainly under-employed. If firms do not shed labour because they want to hold on to trained and experienced workers, and thus they are clearly overstaffed, then the true level of unemployment is disguised. This is more likely in nationalised industries than in profit-seeking private firms. Disguised unemployment was a major problem in the former centrally planned economies.

On the other hand, some of these officially unemployed may not be genuinely unemployed. Some people may have a job as well as claiming benefit fraudulently. Certain other groups of people may wish to claim benefit, but have no real intention of accepting a job if they are offered one. In this category may be some older workers who have effectively retired early, women who wish to stay at home raise a family, or those who just do not wish to work.

The unemployment statistics need to be used cautiously, because they are average figures. A national average disguises many irregularities in the distribution of unemployment. If periods of unemployment were spread evenly across all workers in the labour force during their working lives, the concerns over unemployment would be greatly reduced. However they are not evenly distributed. Some people never suffer unemployment throughout their working lives. Others suffer long periods of unemployment. Differences are often marked geographically, *eg* higher in certain regions of the country, or inner city areas. They may be markedly different by gender, by age, by ethnic origin or by education. As an example, see Figure 3.34 for an illustration of some of these differences in the United States.[8] In Figure 3.34(a) the unequal distribution of unemployment by sex, race and age is shown. The unequal distribution by educational attainment is shown in Figure 3.34(b).

Figure 3.34(a) – Inequality in the Distribution of Unemployment in the United States – by Sex, Race and Age

Unemployment rates, per cent (1992)

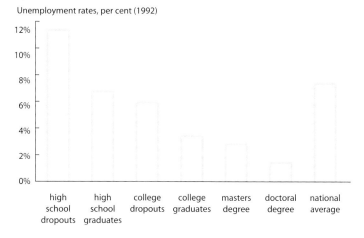

Figure 3.34(b) – Inequality in the Distribution of Unemployment in the United States – by Education

Unemployment rates, per cent (1992)

Source: US Department of Labor

The costs of unemployment – and some benefits

The costs of unemployment fall on the unemployed individuals themselves, their families and friends, society as a whole, and the national economy.

Individuals lose the income difference between their previous wage and any unemployment benefit. They also lose self-esteem, and may suffer ill-health. Families may suffer a loss of income and living standards. This may be accompanied by a worsening of personal relationships, family breakdown, or violence. Society as a whole may suffer the consequences of increased vandalism and crime. The economic output of the individual is also lost to society. The economy will be operating inside its production possibility frontier. Further, if the income of one individual falls, the income of others falls, as a result of his/her reduced spending. Government tax revenue falls, and if the government provides unemployment benefits, government expenditure will rise.

However all unemployment is not all bad. Some unemployment is inevitable as economies change, as new industries grow, and old industries decline. Resources must move out of old 'sunset' industries and into new 'sunrise' industries to produce the changing mix of goods and services demanded. Unemployment which results from the natural and inevitable changes in the economy is known as *the natural rate of unemployment*. When the labour market clears, *ie* there is full employment, there will not be a zero rate of unemployment, rather there will be a positive rate of unemployment. It is this which is known as the natural rate, and is comprised of three types of unemployment; frictional (or search) unemployment, structural unemployment and seasonal unemployment.

TYPES OF UNEMPLOYMENT CATEGORISED BY CAUSE

Frictional (Search) Unemployment

On the particular day of the month that the unemployment rate is measured there will be some people entering, or re-entering, the labour force and other people switching between jobs. It takes time for a worker to find the right job, and for an employer to find the right worker. There is a process of searching, travel, making applications and attending interviews. This is part of the normal process of the labour market working, of the process of resources moving into more productive uses. As such, this type of unemployment is not really a problem. It is rather the inevitable and desirable consequence of a growing and changing economy.

Structural Unemployment

Structural unemployment occurs when the structure of the economy changes. It is similar to frictional unemployment – up to a point. The degree of unemployment, however, is altogether more serious. There is a significant loss of jobs in certain industries. It may be the result of an overall fall in demand for a product – *eg* steel or coal. It may be the result of a shift of production to abroad. In either case a large number of people in one industry may become unemployed. As some industries have a heavy regional geographic location, structural unemployment may also give rise to heavy regional unemployment. Another type of structural unemployment is known as *technological* unemployment. This is where human skills are replaced by machines *eg* clerks by computers, or assembly workers by robots. Large numbers of workers may be structurally unemployed, and often for a long period of time. Whereas frictional unemployment is likely to last for a few weeks, structural unemployment is commonly endured for many months or even years.

Occupational and geographic immobility are problems when the structure of economic output changes. Workers with redundant skills, particularly older workers, find it very difficult to acquire new skills. Textile operatives, coal miners or shipbuilders do not find it easy to switch into computer programming or selling insurance. Regional imbalance means that new jobs are often in a distant location. Many economic and social factors make it difficult to be geographically mobile. House prices are likely to be low in the depressed region and high in the buoyant region. Family, school and social ties may also prevent the unemployed from moving.

Seasonal Unemployment

Some occupations are weather dependent and involve a busy working season and a slack season. Agriculture, forestry, fishing and tourism are examples. The Alaskan crab fishermen will work round the clock in the long summer days and lay up the boat in the dark, cold and stormy winter. Greek hoteliers, waiters and taverna owners will have little sleep or leisure in the summer but have little to do in the winter. (You might ponder on the work pattern of Santa Claus!)

Natural Unemployment, or Equilibrium Unemployment

Frictional, structural and seasonal unemployment are all collectively known as 'natural unemployment'. There will always be some natural unemployment even when the labour market clears, *ie* the demand for labour and the supply of labour is in equilibrium.

A diagram of the labour market is useful to illustrate this. Figure 3.35 shows the aggregate demand for and aggregate supply of labour: that is the total demand and supply of labour in the whole economy. The average real wage is graphed on the vertical axis, that is the average money wage expressed in terms of its purchasing power (*ie* it is adjusted for inflation). The aggregate supply of workers slopes upward – more people will be willing to enter the workforce, rather than doing housework, retiring early, staying on at school, or searching for a better paid job if unemployed. The aggregate demand curve slopes downward. As employers have to pay higher real wages they will economise on the use of labour and substitute capital for labour. The labour market is in equilibrium at w_e where the demand for labour is equal to the supply for labour.

📊 Figure 3.35 – The Labour Market

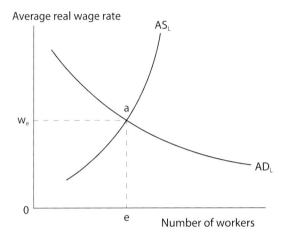

The labour market showing equilibrium, point a, where total demand for labour is equal to the total supply of labour at a real wage of w_e. At any other real wage a shortage or surplus of workers will raise or lower wage rates to w_e.

We have already noted that at full employment, that is when the demand for and the supply of labour is equal at the real wage, there will still be natural unemployment. This is shown as the distance *ab* in Figure 3.36. The line *N* represents the total labour force. AS_L represents those willing to accept jobs at each wage rate. The gap between AS_L and *N* represents those unemployed but not willing to accept the market wage. *N* gets closer to AS_L at higher wage rates as the incentive of higher wages will increase the willingness of the unemployed to accept jobs. Natural unemployment is found when the labour market is in equilibrium. It is also known therefore as equilibrium unemployment.

Figure 3.36 – Natural Unemployment

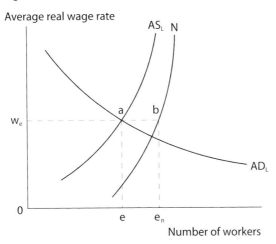

The labour market showing natural unemployment, ie frictional, structural and seasonal unemployment. At equilibrium a, there is natural unemployment of ab.

Disequilibrium Unemployment

If the labour market is not in equilibrium, if something prevents the market from clearing, then further unemployment, *ie* unemployment in addition to natural unemployment, will occur. Such unemployment is known as disequilibrium unemployment to distinguish it from equilibrium or natural unemployment. There are two possible causes of disequilibrium unemployment. These two, classical (or real-wage) unemployment, and demand-deficient (or cyclical) unemployment, are highly contentious. Economists are very divided as to which of these is the true cause of disequilibrium unemployment. It follows that economists are very divided as to what should be done to reduce disequilibrium unemployment.

Classical (Real-Wage) Unemployment

Classical economists believed that the severe unemployment of the great depression in the 1920s and 1930s was caused by labour unions driving real wages above the market clearing rate. Classical economists therefore gave 'real-wage' unemployment its more popular name, classical unemployment. The situation is illustrated in Figure 3.37. Here wages are held at W_1 by labour unions, instead of being allowed to fall to W_e, the market clearing, full employment, wage level. It is argued that unions, by threatening to disrupt production, can force firms to pay higher wages than would be required in a free labour market. Higher real wages cause the demand for labour to fall and the supply of labour to increase. Those workers who have jobs (OQ_2) have high real wages but Q_2Q_1, workers are unemployed.

Figure 3.37 – Real-Wage or Classical Unemployment

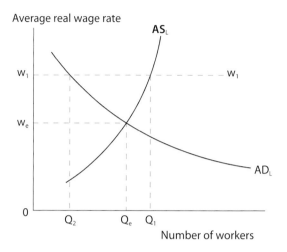

Labour unions, or minimum wage legislation, hold the real wage above the equilibrium level, not allowing the market to clear. Aggregate demand for labour falls to $0Q_2$. Aggregate supply of labour increases to $0Q_1$, $Q_2–0Q_1$ is the level of disequilibrium unemployment. This is in addition to natural unemployment.

It is not only unions which could prevent the market from clearing – the government could do it by acting on behalf of labour. Thus – government imposed minimum wage legislation, would, it is argued, have the same effect.[9] A third possibility is that wages are determined in imperfect markets, and it is the spoken or unspoken agreements between employers and workers which hold wages above market clearing rates.

Demand-Deficient (Cyclical) Unemployment

A major alternative explanation for disequilibrium unemployment is that there is a deficiency of aggregate demand for goods and services, together with a poorly operating labour market. This was first put forward in the 1930s by John Maynard Keynes (see profile), whose achievement was to revolutionise the understanding of macroeconomics, and thus lead to the 'classical' versus 'Keynesian' difference of opinion. Despite an enormous amount of study and research there is still a division of opinion between classical and Keynesian economists to this day.

Disequilibrium unemployment is explained as being the result of two causal factors. The first is that a fall in demand for goods and services, *ie* a fall in aggregate demand, is the reason for the fall in the demand for labour – see Figure 3.38. The second causal factor is that labour markets do not work smoothly. Labour resists wage cuts. Money wages tend to rise easily but resist falling, because workers are not passive commodities, like fruit is in a fruit market. Money wages are said to be 'sticky' downwards. Figure 3.39 illustrates the ratchet effect of money wages. Wages rise easily, but resist falling. Of course prices can change and thereby reduce real wages. Keynesians, however, argue that this only happens slowly and so the labour market does not clear resulting in demand-deficient unemployment. This is the type of unemployment we noted in Section 3.4, arising when there was a recessionary gap. Cyclical unemployment extends across the whole economy, and across all industries.

Figure 3.38 – Demand-Deficient (Cyclical) Unemployment

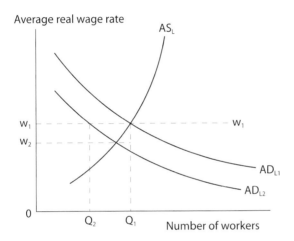

The demand for labour falls from AD_{L1} to AD_{L2} as a result of a fall in the demand for goods and services. However as the labour market is 'sticky' downwards real wages do not fall to W_2, at least, not quickly enough to maintain equilibrium. Disequilibrium unemployment of Q_2–Q_1 results.

📊 Figure 3.39 – The Ratchet-Effect of Wage Changes

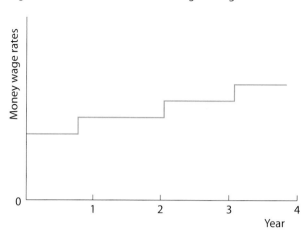

When the demand for labour is strong, money wages rise without resistance. When the demand for labour falls, wage rates resist falling. This is due to worker resistance to wage cuts.

Keynes, the Classicists and the Great Depression

Keynes pointed out in 1935 that Classical economists…'were apparently unmoved by the lack of correspondence between the results of their theory and the facts of observation: a discrepancy which the ordinary man has not failed to observe…

The celebrated optimism of (Classical) economic theory…is…to be traced, I think, to their having neglected to take account of the drag on prosperity which can be exercised by an insufficiency of effective demand. For there would obviously be a natural tendency towards the optimum employment of resources in a Society which was functioning after the manner of the classical postulates. It may well be that classical theory represents the way in which we would like our economy to behave. But to assume that it actually does so is to assume our difficulties away.'

Source: John Maynard Keynes, The General Theory of Employment, Interest and Money. Macmillan. pp 33–34.

Question

Classical economists were arguing in the nineteen thirties that the economy would adjust to the recession, that economies were inherently stable. Unemployment was a temporary phenomenon and would adjust. Why does Keynes say this is unrealistic?

MEASURES TO DEAL WITH UNEMPLOYMENT

Government macroeconomic policy generally aims to reduce unemployment to a minimum. What that minimum level is, what priority unemployment takes when it conflicts with other policy goals, and the method used to reduce unemployment are, however, all highly contentious issues. In this section, a straightforward look at measures to reduce unemployment is undertaken by category of unemployment. The more contentious points are left to the end of Section 3.

Frictional (Search) Unemployment

Frictional unemployment is both inevitable and desirable in a dynamic economy. Nevertheless, government may be able to reduce the friction, (reduce the search time), to enable the labour market to function more smoothly. One way of doing this would be to improve the flow of information between employers and job seekers. The government may also reduce frictional unemployment by reducing state benefits to the unemployed. This increases the opportunity cost of remaining unemployed, and thus increases the incentive to get back to work as quickly as possible.

Structural Unemployment

There are two broad underlying approaches to policies which attempt to reduce structural unemployment: they are a market-orientated approach, and an interventionist approach.

A market orientated approach encourages workers to leave the old industry, leave the depressed region, and move to where the work is. It involves helping workers to retrain to overcome occupational immobility. It may involve cutting wages locally to widen the differential with the more prosperous areas. It may involve an overall cut in welfare benefits to encourage people to move. The increased relative poverty of the depressed region would encourage the price system to shift resources, *ie* encourage workers to move from low wage areas and occupations to high wage areas and occupations.

An interventionist approach accepts that occupational and geographical immobilities are so great that it would take an unacceptable level of poverty over an unacceptable length of time to move workers to new jobs and new locations. Government intervention would then involve direct action to bring jobs to the region.[10] Tax holidays, grants, government-funded retraining schemes, and direct provision of buildings and services may all be used to encourage firms to locate or relocate, and to create new jobs in the areas of high structural unemployment.

Seasonal Unemployment

Areas with high seasonal unemployment may be able to earn sufficient income in the busy season to cushion the slack season. The tourist industry is often well adapted to doing this. However, incomes in the area affected may be considered unacceptably low compared to the rest of the country, *eg* in the south of Italy compared to the north, in the north of Canada compared to the south. Government measures are then very similar to those used to reduce structural unemployment.

The most acute regional income differences in the world are to be found in the poorest countries. The migration from rural areas to urban areas is so large, and so fast at this time, that the problem is overwhelming the ability of many cities to cope with it. This acute problem of regional imbalance will be studied in Section 5 on economic development, under the heading of *rural-urban migration*.

Classical (Real-Wage) Unemployment

The classical view of the labour market is that it is like any other market. If the demand for labour falls the price of labour, the real wage, falls and the market remains in equilibrium. Excepting natural unemployment, unemployment can only exist if the market is not being allowed to work. The solution is to remove the restrictions and *make* the market work. If labour unions are holding wages above equilibrium, the power of unions should be reduced by legislation. If minimum wage laws are preventing the market from clearing, then these should be abandoned. If social legislation raises real wages by compelling employers to pay compulsory social insurance contributions these should be reduced or abandoned. If state welfare benefits lower the opportunity cost of not working so that some unemployed people would prefer to be unemployed than accept the market wage, then state welfare benefits should be reduced.

Demand-Deficient (Cyclical) Unemployment

Where the demand for labour falls because the demand for goods and services falls, classical economists assume (a) that the labour market will adjust wages downwards and if not, (b) the labour market should be made to work, so that it *does* happen. Other economists, following the original analysis of Keynes, argue that there is such resistance to wage adjustment downwards it is unreasonable to expect it to happen. The solution they advocate is for the government to use fiscal policy or monetary policy to raise aggregate demand, and thus raise the demand for jobs. These policies were actively pursued in many industrial countries throughout the 1950s and 1960s. However by 1970 these policies were seen to be creating high inflation and balance of payments problems. They were largely abandoned in favour of classical policies based upon making markets work. With high unemployment persisting through the 1970s, 1980s and 1990s the debate in macroeconomics has been intense. We will return to this at the end of this section.

MULTIPLE CHOICE QUESTIONS – UNEMPLOYMENT

1   If a government wished to reduce structural unemployment the most effective policy would be to

   A   reduce direct taxes.
   B   reduce the minimum wage.
   C   lower interest rates.
   D   increase the mobility of labour.

2   The demand for the product of a domestic industry shifts abroad permanently. This will cause

   A   structural unemployment.
   B   cyclical unemployment.
   C   frictional unemployment.
   D   demand deficient unemployment.

3.6   INFLATION

DEFINITION

Inflation is a sustained upwards movement in the average level of prices. Sustained is an important word, as a once only increase in prices would not be regarded as inflation. Deflation[11] is a sustained downward movement in the average level of prices. Price stability occurs when the average level of prices is moving neither up nor down. The average level of prices is known as the *price level* and is measured by a price index.

Measuring Inflation

The inflation rate is the percentage change in the price level. The formula is:

$$\text{Inflation rate} = \frac{\text{current year's price level} - \text{last year's price level}}{\text{last year's price level}} \times \frac{100}{1}$$

If the price level last year was 130 and this year it is 135 the inflation rate is:

$$\frac{135 - 130}{130} \times \frac{100}{1} = \frac{5}{130} \times \frac{100}{1} = 3.8\%$$

The most common method of measuring the price level is to construct a price index. As there are far too many goods and services to be monitored, a representative sample is recorded. This sample may be imagined as a very large basket of goods and services. The most widely used basket is the one which looks at the prices of retailed goods and services. This is known as the 'Retail Price Index'. Other types of price may be used to construct other price index numbers, *eg* wholesale prices, export prices, wages, and prices of goods most commonly used by certain groups of consumers, like students, or retired people. When the 'inflation rate' is mentioned it usually refers to the change in the Retail Price Index. However, as wholesale prices are the prices which retailers pay when buying their goods, a change in wholesale prices usually feeds through into a change in retail prices. The wholesale price index is, therefore, a good guide to the *underlying rate of inflation* – that is, the likely future inflation of retail prices.

A large number of goods and services are selected as representative of all goods and services, *ie* a representative sample of goods and services. For example in the UK 150,000 prices are recorded for 600 items. Prices have to be recorded in different regions, and in different outlets, and averaged. For example, bottled beer may be sold at different prices in supermarkets and corner shops. Ticket prices for cinemas, theatre and football games will differ in different regions of the country.

Suppose an economy sells only two products: beer and bread. The price of beer increases from 20 francs to 24 francs from year 1 to year 2. The price of bread increases from 10 francs to 11 francs over the same time period.

The two new prices can be expressed relative to the original prices in a number of ways, *eg* as percentages, as decimals, as fractions, or by relating to a base figure of 100. Thus, if the price of a good in year one is assigned the value of 100 as an index number, changes in price could be related to this base year number. For example, if the price of the good increased by 5%, the index would move to 105. If it fell by 1%, the index would fall to 99.

In the case of a 'beer and bread two product economy', we first need to calculate an index for each good separately:

That is: $\dfrac{\text{price year } 2}{\text{price year } 1} \times \dfrac{100}{1}$

$$\text{Beer index} = \frac{24}{20} \times \frac{100}{1} = 120$$

$$\text{Bread index} = \frac{11}{10} \times \frac{100}{1} = 110$$

As there are two goods in the economy an average of the two figures would result in an average price index:

$$ie \ \frac{120 + 110}{2} = 115$$

The price level has moved from 100 to 115. There has been inflation of 15%.

Such an average index, however, gives no weight to the importance of the goods. Each good is treated as of equal importance by averaging the two price index numbers. If bread is in fact much more important to consumers than beer, the price index can be made to reflect the degree of importance, and consequently be much more useful as a statistic. In a consumer society the importance of a good is determined by how much consumers spend on it, the information being obtained from consumer expenditure surveys. Thus, if consumers spend 0.2 of their income on beer and 0.8 on bread, each product index is weighted by these figures to calculate its due importance:

Product	Index	Weight	Weighted price index (Index x weight)
Beer	120	0.2	24
Bread	110	0.8	88
			112

Bread prices are four times as important to consumers as beer prices. The weighted price index shows an average increase in prices now to be 12% not 15%. It is rather as if we had placed five items in our basket: four loaves of bread and one bottle of beer, and then averaged the price increase over the five items.

The Consumer Price Index – USA

The market basket of goods used in constructing the CPI in the US is for a hypothetical household. The index is updated every 10 years. The expenditure pattern graphed below is based upon surveys conducted between 1993 and 1995.

1 housing
2 transportation
3 food & beverages
4 recreation
5 medical care
6 education & communications
7 apparel & upkeep
8 other goods & services

Source: US Bureau of Labor Statistics

Problems of Measurement

A price index does a fairly good job of calculating month-to-month and year-to-year rates of inflation. However, there are some inbuilt problems which increase in magnitude the longer the time period of comparison.

Arrival and Disappearance of Goods

New goods are continually introduced to the market and old goods continually drop out of the market. The basket of goods and services is, therefore, continually changing. The longer the time period of the comparison, the greater the difference in the contents of the two baskets of goods and services. For example, mobile phones, DVDs and internet shopping are all relatively new products. Home-use ciné cameras, black and white television receivers, LP records and metal toys, once everyday products, are now rarely found.

Quality of Goods

Many goods and services can be found over long time periods, but with major differences in the quality of the product. The clothes, cars, telephones, health care and banking services of today are very different from those of the 1960s. To compare the price of a good in two time periods the quality of the good needs to remain constant, yet many price changes are themselves a reflection of quality changes. For example, if the price of a motor car rises, it may be due to general inflation or it may be due to additional equipment *eg* the provision of air-bags.

Choice of Weight

The expenditure pattern which determines the weights used in the price index is an average for the economy as a whole. The spending pattern of particular groups of people, *eg* old people or students, may bear little resemblance to the average and reduce the value of the index to such groups.

The expenditure pattern changes over time, and weights based upon the first year expenditure pattern will not be totally appropriate for the second year. This is especially true for the very goods which change most in price as consumers switch between substitutes. Thus if beef prices increase and lamb prices do not, consumers will switch from consuming beef to consuming lamb. The original expenditure weight will, however, overstate the importance of beef, and thus the effect of the price rise in beef.

COSTS OF INFLATION

Redistribution Costs

Prices are the co-ordinating mechanism in a market. Prices move to reflect changing values and changing scarcities. Prices, therefore, have enormous importance in a market economy. However, prices change not only to reflect relative scarcities, but to reflect inflation as well. If during a period of inflation every single price changed by exactly the same percentage it would have a neutral effect on resource allocation. For example, in 1992 the Polish government reduced the value of the zloty by a factor of 1000. Every single price and every wage was reduced to one thousandth of its previous value. Everyone retained exactly the same relative real income after the change as they did before the change. Inflation does not occur like this however. Prices change arbitrarily. Some prices rise easily, others do not. This distorts the price system. Wrong signals are sent to markets, and resources no longer move according to relative values and scarcities. Thus the price system is itself a victim of inflation. Resources become redistributed arbitrarily, rather than responding methodically to values and scarcities. Three examples of this arbitrariness are given below:

▍ people on relatively fixed incomes will suffer a fall in real income, *eg* those receiving old age pensions, students receiving grants, or those in non-unionised occupations who have little bargaining power over their wages. Those with power to increase their incomes will gain during inflation.

▍ borrowers will gain at the expense of lenders. If individual 'A' borrows $100 from individual 'B' at a 10% rate of interest, 'A' will pay back $110 after a year; $10 being the payment for the loan. If there has been inflation meanwhile, let's say a 10% inflation of prices, the $110 dollars will be worth the same as the original $100 one year earlier. The loan has been free. The borrower has gained at the expense of the lender.

▍ export prices will change relative to import prices. Inflation of domestic prices will make exports more expensive relative to imports. People in the import business will gain at the expense of people in the export business.

In each of these three cases the point to note is not just that resources are redistributed, and that there are gainers and losers, but that the redistribution is arbitrary: it does not follow the normal laws of economic scarcity.

Uncertainty

Inflation increases the sense of uncertainty in the business community. Firms may be discouraged from investing if they find it difficult to predict their revenues and their costs. If investment does fall, then economic growth will fall.

Resource Cost

Extra resources will be directed to cope with inflation and thus reduce more useful production. Two such costs are known rather colourfully as *menu* costs and *shoe-leather* costs. Menu costs are incurred as firms have to change their price lists frequently (literally reprinting menus in restaurants). Shoe-leather costs refer to the time cost of keeping informed about price changes (literally walking from shop to shop to compare prices, in some cases).

The Functions of Money are Eroded

Inflation makes money literally 'worth less'. If inflation is high, the value of money is reduced quickly. If the value of money is eroded then so are the functions of money. Money is used to exchange goods and services. In economies with a high division of labour and specialisation, money is essential to allow the exchange of goods and services to take place. If inflation destroys money, the exchange of goods and services breaks down. Output falls dramatically, as specialisation and the division of labour crumble. There is a reversion to barter and low incomes. Secondly, money is used to save for the future. If money becomes worthless then savings become worthless. Life savings may be destroyed. Such profound changes have many times in the past led to severe social and political unrest. The hyper-inflation of Germany in 1921–3 destroyed its middle classes, and thereby contributed to the growth of extreme Nazi nationalism.

Mademoiselle Zelia – Society Islands

'Some years since, Mademoiselle Zelia, a singer, gave a concert in the Society Islands in exchange for a third part of the receipts. When counted, her share was found to consist of three pigs, 23 turkeys, 44 chickens, 5000 coconuts, besides considerable quantities of bananas, lemons and oranges... as she could not consume any considerable portion of the receipts herself it became necessary in the meantime to feed the pigs and the poultry with the fruit.'

An observation on barter in the absence of money, by W S Jevons in 1898.

Anticipated and Unanticipated Inflation

If inflation is correctly anticipated then many of its worst effects can be eased. It has, for example, been common in many countries in Latin America to anticipate and accept the state of inflation. Many prices, *eg* wages and taxes, are indexed to inflation. If the price level rises, wages and taxes move up in line with the index. Such a system avoids some of the worst redistribution costs, but not the menu and shoe-leather costs. Indexing accepts rather than combats inflation. However it is unanticipated inflation which causes the most serious problems.

Creeping Inflation and HyperInflation

A low rate of inflation, say 2% or 3% a year, is known as *creeping inflation*. A very high rate, 100% and more, is known as *hyper-inflation*. One of the dangers of not controlling low inflation is that it may grow. Final prices and factor prices (especially wages) may chase each other, spiralling ever upwards in rapidly expanding rates of inflation. In 1993 inflation in the Ukraine was 500% and in Brazil 1200%. In the 1920s Austria and Hungary had even higher inflation. Poland's prices went up by two million per cent. The prices in the USSR rose by several billion percent. In Germany, the inflation rate in 1923 reached 7,000,000,000,000 per cent!

Hyperinflation 1945/46 – Hungary

The Hungarian currency in July 1945 was known as the Pengo. The New Pengo followed, defined as 1 million old Pengos. Then came the Milpengo – defined as 1 million New Pengos – and the Bilpengo – worth 1 million Milpengos.

Date	Price Index
15 July 1945	100
30 September 1945	423
30 November 1945	16,801
31 January 1946	77,054
31 March 1946	2,228,900
31 May 1946	11,700,000,000
31 July 1946	136,650,000,000,000,000

Question

Write down the four functions of money.

What would have happened to each of these four functions in Hungary in 1945/6?

CAUSES OF INFLATION

There will be price stability in an economy that has neither inflation nor deflation, when aggregate demand and aggregate supply are in equilibrium. This is illustrated as price level P_e and output level Y_e in Figure 3.40. Consider the situation at price level P_1 – here aggregate demand is greater than aggregate supply. The resulting shortages of goods and services will drive up prices to P_e. Suppliers will respond to the higher prices by producing more, moving up the *SRAS* curve, and buyers will buy less as *AD* responds to the increased price level. This is how inflation is caused. A situation where aggregate demand is greater than aggregate supply drives up prices.

 Figure 3.40 – Aggregate Demand greater than Aggregate Supply

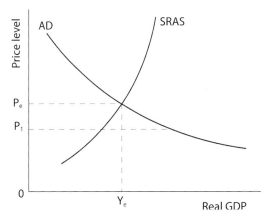

Macroeconomic equilibrium at price level P_e, and output level Y_e, where aggregate demand equals aggregate supply. At price level P_1, aggregate supply is less than aggregate demand. Shortage will drive prices up towards equilibrium.

This situation can occur:

I by a shift rightwards of the *AD* curve
I by a shift leftwards of the *AS* curve
I by a combination of both.

If the shifts persist, *ie* there is a sustained excess demand problem, then there is inflation. The faster the curves shift the higher is the rate of inflation. If the inflation originates by aggregate demand shifting to the right it is called *demand-pull* inflation. If it originates from aggregate supply shifting to the left it is called *cost-push* inflation.

Demand-Pull Inflation

Demand-pull inflation is caused by persistent shifts of the *AD* curve to the right. In Figure 3.41, *AD* has increased from AD_1 to AD_2, raising equilibrium output to Y_{e2} and the price level to P_2. Inflation occurred as the price level increased. If, however, the increase in *AD* was a demand-side shock, *ie* a once only increase in *AD*, the price level will stay at P_2 and the rate of inflation will fall to zero. There must be a sustained increase in *AD* for inflation to continue. For the rate of inflation to rise the *AD* curve must shift even faster to the right.

📊 Figure 3.41 – Demand-Pull Inflation

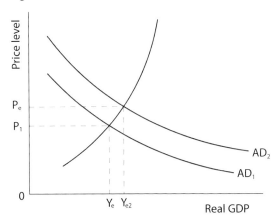

Price level increases by AD shifting to the right, from AD₁ to AD₂. For demand-pull inflation to continue AD must keep moving to the right.

Aggregate demand can increase by a rise in one or more of the components of aggregate demand: consumption, investment, government spending or net exports (*C, I, G, X–M*). Demand-pull inflation is associated with the boom phase of the business cycle, the opposite of the recession phase. Just what sets off an increase in aggregate demand, however, is controversial.

Some economists believe that *AD* increases solely, or mostly, because of an increase in the money supply. Such economists are known as *monetarists*. Other economists believe equally strongly that aggregate demand can increase independently of the money supply. Thus, if government cuts taxes, consumers will spend more, and if business people feel more confident investment will increase. These economists believe that the money supply adapts to the increase in spending. That is, an increase in the money supply is a consequence, not a cause of inflation. There are therefore two explanations of demand-pull inflation: monetarist and non-monetarist. One version of the monetarist version of demand-pull inflation is based on the quantity theory of money.

The Quantity Theory of Money

The quantity theory of money claims that, in the long run, an increase in the quantity of money causes an equal percentage increase in the price level. The theory is based upon an equation, and a concept – the equation of exchange, and a concept called the velocity of circulation.

The velocity of circulation (*V*) is the average number of times a unit of money is used annually to buy goods and services. *V* is best explained by relating it to *GDP. GDP* is equal to the price level (*P*) multiplied by real *GDP* (*Y*). With *M* representing the stock of money, *V* is determined by the equation:

$$V \ = \ \frac{PY}{M}$$

That is, the value of the *GDP* divided by the stock of money is equal to velocity. For example if *GDP* is *$600 billion* and the money stock (*M*) is *$300 billion*, *V* is equal to *2*. Each unit of the *$300 billion* money stock (*M*) must on average be used twice (*V*) to finance a *GDP* (*PY*) of *$600 billion*.

The equation of exchange states that the quantity of money (*M*) multiplied by the velocity of circulation (*V*) equals *GDP*, or: *MV* = *PY*

Given the definition of the velocity of circulation, this equation *must be true*, that is, *MV* ≡ *PY* is an identity.

It is the quantity *theory* of money which is controversial. This claims that increases in the stock of money (*M*) *cause* increases in prices (*P*) *ie* it is increases in money supply which cause inflation. For this to be possible both *V* and *Y* must be constant, or at least quite stable. Monetarists claim that this is so. It is important to supporters of the quantity theory that:

1 The velocity of circulation is not influenced by the quantity of money
2 Potential real *GDP* is not influenced by the quantity of money

If these assumptions are true then a change in the stock of money must bring about an equivalent change in the price level.

Historical evidence does indeed show broadly consistent correlation between increases in the money supply and inflation over the long term. However, correlation is not the same thing as causation. It is indeed possible that increased money growth causes inflation, but it is equally feasible that inflation causes the money supply to expand. That is, an increase in prices causes either the Central Bank, the commercial banks, or peoples' behaviour to change, such that the money supply increases. Another possibility is that some third factor causes both money supply and inflation to increase.

The consensus view is that in the long-term increases in the money supply do indeed *cause* inflation. However the quantity theory is not conclusive in the short run.

Cost-Push Inflation

Cost-push inflation is caused by the *SRAS* curve shifting to the left. An increase in firms' costs, *eg* by wages rising or raw material costs rising, shifts the *SRAS* curve to the left, resulting in a rise in the price level and a reduction in real output – Figure 3.42. A once only rise in prices, a *supply-side shock*, would cause the price level to rise and then stay at the new higher level. For inflation to continue, *ie* for there to be a *sustained* price rise then the *SRAS* curve must shift continuously to the left. For the rate of inflation to *rise* then the *SRAS* curve must be shifting ever faster to the left.

 Figure 3.42 – Cost-Push Inflation

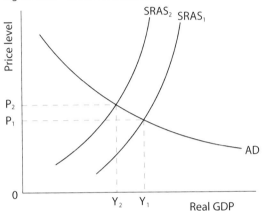

Cost-push inflation – a rise in factor prices shifts the SRAS curve to the left from SRAS₁ to SRAS₂, thereby raising the price level and reducing real output. For cost-push inflation to continue aggregate supply must continue to fall.

It is worth noting that although demand-pull and cost-push both cause inflation, increased *AD* increases output and hence employment whereas cost-push reduces output and employment. If we now go back a step and ask what could cause costs to rise, then there are a number of possibilities. Several of these possibilities involve one or more economic groups growing in power and exercising this power to try to gain a greater share of national output for themselves. These groups include labour, capitalists, foreigners and governments. Types of cost-push inflation take their names from the forces exerted by the relevant groups. These are:

- wage-push inflation. This is where labour unions push up wages independently of the demand for labour.
- profit-push inflation. This is where firms use monopoly power to raise profits independently of consumer demand.
- import-price-push inflation. This is where import prices rise independently of aggregate demand (*eg* OPEC raising oil prices in the 1970s).
- tax-push inflation. This is where taxes are raised.

reduction of finite natural resources will also reduce aggregate supply, *eg* deforestation, over-fishing, the running down of oil or other mineral reserves.

Sometimes two or more of these reasons interact and chase each other upwards, causing an inflationary spiral *eg* wages and profits.

The Interaction of Demand-Pull and Cost-Push

Demand-pull and cost-push may occur together as wages and prices may increase by either *AD* rising, or *AS* falling. Certainly once inflation has started it may be very difficult to separate the two as they chase each other in an upward spiral. For example, aggregate supply may shift continuously to the left as labour unions and companies keep raising costs by competing to stay ahead of one other. At the same time government may increase aggregate demand, with fiscal and monetary policy, to try to reduce the growing unemployment that will arise from the *AS* curve shifting to the left. These shifts can get faster and faster as the economy enters a wage-price spiral. Inflation goes on rising. This is illustrated in Figure 3.42(b).

Figure 3.42(b) – Inflation: a Wage-Price Spiral

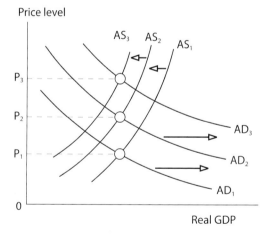

Prices rise and output falls as aggregate supply shifts to the left. Government expands aggregate demand, shifting AD to the right, in an attempt to offset the rising unemployment.

Expectation and Inflation

Workers and firms take the expected rate of inflation into consideration when making decisions. Firms setting prices need to anticipate increases in their costs due to inflation, and to build them into their prices. For example, your school or college may well have set its tuition and accommodation fees for next year or the year after that. They will undoubtedly have made an estimate of the expected inflation rates of teachers' wages, heating costs, bank interest rates and so on. The school will want to increase its prices to cover these expected increases in costs. Labour unions negotiating wage rates for future years will wish to maintain the real purchasing power of their members. They too will estimate the expected rate of inflation. All negotiations on future prices and wages will begin from the base line of the expected rate of inflation. If inflation is expected to be 2%, then employers will want to raise prices by at least this much to cover their anticipated costs. Workers will want at least a 2% increase in their wages to maintain their real income. If expected inflation is 20% negotiations over future prices and wages will begin at 20%. In this way inflation begins to get built into an economy. What determines people's expectations, however, is the subject of great debate amongst economists.

MEASURES TO DEAL WITH INFLATION

One of government's macroeconomic aims is to achieve stable prices. The control and reduction of inflation will however depend on what is causing the inflation. Is it a demand-pull inflation, or a cost-push inflation? If it is demand-pull, is it a monetary phenomenon, or a non-monetary phenomenon?

Demand-Pull

Demand-side policies are used to reduce excess demand. If the excess demand is believed to be caused by excess money, then monetary policy will be used to reduce that demand. Monetary policy uses two main, interlinked tools: the quantity of money, and the price of money, *ie* the interest rate. If aggregate demand is too high because there is too much money, then the answer is to reduce the money supply, or alternatively to raise the interest rate. Raising interest rates encourages saving rather than spending, and raises the cost of borrowing. If borrowing is more expensive, consumer demand for interest-sensitive goods, like consumer durables, will fall. Demand for business investment, and house purchase, will also fall. An important school of economic thought called *monetarism*,[12] believes that all inflation is caused by too much money in the economy. Monetarists believe that the only way to achieve price stability is to control the money supply rigorously. They advocate limiting increases in the money supply to the same level as increases in the real output of goods and services.

Excess demand could be present for non-monetary reasons. That is, consumption, investment, government spending or exports could have increased independently of what is happening to the money supply. In this case, fiscal policy can be used to reduce aggregate demand. Deflationary fiscal policy aims to reduce demand directly rather than indirectly by changing the money supply or interest rates. For example, government spending may be cut. Alternatively, taxes may be raised to reduce the income and spending of consumers.

In the situation illustrated in Figure 3.41 monetary or fiscal policy would be used to slow or stop the movement of the *AD* curve to the right, and hence stabilise the price level.

Cost-Push

Supply-side policies are employed to try to reduce costs. If the power of labour unions is causing wage-push inflation, the power of unions can be reduced by legislation. If the power of big companies is causing profit-push inflation, anti-monopoly legislation can increase competition and reduce prices. Business taxes and government bureaucracy can be reduced to lower business costs. Labour productivity can be encouraged by increasing incentives to improve education and training. Capital and land productivity can be encouraged with tax or subsidy incentives to increase research and development, and to increase investment in new technology.

In the situation illustrated in Figure 3.41 supply-side policies would be employed to slow or stop the movement of the *SRAS* curve to the left and hence stabilise the price level.

MACROECONOMICS
Inflation

MULTIPLE CHOICE QUESTIONS – INFLATION

1 The table below shows the consumer price index for Country X from 1999 to 2003.

Year	Consumer Price Index
1999	109
2000	120
2001	125
2002	140
2003	148

What is the rate of inflation for the year 2002?

A 12%   B 15%   C 25%   D 40%

2 The table below shows the consumer price index for Country Y over a five year period.

Year	% change in RPI
1	+17
2	+9
3	+4
4	0
5	-5

This information shows that the price level
A was at its lowest at the start of the period.
B was at its highest at the start of the period.
C fell throughout the period.
D rose throughout the period.

3 The following information is from Country Z. The money supply is 20 million pesetas, the number of transactions is 10 million, and the velocity of circulation is 4. The quantity theory of money predicts that the average price level will be

A Ptas 4   B Ptas 8   C Ptas 16   D Ptas 20

3.7   THE INFLATION/UNEMPLOYMENT DEBATE

IS THERE A 'TRADE-OFF' BETWEEN INFLATION AND UNEMPLOYMENT?

The *AD/AS* model focuses on changes in inflation and real output. As jobs are linked to output we have been able to work out what would happen to unemployment. In Figure 3.43(a) increased aggregate demand increases prices and real output, and hence reduces unemployment. In Figure 3.43(b) a fall in aggregate demand reduces prices and real output, and hence increases unemployment. In Figure 3.43(c) a reduction in aggregate supply increases prices and reduces output, thus increasing employment. In Figure 3.43(d) an increase in aggregate supply reduces prices and increases real output, and thus reduces unemployment.

In the two examples where aggregate demand shifts, Figure 3.43(a) and Figure 3.43 (b), the price level and real output are positively correlated, that is, they increase and decrease together. However, unemployment rises and falls inversely with output, *ie* is negatively correlated. As more real *GDP* is produced, the number of jobs increases, *ie* unemployment falls. As less real *GDP* is produced the number of jobs falls, *ie* unemployment rises. Price level increases and unemployment are therefore inversely related. When *AD* increases, as in Figure 3.43(a), rising prices will be accompanied by falling unemployment. When *AD* falls, as in Figure 3.43(b), falling prices will be accompanied by rising unemployment.

Figure 3.43(a) – Increase in aggregate demand   Figure 3.43(b) Fall in aggregate demand

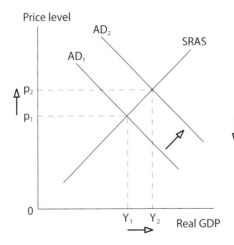

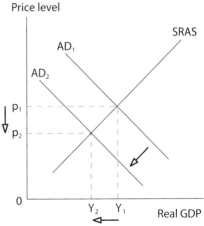

A persistent increase in AD leads to inflation and increasing output, and indirectly to a reduction in unemployment.

A persistent fall in AD leads to deflation and falling output, and indirectly to an increase in unemployment.

Figure 3.43(c)– Fall in aggregate supply   Figure 3.43(d) – Increase in aggregate supply

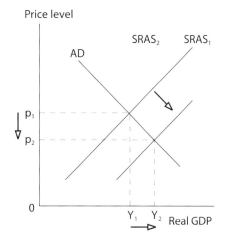

A persistent fall in SRAS leads to inflation and fall-
ing output, and indirectly to an increase in
unemployment.

A persistent increase in SRAS leads to deflation
and rising output, and to indirectly falling
unemployment.

Aggregate demand shifts were central to the work of John Maynard Keynes, writing in the great depression of the 1930s. His 'General Theory' of the economy blamed deflation and unemployment upon insufficient aggregate demand. Keynes argued persuasively that increasing aggregate demand was something governments could and should do. We need a diagram of the full *SRAS* curve to explain the demand deficiency as Keynes saw it: in Figure 3.34 the first section of the curve, when real *GDP* is low, is perfectly horizontal. If aggregate demand shifts to the left over this range of *GDP*, output falls and unemployment rises. As the *SRAS* curve is flat prices are stable. The government can increase *AD* (by fiscal or monetary policy) to increase output and reduce unemployment without raising the price level. In the original Keynesian model the curve was assumed to be 'L' shaped, so that *AD* could increase to the physical limit of production before prices rose. Later modifications produced the upward sloping middle section. The modification seemed to accord better with reality where unemployment and rising prices were found together. This middle section is the *AS* curve shown and used in Figure 3.32 with inflation and output positively correlated (and inflation and unemployment negatively correlated). Governments operated their macroeconomic policies towards stable prices and low unemployment, and many used the model actively for 20–25 years after World War II. Aggregate demand was deliberately manipulated to keep it high – above *AD₂* in Figure 3.44. This experience developed into attempts to 'fine tune' the economy, *ie* the government adjusting the *AD* to obtain the combination of unemployment and inflation which was the most politically acceptable.

Figure 3.44 – The Keynesisan Short Run Aggregate Supply Curve (SRAS), and Aggregate Demand (AD).

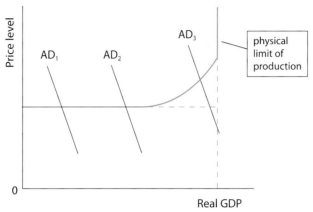

John Maynard Keynes (1883–1946), a Personal Profile

The publication of Keynes's *The General Theory of Employment, Interest and Money* in 1936 was the beginning of modern macroeconomics. Probably no other economist and no other book has had such a profound effect on the subject, and on government macroeconomics policies. In the 1950s and 1960s many governments, including those of the UK and the USA considered themselves to be 'Keynesian' with regard to economics. Keynes' father was a Cambridge University economist, his mother a mayor of the city and a Justice of the Peace. He himself had an outstanding academic career at the elite public school, Eton, and then at Cambridge University. He was a brilliant debater, secretary of the Cambridge Union and president of its famous debating club. He had wide literary and artistic interests and became a prominent member of the Bloomsbury Group, whose membership included Virginia Woolf, EM Forster and Bertrand Russell. In the middle of his life he married a famous Russian ballerina and later built a theatre for her in Cambridge. He was not only an academic at Cambridge, but editor of Britain's most famous economic publication, *The Economic Journal*, Bursar of Kings College Cambridge, author of a huge number of books and articles, and a successful speculator in the commodity markets. At the outbreak of World War I he joined the Treasury and rapidly rose to the top, becoming one of the government's chief advisors at the Versailles peace conference. He was scathing at the punitive peace terms the allies imposed upon Germany. He correctly predicted the severe unrest this would cause in

Germany. His best-selling book *The Economic Consequences of the Peace* made him internationally famous. He became a celebrity figure and his advice was sought on many of the biggest issues of his time. He enjoyed an instant recognition amongst the public and media which possibly no other economist did, either before or since.

Throughout the 1920s Keynes wrote many pamphlets critical of the prevailing laissez-faire economics of his day. With a major depression in the UK, and after 1929 throughout the world, Keynes argued that full-employment was not a natural state, that markets did not clear and maintain a state of full employment. He was strongly opposed by the mainstream classical thinking of that time. Then in 1936, he published his greatest work – one of the truly great books of the twentieth century – *The General Theory of Employment, Interest and Money*. This rather dry and difficult book took the world by storm just as Keynes had predicted. The theory revolutionised macroeconomic thought and became known as 'the Keynesian Revolution'. He showed that unemployment was not just a temporary aberration that would be automatically corrected by the markets. He showed how and why unemployment could and would persist, offering a cogent explanation for the great depression that people were experiencing at that time. Further, he offered a solution. The government had to intervene and increase spending to get the economy back to work. The advice was reasoned, detailed and specific.

Keynes was no left wing opponent of capitalism. He visited Russia more than once and rejected the planned system. However his interventionist policies supported a capitalist system by modifying it. In a world which at that time was replete with dictatorships of the right and communist ideology of the left, Keynes had a profound influence on democratic market based economies. Keynes returned to the British Treasury during World War II and he worked closely with United States advisors on wartime financial assistance plans. After the war he was one of the chief architects of the post war international agreements reached at Bretton Woods which set up the enduring IBRD, the IMF and GATT. Keynes died suddenly and prematurely in 1946 for he undoubtedly still had much to offer the economic world.

Source: John Sloman, Economics, 4th ed, 2000, Prentice Hall

MiltonFriedman, a Personal Profile

Friedman was born the son of an immigrant Hungarian garment worker in NewYork. He was an undergraduate at Rutgers University and a postgraduate at the University of Chicago where he became an economics professor and a member of the famous Chicago school on inflation. Since his retirement from Chicago he has continued to work at Stanford University.

Friedman brought a brilliant and original brain to some of the accepted economic orthodoxies of post war macroeconomics and has challenged many established beliefs. He won the Nobel Prize for his work in 1976. His main thesis is that economies are better off without government interference. That well meaning governments actually cause harm. Laissez-faire and markets are far better at sorting out problems. His best known book (and series of TV films), made with his wife Rose, is 'Free to Choose', an argument that markets give the best solutions.

Another very influential book, written together with Anna Swartz, is 'The Monetary History of the USA', which argues that the Great Depression was not the cause of market failure, as reasoned by Keynes, but the mis-management of the US monetary system. Friedman was a founder member of the school of economists known as monetarists. They have a strong belief in the quantity theory of money, that is, that inflation is directly the result of government expansion of the money supply. Friedman argues that government should only expand the money supply neutrally in line with increases in economic activity.

Source: John Sloman, Economics, 4th ed, 2000, Prentice Hall

Keynesian theory and policy prescription, based upon this inverse relationship between inflation and unemployment, held up well until the late 1960s. Then it all went horribly wrong. In industrial country after industrial country, inflation and unemployment both rose together. Macroeconomics went into a state of crisis. We can, however, now see one explanation for stagflation (a situation of stagnation together with inflation) in Figure 3.43(c). A shift of the short run aggregate supply curve to the left will cause prices to rise and output to fall (and unemployment to rise). Thus when OPEC[13] raised oil prices to very high levels during the 1970s the *SRAS* curve shifted to the left. As other factor prices, including wages, rose competitively to keep pace with rising prices, inflation was sustained. In the early 1970s inflation was in fact worsened by governments, as they expanded demand in the time-honoured fashion to reduce unemployment. With a wage-price spiral shifting *SRAS* to the left and government action shifting *AD* to the right, inflation rose sharply, as shown in Figure 3.43.

As a consequence of this experience in the 1970s, industrial countries have concentrated their policy actions upon shifting the *SRAS* curve to the right. The collective name of such policies is *supply-side economics*. The *SRAS* curve in moving to the right increases output, and thus reduces unemployment, while lowering the price level. This has become the dominant feature of government macroeconomic policy in the 1980s and into the new millenium, *ie* to stabilise prices and reduce unemployment. Government demand management has become rare. (See the boxed reading on Japan for a recent exception – near the end of Section 3.)

So far the *AD/AS* model has been used to discuss the relationship between inflation and unemployment. It would help understanding further to introduce a model which focuses directly upon the inflation/unemployment relationship, rather than indirectly, via changes in real output. A macroeconomic model which does this is the Phillips curve model. However this is not a requirement of the standard level syllabus.

HL EXTENSION

THE PHILLIPS CURVE

In 1957 the New Zealand economist, AW Phillips undertook a study of the relationship between wage inflation and unemployment. His statistics confirmed a strong inverse relationship between the two. That is, high wage inflation was associated with low unemployment, and low wage inflation was associated with high unemployment. As wage costs form a very high percentage of total costs, and are strongly reflected in final prices, the Phillips relationship is more commonly depicted as the relationship between price inflation and unemployment. (This is generally known as the Phillips curve from its graph.) Phillips' initial study, which was of the UK economy, was repeated in other industrial countries and shown to be widely valid.

The Phillips curve is illustrated in Figure 3.45. The curve showed how unemployment and inflation were related in many countries for most of the nineteenth century, and right up until 1957, when Phillips undertook the study. It carried an uncomfortable message for government policy makers. Reducing unemployment below a certain level would cause increasing inflation, *ie* a move from point C to point B or point A. Reducing inflation involved accepting higher levels of unemployment, *ie* a move from point A to point B or point C.

Figure 3.45 – Phillips Curve Relationship between Unemployment and Inflation

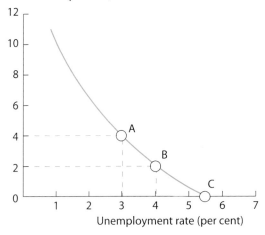

The trade-off shown by the Phillips curve can be linked to the *AD/AS* model explanation used earlier, Figure 3.46. Starting at point A on the Phillips curve, Figure 3.46(b), with low inflation and high unemployment, an increase in aggregate demand from AD_1 to

AD_2, Figure 3.46(a), raises output from point a to point b. The increase in inflation and fall in unemployment are shown as point B back on the Phillips curve Figure 3.46(b). During the 1950s and 1960s governments manipulated aggregate demand, using fiscal and monetary policy, to achieve the most politically acceptable balance between unemployment and inflation. While this situation posed difficult choices, they were to prove mild compared to what was to happen in the 1970s. During the 1970s, countries experienced very high rates of inflation, together with very high rates of unemployment, a situation which gave birth to the new term – *stagflation*. The plotted inflation/unemployment co-ordinates did not fall on the Phillips curve, but way above it and further to the right. A likely explanation for this is that the Phillips curve had shifted. Linking back again to the *AD/AS* model this can be illustrated: Figure 3.47. The *SRAS* curve shifted sharply to the left in the 1970s due to OPEC's action in raising oil prices by very large amounts. Oil is very widely used as a factor input, and so many other product prices rose as a result. As the price level rose, output fell – to point b in Figure 3.47. This inflation was accompanied by a fall in output and a rise in unemployment. For example, in the USA inflation rose from 8.7% to 12.3% while unemployment rose from 4.9% to 5.6%.

📊 Figure 3.46(a), Figure 3.46(b) – AD/AS model Phillips Curve model

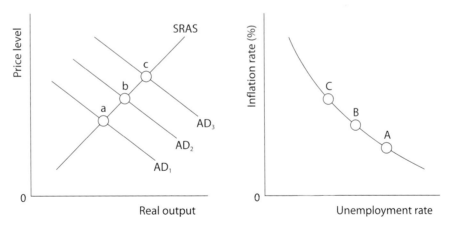

Starting at point A on the Phillips curve, Figure 3.46(b), with low inflation and high unemployment, an increase in aggregate demand from AD₁ to AD₂, in Figure 3.46(a), raises output and the price level from point a to point b. The increase in inflation and fall in unemployment are shown as point B on the Phillips curve.

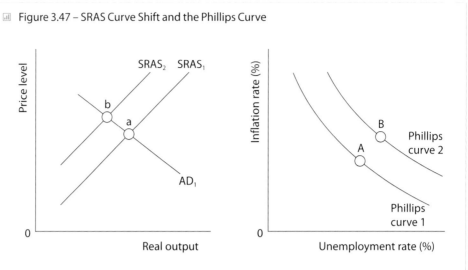

Figure 3.47 – SRAS Curve Shift and the Phillips Curve

SRAS curve shifts to the left due to oil price increases. Phillips curve shifts to the right.

From position *b* on the *AD/AS* graph, government attempts to expand demand to reduce unemployment caused inflation to rise to even higher levels. The increases in output and rising employment were offset by further shifts of the *SRAS* curve to the left, as wages chased prices in a wage-price spiral. The Phillips curve shifted further and further to the right.

A further development of the Phillips curve trade-off between unemployment and inflation is undertaken later in this section again, as an extension to the syllabus for higher level students. Meanwhile we can use the basic theoretical tools to illustrate the following important macroeconomic controversies:

I In the trade-off between unemployment and inflation which problem should be treated as a priority?
I Are the problems of unemployment and inflation better tackled by government, or by market-led strategies?
I What are the uses and limitations of monetary and fiscal policies?

IN THE TRADE-OFF BETWEEN UNEMPLOYMENT AND INFLATION WHICH PROBLEM SHOULD BE TREATED AS A PRIORITY?

This is a difficult question, and there is no single answer. It cannot be answered objectively while economists are divided as to how the macroeconomy works. There has to be greater certainty of knowledge. Then, even if there is agreement that there is a trade-off between unemployment and inflation, as we have shown in this analysis, there will still be subjective judgements as to the relative importance of each problem.

The real core of the objective argument lies in the shape of the *SRAS* curve. To conduct our earlier analysis we took a moderate view of the aggregate supply curve and showed the curve in the short-run to have a horizontal section, an upward sloping section and a vertical section. The consensus view is that economies normally operate on the middle or upward sloping section of the curve. Extreme Keynesians, however, believe the curve to be as in Figure 3.48(a): an L-shaped curve. Extreme monetarists argue that it is perfectly vertical as in Figure 3.48(b). A moderate, consensus view, is of two curves, short run and long run, as in Figure 3.48(c).

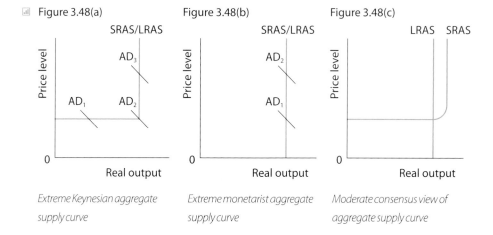

Figure 3.48(a)

Extreme Keynesian aggregate supply curve

Figure 3.48(b)

Extreme monetarist aggregate supply curve

Figure 3.48(c)

Moderate consensus view of aggregate supply curve

a The Keynesian Supply Curve

The curve becomes vertical at full employment Figure 3.48(a). An increase in aggregate demand from AD_2 to AD_3 cannot increase real output. It can only increase the price level. There is no disagreement, therefore, with the monetarists' vertical curve at the full employment level. Keynesians, however, argue that there is a horizontal section of the curve at lower levels of output. They claim that demand can fall to AD_1, with real output falling and unemployment rising, but without the price level falling. They argue that many final prices as well as wages are 'sticky' downwards. Prices and wages will either not adjust to keep the economy at full employment, or the adjustment process will be so slow as to be politically and socially unacceptable.[14]

b Monetarist Aggregate Supply Curve

The monetarist supply curve is assumed to be vertical throughout its whole length at the full employment level Figure 3.48(b). Any movement away from this point will bring an instant adjustment of markets. Thus the labour market always clears at the full employment level. The only unemployment will be natural unemployment. There will be jobs available at the going wage, the unemployed need only to 'get on their bikes' to find it. It may mean steelworkers accepting jobs as barmen, or textile workers being willing to waitress. It may involve labour moving to another part of the country.

c Moderate Consensus Aggregate Supply Curve

This is the modified Keynesian curve in the short run, with the economy normally functioning on the upward sloping middle section Figure 3.48(c). Here unemployment and inflation have a Phillips-type trade-off. In the long run the economy would be on a vertical *LRAS* curve at the full employment level. These were the *AS* curves assumed in the earlier analysis.

We return now to the question of the relative priority government should give to unemployment or inflation. Extreme monetarists would argue that employment is always at the natural rate. Any government attempts to reduce unemployment by expanding aggregate demand can only raise the rate of inflation and leave unemployment unchanged. Government priority should therefore be to control inflation. Strict control of the money supply is the government's central role, in order to give price stability. Monetary and fiscal policy to manage aggregate demand should not be undertaken, as unemployment cannot be increased by changing aggregate demand. Natural unemployment should be tackled by supply-side measures only.

Extreme Keynesians would have no problem with this analysis at full employment, but differ fundamentally below the full employment level. Here aggregate demand can be increased, from AD_1 to AD_2 in Figure 3.48(a) without raising inflation. The economy should be steered to where AD_2 cuts the $SRAS$ curve. Demand management should be undertaken by fiscal policy and monetary policy. A fundamental belief is that markets do not adjust easily, especially the labour market. Government must intervene to manage aggregate demand.

In this climate of uncertainty, the priority choice between unemployment and price control will be influenced by political persuasion. Politicians of the right tend to be supporters of market freedoms and hostile to government intervention. Politicians of the left tend to support government intervention and to be suspicious of market solutions. There is a human tendency to filter out unpleasant truths and to embrace easily those ideas one wishes to hear. In an area of controversy in macroeconomics it is therefore easy for anyone to claim priority for those policies which they wish to believe in.

ARE THE PROBLEMS OF UNEMPLOYMENT AND INFLATION BETTER TACKLED BY GOVERNMENT, OR BY MARKET-LED STRATEGIES?

We have already noted that there is considerable controversy in these areas. In the area of unemployment, for example, we noted that there is considerable disagreement as to whether the market works effectively in the labour market. Are wages 'sticky' downwards? Or does demand-deficient unemployment correct itself quickly by adjusting wages downwards? If the latter, the market wants and needs no government intervention. If it doesn't work because of market imperfections, *eg* labour unions are too strong and are holding real wages above their equilibrium level, or if government legislation on minimum wages or working hours is doing the same, then the answer is to remove the market imperfections. Make the markets work. Weaken the unions or the labour legislation.

If however the labour market does not work because wages are inherently different, that is, wages are not flexible as most other prices are, then it is arguable that government intervention is called for. Keynesian policy in a situation of cyclical unemployment would advocate increasing the aggregate demand for goods and services and thereby increase the demand for labour. This would involve demand management, *ie* using active fiscal and monetary policy.

In the area of inflation we have also met with controversy. Monetarists claim that inflation is always and everywhere caused by expanding the money supply. The government's overwhelming responsibility is to provide sound money. The government should ensure that the Central Bank is set up independently of political control. It should expand the money supply neutrally to match the growth of real output – and no more. Apart from sound money the government should only ensure conditions for the flourishing of markets.

Keynesians believe that inflation can be caused by changes in real variables, independent of the money supply. Thus demand-pull or cost-push inflation can occur independently. Money supply will increase as a *result* of the resulting inflation, *ie* increased money supply is the effect rather than the cause of inflation. Keynesians do agree that large changes in the money supply cause inflation but for regular smaller changes in money supply the relationship between money and prices is much weaker than claimed. Thus Keynesians would advocate direct government action to curb excess demand by deflationary demand management. This would involve fiscal and monetary policy. Cost-push inflation would also be tackled directly by a prices and incomes policy – a policy limiting, by law or consensus, increases in wages and prices.

Thus it is still a subject of debate as to whether government or market-based strategies are best for tackling unemployment and inflation. The consensus view has however swung away from advocating very active government demand management, as in the period from 1946 to the early 1970s. Since that time the consensus has been largely in favour of a market-based approach. In the Western industrial countries the shift has been dramatic. There has been extensive privatisation of the nationalised industries. There has been a greater awareness, and use, of market solutions. There have been greater attempts to control the money supply. There has been very little use of fiscal and monetary policy to manage demand. This move was paralleled and magnified in the late 1980s and 1990s in the USSR and Eastern Europe, as these countries abandoned central planning, the most direct form of government intervention. The former centrally planned economies are undergoing a process of privatisation of ownership, and an adoption of market resource allocation, on an unprecedented scale.

A Global Revolution in Banking

In 1988 the Group of 10, the world's largest economies, signed the Basel Accord, making international banking the first industry to be regulated at international level. The task of financial regulation had become too much for single country central banks. The Basel Accord was concerned with (i) capital adequacy provisions, specifying minimum financial backing for each type of credit risk; (ii) risk assessment, specifying the relative importance of different risks; and (iii) fit and proper rules for management conduct. This agreement was made necessary by a wave of financial reforms which had swept through the banking industry in the mid-1980s as banking globalized. In earlier days different sections of the banking market were separated and regulated, relatively informally in most cases, by central banks. The first European Centre to feel the wind of change was London, with the 'Big Bang' reforms of 1986. Banks were able to become market-makers on the Stock Exchange, Building Societies were allowed to compete with banks and across the globe the entry barriers to particular financial markets came tumbling down. The volume of business multiplied and so did the types of business transacted. New and fancier types of business were transacted. Computerisation increased the speed of business. When futures trader James Neilson single-handedly bankrupted Barings Bank by fraudulent deals on the Tokyo market from his base in Singapore, it was partly because his superiors had little idea of how the complex new markets worked, and Central Banks lacked control and ability to regulate.

WHAT ARE THE USES AND LIMITATIONS OF MONETARY AND FISCAL POLICY?

In a Centrally Planned Economy, government planners are able to take direct action to influence macroeconomic objectives – full employment, price stability, economic growth, and balance of payments. In a market economy most economic activity is under the control of individuals in the private sector. The government, however, is a powerful economic agent, and is able to use indirect methods to affect the private sector and macroeconomic variables like unemployment and inflation. There are two basic economic 'toolboxes' which a mixed economy government can use to steer the macroeconomy in the way that it wishes. These toolboxes are:

1 monetary policy
2 fiscal policy (or budgetary policy)

Monetary Policy

Monetary policy involves changing the money supply and the interest rate in order to affect the macroeconomy. The operation of monetary policy is the major responsibility of the country's Central Bank.[15] If the *GDP* is considered too low or too high, the Central Bank may intervene in order to change aggregate demand and spending in the economy.

Consider a situation where a Central Bank wishes to increase aggregate demand. In Figure 3.49 aggregate demand and aggregate supply (AD_1 and $SRAS$) cut to the left of the full employment level. Left alone, wages would fall shifting the $SRAS$ curve to the right. This would bring unemployment back to the natural rate at a real *GDP* of *$600 billion*. The time it takes for the labour market to adjust may, however, be unacceptably long for social and political reasons. The Central Bank may intervene to speed up the adjustment process. Monetary policy would dictate that it expands the money supply. Increasing the supply of money lowers the price of money, that is it lowers the interest rate.

Figure 3.49 – Monetary Policy to Increase Aggregate Demand

Price level (GDP deflator, 2004 = 100)

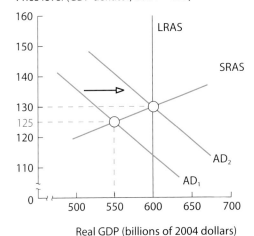

Real GDP (billions of 2004 dollars)

More money and lower interest rates increases aggregate demand from AD_1 to AD_2. This is to keep output at *$600 billion* and employment at the natural rate.

This is because the money market is similar to other markets. It is formed by the demand for, and the supply of money. The price of money is the interest rate. In Figure 3.50 the demand for money (*MD*) cuts the supply of money (*MS₁*), at a quantity of *$500 billion*, and at an interest rate of *5%*. The Central Bank increases the supply of money to *$600 billion* and this lowers the interest rate to *3%*. The increased supply of money and the lower cost of borrowing, both act to increase spending. The aggregate demand curve shifts to the right, to *AD₂* in Figure 3.49.

Figure 3.50 – Monetary Policy to Reduce the Interest Rate

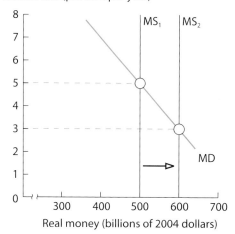

An increase in the money supply lowers interest rates.

If, on the other hand, aggregate demand is too high, at AD$_2$ in Figure 3.51, unemployment rises above the natural rate and the price level rises. Left alone, wages would rise, shifting the *SRAS* curve upwards and to the left, to cut *AD* and the *LRAS* curve at the natural rate of unemployment, at *$600 billion*. This is, however, at a higher price level. To prevent this situation of over-full employment and inflation, the Central Bank can act in order to reduce aggregate demand. In Figure 3.52 the Central Bank reduces money supply from *MS$_1$* to *MS$_2$* simultaneously raising the interest rate to *5%*. The combined shortage of money and the higher cost of borrowing reduces aggregate demand[16] back from *AD$_2$* to *AD$_1$*. Being able to adjust the money supply just sufficiently to keep aggregate demand at the full employment level does, however, require a combination of good luck and good judgement.

⊞ Figure 3.51 – Monetary Policy to Decrease Aggregate Demand

Price level (GDP deflator, 2004 = 100)

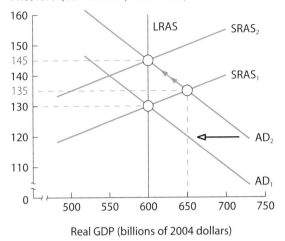

Real GDP (billions of 2004 dollars)

Less money and higher interest rates reduces aggregate demand from AD₂ to AD₁. This is aimed at keeping the price level stable at 130 instead of rising to 145.

⊞ Figure 3.52 – Monetary Policy to Reduce Inflation

Interest rate (per cent per year)

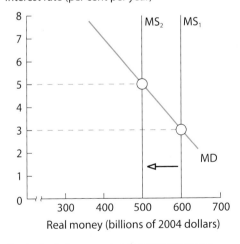

Real money (billions of 2004 dollars)

A reduction in the money supply raises interest rates.

Fiscal Policy

Fiscal policy is the use of tax and government spending measures to affect aggregate demand and the macroeconomy. Whereas monetary policy affects aggregate demand indirectly via changes to the money supply and the interest rate, fiscal policy acts directly on spending. The components of aggregate demand are: consumption, investment, government spending, exports and imports, *ie* $AD = C + I + G + X - M$. Government fiscal policy has considerable influence over two of these, consumer spending (C) and government spending on goods and services (G). If GDP is considered too low, as in Figure 3.49, the government could increase consumer spending by cutting taxes. This would increase consumer disposable income and consumers would spend more. Government spending would have to be maintained so that overall spending increases. That is, the government runs a deficit budget. It spends more than it collects in taxes. This would shift the AD curve to the right.[17] Alternatively the government could increase its own spending without increasing taxes.

If, on the other hand, the GDP and aggregate demand is considered too high and is thus inflationary, as in Figure 3.51, the government could cut consumer spending (C). It could do this by raising taxes, reducing disposable income and spending. It would not raise government spending *ie* it would run a surplus budget so that aggregate spending falls. Alternatively the government could reduce its own spending (G), without reducing taxes *ie* run a surplus budget.

Limitations of Monetary and Fiscal Policies

For many years there has been a fierce and ongoing debate between Keynesian and Monetary economists on the relative effectiveness of fiscal and monetary policies. Keynesian economists regard the economy as inherently unstable. They argue that active government intervention is necessary to maintain full employment and price stability. Keynesians regard monetary policy as relatively ineffective and advocate the use of fiscal policies to achieve stability.

Monetarists, on the other hand, regard the economy as inherently stable. They see the control of the money supply as being the most important factor in determining aggregate demand, and argue that fiscal policy is ineffective. This fierce debate is now largely settled. An intermediate view is the consensus position of most economists. Nevertheless it is interesting to take a brief look at the argument which divided macroeconomists for so many years. There follows a very brief summary of the two most extreme views of the argument to highlight the major issues.

Extreme Keynesians

The extreme Keynesian view is that changes in the government budget have a large effect on aggregate demand and that changes in the money supply have no effect at all on aggregate demand. For this money argument to hold, investment has to be completely insensitive to the interest rate, *ie* the investment demand curve has to be vertical. Alternatively, the demand for money has to be totally insensitive to the interest rate *ie* there is a horizontal demand curve for money.[18] If either of these circumstances prevail a change in the money supply has no effect on aggregate demand. Monetary policy either does not affect the interest rate, or if it does, a change in the interest rate does not affect investment and therefore spending.

Extreme Monetarists

Extreme Monetarists believe that fiscal policy has no affect at all on aggregate demand. On the other hand changes in the money supply have a large effect on aggregate demand. For this to occur, either the demand for investment has to be extremely sensitive to the interest rate *ie* be horizontal, or alternatively, the demand for money curve must be vertical. If the demand for investment is horizontal then any increase in government spending which increases interest rates will displace an equal amount of private investment. The fiscal expansion will be neutralised. (This process is known as 'crowding-out' – a part of the Higher Level extension which follows).

If the demand for money is fixed, *ie* the demand for money curve is vertical, no matter what the change in the interest rate the demand for holding money does not change. Any change in the supply of money is passed on totally as a change in spending.

The Intermediate Position

The intermediate position is that monetary policy and fiscal policy both affect aggregate demand. Following extensive testing of the opposing positions, the intermediate position seems to be the right one. The demand for money is sensitive to the interest rate *ie* the demand for money curve slopes downward. It is neither vertical nor horizontal. The demand for investment is also sensitive to the interest rate, *ie* the demand for investment also slopes downwards. Thus this particular macroeconomic controversy is largely settled. The *AD/AS* model used in this textbook is based upon this consensus intermediate position. There are other macroeconomic controversies, however, and the most debated currently is over the working of the labour market.

MULTIPLE CHOICE QUESTIONS – THE INFLATION/UNEMPLOYMENT DEBATE

Question 1 refers to the following diagrams

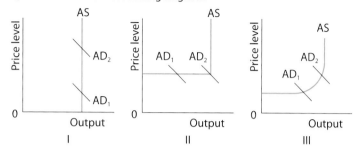

I   II   III

1   Which of the three aggregate supply curves illustrates a Keynsian view of an increase in aggregate demand from AD$_1$ to AD$_2$?

   A   I only   B   I and II   C   II and III   D   I, II and III

2   A governments main macroeconomic aim is to reduce unemployment. Which of the following policies would work against that aim?

   A   A revaluation of the exchange rate.

   B   A lowering of real interest rates.

   C   A cut in direct taxation.

   D   Increased government expenditure on retraining schemes.

3   The question refers to the AD/AS diagram below

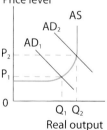

Real output

The shift from AD$_1$ to AD$_2$ could be explained by government action lowering

   I   interest rates.

   II   income taxes.

   III the nominal stock of money.

   A   I only   B   I and II   C   II and III   D   I, II and III

4   In a situation of full employment, if aggregate demand is bigger than aggregate supply the appropriate government policy according to a Keynsian is:

A   an expansionary fiscal and monetary policy.

B   an expansionary fiscal policy and a prices and incomes policy.

C   a contractionary fiscal and monetary policy.

D   a balanced budget and the introduction of supply side measures.

Question 5 refers to the diagram below

Rate of inflation

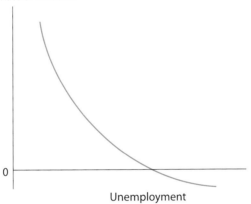

5   A short run Phillips curve like the one shown above is based on the assumption that

A   there are no trade unions.

B   money illusion exists in the economy.

C   there is no change in productivity.

D   governments adopt a policy of demand management.

6   In the macroeconomic circular flow model which of the following is an injection?

A   Taxation

B   Expenditure on imports

C   Saving

D   Expenditure on exports

7   The table below shows how three variables behaved over a two year period in a country X.

Year	Retail Price Index	Money Supply Index	Nominal GDP Index
1	100	100	100
2	115	100	105

It follows that in country X

A   the velocity of circulation has decreased.

B   the rate of inflation has fallen.

C   real income has fallen.

D   economic growth has increased.

8   Which of the following is NOT an instrument of fiscal policy?

A   A relaxation of credit controls.

B   A rise in income tax.

C   A cut in government spending.

D   A rise in subsidies to private industry.

9   According to monetarists, which of the following is would reduce the rate of natural unemployment?

A   Implementing minimum wage legislation

B   Reducing the mobility of labour

C   Increasing the volume of exports

D   Restricting the activities of trade unions

10 Which of the following is the best example of a 'supply side' policy?

A   Increased expenditure on training

B   An increase in direct taxation

C   A reduction in the money supply

D   An increase in the rate of interest

THE INFLATION/UNEMPLOYMENT DEBATE

The actual shape of the aggregate supply curve in an economy is crucial to the effectiveness of fiscal and monetary policy. The shape of the *AS* curve is therefore a central point of controversy between Keynesian economists and monetary economists. Section 3 of the IB course at Higher Level now returns to the wider Keynesian/Monetarist debate. Further theoretical tools are used to illustrate three of these controversies:

I The long run Phillips curve
I Whether 'crowding-out' occurs
I Whether taxes should be used for redistribution or whether the incentive effects of lower taxation are more important

THE LONG RUN PHILLIPS CURVE

In the Core Course (Standard Level) we used the Phillips curve model of the economy. This had an advantage over the *AD/AS* model in focusing attention upon the unemployment/inflation relationship. The *AD/AS* model deals only indirectly with these variables as changes in real *GDP* and the price level. Higher level students now need to develop their understanding of the Phillips curve further. 'Time' and 'expectations' are introduced into the model. The original Phillips curve is renamed the *short run Phillips curve* to distinguish it from the *long run Phillips curve* which is now developed. However we begin by looking at 'expectations'. In our previous study of inflation we noted that there is a difference between *anticipated* inflation and *unanticipated* inflation.

The inflation rate depends partly on people's *expectations* of the inflation rate. When businesses set prices, and when workers and firms negotiate wage rates, they take into account what they expect the inflation rate to be. If inflation is expected to be 5% in the coming year, all those involved in setting prices will want to increase their own prices by 5% at least, in line with inflation. Otherwise they will suffer a drop in real income.

ANTICIPATED INFLATION

If people correctly anticipate inflation, then expected inflation will equal actual inflation at the natural rate of unemployment. In the *AD/AS* model Figure 3.53 there is an increase in aggregate demand from equilibrium. (Equilibrium is where AD_1 cuts $SRAS_1$, on the *LRAS* curve, *ie* at the natural rate of unemployment.)

Figure 3.53

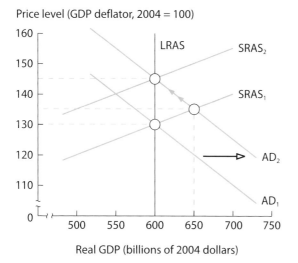

Real GDP (billions of 2004 dollars)

If people correctly anticipate inflation, then expected inflation will equal actual inflation at the natural rate of unemployment. In Figure 3.53 there is an increase in aggregate demand from equilibrium. The AD curve shifts to AD₂. Wage negotiators and other factor owners, however, have correctly anticipated the effect on inflation of the increased demand, and the SRAS curve shifts to the left as factor costs rise, a shift to SRAS₂.

The AD curve shifts to AD_2. Wage negotiators and other factor owners, however, have correctly anticipated the effect on inflation of the increased demand, and the $SRAS$ curve shifts to the left as factor costs rise, a shift to $SRAS_2$. Inflation increases as predicted (to a price level of *145*), but at the same level of real GDP (*$600 billion*). Unemployment remains unchanged at the natural rate. The cause of this inflation has been twofold. It has partly occurred because aggregate demand has increased, and partly because wages and prices increased in anticipation of the demand increase (*ie* the $SRAS$ curve shift). Because the anticipated inflation was correct the price level moved up as anticipated and unemployment remained unchanged.

UNANTICIPATED INFLATION

Inflation may be unanticipated. If, in the earlier example, aggregate demand increased by *more* than expected, then the AD and $SRAS$ curves will intersect to the right of the $LRAS$ curve. That is, real GDP will be higher than potential GDP. Unemployment will be lower than the natural rate.

Cost-push inflation can also be viewed as unanticipated inflation. Say the $SRAS$ curve shifts up to adjust to an expected increase in aggregate demand; but aggregate demand does not increase as much as is expected. The $SRAS$ and AD curves will now intersect to the left of the *LRAS* curve. That is, the actual real *GDP* will be below the potential real *GDP*. Unemployment will be higher than the natural rate.

In conclusion we note that real *GDP* only differs from potential *GDP* when inflation is incorrectly anticipated. Put another way, unemployment only departs from the natural rate when inflation is not anticipated. We can now return to the Phillips curve.

The Short Run Phillips Curve

The short run Phillips curve shows the relationship between inflation and unemployment when:

1 the expected rate of inflation is constant, and
2 the natural rate of unemployment is constant.

The short run Phillips curve in Figure 3.54 shows the inflation/unemployment trade-off at a natural rate of unemployment of *4%* and an expected rate of inflation of *8%*. There is a Phillips curve passing through this point, *a*, in the Figure.

📊 Figure 3.54 – The Short Run Phillips Curve

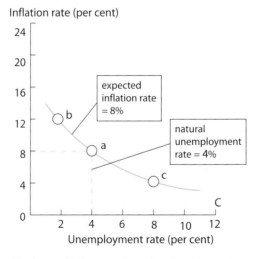

The short run Phillips curve shows the inflation/unemployment trade-off at a natural rate of unemployment of 4% and an expected rate of inflation of 8%. There is a Phillips curve passing through this point, a. If inflation rises above its expected rate, unemployment falls below the natural rate, point b. If inflation is lower than expected, unemployment rises above its natural rate, to point c.

If inflation rises above its expected rate, unemployment falls below the natural rate, point *b*, in the Figure. If inflation is lower than expected unemployment rises above its natural rate, to point *c* in the Figure.

This was the original Phillips curve. The importance of expectations had not arisen when Phillips undertook his study.

THE LONG RUN PHILLIPS CURVE

The *long run Phillips curve* (*LRPC*) shows the inflation/unemployment relationship when the actual rate of inflation is equal to the expected rate of inflation. The long run Phillips curve is vertical at the natural rate of unemployment – see Figure 3.55. This shows that there can be any rate of inflation at the natural rate of unemployment. This correlates with the explanation using the *AD/AS* model previously (Figure 3.53). If the actual rate of inflation is the same as the anticipated rate of inflation the real *GDP* remains at the potential *GDP* level, *ie* at the natural rate of unemployment. This point, the natural rate of unemployment is also known as *NAIRU*, the non-accelerating inflation rate of unemployment. This is the rate of unemployment which will exist when inflation is correctly anticipated and stable *ie* not accelerating.

At each point on the *LRPC* where the expected and actual rates of inflation are equal there is a short run Phillips curve. If in Figure 3.55 the expected rate of inflation falls to *6%* the short run Phillips curve shifts downwards to $SRPC_2$. Let us see what happens if the inflation rate falls, and expectations do not. From a situation of expected = actual inflation of *8%*, aggregate demand is reduced by the government, so that actual inflation falls to *6%*. However, people go on anticipating *8%* inflation. The situation of anticipated inflation being greater than the actual inflation is a situation where real *GDP* falls and unemployment rises above its natural rate. That is, there is a movement *along* the *SRPC* to point *b*, where actual inflation of *6%* correlates with unemployment of *6%*. As unemployment increases the wage rate adjusts down to a new lower expected rate of inflation. The economy is in equilibrium where the expected rate of inflation equals *6%*, the same as the actual rate of inflation at the natural rate of unemployment, point c on the long run Phillips curve.

📊 Figure 3.55 – The Long Run Phillips Curve

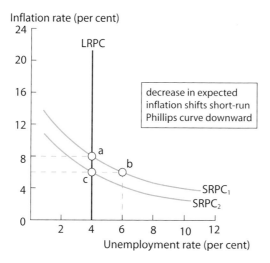

SRPC$_1$ is drawn at an expected inflation rate of 8%. SRPC$_2$ is drawn at an expected inflation rate of 6%. From point a expected inflation remains at 8%, when actual inflation falls to 6%. Unemployment rises to 6% – above the natural rate. Wages will begin to fall. When the expected rate of inflation falls to 6% equilibrium is restored at point c.

If expected inflation rises, the economy will move to a higher Phillips curve. If people underestimate expected inflation there will be a move leftwards along the *SRPC*. Unemployment will fall below the natural rate.

The natural rate of unemployment (*NAIRU*) will change if any of the component parts change, *ie* frictional, structural or seasonal unemployment. If, for example, the natural unemployment rate rose from *4%* to *8%* the long run Phillips curve would appear as a vertical curve at *8%* – see Figure 3.56. Short run Phillips curves would also shift to the right. In Figure 3.56 point *b* is where expected inflation of *8%* is equal to actual inflation of *8%*. The inflation rate is the same, but at a higher level of unemployment.

Figure 3.56 – Increase in Natural Unemployment

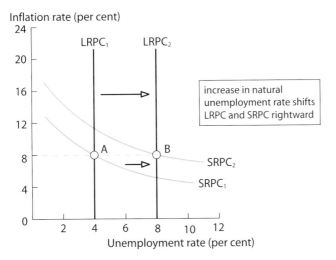

The natural rate of unemployment rises from 4% to 8%. Short run and long run Phillips curves shift to the right. Both points a and b are where expected inflation of 8% is equal to actual inflation of 8%.

THE PHILLIPS CURVE APPLIED TO RECENT EXPERIENCE

Up until the mid-60s the short-run Phillips curve explained the inflation/unemployment relationship very well. During the late 1960s, the 1970s, 1980s and 1990s much higher unemployment and inflation figures were experienced in industrial countries, the situation known as stagflation. The inflation/unemployment co-ordinates as in Figure 3.57 (UK figures) do not fit the original Phillips curve. This is partly because expected inflation became much more important, *ie* the short run Phillips curve shifted up to the right. It is also partly because the natural rate of unemployment shifted.

Figure 3.57 – The Phillips Curve Applied To Recent Experience

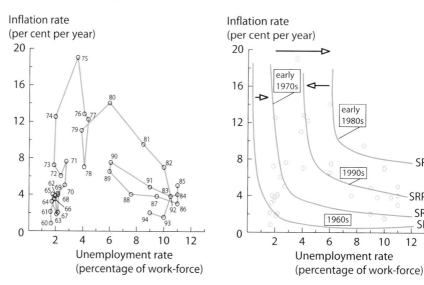

In the UK the cluster of points in the 1960s fits well to the Phillips curve with low expected inflation and a low natural rate of unemployment. The oil price shocks of the 1970s shifted expected inflation rates up and the natural rate of unemployment up to give short run Phillips curves above and to the right of that for the 1960s, explaining the stagflation statistics. With strong government monetary restrictions and supply-side measures in the 1980s, the expected rate of inflation fell. This, together with a fall in the natural rate of unemployment, led to the lower figures of the 1990s.

In the UK for example the cluster of points in the 1960s fits well to the Phillips curve with low expected inflation and a low natural rate of unemployment. The oil price shocks of the 1970s shifted expected inflation rates up and the natural rate of unemployment up to give short run Phillips curves above and to the right of that for the 1960s, explaining the stagflation statistics. With strong government monetary restrictions and supply-side measures in the 1980s, the expected rate of inflation fell. This, together with a fall in the natural rate of unemployment, led to the lower figures of the 1990s.

DOES CROWDING-OUT OCCUR?

At low levels of real *GDP*, Keynesian policy requires the government to increase spending in order to increase aggregate demand and job creation. The question arises as to whether this spending creates *additional* demand, or *replaces* private sector demand. There is an argument that it does replace or 'crowd-out' private sector investment.

Full crowding-out would occur if government spending replaces an equivalent amount of private investment. However full crowding-out will not occur if real *GDP* is less than potential *GDP, ie* the unemployment rate is above the natural rate of unemployment. In this situation there are idle resources which could be brought into employment. Neither would crowding out occur if government spending was on capital goods which were as productive as the private investment which it displaced. Thus government spending on roads, bridges, airports, schools, universities or education might be equally productive to the displaced private investment.

Crowding-out can occur however, when the economy is at or near full employment, if the government increases spending on goods and services by borrowing. That is, the government runs a deficit budget (if the extra spending was paid for by raising taxes, the increase in government demand would be offset by a fall in consumer demand). If the government runs a budget deficit this will increase the demand for loanable funds. The increased demand for loanable funds will raise the interest rate. The higher interest rate will reduce the demand for private investment, *ie* there is a movement along the demand for investment curve – see Figure 3.58. So the increased government borrowing displaces private sector borrowing and crowds out productive investment.

Figure 3.58 – Crowding-Out

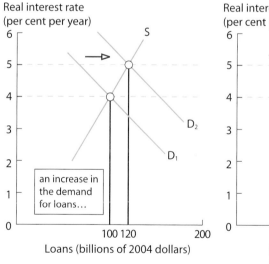

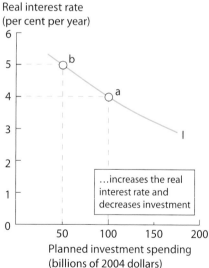

INCREASED GOVERNMENT BORROWING RAISES THE INTEREST RATE. HIGHER INTEREST RATES REDUCE OR 'CROWD-OUT' PRIVATE INVESTMENT

Japanese Fiscal Policy

In 1990/91 Japan began to slide into recession. The Japanese growth rate had slowed down and industrial growth was at an historic low. With a world recession and a rising value of the Yen the Japanese government was worried that there would be insufficient growth of exports, the traditional engine of the Japanese economy, to lift Japan out of the recession. In March of 1992 Mr Masaru Yoshimiti, head of the Economic Planning Agency, announced government measures to halt the decline and to allow the economy to reach its growth target of 3.5% in 1992. The package of economic measures would aim to increase public spending by at least Yen 4000 billion ($26 billion) in the next six months, with immediate effect. The package aimed to increase central government expenditure on public works and local government expenditure on public utilities such as gas, electricity and telecommunications. To allow for the increased spending the Japanese government seemed prepared to allow the money supply to increase. Interest rates were not to be allowed to rise and might even be cut. In other words the fiscal policy package would be backed up by an expansionary monetary policy.

Questions

1   Explain the connection between the government's concern for the economy and its fiscal policy?
2   Some of the increased spending was merely bringing forward spending already intended for later in the year. What would happen if all the increased early expenditure was of this type?
3   Do you see any evidence that the Japanese government has accounted for the problem of crowding out?

SHOULD TAXES BE USED FOR REDISTRIBUTION OR ARE THE INCENTIVE EFFECTS OF LOWER TAXATION MORE IMPORTANT?

Cutting direct taxes to increase the incentive to work and invest is central to supply-side economics. During the last twenty years many governments have reduced high rates of taxation for this reason. High rates of taxation are, however, a central plank in policies to redistribute income. The policy of efficiency conflicts with the policy of equity.

Governments use three main policy instruments to relieve poverty and redistribute income. They are:

| Income taxes
| Transfer payments
| Goods and services in kind

Income taxes may be progressive, proportional or regressive. A *progressive* income tax is a tax which increases with income. More precisely it is the marginal rate of tax[19] which increases with income. As a person's income rises he/she pays a higher tax rate on extra units of income. As lower rates of tax are paid on the first units of income, the average rate of tax paid is less than the marginal rate of tax ($ART < MRT$). A *proportional* income tax is one that taxes at a constant rate irrespective of the level of income. The average rate of tax is equal to the marginal rate of tax ($ART = MRT$). A *regressive* income tax is one that taxes income at a reducing marginal rate as income increases, *ie* the marginal rate of tax is lower than the average rate of tax ($ART > MRT$).

Most governments adopt progressive tax systems as a major tool in redistributing income from high earners to low earners. The process of redistribution, however, affects economic efficiency. Direct taxes reduce the reward to the factors of production and may negatively affect aggregate supply by reducing people's willingness to work, to invest or to take risk.

One economist[20] has likened the process of redistributing income to transferring water from one barrel to another with a leaky bucket. Some of the water leaks out of the bucket as water is transferred. As income is transferred some of it is lost. Several income leakages occur during income redistribution transfer. One of these is the disincentive effect to higher income earners. If they work less and save less due to higher taxes there is less output and income for everyone – rich and poor. Another leakage comes with administrating the scheme. Scarce labour and capital are employed and have an opportunity cost. They could be producing output rather than merely transferring it. There is also a dead-weight loss. A higher income tax reduces the opportunity cost of leisure and there is a substitution out of work into leisure – so output falls. The greater the degree of income equality sought by a society, the greater the resource cost in transferring it. Hence there is a big trade-off between equity and efficiency.

During the 1980s and into the 1990s most industrial countries shifted the emphasis in the trade-off from equity to efficiency. The shift formed part of the move to supply-side economics. Higher rates of income tax were cut very significantly in order to increase the incentive to produce. As a consequence income distribution has widened. (In the USA the process came under the heading of 'Reaganomics' and in the UK 'Thatcher economics', after notable tax-cutting political leaders.) There is no one 'correct' balance between these two objectives of equity and efficiency. The concept of 'fairness' is subjective. The distribution of income is revisited in the concluding part of Section 3 – Indicators of

Development, Poverty and Income Distribution.

THE LAFFER CURVE

Professor Laffer, an economic advisor to American President Ronald Reagan, was a strong advocate of direct tax cuts. He argued that cutting tax rates would both increase output and actually increase the total tax collected by the government. If cutting tax rates causes income to rise through an increased incentive to work, take risks, invest and so on then more tax would be paid on the increased income. Laffer argued that this gain in tax revenue would be greater than the loss incurred by cutting the rate of tax. The Laffer Curve in Figure 3.59 illustrates this. At a tax rate of zero no tax will be collected. As tax rates rise above zero more tax revenue will be collected. The curve will be upward sloping. Eventually the curve will peak (at t_1) and start to fall as higher tax rates discourage work and output falls. The tax revenue will continue to fall, reaching zero at a 100% tax rate where no one will work. The curve may well not be symmetrical of course, it might peak at 40%, 60% or 90%, it is not known. However the idea reinforced the will to cut direct taxes as part of the supply side measures in many countries over the last two decades.

Figure3.59 – The Laffer Curve

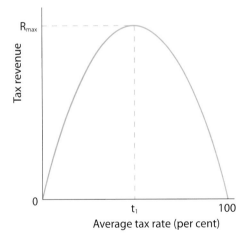

Less Tax – More Work?

A lower marginal rate of tax increases the reward for working and the opportunity cost of leisure. This encourages people to substitute more work for less leisure. This is the substitution effect. However lower tax rates makes people better off. The income effect makes them want to consume more leisure and work less. The net effect of tax cuts is the balance of the income and substitution effects. In the late 1990s existing evidence suggested that the effect of tax cuts on people in work is relatively small. Of more significance is whether people work at all. Tax cuts reduce the costs of working – commuting costs, childminding, foregoing welfare benefits *etc.* Evidence from CV Brown shows negligible effects for men and single women, but some effect on married women.

Prime Minister Margaret Thatcher set out on a major direct tax cutting programme in the UK on the basis that this would supply more work effort. It was the corner stone of the supply-side policy. The tax-free allowance, the amount a worker can earn before paying any tax at all, was increased by 25%. The basic rate of tax, paid by most workers was reduced from 33% to 25%. The top rate of tax, on the very highest income earners was reduced from 83% to 40%.

Questions

1 the substantial cut in the tax-free allowance had led to less than 0.5% of extra hours supplied.

2 the cut to the basic tax rate had no detectable effect.

3 the cuts to top peoples tax rates had a very small effect.
   Source: CV Brown 'Taxation, the Incentive to Work' OUP 1980

MULTIPLE CHOICE QUESTIONS – THE INFLATION/UNEMPLOYMENT DEBATE

1   Increased government spending either *'crowds out'* or *'does not crowd out'* private sector spending. Expansion of the money supply is either *'the main cause'* or just *'one possible cause'* of inflation. Select from the table below that combination which most accurately reflects the Keynsian and monetarist views to an increase in government spending and an expansion of the money supply.

	Effect of increased government expenditure on private expenditure		Effect of an expansion of the money supply on inflation	
	Monetarist view	Keynsian view	Monetarist view	Keynsian view
A	Crowds out	Does not crowd out	The main cause	One possible cause
B	Does not crowd out	Crowds out	The main cause	One possible cause
C	Crowds out	Does not crowd out	One possible cause	The main cause
D	Does not crowd out	Crowds out	One possible cause	The main cause

2   Increased government spending causes interest rates to rise and private sector investment to fall. This is an example of

A   the accelerator.

B   the liquidity trap.

C   crowding out.

D   fiscal drag.

3   A Laffer curve is illustrated below. It shows that

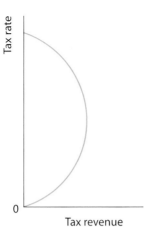

A   tax revenue rises as tax rates increase.

B   tax revenue falls as tax rates increase.

C   tax revenue falls as tax rates fall.

D   tax revenue at first rises with rising tax rates and then falls.

3.8   MEASURING ECONOMIC DEVELOPMENT

We have already noted that 'development' is not an easy concept to define and to measure. Therefore it is common practice to use 'indicators' of development instead. Each of these indicators is chosen as a close approximation to a characteristic which changes markedly during the process of development. For example the infant mortality rate is very closely correlated with the health of the population. Whilst health is a difficult concept to quantify, infant mortality is quantifiable and provides a good indicator of health. Health is also related to nutritional standards and health care provision so these too can be used as indicators of health.

By far the most frequently used single broad indicator of development is the GNP (or GDP) per capita and is the first to be examined here. However there are many shortcomings in using this indicator by itself. These will also be examined.[21] After GNP per capita we will look in turn at other major indicators. The section will conclude with an examination of some composite indicators. These are index numbers formed by combining two or more individual indicators to facilitate comparison, in order to improve over the use of GNP per capita alone.

For convenience of study this is sub-divided as follows

1 GNP/GDP Per Capita
2 Birth Rates, Population Growth And Structure
3 Life Expectancy, Health, Literacy
4 Energy Consumption
5 Rural-Urban Migration and Unemployment
6 Poverty and Income Distribution
7 Composite Indicators

1   GNP/GDP PER CAPITA

GNP per head is usually used as a 'summary index', and is often considered to be the best 'single indicator' of economic well being. The International Bank for Reconstruction and Development, the IBRD, more commonly known as the World Bank, classifies countries into three groups according to their GNP per capita (see Figure 3.60).

Figure 3.60 – World Bank Classification of Countries by GNP Per Capita

Classification	GNP per capita	Number of countries
Low income	$755 or less	64
Lower Middle Income	$756 to $2995	40
Higher Middle Income	$2996 to $9265	51
High Income	more than $9266	51

Source: World Bank: World Development Indicators 2001

Measured by GNP statistics 25% of the people in the world produce over 80% of total output, with 75% of people producing only 20% of output. Since consumption patterns closely mirror production patterns these figures highlight the huge gap between the few rich and the many poor. Figure 3.61 illustrates the gap in GNP per capita for a range of countries selected from each income group.

Figure 3.61 – GNP Per Capita of 12 Nations (1999 $ US)

	Country	GNP per capita	Rank
High income countries	Switzerland	38380	3
	United States	31910	8
	Singapore	24150	22
	Australia	20950	27
	Spain	14800	39
Middle income countries	Argentina	7550	58
	Uruguay	6220	64
	Poland	4070	74
	Slovak Rep.	3770	77
	Malaysia	3390	84
	Botswana	3240	87
	Philippines	1050	133
Low Income countries	China	780	149
	India	440	163
	Bangladesh	370	170
	Sierra Leone	130	204
	Ethiopia	100	207

Source: IBRD, World Development Indicators 2001

Whilst GNP per capita is the most common method of comparing living standards, it is far from satisfactory and attempts are being made to find acceptable methods with fewer problems.

At this stage revise the difference between GNP and GDP which was covered at the beginning of Section 3. This is relevant at this point. Developed countries, home to nearly all the world's multinational companies usually receive net income *from* abroad, that is their GNP is larger than their GDP. By contrast most developing countries make income payments abroad so that their GNP is often smaller than their GDP. Net international payments are *to* abroad. Thus the income gap between rich and poor countries appears smaller than it really is by using GDP rather than GNP figures.

If we now look at really meaningful measures of the living standard of people; whether their lives are short or long, whether they are healthy or not, whether they are educated or not, we can note a very obvious correlation to GNP per capita: see Figure 3.62.

Figure 3.62 – Correlation between GNP Per Capita and Indicators of Living Standards

Country	GNP per capita ($US 1998)	Life expectancy	Infant mortality (1997)	Adult illiteracy
		Male/Female		Male/Female
Congo	110	46/51	92	15/30
Sierra Leone	140	36/39	170	…/…
Mozambique	210	44/47	135	43/75
Uganda	320	43/42	99	25/47
Nigeria	300	52/55	77	31/49
Ghana	390	58/62	66	23/43
Zimbabwe	610	51/54	69	6/12
Colombia	2600	67/73	24	9/9
Mexico	3970	69/75	31	8/12
Argentina	8970	70/77	22	3/4
Australia	20300	76/81	5	Negligible
Japan	32380	77/83	4	Negligible
Denmark	33260	73/78	6	Negligible

Source: World Bank, World Development Report 2000; Tables 1, 2 and 7

There are exceptions to these correlations with GNP per capita however, so do be aware of the limits to defining countries solely by this measure. To illustrate such exceptions Figure 3.63 tables four countries with fairly low-incomes and yet high life expectancy. Three well-off countries with more modest life expectancy are also listed. The exceptions occur because 'other things are not constant'. Poor countries may have relatively high living standards by distributing their income fairly evenly. Brazil by contrast has a very wide distribution of income. Countries getting rich quickly through a 'windfall gain', as in the case of Oman and Saudi Arabia may need more time to raise living standards.

Figure 3.63 – Non-Correlation of GNP Per Capita and Living Standards

Country	GNP per capita ($US 1991)	Life expectancy (1991) Male/Female
China	750	68/71
Sri Lanka	810	71/75
Jamaica	1680	72/77
Costa Rica	2780	74/79
South Africa	2880	62/68
Gabon	3950	52 (average)
Brazil	4570	63/71
Saudi Arabia	7230	69/72

Source: IBRD, World Development Report 1993, Table 1

USES AND LIMITATIONS OF NATIONAL INCOME ACCOUNTS

National income statistics are some of the most useful and widely used figures available to the economist. However, there are problems in measurement and some major deficiencies in the end figure. All students must be aware of these shortcomings before using NI statistics as measures of total final economic output.

Thus GNP per capita is the most commonly used single indicator of the standard of living within a country, and for comparing countries. Indeed 'LDCs' and 'MDCs' countries are defined in this way. However the problems and shortcomings of using GNP per capita as though it were the same thing as standard of living are great. Students must exercise great caution in coming to conclusions when usng these statistics. Some of the major problems of using GNP per capita are now discussed.

NON-MARKET OUTPUT

The national income statistics are an aggregate of all economic activity that is recorded. Any economic output that does not pass through a market is omitted, or is estimated. This has long been recognised as a weakness of the GNP figures, even in their designed function of measuring total economic output. Thus in a developed country many people do unrecorded work *eg* housework, and 'do it yourself' activities. This non-market activity is either ignored, like the output of housewives, or estimated and added in, as for example the 'rent' that the owner-occupier would pay for using his house if he didn't own it!

There is also the deliberate non-declaration of market transactions to evade tax payment. Some widely varying estimates have been made as to the size of the parallel economy. (One method of doing this is to use the difference between declared national income and actual national expenditure, to obtain an estimate of the concealed element of income.)

The problem is magnified when international comparisons between countries are attempted. Different economic behaviour leads to different GNP figures. For example, most Swedish women work in the market place and pay for child care, convenience foods, laundry, and labour saving household appliances. A greater proportion of Spanish women are housewives and care for their families more directly and personally. The statistics suggest a greater output proportionately in Sweden to Spain than is in fact the case.

The difference is more marked the more different is the lifestyle. It is characteristic of many LDCs that a large part of rural output is for 'subsistence'. Thus a large proportion of families in the population may consume a great deal of their own production. These activities are likely to be very extensive compared to an industrialised country, and include growing and preparing food, carrying water and firewood, building accommodation, caring for children and entertainment. There is also a large informal sector (*ie* unrecorded economic activity) in the slums surrounding the cities. Here you will find service activities like bicycle repair, car washing, haircutting, retailing of soft drinks, thieving and prostitution. There will be simple manufacturing of pottery, stoves and other metal products. These activities will recycle every kind of scarce material from tin cans to plastic bags and bottles.

Estimates of these unrecorded activities are open to very large margins of error, and the wide diversity of countries gives a wide diversity of measurement.

The Value of a Housewife or Househusband

How can we put a value on housework, the output of those people whose work it is to look after their own home? That there is output in the form of services is clear – in the form of washing, ironing, shopping, cooking, cleaning, looking after children etc. But how can this non-market output be given a monetary value?

One way is to estimate the value of housework directly. This measures the number of hours of housework done in a week and attributes a cost per hour based upon the market rate to hire someone to do this work commercially.

An alternative method of valuing the services of housewives/househusbands is to price the work that they forgo by not participating in the market place. That is, we measure the opportunity cost to society of these people not working in the formal economy. This then gives a measure for the under-recording of the measured GNP.

MILITARY SPENDING AND INVESTMENT

GNP figures include all forms of production and spending. What is produced, however, is critical to the well being of the population. High levels of military spending have a high opportunity cost in lowering the consumption of civilian goods. High investment also reduces current consumption. Thus two countries with similar GNP per capita figures could have widely varying standards of living.[22]

POLLUTION, IRREPLACEABLE EXTRACTION, LEISURE

Pollution lowers the quality of life. Yet economic activities to reduce pollution add to the GNP. Thus if a new airport creates noise to nearby residents and they double-glaze their windows to reduce noise pollution, the activity of the airport is included in GNP in total. Then an additional amount is included for the defensive double-glazing activity which was not necessary before the airport was built.

No account is taken in GNP tables for the using up of non-renewable resources such as oil, minerals and hardwoods. The extraction of these gifts of nature swell the current national income but deplete the national wealth. They are not sustainable.

Neither is any account taken of increased leisure in GNP tables. Few would disagree that increased leisure is a plus factor in judging standard of living. Yet increased leisure is not accounted for in National Income tables. Indeed more leisure may mean lower GNP as work hours fall.

GNP figures

By standard accounting methods increased road accidents create growth of GNP! Increased road accidents cause output to expand in industries like motor insurance, vehicle repair, vehicle replacement, hospital care and funeral services.

DISTRIBUTION OF INCOME

The GNP per capita figure is an average. Two countries each with an identical GNP per capita could have widely differing degrees of poverty. For example, Hungary has a very even distribution of income, Brazil a very uneven one. Both had a similar level of GNP per capita in 1989. However if we compared the richest 20% with the poorest 20% in each country, the richest Hungarians received three times the income of the poor. In Brazil the figure was 26 times.

This is why pursuing economic growth may, in itself, do nothing to reduce poverty. The growth of GNP in many poor countries may represent the growth in incomes of the richest income earners whilst incomes of the poor stagnate. Average income statistics like GNP per capita will fail to show this.

EXCHANGE RATES

To compare the national incomes of different countries the GNP in the local currency is converted to United States dollars by using the exchange rate. This can be very misleading as exchange rates are often heavily influenced by speculative capital flows. Even if goods and services alone are considered, the exchange rate reflects only those goods and services which are internationally traded. For example, the trade in coffee has a very important affect on the exchange rate of Uganda as it forms 90% of the value of all exports, yet coffee forms only a tiny part of household expenditure by Ugandans.

Moreover, exchange rates are frequently managed by governments. The price of the currency is often very different from its free market value.

CONCLUSION

Despite problems, GNP remains a very useful measure of marketed national output. Its common use to compare living standards, across a wide range of countries, and ranking them like competing teams in a football league – is however, expecting too much of this statistic.

Nevertheless, GNP per capita does correlate reasonably well with more complex definitions of what is meant by 'standard of living'. It represents the best *single* indicator we have. This only serves to highlight the absence of, and need for, a better measure.

2 BIRTH RATES, POPULATION GROWTH AND STRUCTURE

BIRTH RATES

The crude birth rate is one of the easiest ways of distinguishing LDCs from MDCs. The crude birth rate in low income countries as a group is 30 per thousand, twice that of developed countries at 14 per thousand, (see Figure 3.64). Death rates on the other hand have been reduced significantly in LDCs in the last three decades. The natural increase in population, that is the birth rate minus the death rate, is thus much higher in less developed countries than developed countries, at 2% as against 0.5%.

As more than three quarters of the world's population live in the LDCs already (Figure 3.64), and their growth of population is so high, the development problem is growing bigger not smaller. If population were to continue to grow at present rates, by the year 2025 the population of the MDCs will have increased from 1.22 billion (1992) to 1.39 billion, an increase of 0.17 billion. However the LDC population will have increased by 2.95 billion in that time, that is from the current 4.2 billion to 7.15 billion.

Finally the age structure of LDC populations differs from that of MDCs. About one third of the populations of low income countries are under 15 years of age compared to a fifth in high income countries. Even though MDCs have more retired people, the dependency burden, that is the ratio of non-workers to workers, is greater in LDCs. Having such a youthful population has in addition, significant implications for the future population growth.

Figure 3.64 – Population

Region	Estimate (mid-1992)	Birth rate (per 1000)	Death rate (per 1000)	Natural increase[1] (%)	Doubling time[2] (years)	% aged /65+
World	5420	26	9	1.7	41	33/6
More developed	1224	14	9	0.5	148	21/12
Less developed	4196	30	9	2	34	36/4
Africa	654	43	14	3	23	45/3
Asia	3207	26	9	1.8	29	33/5
Latin America	453	28	7	2.1	34	36/5

[1] figures may be inexact due to rounding

[2] at the current rate of increase

Source: 1992 World Population Data Sheet, Population Reference Bureau, Inc.

POPULATION GROWTH

Over the last 50 years world population has grown very rapidly compared to any previous time. Most of this increase is in the Less Developed Countries. High population growth is associated with LDCs and low population growth with MDCs.

A study of population is thus central to a study of development. The issue is by its very nature personal and sensitive, and often gives rise to subjective and prejudiced opinion. World population growth needs to be studied in order to understand its impact upon the process of development. We also look at the process in reverse and ask how population growth is affected by development.

There is considerable disagreement about the effect of population increase upon development. One important reason is that more people provide more output with their labour and minds as well as providing more mouths to feed. However the balance of current informed opinion is that rapid population growth tends to worsen poverty.

There is, however, widespread agreement that it is poverty which causes rapid population growth. Thus any policies aimed at slowing the growth of population must concentrate on the reduction of poverty in order to bring about the desire for fewer children per family. In this regard a better understanding of why people have children is a key to understanding the reasons for population increase. Policies aimed at slowing population growth without tackling its cause, namely poverty, are unlikely to succeed.

The large size of some existing populations, and their present high rates of growth, mean that many governments are actively encouraging a slow down as part of their over-all development plan.

The study of population begins by looking at population statistics to acquire some factual knowledge of population size, distribution and growth.

THE FACTUAL BACKGROUND – A STATISTICAL REVIEW

The history of human population on earth is one of almost continuous growth. However recent growth rates are acting upon a large absolute population base and therefore give unprecedented increases in total numbers of people.

At the end of the hunter-gathering era and the beginning of settled agriculture about 12,000 years ago, the world's population is estimated to have been about 100 million. This had increased to about 1.7 billion at the start of the industrial revolution 200 years ago. By 1945 population had increased to 2.5 billion. By 2000 it had increased to 6 billion and it is estimated to increase to 8.2 billion by 2025.

ABSOLUTE SIZE

Some of the poorest countries in the world are also the most populous. Figure 3.65 shows that seven out of ten of the largest countries are in the Third World, five of them in Asia. Two countries alone account for 37.7% of the world's people, that is, roughly two out of every five people on earth are either Chinese or Indian.

GROWTH OF POPULATION

High population growth is a characteristic of LDCs. All of the twelve large countries (and several smaller ones) which have population growth rates of 3.5% or more are Third World countries. Seven are in Africa and five in the Middle East. Their populations will double in 20 years or less (see Figure 3.66).

Figure 3.67 shows clearly why population is a development issue. The three poor continents, Africa, Asia and Latin America have much faster population growth rates than the industrialised continents of Europe and North America and the countries of the former USSR.

AGE STRUCTURE OF LDC POPULATIONS

Children under 15 form 40%–50% of LDC populations, resulting in a very high dependency ratio of children to workers. Children form only 25% of the population of MDCs, but even with a greater proportion of old people the dependency ratio is much lower. These high numbers of young people will also ensure that population growth will continue, even if the birth rate falls, as there are greater absolute numbers of future parents already alive. This is why demographers can be certain of future population growth even if the size of individual families falls.

Figure 3.65 – The Ten Largest Countries in the World by Population Size (1999)

Country	Population (millions)
China	1261
India	1016
USA	282
Indonesia	210
Brazil	170
Russian Fed.	146
Pakistan	138
Bangladesh	130
Japan	127
Nigeria	127

Source: World Bank: World Development Indicators 2002

Figure 3.66 – Twelve of the Fastest Growth of Population Countries

	Average Annual Growth rate (1990-98)	Doubling time (years)
Jordan	5.2	14
Yemen	4.7	15
Niger	3.9	18
Saudi Arabia	3.9	18
Angola	3.8	19
Turkmenistan	3.6	20
Congo	3.6	20
Uganda	3.5	20
Togo	3.4	21
Nigeria	3.3	22

Source: World Bank: World Development Report 2000

⊞ Figure 3.67 – Population Size, Growth Rate and Doubling Time by Continent

	Size (millions) 1998	Growth rate (percentage) 1990–98	Doubling time (years)
World	5897	1.6	45
Sub Saharan Africa	628	3.0	23
E. Asia & Pacific	1817	1.5	48
L. America & Caribbean	502	1.9	38
M. East & N. Africa	285	2.6	28
Europe & C. Asia	473	0.2	338
South Asia	1305	2.1	34

Source: World Bank: World Development Report 2000

THE FOUR STAGES OF DEMOGRAPHIC TRANSITION

There has been a pattern to the growth of population in the industrialised countries. They have passed through four distinct stages of demographic change. It is instructive to look at the present day LDCs to see whether they too might be passing through the same four stages (generalised birth and death rates of Western Europe are given in Figure 3.68).

⊞ Figure 3.68 – The Four Stages of Demographic Transition in Western Europe

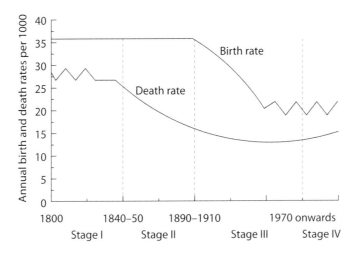

Source: Berelson, World Population: Status Report 1974.

Stage one represents the pre-industrial era, characterised by high birth rates and high death rates and thus a relatively stable population growth. The fluctuating death rate reflects frequent mass fatalities from diseases like typhoid and cholera.

Stage two sees rapid population growth, for whilst the birth rate remains high the death rate falls dramatically. The death rate declines as a result of increased incomes, improved diet and public health measures, such as ensuring drinking water is clean and separated from sewage.

The third stage sees the death rate fall further, with further improvements to diet and public health care. The birth rate continues to decline. As the birth rate is higher than the death rate, the population continues to increase.

Stage four has low birth and death rates leading again to low stable population growth.

There are some similarities with present day LDCs and also some important differences (Figure 3.69).

Figure 3.69 – Demographic Transition in Less Developed Countries

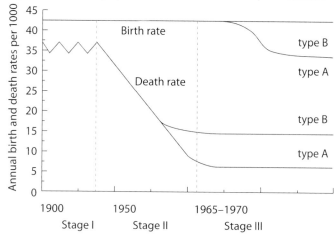

Source: Berelson, World Population: Status Report 1974.

Most LDCs have moved from stage one to stage two and some into stage three. However both birth rates and death rates in stage one are considerably higher than the corresponding ones in the developed countries. Secondly the population increase associated with stage two is over a much shorter time span.

In countries with even income distribution the death rate has fallen to First World levels, and the birth rate is also falling eg Costa Rica, Chile, Sri Lanka, Taiwan and China (type A countries in Figure 3.69).

However in most poor countries the death rate has levelled out at a higher level and the birth rate has remained high (type B countries). This is because in most LDCs there is still widespread poverty.

The real key to lowering the population growth rate is to reduce the birth rate, Figure 3.70. The death rate in LDCs will fall to First World levels (though these are unadjusted for the different age structures *ie* MDCs have ageing populations and LDCs increasing numbers of children, which affects the comparison). However birth rates, whilst falling, remain high at twice that of MDCs.

Figure 3.70 – Comparison of Birth Rates and Death Rates

	Crude birth rates 1960–2000			Crude death rates 1960–2000		
	1960–1965	1980–1985	1995–2000	1960–1965	1980–1985	1995–2000
World	34.0	28.1	23.8	14.4	10.6	8.7
MDCs	20.3	15.9	14.9	9.0	9.7	10.1
LDCs	40.0	32.1	26.2	16.8	10.9	8.3

Source: UN. World Population Trends and Prospects, 1950–2000, New York.

CONCLUSION

High population growth is associated with poverty. Birth rates remain high whilst death rates fall. Certainly GNP per capita is highly correlated with population growth. So is income distribution, however. It is the poverty resulting from one or both of these factors which causes the birth rate to remain high.

3 LIFE EXPECTANCY AND HEALTH

A marked characteristic of a less developed country is the poor health of its people. Whilst the evidence of disease and malnutrition are very visible in a poor country, 'health' itself is too intangible to be measured with any degree of precision.

There are however certain things which can be measured which do give a good 'indication' of whether someone enjoys good health or not. The two most commonly used indicators measure the effective consequences of good or ill health *ie* (1) infant mortality, (2) life expectancy.

Two other widely used indicators of health are measures of known nutritional requirements for the human body *ie* (3) calories per day (4) protein per day. Finally, medical care which aids health maintenance is often measured by: (5) number of doctors, (6) number of hospital beds per 100,000 people. We look at each of these indicators, in turn, below.

1 The infant mortality rate is the number of live-born babies who do not survive to their first birthday out of each thousand babies born in total (see Figure 3.71).

⊞ Figure 3.71 – Infant Mortality Rates and Life Expectancy for Selected Countries

	Infant Mortality per thousand	Life expectancy at birth
World	68	67
More developed countries	6	78
Less developed countries	69	63
Afghanistan	147	46
Somalia	121	48
Zambia	114	38
Pakistan	90	63
Bangladesh	61	61
Bolivia	59	62
Ghana	57	58
Brazil	32	67
China	30	70
Chile	10	76
Canada	5	79
Netherlands	5	78
Sweden	4	79
Japan	4	81

Source: World Bank Atlas 2001; World Bank: Development Report 2000. World Bank Atlas 2002

2 Life expectancy at birth is the average number of years new-born babies can be expected to live if health conditions stay the same. In developing countries life expectancy is lower for all people than it is in industrial countries, Figure 3.71. However it is very much lower for infants and children. In MDCs (more developed countries) deaths of children under five years of age account for 1.3% of all deaths whilst in LDCs (less developed countries) the figure is 10.5% (1986).

The reasons for premature death are poor quality drinking water, poor sanitation, inadequate nutrition for pregnant women and infants, and poor health care provision. Many people fall victim to polio, measles, diphtheria, tetanus, tuberculosis, whooping cough, flu, diarrhoea, pneumonia, typhoid, cholera and malaria. Remedies for these are generally both cheap and effective, and largely account for the marked improvement in the infant mortality rate over the last thirty years. Thus the number of infants surviving their first year of life in LDCs rose from 88% in 1965 to 93% in 1986. This in turn improved the life expectancy from 58 years in 1965 to 67 years in 1986. However whilst the gap is closing there are still areas of very high infant mortality and low life expectancy especially in sub-Saharan Africa. The life expectancy for the poorest 42 LDCs in 1988 for example was 49 years compared to 74 years in the MDCs.

3 Calories per day. Calorie deficiency is a cause of malnutrition. The body has insufficient food to provide energy and to maintain good health. In the selection of countries in Figure 3.72 it can be seen that some countries have 'developed' significantly on this criteria, but others, mainly in Africa have worsened over the 20 years shown.

Figure 3.72 – Daily Calorie Supply per Head

Country	Calories per day	
	1965	1986
United States	3292	3682
West Germany	3143	3519
France	3303	3358
Libya	1923	3585
Saudi Arabia	1866	3057
China	2034	2620
Venezuela	2321	2485
Bolivia	1868	2171
Nigeria	2185	2129
India	2100	2126
Bangladesh	1964	1804
Chad	2303	1733
Mozambique	1982	1617

Source: The World Bank, The Development Data Book

4 Protein per day. Type of food is just as important as quantity of food in the maintenance of good health. Lack of protein for example is a common cause of malnutrition. If a child receives insufficient protein during the mothers pregnancy and the first few years of life, his/her brain cannot fully develop. Protein deficiency is also a common cause of rickets, a softening of the bones. Clearly, therefore, malnutrition has serious implications not just for current health but for the future productivity of a population – the ability to work effectively.

5 Population per physician.

6 Population per hospital bed. Medical care is very scarce in poor countries. Measures commonly used as a proxy for the quality of available health care are the number of people there are per doctor, or per hospital bed. Some of the least well provided countries are contrasted with industrialised countries in Figure 3.73.

Figure 3.73 – Population per Doctor 1990

	Population per doctor				
Less developed countries				Industrial countries	
Rwanda	72990	Ethiopia	32650	Japan	610
Burkina Faso	57320	Ghana	22970	Canada	450
Malawi	45740	Kenya	10130	Austria	230

Source: IBRD World Development Report 1993, Table 28

LITERACY RATES

The greatest efforts of most LDCs have gone into raising levels of literacy, the ability to read and write. However standards still remain very low. Literacy is a development objective in its own right. It is used as an indicator of wider development issues however. It has strong connections with education, openness to change and labour productivity.

There are problems in defining 'adult illiteracy' and there are several working definitions in use. The World Bank defines it as that proportion of the population over the age of 15 who cannot, with understanding, read and write a short, simple statement about their everyday life.

On this definition Figure 3.74 illustrates the magnitude of the problem by income group, with some specific examples.

Figure 3.74 – Adult Illiteracy

	Adult illiteracy	
	Female %	Male %
Low income economies	42	22
Middle income economies	16	10
High income economies	...	...
Argentina	3	3
Costa Rica	5	5
Mexico	11	7
Algeria	14	23
Pakistan	70	41
Bangladesh	70	49
Guinea Bissau	82	42
Burkino Faso	87	67
Niger	92	77

Source: World Bank, World Development Report 2000, Human Development Report 2001

Ram Prasad and Somi – India

Ram Prasad (born around 1962) is the fifth of the six sons of Sagwa. Sagwa died in about 1966 and his elder brother Jabre helped to look after the family. But Jabre seems to have taken some of Sagwa's land under his own name. As a result, of the 27 acres originally inherited jointly by Jabre and Sagwa, Jabre (and his three sons) took about 18 acres, and Sagwa's six sons only had about 9 acres between them. Sagwa's sons were then given 6.5 acres of low-lying land near the Ganges by the state government. But in 1979 the government compulsorily repurchased this land to build a barrage across the river, about 5 kilometres from Dharmnagri. Ram Prasad and his brothers were entitled to Rs 130,000 in compensation, but have only received Rs 20,000 so far, despite regularly bribing the village headman and land revenue officials to pay out what is owed to them. Over time, Ram Prasad has sold about half an acre of the land he inherited, and is now left with one acre of land which he has rented out to his cousin, Ram Kishan.

None of the six brothers is doing very well. One brother, Raja Rao, has TB and depends on his wife's family. Another brother, Dharm Vir, has only one eye and had to borrow money when his wife needed a caesarean section for their second child. He has also mortgaged his land to Ram Kishan, and works as a labourer on a farm about 5 kilometres away. The other three brothers largely support themselves from their own land. The oldest, Sita Ram, has half an acre more than the others, and he and the youngest, Vijai Pal, rent land from others to increase their income. All the brothers do other labouring work when they can get it as well. Ram Prasad and Vijai Pal are better educated than the others, having been to school to sixth or seventh class. So they can read and write Hindi and know the English script as well.

Ram Prasad married Somi in 1980, when she was about 15. Somi comes from a village 25 kilometres away. She now has four children – girls (Siobhan and Sundari) born in 1983 and 1987, and boys (Devinder and Dharminder) born in 1985 and 1989. Since Devinder was born Somi has repeatedly said she would like no more children, but she is scared of sterilisation and Ram Prasad's mother is also against the idea. They have been using condoms since 1990. Somi now spends most of her time looking after the children and doing domestic work. On the occasions when they have milch cattle she has to do the feeding and milking, and the making of dung-cakes. She and her sisters-in-law do not get on well, and none of them helps out with the work of any of the others.

Ram Prasad and Somi would like their children to go to school but have not made any arrangements yet. Siobhan is already eight but it is common for girls to be held back from starting school so they can help their mothers and also start school with a younger brother. Devinder was six when this programme was made and he should have started school. But overall in the village only a third of the 5-9 year old girls are in school, and half of the boys. People have a very low opinion of the state schools. Even though no fees are charged, many parents cannot afford to provide children with decent clothing, school text books, notebooks, pens and pencils. Sending the children to private schools costs at least an extra Rs 50 per month, beyond the purse of the landless and poor peasants. Even so, many poor families do feel that education will help their children to obtain jobs.

Ram Prasad has had little help from his brothers since he left school, and has tried a variety of ways to support himself and his family. When he was 16 or 17 he went to Saharanpur (100 kilometres away) and worked as a kitchen boy to a Punjabi family, who taught him basic middle-class Indian cuisine. He also worked as a cook. Then he worked his own land for a while, getting a government loan for a buffalo (which later died), acting as a watchman for three months a year (at Rs 600 per month) for a small mango orchard nearby, and then cycling a rickshaw in Bijnor town. He paid off half the loan for the rickshaw, but in July 1990 went back to being a cook. In June 1991 Ram Prasad started to ride the rickshaw again, but he had failed to keep up the payments on his old rickshaw and had to start on a new contract with the rickshaw owner. Then he fell sick and was unable to keep up the hire purchase payments on his rickshaw and on a cow he was buying from Somi's brother, so he needed cash urgently. Previously he had rented out his one acre plot to his cousin, Ram Kishan, on a share cropping basis. But he claims he never got his full 50% share of the crop. Then he entered into a new contract with Ram Kishan, renting out his land for five years for Rs 3000 (or Rs 600 per acre per year). Ram Prasad used Rs 1500 to pay off a loan and the other Rs 1500 went on general household expenses. Ram Prasad and Somi eventually decided to go to her mother's village and take up with work as bonded labourers at a brick kiln. They have taken an advance payment on their wages to obtain and feed a buffalo whose milk they will sell. The contract with the brick kiln owners is, however, only for 7 months as the brickworks cannot operate during the monsoon.

Source: Open University; Development Studies Pack.

4 ENERGY CONSUMPTION

The consumption of energy in a country is highly correlated to the degree of industrialis-ation. The poorest LDCs use very little energy, the richest industrial countries use the most. Figure 3.75 shows the per capita energy consumption figures for a range of countries.

Figure 3.75 – Per Capita Energy Consumption for a Range of Countries

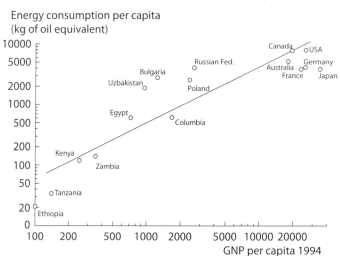

Source: World Bank: World Bank Indicators 1996

5 RURAL-URBAN MIGRATION AND UNEMPLOYMENT

In LDCs a severe unemployment problem is linked with the phenomena of rapid growth of cities. The rural poor flood into the cities continuously expanding the gigantic slum areas surrounding them, as they look for jobs and a better life. Most of these migrants remain unemployed and in poverty however. Figure 3.76 and Figure 3.77 illustrate the speed and size of this urbanization problem. By the year 2015 only two of the fifteen largest cities in the world will be in developed countries.

Figure 3.76 – Total Urban Population Less Developed and More Developed Countries, 1950, 1985, 2000, 2025 (Projected)

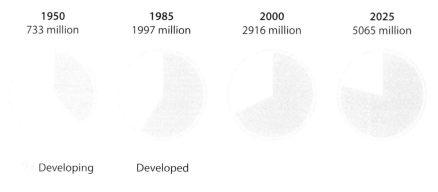

1950	1985	2000	2025
733 million	1997 million	2916 million	5065 million

Developing   Developed

Source: M.Todaro & S. Smith, Economic Development 8th Edition Table 8.1

Figure 3.77 – The World's Fifteen Largest Cities, 1995 and 2015

Country	1995 population		Average annual growth rate (%)	2015 population	
	Rank	Inhabitants (m)	1990–1995	Rank	Inhabitants (m)
Tokyo, Japan	1	26.8	1.41	1	28.7
Sao Paulo, Brazil	2	16.4	2.01	6	20.8
New York, USA	3	16.3	0.34	11	17.6
Mexico City, Mexico	4	15.6	0.73	10	18.8
Bombay, India	5	15.1	4.22	2	27.4
Shanghai, China	6	15.1	2.29	4	23.4
Los Angeles, USA	7	12.4	1.60	–	–
Beijing, China	8	12.4	2.57	8	19.4
Calcutta, India	9	11.7	1.67	12	17.6
Seoul, South Korea	10	11.6	1.95	–	–
Jakarta, Indonesia	11	11.5	4.35	5	21.2
Buenos Aires, Argentina	12	11.0	0.68	–	–
Tianjin, China	13	10.7	2.88	14	17.0
Osaka, Japan	14	10.6	0.23	–	–
Lagos, Nigeria	15	10.3	5.68	3	24.2
Karachi, Pakistan	16	–	–	7	20.6
Dhaka, Bangladesh	17	–	–	9	19.0
Manila, Philippines	18	–	–	15	14.7
Delhi, India	19	–	–	13	17.1

Source: M.Todaro & S. Smith; Economic Development 8th Edition Table 8.2

WHY IS THIS HAPPENING?

In the developed countries there was also rural-urban migration when industrialisation occurred. Labour saving machines and techniques freed labour from the countryside to rapidly growing industries in cities. There was, in effect, a push from the land and a pull from the city encouraging people to migrate.

As LDCs are also characterised by massive rural-urban migration it is tempting to think the same process is occurring. However, there are two crucial differences.

1 Third World agriculture is not modernising and becoming more productive.
2 The demand for urban jobs is far outstripping the supply.

We will look later at why agriculture remains stagnant. Here we ask why sufficient urban jobs have failed to appear, despite periods of rapid economic growth.

Firstly, it should be noted that the urban sector is small relative to the rural sector and therefore its capacity to absorb labour is constrained.

Secondly, the rapid growth of industry has been capital-intensive rather than labour-intensive.

Finally, the supply of labour has been overwhelming due to the rapid growth of population. With falling death rates, more and more young people are surviving to working age.

With such widespread urban unemployment it seems puzzling why so many people continue to migrate, pouring daily into the city slums.

The main economic explanation lies in the wide wage differential between city and country, coupled with the probability of finding work. If income prospects are poor in the countryside there is a temptation to move, especially for the young. If the chance of obtaining work multiplied by the urban wage is greater than the rural wage then it is logical to move. Simplistically, if there is a one in six chance of getting work (or a 100% chance of getting work for 2 months a year), then it is worth moving if the urban wage is greater than six times the rural wage. For young people with their lives ahead of them, the life-time earnings possibilities may well be higher despite massive unemployment. If they are educated, there is a hope that the earnings differential will be greater still and they are even more likely to move.

Most studies show that people migrate for economic reasons and that they are better off as a result.[23] In Botswana for example, the danger of drought is reduced by placing members of the same household in different markets. For similar reasons, daughters in rural India may be married into distantly related families. Studies show that most migrants find a job within a month or two. They also confirm that it is the educated who are most likely to move, and the very poor to remain. However, those remaining may be helped by the reduced labour surplus in the countryside and the remittances sent back from the migrants.

ECONOMIC THEORY AND UNEMPLOYMENT

Standard economic theory is not very useful in explaining the LDC unemployment and economic theory situation.

Keynesian demand-deficiency theory has little relevance in LDCs where economies are characterised by supply-side constraints, (so-called "bottlenecks"), rather than insufficient demand.

Dynamic growth models, like the Harrod-Domar growth model where increased savings and investment creates output and jobs are, as we have already noted, having only limited effects due to the use of (inappropriate) labour saving technology.[24]

Economic theory of market behaviour predicts that employers in LDCs should use abundant labour and economise on scarce capital. However the opposite is often the case. The reason is in part due to prices not reflecting true scarcity values. Capital is often subsidised, through capital grants, interest rate subsidies, tax breaks and so on. Wages may be held artificially high by legislation or labour unions.

POLICIES FOR CREATING JOBS AND REDUCING UNEMPLOYMENT

▌ Correcting the factor price distortions.

▌ "Getting the prices right" is a policy for correcting prices, using shadow prices, to encourage a more efficient use of resources and creating more jobs.[25]

▌ Choosing a more appropriate labour-intensive technology where possible.

▌ Expanding small scale labour-intensive industries, especially in the countryside.

▌ Reducing population growth.

6   POVERTY AND THE DISTRIBUTION OF INCOME

Poverty can be recognised in any country. The poor are those who cannot enjoy the living conditions and activities normal to the society they live in. They are poor relative to the standards of the country. Thus in Canada a family that cannot afford a dishwasher or a car might consider themselves poor, whereas they might be considered well off in many countries of the world. Today's poor in Sweden or Australia would be rich compared to the poor of an earlier generation. In twenty years time someone with a living standard considered adequate today might be considered poor. The poverty line moves up as society's norms move up. This relative poverty will always exist where there is any degree of income inequality.

Relative poverty, however, is distinct from absolute poverty. The latter refers to the ability to just meet the basic physical needs of life; to have just sufficient food, clothing and shelter in order to survive.[26] We would consider a person below this level to live in "absolute human misery" such that his/her health was at risk. It is the high levels of this extreme type of poverty, absolute poverty, which distinguishes LDCs from developed countries. By this standard, one in five people in the world and two in five people living in LDCs are absolutely poor, whereas this type of poverty has been eradicated in developed countries. Over the last decades inroads have been made into reducing the percentage of poor in the world, but as poor populations are increasing rapidly the total number of poor is not falling. Two regions, South Asia and sub-Saharan Africa are home to two thirds of all the world's poor (1998).

The proportion of population below the poverty line and absolute numbers in a selection of individual countries is shown in Figure 3.78.

Figure 3.78 – Percentage of Population below the Poverty Line 2000

	population below the national poverty line (%)	Number of people in absolute poverty (millions)
Bangladesh	36	47
Brazil	17	29
China	5	63
Egypt	23	15
Eritrea	53	2
Haiti	65	5
India	35	356
Madagascar	70	11
Philippines	37	28
Sierra Leone	68	3
Uganda	55	12
Vietnam	51	39
Zambia	86	9

Source: World Bank, World Bank Atlas 2002, pp. 28/29

Poverty and the Distribution of Income

The direct link between per capita income and the numbers living in poverty is income distribution. It is a truism that poverty will be eliminated much more rapidly if any given rate of economic growth is accompanied by a declining concentration of incomes. Equality should however, in my belief, be considered an objective in its own right, the third element in development (after food and a job). Inequalities to be found in the world today, especially in the Third World where there is massive poverty, are objectionable by any religious or ethical standards. The social barriers and inhibitions of an unequal society distort the personalities of those with high incomes no less than those who are poor. Trivial differences of accent, language, dress, customs, etc., acquire an absurd importance and contempt is engendered for those who lack social graces, especially country dwellers. Since race is usually highly correlated with income, economic inequality lies at the heart of racial tensions. More seriously, inequality of income is associated with other inequalities, especially in education and political power, which reinforce it.

Source: Dudley Seers IDS Reprint 106 originally from the International Development Review (Vol. 11, No. 4, 1969).

Question

Consider the above in the context of the country you come from or the one you are studying in. Do you think income inequality has anything to do with other perceived differences between groups? (NB No answer is given to this question in the answer section.)

Income Distribution

	GNP per capita		Percentage share of household income				
	(Current international US dollars 1998)	Year	Lowest 20%	Second 20%	Third 20%	Fourth 20%	Highest 20%
Bangladesh	350	92	9.4	13.5	17.2	22.0	37.9
South Africa	2880	93/94	2.9	5.5	9.2	17.7	64.8
France	24940	89	7.2	12.7	17.1	22.8	40.1

Question

Using data from the table above:

Calculate the income distribution ratios (lowest 40% / highest 20%) for each country.

Comment upon the likely incidence of absolute poverty in each country.

Poverty is of course highly concentrated in countries with low GNP per capita. However these figures are averages and give no indication as to how income is distributed.

The extent of poverty in any country then depends upon two factors:

▌ the average level of income and
▌ the degree of inequality in its distribution.

To illustrate this (Figure 3.79), three pairs of countries with fairly similar GNP per capita figures are shown. Each pair has a markedly different incidence of absolute poverty.

Figure 3.79 – Poverty and Income Distribution

Country	GNP per capita ($US 2000)	Percentage of population in poverty
Zambia	300	86
Bangladesh	370	35.6
India	450	47.0
China	840	4
Brazil	7300	17.4
Latvia	7070	0

Source: World Bank, World Bank Atlas 2002.

In order, therefore, to appreciate the extent of world poverty it is necessary to look at the income gap within individual countries, Figure 3.80. The gap is generally greater in poor countries, though there is no obvious close correlation with the levels of income per capita, as shown above. One way of showing this is to compare the share of the National Income going to the poorest 40% of the population to that going to the richest 20% of the population.

▥ Figure 3.80 – Per Capita Income and Inequality

Country	Year	Per capita GNP ($US 1998)	Lowest 40% (percentage of NI)	Top 20%
Brazil	1995	4570	8.2	64.2
Guatemala	1989	1640	7.9	63.0
Tanzania	1993	210	17.8	45.5
Kenya	1994	330	14.7	50.2
Sweden	1992	26930	24.1	34.5
Hungary	1993	4510	23.7	39.3
United States	1994	29340	15.3	45.2

Source: IBRD World Development Report 2000, Tables 1 and 5.

The pursuit of economic growth has dramatically failed to reduce the widespread poverty of LDCs. It is therefore now widely recognised that attacking poverty directly is an absolute priority of development.

Understanding poverty is an essential prerequisite to understanding a number of other specific development problems. The fast growth of population, rural unemployment, resistance to change by peasant farmers, huge increases in city slums and poor educational standards are all poverty related.

WHO THEN ARE THE POOR?

If governments wish to reduce absolute poverty it is important to be able to identify the poor.

Predominantly, poor people are to be found in the countryside. In Africa and in Asia 75%–80% of the poor live in rural areas. In Latin America the figure is 70%. Most of the remainder live in the giant sprawling slums which surround most Third World cities. As three out of four absolutely poor people live in the countryside, and the rest in city slums intrinsically linked to the countryside through migration, the countryside is where development programmes need to be concentrated.

Amongst the poor themselves, women are often the poorest of the poor, and generally have a lower status than men. This is related to who controls the factors of production. It is usually men who control the land, capital, and technology and receive any school education available. Yet women work long hours in the home as well as in the fields or in the slums.

Development programmes need to target the low status of women, not only because women are poor, but also because of the effect female poverty has on other development problems *eg* birth rates, nutrition and health.

Poverty and Gender

'Poverty is not gender neutral. Women have less access to, and control of, land, credit, technology education and health, and skilled work. Women also suffer discrimination in pay and in access to land, legacies and credit. Though the evidence (in most countries) does not suggest that women are more consumption-poor than men, their control over income is certainly less. It is based on more menial and less self-directed work accompanied by the 'double-day' of care for home and children, frequent pregnancies and frequent child deaths.'

Poverty and Age

'Poverty incidence amongst children is everywhere (in the world) much higher than among adults.'

International Fund for Agricultural Development: Rural Poverty Report 2001

Absolute poverty is heavily concentrated in the poorest countries. Low GNP per capita is highly correlated with widespread poverty. Because of this there have been enormous efforts to raise GNP per capita in LDCs. Indeed economic growth has been the number one government economic policy goal in developing countries. Figure 3.81 illustrates the correlation between low average income and the incidence of poverty.

Figure 3.81 – The Correlation between Poverty and GNP Per Capita

Country	GNP per capita 1991 ($ US)	Percentage of population in poverty	
		urban	rural
Mozambique	70	40	70
Bolivia	750	...	86
Philippines	790	40	54
Guatemala	1000	60	80
Peru	1350	52	72
Uruguay	3470	10	23

Source: IBRD World Development Report 1996.

However, low average income is only one of two factors responsible for absolute poverty. The other, the inequality of income distribution, has been given far less recognition and attention in all but a few LDCs. Remember, GNP per capita is an average figure, it could represent an even spread of income or a highly skewed one, where there are a few rich and many poor. As we shall see later it is a characteristic of many LDCs that they have a very unequal income distribution compared to developed countries. Nevertheless, to date, popular emphasis has been disproportionately focused upon low GNP per capita. Many development economists believe this is a major reason for LDCs concentrating upon policies to raise economic growth without due regard to the distribution of income. The consequence of such policies, even when successful in raising growth rates, has often left poverty untouched because the distribution of income has been untouched.

Poverty differs significantly in countries with similar GNP per capita. One important reason is because of different distributions of that income. Figure 3.82 pairs four countries where the incidence of poverty shows little relationship to the GNP per capita.

Figure 3.82 – Non-Correlation of GNP Per Capita and Poverty

Country	GNP per capita 1992 (US$)	Population in poverty 1992 (%)		Country	GNP per capita 1992 (US$)	Population in poverty 1992 (%)	
		urban	rural			urban	rural
Ghana	460	59	54	Peru	1350	52	72
China	480	–	12	Thailand	2840	7	29

Source: IBRD World Development Report 1996.

Before proceeding further with income distribution we need to look at ways of measuring it.

METHODS OF MEASURING INEQUALITY IN INCOME DISTRIBUTION

The most common way of measuring inequality is to arrange all households in order of incomes, from the poorest to the richest, then to divide the population of households into quintiles, *ie* 5 equal groups of 20%. We are then able to look at the percentage of total income which is earned by each quintile. In an economy with perfect income equality each quintile would earn 20% of total income.

Figure 3.83 compares income distribution estimates for a number of countries against their GNP in 'current international dollars', that is GNP in dollars adjusted for Purchasing Power Parity.

Figure 3.83 – Income Distribution and Purchasing Power Parity GNP per Capita

GNP per capita in current international US dollars (PPP)		Year	Lowest 20%	Second 20%	Third 20%	Fourth 20%	Highest 20%
Low income countries							
Ethiopia	500	1995	7.1	10.9	14.5	19.8	47.7
Sierra Leone	390	1989	1.1	2.0	9.8	23.7	63.4
Nigeria	820	1993	4.0	8.9	14.4	23.4	49.3
Bangladesh	1100	1992	9.4	13.5	17.2	22.0	37.9
Pakistan	1560	1996	9.4	13.0	16.0	20.3	41.2
Indonesia	2790	1996	8.0	11.3	15.1	20.8	44.9
Lower middle income countries							
Philippines	6740	1994	5.9	9.6	13.9	21.1	49.6
Guatemala	4070	1989	2.1	5.8	10.5	18.6	63.0
Thailand	5840	1992	5.6	8.7	13.0	20.0	52.7
Columbia	7500	1995	3.1	6.8	10.9	17.6	61.5
Upper middle income countries							
Venezuela	8190	1995	4.3	8.8	13.8	21.3	51.8
Malaysia	6990	1989	4.6	8.3	13.0	20.4	53.7
Poland	6740	1992	9.3	13.8	17.7	22.6	36.6
Hungary	...	1993	9.7	13.9	16.9	21.4	38.1
Brazil	6160	1995	2.5	5.7	9.9	17.7	64.2
High income countries							
Spain	16060	1990	7.5	12.6	17.0	22.6	40.3
Australia	20130	1989	7.0	12.2	16.6	23.3	40.9
UK	20640	1986	7.1	12.8	17.2	23.1	39.8
Germany	20810	1989	9.0	13.5	17.5	22.9	37.1
USA	29340	1994	4.8	10.5	16.0	23.5	45.2
Norway	24290	1991	10.0	14.3	17.9	22.4	35.3

Source: World Bank; World Development Report 2000, Tables 1 & 5.

Notes

1 The countries are ordered by GNP per capita before adapting figures for Purchasing Power Parity.

2 The figures must be used with caution, as definitions and sources vary between countries.

The statistics in Figure 3.83 show a number of relationships.

1 Middle income LDCs appear to have greater income inequality than very poor countries or high income countries.

2 Income inequality is highest in Latin America.

3 Income inequality was low in Poland and Hungary in the early 1990s, the two countries which were formerly centrally-planned.

The statistics however are not very easy to read in this form. There are therefore other ways of consolidating and displaying the information. One is to construct an income distribution ratio, also known as Kuznets ratio. A second is a Lorenz curve and the third a Gini coefficient.

Income Distribution Ratios (Kuznets Ratios)

The percentage of income earned by the bottom two quintiles are added together and expressed as a ratio of income earned by the top 20%.

$$\frac{\text{bottom } 40\%}{\text{top } 20\%}$$

Thus adding the figures for Brazil we get $\dfrac{2.5\% + 5.7\%}{64.2\%} = \dfrac{8.2\%}{64.2\%}$

The poorest 40% of Brazilians earn only 8.2% of the National Income. The richest 20% earn 64.2% which is nearly 8 times as much as the poorest 40%. (If we used equal quintiles the richest 20% have 64.2/2.5 = almost 26 times the income of the poor). Figure 3.84 shows the income ratios of the countries of Figure 3.84.

Figure 3.84 – Income Distribution Expressed as a Ratio

Low income countries	
Ethiopia	18/48
Sierra Leone	3/63
Nigeria	13/49
Bangladesh	23/38
Pakistan	22/41
Indonesia	19/45
Lower middle income countries	
Philippines	16/50
Guatemala	8/63
Thailand	14/53
Columbia	10/62
Upper Middle Income Countries	
Venezuela	13/52
Malaysia	13/54
Poland	23/37
Hungary	24/38
Brazil	8/64
High income countries	
Spain	20/40
Australia	19/41
UK	20/40
Germany	23/39
USA	15/45
Norway	24/35

Figures are rounded to the nearest whole number.

Adapted from The World Development Report 2000, Table 5.

The greater the disparity between the two figures for a country the greater is the inequality. The closer they are, the greater the equality.

For any given level of average income, poverty will be greater the more unequally income is distributed. Thus Brazil and Malaysia will have more poverty than Poland, all other things being equal.

For any given distribution of income, poverty will be greater the lower is average income. Thus Pakistan has a more equal distribution of income than the United States but more poverty due to the low level of that income.

Lorenz Curves

📊 Figure 3.85 – Lorenz Curve

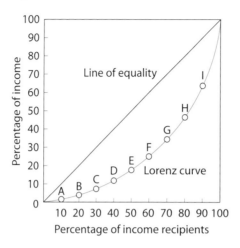

Figure 3.85 shows how a Lorenz curve measures inequality. Along the horizontal axis is plotted the number of income recipients as a cumulative percentage. On the vertical axis is the cumulative percentage of national income received. The axes are on the same scale and are connected to form a square. Thus point A is the co-ordinate of the percentage of income received by the poorest 10% of the population. Point B the percentage of income received by the poorest 20%, *ie* the lowest 10% plus the next lowest 10% and so on. All of the population except for the richest 10% is co-ordinate I. 0% of the population of course receive 0% of national income and 100% of the population receive all the income so the curve starts and finishes in the corners of the square.

A diagonal drawn across the square traces out all the co ordinates of absolute equality. Thus if 10% of the population received 10% of income, 20% received 20%, 50% received 50% and so on all of the points would fall on the diagonal. This serves as a base from which to judge the degree of inequality. When actual figures are graphed, as with points A to I one can see how the resulting curves compares to the straight line diagonal. The more unequal is income distribution the more will the curve bow away from the diagonal. (The case of extreme inequality where 99% of the population received no income and 1% received everything would result in a curve which was represented by the bottom horizontal and right hand vertical axis.)

Figure 3.86(a) – Two Lorenz Curves

Figure 3.86(b) – Gini coefficient

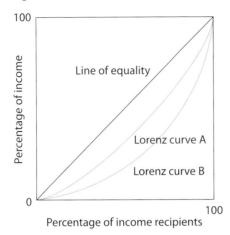

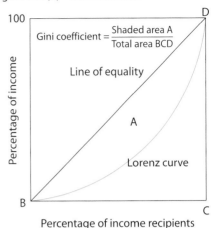

Figure 3.86(a) shows two curves for comparison. The relatively flat curve shows a fairly equal distribution of income and the very bowed curve a very uneven distribution of income. It would be a useful exercise if you drew your own Lorenz curves from the data given in Figure 3.83 choosing two countries with widely different income distributions, say for example Poland and Brazil.

Gini Coefficients

A Gini coefficient is a simple way of showing inequality by converting the Lorenz curve into a single statistic. The area between the diagonal and the Lorenz curve is divided by the total area of the half square in which the curve lies. In Figure 3.86(b) the Gini coefficient is the ratio of the shaded area A and the area BCD.

6 COMPOSITE INDICATORS

There have been a number of attempts to modify GNP figures. Some have been desired to correct weaknesses of international comparison *eg* the Purchasing Power Parity method described below. Others attempt to construct more meaningful indicators of welfare. There are presently several indices which attempt to quantify and compare more comprehensive measures of the standard of living than GNP alone. Some are restricted to weighted indices of quantifiable features, such as the infant mortality rate and the literacy rate. Others are more ambitious in scope, and correspondingly more subjective. For example there are some which attempt to compare 'political freedom', 'freedom of the press', 'women's rights' and 'pollution'. The Human Development Index (HDI) is an example of the former, and the Human Suffering Index of the latter.[27] They are included here as readings.

The Human Development Index

The Human Development Index measures the average achievement in a country in three basic dimensions of human development.

▎ A long and healthy life as measured by life expectancy at birth

▎ Knowledge, as measured by the adult literacy rate (2/3 weight), and the combined primary, secondary and tertiary gross enrolment ratio (1/3 weight).

▎ A decent standard of living, as measured by GNP per capita (PPP US$).

An index is created for each from 0–1 with minimum and maximum values in Figure 3.86.

Figure 3.86 – Human Development Index

	Maximum value	Minimum value
Life expectancy at birth (years)	85	25
Adult literacy rate	100	0
Combined gross enrolment rate	100	0
GNP per capita (PPP US$)	40000	100

HDI is a simple average of values (Figure 3.87).

Figure 3.87 – Sample HDTs

High Human Development		Medium Human Development		Low Human Development	
Norway	.939	Mexico	.790	Pakistan	.498
Australia	.936	Malaysia	.774	Nigeria	.455
Canada	.936	Philippines	.749	Uganda	.435
USA	.934	Egypt	.635	Gambia	.398
Argentina	.842	India	.571	Ethiopia	.321
Chile	.825			Niger	.724
Costa Rica	.821			Sierra Leone	.258

The Human Development Index

The HDI combines life expectancy, literacy and purchasing power into a single measure to rank countries by the quality of life their citizens enjoy, rather than the amount of GNP their economies produce. It has been developed under the United Nations Development Programme by a team of development economists led by Dr Mahbub ul Haq. It is intended to show that wealth and social progress do not necessarily go together. It shows that some countries have successfully translated relatively low levels of economic growth into human progress while others have conspicuously failed, despite high rates of economic growth.

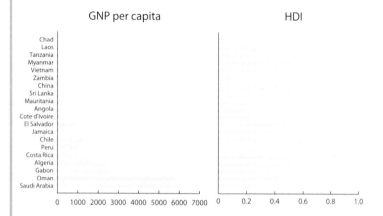

A comparison of HDI and GNP rankings proves this. Gabon for instance, with a GNP per capita higher than Uruguay, has a much lower HDI ranking which reflects its relative failure to translate its oil earnings into high levels of human development.

The HDI could be considered a 'statistic with a human face', but it does have its drawbacks. Like GNP per capita figures, it masks disparities in life expectancy, literacy and income between rural and urban areas, females and males, and rich and poor. It also fails to take into account the amount of money being invested in human development in areas such as health and education.

Another criticism is the failure of the HDI to take into account political freedom and human rights, now widely accepted as an essential prerequisite for development. Aware of this shortcoming, the authors promise in future editions of the Report to devise a quantitative measure for human freedom which would include "free elections, multi-party political systems, uncensored press, adherence to the rule of law, guarantees of free speech and so on".

Adapted from an article by Ross Hammond on the Human Development Report (1990) UNDP, Oxford University Press.

The Human Suffering Index

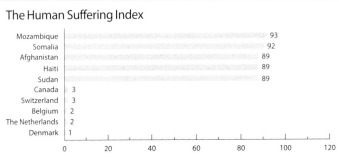

10 indicators of human well being: life expectancy, daily calorie supply, access to clean water, infant immunisation, secondary school enrolment, per capita income, rate of inflation, communications, technology, political freedom, and civil rights. The index assigns a value of 0–10 to each indicator with 10 points reflecting the highest level of suffering and 0 the lowest. Source: Washington based Population Crisis Committee (PPC).

Almost three-quarters of the world's population live in conditions that tax human endurance, and the gap between rich and poor countries is widening, according to a new index of human misery.

The index, published today, ranks countries on a table of human suffering based on ten measures such as access to clean water, adequate food and education. Mozambique has the highest levels of human suffering, followed by Somalia, Afghanistan, Haiti and Sudan. The five countries with the least human suffering are Denmark, Holland, Belgium, Switzerland and Canada. America ranks 8th and Britain 22nd.

The Washington-based Population Crisis Committee, publishers of the index, says that in nine countries, mostly in Africa, access to clean water has declined since 1987. The committee, a privately funded organization, ranked 141 countries on the basis of ten indicators of well-being, life expectancy, daily calorie supply, access to clean water, infant immunisation, secondary school enrolment, per capita income, rate of inflation, the number of telephones per 1000 people, political freedom and civil rights. The index assigns a value of 0–10 to each indicator with 10 reflecting the highest level of suffering and 0 the lowest.

Less than one-sixth of the world's population, 800 million people, live in conditions of minimal human suffering with a score of 24 or below. More than 430 million people live in conditions of extreme suffering with a score of 75 and above and a further 3.5 billion in conditions of high suffering, scoring over 50. Mozambique's total of 93 is the highest. Denmark has a score of one.

"The 1992 index shows that an appalling three-quarters of the world's people live in countries where human suffering is the rule, rather than the exception", said Dr Sharon Camp, editor of the index. "Both the numbers and the proportion of people in these countries are up significantly from five years ago. The development gap between the world's rich and poor has widened." (See table)

Reprinted from "The Times" 18th May 1992

THE GNP AND PURCHASING POWER PARITY

The IMF now constructs tables to compare GNP using purchasing power parities (PPP) instead of market exchange rates, The PPP takes account of the local buying power of the currency. Instead of regarding one dollar as of equal purchasing power in, for example, India and Switzerland, the new tables reflect the different purchasing powers of different countries.

The results, now published for comparison by the World Bank are quite staggering, raising the measured level of GNP per capita of many countries dramatically. The table of GNP per capita (Figure 3.88) shows that the PPP measure results in a multiple of the exchange rate measure, for example in China, India, Indonesia, Thailand, Pakistan, Egypt and Malaysia. The PPP measure accords more realistically with other evidence on living standards.

Equally dramatically, the second table (Figure 3.89) shows how the total GNP measured in this manner places several Third World countries amongst the biggest economies in the world.

Figure 3.88 – Developing Countries

Country	GNP per capita $ (1998)	
	Market exchange rates	Purchasing power parity
China	750	3220
India	430	1700
Brazil	4570	6160
Mexico	3970	8190
Indonesia	680	2790
South Korea	7970	12270
Thailand	2200	5840
Pakistan	480	1560
Argentina	8970	10200
Nigeria	300	820
Egypt	1290	3130
Philippines	1050	6740
Malaysia	3600	6990

Source: World Bank, World Development Report 2000, Table 1

📊 Figure 3.89 – The World's Largest Economies 1998

Country	$ billions
United States	7923
China	3984
Japan	2928
Germany	1709
India	1661
France	1312
United Kingdom	1219
Italy	1163
Brazil	1021
Mexico	786
Canada	736

Source: World Bank, World Development Report 2000, Table 1

Not only do the poor countries have a low income absolutely and relatively, but the gap between the rich and the poor nations is widening in many cases.[28] Many LDCs have achieved reasonable growth rates of GNP but have the potential benefits to living standards negated by large increases in population. In much of sub-Saharan Africa for example the population growth rate is higher than the GNP growth rate resulting in the GNP per capita actually falling.

Spot the Country!

📊 Table 1: GNP Per Capita For Fourteen Selected Countries (US $ 1990)

Country	GNP per capita
Tanzania	110
Uganda	220
Sierra Leone	240
China	370
Sri Lanka	470
Cameroon	960
Thailand	1420
Brazil	2680
Republic of Korea	5400
Saudi Arabia	7050
Singapore	11160
United Kingdom	16100
Germany	22320
Japan	24430

Table 1 shows 14 countries ordered by their GNP per capita.

Table 2 shows the same 14 countries but mixed randomly and labelled A to N.

📊 Table 2 - Indicators of Development

Country	Adult literacy rate (%) 1990	Tertiary enrolment ratio (%) 1988-9	Life expectancy (years) 1990	Infant mortality rate (per 1000) 1989	Av. annual population growth (%) 1980-90	Labour force in industry (%) 1986-9
A	73	2	70	29	1.4	14
B	88	8	74	7	2.2	29
C	99	24	76	8	0.2	20
D	21	1	42	147	2.4	14
E	93	16	66	27	1.8	6
F	54	3	54	88	3.0	5
G	62	12	65	65	4.7	14
H	65	0	54	115	3.1	5
I	99	31	79	5	0.6	24
J	96	39	70	17	1.1	27
K	88	4	71	19	1.4	12
L	99	34	75	7	0.1	30
M	81	11	66	57	2.2	16
N	48	1	52	117	2.5	4

Source Human Development Report 1992, World Development Report 1992.

Table 2 shows 6 characteristic indicators which are widely used to define development and underdevelopment. If GNP per capita is a good measure of development then it follows that you should be able to identify many of the countries listed in Table 1.

To do this exercise create a blank table in your note-book, with 14 rows and 6 columns plus the headings of Table 2 and the column of countries, A to N. Take one column of figures at a time and divide it into three groups high (H), low (L), and medium (M), to represent characteristics of countries with high, low and medium levels of income.

At this point you may wish to go ahead and complete the table. However if you want further guidance you can use the division the author made (which is of course subjective). A compromise would be to copy the first column or two to get the idea, and then attempt your own classification with the remaining columns.

Taking literacy first, the data is divided into three groups with the high group "cut off point" taken as 88%. The low group is taken as those of 65% or less. Thus on this division B, C, E, I, J, K and L are considered high; D, F, G, H and N low; and A and M medium.

Tertiary education (education beyond compulsory school age) is also divided into the three groups, with C, I, J, and L classified as high; A, D, F, H, K and N classified as low; leaving B, E, G and M in the middle.

The other divisions made by the author are shown in Table 3

📊 **Table 3**

	High income	Low income
Life expectancy	> 70	< 60
Infant mortality	< 10	> 50
Population growth	< 1.5%	> 3.0%
% labour in industry	> 20%	< 10%

Table 4 shows a summary based upon his judgement.

Table 4

Country	Adult literacy	Tertiary enrolment	Life expectancy	Infant mortality	Growth of population	% of labour in industry	Summary
A	M	L	H	M	H	M	2H, 3M, 1L
B	H	M	H	H	M	H	4H, 2M
C	H	H	H	H	H	H	6H
D	L	L	L	L	M	M	2M, 4L
E	H	M	M	M	M	L	1H, 4M, 1L
F	L	L	L	L	L	L	6L
G	L	M	M	L	L	M	3M, 3L
H	L	L	L	L	L	L	6L
I	H	H	H	H	H	H	6H
J	H	H	H	M	H	H	5H, 1M
K	H	L	H	M	H	M	3H, 2M, 1L
L	H	H	H	H	H	H	6H
M	M	M	M	L	M	M	5M, 1L
N	L	L	L	L	M	L	1M, 5L

Summary of Categories based on Development Indicators

Can you identify the fourteen countries from these summaries? When you have attempted it, compare with the actual list in the Answers Section.

(This exercise was first printed in the Economic Review Vol 10 No. 3 February 1993 as part of the article 'Can we measure economic development' by Peter Smith.)

MULTIPLE CHOICE QUESTIONS – MEASURING ECONOMIC DEVELOPMENT

1   The Human Development Index includes which of the following measures?

   I   Income levels

   II   Life expectancy rates

   III   Literacy rates

   A   I only   B   I and II   C   II and III   D   I, II and III

2   Which of the following is a typical characteristic of an LDC?

   A   High population density.

   B   A lack of natural resources.

   C   Even income distribution.

   D   Low productivity in agriculture.

3   If the savings ratio, labour productivity and income distribution is compared between more developed countries and less developed countries we generally find that in MDCs...

	Savings ratios are...	Labour productivity is...	Income distribution is...
A	higher	lower	more equal
B	lower	higher	less equal
C	higher	higher	more equal
D	lower	lower	less equal

4   What does 'absolute poverty' mean as against 'relative poverty'?

   A   Purchasing power varies from country to country.

   B   The standard for judging the poverty level has changed over time.

   C   There is a certain quantity of food, shelter and clothing which people need in order to live.

   D   The standard of living of the poor is compared with those in their own country rather than with those in other countries.

5 The growth of huge urban slums in LDCs is associated with the

A shortage of labour in the urban areas.

B provision of high quality social housing by city authorities.

C low productivity in the rural areas.

D low mortality rates.

6 Which of these combinations of birth rates and death rates is most likely to be found in the very poorest LDCs?

	Death rate (per 1000 population)	Birth rate (per 1000 population)
A	3	5
B	20	60
C	15	45
D	40	40

7 Absolute poverty in any particular country, is measured by estimating the amount of money

A earned by the poorest 20% of the population.

B spent on goods and services by an average family.

C needed as food aid.

D needed to buy a minimum level of subsistence.

8 A country's long term growth and development could be measured by regarding which of the following?

I   Real domestic investment.

II   Real consumption per capita.

III Real GNP per capita.

A I only   B I and II   C II and III   D I, II and III

9 Which of the following are characteristics of LDCs?

I   Low productivity in agriculture.

II   A rapidly expanding urban population.

III A high dependence on the production of primary products.

A I only   B I and II   C II and III   D I, II and III

10 The use of GNP per capita measured in current US dollars rather than purchasing power parity, makes the majority of LDCs appear to have a

A   lower GNP per capita than is actually the case.

B   higher GNP per capital than is actually the case.

C   higher degree of income inequality than is actually the case.

D   larger primary sector than is actually the case.

11 US dollars are used to convert the GNP per capita of all countries to allow international comparison. Which of the following is not a valid criticism of using the exchange rate to do this? Exchange rates

A   ignore goods which are not traded internationally.

B   may be managed by governments.

C   are heavily influenced by speculative flows.

D   take no account of income distribution.

12 Which of the following indicators is included when constructing the human development index?

A   Access to medical care.

B   Literacy rate.

C   Access to clean water.

D   Inflation rate.

Notes

1　As gas, electricity and water are metered, to measure household consumption.

2　A process known as deflation. As this is uncommon the term deflation more often describes the action of deliberately reducing overall demand in an economy by the government.

3　Dudley Seers, The Meaning Of Development, International Development Review (Vol. 11, No. 4, 1969) and IDS Reprint 106, University of Sussex, UK.

4　Michael Todaro, Economics for A Developing World, 3rd ed, Longman, 1992, p102.

5　You will learn more about price index numbers in Section 3.4.

6　The shift in aggregate supply is further expanded under the heading 'Causes of Economic Growth' in Section 5.

7　Calculating forward from past information.

8　1992 figures.

9　In either case unemployment would be somewhat less severe in practice as higher wages will increase aggregate demand, and shift the demand curve for labour to the right.

10　This is sometimes called a policy of taking 'work to the workers'. This is in contrast to the policy of taking 'workers to the work' under a market-orientated scheme.

11　Deflation does sometimes occur in practice but rarely compared to inflation, and the term is more often used to describe a slow down in the growth of output.

12　see monetarists, above.

13　An international cartel of oil producers and exporters.

14　Because unemployment would remain high.

15　Some Central Banks are independent of the government, others are under the direct control of the government.

16　The Quantity Theory of Money, which was considered previously in this Section, is a limited version of this model which works in some situations.

17　Higher Level students will be able to link this to the multiplier effects of changing AD.

18　A situation known as a 'liquidity trap'.

19　The amount of tax paid on the last dollar of income

20　Arthur Okun, Equality and Efficiency: The Big Trade Off, Brookings Institution 1975.

21　Note the link to Section 3.2, 'Uses and Limitations of National Income accounts'.

22　Military spending is very high in a number of LDCs, eg in Pakistan, North Korea and countries of the Middle East.

23　World Development Report, 1990, p62

24　The Harrod-Domar growth model shows the growth of GDP (g) to depend upon the savings rate (s) divided by the capital-output ratio (k), that is g=s/k.

25   A shadow price is calculated to reflect the true scarcity of the factor. Thus shadow prices of capital are likely to be higher that their actual subsidised prices and shadow wages lower.

26   A figure of $370 US a year at constant 1993 values and adjusted for local purchasing power (PPP) is used - this is roughly 'a dollar a day'.

27   HDI is part of the IB syllabus, the HSI is not.

28   Global income disparity between the richest 20% and the poorest 20% of population in the world from 1960-2000 (richest:poorest): 1960=30:1, 1980=45:1, 2000=70:1 Source: UNDP, Human Development Report 2001

Section 4

International Economics

4.1   REASONS FOR TRADE

INTRODUCTION

Trade has the ability to raise the standard of living and make those who trade better off. International trade has the same effect as domestic trade. The economic principles that improve the living standard of one Canadian who trades with another are exactly the same principles that improve the living standard of a Malaysian who trades with an Australian. International trade has the ability to make all those involved in it economically better off. Indeed, the marked rise in global living standards over time can be shown to have come from the benefits of increased trade. This has been dramatic in the last half-century for those living in the industrialised countries. Section 4.1 begins by looking at the economics of these trading gains. Certain groups of producers, however, may well suffer lower living standards from increased international trade, and thus campaign for protection from imported goods and services. There are a few valid arguments for protecting trade and many invalid ones. The case for protection is examined in Section 4.2.

Free trade is one of the greatest sources of economic well being. Yet in every country foreign trade has, at times, been hated and reviled by sections of the population. If you consider the area of the world you are living in now, you are likely to find strong trade-related protests appearing in the news media. Why should international trade be so feared when it can be shown to be beneficial? A clue to this apparent paradox can be found by considering who benefits and who loses from the increase in foreign trade. The beneficiaries are the millions of consumers who vote quietly and unobtrusively with their dollars, as they make gains in price, quantity, quality and choice. The losers, however, are likely to be a relatively small group of producers compared to the size of the consumer group. Whereas each consumer is likely to gain a relatively small amount from each import purchased, compared to their total expenditure, producer groups are likely to lose a great deal. They might lose their jobs, their livelihood, their company, even a whole way of life. With a great deal to lose it is worth their while campaigning for protection by lobbying, demonstrating and taking direct action. As the producers are all in the same trade, they are highly concentrated and organised compared to the millions of scattered beneficiaries: the consumers. In addition, it is not difficult to stir up distrust and hatred of foreigners. The government will need to be strong and unbiased to take a balanced view of benefits and costs when the lobbying pressure may be so uneven. It is the job of economists to highlight these costs and benefits as objectively as possible.

In Section 4.3 there is an examination of the recent growth of trading blocs, where freer trade is encouraged within a protectionist group of neighbouring countries. A trade bloc may take the form of a Free Trade Area, a Customs Union, or a Common Market.

Gains from Trade

Trade has the potential to make people economically better off. There are four powerful economic reasons for this. They are:

| The theory of comparative advantage
| Economies of scale
| International competition
| The spread of modern technology

There are, in addition, some non-economic reasons. Each of these economic and non-economic reasons is now treated in turn.

Comparative Advantage

Countries are endowed with different resources, including populations with different skills. According to well established economic theory, countries should specialise in those goods in which they have a comparative advantage. The theory of comparative advantage proves that, under certain assumptions, global output can increase through trade and can benefit all nations. A country is able to consume beyond its own Production Possibility Frontier, whereas without trade its consumption is limited to what it can produce, *ie* its consumption is bounded by the PPF.

This theory is the key to this section on trade, an important and powerful argument for trading. In terms of your course, and this textbook, this is the first time that you have met the theory of comparative advantage. Detailed study of it is a requirement of the Higher Level course only. It is important to be reminded, however, that even without the theory of comparative advantage there are still other powerful economic arguments in favour of specialising and trading. The three arguments which follow are brief summaries only. That is because they have all been examined elsewhere in this course. Nevertheless they give further reasons why trade will lower prices and increase output, and thus increase economic welfare.

> David Ricardo
>
> 1772-1823
>
> David Ricardo was born in Amsterdam, the son of a Jewish broker, and moved to England when he was thirteen. He became a broker himself at fourteen, and became immensely wealthy. He retired at a young age and entered Parliament where he became a noted debater. He was inspired to understand economics by reading the Wealth of Nations. His own major book, the Principles of Political Economy and Taxation was published in 1817. This book became a major influence on the development of economic theory over the next half-century. The Law of Comparative Advantage which he first explained in this book is still valid today.

Economies of Scale

The theory of long run costs shows that firms frequently gain economies of scale as they grow. The average cost of production falls as production increases. A limiting factor to economies of scale is, however, the size of the market. A company limited to its domestic market may not be able to benefit from economies of scale. Small island economies have always been heavily involved in trade for this reason. However, even quite large industrial countries may gain from specialisation in high fixed-cost industries, *eg* in civilian and military aircraft production. Thus the two giant US aircraft producers, Boeing and McDonnell Douglas, merged in 1997 in order to sell more efficiently in the global market. The European Airbus and the Eurofighter can only be produced at an economic cost with the co-operation of several large European industrial countries in order to guarantee a sufficiently large market. Contrast this with Sweden's production of high-tech military planes in order to maintain military neutrality during the cold war years. Economically this was very expensive for Swedish taxpayers in a domestic market of only 8 million people.

Increased International Competition

Standard theory of the firm shows that where there are barriers to entry to a market, firms have the potential to reduce output and raise prices. Under certain conditions, which are commonly found, monopoly is inferior to competition in terms of output, price and allocative efficiency. That is, consumers would be better off with increased competition. Being open to international trade may well increase efficiency in industries which would otherwise enjoy domestic monopoly. For example, while car manufacturing would be considered monopolistic or oligopolistic within national boundaries, in practice the international trade in cars ensures a very competitive market with low prices and high output.

The Spread of Modern Technology

Best practice in production techniques spreads rapidly with international trade. Some innovative ideas are embodied within traded products and others are transferred when multinational companies locate abroad. Gains in efficiency, *ie* lower prices and increased output, can come from more productive ways of working. For example, the rapid spread of technology from the United States and Japan in recent years has increased output in many other countries.

Other Benefits of International Trade

Consumer choice is prized by most people. Even where trade does not lower prices and increase total consumption, greater variety and choice is still valued by consumers. For example, foreign holidays, foreign food, foreign cars, and foreign education are all valued for their novelty, even where domestic products are available at similar prices.

In addition, there may well be political and social gains from increased international trade. The increased trade between member states of the European Union is secondary in the minds of many of its proponents to the reduced likelihood of further European wars. There is enormous political significance in the increased international trade between China and the rest of the world, as there is between the former Soviet Union and the West. Closer to home, the International Baccalaureate Organisation justifies trade in education as much in terms of social and political advantage as in terms of economic gain.

THE THEORY OF COMPARATIVE ADVANTAGE

Having listed the gains to be made from countries specialising and exporting in exchange for imports, we need now to consider what goods and services a country should specialise in. Let us first deal with the obvious case. That is, where Country A can produce a product using fewer resources than Country B. Country B can produce a different product with fewer resources than Country A. They specialise and trade. This is known as a situation of *absolute* advantage. Each trading partner has an absolute advantage over the other in different products. This explains why Australia can export beef and beach holidays to Japan, and import computers and cameras in exchange.

If each country uses its scarce resources to specialise in its absolute advantage industries, it can then exchange part of the output for the different products of other countries. This will be cheaper than diverting resources to their production at home.

However it is possible to show that even if one country has an absolute advantage in all industries over a second country, it can still benefit from specialising and trading. Both countries should specialise in the product(s) in which they have a *comparative* advantage. They can both enjoy a higher material standard of living. The law of comparative advantage is one of the oldest and most powerful in economics. Yet there are many spurious protectionist arguments that either fail to acknowledge this theory, or deliberately ignore it. The Law was first formulated by David Ricardo in the early part of the nineteenth century. It states that all countries can benefit from trade if they specialise in goods in which they have a comparative advantage.

A country has a comparative advantage over another country in the production of a good if it can produce it at a lower opportunity cost than the other country. That is, it has a comparative advantage in producing a good, if it has to forego less of other goods than the other country does.

To demonstrate the law of comparative advantage, a simple model of the world is utilised. It is assumed that there are only two countries; and only two products. Furthermore, it is assumed that there are no transport costs and there is full employment. These and certain other implicit assumptions can be examined again when the simple model is better understood. Some of the assumptions, *eg* that there are only 2 countries, 2 products and no transport costs are easily accommodated to a real, complex world of many products and many countries. Some others, like the assumption of full employment, cannot be easily accommodated and leave real reservations about the theory. That is, some of the unrealistic assumptions of the model weaken its validity and application to the real world. These are examined later as part of the case for protectionism.

Assume now, that with a given combination of resources, Country A can produce either 10,000 units of food or 5,000 units of machinery. Thus, the opportunity cost of producing 10,000 units of food is 5,000 units of machinery. There is an opportunity cost ratio of food to machinery of 1:0.5, *ie* for each unit of food produced half a unit of machinery is sacrificed. For each machine produced 2 units of food are sacrificed. This can be shown as a Production Possibility Frontier. In Figure 4.1a, Country A can produce 10,000 units of food if it produces no machines. It is at point a. Alternatively it can produce at b, using all of its resources to produce 5,000 machines, but producing no food. The country can also produce any combination of the two goods bounded by the Production Possibility Frontier (PPF). For example it could produce 6,000 units of food and 2,000 units of machines, at point c, or 3,000 units of food and 3,500 machines, at point d. As it is at full employment it will not produce inside the PPF. It also cannot produce outside its PPF. If the country tries to be self-sufficient and does not trade, its consumption has to be limited to its own domestic production. In other words the Production Possibility Frontier is also the Consumption Possibility Frontier. A consumption combination of 7,500 units of food and 2,000 machines, at point x, is therefore impossible.

Figure 4.1a

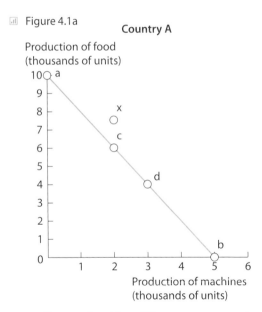

Country A

Country B, with a different resource endowment, can produce either 4,000 units of food or 4,000 units of machinery. The opportunity cost of 4,000 units of food is the 4,000 units of food foregone. There is an opportunity cost ratio of food to machinery of 1:1. For each unit of food produced one unit of machinery is sacrificed, and for each machine produced 1 unit of food is sacrificed. This is also shown as a Production Possibility Frontier in Figure 4.1b. Country B can produce 4,000 units of food if it produces no machines, at point a. Alternatively it can produce at b, using all of its resources to produce 4,000 machines but no food. This country can also produce any combination of the two goods bounded by the Production Possibility Frontier. For example, it could produce 3,000 units of food and 1,000 units of machines, at point c or 2,000 units of each, at point d. It will not produce inside the PPF, as it is at full employment. It is of course impossible to produce outside its PPF. If the country does not trade, its Production Possibility Frontier is also its Consumption Possibility Frontier. A consumption combination of 2,500 units of food and 2,000 machines, point z, is therefore impossible.

Figure 4.1b

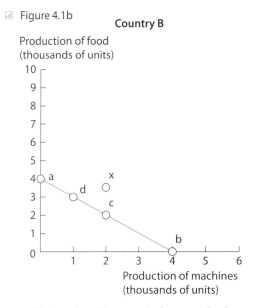

Country B

Notice that Country A has an absolute advantage in producing both food and machines. However the production of either has an opportunity cost. It can be shown that making one of the products has a higher opportunity cost than the other product, compared to Country B. It has a comparative advantage in one of them.

Country B, on the other hand, has an absolute disadvantage in both goods. However, because the opportunity cost of producing the goods is different to Country A, we will be able to show that it has a comparative advantage in one of these goods. To understand this it helps to set the opportunity costs out as a table as in Figure 4.2.

Figure 4.2 – Opportunity Cost and Comparative Advantage

Country	Production of food ('000 units)	Production of machines ('000 units)	Opportunity cost of food (in terms of machines)	Opportunity cost of food (in terms of food)
A	10	5	0.5	2
B	4	4	1	1

The opportunity cost of producing food in A is less than it is in Country B (0.5 of a machine in Country A, as against one machine in Country B). Because the opportunity cost of food is lower in Country A, it is said that Country A has a comparative advantage in the production of food. The opportunity cost of producing machines in Country B is less than it is in Country A (only 1 unit of food whereas 2 have to be sacrificed in A). Because the opportunity cost is lower in Country B, it is said that B has a comparative advantage in producing machines. Country B even though absolutely inferior is comparatively superior in producing machinery. It can now be shown that if each country specialises in its comparative advantage, total world output of both products will rise. If this extra output is shared both countries will be better off. Figure 4.3a shows one possible outcome. In the first case each country is self-sufficient by devoting exactly half of its resources to food and half to machines. Adding the two countries together gives the total world output of each product: 7,000 units of food and 4,500 units of machinery. In the second case, Figure 4.3b, each country specialises; according to comparative advantage, with Country A shifting resources into food and out of machines, and Country B doing the opposite. Here, as just one possible resource reallocation, it is assumed that Country A moves 80% of its resources into food production and leaves 20% of its resources in machine production. Country B totally specialises; putting 100% of its resources into the machine industry and therefore producing no food. Total world output of food rises to 8,000 units. The total world output of machines rises to 5,000 units. World output has increased by specialising, as the law of comparative advantage predicts.

Figure 4.3a – Before Specialisation

Country	Total production of food (units)	Total production of machines (units)
A	5,000	2,500
B	2,000	2,000
World	7,000	4,500

Figure 4.3b – After Specialisation

Country	Total production of food (units)	Total production of machines (units)
A	8,000	1,000
B	–	4,000
World	8,000	5,000

World output increases as countries specialise in the industries in which they have a comparative advantage. Country A has the lower opportunity cost of producing food, and Country B has the lower opportunity cost of producing machines. A specialises in food, B specialises in machines. More is produced in total. If they now trade it is possible for them both to be better off.

The two countries can now trade. Country A will export food and import machines. Country B will export machines and import food. The rate at which they exchange is known as the terms of trade. Country A can exchange food domestically for 0.5 machines, so any international terms of trade better than 1:0.5 will make it better off *eg* 1:0.6; 1:0.7; 1:2 ; and 1:10. The more machines obtained in exchange for one unit of food the more favourable are the terms of trade for Country A. However, the lower limit is the domestic opportunity cost ratio 1:0.5. Country A will not trade for less than 0.5 of a machine. After all, it can get this much at home by giving up a unit of food.

There is, however, also an upper limit to how many machines Country A can get for a unit of food. This is determined by the opportunity cost ratio of food in Country B. Domestically, Country B can obtain a unit of food by giving up one machine. It is not therefore going to be willing to give up more than this internationally. Thus the terms of trade of 2 machines to 1 unit of food or 10 machines to 1 unit of food are just not on offer by Country B. The domestic opportunity cost ratio 1:1 is the limit. However, any ratio better than this will benefit Country B. Thus giving up 0.9 machines for a unit of food is better than giving up 1 machine, as it has to do domestically. 0.8:1 is even better; 0.7:1 better still. We have already noted that there is a limit set by Country A's own opportunity cost ratio, *ie* 0.5:1. The terms of trade are therefore going to lie somewhere between these two ratios. Where it lies in practice depends upon the relative bargaining power of countries A and B.

Let us say that the terms of trade are settled at 1 unit of food for 0.8 machines, which looked at the other way round is 1 machine to 1.25 units of food. Clearly these terms of trade are acceptable to A and B as they are both getting better terms of trade than if they diverted resources at home. In Figure 4.4a and Figure 4.4b the original Production Possibility Frontiers are redrawn (*ie* before trade), and the new Consumption Possibility Frontiers are added. These consumption possibilities have only become possible by specialising and trading. In Country A the slope of the line has changed and shifted to the right from 1:0.5 to 1:0.8. In Country B the slope of the line has changed and shifted to the right from 1:1 to 1.25:1. Both countries can consume more by trading than they can consume by being self-sufficient. Notice in particular that points x and z, which were not previously possible because they were beyond the PPF, are now possible due to specialisation and trade.

Figure 4.4a

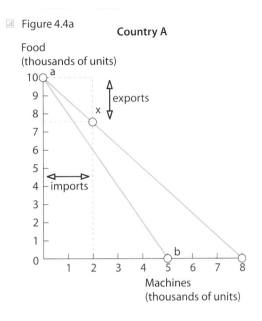

Country A

Food
(thousands of units)

Machines
(thousands of units)

Figure 4.4b

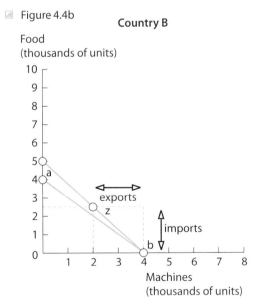

Country B

Food
(thousands of units)

Machines
(thousands of units)

In Figure 4.4a Country A has specialised totally in food, producing 10,000 units. It con-sumes 7,500 units of food and exports 2,500 units to Country B. With terms of trade of 1:0.8 it receives 2,500 × 0.8 = 2,000 units of machines in return. That is, it imports 2,000 units of machines from Country B. In Figure 4.4b Country B has specialised totally in machines, producing 4,000 units. It consumes 2,000 units of machines and exports 2,000 units to Country A. With terms of trade of 1:1.25 it receives $2,000 \times 1.25 = 2,500$ units of food in return. That is, it imports 2,500 units of food from Country B. Both countries are consuming more with trade than without trade.

Exactly the same principle of comparative advantage supports individuals specialising and trading with each other. A senior barrister may also be able to bake excellent bread. However, her comparative advantage will lie in the courtroom. The opportunity cost of taking a morning off to bake bread will be very high. Other things being equal it would be better to practise the law and trade a few minutes of her expensive time for the lower cost specialised time of the local baker.

Comparative Advantage

The notion of comparative advantage was developed by David Ricardo in 1817, a development of the free trade ideas of Adam Smith which were published in the Wealth of Nations 40 years earlier. According to the Theory of Comparative Advantage, countries should specialise in the things they do best and exchange them for things other countries do best. In this way output and income are increased for all those who participate in trade.

Questions

'A country which can produce all products better than another has a comparative advantage in everything. It is better off being self-sufficient.'

1   Correct?
2   If not, why not?

COMPARATIVE ADVANTAGE AS AN EXPLANATION OF TRADING PATTERNS

Given that the assumptions of the theory are valid, the law of comparative advantage shows that countries will be better off by specialising and trading, than being self-sufficient. A question then arises as to which goods and services a country should produce itself and which goods are best imported. In other words, how in practice should one expect to identify comparative advantage.

A country's comparative advantage will depend upon its resource endowment. That is, some factors of production will be relatively scarce, others will tend to be relatively abundant. Notice in particular the word relatively. We have already noted that this is not the same as absolutely. Thus a rich country that is absolutely endowed with more of all resources than a poor country will still be relatively better off in some resources than others. As long as domestic opportunity costs are different comparative advantage will exist and so will potential trading benefits between the two countries.

All countries are likely to have factors of production which are relatively abundant and others which are relatively scarce. Each country will tend to have a comparative advantage in those goods which are intensive in their use of an abundant factor. Countries with an abundance of land like Australia, New Zealand and Canada specialise in meat and grain production because they are land-intensive activities. With land being abundant, land costs will be relatively low, compared to, say, labour or capital costs. Prices of grain and meat will therefore be relatively low compared to land-scarce countries. The resource endowment is different in Belgium, Hong Kong and Japan. These countries do not have a comparative advantage in grain production and animal ranching. Labour-intensive activities *eg* making clothes, and assembling manufactured goods like computers and television sets, will be the comparative advantage choice of countries with abundant labour. The rapid economic growth in the Asia-Pacific Rim countries – Hong Kong, Taiwan, Singapore, South Korea, Malaysia, The Philippines and China – is partially due to labour abundance in Asia. The price of labour is generally low and goods which require a lot of labour are therefore relatively cheap. Japan, Europe and North America have high capital endowment, many scientific research institutes and a highly educated workforce. Consequently comparative advantage products tend to be capital-intensive and use advanced technology. Mediterranean countries and the West Indies are endowed with beaches, sunshine, and proximity to large, high-income populations. They have relatively low opportunity cost in providing beach holidays within the tourist industry.

The effect of such trade between countries is to equalise factor prices. For example, the demand for labour will rise in labour-abundant countries like Taiwan and South Korea as they specialise in labour-intensive goods. This will pull tend to pull wages up towards those of the higher wage countries. Conversely this explains the resistance to foreign trade from workers in non-comparative advantage domestic industries. Wages will tend to fall in those industries as the demand for labour-intensive goods transfers from domestic products to imported products. The returns on land and capital will also tend to equalise with trade.

1 German worker = 2 Americans = 5 Taiwanese = 128 Chinese!

Hourly Labour costs in Manufacturing (US$)			Hourly Labour costs in Manufacturing (US$)		
	1985	1995		1985	1995
Germany	9.60	31.88	Chile	1.87	3.63
Japan	6.34	23.66	Poland	na	2.09
France	7.52	19.34	Hungary	na	1.70
United States	13.01	17.20	Argentina	0.67	1.67
Italy	7.63	16.48	Malaysia	1.08	1.59
Canada	10.94	16.03	Mexico	1.59	1.51
Australia	8.20	14.40	Czech Republic	na	1.30
Britain	6.27	13.77	Philippines	0.64	0.71
Spain	4.66	12.70	Russia	na	0.60
South Korea	1.23	7.40	Thailand	0.49	0.46
Singapore	2.47	7.28	Indonesia	0.22	0.30
Taiwan	1.50	5.82	China	0.19	0.25
Hong Kong	1.73	4.82	India	0.35	0.25
Brazil	1.30	4.28			

Source: Morgan Stanley – August 1996

The table shows the total costs of hiring one manufacturing worker for one hour. It includes all taxes and benefits, *eg* paid holidays and paid sick leave. The comparison is made using average exchange rates for 1995. The very high wage costs in Germany in 1997 caused the prestigious car maker Mercedes to announce that it would shift production out of Germany unless car workers agreed to a reduction in benefits. In January 1997 South Korea suffered severe clashes between workers and the police, as the Government sought to end 'job for life' guarantees and to demand greater wage flexibility. Compare wages within these two countries in 1995 and 1985, and then with other countries, to offer an explanation for these events. In 1985 Europe, Japan and the USA were worried about the loss of manufacturing jobs to NICs like Hong Kong, South Korea and Taiwan. Governments in the NICs are themselves now worried, as their wage costs have risen due to their success. They are now losing manufacturing jobs to China and to India.

Question

1   Which was the highest wage-cost country in 1985?

2   How has this changed in comparison to Germany and Japan?

3   Calculate the relative wage cost ratios between the US, South Korea and China for both periods. Note how they have changed.

SOME LIMITS TO SPECIALISATION

In practice countries do not specialise totally, as in the model of comparative advantage. There are limits to specialisation. One reason is that opportunity cost is not constant in the real world. Take France as an example. The opportunity cost between land-intensive products and capital-intensive products will change as specialisation proceeds. If France has a comparative advantage in capital intensive, high technology goods its resources will move out of agriculture and into industry. The poor soils and steep hillside areas have a low marginal product and thus a low opportunity cost to the production of more industrial goods. As the transfer continues, however, more increasingly productive farmland will be sacrificed, at increasingly higher opportunity cost. In practice France will produce a mixture of goods. It will continue to produce farm goods, on its most productive farm land. This is why in practice trade debates are never about total specialisation. They are about producing a little more of some things and a little less of others; a debate about the balance of the product mix. The Production Possibility Frontier is not a straight line, but a curve convex to the origin. As the country moves further towards total specialisation, so the opportunity cost of any one product rises and its comparative advantage reduces.

Transport costs are ignored in the model, but they do place limits on trade in practice. It could well be that Australia has a comparative advantage in producing certain low-cost, heavy, bulky goods like road-stone, cement or bricks. With long distances to foreign markets, however, these goods are unlikely to be traded internationally. Yet the omission of transport costs do not weaken the theory of comparative advantage. This is because the measure of opportunity cost in practice is price. Consumers don't consider the physical opportunity cost of competing goods, they look at the price. The price of a good includes a provision for transport costs, just as it does for every other cost. Thus, if a consumer shops for a new pair of trainers, and the range of goods on offer has been manufactured variously in the USA, The Philippines, Taiwan, Portugal and Brazil, the consumer is no more concerned with transport costs than with any other cost. Rather she or he directly compares the retail prices of the shoes.

Another limit to the trade in goods and services is the mobility of the factors of production. It is in the self-interest of the owners of the factors of production to move them to the highest-paid locations, that is, where there is relative scarcity of that factor and hence a high reward to it. Thus, in the absence of restrictions, labour would tend to move from low-wage countries to high-wage countries. Capital would move from capital-abundant countries to capital-scarce countries. It is a feature of the late twentieth century that capital investment is doing just that, much of it directed by the owners of multinational companies. However, governments are far more strict on the movement of people. Immigration rules are rigorously enforced. This is in marked contrast to the large-scale migration of people in the nineteenth century.

Despite the arguments in favour of trade in goods and services, governments do restrict trade. This is because there are other assumptions of the model which do not reflect real world problems. There are, for example, dangers from being over-specialised. In addition, the existence of unemployment is relevant. These will be examined when the reasons for protectionism are considered in Section 4.2.

THE MAJOR PATTERNS OF WORLD PRODUCTION AND TRADE

TRADE VOLUME

The United States is easily the world's biggest trading nation, its total imports being almost double those of any other country. The link between high National Income per capita and trading activity is clearly shown in Figure 4.5. Europe, North America and Japan combine high per capita GDP with high trade volumes and values. Africa's poverty is accompanied by low levels of foreign trade. Yet Mexico and China are major trading nations which also have widespread poverty, so the link is not a simple one. Exports of primary materials (such as mineral ores, crude oil or unprocessed cereals) are less beneficial to a country than exports of value added goods. About 40% of Africa's merchandise exports are oil and gas, whilst minerals and non-ferrous metals account for another 5%. Fully 70% of Middle East merchandise exports are comprised of oil and gas.

Figure 4.5 – The World's Biggest Traders

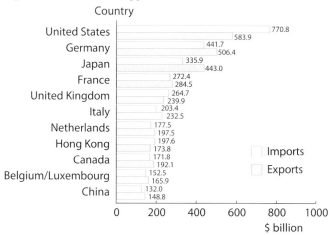

Source: WTO Understanding Global Issues (1997)

These eleven countries account for almost 70% of all international trade. Notice the high degree of correlation between high income and international trade.

A great deal of trade in the modern world involves goods whose components cross international borders several times before reaching the consumer. For example, half of China's exports in 1995 came from factories which were processing and assembling imports. Mexico's maquiladora (or 'make-up') factories accounted for a full 40% of that country's exports in 1995.

Foreign direct investment (FDI), once regarded as an alternative to the export trade, is very closely related to trade globalisation. FDI is concentrated in the rich world (over 70%), and in Asia. It is significant that out of some $80 billion of FDI to developing countries in 1994, only $4.5 billion went into Africa.

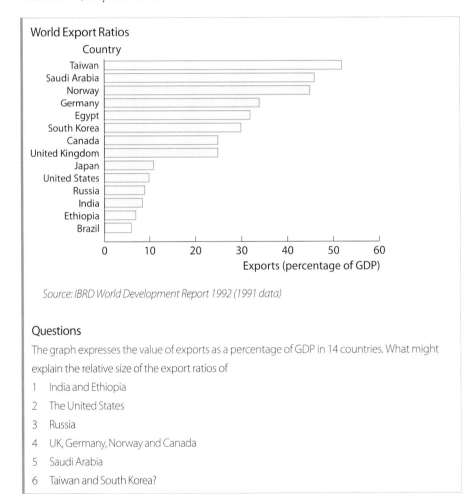

Source: IBRD World Development Report 1992 (1991 data)

Questions

The graph expresses the value of exports as a percentage of GDP in 14 countries. What might explain the relative size of the export ratios of

1   India and Ethiopia

2   The United States

3   Russia

4   UK, Germany, Norway and Canada

5   Saudi Arabia

6   Taiwan and South Korea?

GROWTH OF WORLD TRADE 1950 – 1995

In real money terms, the value of world trade has grown 15-fold in the last 40 years, and it continues to grow (see Figure 4.6). The nature of the trade has also changed. Forty years ago trade was dominated by agricultural produce, fuels, textiles and heavy manufactured goods. Over the years, processed foods, high-tech consumer products, clothing and services have become more important in the trade mix. In 1995, for example, international tourism receipts exceeded $370 billion and the trade in banking and insurance services expanded rapidly in order to sell to the global market. Shipments of semi-conductors reached $155 billion in 1995, and 60 million personal computers were exported internationally.

Figure 4.6 – Growth of World Trade 1950–1993

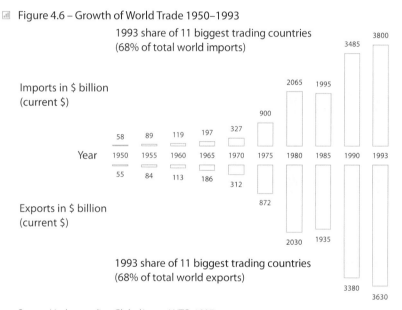

Source: Understanding Global Issues, WTO, 1997.

The Growth of International Crime

A feature of the modern world is the spread of international, cross-border crime. Crime flourishes in civil wars and in other chaotic and lawless situations. As civil wars have become the most common form of modern warfare, and modern transport and communications networks are so efficient, there have been greatly increased opportunities for international crime. This is an area that the WTO currently has on its future agenda. There is a need for a properly policed trading system, covering physical goods, services, and money, and the development of stronger links with Interpol.

THE UNEVEN DIRECTION OF TRADE

The great majority of import and export transactions are carried out by the industrialised countries As we noted before, trade is markedly a function of income. The poor buy and sell little. (If you are studying in an international school which charges fees, *ie* is trading in services, reflect for a moment on the income backgrounds of students in your school. The students are from the rich industrial countries, or the rich sector of an LDC are they not?) Figure 4.7 shows that the largest amount of world trade takes place amongst industrial countries themselves. The intra-country trade amongst the less developed countries is small. LDCs produce relatively little that is demanded by other LDCs. Exports, dominated by primary goods, go mainly to developed countries. Imports, mainly manufactures and some services, come from developed countries. Figure 4.7 shows exports to developing countries exceed imports from developing countries by a substantial margin, adding to the debt burden on poorer nations. The intra-country trade of the transitional economies should grow as they specialise to comparative advantage, but at present is a tiny fraction of world trade. This uneven pattern of trade is, however, changing. Trade in Asia and Central Europe has been growing much faster than in Western Europe and North America. In the 1990s, the Newly Industrialised Countries (NICs) of Asia, the so-called 'Asian Tigers', Hong Kong, South Korea, Malaysia, Singapore, Taiwan, and Thailand, saw average annual export growth of 11% (compared with 1% for Japan and 4.5% for Western Europe). However this was followed by the Asian crisis and recession of the late 1990s. Asia as a whole had an average growth of exports of 7.5% a year from 1990 to 1995. A large amount of the increased exports of the NICs are of manufactured goods.

Figure 4.7 – The Uneven Direction Of Trade

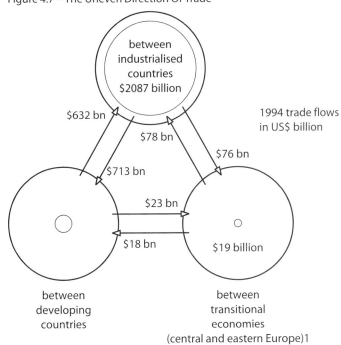

Source: Understanding Global Issues, WTO, 1997.

TRANSNATIONAL/MULTINATIONAL CORPORATIONS

A Transnational or Multinational corporation (TNC or MNC) is a company which has production facilities in at least two countries, *ie* it produces in a second country to its home base, not merely exports to it. Many multinationals produce in several countries and have an internationally orientated management. The largest MNCs control resources larger than middle-size economies (turn to the Figure 5.18 comparing countries to companies in *Section 5 – Foreign Direct Investment and MNCs*, to see just how huge the biggest MNCs are).

The growth of multinational companies took off after World War II and continues to accelerate. This growth of MNC activity explains the parallel increase in foreign direct investment (FDI), investment specifically directed from abroad. Early records are incomplete but, according to UN estimates, by 1970 there were 7,000 MNCs, of which 50% were based in the US or UK. In the early 1990s there were 35,000 MNCs with the US, Japan, Germany and Switzerland controlling 50%. Most MNCs are owned by shareholders in rich industrialised countries, although an interesting development in the 1990s is the rise of large MNCs owned by companies in the NICs, like South Korea and Taiwan.

By 1990 the largest 100 MNCs owned $13,100 billion of assets, of which a third were located outside the domestic economy of the country. An estimated 50% of all industrial production (excluding the former centrally planned economies) was produced by these 100 companies in 1990, and that their activities accounted for 40–50% of world trade.

REASONS FOR THE GROWTH OF MNCs

A number of reasons have been put forward for this growth in the international ownership of production. Early examples in the post-war years did seem to be satisfactorily explained by neo-classical market theory. That is, companies were locating abroad as a means of attaining the highest return on capital. Most investment latterly, however, has been between similar rich economies. In addition it is not necessary to retain ownership for returns on capital. Other explanations for the growth of MNCs have been sought. One explanation within the mining and energy MNCs has been the need to secure their supply lines of raw materials. For some manufacturing MNCs the need to locate within restrictive trade barriers has been a determining factor. That is, if protection seeks to keep out exports, the exporter can circumvent the barriers by relocating a production unit inside the country, so that its products are treated as domestic ones. A third explanation lies with 'Product life theory' which stresses the need to sell to ever larger markets when new products are fully developed and become price elastic. Firms need to sell high volumes and limited domestic markets limit sales.

Locational advantages are also important. Low wage levels, low taxes and high education levels might be important. Many host countries exaggerate these by offering export processing free zones with tax, infrastructure, subsidy and labour advantages. Some companies locate in order to be close to a large market to reduce transport costs, or to benefit from local low-cost sub-contracting of parts. An explanation of why ownership is retained within the company has to be sought as firms could otherwise license foreign producers to produce for them. Of course many do, and others set up joint partnerships with domestic firms. This latter is favoured where there is local uncertainty, as for example in much of Eastern Europe during the transition period. It is also often demanded by the host nation *eg* Malaysia insists on it, to retain greater control within the domestic economy. A common reason for companies wishing to retain control of production is, however, to retain and control the production technology.

CONSEQUENCES OF THE GROWTH OF MNCs

The reasons producers have increasingly sought out direct international investment opportunities are outlined above. There has truly been a globalisation of markets. Consumers have benefited from lower prices of many manufactured goods as the benefits of comparative advantage have reduced prices. This has been very marked in the manufactured goods which have been increasingly produced in low labour cost Asia-Pacific Rim countries. Consumer choice has increased, at least for those in industrial countries with the incomes to benefit. Thus, for example, the variety of foodstuffs on offer has increased enormously, and seasons play an increasingly smaller part in the year-round availability of fresh produce.

The potential to move production from high wage-cost countries to low wage-cost countries has strengthened the bargaining position of First World employers and weakened that of employees. Trade Union demands and government social legislation can be circumvented by companies moving, or even threatening to move, out of the country concerned. The least educated and least skilled in the developed countries have become the most vulnerable to job losses to low wage, low tax, low social protection countries. Globalisation has increased the need for worker flexibility and increased the premium on education and training.

The governments of host countries generally regard themselves as beneficiaries of the process. Inward investment creates jobs, income, education and training, tax revenue, access to world markets and technology transfer. In addition, there are further multiplier advantages to the original investment. Many governments are so keen to attract foreign companies that they offer subsidies and tax advantages to help lure inward investment. In Section 5, while acknowledging the generally beneficial effects of the MNCs on growth, we will be much more critical of their effect on development. This is to say, modern technology may be capital – rather than labour – intensive, tax payments may be low, profits may be largely expatriated, and political power may lie too heavily with the giant MNC rather than the government.

One problem peculiar to the MNCs activities is that of transfer pricing. Roughly a quarter of all of the MNC trade is between branches of the same company, as parts are manufactured in separate factories and moved to assembly in factories elsewhere. Company accountants seeking to minimise tax bills set their internal company prices so that the highest value added work appears to be done in the countries with the lowest tax rates. This may well effectively defraud local governments of taxes on work done in their own country if compared with the market prices that would be used between separately owned companies. Local businesses too object to this process, as it means that their own taxes are disproportionately larger. In fact this highlights a general problem with the development of multinationals. They can escape regulation from particular nations. Over time, nations and the institutions within them, like labour unions, have developed laws and agreements to control or balance the excesses of private companies. The multinational corporation is not matched with a powerful global government, or global union structure to oppose it and reduce the worst excesses. This is also true of any environmental damage they cause, which is likely to be large just because of their size. Environmental pressure groups like Greenpeace and Friends of the Earth have themselves adopted a multinational structure in order to confront polluting multinational companies.

Hoover and Grundig Relocate

In 1993 the US vacuum cleaner company Hoover decided to close its French factory and move to Scotland. Scottish workers were cheaper and had agreed to more flexible working conditions than the French. At the same time the TV factory owned by Grundig decided to shift its operations from France to Austria. Furious French workers marched on Brussels demanding that the EU prevent these relocations, which would cause major regional job losses. The EU was powerless under its own rules to prevent the movement of capital, even if it wanted to. Global markets are conducive to quick shifts in direct foreign investment. However, labour forces are not very mobile and have become more vulnerable to international shifts of capital.

MULTIPLE CHOICE QUESTIONS – GAINS FROM TRADE – HL EXTENSION

1   The following factors allow countries to specialise and trade except

   a   countries having different factor endowments.

   b   goods having different opportunity costs of production.

   c   some countries being able to produce more goods and services than other countries.

   d   some countries having no mobility of factors between industries.

Question 2 refers to the diagram below

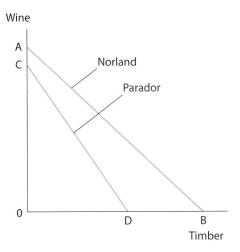

2   According to the theory of comparative advantage

   A   Parador has an absolute advantage in both wine and timber.

   B   Parador should export wine.

   C   Norland should export wine.

   D   No trade should take place.

3   With a given amount of resources, Atlantis can produce more food and more machines than Sparta. Which of the following statements may be true?

   I   Atlantis can benefit from importing machines.

   II   Sparta has a comparative advantage in producing food.

   III Output of either food or machines can be increased through specialisation.

   A   I only   B   I and II   C   II and III   D   I, II and III

4   The theory of comparative advantage shows that two countries can be better off by specialising and trading except when

   A   one country can produce all goods more efficiently than another.

   B   each country has an absolute advantage in at least one good.

   C   the opportunity costs of producing each good are the same in both countries.

   D   the pattern of demand is the same in both countries.

5   Disneyland (D) and Oz are two countries that each produce wine and textiles. (No other country produces these products.) The diagram below shows the production possibility curves of the two countries.

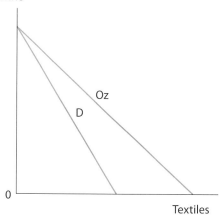

   If the two countries trade, we can expect

   I   Disneyland to specialise in wine.

   II   the total world output of wine to increase.

   III Oz's consumption of textiles to fall.

   A   I only   B   I and II   C   II and III   D   I, II and III

6   A major reason for international trade gains is that different countries have different

   A   economic systems.

   B   currencies.

   C   opportunity costs of production.

   D   levels of aggregate supply and demand.

7   The behaviour of multinational companies in LDCs has attracted criticism for

   I   escaping domestic taxation.

   II causing environmental damage.

   III hindering economic development.

   A I only   B I and II   C II and III   D I, II and III

8   Which of the following is likely to encourage the spread of multinational companies?

   I   Substantial barriers to international trade.

   II Substantial differences in labour costs between countries.

   III Limited size of individual national markets.

   A I only   B I and II   C II and III   D I, II and III

9   In the diagram below P_w is the world price for fibre optic cable. LRAC is the long run average cost curve of a company that manufactures fibre optic cable.

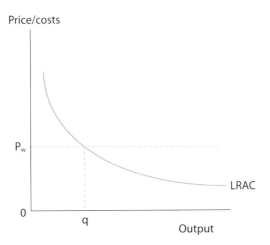

The company finds it easier to sell fibre optic cable when output exceeds Oq because it

   A grows beyond the minimum efficient scale for international trade.

   B gains from decreasing returns to scale.

   C gains from the law of diminishing returns.

   D gains from increased competition.

4.2   PROTECTIONISM

Protectionism is the act of imposing trade barriers to protect the income of domestic producers. Free trade is a situation where there are no trade barriers at all. Although it can be conclusively shown that there are enormous economic benefits from international trade, countries do frequently restrict trade. Politicians, who have the ability to erect trade barriers, are constantly having to make marginal decisions on trade in particular industries. Should trade be more open or more protected?

What are the arguments used to justify protectionism? Are these arguments valid? It is the job of the economist to make the government, and society, aware of the relative economic benefits and relative economic gains of more or less trade. First, however, we look at some of the methods of restricting trade. This will serve to highlight once more the economic losses of protection, alongside any gains.

TYPES OF PROTECTIONISM

The main explicit types of protectionism are; embargoes, tariffs, quotas and subsidies. There are also indirect ways of restricting trade. The main ones are; Voluntary Export Restraints (VERs), exchange rate controls, import licences and administrative barriers.

Embargo

This is a total ban on trade. It may be imposed from outside the country or by a domestic government itself. Imposition from the outside is likely to be for political or military reasons. Thus it might be done to put pressure on a regime abusing human rights, for example. Figure 4.8a shows the market situation of an embargoed good, *ie* one that is not traded. If there is an embargo, the whole supply of the good has to be domestically produced, shown by the supply curve S1. The market clears at A; p1 and q1 are the domestic price and domestic quantity of the good. Thus during the UN embargo on arms during the apartheid era in South Africa, domestic arms producers there flourished. An embargo is most effective where the country cannot easily produce the embargoed goods itself, or only at very great cost.

Figure 4.8a – No Trade: an Embargo

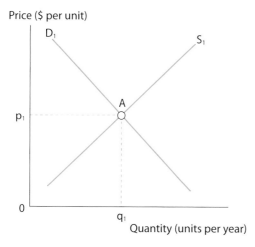

When a good is embargoed the whole supply has to be domestically produced. The market clears at A; p_1 and q_1 are the domestic price and domestic quantity of the good.

There may be a self-imposed ban on the trade in particular goods, for example, on guns, narcotic drugs or endangered species. In these cases the internal market also is likely to be suppressed.

Figure 4.8b shows the situation after the removal of an externally-imposed embargo and the benefit to consumers of free trade. The world price is $0p_2$. Domestic supply will be $0q_d$, supplied by the most efficient domestic firms, that is, those who can produce at a lower price than the world price. However imports flow in at price p_2, as merchants can undercut domestic producers. The supply curve becomes elastic (horizontal) at this price. It cuts the demand curve at B. Trade has benefited consumers by lowering prices and increasing quantity consumed. The losers are the domestic producers. They either do not produce at all, or produce at a lower price than before trade.

📊 Figure 4.8b – Free Trade

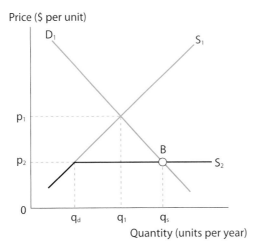

With world price at p_2 free trade will give a domestic supply of $0q_d$. Imports enter at price p_2, and the supply curve is elastic at this price, cutting the demand curve at B. Trade benefits consumers by lowering price from p_1 to p_2 and increasing the quantity consumed from q_1 to q_s. Domestic producers now sell less and at a lower price.

Tariffs

A tariff is a tax on imports. This could be a specific tariff, or an ad valorem tariff. Just as ad valorem taxes are more common than specific taxes, in order to allow for inflation, so ad valorem tariffs are more common than specific tariffs. In some cases tariffs may be variable, *eg* in the European food protection programme. Duties are varied to bring them up to a certain bench-mark level determined by domestic prices. What you learned about indirect taxes and elasticity is useful here. A tariff (which raises the price of a good) will be more effective the more price elastic in demand the good is. You will see in Section 5 that Less Developed Countries often use tariffs as a source of government revenue, as there is little other cash income to tax. In this case, the more price inelastic in demand the traded product is, the higher will be the revenue collected.

Figure 4.8c shows the effect of imposing a tariff compared to a situation of free trade. A tariff raises the supply curve vertically by the amount of the tariff, exactly as an indirect tax does. The supply curve has thus moved from S_2 to S_3 giving a new equilibrium at point C. The tariff has benefited domestic producers. An extra amount, $q_d\,q_t$, is now produced domestically and those who were already producing $0q_d$, now receive a higher price than before; $0p_3$ rather than $0p_2$. However, consumers lose out. They pay a higher price, and receive less of the good. Incidentally, the government gets a revenue from the tariff. This is equal to the tariff times the amount imported, shown by the rectangle *xyzC* in the diagram.

Figure 4.8c – Imposition of a Tariff

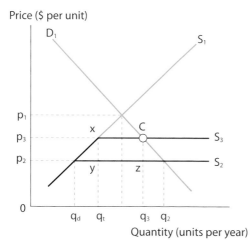

Price ($ per unit)

A tariff raises the supply curve from S_2 to S_3 with equilibrium at point C, quantity q_3 and price p_3. An extra amount, q_dq_t, is produced domestically at a higher price p_3 rather than p_2. Consumers pay a higher price, and receive less of the good than under free trade. The government collects revenue of xyzC.

Quotas

A quota is a physical limit imposed upon the amount of goods which may be imported. Thus it will be expressed in terms of numbers of cars or tons of beef.

Figure 4.8d shows the effect of a quota. The supply curve begins like that of free trade in Figure 4.8b; $0q_d$ is produced domestically and imports start to flow in at price p_2. However, only the quantity specified by the quota restriction can be imported: q_dq_q in Figure 4.8d. As nothing more is allowed to be imported, the supply curve reverts to the domestic supply curve. This forms an equilibrium with demand at point *D*. The quota has raised the price and reduced the consumption of the product.

📊 Figure 4.8d – Imposition of a Quota

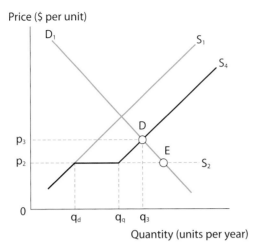

$0q_d$ is produced domestically and imports enter at price p_2. However only the quota can be imported, q_dq_q. At q_q supply reverts to the domestic supply curve. Equilibrium is at D. The quota has raised the price and reduced consumption compared to the free trade equilibrium E.

Subsidies

Subsidies can be applied to domestic goods to lower domestic prices and make them more competitive with imported goods. Figure 4.8e shows the effect of giving a subsidy to domestic producers of the good to help them to compete with cheaper imports. A subsidy shifts the supply curve down by the amount of the subsidy (review the imposition of a subsidy in Section 2.1). The supply curve moves from S_1 to $S_{subsidy}$. This reduces the costs of domestic producers, so that more of them can compete with imports. $0q_d$ is now produced domestically and the amount imported falls to q_dq_s. Consumers pay the same price and receive the same quantity: point E in the diagram.

Figure 4.8e – The Effect of a Domestic Subsidy

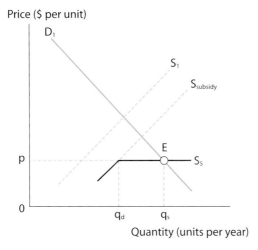

A subsidy shifts the supply curve down by the amount of the subsidy, from S_1 to $S_{subsidy}$. $0q_d$ is now produced domestically and the amount imported falls to q_dq_s. Consumers pay the same price and receive the same quantity at point E.

Subsidies can also be placed upon exports. This lowers their price to below their true production cost and therefore makes them cheaper to overseas consumers. It is effectively protecting the domestic industry from foreign competition, but it is doing it in the foreign market place. It is then foreign producers who are affected by the artificially low prices. This practice of selling abroad below the cost of production is known as dumping. Dumping is regarded as an unfair practice by the WTO, which legitimately allows trade barriers to be erected against dumping. Because of this many producers claim that dumping is happening whether it is or not, much as football players will claim a foul has been committed, even when they know it has not.

Voluntary Export Restraints and the US Steel Industry

After World War II the giant US steel companies were a symbol of US industrial power. By the early 1980s they were in serious decline. Low-cost foreign producers were taking an ever increasing share of the US and world markets. By 1992 the US companies had halved the number of man hours it took to produce one tonne of steel. How had this remarkable transformation occurred? After several American lawsuits claiming foreign 'dumping' of steel, the US negotiated a series of Voluntary Export Restraints with Japan, the EU and Korea. Foreign imports were restricted by 'voluntary' quotas while the industry was rationalised. The protection was, however, estimated to have cost American consumers $7 billion.

Even so, one of the first acts of the 2001 George W Bush administration was to impose direct restrictions on imports of steel.

Question

Why would protection cost consumers $7 billion?

Voluntary Export Restraints

The General Agreement on Tariffs and Trade (GATT), renamed the World Trade Organisation (WTO) in January 1995, forbids countries to apply tariffs and quotas in all but a few explicit exceptional circumstances, like dumping. Countries therefore try to get around the rules by inventing new restrictions. The Voluntary Export Restraint (VER) is just such an example and has flourished in the last twenty years. This has been a time of world recession and therefore a time of strong lobbying for protection by pressure groups. A VER is where an exporting country agrees to a voluntary quota of exports into a second country. Japan, for example, 'agreed' to such restrictions on automobiles, steel and computer chips requested by the USA and Europe. The economic effect is just like that of an imposed quota, as in Figure 4.8d. Consumers end up paying more for less.

Exchange Controls

Exchange controls are a form of protection. The government limits the amount of foreign currency available to importers, or to citizens wishing to travel abroad, or to companies wishing to invest abroad.

Import Licensing

This is a form of rationing. A licence, or permission to import, has to be obtained from the government. Import licensing is often used in conjunction with currency exchange controls.

Administrative Barriers

Administrative barriers can be set up which make it expensive for importers to compete. For example a country may set certain safety, health or environmental requirements on products. All domestic producers will have to meet the domestic legal requirements. As their costs will rise uniformly, their own competitiveness relative to each other remains unchanged. However, the new legal requirement will discriminate against foreign products produced to different standards. The cost of changing products for goods exported to one particular country will be relatively high for foreign producers, and they may therefore be effectively prevented from exporting.

All Roads Lead to Poitiers

One of the more celebrated examples of bureaucratic protection was that concerning video recording machines in the 1970s. Japanese productivity was more than a match for the European producers of the early video recording machines. On top of this the French government found itself relatively powerless against the influx of Japanese imports, because it was restrained by the rules of GATT. It therefore decreed that all VCR imports had to be processed at Poitiers, a tiny inland town miles and miles from the major container ports of Le Havre and Marseilles. Giant container trucks were soon gridlocked on the small roads around Poitiers, while the one official on duty slowly processed the many necessary papers before and after his long lunch-break.

ARGUMENTS FOR PROTECTIONISM

Exploitation of Third World Workers

It is often argued that consumers in rich countries should not buy goods made by workers in very poor countries. These workers may be paid no more than a dollar a day sewing clothes or weaving carpets. For example, the maquiladoras of Latin America, assembling goods for northern markets, have some of the worst labour and environmental conditions in the world. In the worst cases workers may earn as little as $2 a day for a 12 hour shift in a factory.

Question

Buying goods from firms that employ such workers is wrong and should be discouraged, should it not?

Child Labour and Free Trade

The United Nations agency on labour, the International Labour Organisation (ILO), has laid down the minimum working age for children as 15 years. Yet world-wide there are probably about 200 million children under this age employed. In a First World country this would be regarded as gross exploitation of children, yet in many poor countries child labour is seen as a normal part of family life. Children work alongside their parents and other relatives in extended family businesses. However, less fortunate children are found in factories, fields and mines. Many are virtual slaves to their employers, some trapped in crime and prostitution by adults. A worldwide legal ban sounds like a good idea on behalf of such children. However, it may make matters worse if it further impoverishes hard-pressed families. It is the causes of the poverty which lead to children being vulnerable which need to be addressed.

Such a scheme is found in Bangladesh in the garment industry, where child labour has been commonplace. The Bangladeshi government, working with UNICEF and the ILO, have come up with a scheme to phase it out, in one of the poorest countries in the world. Children will not be allowed to work in the garment industry, but will be paid the equivalent in wages to stay on at school. Their jobs are offered to other family members before being offered to anyone else. Financial aid will be provided by the Bangladeshi and US governments.

Questions

1   What are the relative merits of a ban on child labour?
2   What are the advantages of the Bangladeshi scheme?

The main arguments against protectionism have already been studied. They are the arguments for free trade, *ie* comparative advantage, economies of scale, increased competition and the spread of technology. Here we examine the case for protection.

1 The Assumptions of Comparative Advantage are Unrealistic

The theory of comparative advantage is only as good as its assumptions. Any divergence from the assumptions of the model weakens the power and applicability of this elegant textbook theory. In practice, reservations about the applicability of trade theory are strongest in the distorted markets of less developed countries. Some of these reservations are outlined here as possible reasons to limit international trade by protection.

The model assumes that opportunity cost is static. In practice it is dynamic, some of the most important factor inputs determining quality levels are intangible: science, technology and skills. (By studying the International Baccalaureate course for two years you are currently changing your own education skills and hence your comparative advantage in the market place.) Trade based on present comparative advantage may lock the LDC into low-skilled, labour-intensive production, whilst MDCs continue to grow from the dynamic of high-tech production. Japan, Hong Kong, Singapore, Taiwan and South Korea are examples of countries that have deliberately engineered their comparative advantage during the second half of the twentieth century, with outstanding results for trade and standards of living.

The model does not allow for uncertainty and risk. In practice, concentration on a few primary commodities does subject the LDC to considerable risk. Zambia's dependence on copper and Cuba's on sugar are two of many examples of high specialisation in LDCs. This is risky for the following reasons:

1 Commodities are notoriously income-inelastic in the long term, and are subject to price fluctuations in the short term.
2 Many synthetic substitutes have been developed to replace primary products, *eg artificial fibres for natural fibres.*
3 First World countries protect their own primary sectors against cheaper imports, *eg* the Common Agricultural Policy of the EU.

Due to the risks of over-specialisation, most LDCs would gain from the diversification of their production, with long run gains likely to exceed the short run losses by far. This issue is further addressed in Section 5.

Sino/Japanese Dispute over Steel

In February 1993 The Wall Street Journal reported that Japan would impose high tariff barriers on cheap Chinese steel imports. Duties of between 5% and 27% would be imposed upon the steel exports of over 100 Chinese producers. 'Dumping' was the justification given by the Japanese government to impose protection. China's share of the Japanese market had increased from 17% in 1989 to 39% in 1991.

Questions

1   Which groups of Japanese will be hurt, and which will be helped by the tariffs?
2   What is meant by 'dumping' in the context of foreign trade?

In the model prices reflect opportunity cost. Decisions to import and export are based on relative prices in the real world. Prices are therefore taken to reflect the opportunity costs of production. However, it is only under conditions of perfect competition that relative prices reflect opportunity costs. Prices in reality are considerably distorted by firms. Under conditions of imperfect competition, firms are price makers and can influence prices. Governments also distort prices by applying indirect taxes and subsidies. Finally, prices are based upon private costs and benefits and rarely reflect social costs and benefits. An example of this last type of price distortion is the market for reprocessing plutonium in the UK. The company, British Nuclear Fuels, has a comparative advantage in processing spent plutonium rods at its Sellafield plant. Used fuel is transported there from as far away as Japan. However, environmental pressure groups argue for restriction on the grounds of the potential social costs of this trade.

In the model there is no consideration of who gains from trade. Exports from LDCs are frequently produced by foreign-owned plantations and factories. A large proportion of trading gains may thus accrue to citizens of industrialised countries as the owners of exporting firms in LDCs. The poor are not likely to benefit very much.

In the model full employment is assumed. Countries operate on their Production Possibility Frontiers. Increased production of one good has an opportunity cost in goods foregone. It is characteristic of many countries, and especially of LDCs, that unemployment and under-employment are high. So increased domestic production may well be gained at zero or low opportunity cost, while badly needed jobs are created for the rural poor.

The model does not allow for economies of scale. Developing countries may find that industries in which they might have comparative advantage in the future are at present effectively protected by the economies of scale of the giant multinational companies.

In order to allow the development of new industries for the reasons outlined above, protection may be required during the period of transition. This known as the infant industry argument.

2 Anti-Dumping

Under WTO rules, countries are allowed to impose trade restrictions on products which are being 'dumped'. Dumping is when a product is exported at a price lower than its production cost . Of 160 anti-dumping investigations carried out by the GATT/WTO in the year 1994/5, 27 were against China, 17 against the EU or its member states and 10 against South Korea. Other countries accused of dumping included Indonesia, Thailand, the US, Russia, Brazil, Taiwan and Mexico.

3 Infant Industry Argument

The infant industry argument claims that protection is essential for industry to develop within LDCs. Many manufactures and services are produced at low cost in the developed nations because of the presence of economies of scale. A new baby industry in an LDC would find it impossible to compete, for at low units of output its costs would be high (at point *a* in Figure 4.9). By protecting the infant industry with trade barriers it can be guaranteed a captive market. The industry can then expand and move down the cost and learning curves. When the infant has grown to adulthood (point *b* in Figure 4.9), the barriers are removed and it competes equally. There have been many attempts to do this in LDCs, and many failures. One of the successful examples is the development of the Proton automobile company in Malaysia. There are, however, many dangers of creating infant industries. We will return to them in Section 5.

Figure 4.9 – Infant Industry Argument

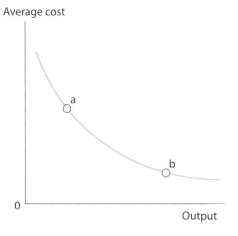

An infant industry with high costs, point a in the figure, is protected. The industry can then expand and move down the cost curve. At adulthood, point b, the barriers are removed.

4 Declining Industries

Similar reasoning is sometimes used in developed countries to protect old declining industries. This is known as the senile industry argument; where potential comparative advantage industries have declined and are not making enough profit to invest and modernise. Firms in these industries then argue for a period of protection to enable them to rationalise their production. For example the United States steel and automobile industries both successfully lobbied for protection on senile industry grounds. Most economists would argue, however, that the market is better at spotting investment and reinvestment opportunities than government, and that protection in developed countries for this reason is likely to be harmful.

5 Protecting Employment

Protection may be extended to declining industries to cushion them from the structural unemployment that results from rapid change. Even where it is recognised that the industry is in terminal decline, *ie* it has permanently lost its comparative advantage, the social and economic suffering of the affected workers may justify some temporary protection. Consumers pay the cost in terms of higher prices, by being denied cheaper imports.

6 Balance of Payments Disequilibrium

Protection may be used as a means to overcome a deficit in the balance of payments. Under certain specialised exchange rate circumstances a country may restrict imports in order to reduce a deficit in its balance of payments. This is considered under Section 4.5 'Exchange Rates', (a Higher Level topic).

ARGUMENTS AGAINST PROTECTIONISM

1 Higher Prices

The most powerful argument against protectionism is the loss of comparative advantage. The prices of goods and services to consumers will be higher. As a consequence of that, their incomes will buy less of all goods. And it is not just the prices of traded goods and services that are affected. Non-traded goods and services that use imported goods and services as inputs will be more expensive. There will be both down stream and up stream effects on other goods and services. For example, say an LDC were to offer infant industry protection to its agricultural machinery industry. 'Up stream', farmers, as the users of tractors, are denied cheaper (and probably superior) imported tractors. Farm costs will be higher than with free trade. 'Down stream', agricultural produce, *eg* wheat, will be more expensive and less competitive in domestic markets, hitting consumer spending again. In addition agricultural goods will be less competitive as exports to foreign markets.

2 Identifying the Infant Industries

There is the danger that the government will protect the wrong industries. Governments are not noted for having the entrepreneurial insight to see which industries will flourish in the future, and which will decline.

A Tax of 9900%!

Many developing countries have tried to save foreign exchange by putting very high import tariffs on luxury items. Ironically this affords a high level of protection to domestic producers of those goods. In 1966 the effective rate of protection on perfume in Brazil was a massive 8500%. Around the same period, Pakistan's protection of silk was 9900%. In the Philippines it was 2300% for electric lamps, and in Argentina 380% for textiles. In Mexico protection was 212% on cars.

Question

Assume that the countries above wish to have higher spending on necessities to help development programmes, and lower spending on luxuries for the wealthy. Why is high protection likely in practice to lead to *greater domestic production of luxuries?*

4.3   TRADE AGREEMENTS

> ### Case for Open Trade
>
> 'The economic case for an open trading system, based upon multilaterally agreed rules, is simple enough and rests largely upon common sense. Liberal trade policies which allow the unrestricted flow of goods, services and productive inputs multiply the rewards that come with making the best products, with the best design at the best price.
>
> But trading success is not a static thing. Competitiveness in particular products can move from company to company. For as much as the trading system is allowed to operate without the constraints of protectionism, firms are encouraged to adapt in an orderly and relatively painless way. The alternatives, of import protection and perpetual government subsidies, lead to bloated, inefficient companies supplying consumers with outdated, unattractive products. Ultimately, factories close and jobs are lost despite protection and subsidies. If other governments pursue such policies overseas, markets contract and world economic activity is reduced. One of the objectives of the WTO is to prevent such a self-defeating and destructive drift into protectionism.'
>
> *Source: WTO 'Trading into the Future'*

WORLD TRADE ORGANISATION (WTO)

International trade suffered a severe set-back in the first half of the twentieth century. The inter-war period saw a dramatic shrinking of world trade, and the erection of high protectionist barriers. During the three years following the Wall Street Crash, the volume of trade in manufactures fell by a third. The whole world was worse off, mainly as a consequence of the loss of comparative advantage. It was important therefore that when peace returned after World War II, international trade should be allowed to flourish.

The General Agreement on Tariffs and Trade (GATT) was signed at Bretton Woods in 1947 (at the same time as the IBRD and the IMF were set up). There were 23 signatory countries at that time. In 1991 GATT was renamed the World Trade Organisation. Today there are over 100 member countries covering more than 90% of world trade. Large tariff reductions are gained immediately by new countries upon joining the WTO due to the 'Most Favoured Nation' clause. This states that the most preferential tariff offered to any member country can be claimed by every other member country. The WTO forbade the use of quotas (except in agricultural goods) and placed restrictions on when tariffs might be used. Special allowances were made for LDCs, enabling them to protect trade more easily, in recognition of their need to develop.

WTO members meet periodically to negotiate reductions in trade restrictions. There have been eight such rounds, the most important being the Kennedy Round (1964–7), the Tokyo Round (1973–9) and the Uruguay Round (1986–93). The first two rounds led to tariff reductions of over 30% in each case. However the last, the Uruguay Round, was the most comprehensive, tackling agricultural protection and the trade in services for the first time.

The present round, the Doha round, began in November 2001 and is scheduled to complete in 2004. Agriculture is again a major item on the agenda. Rich countries spend more than $1 billion a day on subsidies, a sum greater than the entire GDP of sub-Saharan Africa. Services are also high on the agenda. Services make up 60% of world output but only 20% of world trade so there is great scope here for trade gains. Intellectual property rules are likely to be strengthened. Finally the use of 'anti-dumping' claims as an excuse to restrict trade is likely to be curtailed. The negotiations are likely to be very tough in the face of protectionist instincts at a time of world recession.

There has been an increased need for the discipline and policing of the WTO in the last 20 years. Following a spectacular increase in world trade, the oil price increases of the 1970s and the recession of the 1980s, countries were very tempted to restrict trade. With rules governing the imposition of tariffs and quotas the favourite weapons had to be more oblique. Thus subsidies, health and safety standards, and administrative delays on imports were widely used. The imposition of voluntary quotas (VERs) became commonplace during the 1980s, especially by North Americans and Europeans, reacting against their balance of trade deficits in manufactures with Japan.

The Uruguay Round

One hundred and five countries took part in the round of trade negotiations, named after the host country Uruguay. They began in 1986 and were originally due to be concluded in December 1990. There was a great deal of hard bargaining, however, and the negotiations staggered on until December 1993. The negotiations threatened to break up without agreement on several occasions, as member countries were very reluctant to give up existing protectionist policies, especially in agricultural products. The aim of the Uruguay Round was to include virtually all goods and services in the negotiations. Tariff levels were only 5% at the outset of the Uruguay Round, compared to 40% in 1947. One aim was to reduce these levels by a further third. Agreement was sought to reduce and eliminate the many non-tariff barriers which had grown up. Rules were to be tightened and made more restrictive on the use of: (i) subsidies, (ii) restrictions used for balance of payments reasons and (iii) restrictions used for anti-dumping reasons. Large product groups which were previously exempt were now included. These were: natural resource-based products, tropical products, agriculture, textiles and clothing. Also included for the first time was the growing international trade in both services and intellectual property.

These were very ambitious targets. The real stumbling-block was the level of suspicion between the USA and the European Union. The USA, Australia and a few others called for a 75% reduction in EU farm protection policies. The EU would offer only 30%. After two further years of negotiation the EU offered to reform its farm support system (CAP) and an agreement was signed between the USA and the EU. Even then France tried to reopen the negotiations on behalf of her farmers and (as stated above) it was not until December 1993 that the Uruguay Round was finally concluded.

The WTO deal is calculated to add $213 billion per year to the global economy from tariff reductions alone, and of that $190 billion from agriculture. If the non-tariff barrier gains were to be included the figure would be higher. The main beneficiaries of the agreement will be the developed countries, because they trade most and protect most. The gains will be especially high in agriculture – from lower prices and increased outputs. The largest gainers will be the EU, EFTA, the ASEAN countries and Japan. However, while the increased global output is immense at $213 billion, the potential gain from total free trade is estimated to be more than double that, at $450 billion. There is therefore still some way to go towards a world of free trade.

ECONOMIC INTEGRATION

At the same time as the WTO has been attempting to free up trade globally, regionally based groups of countries have formed limited areas of freer trade by integrating economically. There are three main types of trading bloc; free trade areas, customs unions and common markets. These are playing an increasingly important role in international trade. Figure 4.10 shows a model of progressive forms of integration. Five countries are each represented by a letter; A to E. In diagram (i) each country has its own fence or boundary to every other country. Each country is 'sovereign'. There is no integration at all. In diagram (ii) the three countries A, B & C have formed a free trade area. This is represented by the inclusive boundary fence. Within this boundary goods and services move freely. However, each country retains its own sovereignty with respect to outside countries, D and E. Note that in a free trade area a way has to be devised to prevent imports entering the country with the lowest trade barrier and then moving onwards freely to those member countries with higher trade barriers. In diagram (iii) there is a customs union – a unification of customs or trade policies. The individual country barriers have disappeared and the countries are no longer sovereign. They are represented at trade discussions by a supra-national organisation, *eg* as the EU was at the Uruguay Round. A common market, as in diagram (iv), is a customs union for trade and something else in addition. It is an area with free movement of the four factors of production: land, labour, capital and enterprise. So that not only can goods and services move freely, but the factors of production can too. Finally, groups of countries can integrate more than their trade policies alone. An economic union is where a group of countries, having formed a common market, adopt common economic policies, *eg* a common agricultural policy, a common fisheries policy, a common transport policy, a common energy policy. They could then adopt a fixed exchange rate between members to facilitate the workings of these common policies. This exchange rate system could then further integrate into a common currency within the integrated area, abandoning individual national currencies. Common macroeconomic policies might be adopted towards inflation and unemployment. The countries will by then have given up a very significant degree of sovereignty in exchange for integrated economic behaviour. The ultimate act of integration would be to adopt common political policies and thus become a political union, a federation of states, rather than remaining sovereign countries.

Figure 4.10i to 4.10iv Forms of Economic Integration

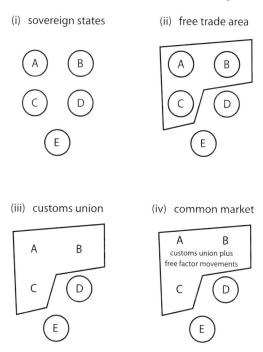

(i) sovereign states

(ii) free trade area

(iii) customs union

(iv) common market

As always, models do not reflect reality completely, but we can try to place existing major economic groups into this model. Amongst the developed countries, the European Union is the most integrated. Another group EFTA, the European Free Trade Area, began with a large number of members 30 years ago but has dwindled as members have left to join the EU. In 1993 NAFTA was formed, consisting of the United States, Canada and Mexico, a vast free trade area in terms of spending power. ASEAN, the Association of South East Asian Nations, is a powerful group of newly industrialised countries co-ordinating their trade policies. The Latin American Integration Association has developed from the Latin American Free Trade Area (LAFTA). Amongst other LDC groups are the Andean Pact, the Central American Common Market, the Caribbean Community (CARICOM) and the Economic Community of West African States (ECOWAS).

Regional Trading Blocs

APEC (Asia Pacific Economic Co-operation group), which includes the six ASEAN countries plus China, Japan, South Korea, the United States and eight other Pacific Rim countries. There is talk of a Western Hemisphere free trade area and even a North America / EU free trade area.

ASEAN (The Association of South East Asian Nations) – Brunei, Indonesia, Malaysia, Philippines, Singapore and Thailand – have agreed to develop a free trade area, as have the members of APEC.

EU (European Union). The biggest, and by far the most closely integrated, trading bloc. Operates a customs union and a single market with, in theory, complete freedom of movement of goods and services, capital and people. Has a wide range of social and environmental measures. Members of the EU are Austria, Belgium, Denmark, Finland, France, Germany, Greece, Italy, Ireland, Luxembourg, Netherlands, Spain, Sweden, Portugal and the UK. In December 2002 it was agreed to increase membership by 10 with the inclusion of Cyprus, the Czech Republic, Estonia, Hungary, Latvia, Lithuania, Malta, Poland, Slovakia and Slovenia.

Mercosur. South American Common Market. A free trade area involving Argentina, Brazil, Paraguay and Uruguay, with Chile a recent addition and Bolivia hoping to join soon.

NAFTA (North American Free Trade Area). Links the economies of Canada, Mexico and the US and liberalises trade between them. Weak social and environmental measures.

Russia, Belarus, Kazakhstan and Kyrgyzstan have formed a customs union as part of their closer economic integration. There are regional 'free trade areas' in Africa, Latin America, the Caribbean and Asia, but none is closely integrated as yet. The question for the future is whether regional free trade areas will serve to complement the global system, reinforcing the move towards open trade, or evolve into protected 'fortress-style' trading blocs.

NAFTA and Free Trade

Critics of free trade have argued that NAFTA and liberalisation led to the spectacular collapse of the Mexican economy at the end of 1994. Others point to the long period of protectionism which made Mexico's industries uncompetitive, and its public sector too big a drain on the budget. The ambitious challenge facing Mexico was the rapid change from a closed to an open economy, while simultaneously moving from an authoritarian one-party rule to democracy. Speculative 'hot money' which had flowed into Mexico in anticipation of NAFTA benefits quickly evaporated as political instability followed the assassination of the man expected to be Mexico's next president. It took a $50 billion support package – quickly engineered by the US, which provided $20 billion – to restore confidence. But social division and political uncertainty remain. Real wages have gone down, and unemployment has risen, particularly in the rural areas. It is still too early to judge the overall success of the NAFTA experiment. So far the biggest winners seem to be the maquiladora (assembly factories) established in Mexico, many of them in the north and close to the US border. The 50% devaluation of the peso in December 1994 has made such operations even more profitable for foreign owners. The hope is that, in the long term, all three member countries of NAFTA will benefit from the increase in mutual trade. However, it already seems clear that NAFTA should have been bolstered by stronger social and environmental programmes to offset the sudden impact of free trade.

Source: Fairer Global Trade? The challenge for the WTO.

HL EXTENSION

TRADE CREATION AND TRADE DIVERSION

The increased trade which is likely to follow the creation of an integrated free trade area will not all be totally beneficial. A distinction has to be made between trade creation and trade diversion, that is, new trade and trade which has been re-routed from elsewhere. Trade creation causes total economic welfare to increase as a result of the new trade grouping. If a member country was formerly protecting an inefficient industry, then consumers would have been paying higher prices and receiving lower outputs than with free trade. If on joining a trade area lower cost goods now become available from another member country, prices will fall and quantity consumed will rise. There will have been trade creation, namely, an increase in output due to trade.

On the other hand, a country may have already been benefiting from low cost goods on the world market before entry to the group. It is possible that, as members of an integrated group with a common external barrier, consumers can now buy the product from another member country more cheaply than outside. In this case trade is said to have been diverted. Consumers are switching to a higher cost, comparative disadvantage producer due to the distorting effect of the relative tariffs. Trade has been diverted from the external comparative advantage producer and, other things being equal, there is a loss of economic welfare. For example, when the UK joined the EC in 1971 it was already buying food at world prices from New Zealand, Argentina and the USA. Within the highly protected Common Agricultural Policy of integrated Europe, tariffs made these products expensive compared to domestic produce from within the UK itself, France, and Italy. Trade was therefore diverted from low cost to high cost producers.

MULTIPLE CHOICE QUESTIONS – PROTECTIONISM AND TRADE AGREEMENTS

1 All of the following are justifications for imposing a quota on imports except

A to prevent dumping.

B to protect infant industries.

C to raise tax revenues.

D to support a strategic industry.

Question 2 refers to the diagram below, a country's market for steel.

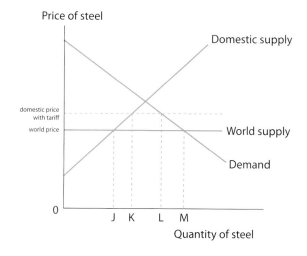

2 The country imposes a tariff on steel imports. After the tariff is imposed steel imports change from

A 0J to 0K   B JM to KL   C KM to JL   D 0L to KM

3 Three countries form a free trade area. This will aim to

A establish a common external tariff with non-member countries.

B abolish trade restrictions between member countries.

C integrate the monetary systems of member countries.

D protect the incomes of domestic agricultural producers.

4   A customs union benefits its members because it

    A   produces economies of scale.

    B   stimulates trade with members.

    C   encourages suppliers from low cost countries.

    D   leaves members to set their own external tariffs.

5   Which of the following is a characteristic of a customs union but not a characteristic of a free trade area?

    A   A common currency.

    B   A common external tariff.

    C   The free movement of labour.

    D   A common tariff between member countries.

6   The main function of the WTO is to

    A   provide economic aid to LDCs.

    B   stabilise exchange rates.

    C   provide loans to LDCs.

    D   reduce the level of protection in world trade.

7   The rules of the WTO allow tariffs to be imposed where

    A   imports threaten jobs in domestic industry.

    B   imports cause domestic producers' incomes to fall.

    C   imports are sold at a lower price than their production costs.

    D   tariffs are a source of government revenue.

8   Gormenghast imports wheat at a lower price than its own domestically grown wheat. The imposition of a tariff on imported wheat should increase

    I   domestic production.

    II   economic efficiency.

    III consumer welfare.

    A   I only   B   I and II   C   II and III   D   I, II and III

9   A quota can be used in placeof a tariff for all of the following reasons except

   A   to protect a declining industry.

   B   to protect an infant industry.

   C   to prevent dumping.

   D   to raise tax revenue.

10 A Taiwanese car assembly factory is built in Canada, a member of NAFTA. Which of the following is NOT a valid reason to explain the action of the Taiwanese company?

   I   Avoidance of a common external tariff on goods made in Taiwan.

   II   Opportunities to exploit factor costs different from those in Taiwan.

   III Access to an enlarged market without internal barriers.

   A   I only   B   I and II   C   II and III   D   I, II and III

4.4   BALANCE OF PAYMENTS

The balance of payments is a country's account with the rest of the world. All the transactions between citizens and organisations of a country and foreigners and foreign organisations are recorded as the balance of payments. By way of illustration Figure 4.11 shows a summary table of the balance of payments of the USA in 1992. The account has two main sections: the current account and the capital account. The current account records all trade on a day-by-day basis, that is, goods and services which are continuously traded. The capital account records transactions in external assets and liabilities.

Figure 4.11 – the Balance of Payments Account of the United States, 1992

	Item	Amount ($ billions)
1	Merchandise exports	439
2	Merchandise imports	(535)
	Merchandise trade balance (or Visible balance) (items 1-2)	**-96**
3	Service exports	178
4	Service imports	(123)
5	Income from US overseas investments	109
6	Income outflow for foreign US investments	(99)
7	Net US government grants	(14)
8	Net private transfers and pensions	(17)
	Current Account Balance (items 1-8)	**-62**
9	US capital inflow	80
10	US capital outflow	(48)
11	Increase in US official reserves	3
12	Increase in foreign aid assets in US	40
	Capital Account Balance (items 9-12)	**75**
13	Statistical discrepancy	(-13)
	Net balance (items 1-13)	**0**

Source: US Department of Commerce

The Current Account

The current account is itself split in two. The first part is known as the merchandise trade account, or visible account, which records the trade in goods. The second part is known as the invisible account, recording the trade in services.

In 1992 the $ billions of merchandise exports in the US totalled $439 billion, and merchandise imports $535 billion. This gave a deficit on the Merchandise Trade Balance of minus $96 billion. That is, visible imports were $96 billion more than visible exports in 1992.

Service exports, the export of services like films, tourism, banking and insurance were, however, larger than service imports. Income from American assets owned abroad was also larger than income paid out to foreigners owning US investments. The current account balance is a sub-total of the balance of payments. It includes the merchandise trade, the trade in services, investment income flows, government grants and private transfers (e.g. wages sent home by foreigners working in the United States). The current account balance is the most comprehensive summary of current trade relations. In 1992 the US had a current account deficit of $62 billion.

The Capital Account

The deficit of the current account is offset by the surplus of the capital account. The capital account is a record of asset transactions across international borders. The US capital inflow is the sum of all foreign purchases of long-term and short-term capital assets. Long-term assets are American companies, farms, or shops bought by foreigners. Short-term assets are American bonds and bank deposits. This gave a total inflow of spending of $80 billion in 1992. $48 billion of US spending went abroad in the same period to buy foreign assets. In addition, the US and foreign governments bought and sold dollars, giving an increased inflow of another $43 billion (items 11 & 12). Item 13 is a difference figure between the transactions in and out which were not recorded. There are large numbers of these transactions. However, as the Central Bank has a monopoly over all foreign exchange transactions, the total amount of foreign exchange is known.

The capital surplus has to balance the current deficit. The demand for every dollar has to be matched by an equal supply.

Net balance of payments = current account balance + capital account balance = 0.

The current account indicates whether a country is paying its way day-by-day, showing whether it is exporting sufficient domestic goods and services to pay for its imports of foreign goods and services. All countries cannot have positive current accounts. The surplus of one country has to be balanced by the deficit of another. Over a long period of time it would not even make sense to export more than was imported. It would be rather like working for someone else for no payment. Exports are useful only for the imports for which they can be exchanged.

Several years of negatives in a row on the current account might start to give concern. Even then, it would depend upon a more detailed analysis. If the country were consistently consuming more than it was producing, there would be grounds for concern. If, on the other hand, a country were importing capital equipment, a deficit could be highly acceptable, as future output would be likely to increase as a result. China is a country presently in this situation, importing large volumes of capital investment goods as its economy expands. There is a parallel in the way many young adults run negative balances while they are at college. It makes sense if, as a result, their productivity and earning power increase in the future.

The merchandise trade figures are usually the most readily available, and are published monthly. Aside from their own intrinsic importance as a record of visible transactions, they act as an indicator, or barometer, of what is likely to be happening in other less accessible parts of the account.

Japanese Surpluses 1981–1989

The current account of Japan's balance of payments showed large and increasing surpluses from 1981 to 1987, and falling but still positive surpluses thereafter. This meant that Japan's exports were increasing at a far greater rate than her imports. This surplus attracted a good deal of international criticism, especially from countries with large and growing trade deficits like the United States. At the same time Japan's net outflow on the capital account increased massively. This illustrates one of the characteristics of the balance of payments system. Current account surpluses lead, by definition, to increased assets in the form of claims on foreign countries.

Questions

1   Why should Japan's surpluses attract criticism from its trading partners?
2   What is the connection between the current account surplus and the outflow on the capital account?

MULTIPLE CHOICE QUESTIONS – BALANCE OF PAYMENTS

1 The domestic demand for goods and services in Zanadu is lower than the domestic supply. Zanadu's balance of payments account is likely to show this as

A a visible trade deficit.

B a current account surplus.

C a capital account surplus.

D an invisible trade deficit.

2 Which of the following will appear as negative on the current account of the balance of payments?

A The purchase of domestic airline services by a foreign resident.

B Spending overseas by domestic residents when on holiday.

C The export of coal.

D The receipt of interest on overseas shares held by domestic residents.

3 Which of the following statements is correct?

A The current account records trade in goods only.

B The capital account records trade in capital equipment.

C The sum of visible and invisible trade must be zero.

D The current and capital accounts, including official financing, must sum to zero.

4 The balance of payments of Sparta is shown in the table below.

	$ million
Exports of goods	220
Imports of goods	220
Exports of services	120
Imports of services	100
Net capital transfers	40

The current account balance is

A -$40 million.   B -$20 million.   C zero.   D +$20 million

5   The balance of payments of Phoenicia is shown in the table below.

	$ million
Exports of goods	35
Imports of goods	45
Exports of services	25
Imports of services	15
Net capital transfers	30

The current account balance is

A -10   B 0   C +20   D +30

6   Which item would appear as a plus on 'invisibles' in the balance of payments of Nania?

A   Imports of goods.

B   An increase in foreign exchange reserves.

C   Tourist visits to Narnia by foreigners.

D   Inflows of capital.

7   The overall balance of payments of a country will

A   sometimes balance.

B   always balance.

C   be negative.

D   be positive.

8   The table below shows some information about the UK economy.

	Year 1	Year 2	Year 3
	(£ billion)		
Exports of goods	-300	+200	-150
Net capital transfers	-100	+500	+100

In each of the three years the invisible balance was

A   in surplus.

B   sometimes in surplus and sometimes in deficit.

C   in equilibrium.

D   in deficit.

9 In the balance of payments accounts of the two countries, Kernow and Gaul, which of the following would be a change in Kernow's external assets?

A Imports of consumer goods from Gaul to Kernow.

B Exports of machinery from Kernow to Gaul.

C Expenditure in Gaul by tourists from Kernow.

D The purchase of a bond by a Gaul resident from a Kernow resident.

10 The following would all appear in the current account of the balance of payments except

A Transfers abroad by immigrant workers.

B Interest and dividend payments to foreign shareholders.

C The purchase of a foreign hotel chain.

D Receipts from tourism.

4.5   EXCHANGE RATES

DETERMINATION OF EXCHANGE RATES

In a market exchange rate system, the rate of exchange is determined solely by the forces of demand and supply. This is known as a floating exchange rate system, with the currency floating freely up and down. The total demand for a currency is, of course, the sum of all the individual demands for it. These demands have already been categorised into groups in the Balance of Payments as the demands for: goods, services, capital transactions and changes in reserves. Assume now that there are just two countries, Canada and Mexico. We can then look at the demand and supply of Canadian dollars (*C$*) in terms of Mexican *pesos* to illustrate how an exchange rate is determined.

When Mexican importers wish to buy Canadian goods, for example wheat or tractors, they will demand Canadian dollars in the foreign exchange market. The Mexican demand for Canadian services, *eg* for tourism, study or business trips to Canada, will also cause there to be a demand for Canadian dollars. If a Mexican manufacturing company wishes to set up factory in Canada, it too will demand Canadian dollars. Mexican speculators expecting an upward movement in the Canadian dollar will demand dollars.

The lower the price of the *C$* the more will be demanded. The cheaper the *C$* is to Mexican traders the cheaper are Canadian goods, services and assets. Therefore the demand curve for the dollar will slope downwards.

The supply of Canadian dollars into the foreign exchange market comes from Canadians wishing to buy Mexican goods, services and assets. To buy Mexican manufactures, or a Mexican holiday, Canadians demand *pesos*. When they buy *pesos* they pay for them with Canadian dollars. The higher the *C$/peso* exchange rate the more *pesos* will be bought and the more dollars will be supplied. This is because the price of Mexican goods, services and assets are cheaper in Canadian dollars the higher is the price of the *C$*. Thus the supply curve of Canadian dollars will slope upwards against its exchange rate.

The equilibrium exchange rate will be where the demand for dollars matches the supply of dollars. In Figure 4.12 this is at an exchange rate of *C$1 = 100 pesos*.

Figure 4.12

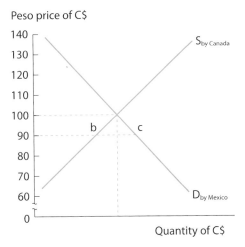

Peso price of C$

If the exchange rate were below the equilibrium, say at an exchange rate of *C$1 = 90 pesos*, the demand for *C$* in the foreign exchange dealing rooms would be greater than the supply of dollars on offer. There would be an excess demand for *C$*, of *bc* in Figure 4.12. Dealers wanting to earn commission by exchanging money will have to raise the offer price for the *C$* to encourage a greater supply, and to reduce the excess demand. They would keep doing this until the equilibrium point is reached. Similarly if the exchange rate were above the equilibrium, say at an exchange rate of *C$1 = 110 pesos*, there will be an excess supply. Dealers will lower rates to encourage demand and reduce supply. In practice the process of reaching equilibrium is very rapid; exchange rates adjust to small gaps in rates minute by minute. This is a market that barely sleeps, following the sun around the globe. As foreign exchange markets close in Europe, they are already open in eastern North America. They then move on to the west coast of North America, then to the dealing rooms of the Far East, the Middle East, and then back full circle to Europe again.

Juggling in the Foreign Exchange Market

A chain of electrical retailers based in Switzerland wishes to buy *1,000 television sets from Sony of Japan at a cost of 40,000 Yen each, ie at a total cost of 40 million Yen. It will need to buy Yen from the foreign exchange market in order to pay Sony. The firm will phone several Geneva-based banks to get quotes for the price for Yen. Each bank, in competition with the others, will wish to earn the commission on the business and seek to offer a higher rate than the other banks. The higher the Yen/Swiss franc rate, the more Yen the importing firm will get for its money. Thus a rate of Yen 198 = Swf 1 is better than a rate of Yen 195 = Swf 1. The bank that wins the business will then have to set about buying 40 million Yen. To do this it will have to offer Japanese who are selling Yen a sufficiently low exchange rate. The lower the Yen/Swf rate the more attractive it is for Japanese to buy Swiss francs. For a Japanese wanting to exchange Yen for Swiss francs a rate of Yen 195 = Swf 1 is better than a rate of Yen 198 = Swf 1. The dealers are thus in a delicate balancing position at the centre of the market. They must offer a high enough rate to gain the importer's business and a low enough rate to obtain the required amount of Yen. The dealers are therefore constantly juggling exchange rates to balance the demand for, and supply of, each currency.*

Question

A Singaporean food processing company wishes to import wheat from Australia. How will a Singaporean foreign exchange dealer respond to a quote for Australian dollars?

CHANGES TO A FLOATING EXCHANGE RATE

Unless a government intervenes, the changing forces of demand and supply will cause the exchange rate to change. In Figure 4.13 a fall in demand for C$ is shown as a shift of the demand curve from D_1 to D_2. An increase in supply of C$ is shown as a shift of the supply curve from S_1 to S_2. In both cases the exchange rate of the C$ will fall. Any fall in the price of a currency is called a depreciation. A rise in an exchange rate is known as an appreciation. There are a number of things which can cause the demand and supply of a currency to appreciate or depreciate as in Figure 4.13. The major ones are examined here and then more fully in the HL Extension to the topic.

Figure 4.13

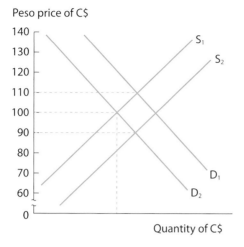

Shifts in the demand and supply of a currency cause the currency to appreciate and, as in this case, depreciate.

A Change in Incomes

It was noted in the macroeconomic study in Section 3 that imports are a function of income. If a country's National Income increases then its demand for imports will increase. Thus the supply of its currency will increase and the exchange rate will depreciate. If, however, foreign incomes rise, demand for the country's exports will increase. The demand for its currency will increase, and the exchange rate will appreciate. So, if Canadian incomes rise, the demand for imports, and hence the supply of dollars will rise. The C$ will depreciate. If Mexican incomes fall then the demand for Canadian goods and hence dollars will fall. Again, the C$ will depreciate.

A Change in Relative Prices

Inflation in a country will affect the exchange rate. As the price of goods and services rises imports become relatively cheaper and exports become relatively dearer. Thus the supply of the currency will rise and the demand for it will fall. Both of these forces will put downward pressure on the exchange rate.

So, if Canadian inflation is higher than Mexican inflation, then Canadian exports will become less competitive. The demand for Canadian dollars will fall. At the same time Mexican imports will become relatively cheaper for Canadians, and the supply of C$ will rise. The C$ will depreciate.

A Change in Relative Investment Prospects

If conditions in a country change, such that investors raise their expectations of a high return on their capital, foreign investors will demand more currency to enable them to invest. This will raise the exchange rate.

If investment prospects become better in Mexico relative to Canada, the demand for Canadian dollars will fall. At the same time the supply of Canadian dollars will rise as Canadian investors buy more pesos. The C$ will depreciate.

A Change in Relative Interest Rates

Investors move money around the world to seek the highest return on their funds. If interest rates rise in one country, then its saving rates become relatively more attractive than before, and the saving rates of other financial centres less attractive than before.

For example, if Canadian interest rates fall there will be less demand for C$. This is because fewer people will wish to hold their money in Canada. As Mexican interest rates will be relatively higher than before, there will be a greater demand for pesos, and hence a greater supply of dollars. The C$ will depreciate.

Speculation

Speculators may believe that there will be a change in the exchange rate. Professional speculators in currency, and traders who want to choose the most favourable time to buy or sell, will try to anticipate an exchange rate movement.

Say for example they think the C$ is overvalued and is due to fall. People holding C$ will rush to sell, and the supply of C$ will increase. People wanting to buy C$ will delay purchases, and hence delay demand for the C$. Demand for the C$ will fall.

It is in fact speculative activity which causes most of the day-to-day changes in exchange rates. The amount speculated is very large, perhaps as much as *80%* of all dealing on any one day. It is trading changes, however, which determine the long-term value of an exchange rate.

Use of Foreign Reserves

If a government is nervous about large swings in the exchange rate, it may intervene to try to bring greater stability. One way of doing this is to buy or sell its own currency, using reserves of gold and foreign currencies. When a government intervenes in a floating system like this, there is no longer a pure or clean float. A floating system where the government does intervene is known as a dirty float. Since 1972 many countries have operated a dirty float.

If, for example, the Canadian government wants to support the Canadian dollar to save it from falling, it can enter the market and buy C$. It would do this with foreign currencies from the reserves account. This will increase the demand for the *C$*, shifting the demand curve to the right. The *C$* would appreciate.

HL EXTENSION

PURCHASING POWER PARITY – THEORY OF EXCHANGE RATES

Purchasing power parity (PPP) exists when a given amount of currency will buy exactly the same bundle of goods, in each of two countries, at the current exchange rate. For example if *£1 = $2*, then purchasing power will exist if a specific bundle of goods costing *£10* in the UK can be bought in the USA for *$20*. It would not exist if it cost *$15* or *$22* in the US. The purchasing power parity theory holds that movements in relative inflation rates will be exactly offset by movements in exchange rates. Thus if the UK inflation rate was *4%*, and the US inflation rate was only 2%, prices in the UK would be rising on average by *2%* relative to US prices. This would affect the balance of trade. British goods would become less attractive to Americans by becoming more expensive. They would then demand fewer pounds. American goods become more attractive to British consumers, who would increase their supply of pounds. With demand for pounds falling and supply of pounds increasing in the foreign exchange market the pound will depreciate. Purchasing power parity theory argues that the exchange rate will fall in line with inflation – in this case by *2%* to offset the domestic inflation difference.

[handwritten: "what the ex rate should be" above Implied PPP column; "% of change" above last column]

Country	Big Mac prices in local currency	Big Mac prices in dollars	Implied PPP of the dollar	Actual $ exchange rate	Local currency under (–)/ over (+) valuation, %
United States	$2.32	2.32	–	–	–
Argentina	Peso 3.00	1.29	1.29	1.00	+29 _[handwritten: over inflated]_
Australia	A$ 2.45	1.82	1.06	1.35	-22
Austria	Sch 39.0	4.01	16.8	9.72	+73
Belgium	BFr 109	3.84	47	28.4	+66
Brazil	Real 2.42	2.69	1.04	0.9	+16
Britain	£ 1.74	2.80	1.33	1.61	+21
Canada	C$ 2.77	1.99	1.19	1.39	-14 _[handwritten: under value]_
Chile	Peso 950	2.40	409	395	+44 _[handwritten: over valued]_
China	Yuan 9.00	1.05	3.88	8.54	-55
Czech Rep.	CKr 50.0	1.91	21.6	26.2	-18
Denmark	DKr 26.75	4.92	11.5	5.43	+112
France	18.5 Ff	3.85	7.97	4.8	+66
Germany	M 4.80	3.48	2.07	1.38	+50
Hong Kong	HK $ 9.50	1.23	4.09	7.73	-47
Hungary	Forint 191	1.58	82.3	121	-32
Indonesia	Rupiah 3,900	1.75	1,681	2,231	-25
Israel	Shekel 8.9	3.01	3.84	2.95	+30
Italy	Lire 4,500	2.64	1,940	1,702	+14
Japan	Yen 391	4.65	169	84.2	+100
Malaysia	M $ 3.76	1.51	1.62	2.49	-35
Mexico	Peso 10.9	1.71	4.7	6.37	-26
Netherlands	FL 5.45	3.53	2.35	1.55	+52
New Zealand	NZ $2.95	1.96	1.27	1.51	-16
Poland	Zloty 3.40	1.45	1.47	2.34	-37
Russia	Rouble 8,100	1.62	3,491	4,985	-30
Singapore	S$ 2.95	2.10	1.27	1.4	-9
South Korea	Won 2,300	2.99	991	769	+29
Spain	Ptas 355	2.86	153	124	+23
Sweden	SKr 24.0	3.54	11.2	7.34	+53
Switzerland	SFr 5.90	5.20	2.54	1.13	+124
Taiwan	NT$ 65.0	2.53	28	25.7	+9
Thailand	Baht 48.0	1.95	20.7	24.6	-16

Source: The Economist, April 15 1995

The Price of a 'Big Mac'

Purchasing Power Parity theory claims that, if the exchange rate is at its equilibrium value, an identical good should cost the same in each country. In order to put this theory to the test, the Economist magazine chose an homogenous good, a McDonald's Big Mac. The beefburger is homogenous because it is prepared to the same recipe world wide. Since 1986 the Economist has published its 'Big Mac' Index. The table below shows the 1995 figures. The first column gives the price in local currency. The second gives the dollar price using the actual exchange rate. The implied PPP of the dollar obtained by dividing the local dollar price by the US dollar price is given in column 3. This would be the exchange rate if the Big Mac actually was the same price in each country. If this implied rate is now compared with the actual exchange rate (column 5) we can see whether the exchange rate is over-valued or undervalued according to the Big Mac Index. The second column shows that the cheapest Big Mac is in China, and the dearest in Switzerland. Column 6 tells us that China has the most undervalued currency and Switzerland the most overvalued. According to the table, as many countries are undervalued as are overvalued. However, many of the world's major currencies appear overvalued against the dollar, *eg the Yen, DM and Ff. The index does have some weaknesses. The PPP theory applies to traded goods, but Big Macs are not internationally traded. Also local cost conditions affect prices, for Big Macs are made of local ingredients even if they are to a standard recipe.*

MULTIPLE CHOICE QUESTIONS – EXCHANGE RATES

1 Which one of the following features indicates that a country has a floating exchange rate?

A   The country is not able to pursue an independent monetary policy.

B   Movements in the country's exchange rate will affect the interest rate.

C   The foreign exchange reserves of the country do not alter greatly.

D   Short run fluctuations in the exchange rate are subject to government intervention.

2   Refer to the diagram below.

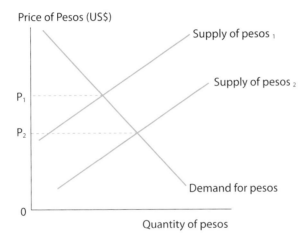

Price of Pesos (US$)

A change in the exchange rate from P_1 to P_2 could be caused by

A   Mexican interest rates rising faster than American interest rates.

B   Mexican migrant workers in the US sending money home.

C   American tourists visiting Mexico.

D   American banks receiving deposits from Mexican investors.

3   A country's exchange rate depreciates, other things equal there will be an immediate

A   fall in the rate of inflation.

B   adverse movement in the terms of trade.

C   favourable balance of payments.

D   rise in export prices.

4   Which of the following is likely to cause an appreciation of the Philippine peso against the Japanese Yen?

   A   The rate of inflation is faster in the Philippines than in Japan.

   B   The rate of inflation is faster in Japan than in the Philippines.

   C   The level of unemployment in Japan has increased.

   D   The level of direct investment in Japan by the Philippines has increased.

5   Jamaican dollars will appreciate against the US dollar if

   A   inflation increases more rapidly in the US.

   B   productivity increases more rapidly in the US.

   C   interest rates rise in the US.

   D   The US central bank buys dollars.

6   It is a characteristic of floating exchange rates that they lead to an increase in

   A   the number of countries with balance of payments deficits.

   B   uncertainty about future import prices.

   C   the need to keep foreign currency reserves.

   D   government intervention on foreign exchange markets.

HL EXTENSION

7   In the USA a bundle of goods costs $300. The same bundle of goods in the UK costs £200. There is purchasing power parity if

   A   the inflation rate is the same in both countries.

   B   the interest rates is the same in both countries.

   C   the £/ $ exchange rate is £1 = $1.5.

   D   the £/$ exchange rate is £1 = $1.

4.6   BALANCE OF PAYMENTS PROBLEMS

CONSEQUENCES OF IMBALANCES

In this section we bring together a number of the external items (international items) that we have now studied separately: trade, protection, the balance of payments and the exchange rate. The link between the external balance and the internal balance of the macroeconomy will also be made, that is the effect of imbalances on the balance of payments upon: growth of output, employment, and inflation.

CHANGES IN EXCHANGE RATE

We have already noted the major changes which determine the value of the exchange rate. These changes will also show up as changes in the record of international transactions, *ie* the Balance of Payments.

A Change in Incomes

Changes in relative incomes will have a direct effect upon the trade in visibles and invisibles, and alter the current account balance. Thus a rising domestic income is associated with increasing import spending and a worsening of the current account balance. This in turn will cause the exchange rate to depreciate. A recession in National Income will cause import spending to fall, and the exchange rate to strengthen. Rising world incomes will increase the demand for exports. As a result the balance of payments on current account will become more positive. The increased demand for currency causes the exchange rate to appreciate. A world recession will reduce the demand for exports, reduce the current account balance and depreciate the currency.

A Change in Relative Prices

A change in the relative inflation rate will have similar effects. Thus, if a country has a high inflation rate relative to its main trading partners, it will export less to them and import more from them. The current account section of the balance of payments will worsen, and the currency will depreciate. Conversely, a falling inflation rate will strengthen export sales and reduce the spending on imports. This will improve the balance on the current account and strengthen the exchange rate.

A Change in Relative Investment Prospects

Changes in relative investment prospects will affect flows of long-term capital and therefore affect the balance of payments on the capital account. A country with good investment prospects will attract foreign investment and capital will flow in. The increased demand for currency strengthens the exchange rate. There will be corresponding outflows from the capital account of countries where the funds originate. In these countries the balance of payments will weaken and the currency depreciate.

A Change in Relative Interest Rates

Changes to a country's interest rate have a marked effect on short-term capital flows. Thus an increase in the interest rate will increase the demand for bonds and bank deposits in that country by foreigners. This will show up as a capital inflow on the capital account of the balance of payments. The strengthening of the balance of payments will coincide with a strengthening of the exchange rate. Similarly, a fall in the interest rate will cause short term capital to be transferred abroad, the capital account to weaken, and the exchange rate to depreciate. Governments have to be concerned not only with their own interest rate but those of foreign countries. An interest rate change in another country alters the relative amount of interest to be earned in the domestic economy. This will affect the balance of payments and the exchange rate in exactly the same way as a change in the domestic interest rate.

Speculation

The capital account and the exchange rate will be affected if speculators believe there will be a change in the exchange rate. Speculation is the act of buying or selling in order to make a gain in the difference in prices. Speculators are very active in foreign exchange markets. In practice huge amounts of speculative money move at very short notice, trying to gain on small anticipated changes to the exchange rate, or the interest rate. Very large sums of money can therefore shift between countries in a very short space of time. This affects the inflow and outflow of short-term capital and raises and lowers exchange rates respectively.

Use of Foreign Reserves

Finally governments actively using reserves affect both the balance of payments and the exchange rate. If the government is aiming to stabilise the exchange rate, it will buy or sell currency from its foreign reserves. This item in the capital account will therefore decrease if the central bank (the government's agent in currency dealing) is buying, and increase if it is selling. If the government operates a managed exchange rate policy (Part of the Higher Level syllabus only) then the central bank will be using its foreign reserves actively to maintain the exchange rate within the exchange rate band.

CHANGES IN THE EXTERNAL BALANCE, AGGREGATE DEMAND AND THE DOMESTIC MACROECONOMY

There is a strong relationship between the external balance, *ie* the balance of payments, and the internal balance, *ie* aggregate demand. Aggregate demand (*AD*) in an economy consists of *C + I + G + (X-M)*.

Any increase in export spending (*X*) will increase aggregate demand. A fall in export spending will reduce aggregate demand. An increase in import spending (*M*) will reduce aggregate demand and a fall in import spending will raise aggregate demand. The external balance therefore affects the domestic economy. A change in the external balance will change aggregate demand, which acts through the multiplier to raise or lower National Income. Thus the actual growth of National Income (*NI*) is affected. An increase in the net external balance (*X-M*) will increase *NI*. A National Income increase will either reduce unemployment or increase inflation, depending on how close to the full employment level the country is. A fall in the net external balance *(X-M)* will reduce National Income. A fall in *NI* will either increase unemployment or reduce inflation, depending on how close to the full employment level the country is.

Countries resorting to Protectionism

A major benefit of a floating exchange rate system is that imbalances in the balance of payments will adjust automatically. A country running a balance of payments deficit, for example, will find its currency sliding down in value. As the currency depreciates so its exports become cheaper, and its imports become dearer. As export sales increase and import demand falls this will tend to restore equilibrium to the balance of payments.

If, on the other hand, a country has locked itself into an exchange rate mechanism that does not allow the currency to adjust, then its government must act to restore balance by some other method. One possibility in theory is to impose import controls. GATT made a few exceptions to allow members to do this temporarily, but generally it was strictly against the rules. This precluded most of the industrial countries from using protectionism for balance of payments reasons. Currently the WTO is tightening up even further on the rules, *eg* LDCs are now included as well. Protectionism is always deeply unpopular with the trading partners whose products are affected, and retaliatory action is a distinct possibility. Other methods of correcting balance of payments deficits are examined in the higher level extension which follows.

Question – Exchange Rates

The figure shows the demand and supply of South African rand. The D and S curves are the original demand and supply curves respectively.

Price of Rand

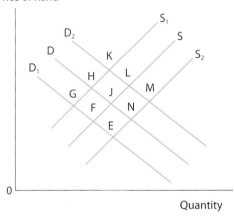

Quantity

1 At which point (E to N) is the market in equilibrium?

2 Starting each time from the original equilibrium position, which point will the market be most likely to move to in the short term if there is:

   a an increase in exports?

   b an increase in imports?

   c a rise in the number of take-overs of Lesotho companies by South African companies?

   d a belief that the value of the rand will increase in the future?

   e a fall in interest rates in the South African money markets?

   f the discovery of a large new gold-field to the north of Johannesburg?

   g an increase in the number of tourists from Europe, North America, and Japan?

   h a sharp increase in the South African rate of inflation?

   i intervention selling by the SA government in the foreign exchange market to reduce fluctuations of the rand?

THE LONG RUN APPRECIATION AND DEPRECIATION OF A CURRENCY

Changes in International Trading Patterns

Over the longer term, changes in trading patterns affect the value of the exchange rate. These changes include changes in consumer tastes, changes in the nature and quality of goods, and the changes in relative costs of production in different countries. These changes are gradual, unlike the speculative movements which cause wide swings in exchange rates. Figure 4:14 shows the long-term trends of five major currencies against £ Sterling from 1980 to 1996. Consider as an example the increase in trade in German goods in the decades since World War II. The successful export sales of companies from Germany led to a steady long-term appreciation in the Deutschmark. Compared to £ Sterling, the German currency rose in value from *DM 4.23 = £1* in 1980 to *DM 2.26 = £1* in 1995. The factors which affect long-term competitiveness of countries are the same factors which affect economic growth. These were examined in Section 3.

Figure 4:14 – Long Term Exchange Rate Movements: £ Sterling 1980-1996

	US dollar	French franc	Japanese yen	German mark	Italian lira
1980	2.33	9.83	526	4.23	1992
1981	2.03	10.94	445	4.56	2287
1982	1.75	11.48	435	4.24	2364
1983	1.52	11.55	360	3.87	2302
1984	1.34	11.63	317	3.79	2339
1985	1.30	11.55	307	3.78	2463
1986	1.47	10.16	247	3.18	2186
1987	1.64	9.84	237	2.94	2123
1988	1.78	10.60	228	3.12	2315
1989	1.64	10.45	226	3.08	2247
1990	1.79	9.69	257	2.88	2133
1991	1.77	9.95	238	2.93	2187
1992	1.77	9.33	224	2.76	2163
1993	1.50	8.51	167	2.48	2360
1994	1.53	8.49	156	2.48	2467
1995	1.58	7.87	148	2.26	2571
1996	1.53	7.71	163	2.25	2407

Source: Economic Trends. Office of National Statistics, UK

Question:

How did the pound change against the dollar, the yen, and the lira over this time period? What conclusions can be drawn about the movements of these three currencies?

GOVERNMENT INTERVENTION

Both floating and fixed exchange rates have advantages and disadvantages. In practice, governments usually opt for some compromise between the two extremes. Two such systems are the adjustable peg and the dirty float. The adjustable peg system was the major exchange rate system from 1945 to 1972, and the dirty float has been the dominant system since then. Before looking at how these two compromise systems work, the main advantages and disadvantages of fixed and floating rates are first examined.

FIXED EXCHANGE RATES – ADVANTAGES

Certainty. On the microeconomic side, an exchange rate movement alters every single export and import price. Thus when a currency appreciates all export prices rise to foreigners, and the demand for exports falls. By the same token all import prices fall, and importers enjoy lower prices. When an exchange rate depreciates exporters gain and importers lose. Investors are also affected by increased uncertainty. Profits returning from foreign investments may be boosted by a currency change but they may also be reduced. It is the uncertainty that many traders do not like. Business people specialise in the risks of their trade but exchange rate movements are totally beyond their control. The main calls to stabilise or correct a currency are usually to be found from business.

Increased trade. If it could be shown that businesses were more willing to trade due to the increased certainty of a fixed exchange rate, then it could be argued that there would be benefits to increased trade. That is there would be welfare gains from comparative advantage etc. There is no conclusive evidence that this is so. In the period since 1972 there have been very large changes in exchange rates, and yet there has been a simultaneous rapid expansion in international trade.

Speculation. As the exchange rate is fixed there is no place for speculation to de-stabilise the exchange rate. Against this, however, it must be said that in periods of devaluation and revaluation a managed exchange rate is very unstable and huge gains are made by speculators. This is because the direction of change of an undervalued or overvalued exchange rate is fairly obvious.

Discipline. This is one of the major macroeconomic arguments claimed for fixed exchange rates. A government which inadvertently expands demand, or does so deliberately to court popularity (*eg* to win an election), will be disciplined by the system.

If the government over-expands the money supply the extra demand will cause the current account of the balance of payments to move into deficit. The fall in interest rates which would accompany an expansion of the money supply would cause an outflow on capital account. Both measures lead to balance of payments deficits. The government will be forced to take measures to correct it, *ie* deflating the economy by monetary or fiscal means.

Expansionary fiscal policy would increase aggregate demand. This would lead to an increase in imports, a deficit on the balance of payments and again a need to deflate the economy.

Inflation. Changes in import prices will not occur due to exchange rate fluctuations. Therefore they cannot threaten internal inflation.

FIXED EXCHANGE RATES – DISADVANTAGES

Reserves. To operate a fixed exchange rate system large stocks of gold and reserves have to be held to be able to intervene in the market and support the currency.

Domestic policy is dictated by the world economy. Inflation is dictated by world inflation rates. This is because domestic monetary policy is neutralised. Any attempt to reduce money growth and raise interest rates will be met by an increased surplus on the balance of payments. The current account will go into surplus as the reduction in aggregate demand reduces imports. The capital account will go into surplus as a result of higher interest rates attracting a greater inflow of capital. The expansion of the money supply will return inflation to world levels.

No automatic adjustment. With a fixed exchange rate there can be no automatic adjustment. This becomes serious for major supply side shocks, like the oil price increase of the 1970s.

FLOATING EXCHANGE RATES – ADVANTAGES

Auto-correction. The balance of payments is self-correcting. It requires no government intervention, so there is no scope for the government to apply incorrect policies.

No reserves/no liquidity shortage. There is no central bank intervention, and therefore no foreign reserves are required. Currency is exchanged at the prevailing exchange rate. International trade is thus financed without foreign reserves and there can be no shortage of international liquidity.

Freedom to make domestic policy. The country is not locked in to unacceptably high world interest rates. The government is therefore free to pursue its own domestic policies. It can choose its own level of aggregate demand, for example, to suit its own unemployment level, and leave the exchange rate to adjust the effects on the balance of payments. This is a major macroeconomic advantage.

Smooth exchange rate changes. There are no large discrete jumps of exchange rate such as occur at times of exchange rate re-alignment, *ie* devaluation and revaluation in a fixed system.

Speculation may be reduced. As exchange rates are free to move either way, many speculative purchases will cancel each other out. Speculators are anyway, gambling against each other and not the central bank.

FLOATING EXCHANGE RATES – DISADVANTAGES

Increased uncertainty. Businesses prefer to know the exchange rate when they make trading decisions. A floating rate adds to their uncertainty. Forward markets enable firms to escape some of this risk. However, with long-term investment that is not possible and so increased uncertainty may reduce international investment flows.

Increased speculation. Although speculation can be stabilising it can also lead to violent fluctuations in an unstable world with large sums of footloose, or hot money. In the last 20 years there have been considerable fluctuations in exchange rates and 'overshooting' of the long- term average exchange rate.

Lack of discipline. The government can pursue irresponsible inflationary policies and firms and labour unions can drive up wages knowing the exchange rate will adjust to the ensuing inflation. The depreciation of the currency caused by such behaviour will itself fuel inflation further by driving up import prices.

The advantages and disadvantages of the two extreme types of exchange rate system are summarised in Figure 4.15.

Figure 4.15 – A Comparison of Fixed and Floating Exchange Rate Systems

	Fixed	Floating
Advantages	1 Stable exchange rates provide a basis for business expectations	1 Automatic adjustment of imbalances
	2 Stability encourages increased trade	2 Reduced need for reserves – in theory no need for reserves at all
	3 Reduced danger from exchange rate speculation	3 Relative freedom to make internal economic policy
	4 Discipline is imposed on internal economic policy	4 Exchange rate changes smoothly
	5 Domestic price stability is not endangered by import price changes	5 May reduce speculation as rates move freely up or down
Disadvantages	1 Large reserves are required	1 Increased uncertainty for traders
	2 Internal domestic policy is largely dictated by external factors	2 May increase speculation and overshooting of long term exchange rates
	3 No automatic adjustment – danger of large changes in rates	3 Lack of discipline over the domestic economy

MANAGEMENT OF EXCHANGE RATE MOVEMENTS

Maintaining a totally fixed exchange rate would cause a government to intervene in the market continuously and is a rather unrealistic option. Governments also find it impossible not to intervene in floating exchange rate systems due to the pressures set up by exchange rate movements. Managing an exchange rate somewhere between being fixed and floating is, however, a practical possibility. Indeed most exchange rates in the world were managed from 1945 to 1972. The system of management was known as the Bretton Woods System, or the IMF System. The IMF was established (at a post World War II conference in Bretton Woods, New Hampshire) to manage post-war exchange rates. The European Exchange Rate Mechanism (ERM), which tied several EU currencies together in preparation for full monetary union, was similar in the way it worked. The most commonly used type of managed system is the adjustable peg – see Figure 4.16. A central exchange rate is chosen, for example point *'a'* in Figure 4.16, and the government then pledges to maintain that rate. Usually some flexibility is built in by allowing the rate to move freely within an exchange rate band. The band is expressed in percentage points centred on the peg. The top of the band is known as the ceiling, and the bottom the floor. The central bank regulates the exchange rate. If the rate threatens to rise out of the band, *ie* go through the ceiling, the central bank can sell currency or lower interest rates in order to depreciate the currency. If the rate threatens to fall out of the band, *ie* drop through the floor, the central bank can buy the currency or raise interest rates in order to appreciate the currency.

Figure 4.16 – Adjustable Peg Exchange Rate System

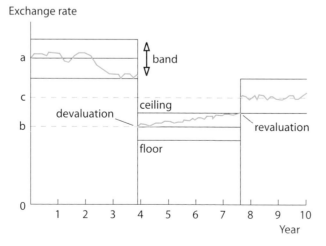

Figure 4.17 and Figure 4.18 illustrate central bank intervention in the foreign exchange market to maintain stability. If say under the old ERM system the central rate of the French franc to the deutschmark was established at *4ff = 1dm*. Say a *1%* fluctuation was allowed, giving a permissible currency band of *3.96* to *4.04* francs to a deutschmark. In Figure 4.17 an increased supply of francs threatens to lower the exchange rate to a position below the band. The central bank of France, and probably the central bank of Germany too, would intervene and buy francs by selling marks to raise demand and keep the rate within the band. Other things being equal, they would need to buy up *b-d* francs per day. If the foreign reserves were insufficient the central bank of France would consider raising interest rates to attract purchases of francs on the capital account and thus appreciate the franc. In Figure 4.18 an increased demand for francs threatens to raise the exchange rate to a position above the band. The central banks would intervene and sell francs to increase the supply of francs and keep the rate within the band. Other things being equal, they would need to sell *b-d* francs per day.

📊 Figure 4.17 – Intervention Buying of Currency in a Managed Exchange System

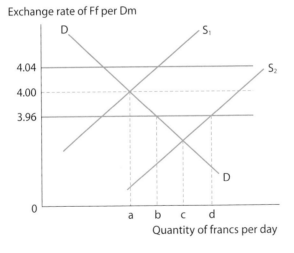

The French franc is pegged to the deutchmark at 4ff = 1Dm. It is allowed to fluctuate within a 1% band either side of the central rate ie between 3.96 and 4.04. From an initial equilibrium where S1 cuts D at 4.00 Ff, supply of francs shifts to S2. The resulting equilibrium at c is outside the permissible band. The Central Banks in the system will intervene and buy b-d francs to keep the exchange rate from falling below 3.96 at B.

Figure 4.18 – Intervention Selling of Currency in a Managed Exchange System

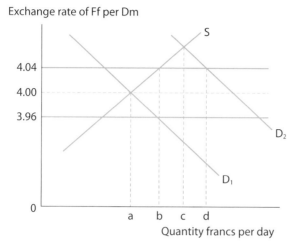

Exchange rate of Ff per Dm

The French franc is pegged to the Deutchmark at 4Ff = 1Dm. It is allowed to fluctuate within a 1% band either side of the central rate ie between 3.96 and 4.04. From an initial equilibrium where S cuts D1 at 4.00 Ff, demand for francs shifts to D2. The resulting equilibrium at c is outside the permissible band. The central banks in the system will intervene and sell b-d francs to keep the exchange rate from rising above 4.04 francs at d.

In the long term, to prevent an exchange rate falling, there is the theoretical possibility of imposing import restrictions. It has already been already noted, however, that the WTO agreements and the threat of retaliation severely limits the potential of this option.

The main alternative for a government in the long-term is to deflate its domestic economy to reduce import spending. Thus the government would use monetary and/or fiscal policy to deflate national income. The demand for imports is markedly a function of national income and so import spending would fall. Export demand, being determined abroad, would not be affected by the fall in income and thus the balance on current account would improve. The demand for currency would remain unchanged while the supply of currency was reduced. The supply curve will shift to the left and will therefore remain within the exchange rate band.

If this option failed, the country would have to acknowledge that its exchange rate was fundamentally over-valued or under-valued. In this case it would pull out its peg and set it at a new level, one it could more realistically maintain. If the peg is lowered, *ie* the exchange rate is pegged at a lower price, the process is known as a devaluation. In Figure 4.16 this is shown as a move from point a to point b. The currency is devalued with respect to other currencies in the system. As long as the other currencies themselves are not devalued, the first currency will have depreciated in value. Other things being equal, this will increase its revenue from exports and reduce its expenditure on imports. If the peg is raised, *ie* the exchange rate is pegged at a higher price the process is known as revaluation. In Figure 4.16 this is shown as a move from point *b* to point *c*. The currency is revalued with respect to other currencies in the system. As long as the other currencies themselves are not revalued, the first currency will have appreciated in value. Other things being equal, this will reduce revenue from exports and increase its expenditure on imports.

'DIRTY FLOAT'

A dirty floating system of exchange rates is basically a free floating system, but with some government interference. The central bank will intervene from time to time to prevent excessive exchange rate fluctuations. It is thus a form of 'managed flexibility'. Under this system the government does not attempt to maintain any pre-announced exchange rate, but rather it seeks to allow an 'orderly adjustment' to major changes in demand and supply, while preventing the excesses of the violent short-term swings which are mainly the result of speculation. The most used method of dampening these swings is by buying and selling from the foreign reserves account. This can be reinforced by adjusting the interest rate in order to influence speculative activity on the capital account.

EXPENDITURE SWITCHING AND EXPENDITURE CHANGING

This section extends the previous analysis of government attempts to correct the balance of payments under a managed exchange rate system. The two basic long-term methods of adjustment are (a) expenditure switching and (b) expenditure changing. Expenditure switching (a) is persuading people to switch expenditure between foreign and domestic products by changing their relative prices. Expenditure changing (b) is changing the total amount spent on imports by altering incomes.

a Expenditure switching

A blunt instrument here is the imposition of tariffs or other restrictions to reduce the size of the import bill and thus improve the balance of payments. Subsidising exports has a similar effect. It was possible for LDCs to do this under the old GATT agreement – but very difficult for the main industrialised nations: it is after all against the principles of free trade. Retaliation is highly likely and international agreements like GATT have been negotiated exactly for this reason. Tit-for-tat retaliation quickly ensures that the benefits of international trade are lost. The new WTO agreement has now included LDCs under the umbrella, making it very difficult for them to use trade restrictions for balance of payments reasons also. The alternative is to encourage expenditure switching by changing the exchange rate. Thus a balance of payments deficit can be corrected by devaluing the currency (and a surplus by revaluing the currency). If the currency is devalued all imports become more expensive and all exports become cheaper at a stroke. Subject to certain conditions with respect to elasticities of demand for exports and imports (covered later in this section), the balance of payments will improve. This is such an easy and tempting alternative to countries in a managed system, that rules are devised to prevent it happening except when there is general agreement among all the members that a particular currency is fundamentally, and long-term, over-valued or under-valued. Otherwise there is a risk of competitive devaluation occurring.

b   Expenditure changing

Deflationary policies are used to reduce National Income. This will reduce aggregate demand, including expenditure on imports, which is the object of the action. The larger the marginal propensity to import the bigger will be the fall in imports. The supply curve of the currency will shift to the left, appreciating the currency and maintaining its value. There must be a consideration of internal as well as external balance here. A deflation to correct the balance of payments could well worsen unemployment and growth in the domestic economy. On the other hand if the economy were suffering inflation, the move could help both the internal and the external balance. The deflation to reduce the balance of payments deficit would reduce the domestic inflation. Exports will become cheaper compared to competing foreign goods, and imports relatively more expensive compared with home-produced alternatives. Foreign consumers will switch to domestic exports. The more elastic the demand for exports the greater will be the switch. Domestic consumers will switch to home-produced goods. Again the more elastic the demand for imports the greater will be the switch. In both cases demand will be more elastic the closer domestic goods are as substitutes for foreign goods.

Deflation is, however, likely to affect interest rates and thus the capital account. For example, if restrictive monetary policy is used to reduce income and imports, the corresponding rise in interest rates will attract inflows on the capital account.

HL EXTENSION

COMMON CURRENCIES AND MONETARY INTEGRATION

A country can peg its currency against another currency while allowing it to float against other currencies. A group of countries fixing their currencies against each other, but letting the group of currencies float against all other currencies, is known as a currency bloc. The European Monetary System (EMS) was just such a system.[2] Most of the EU countries kept their currencies within a narrow band. The main band was originally 2.25% around a central rate, *ie* 4.5%. This widened in late 1992 to a +/- 15% band, after turmoil in the exchange markets left many countries unable to maintain the exchange rate. The central rate of the bloc floated against the dollar, the yen and other world currencies.

If a currency threatened to break out of the band, central banks of the EU intervened in the market, buying or selling to maintain the currency within the band. Like the Bretton Woods system this was a compromise; a managed exchange rate system between a fixed and floating system.

In order to consolidate further the separate economies of the EU, a single European currency, the Euro, was created on 1st of January 1999 and a new European Central Bank (ECB) was set up to manage the currency. There followed a period of dual legal tender, until individual national currencies were withdrawn totally in July 2002. The main opportunity cost of this was the loss of sovereignty by individual member states over their own monetary policy, the main macroeconomic tool to control the domestic economy. A reading is included here to assess the major costs and benefits of European Monetary Union (EMU).

The Costs and Benefits of EMU

European Monetary Union (EMU) took place on the 1st of January 1999. Member countries gave up their national currencies and began to use the new European currency, the Euro. Members also gave up their individual ability to manipulate money supply, *ie* to control their own monetary policy. This is now done Europe-wide by the European Central Bank. Some countries struggled to meet the conditions required to join, and some decided not to join because they didn't wish to. In the event the transition to the new currency proceeded smoothly. It is still too early to assess the economic effects of joining but the potential benefits and costs are reviewed here.

Potential Benefits

1   Price stability

Price stability is the primary objective of the new European Central Bank (ECB), which took over from the Central Banks of the member countries. The German Bundesbank is the model that the new bank emulates. The Deutschmark had remarkable stability and strength due to sound management by the Bundesbank. This in turn owed a lot to two factors: a determination never to repeat the enormous hyperinflation of 1921, and the bank's independence from political interference. Opponents to EMU argued that EU countries could themselves gain stability by making their own central banks independent, without signing up to one common bank. Secondly there is no guarantee that the low German rates of inflation will continue to be enjoyed. As all member countries vote proportionately, European inflation might be at a common higher average rate.

2   Increased cross-border trade and investment flows

The elimination of transaction costs. Estimates of pre-Euro exchange rate costs put the loss at between 0.3% and 0.4% of European Union GDP. That is a sum of 20–25 billion Euros. Savings to individual countries are of course proportional to their trade. Thus it is important to Ireland and the Netherlands, with trade greater than 50% of GDP, and less important to Italy and Spain, with trade less than 20% of GDP.

The elimination of exchange rate uncertainty. It is widely held that exchange rate swings reduce trade, and consequently the benefits arising from trade. In practice it has been hard to find evidence to support this. The existence of forward markets is perhaps one reason. It appears more likely that exchange rate swings increase the risk of cross-border investment, however, as risk is a very important consideration in any investment. EMU might therefore benefit investment, if not trade. All estimates are based on current trade flows. If trade were to increase because of EMU, which is likely, all gains would be greater.

Potential Costs

1 Structural differences between members

   The different economic structures of countries may make it difficult to operate the single currency. This has been partly anticipated by the conditions of the Maastricht Treaty, which are designed to harmonise certain economic conditions, *eg* interest rates, exchange rates, inflation rates, public sector deficits and debt ratios. The potential problem is that different countries may react differently to EU monetary and fiscal policies that are designed to reduce demand-side and supply-side shocks. Thus countries differ in their reliance upon manufacturing, in the relative size of their firms, in whether they import or export oil, in the significance of their trade with non-EU members and in the structure of household debt. As an example of debt structure, consider the effect of an interest rate change on a country like the UK, where most debt is variable with the interest rate, and Germany, where most debt is at a fixed interest rate.

2 Fiscal transfers

   There is uncertainty as to the degree of fiscal transfer that will be needed between the member countries in order to cushion economic shocks. Spain's unemployment, for example, is four times that of Germany (in 1997). On the other hand, there were already significant fiscal transfer from the rich northern countries to the poorer southern regions before EMU.

3 Transitional costs

   i   There have been transitional costs borne by households and businesses. These include replacing notes and coins, tills, vending machines, computer systems, price lists and legal contracts.

   ii   Uncertainty costs. These are the costs caused by uncertainty in some countries whether or not to join.

Conclusion

The economic arguments are not conclusive. With the balance of benefits and costs finely weighed, the argument is now lying in the political arena in those countries not already fully committed. Most members of the EU, 12 countries, have in fact joined, the other three, Denmark, Sweden and the UK may join later. At present there is a two-tier system.

Source: Adapted and updated from: 'Report on EMU'. Coopers and Lybrand, Accountants (1997).

ELASTICITIES, EXCHANGE RATES AND THE MARSHALL-LERNER CONDITION

In the preceding sections it has been assumed that a depreciation of a currency, by reducing export prices and increasing import prices, would automatically improve the balance of payments. (Vice versa of course for a currency appreciation.) The assumption implied that the demand for exports and the demand for imports are both elastic. In this section elasticity is examined more closely to see what impact it has on the process of exchange rate adjustment and the balance of payments.

Note that when an exchange rate changes it is merely a *price* that is changing. Whether the balance of payments improves or deteriorates depends upon a *value* change, that is, the product of price times *quantity*. The connection between price and quantity is the price elasticity. Regarding a depreciation of the currency, consider first the elasticity of demand for exports, and then the elasticity of demand for imports. Currency depreciation makes export prices cheaper. If the elasticity of demand for exports is unity, then an exchange rate movement (price change) will be exactly offset by the quantity change in the volume of exports. An exchange rate depreciation leaves the balance of payments unchanged. If the demand for exports is price-inelastic then an exchange rate depreciation (price fall) will have a proportionately lower effect on the volume of exports demanded, and the balance of payments will deteriorate. The lower the elasticity of demand for exports, the greater the deterioration of the balance of payments. If demand for exports is price-elastic, then a depreciation of the exchange rate will improve the balance of payments. This is because a fall in export prices causes the volume of exports to increase more than proportionately. So, the higher the price elasticity of demand for exports, the greater the improvement on the balance of payments.

Currency depreciation makes imports dearer. If the elasticity of demand for imports is unity, then an exchange rate depreciation will leave the balance of payments unchanged. If imports are price-inelastic in demand, the increase in the price of imports will have a proportionately smaller effect in reducing the volume of imports. As the price has risen proportionately more than the quantity has fallen, the expenditure on imports rises (*price x quantity*). The balance of payments deteriorates. The lower the price elasticity of demand for imports the bigger is the fall in the balance of payments. If the price elasticity of demand for imports is elastic then the exchange rate depreciation will cause a more than proportionate fall in imports. Consequently the balance of payments would improve.

Of course a change in the exchange rate affects exports and imports simultaneously. Thus if the demand for exports and the demand for imports are both elastic, there will be a very significant improvement in the balance of payments.

Whether goods or services which are traded are elastic or inelastic in demand depends mainly on the number of close substitutes they have, the proportion of income spent on them, and the length of the time period under consideration.[3] Many manufactures, like cars and machines, do have close domestic substitutes for traded goods (at least in the industrial countries). The demand for both exports and imports in industrialised countries is therefore likely to be elastic. This is not the case for LDCs which, with a small manufacturing base, are likely to have much lower elasticities. There is far less chance of substituting domestic goods for foreign goods in LDCs.

The opposite is true, however, for energy and raw materials. They are likely to be price-inelastic in demand. The industrialised countries are likely to have fairly low elasticity of import demand for coffee, tea etc. with poor availability of domestic substitutes. This is also likely to be the case for oil and raw material inputs. These are likely to form only a relatively small percentage of finished product costs, which reinforces inelasticity.

In general a depreciation will improve the balance of payments if elasticities are high, and worsen it if low. Specifically, it is possible to calculate the combined effect of a depreciation on the export and import bills jointly. If the combined elasticities are greater than one, a depreciation will improve the balance of payments, ie $PED_X + PED_{M1}$. This is known as the *Marshall-Lerner condition*. If the combined elasticities equal unity, ie $PED_X + PED_M = 1$, then the balance of payments remains unchanged. If the combined balance is less than one, ie $PED_X + PED_M$, then a depreciation will worsen the balance of payments. For a country with negative balance of payments problems, a depreciation of the currency will be more effective the higher is the combined elasticity of demand for exports and imports. For a country with a combined elasticity of less than one, the balance of payments would worsen with a depreciation. In this case appreciation of the currency would be the best way to improve the balance of payments.

THE J-CURVE EFFECT

When a devaluation of a currency occurs the balance of payments is likely to worsen before it improves. Figure 4.19 illustrates the net exports on the balance of payments. The country is running a deficit. At a point in time, t_1, the currency is devalued. Even with combined elasticities greater than one, ie the Marshall-Lerner condition being satisfied, the balance of payments worsens before recovering and then improving. The graphed shape of the fall and subsequent rise of the external balance, as in Figure 4.19, gives the name to this phenomenon. It is known as the 'the J-curve effect'.

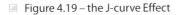

Figure 4.19 – the J-curve Effect

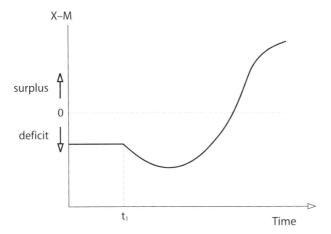

The explanation lies with the elasticities of demand for exports and imports. Time is important in the determination of elasticity. It takes time for traders to adjust, *ie* the Marshall-Lerner condition is not immediately satisfied. Although exports become cheaper immediately upon devaluation, it takes time for foreign consumers to change their consumption habits. It also takes time for domestic producers to produce more, and to set up supply lines abroad. Similarly, although imports become instantly more expensive, it takes producers time to find domestic substitutes and switch to them. Thus upon devaluation more has to be paid for imports while few extra exports are sold, so the balance of payments deteriorates. With the passage of time, traders adjust, and the balance of payments improves.

MULTIPLE CHOICE QUESTIONS – BALANCE OF PAYMENT PROBLEMS

1   Reasons for the worsening terms of trade for the poorest LDCs include

   I   weak demand for primary goods.

   II rising prices for manufactured goods.

   III high income elasticity for primary products.

   A I only   B I and II   C II and III   D I, II and III

2   Country X joins a managed exchange rate system at a par rate higher than its existing floating exchange rate. Which of the following is/are likely to fall?

   I   Interest rates.

   II Holdings of official reserves.

   III The current account balance.

   A I only   B I and II   C II and III   D I, II and III

3   A 'hard' currency is one that is

   I   convertible into other currencies.

   II used as a form of international liquidity.

   III backed by gold when it is issued.

   A I only   B I and II   C II and III   D I, II and III

4   A country's inflation rate increases as a consequence of the depreciation of its currency. What might have caused this?

   I   Domestic producers meeting more competition from foreign producers.

   II The costs of domestic producers rising.

   III The price of imports rising.

   A I only   B I and II   C II and III   D I, II and III

HL EXTENSION

5   Compared to floating exchange rates, fixed exchange rates reduce the need for

   I   importers to purchase currency in advance of receiving goods.

   II government to correct a balance of payments disequilibrium.

   III foreign exchange reserves.

   A   I only   B   I and II   C   II and III   D   I, II and III

6   A government has the exchange rate as its main economic target variable. As a consequence it cannot have an independent short run target for the rate of

   A   inflation.   B   taxation.   C   interest.   D   economic growth.

7   The features below are all advantages of an adjustable peg exchange rate system except

   A   reducing uncertainty for traders.

   B   reducing currency speculation.

   C   disciplining government domestic economic policy.

   D   ensuring smooth long-run changes in the exchange rate.

8   Suppose the euro appreciates against the Canadian dollar. How would this affect an Italian company's earnings from exports to Canada if the price elasticity of demand is unity?

	Company earnings in Canadian dollars	Company earnings in euros
A	Constant	Increase
B	Constant	Fall
C	Increase	Constant
D	Fall	Increase

4.7   TERMS OF TRADE

It was in studying the theory of comparative advantage that the concept of terms of trade was first encountered. The rate at which machinery traded for agricultural goods was called the terms of trade: *eg* two units of agricultural produce for one unit of machines. The international terms of trade is the rate at which exports will trade for imports. This is clearly important to a country. The more imports it can obtain for each unit of exports, other things being equal, the better off it will be.

International trade is, however, rarely bartered, *ie* goods are not often exchanged in terms of physical units. In practice trade is conducted through the use of prices. The terms of trade are therefore expressed in terms of a ratio of average export prices to average import prices. If export prices rise relative to import prices, the terms of trade 'improve'. If import prices rise relative to export prices the terms of trade 'worsen'. However these are price movements only. They tell us nothing about how the volume of trade changes as a result of the price changes. The volume will depend upon the elasticities of demand for exports and imports, as noted previously.

So whether a change in the terms of trade improves or worsens the balance of payments depends on the combined elasticities of demand. Thus an 'improvement' in the terms of trade will worsen the balance of payments if demand for exports is elastic and if the demand for imports is elastic. In other words if the price of exports rises relative to imports, export volumes will fall more than proportionately, worsening the trade balance. Imports will increase more than proportionately, also worsening the trade balance. The terms 'improve' and 'worsen' refer only to relative prices, not to whether the net effect is good for the balance of payments or not.

Changes to a country's terms of trade will affect not only its external economy but also its domestic economy. Changes in total export spending brought about by a change in the relative price of exports will shift the aggregate demand function of a country. The domestic multiplier will increase the magnitude of the change on its national output, its employment and its inflation rate (review Section 3). Similarly, a change in import spending (price times quantity) will affect withdrawals from the circular flow, *ie* change the aggregate demand function in an economy – again with multiplier effects on output, employment and inflation. Any change to inflation caused by a change in aggregate demand would, of course, be a change in demand-pull inflation. Inflation can be affected from the cost-push side also. If demand for imports is relatively inelastic, then a change in import prices will raise the cost of raw materials of intermediate goods and of final goods, all of which will all affect the Retail Price Index.

MEASUREMENT OF TERMS OF TRADE

The terms of trade are an average of export prices divided by an average of import prices. Constructing the averages is done in a similar way to the construction of the Retail Price Index (Section 3). A selection of the main export prices are *weighted* according to their importance. The degree of importance is itself determined by the percentage of total export expenditure on the good. This weighted index is set to 100 in the *base year*, the reference point for future changes. A weighted index of the main import prices is also compiled. This too is set to 100 in the base year. The terms of trade are themselves an index number, derived from the export and import price index numbers as follows.

$$\frac{\text{Index of export prices}}{\text{Index of import prices}} = \frac{100}{1} = \text{Terms of trade}$$

Thus in the base year the terms of trade are: $\dfrac{100}{100} \times \dfrac{100}{1} = 100$

As export prices and import prices change the terms of trade can be recalculated. For example, assume that over the next year the weighted average of export prices rise by 8% and the export price index therefore moves to 108. Over the same period assume that the weighted average of import prices rises by 4% *ie* the import price index moves to 104. The terms of trade are calculated as:

$$\frac{108}{104} \times \frac{100}{1} = 103.85$$

The terms of trade have 'improved'. That is, a given basket of exports will now buy more imports. However, do remember the earlier caution – it is only a price relationship which has improved. Whether or not the balance of payments has improved depends on the elasticities of demand for exports and imports.

As a second example assume that the export price index fell from 100 to 98 in the first year, and the index of import prices remained constant at 100. The terms of trade are:

$$\frac{98}{100} \times \frac{100}{1} = 98$$

The terms of trade have 'worsened' from 100 to 98. Again this is not necessarily a bad thing – it is a price relationship, and the consequences for the balance of payments depend on the elasticities.

CAUSES OF CHANGES IN THE TERMS OF TRADE

The 'terms of trade' expresses a price relationship. Anything that changes relative prices will therefore change the terms of trade. In the short run, day-by-day changes to a floating exchange rate will cause the relative prices of exports and imports to change. These short run changes are dominated by capital movements and they can be very large, as speculators and dealers react to interest rate changes and anticipated exchange rate movements. In the long-term it is the movement in domestic prices which determines the trend of exchange rates and the terms of trade. Domestic prices are themselves determined by the domestic inflation rate and productivity. It is the 'relative' inflation rate which is important for international trade, *ie* whether domestic prices are rising more or less quickly than those of the main trading partners. If, for example, export prices are rising more quickly than import prices due to a relatively higher domestic inflation rate, then the terms of trade will improve. If foreign inflation is higher the terms of trade will worsen.

Relative productivity will also determine how domestic prices move relative to foreign prices. Productivity is the amount of output produced per worker per year and per hour. The higher the productivity the lower prices will be. So countries with high productivity will produce lower cost goods than others and their export prices will rise less quickly. Exports will be relatively more attractive as the terms of trade fall. Going back a step further, the factors which determine productivity will be those same factors listed as 'supply-side' measures in Section 3, and to be treated again and more fully under the 'causes of economic growth' in Section 5.

VOLATILITY OF THE TERMS OF TRADE FOR LDCs

The terms of trade can fluctuate considerably, in particular for LDCs, due to their dependence on just a few primary exports. Demand for primary products tends to be very price-inelastic. Supply also tends to be very price-inelastic. Further, primary industries are subject to frequent supply-side shocks (especially true of agricultural goods) and demand-side shocks (especially in mineral extraction). The combination of shifting supply and demand and price inelasticity causes wide price fluctuation.[4] Because prices can change rapidly, and the demand for primary goods is price-inelastic, the earnings from exports can be very volatile and unpredictable. This makes it difficult for LDC governments to plan ahead.

A second characteristic of the terms of trade of LDCs is their long-term decline (oil exporters excluded). Again, the problem originates in their general dependence on primary commodities. Primary commodities tend to be inelastic to income as well as to price. Thus, as world income grows, demand for such commodities grows hardly at all. This is in contrast to the income-elastic demand for manufactures and services. Therefore increases in world income puts upward pressure on the prices of manufactured and service imports of LDCs, without correspondingly raising the prices of their exports. The terms of trade move against the LDCs. In 1991 the terms of trade for developed market economies were 92% of their 1960 level. By contrast, those for developing countries were only 68% of their 1991 level. The terms of trade movement against LDCs is illustrated with figures in Section 5.

Terms of Trade and LDCs

The developing countries, heavily dependent on primary commodity exports which often have widely fluctuating prices, suffered a marked deterioration in the terms of trade in recent decades. With 1987 as the base year, the index fell from 100 to 71 in 1993. For Africa it fell to 59.

Question

What effect would the fall in terms of trade have had upon imports?

MULTIPLE CHOICE QUESTIONS – TERMS OF TRADE

1 Which of the following is most likely to accompany an increased deficit on the current account of a country's balance of payments?

A domestic consumption.

B exports.

C foreign currency reserves.

D saving.

2 Which of the following will reduce the inflow of speculative funds into Country X?

I   A fall in Country X's interest rates.

II   An appreciation of Country X's currency.

III An increasing Balance of Payments surplus in Country X.

A I only   B I and II   C II and III   D I, II and III

3 If a country's terms of trade have improved it means that

A price ratios of particular products in various countries have changed.

B ratios of exchange rates have changed.

C the balance of exports and imports between two countries has changed.

D the ratio of export prices to import prices has changed.

HL EXTENSION

4 Country Y operates in a world without trade restrictions. Y's exchange rate depreciates. Which combination of elasticities below is most likely to improve the balance of trade in country Y?

A Import elasticity 0.3, export elasticity 0.3

B Import elasticity 1.2, export elasticity 0.8

C Import elasticity 0.5, export elasticity 2.0

D Import elasticity 1.5, export elasticity 2.5

5   The exchange rate of four countries A, B, C and D each depreciates by the same amount, 10%. The price elasticity of demand for exports and imports in each country is listed below. Which country is likely to have the strongest improvement in its balance of payments?

	Exports	Imports
A	0.8	1.3
B	2.6	1.7
C	1.9	0.8
D	0.3	0.2

6   The export and import prices in four countries A, B, C and D change as follows. Which country experiences a worsening of its terms of trade?

	Export prices	Import prices
A	Rise by 5%	Fall by 6%
B	Fall by 6%	Fall by 5%
C	Rise by 6%	Fall by 5%
D	Rise by 6%	Rise by 5%

7   Country X devalues to improve a balance of payments deficit? Which of the following conditions would help to achieve this?

I   The country has spare productive capacity.

II   The demand for exports is price-elastic.

III The demand for imports is inelastic.

A I only   B I and II   C II and III   D I, II and III

8   Country Y finds that its imports increase as incomes rise. It could reduce a deficit on the current account of the balance of payments by

A   cutting interest rates and taxes.

B   deflating the economy.

C   a revaluation of the currency.

D   reducing tariffs and quotas.

9 The export prices of a country rise whilst its import prices fall. The volume of exports and imports remains constant. Other things equal what will happen to the terms of trade and the balance of trade?

	Terms of trade	Balance of trade
A	Improve	Improve
B	Worsen	Worsen
C	Worsen	Improve
D	Improve	Worsen

10 A country's terms of trade change from 143 to 146. It follows that the

A   total value of exports has risen.

B   total value of imports has risen.

C   average price of imports has risen relative to the average price of exports.

D   average price of exports has risen relative to the average price of imports.

11 The New Zealand dollar (NZ$) appreciates against the Australian dollar (A$), from a rate of NZ$1 = A$1 to a rate of NZ$1 = A$1.20. As a result the volume of New Zealand exports to Australia falls by 20%. Other things equal, the elasticity of demand for New Zealand exports is

A   0.25   B   0.70   C   1.00   D   1.40

12 A country has an index of import prices of 125 and an index of export prices of 175. Its terms of trade are

A   1.4   B   50   C   71.43   D   140

13 The table below shows indices of export and import prices for a country in 1998 and 2003.

	1998	2003
Index of export prices	100	172
Index of import prices	100	183

From this information it follows that between 1998 and 2003 the

A   current balance increased.

B   terms of trade worsened.

C   current balance fell.

D   exchange rate depreciated.

14 A country's exchange rate depreciates. Which combination of price elasticities will lead to the greatest increase in the balance of trade?

	Price elasticity of demand for exports	Price elasticity of demand for imports
A	2.3	1.8
B	2.3	0.4
C	0.2	1.8
D	0.3	0.2

15 Non-oil LDCs that export primary products and import manufactures and services are likely to experience the following changes to their terms of trade and exchange rate.

	Terms of trade	Exchange rate
A	worsen	depreciate
B	worsen	appreciate
C	improve	depreciate
D	improve	appreciate

Notes

1   For HL Students – this is formally defined as marginal cost. In practice it is usually difficult to know this and the definition is more generally that of average cost.

2   The system preceded the establishment of a single European currency, the Euro, in 1999

3   This was covered in Section 2.1 'The determinants of elasticity'.

4   This is shown in more detail in Section 5.

5   UNCTAD. Handbook of International Trade and Development Statistics.

Section 5

Development Economics

5.1   SOURCES OF ECONOMIC GROWTH AND DEVELOPMENT

Output is a function of inputs, Figure 5.1. For output to grow, either the quantity of inputs must grow or the quality of those inputs. In other words there must be increased amounts of land, labour, capital and enterprise or the existing land, labour, capital and enterprise must become more productive.

Figure 5.1

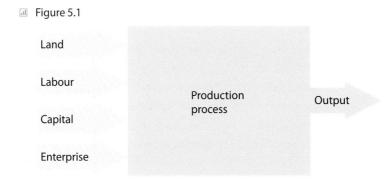

QUANTITY OF INPUTS – THE FACTORS OF PRODUCTION

LAND/NATURAL RESOURCES

Increases in farm land could increase output. In some parts of Latin America and Africa there is still abundant land – but with rapid population growth it is becoming increasingly rare. More characteristic is a situation of diminishing returns brought about by an expanding population upon a fixed area of land.

The term 'land' in economics embraces all natural resources however, not just farm land. Many LDCs have sun, sea and beaches as natural resources which may boost the economy via tourism. The discovery of new mineral sources in an LDC could lead to 'windfall' economic growth, like that caused by the discovery of diamonds in Botswana. A dramatic illustration of increased mineral wealth has been in those countries with oil reserves. When oil prices rose significantly in the 1970s many Third World countries gained large 'windfall' increases in income and foreign exchange. This was especially marked in the countries with big oil reserves and small populations such as Saudi Arabia, Oman and Kuwait which now have very high GNP per capita.

There are many LDCs with fertile land and abundant minerals that remain poor. Having good natural resources is clearly helpful but is not a requirement for becoming rich. Much more important are the human resources which create wealth. There are poorly resourced countries, Hong Kong and Singapore for example, which have a high income and standard of living. Nevertheless where there is an almost complete absence of favourable natural resources, as in much of the Sahel belt of Africa, there are undoubtedly great problems to overcome.

LABOUR

Increases in labour supply can increase economic growth – for example through an expanding population leading to an increased number of young people moving into the work force. In addition, increased population may stimulate the market through increased demand. However an increase in population also means an increase in the number of consumers and in many low income countries population growth may slow the growth of per capita income if there is an existing surplus of labour. We have already noted that increased GNP per capita is the result of subtracting the population growth rate from the GNP growth rate. A look at the statistics in the World Development Report will show that high population growth in many LDCs has reduced the growth of income per capita markedly, and in some nations there has even been a fall in GNP per capita.

CAPITAL

The increase in the stock of capital goods is more universally important. Capital can be directly productive as in the form of new factories, machines, tractors and other equipment. Alternatively it may be indirectly productive as in the provision of roads, railways, harbours, electricity, water and sanitation. This latter type of supporting, or facilitating, capital is called infrastructure.

Different forms of capital investment affect productivity differently. For example an increase in the number of dwelling houses will not have the same effect on the GNP growth as an increase in the number of factories. Generally, though, the size of the capital stock is highly correlated with output, and the growth of investment highly correlated with the growth of GNP.

The act of investment, that is the creation of capital goods, ultimately involves an act of saving. Thus the opportunity cost of capital creation is lower consumption, which for an LDC may present problems. For people on very low incomes, with consumption levels close to subsistence levels, saving represents very real hardship. Indeed significant lowering of consumption may not be possible. This is another of those 'vicious circles of poverty' which bedevil poor people everywhere. See Figure 5.2.

⊞ Figure 5.2

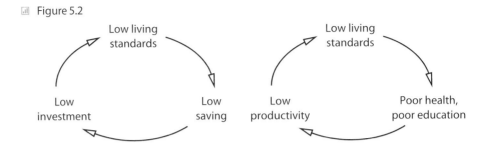

A further problem for many LDCs concerns the appropriate factor mix, the appropriate technology. Most capital goods are developed in the relatively labour-scarce rich countries. Labour is expensive in the industrial countries. Most capital is therefore designed to be labour-saving. Many of the poorest countries are labour-abundant, however. Labour is therefore cheap, whereas imported capital is expensive. It is economically efficient to use more labour and less capital in the factor mix than it is in a Developed Country.

In addition development involves creating jobs and income for the poor. Capital-intensive development may displace workers and do little for unemployment. Poverty is not directly reduced as the factor rewards go to capitalists and foreign firms rather than to indigenous workers. The poor are by definition in the latter group. Thus whilst increased use of modern imported capital is likely to cause GDP per capita to grow, it might also be anti-developmental in effect.

QUALITY OF INPUTS – THE FACTORS OF PRODUCTION

Identifying precise quantitative relationships between factors which cause growth is notoriously difficult. However major studies of growth do conclude that more than half of all economic growth, and perhaps as much as three quarters, is attributable to improvements in the quality of factors of production; improved knowledge, higher efficiency, better education and new technology.

QUALITY OF AGRICULTURAL LAND

A study of land and agriculture is central to any study of development. This is because most of the world's poor live in the countryside. Three and a half billion of the world's six billion people live in rural areas, and two thirds of these make their living from agriculture. Land therefore has enormous significance to production and to the reduction of poverty in poor countries, much more so than in rich countries. With a few exceptions agricultural land is fixed in supply. Growing population and fixed land leads to a classic 'Law of Diminishing Returns' situation. In Figure 5.3 manufacturing output is growing at a regular rate. However as land is fixed in supply, increases in labour to the land results in smaller and smaller incremental outputs of food.

Many of the specific problems that need to be tackled under development programmes have their origins in the countryside. Problems of widespread absolute poverty, inequality, rapid population growth, rural-urban migration and rising unemployment all originate from weaknesses in the agricultural sector. Increasing the productivity of land has therefore become a major developmental objective of most countries with significant poverty. Irrigation, drainage, use of fertilizers and pest control, are potential sources of economic growth which are also likely to be highly effective in reducing poverty. The effect of such measures, for example the use of high yield grains (which has become known as the Green Revolution), is to shift out the Production Possibilities Frontier as in Figure 5.4.

Figure 5.3

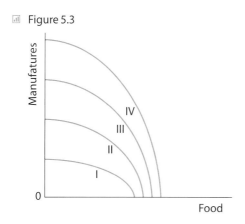

With fixed land, diminishing returns operates upon food production as population increases.

Figure 5.4

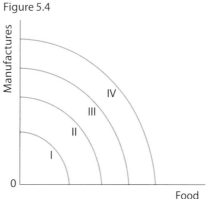

Improving the quality of land, ie productivity, enables the food supply to increase.

AGRICULTURAL OUTPUT

Agricultural output in LDCs has been growing very slowly over the last 30 years. The output performance has been very poor compared to gains in industrial output, and when the increases are divided by a rapidly growing population, the per capita outcome is dismal. The reasons are as follows:

1   Productivity in agriculture is especially low, so large numbers of workers on the land are producing a relatively small share of the GNP, Figure 5.5. With a few exceptions agricultural land is fixed in supply. Growing population and fixed land leads to a classic 'Law of Diminishing Returns' situation.

⊞ Figure 5.5 – Output and employment in Developing World Agriculture, 1995

Region	Percentage of labour force in agriculture	Output of agriculture as percentage of GDP
South Asia	64	30
East Asia (inc. China)	70	18
Latin America	25	10
Africa	68	20

Source: World Bank, World Development Report, 1997

2 Severe droughts and famines have occurred in Africa and South Asia in recent years exacerbating the long term downward trend in productivity.

3 Large price increases in food and fertilizers following the oil crisis of the 1970s further worsened the plight of the rural poor. Poor people already spending as much as 80% of their incomes on food were faced with 100% increases in the price of wheat, maize and rice.

4 Food supply is particularly precarious throughout Africa as Figure 5.6 shows. Over twenty African countries live under the threat of starvation and one in three Africans suffers from malnutrition.

⊞ Figure 5.6 – Index of Per Capita Food Production in Africa 1970-94

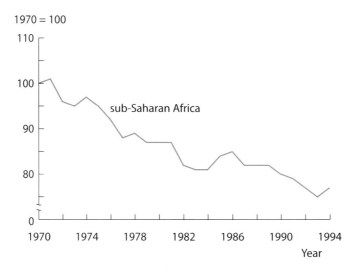

Source: World Resources Institute, World Resources 1996-97, OUP

A major reason for the appalling rural situation has been neglect. Until recently, government policy emphasis has been upon urban/industrial development. 'Trickle-down' benefit to the rural poor has not occurred. A visitor to a Third World country is in effect likely to see two countries and two economies; a modern urban industrial sector and a primitive traditional rural society with vast urban slums separating the two worlds. For this reason LDCs are often described as 'dual economies'.

THE NATURE OF FARMING IN THIRD WORLD COUNTRIES

Farming in LDCs is entirely different from farming in the First World. In an industrial economy a farm is run like a business. Farming is scientific, efficient and highly productive with only a few farmers supporting large populations. Thus in the UK only 2% of the population farm all the land, aided by machines and modern technology. In the United States one farmer supports on average 80 families.

Farming in LDCs is not just an occupation, it is a whole way of life. Peasants are faced with very high risks, not risks of profit and loss, but of life and death. Their major aim is to survive. It is of paramount importance for farmers to avoid risk. Taking risk in a developed country may lead to economic loss or bankruptcy, taking risk in LDC farming may result in absolute poverty and loss of life. Standard economic theory of the firm based upon assumptions of profit maximizing (or sales, or growth or market share), are irrelevant in understanding peasant agriculture. A study of risk avoidance is more helpful in understanding peasant behaviour. We will return to this later.

In LDCs the technology and the way of life in rural villages has changed little over hundreds of years. Land plots are very small, technology is primitive and productivity is very low. One recent change, however, which has brought rural poverty to the fore in developing countries is the rapid growth of population in the countryside as death rates fall, and birth rates remain stubbornly high.

QUALITY OF LABOUR – HUMAN RESOURCES

Education and Training

The quality of labour, is also seen as a major source of potential growth. The basic skills of reading and writing are so taken for granted in most MDCs it is easy to overlook how vital they are to the functioning and productivity of an economy. Most LDCs have made an enormous effort to provide universal primary schooling for children. Increased use of capital and technology demand workers trained in the skills to use them; to service tractors and water pumps, to install electricity to use word-processors and run hotels. Spending on education requires giving up spending on other things, *ie* there needs to be saving. Thus education is another form of investment. This is known as human investment or human capital to distinguish it from physical investment or physical capital.

Kerala – a Model for Development?

📊 Table 1: Comparative GNP And Welfare Indicators

Development Indicator	India (1986)	Kerala (1986)	Malaysia (1987)
GNP per capita (US$)	290	<200	1810
Infant mortality rate	96	27	24
Life expectancy (male)	55	67	68
Life expectancy (female)	54	70	72
Birth rate	33.6	22.4	31
Death rate	11.9	6.2	6
Literacy rate	36	70	–

Source: The Open University (UK), Development Studies Pack 1994 and IBRD Development Report 1989

The state of Kerala is situated in the south west of India. It is a very poor, densely populated agricultural state with a long coastline. With a GNP per capita of less than $200 Kerala is amongst the poorest places on earth. However the standard of living in Kerala is very much higher than the raw income figures would suggest, Table 1.

What is the explanation for these remarkably high welfare indicators? A number of historical and social factors have enabled the people of this state to do a great deal towards helping themselves. This includes an openness to the rest of the world, a diversity of religious experience, active trade unions and socialist inclined governments, and perhaps most important, the high status accorded to women. It was the role of women, which by cutting across strongly rigid caste barriers gave the flexibility essential for change. This was originally based on a system of matrilineal descent, with property passing from mother to daughter rather than the more usual father to son. The focus of women's attention being more naturally centred on birth, child care, family health and nutrition has directly influenced standards of living, as the statistics above testify. Girl babies are valued as highly as boy babies. They do not have their marriages arranged and can re-marry after divorce. A high percentage of women are educated, from primary to university level, and hold many important leadership roles in society. Literacy is very high and Keralan people are able to take an active role in pushing for reforms. Many organizations exist to improve the lives of ordinary people *eg* production co-operatives, and community associations for health care, family planning and housing. The very high level of primary health care is founded on an extensive network of health centres throughout the countryside. Food is subsidised and rationed at low prices to ensure a basic nutritional level is available to all.

> ### Questions
>
> 1 How does the passage above relate to the concept of 'income distribution'?
>
> 2 In contrast to Kerala, women's status in society in LDCs often does differ markedly from men's status. What instances of this are you aware of? (open question)
>
> 3 Using a demand and supply diagram show why low food prices require food rationing and subsidies.

Social and Cultural

A good deal of interest centres upon identifying social and cultural factors which are resistant to change and those which are believed to be conducive to attitudes in favour of change, modern methods and scientific progress. These will regard family structure, tribal structure, caste and religion for example. A great deal has been written about the fact that until Japan developed, all industrial countries were based upon Protestant religions where reward in an after life depended upon success in life on earth. A good deal has been written about the nuclear family being more willing to change that the extended family as the rewards of any effort accrue to the small group rather than being shared.

Entrepreneurship

Entrepreneurial skill is important in generating output and growth. Yet it is difficult to know how to produce entrepreneurs. The supposed scarcity of entrepreneurs was one reason for government involvement in economic activity in poor countries. However it is also claimed that there is a wealth of risk taking expertise in small scale businesses in the informal sector. Promoting small scale industry has been a popular development idea proposed for example by Ghandi in India's early independence years to Schumacher in the book "Small is Beautiful". The official encouragement of small businesses would encourage the development of small scale entrepreneurs as well as getting income and jobs to the poorest people in the countryside and slums.

QUALITY OF CAPITAL – TECHNOLOGICAL PROGRESS

This is undoubtedly a very important factor in creating economic growth. Capital, important in itself in quantity, has an enhanced importance, for technological change is frequently embodied within new capital. New ideas and inventions and applications of science, often find their way into productive processes via new capital goods. New markets which motivate the economy to expand, are also often the result of technical change.

We have already noted, however, that most technological innovation occurs in rich countries and may not be appropriate if the overriding concern is to develop, *ie* reduce poverty, rather than merely to cause average income to grow. For development to occur directly there is an urgent need to create and develop appropriate technologies in labour abundant countries to make the best use of scarce investment and foreign exchange earnings.

The IT Group

This charity, the Intermediate Technology Group, was set up specifically to address the enormous gap between primitive traditional technologies and modern First World technologies. A clear reason for low output and low productivity in LDCs is the primitive technology used. Human muscle power and draught animals have been replaced by machines, lorries, tractors and ships in the industrial world. However to leap from one technology to the other may not be appropriate, even if it is possible. The gap between a plough pulled by an ox to a modern computer aided tractor is immense.

Dr Fritz Schumacher, who founded the Intermediate Technology Group, argued 35 years ago that billions of dollars of aid, in the form of large scale, high technology projects, far from helping the poor was creating dependence. He argued for a half way, or intermediate technology so that the poor could help themselves.

Modern western technology is highly capital intensive, designed for high wage economies. Its use in LDCs may well destroy jobs which the poor need. The work of one bulldozer, or one combine harvester can replace the work of hundreds. LDC government policies and aid packages in the past have too often distorted decisions in favour of modern technology and against the low tech small scale projects, which relative prices would dictate. The IT Group seek to rediscover or re-invent intermediate technologies which advance production from the primitive without leaping to the unattainable or undesirable in one fell swoop. Local labour skills and local material are used wherever possible. Pumps which can be repaired at the village level by a blacksmith can be kept running indefinitely whereas a modern imported machine is useless without costly imported spares, skilled maintenance and repair.

In Nepal people were trekking for days to fetch kerosene for their lamps and women spent up to five hours grinding a single day's corn, yet potential hydro power is abundant. IT developed a simple micro hydro power unit which transforms the life of the poor. In Sri Lanka they taught women how to process the fruit they grew into juice and jam, doubling their income from the "value added". In Kenya IT developed a simple clay stove that uses less scarce firewood, and hence the need to carry wood so frequently. The stove also greatly reduces smoke pollution and thereby improves the health of women and children. They are widely available to the poor because they cost a little more than a dollar, and are made locally by IT trained workers which generates income and jobs.

INSTITUTIONAL FACTORS

Saving and Investment

The rate of saving is critical to enable investment in physical or human capital. This is a major problem for the poorest countries. Saving is a function of income (see Section 3), poor countries have low income by definition and so saving is low. Rich families in today's LDCs are often perceived as having high propensities to consume in contrast to the high regard for saving in the early years of the present day MDCs. One common solution has been to raise high taxes from which the government tries to save and invest.

Role of the Financial Institutions

In MDCs the role of the financial institutions is critical in enabling the economy to function. There is reliance on controlling the money supply and the interest rate to operate monetary and fiscal controls over the macroeconomy. Many institutions such as savings banks, investment banks and the stock exchange collect savings and allocate credit in a smooth seamless operation. They are typically found in every corner of the economy. However this happens in very few LDCs. Banks are often the overseas branches of foreign MNCs and operate mainly for the modern and foreign trade sectors. They cater for medium and large companies in the formal sector operating rather like banks in the MDCs. This is just another aspect of the dual economy. There is little banking on behalf of small farmers and traders. This is a very big problem in LDCs. Street vendors, small shopkeepers and farmers are not catered for by the formal money sector and for credit fall back onto the unorganised informal credit market. They are likely to borrow from family, money lenders and loan sharks. With little collateral these traders may have to pledge their land or animals incurring a very high risk upon failing to repay. With interest rates as high as 20% per day in some cases the situation is appalling in terms of sensible financial channelling of funds into profitable investment.

Development banks have been very successful in the last half century. From small beginnings there are now hundreds of them scattered across the developing world. These set out to redress the shortfall of commercial banks who favoured short term credit and existing established businesses. The development banks set out to aid longer term investment projects which aid growth and development. They tap into foreign sources of funds as well as domestic, borrowing from the large aid agencies such as USAID and the World Bank. They are often very involved in the management and oversight of the projects that they lend to. However these banks do not cater for the poor. Small traders and farmers are too tiny to come under their remit.

To encourage small business is important. They represent a very large section of the economy. Growth here is likely to also help development as these are poor people.

Typically small traders are looking for loans less than $500, farmers to improve their land or to tide them over seasonal fluctuations, small traders to purchase stock, small manufacturers to invest in machinery. Many informal savings and credit associations have grown up to address this market although a great deal more is needed. These may group together to borrow a substantial sum which is then sub-divided and administered by the group with the whole group taking responsibility for repayment. The most famous of these are the Grameen rural banks which began in Bangladesh in 1976 and have since spread over the whole of that country and to many others as well. Customers are groups of five people. Loans are initially made to two members only and payments must begin before loans are made to anyone else. Seventy-five per cent of the customers are women, typically amongst the poorest people on earth.

They support and discipline each other in managing their loans. The loans are frequently used to buy livestock. The repayment record shook the financial world, being far superior to that of regular Bangladeshi commercial banks, with 99% of all loans being repaid within two years.

MULTIPLE CHOICE QUESTIONS – SOURCES OF ECONOMIC GROWTH AND DEVELOPMENT

1 Capital deepening rather than capital widening is more likely to lead to

   A gains in labour productivity.

   B an unchanged capital to labour ratio.

   C the spread of existing technology.

   D the creation of a leading sector in the economy.

2 Which of the following economic principles is most likely to explain low labour productivity in subsistence agriculture in LDCs?

   A Profit maximisation.

   B The theory of comparative advantage.

   C Economies of scale.

   D The law of diminishing returns.

3 Which of the following would allow an LDC to invest more than it saves?

   I   Borrowing from the World Bank

   II   Receiving foreign aid

   III Selling assets to multinational companies

   A I only   B I and II   C II and III   D I, II and III

4 Development using 'appropriate technology' in Bangladesh, India or Pakistan is most likely to use

   A capital-intensive manufacturing processes.

   B extensive switching of resources into research and development expenditure.

   C labour-intensive manufacturing processes.

   D large-scale plants.

5 Labour-intensive production is likely to be the most appropriate technology for development in an LDC because

I   foreign exchange is scarce.

II labour is abundant.

III capital is scarce.

A I only   B I and II   C II and III   D I, II and III

An Economic Profile of Bangladesh

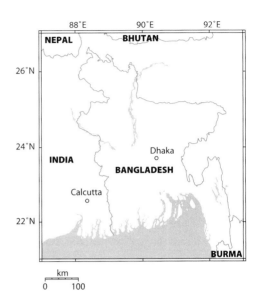

Geographic, Social and Economic Indicators

Capital city:	Dhaka
Area:	143,988km^2
Population:	130 million (2000)
Population (average annual growth rate):	1.9% (1990–1998)
GNI per capita:	US$380 (2000)
GNI per capita (PPP):	US$1650 (2000)
GNP per capita (average annual growth rate):	3.2% (1990–2000)
Agriculture as share of GDP:	26% (2000)
Exports as share of GDP:	12% (2000)
Life expectancy at birth:	58 (1997)
Under age 5 mortality rate (per 1000 live births):	89 (1999)
Adult illiteracy rate (age 15+):	Male 51%, Female 74% (1997)
Human Development Index:	0.470 (low) (1999)
Population living on less than US$PPP a day:	291.% (1996)

Bangladesh

Bangladesh has for decades been one of the poorest of the poor, the 'basket case of Asia'. With the world's highest rainfall it has been subject to flooding and other natural disasters with serious famines recurring with regular frequency. For the last decade Bangladesh has taken measures to pull it up and away from the very bottom of the pile. There are grounds for cautious optimism.

Three quarters of the population live in the rural areas. Subsistence farming is the main activity and rice and jute are the main crops. Rural infrastructure is very poor, the economy is one of the poorest in Asia with $380 per capita, just over a dollar a day per head on average. Income distribution is very even by LDC standards, but as the level of GDP is so low there is widespread absolute poverty. Population growth is high. Unemployment and underemployment are very high at over 20%. The labour force is unskilled and uneducated. There is a low savings rate and a large balance of payments deficit with foreign aid filling external and internal spending gaps.

Bangladesh has however made significant progress in the last decade with the growth of GDP per capita averaging a respectable 3.2% between 1990 and 2000. Exports have increased due to government promotion and better exchange rate management. Government budget deficits have also been reduced. The government has decentralised decision making more and increased the use of price incentives to raise production. Population growth has fallen through the spread of family planning and raising living standards of the very poor. Major government aims include increased food production and better access to food by the poor. The spread of micro credit schemes like that of the Grameen Bank have been significant in assisting the poorest women.

Source: Adapted from: M. Todaro & S. Smith, Economic Development 8th Ed. 2003; and World Bank, World Bank Indicators 2001

An Economic Profile of China

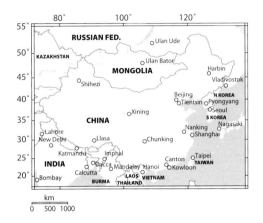

Geographic, Social and Economic Indicators

Capital city:	Beijing
Area:	9,600,000km^2
Population:	1.26 billion (2000)
Population (average annual growth rate):	1.1% (1990–2000)
GNI per capita:	US$840 (2000)
GNI per capita (PPP):	US$3940 (2000)
GNP per capita (average annual growth rate):	9.2% (1990–2000)
Agriculture as share of GDP:	16% (2000)
Exports as share of GDP:	23% (2000)
Life expectancy at birth:	70 (1997)
Under age 5 mortality rate (per 1000 live births):	37 (1999)
Adult illiteracy rate (age 15+):	Male 9%, Female 25% (1997)
Human Development Index:	0.714 (medium) (1999)

China

In area China is only surpassed by Russia and Canada, although due to mountains and deserts only 10% of China is agricultural land and 90% of the population live on just 16% of the land. The sheer number of people gives China a huge significance in terms of effect on the world economy and environment. China has brought down its population growth rate from 2.3% in 1973 to its present day 1% – a massive change. At this rate population will still grow to 2 billion by 2050. If the one child policy were totally adopted the country would have a zero growth rate of population by 2010 with a population of 1.4 billion.

China has alternatively enjoyed and endured huge reversals of fortune since the Communist party took over the running of the country in 1949. The government fairly quickly re established law and order over the dislocated country and made good inroads into rural poverty and unemployment. From 1952 China adopted Soviet style central planning, with help from the Soviet Union, and redirected investment into a rapid build up of heavy industry including defence industry. Economic growth averaged 5.7% but was not higher due to dislocations. The Great Leap Forward of 1957–60 accelerated collectivisation in the countryside, eliminated wage incentives and created 'backyard steel plants'. The result was a famine which killed 15–30 million people and plunged China into economic depression. The Sino-Soviet fall out led to a withdrawal of Russian assistance and technicians. China then reinvested in agriculture to gain 'self-reliance'. This time the Cultural Revolution (1966–76) wreaked havoc with the economy totally disrupting education, training, science and foreign trade.

In the mid 1970s with the death of Chairman Mao, the arrest of the gang of four and a new government under Deng Xiaoping China became more pragmatic and less ideological. The Four Modernisations programme aimed to accelerate progress in agriculture, industry, technology and national defence. The 10 year plan called for a massive import of western plant and technology.

Source: Adapted from: M. Todaro & S. Smith, Economic Development 8th Ed. 2003; and World Bank, World Bank Indicators 2001

5.2   GROWTH AND DEVELOPMENT STRATEGIES

Some Successes...

"Between 1990 and 1998 the proportion of people living in extreme poverty fell from 29% to 23% – 150 million in China"

Source: World Bank Indicators 2001, President James D. Wolfensohn in the forward

Less Developed Country governments have difficult decisions to make in their efforts to encourage development. The problems of scarcity and choice are very evident. In this Chapter we look in turn at several potential strategies for policy makers. They are organised in sub-sections as follows:

1   Harrod-Domar growth model
2   Structural transformation or dual sector model
3   Foreign Trade
4   Aid
5   Foreign Investment/Multinational Companies
6   Export Promotion versus Import Substitution
7   Population Policy
8   Agricultural Policy
9   Demand Management/Supply-Side Policies and Markets versus Planning
10   The role of International and Domestic Financial Institutions

1   HARROD-DOMAR GROWTH MODEL

This model of growth focuses upon the constraint imposed by shortages of capital in LDCs. Economies need capital (K) to produce GNP (Y). The amount of capital required to produce output is known as the capital-output ratio (K/Y = k). Thus if $3 billion worth of capital is required to produce an annual output stream of $1 billion the capital output ratio is $3 billion/$1 billion *ie* k = 3. It is assumed that to increase output (DY) capital is required in the same ratio k. If it is also assumed that the national savings ratio (s) is a constant proportion of national income, say 6%, and that the only source of new investment is domestic savings, then we can construct the following simple model of growth:

1   S = sY   saving (S) expressed as a proportion(s) of national income (Y)

2   I = ΔK   net investment (I) is the change in capital stock (DK)

but K/Y = k, the capital-output ratio or ΔK/ΔY = k, which rearranges to

$$\Delta K = k\Delta Y$$

3 S = I savings (S) must equal net investment (I)

but from equation 1. we know that S = sY and from equations 2 and 3 we know that I = ΔK = kΔY,

therefore we can rewrite the saving equals investment identity as

4 S = sY = kΔY = ΔK = I   or simply as

5 sY = kΔY dividing both sides first by Y and then by k we obtain

$$6 \quad \frac{\Delta Y}{Y} = \frac{s}{k} \quad \text{or} \quad g = \frac{s}{k}$$

This is the simple Harrod-Domar growth model. The rate of growth (g), the percentage change in national income is shown on the left hand side of the equation. It is shown to depend upon the national savings ratio, s, and the capital output ratio, k. Thus in the absence of any government activity the rate of growth is a positive function of the savings ratio. The more an economy can save and invest the higher will be its economic growth. Also we note that economic growth is negatively related to the capital-output ratio, k.

So, a strategy for an LDC is simply to increase the proportion of the national income that is saved. If we assume initially that the capital-output ratio is 3 and the saving ratio is 6% then the economy can grow at 2% because

$$g = \frac{s}{k} = \frac{6\%}{3} = 2\%$$

Now if saving could be increased to say 21% through reduced consumption or increased taxes then GNP growth could increase to 7%

$$g = \frac{s}{k} = \frac{21\%}{3} = 7\%$$

If the country cannot raise its saving sufficiently to reach the desired growth rate then an additional possibility is for foreign direct investment or foreign aid to plug the 'savings gap'.

However whilst increased saving (and investment) may be necessary, it is not sufficient for growth. Many of the complementary factors required for growth may well be absent or lacking in an LDC, the necessary structural, institutional and social conditions eg money markets, transport networks, skilled labour, managers and efficient administrators. Finally growth of course may not lead to development.

2 STRUCTURAL TRANSFORMATION OR DUAL SECTOR MODEL

This model is based on transforming a poor largely rural subsistence economy to a modern industrial economy by labour transfer from the large rural sector to the small urban sector. The rural sector has surplus labour, the population being so large in rural areas that labour has zero marginal product.[1] Labour moving out of the rural sector has no effect on output there. Labour is induced to move by the highly productive and high wage urban industrial sector. A wage about 30% higher than the low subsistence income is assumed to be sufficient to induce the rural-urban migration. The labour surplus is so large that the urban factories can induce an endless supply of labour at this wage. Capital investment in the modern sector can therefore earn large profits due to the low wages of labour. This is the source of continuing funds for capital investment and the process of increasing output and rising employment. The process of self-sustaining growth will continue until all the surplus labour is absorbed and further transfers of labour begin to reduce agricultural output and increase the cost of food. The process will then be complete and the economy will have transformed from a low wage surplus labour rural economy to a modern urban industrial economy.

This model is also known as the Lewis dual sector model after Nobel economist W Arthur Lewis who formulated it in the 1950s. The model still has many adherents today, especially amongst American development economists. The model does fit fairly well with the historical experience of present day industrial countries, but has a number of weaknesses with respect to present day LDCs.

The model assumes that investment continues to create jobs and attract surplus labour. In practice the technology employed is modern and labour saving. The model assumes that the rich capitalists reinvest their large profits. It does not allow for the alternatives of the profits being invested abroad, capital flight and conspicuous consumption. In addition the model is one of growth and not of development. It is based on profits accumulating to a small number of the rich and the maintenance of a large number of relatively poor. Further, the assumption that there is a large pool of surplus labour with zero productivity has been undermined by research that concludes that with a few exceptions this is not true. In addition wages in the urban sector have not remained low despite surplus labour. A number of things conspire to raise wages of the employed. Union activity, civil service pay scales and the hiring practices of multinational companies cause urban wages to rise rapidly even with large open urban unemployment.

3 FOREIGN TRADE

World Trade Patterns

The value and volume of world trade expanded rapidly from 1964 to 1987 but has since stagnated due to the global recession, increased protectionism and Third World debt. Figure 5.7 shows international trade dominated by developed countries. About 70% of world exports are from developed countries, 20% from LDCs and 10% from the (former) socialist countries.

Figure 5.7 – Structure of World Merchandise Trade (Percentage)

Trade Structure	Exports		Total Primary		Manufactures	
Country group	1964	1987	1964	1987	1964	1987
World (billion current $)	172.2	2491.5	85.2	775	84.5	1633
World (index)	100	100	100	100	100	100
Developed market economy	68.1	69.7	52.9	53.3	83.3	78.2
Socialist	11.8	10.2	11.2	13.6	12.2	7.2
Developing	20.1	20.1	36	33.1	4.5	14.7
Least developed	1.4	0.3	2.3	0.7	0.1	0.1

Source: UNCTAD, Statistical pocket book, 1989, Adapted from Table 2.4.

The table also shows how, since the 1960s, the proportion of world trade going to the LDCs remained around 20% of the total, however, this disguises significant differences between LDCs. Both the NIC and the oil exporters have experienced fast growth. Other LDCs have stagnated, and the proportion of trade going to the least developed countries has fallen substantially. Trade problems for LDCs are both long term and short term. More recent statistics do show a marked shift to manufactures as a proportion of exports from developing countries. However these figures disguise the fact that a small number of successful NICs dominate the trade. Thus South Korea and Taiwan together exported more manufactures in 2000 than the rest of Asia, Africa and Latin America combined.

LONG TERM

The long term trend in international trade away from poor countries stems from the fact that they mainly export primary goods, and import manufactures and services. Figure 5.8 illustrates this dependence upon primary exports (food, raw materials, minerals) in a selection of developing countries. Figure 5.8 also contains some developing countries; India, Malaysia and Mexico, that have developed a manufacturing base, and finally includes the USA and Japan for comparison.

📊 Figure 5.8 – Dependence of Developing Countries upon Exports and Primary Commodity Exports as a Percentage of total Merchandise Trade

Country	Exports as a % of GDP	% share of Primary commodities	%age share of Manufacturers
Nigeria	49	99	1
Venezuela	27	88	12
Togo	25	82	18
Kenya	16	77	23
Philippines	53	59	41
Brazil	9	46	54
Indonesia	41	46	54
India	9	24	76
Malaysia	110	20	80
Mexico	29	15	85
United States	8	17	83
Japan	10	6	94

Source: World Bank, World Development Indicators, World Development Report 2002, Tables 2 & 3

Many LDCs are highly dependent upon a small range of agricultural goods or non-oil minerals. The following countries for example have more than 40% dependence upon either a single export, or two exports: Burkina Faso (cotton), Chile (copper and metal ores), Cuba (sugar), Ethiopia (coffee), Jamaica (minerals), Kenya (tea and coffee), Malawi (tobacco), Mauritania (iron ore), Panama (fruit), Papua New Guinea (gold and metal ores), Paraguay (vegetable oil and cotton), Seychelles (fish), Sierra Leone (precious stones) and Uganda (coffee).

This trade structure leads to three problems:

1 slow growth of exports
2 fast growth of imports
3 worsening terms of trade

1   Slow growth of exports is itself due to:

i   *Low income elasticity of demand.* Most of these primary products have a low income elasticity of demand. The quantity of food consumption is constrained by biological necessity, and population growth in rich countries. Increased incomes are spent on manufactures and services. The small increases in expenditure on food tend to reflect processing and packaging rather than on increased quantities of raw materials. Similarly, spending on more sophisticated or luxury products often involves little increase in demand for raw materials.

ii *Agricultural protection.* For the very reasons outlined in i) above, farmers in developed countries have gained increased trade protection from their own governments since World War II, in the USA, the European Union and Japan. Thus subsidised European beef, which costs twice as much to produce as beef from Argentina, Brazil and Uruguay is enormously significant to potential exports from these LDCs. The case of subsidized sugar is even worse for LDCs and is estimated to be worth a third of all foreign aid money in lost export revenue. Reducing barriers to agricultural trade proved the most difficult obstacle in the Uruguay Round of GATT negotiations, and almost wrecked agreement on the whole package of trade gains.

iii *Synthetic substitutes.* Many raw materials have faced declining markets due to the development of synthetic substitutes. Timber, metal, cotton, wool, rubber, jute, sisal and hemp all have widely used synthetic substitutes.

iv *Miniaturization.* Many modern technologies, like the transistor and the microchip have enabled many products to become smaller, thus economizing on raw materials.

v *Low price elasticity of demand for primary products.* The fewer substitutes there are for a product the less price-elastic it will be. The demand for primary products to any one country is likely to be very price-elastic as there are often several other countries producing close substitutes. For example, tea and coffee are produced in many LDCs and each country is likely to try to produce as much product as possible. The nature of primary products, however, leads to them being very price-inelastic overall. There are few substitutes for food and many minerals. Commodities are sold on world markets according to the laws of supply and demand. As countries individually increase their output, world price falls markedly. For example at this time (2002/2003) coffee prices have plunged due increased output by new suppliers like Vietnam.

There have been many attempts at maintaining prices by establishing International Commodity Agreements. These have also been used to try to combat the short term problem of price instability.

2 Fast growth of imports is itself due to:

i *High income elasticity of demand for imported manufactures and services.* As LDCs experience economic growth, there is a marked increase in demand for capital goods and consumer goods. As a result of income inequality, the richer groups have a high demand for products which are largely produced in the industrialised countries.

ii   *Low price elasticity of demand for imported manufactures and services.* As there are few
domestic substitutes for the capital and consumer goods imported, they tend to be
price-inelastic. Therefore import prices tend to be maintained or increased, despite falling export prices.

3   Worsening terms of trade

The prices of exports and imports are as important as the volumes or quantities bought
and sold.[2] Historically, the terms of trade for many LDCs has declined against MDCs as
prices for primary commodities fall relative to manufactures and services, for the reasons
outlined in (i) and (ii) above. This decline was particularly marked in the 1980s. However,
the dramatic rise in oil prices in the 1970s substantially increased average primary prices.
(This had such a skewing effect on the average figures, that since that time oil and non-oil
prices have been recorded separately). Figure 5.9 graphs terms of trade figures for commodities excluding oil, illustrating the very substantial fall in export prices relative to import prices.

Figure 5.9 – Real Non-Oil Commodity Terms of Trade 1977–1998

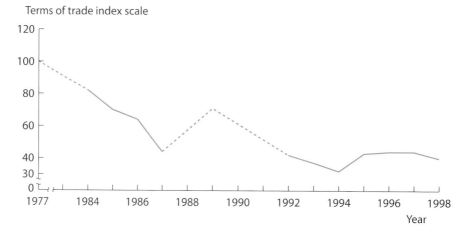

Source: IMF, The World Economic Outlook 1994 and 1998

Some agricultural commodities and metals were hit particularly badly. Therefore in
certain highly specialised countries, the terms of trade have fallen a very long way. For
example between 1960 and 1980 they moved for Bangladesh (jute) from 201 to 84, for Sri
Lanka (tea) from 203 to 93 and for Liberia (rubber) from 255 to 71.

SHORT TERM

Commodity price fluctuations. The prices of primary products tends to fluctuate considerably in the short term. Foreign exchange earnings on the current account can therefore vary considerably and make development plans uncertain as governments are unable to predict income.

For the causes of price fluctuations we need to look at price elasticity of demand and supply and shifts in demand and supply. We have already noted that demand for primary products tends to be very inelastic. The nature of farming and mining also leads to short term inelasticity of supply. Thus, if there is a shift in supply or demand, the effect on price is marked (see Figures 5.45 and 5.46). Sudden shifts in supply in agriculture, supply 'shocks', are common due to drought, flood, pests and disease. With minerals the shifts are more likely from the demand side. Many minerals are used extensively in making capital equipment, and investment demands are notoriously volatile in rich countries due to trade cycle and accelerator effects.

 Figure 5.10

Figure 5.11

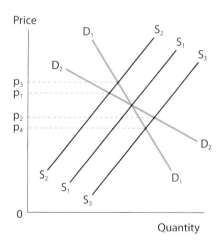

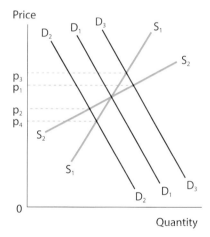

Countries with high dependence on one or two primary commodities are especially vulnerable to wide market price fluctuations such as Zambia (copper), Bolivia (tin) and Ghana (cocoa). In Figure 5.10 the demand curve D_1 represents a good with a lower price elasticity of demand than a good with demand curve D_2. Supply 'shocks' are represented by the supply curve moving between S_2 and S_3, causing much wider price fluctuations to the less price-elastic good than to the more elastic one (p_3p_4 compared to p_1p_2).

In Figure 5.11 the supply curve S_1 represents a good with a lower price elasticity of supply than a good with supply curve S_2. Demand 'shocks' are represented by the demand curve moving between D_2 and D_3 causing much wider price fluctuations to the less price-elastic good than to the more elastic one (p_3p_4 compared to p_1p_2).

INTERNATIONAL COMMODITY AGREEMENTS

There have been many schemes which have attempted to either raise commodity prices or to stabilize them. Raising prices tends to be popular with producers whilst consumers prefer either price stabilization or free markets. Attempts to raise prices involve restricting supply of the product by forming a producers' cartel and issuing quotas. Prices are stabilized by operating a buffer stock and buying or selling to reduce price movements.

RAISING PRICES BY QUOTA RESTRICTIONS

Historically, few countries have had monopoly power over a commodity, so the first step in restricting output is to form a cartel, a single selling organization for a group of producers. The cartel then issues quotas, a percentage allocation of the total supply they will permit to be supplied. These quotas are usually decided according to some historical production pattern. When price needs to be maintained members are ordered to restrict output in line with their quota allocation.

Thus in the diagram (Figure 5.12) the cartel would restrict supply from S_1 to S_2 raising the price from p_1 to p_2. If demand for the product was price-inelastic the total revenue will increase from $0q_1ap_1$ to $0q_2bp_2$. Sugar, tin, coffee and rubber are a few of many quota schemes. Market forces act in various ways to undermine such schemes and few last long.

📊 Figure 5.12 – A Commodity Cartel

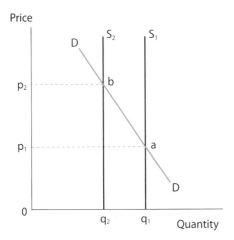

Some of the major weaknesses of quota restriction schemes are as follows:

i   Cheating by members. Success in raising prices makes it attractive for members to sell more at the high price. The more is produced, the further supply increases, and the price falls back towards P_1.

ii Increase in supply by non-members. Again the incentive to produce more is triggered by the high cartel price.

iii Economizing in the use of the product (*eg* using thinner tin coatings on steel cans, aluminium recycling) and the development of substitute products by firms producing consumer goods (Figure 5.13). The search for these is highly likely to be triggered by the new high fixed price.

Figure 5.13 – Substitute Products for Primary Commodities

Primary commodity	Substitute	Primary commodity	Substitute
Aluminium	Plastic	Jute	Plastic
Cocoa	Artificial chocolate flavouring	Rubber	Plastic
Copper	Plastic, glass fibre	Sugar cane	Fructose, sugar beet
Cotton	Synthetic fibres	Wood	Metal, plastic

AN EXCEPTION: THE OIL CARTEL

The cartel in exported oil, the Organization of Petroleum Exporting Countries (OPEC) succeeded where many other cartels failed. There were a number of reasons for this. The political will and unity of the major exporters was intensified dramatically by the Yom-Kippur war of 1973, and this over-rode the temptation to cheat. The supply of the product could be easily reduced by simply keeping it in the ground. Compare this to trying to restrict fresh meat or bananas. The price elasticity of demand for oil was very low in the short run, as vehicles, machines and heating systems could not quickly change their energy source.

Oil prices rose from US$3 a barrel before the war to US$12 to US$13 a barrel in the mid–70s. When Iran and Iraq, two big OPEC producers, went to war with each other in 1979 the other OPEC members did not replace their oil quotas by pumping more themselves. Oil prices soared. At their peak oil touched US$34 a barrel. As demand was price inelastic there was a massive transfer of spending from consumers to OPEC members. Relatively poor Middle Eastern countries became rich beyond belief.

STABILIZING PRICES BY KEEPING A BUFFER STOCK

Producer countries argue that it is difficult to plan tax revenue and import payments if there is major uncertainty over export prices. Consumers too may prefer price stability. However producers and consumers are diametrically opposed over price levels. The main proponent of price stability schemes has been the United Nations Conference for Trade and Development (UNCTAD). There have been International Agreements for tin, coffee, cocoa, tea, natural rubber, sugar, jute and tropical timber.

Buffer stock operation requires a buffer stock manager who buys and sells in the market to manipulate demand and supply in order to stabilise the price. Thus in Figure 5.14 the price is contained within a price band with a ceiling price and a floor price. In this example it is demand which shifts. If market demand were to fall to D_1 then the manager would act to prevent the price falling below the price floor. Thus the manager would buy ab to keep the price from falling. If demand increased to D_2 the manager would sell from stock.

Figure 5.14 – a Buffer Stock

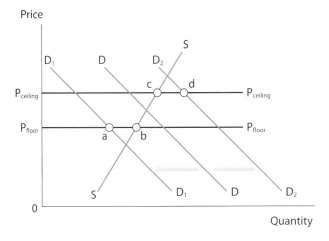

There are problems in operating buffer stocks. Perishable goods are very expensive to stock. Managers need large stocks and cash reserves to be effective, or the scheme will collapse. If the scheme fails to choose a median price because for example producers want to maintain a higher than market price, or the trend price falls, then the stock manager will be buying more often than selling, and building up a large, expensive stockpile.

There are also doubts as to whether there is the need for buffer stock price stabilization at all. It is possible that, if left to market forces, speculative buying and selling may automatically dampen price fluctuations. More fundamentally, some economists are not convinced that price fluctuations are always damaging. Finally, the beneficiaries of price stabilization are not necessarily the poor, and any transfer of resources from consumers to the poor might be more effective if carried out directly.

4   FOREIGN AID

Most LDCs have a deficit on the current account of the balance of payments, which therefore requires a surplus on the capital account to finance it. Private investment from MNCs is one major source of foreign exchange. Another is aid which is either transferred by public bodies, Official Development Assistance, or unofficially.

ODA itself can be divided into two types:

1   Bilateral aid – which is given by individual governments, and
2   Multilateral aid – which is given by multilateral agencies (*eg* the World Bank, the Regional Development Banks and the UN Agencies).

Unofficial aid is aid provided by organisations that are not government bodies. These are commonly known as NGOs, short for Non Governmental Organizations. Some of these are international for example, Red Cross, Oxfam and the churches. Others are indigenous to countries and regions *eg* in India there are almost 10,000 NGOs.[3]

THE AMOUNT OF AID

Between the years 1960 and 1991 ODA has increased from $4.6 billion to $55.5 billion. However when these figures are adjusted for inflation the real value of aid has only increased by 160%. Even more significant, however, is ODA expressed as a percentage of the developed countries' GNP. This actually declined from 0.51% to 0.33% over this period.[4] Developed countries have become less, not more, generous in their giving. The two major international enquiries into development since World War II, The Pearson Report and the Brandt Report, both recommended a target of 0.7% of GNP to be given as ODA. Very few countries exceed this recommended figure.

Among OECD members, the United States is the largest donor in terms of volume; it provided $11.3 billion in aid in 1991, see Figure 5.15. Japan with $10.9 billion, was the next largest provider of total aid. However, the United States is near the bottom among OECD donors when aid is calculated as a proportion of GNP – the figure is only 0.20 per cent. At the other extreme, United Arab Emirates, Saudi Arabia and the Nordic countries give large percentages of GNP.

Figure 5.15 – Official Development Assistance From OECD Members

Figure 5.16 – Development Assistance as a Percentage of Donor's GNP

Flows of aid from DAC[5] member countries ODA

Country	Millions of US $ in 1999
Japan	15323
United States	9145
France	5637
Germany	5515
United Kingdom	3401
Netherlands	3134
Italy	1806
Denmark	1733
Canada	1699
Sweden	1630
Norway	1370
Spain	1363
Australia	982
Switzerland	969
Belgium	760
Austria	527
Finland	416
Portugal	276
Ireland	245
Greece	194
New Zealand	134
Luxembourg	119

Flows of aid from DAC member countries ODA disbursed as % of GNP

Country	1990	1999
Denmark	0.94	1.01
Norway	1.17	0.91
Netherlands	0.92	0.79
Sweden	0.91	0.70
Luxembourg	0.21	0.66
France	0.60	0.39
Japan	0.31	0.35
Switzerland	0.31	0.35
Finland	0.65	0.33
Ireland	0.16	0.31
Belgium	0.46	0.30
Canada	0.44	0.28
New Zealand	0.23	0.27
Australia	0.34	0.26
Germany	0.42	0.26
Austria	0.25	0.26
Portugal	0.24	0.26
Spain	0.20	0.23
United Kingdom	0.27	0.23
Italy	0.31	0.15
Greece	–	0.15
United States	0.21	0.10

Source: IBRD, World Development Report 2001, Table 21.

Aid from the multilateral development banks totalled about $5 billion in 1988. The United Nations assistance agencies, such as the United Nations Children's Fund, the United Nations Development Programme, and the World Food Programme, provided about $3.8 billion.

NGOs in industrial countries gave $5.5 billion to developing countries in 1987.

DIRECTION OF AID

A few bilateral donors – the Nordic countries, for example – emphasise the reduction of poverty in their giving. However, less than half of all ODA goes to the poorest countries. Most aid has in practice been based upon the military and political interests of the donor, and goes to relatively well off LDCs. With the ending of the Cold War and the reduction of global tension there is now a major opportunity to target development needs directly. The early 1990s however have seen a worsening situation for the countries of the South. This is partly as a result of large aid flows being diverted to former Communist countries.

Figure 5.17 illustrates how little correlation there is between poverty, as measured by low per capita income, and the amount of official aid received by the country.

Figure 5.17 – Per Capita Aid Receipts and Per Capita Income 1991 (US$)

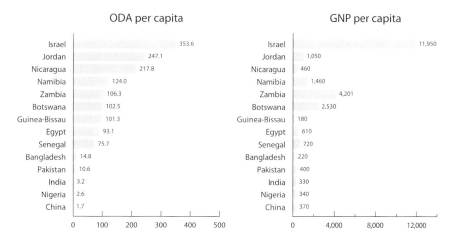

Source: IBRD, World development Report 1993.

Aid – Question

Suggest reasons for the amounts of aid given per capita to the countries in Figure 5.17.

Some aid is given for moral and humanitarian reasons such as for emergency food relief programmes, but political motivation is by far the most important reason. Thus US aid from the 1940s to 1990 was mainly directed at containing communism, by supporting strategically placed countries, such as Egypt and Israel. Over the same period Soviet aid programmes were politically motivated in support of communism. French and British aid goes disproportionately to their former colonies, and OPEC aid mainly to other Arab countries.

Multilateral agencies generally give more weight to development criteria. The World Bank and the IMF are very influential in influencing domestic policies of the recipients by imposing strict conditions to aid. This conditionality attached to assistance from the development banks is a major source of disagreement between the agencies and the recipients, who view the conditions as interference in their domestic policies.

Non Governmental Organizations are often strong in the field, dealing directly with poor people in villages and slums rather than with government departments at a national level. They tend to attack poverty directly, often working with local groups to achieve development by the poor rather than for the poor. The international NGOs also have major educational and publicity functions, keeping development issues to the forefront in the industrial world, educating the public on the issues, and lobbying governments.

THE ARGUMENT FOR AID

The most often quoted reasons for aiding LDCs are economic. Aid can be used to fill resources 'gaps'. Thus foreign aid can fill the foreign exchange gap, allowing LDCs to import more capital (closing the capital gap) which then combines with the relatively abundant resources of labour and land (raw materials) to increase economic growth. Growth will increase income, which will increase savings which will generate further growth and development.

In addition, Technical Assistance helps to fill a personnel gap and ensures good use of aid funds. Technical Assistance is subsidising the transfer of people with particular skills such as engineers, farmers, nurses and teachers.[6]

Most developmentalists would argue that aid should be allocated according to a country's ability to use funds wisely and productively. Yet in practice it has little to do with this. Aid is typically a low priority, residual in donor country budgets and few recipients have any say in the matter. Economic motivations are more likely to fulfil the self-interest of the donor. Where income and jobs are created in the donor country, offering aid is much more likely to win votes for politicians. Therefore *tied aid* is very common and limits purchases to the donor country. This is a 'second best' option to shopping around for the cheapest capital. In Pakistan, for example, the cost of 'transporting' aid by ships of the donor nations (the donors made it a condition to use their own shipping companies) was 50–115 per cent higher than the cheapest available.[7]

Aid is further criticised for maintaining income inequalities in LDCs. The emphasis on capital aid projects fosters the rich, the capitalist, the city dweller. It does little directly for poverty that is rural and labour based. In addition, the modern labour saving technology is often criticised as being inappropriate.

Aid can allow a country to postpone necessary reforms. A number of countries have allowed food aid to depress local food prices and reduce incentives for local farmers. It has allowed essential investments in the rural sector to be postponed. It can displace local saving, local trade and local capital formation.

Due to its political and military basis, aid has been detested by some because it increased the power of dictators and despots who were better able to repress the poor and prevent change from happening. With the ending of the Cold War the case for supporting such regimes has greatly reduced and many are being ousted *eg* the kleptomaniac President Mobutu of Zaire who has robbed that rich country into destitution.

In addition many argue that aid is a very poor substitute for trade. "Trade not aid" is a popular slogan which requires developed countries to remove the many trade restrictions on manufactures like textiles. The ability to earn a living would reduce poverty and the need for aid.

How to Help Africa?

To grasp the scale of Africa's poverty, consider this statistic; the combined GNP of the entire continent south of the Sahara is less than that of Holland. Worse, Africa is slipping. "Sub-Saharan Africa", reported the World Bank earlier this year, "is the only region in the world likely to experience an increase in poverty over the next decade". Worse again Africa has missed out entirely on the new vogue for private investment in the poor world. For the rest of the decade – and probably beyond – it will have to rely for foreign capital almost entirely on aid.

Two different trends are clasping Africa in a pincer-like hold. One problem is that rich-world priorities have shifted. The ending of the Cold War has eroded the desire to buy friends in Africa. Whenever African leaders gather – they fret about 'marginalization' the fact that investors and aid donors from the rich world are losing interest in Africa in favour of the emerging markets of Eastern Europe or of poverty closer to home.

The other grip on the continent comes from the multilateral institutions, mainly the World Bank and the IMF. The Bank says last year's drop in lending happened because the sums set aside for Sub-Saharan Africa in 1992 – chiefly because of drought there – were unusually high. But there is a more troublesome trend. The Bank finds itself increasingly unable to hand out the cash for African countries embarked on economic reform, because so many fail to meet the targets – shrinking budget deficits, reducing inflation – agreed with the IMF.

Much of the drop in the Bank's total lending to Africa was due to the absence of lending to Nigeria and Cote d'Ivoire. Both in the last few years have failed to meet the demands of the Fund and the Bank to get their economies into shape. So aid has been denied. And since IMF support is needed for a country to win debt relief from other creditors – the Fund and the Bank do not write off debts – the burden of offending countries continues to pile up. There could be an unexpected benefit in this foreign-aid squeeze. It is forcing some creditors and donors to reassess what the purpose of their giving should be. Unshackled from Cold War needs, can government aid be aimed more purposefully at helping Africans lift themselves out of poverty? Only a tiny share of aid – less than 10%, according to UNICEF – goes directly to things that help the poor primary health care, basic literacy and education (especially for women), clean water, family planning.

Though in bilateral aid to Africa grants now outrun loans, the money is rarely an unconditional gesture of generosity. Most is tied to purchases from the donor country; some of this is a thinly disguised direct subsidy to specific contracts. Only 5 of the 20 top donors, according to a recent report by Action Aid, a British Aid agency, tie less than half their aid. France ties 60%, Britain 75%, Italy 90%. Virtually all American "food aid" goes into buying up America's farm surpluses, chiefly of wheat.

Even those donors that do not officially tie much aid, such as Japan, often reach unofficial agreements that have the same effect. Limiting the buyer's choice, tied aid is nearly always inefficient. It can also hamper the development of local skills. Oxfam claims that 100,000 consultants from rich countries are now working in Africa, many doing jobs that could be done by Africans. To spend more aid on what Africa's poor really need – rural credit schemes, basic health care – would, however, mean fewer of the grand infrastructure schemes that so interest the world's business lobbies. A likely tale.

Source: Adapted from The Economist September 25th 1993 pp 69-70

5   FOREIGN INVESTMENT/ MULTINATIONAL COMPANIES

The rapid expansion of private direct foreign investment into LDCs since the 1960s and 1970s has been largely due to the activities of the multinational companies. A multinational company (MNC), or transnational company (TNC), is a firm that owns production units in more than one country. They are mainly based in North America, Europe and Japan *ie* they are owned and controlled outside the LDCs. Furthermore, many of them are enormous in size and control more economic resources than the whole GNP of many countries, as Figure 5.18 illustrates.

Figure 5.18 – the size of MNCs (Sales 1999) compared to the GNP (1998 $) of a selection of countries

Country/MNC	$ billion
United States of America	7921
Brazil	4570
China	750
General Motors (US)	176
Ford Motor Co (US)	163
Exxon	161
Norway	152
Daimler Chrysler (Germany)	151
Thailand	134
Toyota (Japan)	120
General Electric (US)	112
Royal Dutch/Shell (UK/Neth)	105
IBM (US)	88
British Petroleum (UK)	84
Philippines	79
New Zealand	56
Bangladesh	44
Total Fina (France)	40
Zimbabwe	7
Zambia	3

Source: UNCTAD, World Investment Report, 2001, World Bank, World Development Report, 2000.

American-owned MNCs account for about half the investment total, with MNCs from Europe, Germany and Japan making up most of the balance. They have concentrated within the richer LDCs, such as Brazil, Mexico, Argentina, Indonesia and Hong Kong, although they are present in almost every LDC. These companies bring not just finance, but technology, managerial skills, market openings and new life styles.

Figure 5.19 gives the total value of direct foreign investment into LDCs, 1970 to 1999. Most of this will be accounted for by multinational activity. The major recipients of the foreign direct investment is then given for 1997.

⊞ Figure 5.19 – Foreign Direct Investment into Developing Countries (1970–1999) and the major recipients in 1997

Foreign Direct Investment		Major Recipients of FDI, 1997	
Year	Total Net FDI (billions of US $)	Recipient	FDI received (as a % of total FDI to low/middle income LDCs)
1970	3.1	China	21
1980	10.9	Brazil	18
1990	23.7	Argentina	13
1991	35.1	Mexico	6
1992	42.5	South Korea	5
1993	53.2	Chile	5
1994	78.1	Poland	4
1995	96.3	Thailand	3
1996	118.9	All other LDCs	
1997	119.4	(low/middle income LDCs)	25
1998	170.9		
1999	185.4		

Source: UNDP, Human Development Report, 1994, World Bank 2001 World Development Indicators

The two central characteristics of MNCs, their large size and foreign ownership, has led to substantial disagreement over the desirability of their role in Developing Countries. The division of opinion is once again the 'growth versus development' argument. Thus the debate centres on different value judgements about the meaning of economic development.

MNCs AND ECONOMIC GROWTH

The injection of direct foreign investment increases the national income of the receiving country. GNP, investment, saving and manufacturing all grow. There is also broad agreement that MNC investment can break crucial supply-side bottlenecks in LDCs.

Thus LDCs characteristically have supply 'gaps' in saving, foreign exchange, taxes, technology and human skills. MNCs, by locating within a developing country, can help to break these growth restraints, bringing in investment, foreign exchange, management skills, technology and access to markets. Their activities generate jobs, saving, tax revenue and exports.

The narrow economic case for private foreign investment is not unchallenged. In practice MNCs are monopolistic or oligopolistic and therefore subject to criticism on efficiency grounds. One specific MNC practice is that of transfer pricing and development. This is the setting of internal prices within branches of an MNC such that when components are shipped between branches the total tax bill is minimised. This is likely to work against the ability of governments to collect taxes from MNCs. In addition, competing LDC governments may offer concessions on taxes, subsidies and protection such that the benefits of investment are greatly reduced.

However, whilst there is some disagreement as to how much an LDC benefits economically compared to the MNC, the real debate is focused upon the impact these giant foreign companies have upon development.

MNCs AND DEVELOPMENT

There is no doubt that MNCs exert a marked impact upon the host economy. Whether their presence aids or hinders development is controversial. In practice the growth potential from capitalist MNC activity needs to be examined alongside the development needs of the country, to assess the relative costs and benefits. That MNCs are potentially anti-developmental is based upon the following arguments. MNCs:

- widen the inequality between rich and poor by developing a modern high wage sector.
- market inappropriate, sophisticated products for elite groups, using the advertising techniques of oligopoly to create desire for these products.
- widen the rural-urban divide by locating in the cities and as a consequence encourage further rural-urban migration.
- use modern technology which, being capital intensive, is inappropriate for labour abundant countries, and does little for jobs and incomes of the poor.
- can use their immense size and consequent power to influence governments into anti-developmental activities.
- may inhibit the development of local enterprise.

6   EXPORT PROMOTION VERSUS IMPORT SUBSTITUTION

Having looked at some of the main theoretical arguments for and against free trade and then studied the existing trade situation, we now go on to examine government policies towards trade and exchange rates. This is an area of very active debate between 'export promotion' free traders on the one hand, and 'import substitution' protectionists on the other. It is another facet of the 'markets versus intervention' debate which pervades so many economic topics.

All the developed countries are industrial. LDCs therefore see the need to produce more manufactures themselves rather than depend, as at present, upon primary products. However, severe balance of payments restraints prevent LDCs buying all the imported manufactures they need to industrialise.

Governments must therefore choose between trade policies which:

1   encourage exports to pay for the needed imports, or
2   discourage imports, whilst developing substitute domestic products.

In practice, governments operate a mixture of free trade and protectionist policies.[8] However, choices must be made and a large number of LDCs have opted to protect many of their industries in the interest of growth and development. Other LDCs have opted for relative openness to world trade. Here we identify the policies and examine some of the main economic advantages and disadvantages of each.

EXPORT-PROMOTION (E–P)

Export-promotion policies encourage free trade in goods and the free movement of capital and labour. Multinationals are encouraged, together with their technology and products. In practice it is manufactures which are likely to be promoted, rather than primary products which are subject to the problems discussed in Section 3.

The theoretical justification for export-promotion is the increased output and growth arising from trade *ie* comparative advantage, economies of scale, increased competition and modern technology. Proponents of E–P reject the higher prices and lower output of the protection option (see Figure 5.20).

Figure 5.20 – The Effects of Imposing a Tariff

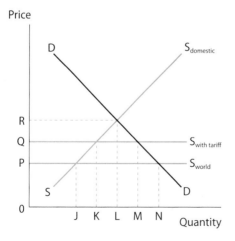

If the world price of a good is OP, a tariff of PQ will shift the supply curve upwards from S_{world} to $S_{with\ tariff}$.
Domestic consumption will fall by MN whilst domestic production will rise by JK. Imports will fall from JN to KM.

The practical justification for E–P is the large measure of success that some E–P countries have had in recent decades. The high economic growth of the 'Asian tigers' of the Pacific Rim – South Korea, Taiwan, Singapore and Hong Kong – are especially important as models to emulate. Some other nations which are export promoting are Brazil, Chile, Malaysia, Thailand and Turkey. Many of these countries have transformed themselves from LDCs towards being developed countries, earning the intermediate collective title of NICs, Newly Industrializing Countries. In the first half of the 1990s many Asian countries, including China, were experiencing very rapid growth through policies which embrace openness in trade.

A problem with E–P has been the protectionism of the developed countries. This has been strong in just those labour intensive manufactures, such as textiles and footwear, where LDCs have comparative advantage. These industries tend to threaten the poorest workers in declining industries in MDCs. One might argue that the more countries which produce these products the stiffer the protectionist resistance. However, this ignores the dynamic of the raised incomes in the NICs which become important markets themselves. Certainly, the growth of intra-LDC trade would be a way around First World trade barriers. Many current observers see South East Asia becoming a very important trading area in its own right within a decade. Latin America has already a high number of middle income countries and, given favourable political conditions, could also flourish. The North American Free Trade Area, very significantly includes Mexico with two of the richest countries in the world, Canada and the USA and could well expand further south. Most of Africa, however, remains very poor and non industrial.

Import-substitution (I–S)

Import-substitution policies encourage self-reliance in the production of manufactures. Tariff barriers are erected against imports to protect the home market. Factor movements of capital and labour are also restricted. Multinationals with inappropriate products, advertising and technologies are restricted.

The theoretical justifications for import substitution (I–S) policies lie in the critique of free trade theory; unrealistic assumptions that do not account for unemployment, changing comparative costs, distorted prices, inappropriate technology and the risks of over specialisation. The 'infant industry' argument is often invoked to justify restrictions on trade (see Figure 5.21). The balance of trade improves with the restriction of imports. When the protected infant industries mature and have become low-cost large producers, tariffs can be removed and industries can then compete with foreign imports, or begin to export themselves.

Figure 5.21 – Infant Industries

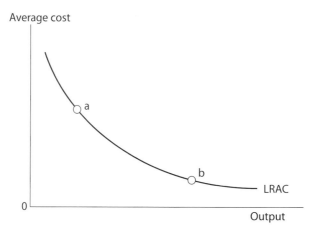

The proponents of the infant industry argument claim that protection is essential for industry to develop within LDCs. Many manufactures and services are produced at low cost in developed countries through economies of scale. A new 'baby' industry would find it impossible to compete at low units of output as its costs would be high (point 'a' in the diagram above). By protecting the infant industry and thus guaranteeing it a captive market behind trade barriers, the industry can expand and move down the cost and learning curves. When the infant has grown to adulthood (point 'b' in the diagram), the barriers are removed and it competes equally.

In practice import-substitution would be undertaken in stages. A country with little manufacturing experience first protects final stage assembly industries, and simple consumer goods industries. Later it progresses to building components and more sophisticated manufactures. Tax and investment incentives are used to gain the co-operation of foreign companies.

The practical experience of I–S strategy has not been very successful. Most of the countries adopting it have experienced very low growth compared to the strongly outward oriented countries. Protectionist countries include Argentina, Bolivia, Peru, Bangladesh, Ghana and Zambia. India, formerly one of the most protectionist countries, is currently dismantling its bureaucracy and relying more on markets.

Infant industries once protected from the rigour of competition often never grow up. They remain high cost and inefficient. This has cost implications for "forward linkage" industries for example, if tractor production is protected then farmers cannot use cheaper foreign tractors to lower the cost of their own products. Moreover, the poor may gain little. Major benefits may instead accrue to wealthy local manufacturers, and to foreign firms located inside the tariff walls.

As capital goods and intermediate products are often subsidised, industries tend to be capital intensive rather than labour intensive, negating comparative advantage. Exchange rates are often held artificially high to encourage the use of imported capital and intermediate goods. This works against raising the incomes of the poor, however, by discouraging labour intensive production and making agricultural exports more expensive.

India's About Turn on Protection

From its independence in 1949 to 1990 India pursued a strong policy of economic self-reliance. The country, standing apart in economic isolation from the rapid changes occurring in the Asia-Pacific rim countries to the east, became a backwater for international trade. It had the world's highest import duties and Indian domestic industry sheltered inefficiently behind the tariff barriers. However by 1990 India had accrued a massive international debt, even the servicing of the debt was proving difficult at $7 billion a year a full third of all export earnings. The National Debt was also very large and the government could only pay the interest by continually increasing the budget deficit and thereby continuously fuelling inflation. In 1991 Premier Rao introduced sweeping reforms to India's foreign trade policy. Restrictive regulations were swept away. Foreign ownership in joint enterprises, and foreign technology were welcomed, *eg* India now has a very competitive software writing industry. India could become the next NIC after China. However it does still have a huge legacy of bureaucrats and officialdom to get rid of first.

Question

1   What arguments might have been use to support protection and self-sufficiency?
2   What is meant by 'servicing' the debt?

7   POPULATION POLICY

With an acute shortage of savings available for investment, governments and development agencies have to make choices in their investment strategies. A good deal has already been written here about the choice between growth and development. The emphasis upon growth in the first four decades of development has seen a marked favouritism towards physical capital accumulation. Governments have priced capital so that it would be extensively used. The countries which have favoured human investment in education and health care, over capital investment are rarer. In this section we look at two specific investment programmes which have a degree of urgency in many poor countries, both of them likely to have a very high pay-off in reducing poverty. They are the investments into population policy and agricultural policy.

Population and Investment

The main cause of population growth in LDCs is the high birth rate. Birth rates remain high even though death rates have fallen. In addition birth rates are much higher than they were in the pre-industrial years of the high income countries. This is because a larger proportion of girls marry, and because they marry at a younger age. Thus a greater proportion of women have children, and they have more years in which to have children. Death rates, on the other hand, have fallen dramatically. This is largely due to inexpensive improvements in public health and nutrition.

Life expectancy in LDCs has increased significantly in many LDCs in the last few decades, with the greatest reason being the improvement in the infant survival rate. Figure 5.22 illustrates just how marked this has been for the three decades between 1965 and 1997 in a selection of countries. The figures also contrast this with the devastating impact of aids in countries of Africa.

Figure 5.22 – Changing Life Expectancy in Selected LDCs

Country	Life Expectancy at birth (years)		
	1965	1986	1997
Guatemala	49	61	64
Mexico	59	68	72
Jordan	50	65	71
Oman	43	54	73
Mozambique	37	48	45
Zambia	44	53	43

Source: IBRD, The Data Development Book, World Development Report 2001

Why do the peoples of LDCs tend to have so many children? If we can answer this question we are on the way to understanding what conditions are required for birth rates (fertility rates)[9] to fall, and hence how to influence the growth of population.

FERTILITY RATES AND THE NATIONAL INCOME PER CAPITA

High fertility rates are associated with low income per capita and low fertility rates with high income per capita. There is little evidence, however, of causality. Fertility rates vary significantly with incomes because they are average figures and say nothing about the distribution of income. Figure 5.23 illustrates this wide diversity of fertility rates at different levels of income. Notice how wide the spread is at any per capita income level.

Figure 5.23 – Fertility Rate and National Income per Capita

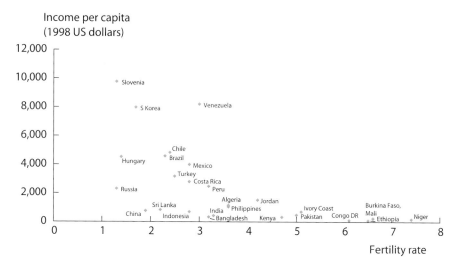

Source: World Bank, World Development Indicators, World Development Rpt. 1999/2000, Tbls. 1 & 7

In fact there is little significant correlation between fertility rates and any macro-economic variables, like GNP per capita, or growth of GNP per capita.

A MICRO APPROACH – FAMILY SIZE AS AN ECONOMIC DECISION

A micro approach to population growth throws more light onto why many of the poor are motivated to have large families. Recent theory argues that the number of children a couple have is a rational decision involving an assessment of the relative costs and benefits of children. The motivation for having children is complex. Economic reasons alone cannot explain why families have children, but they are an important consideration. Given that this is so, the theory of demand can be applied to the family demand for children. Demand is regarded as a rational decision and children are treated as though they were consumer or investment goods.

The first two or three children are not explained in this way, and are assumed to be determined by cultural and psychological factors. However, additional children are seen as being determined by family preference for a certain number of surviving children (often males), the costs and benefits of those children, and the level of family income.

The economic benefits of children are those of an investment; for labour on the farm, or for security in old age. The two main economic costs of having children are:

- the direct costs of feeding, clothing and education
- the opportunity cost of the mother's time in rearing children

According to standard theory of consumer demand, increasing the 'price' or cost of children should reduce the demand for children. This could be the result of:

- an increase in direct costs such as charging school fees for the third and subsequent children
- raising the opportunity cost of having children, primarily by providing more education for girls and more jobs for women
- reducing the benefit of children by raising the legal age of work
- reducing the benefit of children by setting up pension and sickness schemes to reduce the need for family support in old age

Evidence from a number of countries including the Philippines, Chile, Taiwan and Thailand provide support for the effectiveness of this approach. Higher female employment and higher school attendance for both males and females are associated with lower fertility. In addition there is a strong relationship between the decline in child mortality and fertility. Thus improved health care and nutrition increases the chances of children surviving and reduce the need for subsequent births. Higher incomes seem to encourage a few 'high quality' children rather than many 'low quality' children.

Where the majority of the population, and especially the very poor, share in the benefits of development there will be the greatest effect in lowering the fertility rate.

Population and Family Planning in China

Since 1971, China has made unique progress towards gaining control over the growth of its massive population. By doing so it has not only made a large numerical impact on the total population of the globe but has also provided important lessons for other low income countries interested in fertility reduction. But some of the techniques used to reduce the number of births in China may not be transferable to other political and cultural settings, and others would not be widely acceptable because of the loss of personal freedom they involve.

Population policy in China has been anything but constant. After the Communist take over in 1949, Chairman Mao Zedong repeatedly asserted that 'revolution plus production' would solve all problems, with no need to limit population growth. China's first census, conducted in 1953, revealed such a large population (nearly 600 million) that it shook this complacency. But birth control campaigns from 1956–1958 and from 1962–1966 had only limited results and were limited by Mao's famous policy reversals, the Great Leap Forward of 1960 and the Cultural Revolution of the late 1960s. Only in 1971 was a serious and sustained effort launched. At that time the crude birth rate, already reduced by the disruptions of the Cultural Revolution, stood at 30. By 1983 it had been cut to 19.

The 'planned births' campaign of 1971 was reportedly launched at the personal initiative of Premier Zhou Enlai. It established three reproductive norms later marriage, longer spacing between births, and fewer children. To implement these norms, the highly committed post-Mao leadership set birth targets for administrative units at all levels throughout China. Responsibility for achieving these targets was placed in the hands of officials heading units ranging from provinces of 2 to 90 million people down to production teams of 250 to 800. The national government held information and motivation campaigns to persuade people to have fewer children, but it was left to officials to fill out many details of the program and finance much of its cost. A wide range of contraceptives was offered and family planning was closely linked to efforts to improve child and maternal health care.

While national spokesmen maintained that participation in the program was voluntary, local officials with targets to fulfil often applied pressure. At the production-team level, birth planning became intensely personal, as couples were required to seek approval to have a child in a particular year. (The application could be accepted, or they might be asked to wait for a year or two.) Such extreme methods seem to have worked and been reasonably well accepted in China, presumably because of its cohesive social structure and strong government authority from the national down to the neighbourhood level.

The most popular form of birth limitation in China has been the intra-uterine device (IUD). Two other major forms have been abortion and sterilization of both women and men.

The wan xi shao campaign lowered fertility, but population projections continued to be a matter of concern and in 1979 the 'one child' policy was promulgated. Couples were now told that 'only children are better children' and urged to take a pledge to stop at one. Those who do so often receive special incentives, such as an income supplement, extra maternity leave, and preferential treatment when applying for public housing. The 'one child' campaign flies in the face of traditional son-preference by asking half of China's couples to stop reproducing before they have had a male child, and appears to have been associated with some resurgence of female infanticide or neglect of girl babies, but it did succeed in reducing fertility to the replacement level by the mid-1980s. The target is now to stabilize the population at about 1.2 billion early in the twenty-first century.

Although some aspects of China's population program will doubtless remain unique, countries interested in strengthening their own programs could learn from China's strong information activities, its use of a wide range of contraceptive methods, and its decentralization of many aspects of planning and implementation to local authorities.

Source: Gillis, Perkins, Roemer, Snodgrass, Economics of Development, W.W. Norton & Company.

Family Planning Buffaloes and Vasectomy Festivals in Thailand

Thailand is the home of one of the most successful and effective family planning programs in the world. The program relies on the use of media, economic incentives, and community involvement to increase the use of contraception. Thailand's striking approach stresses the immediate practical benefits from lowered fertility and uses methods that mix humour and audacity. The program is run by an NGO, the Population and Community Association (PDA), with the support of the Ministry of Health.

The Community Based Family Planning Services (CBFPS), a PDA program, was initiated in 1974 and now reaches more than 16,000 villages and 17 million people – one third of the nation's population. The key message links population growth to low standards of living and family planning to economic gains. To convey this message, taboos surrounding birth control had to be broken down. Birth control carnivals, games, condom-blowing balloon contests, raffles, village fairs, and weddings have served as occasions for promoting family planning joyfully.

Vasectomy marathons are held on Labour Day and on the king's birthday. In 1993 a team of forty doctors and eighty nurses performed a record-breaking 1,190 vasectomies during the one-day festival. The PDA also delivered free, convenient and efficient vasectomy services in clinics and mobile units. Between July 1980 and June 1984 it performed 25,412 vasectomies.

Registered family planners may also rent cattle for plowing their fields – family planning buffaloes – at half the regular price. They are encouraged to market some of their products through the CBFPS at prices about 30 per cent higher than regular middlemen offer and to buy fertilizer and seeds at 30 per cent below local market prices. Under a similar program villagers who practice contraception may have their goods transported to the marketplace at a discount or may receive free piglets.

In 1985 about 60 percent of all Thai couples practised some form of birth control. The total fertility rate fell from 6.1 in 1965–70 to 2.8 in 1985, as against an average 4.1 for lower-middle-income countries.

Source: IBRD, World Development Report 1990

Questions

1   What does it mean to say that the 'fertility rate' fell from 6.1 in 1965-70 to 2.8 in 1985? (last paragraph in Thailand reading)
2   Is there any significant difference in how family limitation is organized in Thailand and China?
3   List economic incentives and disincentives to have fewer children in both Thailand and in China.

POPULATION POLICY MEASURES

Even though there is still some dissent from the notion that population growth has a negative effect on development, most LDCs are in favour of lowering the rate of population increase. Asian countries in particular have been active in implementing policies, with China the most successful country in slowing growth (see reading – Population and Family Planning in China).

Which government policies are likely to be most effective?

Lowering fertility can only ultimately be achieved by 'development', that is by eliminating absolute poverty; reducing income inequality; expanding education and jobs (especially for women); bringing modern preventive medicine and public health to the poor (especially clean water and sanitation); improving nutrition to lower infant mortality; and widening social service benefits to the poor. Governments might also implement direct family planning policies, together with these development policies, in order to speed up the process. Such policies may include: persuasion through education and advertising; family planning programmes to provide health and contraceptive advice; and offering economic incentives for restricting family size.

Developed countries also have a major role to play. For whether populations are regarded as too high or too low is measured against the resources available. Yet 20% of the world's population uses 80% of the world's resources. The USA alone, with 6% of the world's population uses 40%. If resources were freed (or resource prices eased), by developed nations moderating their life styles, this would aid the developing countries ability to raise their own standard of living.

In addition, increased determination, and therefore increased practical measures, to help poor countries to develop, would assist in slowing population increase. Practical incentives could include more financial assistance, lower trade barriers and help with appropriate technological research.

Population Policy in Pakistan

Unusually for a former cabinet minister, Mahub ul Haq is happy to talk about where he went wrong. It happened, when as minister of planning and finance in Pakistan for most of the Eighties, he tried to curb its rapid population growth with a contraceptive campaign. "I decided that this had to have the top priority in our development plans, and so, in a most unusual step for a finance minister, I announced that there would be no limit to the money to be spent on family planning programmes," he said. "I set out to saturate the villages with condoms. We got them into every shop. I had people design the most attractive dispensers so that as each condom was sold another would fall into position. People were fascinated just to watch them."

He got round an official ban on advertising condoms on radio and television by the ingenious device of calling them "Sathi", meaning companions. So his widely broadcast slogan came out as the apparently innocuous "Take a companion with you." "I thought such an initiative was going to go down well in history," said Dr. ul Haq, now one of the most senior officials in the United Nations Development Programme "but it was my greatest policy disaster. Despite the campaign the population growth rate actually went up!" To this day Pakistan has one of the lowest uses of contraceptives in Asia, and its population is set to more than double to 260 million in the next 30 years.

The story serves as a cautionary tale for the 15,000 people due to attend the controversial UN International Conference on Population and Development, which opens in Cairo this week. It is being billed as the world's last chance to contain the population explosion. The UN Population Fund, which is organising the conference, estimates that, by the year 2025, the world will have nearly 8,500 million people, about half as many again as today. It will be a world that has been transformed even within our own lifetimes. Some 84 per cent of the population will live in the Third World, more than 40 per cent in China and the Indian subcontinent alone. In 1950 Africa had about half as many people as Europe; by 2025 it will contain more than three times as many.

But what is to be done? The conference has created a strange alliance – between the Pope and militant Islamic leaders. The pontiff has publicly attacked the conference more than 15 times since March, charging that it is attempting to "destroy the family", and reaffirming his opposition to contraception and abortion. He has upbraided President Bill Clinton, who has reversed Republican policies on population control, and has written to all heads of government, urging each to "bring your conscience to Cairo". The Holy See, which will participate in the conference as a member of the United Nations, has been recruiting allies. Argentina has publicly declared its support for the Vatican line, and is expected to be joined by a group including Nicaragua, the Ivory Coast, Malta, Senegal, Venezuela and Morocco.

Earlier this month, the Vicar of Christ secured a promise of collaboration from Mohammad Hashemi Rafsanjani, the deputy foreign minister of Iran and the president's brother. Muslim League officials have denounced parts of the draft conference resolution as "repulsive" while the Secretary General of the International Muslim Youth organisation has proclaimed a religious duty to ensure the conference fails. One leading fundamentalist in Cairo goes further. Some people, he said last week, may be prepared to kill for the cause. "If the West is afraid of blood it should stay away." Yet, despite the dubious alliance, the Pope is trying to make an important point. It is that successful population policies result from economic development, education and health care – not from family planning programmes. And the story of Mahbub ul Haq and Pakistan's contraception programme suggests that the Pope is half right.

The evidence indicates that social factors are indeed the most powerful in controlling population, and contraception without them can prove as useless as in Pakistan. As Dr ul Haq says "We have got to put development back on to the population agenda." But it also shows that formal family planning programmes are important, and that the most effective progress is made when both these elements are combined.

It took the whole of human history until the early 19th century for the world population to reach a single billion (there are thought to have been some 150 million people alive at the time of Christ). The second billion was clocked up at the end of the 1920's. The third arrived in 1960, the fourth in 1976, the fifth in 1987. There are now some 5.7 billion people on the planet and there will be 6 billion in less than 4 years.

Every year nearly 90 million more people – the population of Mexico or of the whole of northern Europe – crowd the human race. At present rates, population will double again to more than 11 billion in just 40 years. And the growth is concentrated in the areas least able to cope with it. Last year 94 per cent of the increase was in developing countries.

However the main drain on the earth's resources and threat to the environment comes from the rich. A baby born in Europe or America will consume about 40 to 50 times as many resources during its lifetime as its counterpart in Asia or Africa. Population growth in the United States in the next 30 years, it has been shown, will have more effect on the environment than the increase in numbers in India and China combined. Professor Paul Ehrlich writes "The relatively small population of rich people accounts for roughly two-thirds of global environmental destruction. From this perspective, the most important population problem is overpopulation in the industrialised nations. There are, in fact, too many rich people."

New figures, also published this month, show that the richest fifth of the world's people have increased their share of the world's wealth from 70 to 83 per cent over the last three decades, while the meagre proportion divided amongst the poorest fifth has been cut by nearly half – to just 1.4 per cent.

But won't Third World development simply create more rich people and greater pressure on world resources than the billions of poor people that inhabit Africa and large parts of Asia? The answer is no. It is the super rich (with high consumption and pollution) and the very poor (who are forced to overuse land and cut down trees for fuel) who cause the most environmental damage. A fairer sharing of wealth would ease the pressure at both ends of the spectrum.

Despite the Pope, a dramatic increase in contraception has brought about much of the decrease in the growth rate. More than half the Third World women of childbearing age now use it, up from a fifth in 1960. Even the pontiff's own followers now ignore his strictures. More than half of Mexico's married women use modern family planning, while Brazil is the world's fourth largest manufacturer of contraceptive pills. But contraception only comes into its own when parents cease to want big families. In poor societies there are good reasons for lots of children. They are economic assets, doing useful work for the family from the age of six or seven, and often producing more than they consume well before they reach their teens. They provide security in old age. Where infant mortality is high, parents need to have lots of babies to ensure that enough survive. Many countries from Costa Rica to China, Columbia to Thailand, and Sri Lanka to Chile have cut their population growth rates dramatically by combining family planning with development.

Tackling the remaining, and still acute, population crisis will demand a similar mix of measures. The UN Population Fund estimates that there are still 120 million Third World women who wish to avoid pregnancy, but do not have access to modern contraception. Meeting that unmet demand would bring the world nearly halfway towards achieving the "replacement fertility rate" – roughly two children per woman – that will eventually stabilise world population.

But the crisis will not be defused unless the world tackles the main root of population growth – poverty. This need not cost huge sums of new money, but will entail a reordering of priorities.

The UN Development Programme calculates that the world could achieve universal primary education, halve adult illiteracy, eliminate malnutrition, and provide everyone with safe drinking water and sanitation, family planning services and access to credit by a "20/20 Compact". This would require developing countries to devote 20 per cent of their budgets (instead of the present 13 per cent) to these goals, while industrialised countries would earmark 20 per cent of their aid (instead of the present 7 per cent) to achieving the same objectives.

Everyone, including the Pope, agrees that one measure, above all, would make a world of difference – increasing the education of women. In country after country this has proved the most crucial factor of all. In countries as diverse as Brazil and Zimbabwe, women with little or no education have an average of six or seven children each, while those who have been to secondary school limit themselves to two or three.

> Dr Nafis Sadiq, the Secretary General of the Cairo conference, says "If we had paid more attention to empowering women 30 years ago, and had listened to their needs, we might well have been ahead of the game as far as population numbers is concerned." Mahub ul Haq, reflecting on his experience in Pakistan, agrees. "What went wrong was that female literacy in the villages was only 6 per cent. If I had to do it all over again, I would put almost all the money into educating women."
>
> *Source: 'Independent on Sunday' newspaper, 28 August 1994*

8   AGRICULTURAL POLICY

A Third World farm is not just a business, but a way of life. Policies to change agriculture will therefore need to extend to changing the whole social, political and institutional structure of rural society. Otherwise it is likely that agricultural reform will not take place. Alternatively, it may just widen the gap between the few wealthy landowners and the mass of poor peasants.

The gap between the low productivity subsistence farms of LDCs and the high productivity, specialized cash crop farms of industrialised countries is enormous. Risk is very high in switching from subsistence to cash crops. Dependence upon other people for inputs like fertilizer, irrigation and seed; the price fluctuations of inputs and output; marketing; the transport of inputs and output; and the availability of credit are just some of the new variables with increased risk. Poor farmers close to survival levels are behaving entirely rationally in not undertaking that risk. That is because a poor harvest results not only in financial loss but loss of land, livelihood and ultimately life. The poor therefore continue with well tried, low risk, traditional methods even though these result in low output. A low average product with low variance is logically better than a higher average with greater variance. It is richer farmers and bigger landlords who can afford to take the risk of new methods. Ironically, it is their increased prosperity as a result of modern farm methods which has often widened the gap between rich and poor in LDCs.

There is a valuable intermediate stage of production between subsistence farming and modern farming known as diversified or mixed farming. The aim is to have a surplus to sell, to raise the consumption and living standards of the family, or to allow investment in the farm. By diversifying, the farmer can provide greater security from the failure of a single staple crop.

For example: new cash crops could be introduced to back up the staple subsistence crop such as fruit, vegetables, coffee, tea, animals or poultry. These might be introduced if there are slack periods in the farm year, times when there is disguised unemployment. Alternatively, better seeds, fertilizers or irrigation might give higher yields of the staple crop, allowing land to be freed for cash crops. In Africa, where there are often labour shortages during the peak seasons of weeding and harvesting, simple labour saving machinery would raise output. Modern western farm machinery, however, would be anti-developmental as it is in the main labour-saving. Jobs need to be maintained or created to help the poor who have only their labour to sell.

Certain parallel changes are essential to success, factors such as reasonable and reliable access to credit, fertilizers, water, crop information and marketing facilities. The incredibly high yielding grains of the Green Revolution had very limited success with the most needy because of the absence of one or more of these complementary factors or conditions. The major beneficiaries were generally the better off.

A further major factor which explains resistance to change, is the reluctance to improve land which is leased or rented. In any reform the farmer's family must largely benefit from the changes. In Latin America, for example, land ownership is the single biggest determinant of inequality of income. There is widespread agreement amongst developmentalists that land reform is essential to development.

Finally, it is important that development in the rural areas is seen as a whole. Many of the problems are inter-related and need tackling on a broad front simultaneously. Thus a package of policies need to address health, nutrition, housing, education, employment, social services and income inequality. The low productivity of agriculture is just one part of the extensive problem of rural poverty. In addition, the growth of slums and unemployment are also largely caused by rural poverty. Solutions must, therefore, focus on development of the countryside.

9   DEMAND vs SUPPLY-SIDE, MARKETS vs PLANNING

DEMAND MANAGEMENT VERSUS SUPPLY-SIDE

The absence of a proper functioning financial market precludes any use of money management policies to control the macroeconomy. The industrial country debate about rational expectations and supply-side policies is also rather irrelevant. In the broadest sense policies are all on the supply side, as it is acute shortages and supply-side constraints which characterise LDCs. Demand deficiency, the Keynesian perception of many industrial countries' macroeconomic problems, is not the problem in countries with very high propensities to consume, and with too little saving, not too much. However, government attempts to mobilise resources for development must come from fiscal policy. Taxation, or rather, very low levels of taxation, have been used extensively to attract foreign investment but the main function of taxation is to raise revenue for development programmes.

The restructuring programmes of the IMF and IBRD have meant very considerable changes for government fiscal policy. These have required major cut backs in spending, especially on social services, and required raising and improving tax collection. Direct taxes represent a very small part of the tax revenue, about 25% compared to 50% in industrial countries. Indirect taxes are the major source of revenue, taxes on exports and imports and various sales taxes. Typically, only 3% of people in LDCs pay any income tax compared to about 70–80% in MDCs. LDC tax systems are not progressive. The very rich control power and are thus able to find loopholes to avoid paying tax. Property is very unevenly skewed in ownership and by nature inelastic in its supply. It is an obvious good potential source of income for governments. At the moment it is not being exploited. This has a lot to do with the distribution of power.

FREE MARKETS VERSUS PLANNING

A great deal of hope and trust was invested into economic planning in the three decades from the 1950s. Almost all LDCs produced development plans and published these as documents of intent every five years. The plan would indicate the direction in which the government wished the economy to move, and the changes that were necessary to do so. Few plans achieved their aims, however, and considerable disillusionment with planning has set in. Following the collapse of the centrally planned economies of Eastern Europe, much of the overall planning by LDCs has also been abandoned. There has been a wide-spread adoption of free market policies to take their place. Despite this, planning is likely to retain a degree of importance to developing countries as a new balance with markets is established. The Asian NICs, whose remarkable success has been widely attributed to market competition, especially in manufactured exports, do in fact combine their market freedom with quite rigorous planning in other sectors of their economies.

Planning and techniques of planning in general were covered in Section 2. Development plans usually have the overall aim of increasing economic growth and raising the standard of living. The economic plan is at the heart of this and involves the setting of quantitative targets for the economy to be reached over a specific time period.[10]

Increasing the overall growth of the economy involves planning for each sector of the economy to grow; agriculture, industry, transport, energy, education and so on. The aim of the plan would be to show how this could be done. The planners also have to ensure that the plan targets are consistent, that is, they can be achieved and do not conflict.

Most development planning has been in the context of a mixed economy, with private and public ownership. (India for example has been planning since independence in 1949.) Such planning was thought to be eminently suitable for LDCs. They often do have a need to transform the structure of their economies as well as to use their scarce resources efficiently. In addition, the planning exercise is relatively simple compared to an industrialised economy, as the number of products which need planning are few.

PLANNING RATIONALE IN LDCs

The main argument for using development planning is that of market failure. The poor structure of markets, (or their complete absence in many LDCs), leads to incorrect price signals, the market guide to resource allocation. These incorrect prices then lead resources into non-optimal uses. Capital, labour and foreign exchange for example may be used very inefficiently considering their true opportunity cost to society.

Unless guided, investment projects may allocate scarce resources to socially non-optimal uses. Economic growth is not the same as development. Thus planning can adjust economic decisions to take account of externalities such as job creation, poverty alleviation or the production of necessities. Finally planning can act as a psychological stimulant to the development process by focusing national attention onto development problems.

Why then is planning being abandoned in the 1990s?

THE FAILURE OF PLANNING

There are a number of causes for the crisis in planning. Some centre around the fact that many of the theoretical reasons for planning have been weakly supported in practice. Instead of plans setting factor prices to encourage the use of labour the very opposite has happened and the use of capital has been subsidised. Instead of incomes being generated in the countryside the opposite has happened and urban areas have grown much richer encouraging severe rural urban migration problems. Job selection procedures have led to the overvaluation of education and the over-subsidy of the higher stages of education. Import-substitution policies have overprotected inefficient industry.

In addition planning rhetoric has been much greater than the ability to deliver. Plans have been overly ambitious with scant regard for limited resources and conflict between aims. Data has been weak and inaccurate. There have been internal and external shocks to LDCs which could not be planned for, the most severe being the oil price rises of the 1970s. There are institutional weaknesses in government and planning bodies. Finally there has been a lack of political will. Planning involves taking a view of the whole economy over a long period of time. Established elites and established practices have to be tackled. Many Third World leaders have taken a partisan view rather than a national view. Indeed there are many very corrupt leaders who have used their power mainly to become very rich themselves.

As a result of the growing disenchantment with planning many economists, finance ministers and heads of major international financial institutions, like the World Bank and the IMF, have increasingly advocated using the market mechanism for increasing efficiency and growth in LDCs. The conversion of almost all former "second world" planned economies to a market transition has been a powerful factor. In addition the success of the market sector of the NICs has been seen as an example to follow. The growth of the public sector in LDCs has been accompanied by waste and inefficiency. However abandoning planning does not necessarily mean that markets will automatically spring up in their place. The operation of the invisible hand of the market actually presupposes certain conditions. Many of the former centrally planned economies of Eastern Europe bear testimony to this as they pass through a very difficult period of adjustment. Fraud, corruption and monopoly do not just disappear with the wave of a magic market wand.

THE PRE-CONDITIONS FOR A MARKET ECONOMY

A list of institutional preconditions for the operation of private markets would include:

▮ trust – in banks, insurance companies and other suppliers
▮ law and order – to enforce contracts
▮ security of persons
▮ property rights
▮ a stable currency
▮ honest government
▮ independent judiciary

Some of the cultural requirements are:

▮ rationality as against tradition
▮ freedom in the availability of information rather than favouritism
▮ social mobility, and altruism to protect those not able to compete in a market (*ie* a social safety net).

It is still too early to see how successful the move to markets will be. It is likely that the poorest countries, *eg* those in much of Africa, are going to need to use planning more than middle income countries. It will also partly depend upon the individual country concerned. However many LDCs have serious barriers to markets functioning well. Some of the important imperfections are: the lack of information and uncertainty; the absence of real competition, as in many countries monopoly is the norm; the presence of substantial externalities *eg* in health and education provision, and the widening of an already wide distribution of income.

The success of future development will probably depend more upon using a judicious mix of planning and markets, and knowing in which areas of the economy to use which method. The real success of Singapore, South Korea and Taiwan has been in the blending of the techniques. Market forces have been given considerable play in industry and export markets whilst planning has been active in areas like education, housing, infrastructure and health care.

How Free are the Tigers – Asia?

The dramatic success of the Asian Tigers, or Dragons, is often trumpeted as a triumph of laissez-faire capitalism. These Newly Industrialised Economies (NICs), have transformed themselves from poor backward economies into modern industrial states in a relatively short period of time – 30/40 years. They are, therefore important as case studies for other LDCs hoping to grow and develop.

A marked characteristic of the transformation has been their concentration upon market-based manufactured exports. These have been produced by capitalist companies, often MNCs. Clothing, toys, ships, TVs, cars, cameras, and computers are just some of the product markets which were successfully developed or captured from the older manufacturing centres of the USA and Europe.

The governments of the NICs have been widely involved in this remarkable transformation, although this has not always been recognised and acknowledged beyond the Pacific Rim countries themselves. Researcher Tony Yu of the University of New South Wales, Australia, published findings in 1997, which highlighted the crucial role of government to the growth and development of the Asian NICs. Far from a success for orthodox economic policies alone, of free markets and deregulation, governments were, and are, major players. He describes their behaviour as that of 'result-orientated entrepreneurs'. Governments have been pro-active and dynamic in the development process.

In Hong Kong, perhaps the least regulated country in the world, the government role has been facilitative rather than directive. Nevertheless it has provided the political stability and the social cohesion which are so important to the development of flourishing free markets. Thus, subsidised housing, free education and social welfare have played an important part in Hong Kong's development.

In the other three countries government has been more directly involved in industry itself. Singapore, South Korea and Taiwan have consistently targeted specific industries, and even specific firms for assistance, always with an eye on the export markets and the utilisation of the best available technology internationally. This has been in addition to the provision of infrastructure like roads and housing and massive investment into human capital formation with broad-based health care and education programmes.

These countries recognised the dangers of state intervention but also recognised the shortcomings of unfettered market capitalism. They have sought to combine the best elements of both.

10 THE ROLE OF INTERNATIONAL AND DOMESTIC FINANCIAL INSTITUTIONS

Two institutions dominate the financial arrangements of countries internationally, the International Monetary Fund (IMF) and the International Bank for Reconstruction and Development (IBRD) – The World Bank. The two institutions were set up as the result of a meeting in Bretton Woods, New Hampshire, USA during the closing stages of the war. The Allies wanted a global structure for ordering exchange rates and foreign trade to prevent a repeat of the disastrous inter-war period. During the Great Depression, and of course the war itself, foreign trade shrank as countries scurried into protectionism. The IMF and IBRD were financed and controlled by their member governments. (Today there are about 140 member countries of each, with voting rights according to economic size and contributions.)

The IMF was charged with managing a system of exchange rates and holding currency reserves to aid countries with temporary balance of payments problems. The IMF system, or Bretton Woods system, as it was known, operated a managed exchange rate system from 1946 to 1971, when it collapsed. Refer to Section 4 on exchange rate systems. Since then it has found a new role directly concerned with LDCs.

The IBRD or World Bank was initially set the task of providing the loans for reconstructing war-torn Europe and Japan. The remarkable success of the Marshall Plan meant that this was completed in the 1950s. The IBRD has been wholly involved with development ever since. The influence of the World Bank is enormous. Its role has been evolving and is still evolving. Both institutions have vociferous critics.

INTERNATIONAL MONETARY FUND (IMF)

It was the international indebtedness of many LDCs following the oil price rises of the 1970s that led to a new role for the IMF. Many Third World countries were close to crisis with huge international debt, rapid inflation, balance of payments deficits and large government debt. In this situation private commercial credit to these countries rapidly dried up. The IMF was instrumental in restructuring the debt to allow the functioning of the affected economies. They did this typically by putting together a finance package. This would involve the co-operation of three partners, the IMF, the LDC government, and private foreign commercial banks. The IMF would offer some concessional credit on strict conditions. The government in agreeing to the restructuring of the country's economy to meet these conditions, would then open the way for commercial credit to flow. The private financiers would be reassured that the economy would become sound again due to the involvement of the IMF. Refusal to restructure the economy would prevent the country from receiving the IMF's approval and therefore access to world financial markets. The power of the IMF over the governments of developing countries has thereby increased enormously. The details of the macroeconomic restructuring are covered in

Section 5.3. The set of conditions for help is known generally as a policy of conditionality. Many of these conditions have affected the poor harshly. Withdrawal of subsidies and the cutting of development programmes have aroused intense dislike of the restructuring programmes from many other international agencies whose priorities are for the immediate relief of poverty. They have seen considerable de-development amongst the poor as a result of the macroeconomic restructuring insisted upon by the IMF.

INTERNATIONAL BANK FOR RECONSTRUCTION AND DEVELOPMENT (IBRD) – THE WORLD BANK

The role of the World Bank has also been evolving, although less dramatically than that of the IMF, its sister organization with neighbouring headquarters in Washington. The IBRD was charged with promoting economic growth and prosperity by sourcing funds for investment. The IBRD, with the financial backing of all its member governments, has been able to attract lenders from the rich countries. The organizations and governments in LDCs would not have been able to do this themselves. The IBRD has then on-loaned into LDCs, with technical advice and stringent conditions to ensure loan repayment. Initially, much of its lending was to provide infrastructure in LDCs, roads, power, harbours, bridges, airfields *etc* much as it had done in Europe after the war. However this was less successful in poor countries in encouraging economic growth due to the many supply-side barriers present. Lending diversified in the 1960s and 1970s into individual productive projects. These increased particularly in agriculture, especially the development of cash crop farming for export. One major success was aiding India's Green Revolution. It changed India from being dependent on food aid to becoming a food exporter itself.

Stringent conditions in its own mandate prevented the IBRD from lending directly to commercial concerns without government oversight. As a result, the International Finance Corporation (IFC) was established in 1956 to undertake the more commercial loans. This support to private business has aided economic growth and complements the broader work of the IBRD. The IFC is not strictly part of the IBRD although it shares the same headquarters and staff.

The emphasis of both agencies has been on economic growth not the more broadly defined development. The IBRD set up a separate agency to deal with transfers to the very poorest countries. This is the International Development Agency (IDA), and is formally part of the IBRD. The aims of the IDA are very similar to the rest of the IBRD, however the terms of credit are different. Only the very poorest countries qualify, those under a very low level of GNP per capita. They are then eligible for credits on concessional terms *ie* with an aid element. This usually takes two forms, the loans are interest free and they have a much longer pay back period so that repayments are smaller and more manageable. They currently are financing a large programme for Africa.

The World Bank has other, broader, functions. It sponsors research, provides statistics information, education services, and technical support to its lending.

View from the UN	View from World Bank
On Globalization Increased global competition does not automatically bring faster growth and development	**On Globalization** There is a positive link between freeing markets and trade and the eradication of poverty in the long term
On impact of trade on wages for unskilled workers In almost all of developing countries that have undertaken rapid trade liberalisation, unemployment has increased and wages have fallen for unskilled workers	**On impact of trade on wages for unskilled workers** There is no evidence to justify fears that free trade pushes down wages for unskilled workers in developing countries.
On world growth Growth in the world economy this year will again be too slow to make a significant dent on poverty in developing countries. *Trade and Development Report 1997, UNCTAD*	**On world growth** The prospects for the global economy are the most promising for many decades for growth and for poverty reduction in the developing countries *Global Economic Prospects 1997, World Bank*

The World Bank is very influential. It also has vociferous critics. The emphasis on microeconomic projects and on hard commercial growth projects has been criticised by those who would wish to see more resources going into broad development projects, into education, health and poverty alleviation. The criticism has grown sharply since the IMF, together with the World Bank, has been involved with LDC structural adjustment programmes. These programmes have caused infant mortality rates to rise in some countries, have increased unemployment, and increased poverty, as food subsidies and primary health care programmes have been cut. The policies are seen as anti-developmental by many other agencies, like UNICEF for example, which has been very concerned to see the condition of the world's children worsen. The United Nations Development Programme (UNDP) produced the Human Development Index in 1990 to help focus efforts on a more meaningful measure of development than the narrow GNP growth. The HDI shows that the IBRD/IMF restructuring policies are anti-developmental. The World Bank has become more outspoken in defence of the poor affected by these programmes, but for many has a long way to go in actually introducing its own policies to reduce the worst effects of these on poor people.

In the last two decades the IMF and the IBRD have come to work much more closely together. The IMF became involved with domestic restructuring as a necessary condition for its own external policies to succeed. Meanwhile the IBRD has become involved in the International dimension to allow its microeconomic projects better chance of success.

The two agencies are working more and more closely as they become involved in the same sets of negotiations.

Structural Adjustment in Ghana

Ghana has been hailed as a model for structural adjustment policies. The West African state has been subject to two decades of IMF and World Bank liberal economic policies. However the poor have become poorer and the government more indebted than ever to foreigners. Since the late 1990s the IMF and the World Bank have softened their approach, replacing structural adjustment with poverty reduction strategies. Despite this the fundamental market economics has unchanged harsh effects on the poor.

Nothing comes free, Ghana is a 'cash and carry' society. Health care, education, clean drinking water and sanitation must all be paid for. In many developed countries these are recognized as merit goods and subsidised, often to the point of being free to the end user.

Ghana's biggest export earner is gold, the country was formerly known as the Gold Coast. Two thirds of Ghanaian land is under concession to free market mining companies. Everywhere there are large holes in the ground, giant discarded pits where villages once stood and now nothing can grow. Villagers have been forced off their land. The derisory cash compensation is no replacement for their loss of livelihood. In the village of Dumasi, a Canadian owned mining company is blasting rocks in an open-cast pit less than 100 metres from the huts.

Mary Agyekum breaks stones with a small flint hammer looking for gold. Under a hot sun she sits on the ground for 10 hours a day. Usually she is helped out by some of her six children. They have to take it in turns to go to school, as daily fees must be paid. Mary earns about 20,000 cedis ($3) a week.

The Agyekum family begin their day with a trip to the town's public toilet, recognizable from a long way off by the smell. A woman sits in a booth outside. It costs 100 cedis for each person. If she has run out of money Mary might beg to take in one or more of the children for free. Her life she says 'is full of shame'.

They will then visit a borehole where they pay 250 cedis for a bucket of water. They typically afford four buckets a day for cooking, washing and drinking. She now has only about $1.50 a week left for food and for school fees. The two children she still sends to school are turned away by the teachers if she has not paid the fees on time. School drop out rates and illiteracy are increasing in Ghana.

At the regional hospital in Tarkara cholera patients lie on the floor right next to post natal patients. Each visit must be paid for as must any surgery, gloves, blood, drugs, anaesthetics, gauze and cotton wool. Patients, and even dead bodies, are not released until the bill is paid. Meanwhile the multinational companies make millions from mining this area. They are attracted both by tax free 'holidays' on profits for periods of up to ten years and by minimum regulation on their activities.

There is a genuine regard here for the United States and the former colonial power Britain. People have been shocked by the senseless attacks on New York and Washington on September 11. However political opposition is fomenting at grass roots level against policies of western financial institutions which maintain the grinding poverty and powerlessness of the very poor.

Source: BBC Correspondent 2 Nov, 2001 – www.bbc.co.uk/correspondent

PRIVATE SECTOR BANKS

Banks in LDCs are often the overseas branches of foreign MNCs and operate mainly for the modern and foreign trade sectors.

These banks and the other commercial banks operate in the modern sector of the economy channelling finance to medium and large scale firms. Small firms do not have the collateral to borrow from these banks and resort to the informal market. Small traders borrow from family members and money lenders. The latter charge very high rates of interest to small poor borrowers to cover administration and risk. There is a real absence of banking services for the poor. In some areas micro-credit schemes are addressing the banking needs of the very poor. The Grameen Bank is the best known example of a micro-credit scheme.

Micro Credit – The Grameen Bank of Bangladesh

In 1974 a famine in Bangladesh killed 1.5 million people. A professor of economics at Chittagong University, Mohammed Yunus, was so appalled he turned his attention to studying the poverty around him. How could it be that people who worked 12 hours a day, 7 days a week could still not earn enough even to feed themselves? The critical factor he noted was the absence of capital. If the poor owned even just a little capital; a small plot of land, some chickens, a calf or a goat, they could raise their standard of living a little higher than subsistence. However the most important barrier to the poor owning anything was their inability to borrow. The banks existed only in the towns and operated on behalf of higher income families and businesses. Credit from money-lenders was as high as 10% a month, or even 10% a week. Effectively there was no source of credit for the poor. When Professor Yunos started making loans from his own savings and then from the University he was told that he was foolish and that the poor would not repay the loans. Between 1976 and 1979 he made loans to 500 borrowers, 94% of them women. Borrowers were required to form small groups and the group was responsible for deciding whose turn it was to borrow. Loans were small, $20 –$50, but interest rates were low, and the repayments were in small instalments. There was a 95% repayment success rate, far higher than the formal banks achieved. The scheme, named the Grameen Bank, spread not only across rural Bangladesh but into the cities and has since spread to many other countries. It has undoubtedly improved the lives of thousands and thousands of the world's poorest people.

Islamic Banking

Banks that operate under Islamic Law act as a market place for borrowers and lenders as do non-Islamic banks. However they do not charge interest on loans or pay interest on deposits. The Koran prohibits interest charges on loans. Instead they take a percentage of the borrowing firm's profits, a pre-determined percentage, until the loan is repaid. These profits are then shared with the depositors. Since the oil price rises of the 1970s over one hundred new Islamic banks have opened, most of them in the Middle East. The banks charge fees for other banking services such as checking accounts, travellers checks and trade-related services.

Growth of deposits in the Islamic banks has often been greater than the growth of demand for funds to invest locally. They have therefore been on-lent to traditionally run banks. The funds can then be loaned commercially but are subject to moral restrictions dictated by Islam. Thus these funds cannot be used to buy interest bearing securities or loaned to firms dealing in arms, alcohol, gambling or pork. The Islamic banks are thus able to meet both their profitability requirement and the religious requirements of their depositors.

MULTIPLE CHOICE QUESTIONS – GROWTH AND DEVELOPMENT STRATEGIES

1 Which of the following strategies is most likely to be used by an LDC committed to develop by using *appropriate technology*?

A Encouraging large scale production in rural areas.

B Using capital intensive methods of production.

C Using technology which yields the greatest rate of return, allowing for local costs of the factors of production.

D Spending on high technology research and development projects using international finance.

2 A consequence of India adopting export-promotion in favour of import-substitution is that it

A will become more self-sufficient.

B will find that its exchange rate becomes over-valued.

C will increase supplies of hard currencies.

D will encourage the use of parallel markets.

3 IMF structural adjustment programmes are criticised for

A leading to severe short run declines in living standards.

B encouraging the adoption of protectionist measures in LDCs and CPEs.

C promoting labour intensive industries.

D redistributing income from the rich to the poor.

4 An IMF structural adjustment programme for an indebted LDC is likely to involve

I expansionary fiscal and monetary policy to increase aggregate demand in the economy

II supply-side reforms to expose more of the economy to market forces.

III floating exchange rates and a more open trade policy.

A I only   B I and II   C II and III   D I, II and III

5 An export-orientated development strategy enables an LDC to

   I   build up reserves of hard currencies.

   II take advantage of economies of scale.

   III become more self-sufficient.

   A I only   B I and II   C II and III   D I, II and III

6 An LDC government subsidises certain manufactured goods to promote exports. The short run effect of this is likely to include

   I   lower profits.

   II more specialisation among manufacturing employees.

   III higher incomes.

   A I only   B I and II   C II and III   D I, II and III

7 An American owned MNC opens a game lodge for tourists in an area of Africa with very high unemployment. Which of the activities associated with the investment would generate the greatest positive externalities for development?

   A Company paid training courses for local people in hotel work.

   B The importing of America foodstuffs for use in the lodge restaurant.

   C The use of modern American equipment in the kitchen.

   D Tax incentives from the Less Developed Country's government to encourage the investment.

8 IMF aid packages to indebted LDCs are not likely to include

   A a reduction in import controls.

   B a reduction in government subsidies.

   C an appreciation of the exchange rate.

   D reduced government spending.

9 As a development strategy an LDC is likely to use 'import-substitution' where

   I   industrialisation is believed to be the key to growth.

   II there is a shortage of foreign currency.

   III there is slow growth in primary exports.

   A I only   B I and II   C II and III   D I, II and III

10 As a development strategy 'import-substitution' is often criticised because it

   A encourages free trade in goods.

   B replaces high cost imported products with low cost domestic products.

   C leads to higher prices and lower outputs.

   D encourages inward investment by foreign MNCs.

11 Which of the following reasons does NOT justify using economic and social planning for development?

   A Because no country has industrialised without government planning.

   B Because economic growth is not the same as development.

   C Because market failure in LDCs often leads to incorrect resource allocation.

   D Because planning takes account of externalities.

12 According to the Harrod-Domar growth theory, a country with a savings ratio of 8% of GDP and a capital-output ratio of 2 would have economic growth of

   A 2%   B 4%   C 8%   D 16%

An Economic Profile of South Korea

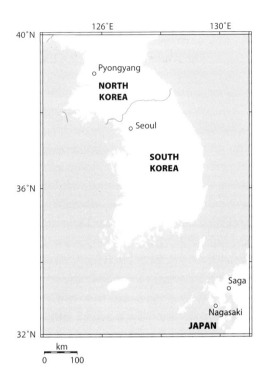

Geographic, Social and Economic Indicators

Capital city:	Seoul
Area:	98,500km^2
Population:	47 million (2000)
Population (average annual growth rate):	1.0% (1990–2000)
GNI per capita:	US$8910 (2000) – $100 (1963)
GNI per capita (PPP):	US$17,340 (2000)
GNP per capita (average annual growth rate):	4.7% (1990–2000)
Agriculture as share of GDP:	5% (2000)
Exports as share of GDP:	38% (2000)
Life expectancy at birth:	72 (1997)
Under age 5 mortality rate (per 1000 live births):	9 (1999)
Adult illiteracy rate (age 15+):	Male 1%, Female 4% (1997)
Human Development Index:	0.875 (high) (1999)

South Korea

South Korea is perhaps the world's best example of a country which developed from widespread poverty as a very poor LDC to a high income country and member of the OECD in a single generation. There are of course a raft of reasons for the transformation but the key engine of the process has been international trade.

In 1945 Korea was divided and remains so today (2002). The communist North inherited most of the mineral wealth, the hydroelectricity and the heavy industry left by the Japanese occupiers. The South was predominantly agricultural, had a large uneducated workforce and a GDP per capita much lower than the North. The 1950 Korean war caused widespread disruption to both Koreas and a flood of refugees to the South. How then did South Korea transform from one of the world's poorest countries in the 1950s to a World Bank designated 'high income country' in just 40 years?

The government introduced sweeping economic reforms in the 1960s with the stress on exports and labour intensive industries. A key feature was the close co-operation between government planners and the private sector with heavy investment in education, health and housing accompanying the private sector business drive. Education combined with high saving and capital accumulation led to a dramatic increase in labour productivity. A very industrious, literate and educated population is now South Korea's most valuable resource. Note that development has been broad across the whole population and not confined to a rich urban sector as occurred in so many other LDCs. Amongst its package of reforms the government tackled the currency, the financial institutions, and land tenure. Its sights were set on expanding exports and jobs in light industry.

GNP rose by 10% a year between 1963 and 1978. Population growth declined throughout the period to 1.7% leading to a twenty-fold increase in GNP per capita. After internal disruptions and the oil crisis, South Korea got back on track again in the 1980s to attain the second highest growth of per capita income in the world for a decade (7.5%, second only to Thailand). Export growth shifted from labour intensive light industry eg textiles and footwear to skill-intensive, high quality production eg autos and electronics.

The 1997 Asian currency crisis has hit Korea very badly with many bankruptcies, severe unemployment and negative growth. The world slump is still affecting South Korea in 2002 although the analysts long term view is that South Korea will still re emerge as one of the major world economies.

Source: Adapted from: M. Todaro & S. Smith, Economic Development 8th Ed. 2003; and World Bank, World Bank Indicators 2001

5.3   BARRIERS TO ECONOMIC GROWTH AND DEVELOPMENT

INSTITUTIONAL BARRIERS

Why then, have so many present day LDCs failed to grow and develop in a similar way to the developed countries? Are there barriers which can be identified which prevents the GNP per capita from growing significantly?

The early growth models focused attention upon the physical economic conditions necessary for growth; the need to increase savings, investment and GNP. However whilst these conditions are indeed necessary, they are by no means sufficient to ensure growth.

In addition, it is a requirement that attitudes and institutions become flexible and willing to change, both within LDCs and by developed countries in their relations with LDCs.

Further, we need to recognize that many of the conditions facing today's LDCs are different from the pre-industrial conditions of the high income countries. This is especially true of the poorest of the LDCs.

1   Attitudes and Institutional Resistance to Change

Political stability is an essential requirement to political growth; yet so is flexibility, for growth by definition demands change. It is inevitable that stress and conflict will occur within a country during periods of rapid change. The interests of existing power groups may be challenged. Power may shift between groups; for example, from land owners to tenant farmers, industrialists or civil servants.

Tension can lead to political instability which in turn can lead to fighting. Between the end of World War II and 1989, there were 127 armed conflicts around the world. All but two of these were in Less Developed Countries.[11]

Many countries have only gained independence as nations since World War II (some as late as the 1960s), and thus have had little time to develop a national identity allied with popular development policies.

In contrast, developed countries were nation states well before industrialisation. They had time to develop a broad consensus of attitude towards 'modernisation'. Their populations had time to adapt to 'modern' concepts such as rationalism, scientific thought, individualism, social and economic mobility, and the work ethic. Modern scientific thought developed in the countries of Europe, and the new world countries peopled by them, forming a small world of broadly similar cultures where people and ideas circulated freely (although Japan is of great interest historically as being a marked exception to this).

These material and cultural values which have been closely associated with economic growth are largely alien to many contemporary Third World countries.

A World Government?

"Mankind's problems can no longer be solved by national governments. What is needed is a World Governfment".

Professor Jan Tinbergen, 1969 Nobel Prize in Economics.

Question

What do you think Tinbergen might mean by his statement above?

Vested interests in industrial countries may equally hold back change and growth in LDCs. In dealings between the institutions of LDCs and the developed countries, power lies with the rich. Many Third World economists believe this to be a major constraint and argue that the political dependency of colonization has merely been replaced by an economic dependency.

Thus, most technological transfer is controlled by huge multinational companies (MNCs) which are First World owned. International trade and international finance are both dominated by developed countries.

International economic relations, (set up at Bretton Woods in 1946 and consisting of the IBRD, the IMF and GATT), largely maintains the power of the industrialised countries. These structures, which form the present 'International Economic Order', are seen as constraints on growth by the poor and have led to repeated demands by the LDCs for a New International Economic Order.

2   Differences between the LDCs and the MDCs in their own Pre-industrialization Period

Physical Differences

Many LDCs are poorly endowed with natural resources, with middle-eastern oil states the marked exception. Africa and Latin America have more minerals than Asia, though they do often depend upon the heavy investment of foreign MNCs to extract them.

Almost all MDCs enjoy temperate climate, whereas LDCs tend to be tropical or sub-tropical. These extremes of heat and humidity affect soil quality.[12]

Population Differences

In many countries populations are already much larger, and population densities much greater than ever they were in pre-industrial developed countries. The growth of population also, is much faster than ever it was in MDCs.

Finally, although there are large movements of political refugees, war victims and boat people, international migration has largely disappeared, especially for the poor and uneducated. This is in contrast to the developed countries where migration had acted as a safety valve for expanding populations. Between the years 1846 and 1939 over ten million Europeans emigrated to the United States, Canada, Australia, New Zealand and elsewhere.

Economic Differences

Income per capita in pre-industrial MDCs exceeded that of today's LDCs, especially the very poorest ones. Furthermore, the inhabitants of pre-industrialised MDCs were generally better educated and more skilled than their counterparts today in Less Developed Countries.

Countries in the 19th Century enjoyed free trade and free capital movements as well as international migration of unskilled surplus labour. Rapidly expanding export markets were seen as 'the engine of growth' for manufacturing industry. In contrast, LDCs today face formidable difficulties in generating such rapid growth based on exports:

The terms of trade have moved steadily against LDCs, so it takes ever more exports to buy the same quantity of imports.

As most science and technology is dominated by the rich countries, LDCs rarely develop new and improved products. Indeed, even their primary products may be replaced as synthetic materials are developed. For example there are substitutes for jute, hemp, cotton, rubber and timber.

Where LDCs have a distinct comparative advantage in secondary production, such as in textiles, shoes and light manufactures, developed countries have frequently resorted to protectionism.

Technological Differences

Developed countries were scientifically and technologically ahead of the world when they developed. Today an estimated 95% of Research and Development is still concentrated in the rich countries. Technology is capital-intensive as befits high wage economies. Production methods that use capital sparingly, and labour intensively, may well be more appropriate in the capital scarce, labour abundant economies.

As income, and not need, determines demand, the priorities of the rich dominate research. Products may be quite sophisticated, whereas simple products and simple designs may be more appropriate for low-income markets.

Poverty in England in the 1800s

Every great city has one or more slums, where the working class is crowded together. True, poverty often dwells in hidden alleys close to the palaces of the rich; but, in general, a separate territory has been assigned to it, where, removed from the sight of the happier classes, it may struggle along as it can. These slums are all pretty well equally arranged in all the great towns of England, the worst houses in the worst quarters of the towns; usually one or two-storied cottages in long rows, perhaps with cellars used as dwellings, almost always irregularly built. These houses of three or four rooms and a kitchen form, throughout England, some parts of London excepted, the general dwellings of the working class. The streets were generally unpaved, rough, dirty, filled with animal and vegetable refuse, without sewers or gutters, but supplied with foul, stagnant pools instead. Moreover, ventilation is impeded by the bad, confused method of the building of the whole quarter, and since many human beings live crowded into a small space, the atmosphere that prevails in these working-men's quarters may readily be imagined. Further, the streets serve as drying grounds in fine weather; lines are stretched across from house to house, and hung with wet clothing.

The houses are occupied from cellar to garret, filthy within and without, and their appearance is such that no human being could possibly wish to live in them. But all this is nothing in comparison with the dwellings in the narrow courts and alleys between the streets, entered by covered passages between the houses, in which the filth and tottering ruins surpass all description. Scarcely a whole window-pane can be found, the walls are crumbling, door frames are loose and broken, doors of old boards nailed together, or altogether wanting in this thieves' quarter, where no doors are needed, there being nothing to steal. Heaps of garbage and ashes lie in all directions, and the foul liquids emptied before the doors gather in stinking pools. Here the poorest of the poor, the worst paid workers with thieves and the victims of prostitution indiscriminately huddled together, the majority Irish, or of Irish extraction, and those who have yet sunk into the whirlpool of moral ruin which surrounds them, sinking daily deeper, losing daily more of their power to resist the demoralizing influence of want, filth, and evil surroundings.

Source: F Engels, "The Condition of the English Working Class".

Poverty in India in the 1950s

Haresh laughed. 'Stop here' he shouted at the rickshaw-wallah. Over Kedarnath's protests, he got him to dismount, and the two of them entered the warren of stinking paths and low huts, led by their noses towards the tanning pits.

The dirt paths stopped suddenly at a large open area surrounded by shacks and pockmarked by circular pits which had been dug into the ground and lined with hardened clay. A fearsome stench arose from the entire zone. Haresh felt sick; Kedarnath almost vomited with disgust. The sun shone harshly down, and the heat made the stench worse still. Some of the pits were filled with a white liquid, others with a brown tannic brew. Dark, scrawny men dressed only in lungis stood to one side of the pits, scraping off fat and hair from a pile of hides. One of them stood in a pit and seemed to be wrestling with a large hide. A pig was drinking at a ditch filled with black stagnant water. Two children with filthy matted hair were playing in the dust near the pits. When they saw the strangers they stopped abruptly and stared at them.

Source: Vikram Seth, "A Suitable Boy" (p. 215), Phoenix. A novel set shortly after Indian independence.

Question

From the two passages above is it possible to compare poverty today with poverty in England in the 1800s?

INTERNATIONAL TRADE BARRIERS AND ADVERSE TERMS OF TRADE

International trade barriers and adverse terms of trade are barriers to development which have been previously covered.

One Lump or Two? – Brazil

Brazil solved two trade problems with one move in the 1970s, in a policy of import substitution of domestic sugar for imported oil. Brazil with virtually no oil of its own was hit badly by the OPEC oil price increases. At the same time EU protection of sugar encouraged European farmers to produce sugar cane which hit the Brazilian sugar cane producers badly. With government sponsorship Brazil distilled sugar into alcohol and converted cars to run on sugar alcohol. The scheme was a big success initially. Later the price of oil slumped and the terms of trade again moved in favour of using cheap oil and against dearer sugar.

INTERNATIONAL FINANCIAL BARRIERS

International Indebtedness

The problem of international indebtedness has created an enormous problem for the welfare of many LDCs, and threatens the whole international financial system. The problem continues into the 1990s and is still to be resolved.

The debt problem began with the two major oil crises of the 1970s. Up to this time most LDCs were used to experiencing deficits on the current account of the balance of payments, because primary exports typically grow slowly and manufacturing and service imports grow rapidly. Before the debt crisis this gap would be covered by inflows on the capital account of private investment plus foreign aid.

Traditional sources of loans and aid did increase to partly finance the trade gap. However, a new source of loans was now available in the form of petro-dollars. This was part of the vast export earnings of the OPEC countries, deposited in Western banks, and now seeking profitable investment opportunities. With the industrialised world in recession, and rapidly expanding LDCs anxious not to hinder their growth, the money poured into the latter. From 1975 to 1979 the external debt of LDCs doubled. On the surface there seemed to be little to be worried about. Oil prices declined again, and exports continued to fuel economic growth. With relaxed monetary policies in the developed countries nominal interest rates were low, and because of high inflation real interest rates were very low or negative.

However, the seeds of the ensuing Third World debt crisis had been sown. Not only had the total amount of debt grown, but, just as important, the nature of the debt had changed. Whereas previously most loans were soft loans, that is they were on concessional terms from governments and international institutions, the new borrowing was from commercial banks at market interest rates *ie* non-concessional hard loans.

The second oil shock of 1979, however, marked the beginning of the crisis proper. The second round of large oil price increases again affected import bills, both directly and indirectly, through the oil induced inflation of industrial imports. The developed countries reacted to this second world recession with severe deflationary policies, and in particular used monetary policies to attack the attendant inflation. As incomes fell so did imports, and hence the exports from LDCs. As money supply was tightened interest rates soared, and as inflation fell, real interest rates increased markedly. A large proportion of loans were now subject to variable market interest rates. The LDCs, holding large debts, faced massive debt servicing problems and were unable to finance them as export sales plummeted.

📊 Figure 5.24 – Severely Indebted Countries

Country	Total debt outstanding 1999 (US $ billion)	Total debt/GNI (ratio %)	Total debt/exports (ratio %)
Argentina	148	56	456
Bolivia	6	37	193
Brazil	245	33	339
Burundi	1	96	1072
Cameroon	9	76	292
Ecuador	15	76	211
Guinea-Bissau	1	347	1222
Indonesia	150	113	255
Ivory Coast	13	117	220
Madagascar	4	80	304
Malawi	3	84	246
Nicaragua	7	271	475
Nigeria	29	91	185
Peru	29	63	354
Sierra Leone	1	136	1234
Sudan	16	172	1717
Syria	22	146	377
Venezuela	36	38	156

Rounded to the nearest whole number.

Source: World Bank, World Development Indicators, 2001.

To escape the ensuing restrictions at home funds fled from the worst affected countries. Capital flight was so great that an estimated 30 cents in every dollar borrowed during this period was sent back out of the debtor countries to be reinvested overseas for higher returns and lower risk.

Figure 5.24 lists eighteen severely indebted countries (SICs). A small number of countries: Brazil, Mexico, Argentina and Indonesia account for 60% of the total outstanding debt. However, proportionately, many small economies were hit very badly. The second and third columns of Figure 5.24 illustrate this, where total debt is expressed as a ratio to GNI and to total exports.

Countries unable to service debts from export earnings were increasingly forced to reschedule them. This involves renegotiating the loan with the lender, usually to extend the repayment period. Rescheduling is a short term holding measure, however, not a solution to the basic problem. In the longer term, LDC governments have had to make major structural reforms, often guided by the IMF, in order to obtain help and sanction for the rescheduling.

IMF-Stabilization Policies

These policies form a package which is centred on an increased use of the market mechanism, devaluation of the exchange rate, and deflation of the economy.

- Market oriented supply-side measures are aimed at increasing output and investment, including foreign investment.
- Trading measures include devaluing the official exchange rate to encourage exports and discourage imports. Deflation of the economy through tight monetary and fiscal policies is aimed at reducing government deficits, inflation and interest rates.

The deflationary policies with increased taxation and deep cuts in government spending have been politically very unpopular with the poor and low income groups, who have seen large cuts in welfare spending. Development programmes have therefore been seriously hampered by the international debt problem. Today, restructuring measures and lower interest rates have eased the problem a little, but the debt is only likely to be reduced as and when the world recovers from the recession, and trade increases.

Non-Convertible Currencies

Most developing countries use fixed exchange rates rather than floating exchange rates. That is, they are not freely convertible through a market. These 'Official Exchange Rates' are often set above the market rate, that is, they are overvalued (Figure 5.25).

Figure 5.25 – Official Exchange Rates: overvalued

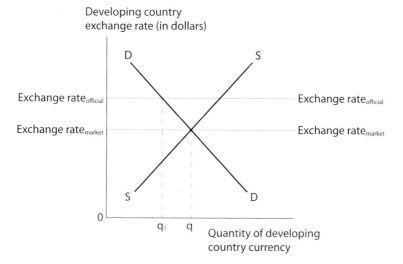

The majority are fixed in terms of the US dollar as most traded products are priced in US dollars. Exporters have to sell the dollars they earn at the 'Official' rate. They therefore receive less local currency for their dollars than the true market value, receiving q_1 local currency rather than q (see Figure 5.25). This, in effect, is a tax on exporters. As a large percentage of exports are primary products it is primary producers who tend to be the ones penalised. On the other hand, by making foreign currency cheap, imports enjoy a subsidy. This is a further example of price distortion – see "getting the prices right".

If on the other hand the official exchange rate is set below the market equilibrium there will be a shortage of foreign currency (Figure 5.26).

Figure 5.26 – Official Exchange Rates – undervalued

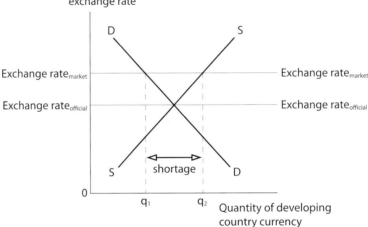

As with all fixed prices below market equilibrium there is excess demand. The usual solution is to use 'Exchange controls', that is, quotas or licences to ration the scarce foreign exchange. This, unfortunately, can allow scope for corruption, evasion and parallel markets in foreign currency.

The solution to an over (or under) valued currency is to devalue (or revalue) it or more generally to set it free to float. (Note: this is often one of the major conditions imposed by the IMF on heavily indebted countries wanting help to reschedule their debt.)

OTHER FACTORS

Unequal distribution of income – this has been covered previously.

Formal and Informal Markets

Most developing countries have not one but two distinct economies. They are often known as dual economies. If you visit any major LDC capital in the world the chances are that the airport and central business district are modern and fairly similar to First World capital cities. Drive away from the centre, however, and you will notice a dramatic contrast. Third World cities are surrounded by huge, densely populated sprawling slums. Rio de Janeiro, Bombay, Johannesburg and Manila all follow the pattern. The poverty is more striking than in the countryside because it is so concentrated; alleyways with washing drying, children playing amongst rubbish and sewage. Often the smell of decay is powerful. Little wonder that many authorities would like to see slums removed as an eyesore. Judge what you see with your economist's eye, however, and you might arrive at a surprisingly different conclusion. The slums are the base for intensive small scale economic activities. These activities follow the basic economic laws of scarcity, and as a result are some of the most economically efficient activities you are likely to find in the city. See the Case Study on Informal Markets.

The Informal Sector

In the city streets of an LDC the streets will be packed with people performing all kinds of work. There will be very many traders with tiny market stalls of little more than a table and fabric roof to keep off the sun and rain. Some traders may merely lay their goods out on the road or sidewalk perhaps on a cloth reminiscent of biblical times. Stalls will sell cloth, T-shirts, pots and pans. Others will sell fruit drinks by the roadside. There will be peddlers selling as they walk; straw hats, sandals, beads, basket work, newspapers, flowers. Some will be selling services, haircuts, car washing, windscreen cleaning, car parking, bike repair and shoe cleaning. At night prostitution will be very evident. There will be porters, rickshaws, motorcycle transport, money lenders, drug traffickers and thieves. Children will be selling single cigarettes from the packet. There will be street musicians, beggars, and photographers with parrots or monkeys to sit on your shoulder. In some areas people will be busy fashioning all kinds of products from metal; simple cookers, chicken feeders and pans. Another area will have woodworkers or leather workers busily toiling by the roadside. Bottles will be collected and reused, as will all plastics, containers and cans. Some will make the building materials for the shacks of the shanty town. Rubber tyres will be cut to make long lasting soles for cheap footwear. Tin cans will be fashioned into exhaust pipes and mufflers. Every scrap of material; wood, metal and plastic, is recycled and reused.

All this activity is unrecorded and outside the formal sector of the economy; as such it is known as the informal sector. It is all likely to feel very alien to someone from the industrial north.

Question

Bearing in mind the relative scarcity of factors of production in LDCs, would you say that the activities of the informal sector, are economically efficient?

Lack of Infrastructure

Infrastructure is the whole web of facilities which need to be in place for productive industry to flourish. Roads, railways, gas, electricity, telephones, water, sewage, schools, hospitals and houses. These are commonly found in density in urban areas of LDCs and are a major reason for businesses to locate in the existing cities. This of course worsens existing rural-urban migration. Some cities in the Third World have social infrastructure so overburdened *eg* housing, sewage, refuse disposal, that they are threatened with collapse. However the real shortage of infrastructure is in the countryside. More investment has to take place in the countryside to stem migration and do something directly for rural development.

Open Unemployment, Underemployment and Disguised Unemployment

Open unemployment is commonly 10–20% of the workforce in LDCs. Even so this underestimates the true problem as disguised unemployment is very widespread. Thus there are many people who appear to be working, but who are in fact producing very little, that is, their marginal product may be close to zero. For example, more and more family members may become absorbed onto a family smallholding, all apparently employed, but if some workers were removed total product would not fall much. In this case unemployment is disguised or hidden. There is also underemployment where people have jobs for only a few hours a week or a few days a month, or a few months a year.

Adding together open unemployment, underemployment and disguised unemployment the problem is massive, much greater than that experienced in any developed country. In addition, there is rarely the support of a welfare state. There is no social security safety net, rather a situation of widespread poverty. Furthermore many of the unemployed are young and educated. As they have expectations of jobs, and are articulate, they are politically a potentially explosive force.

MULTIPLE CHOICE QUESTIONS – BARRIERS TO ECONOMIC GROWTH AND DEVELOPMENT

1   What is meant by 'capital flight'?

   A   The transfer of money by the elite in LDCs to safe havens in MDCs.

   B   The movement of 'hot money' between major financial markets in MDCs.

   C   Investment by multinational companies in LDCs.

   D   The repayment of debt by governments of LDCs.

2   Which of the following has not been a contributory factor in causing the 'third world debt crisis'?

   A   Raised interest rates in high income countries.

   B   Enthusiastic lending by private banks.

   C   The use of borrowed funds in the service sector of LDCs.

   D   The growth of spending by tourists from high income countries.

3   Which of the following actions by the government of an LDC will help to discourage 'capital flight'?

   A   Remove controls on the international movement of capital.

   B   Increase investor confidence in local capital markets.

   C   Allow the exchange rate to fall.

   D   Lower interest rates.

4   When wealthy families in LDCs transfer money to institutions in MDCs for security reasons this is best described as

   A   inward investment

   B   capital flight

   C   debt servicing

   D   restructuring

5 The terms of trade have worsened for most non-oil LDCs over the last 50 years. Which of the following is NOT a contributory reason?

A The major exports of non-oil LDCs have a high income elasticity of demand.

B Many developed countries have protected their primary sectors.

C Synthetic substitutes have reduced the demand for many raw materials.

D Many modern manufacturing techniques economise on raw materials.

6 A barrier to economic growth in many LDCs is

A rapid population growth.

B lower trade barriers.

C foreign investment by MNCs.

D a relatively high savings ratio.

7 It is a barrier to economic growth in many LDCs that

I the price elasticity of demand for primary products is high.

II the terms of trade tend to move against primary products.

III the prices of primary products are volatile.

A I only   B I and II   C II and III   D I, II and III

8 Non-oil producing LDCs have slow economic growth partly because

A their exports have grown so fast.

B their citizens do not wish to buy manufactured products.

C their terms of trade index has increased.

D prices of manufactures have risen faster than prices of primary products.

9 Middle income LDCs which have prioritised economic growth over the last 50 years have often done so at the expense of

A higher GNP per capita.

B greater industrialization.

C more even income distribution.

D greater urbanisation.

An Economic Profile of Nigeria

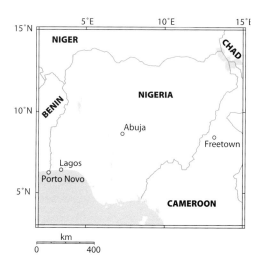

Geographic, Social and Economic Indicators

Capital city:	Abuja
Area:	9,600,000km^2
Population:	127 million (2000)
Population (average annual growth rate):	2.8% (1990–2000)
GNI per capita:	US$260 (2000)
GNI per capita (PPP):	US$790 (2000)
GNP per capita (average annual growth rate):	−0.4% (1990–2000)
Agriculture as share of GDP:	39% (2000)
Exports as share of GDP:	17% (2000)
Life expectancy at birth:	47 (1997)
Under age 5 mortality rate (per 1000 live births):	151 (1999)
Adult illiteracy rate (age 15+):	Male 31%, Female 49% (1997)
Human Development Index:	0.455 (low) (1999)

Nigeria

The most populous country in Africa, Nigeria exhibits most of the common characteristics of an LDC. Eighty five per cent of Nigerians live in rural areas, most exports are primary products, population growth is rapid, poverty is widespread, unemployment is high and increasing. Politically the country is unstable because of tribal and ethnic conflicts. There are 250 ethnic groups. The north is dominated by the mainly Muslim Hausa-Fulani, the south-east by the Catholic Ibos and the south-west by the half Muslim and half Christian Yorubas. Religious and ethnic problems have exacerbated economic and social inequalities between regions since independence from Britain in 1960. Regional income disparity is high. Corruption and mismanagement are widespread in Nigeria.

At independence Nigeria was mainly an agricultural producer, a major exporter of cocoa, groundnuts and palm oil. It was one of the poorest countries in the world with a GDP per capita in 1968 of $90. Since the 1970s oil has dominated, providing 30% of GDP, 90% of exports and 70% of federal tax revenue. Based on its oil wealth Nigeria embarked on a decade of rapid industrialisation and major restructuring of the economy. GDP per capita grew by more than 1000% between 1968 and 1980 to $1020.

However the Nigerian economy then went into major decline with GDP per capita falling back to very low levels. Falling oil prices were partly to blame, the rest was due to massive mismanagement and corruption. Nigeria was too ambitious in its industrialisation plans, borrowed excessively and neglected its agricultural sector. One of the consequences of rural poverty is the 3% population growth rate. Another is the mass migration to the cities causing high urban unemployment.

Source: Adapted from: M. Todaro & S. Smith, Economic Development 8th Ed. 2003; and World Bank, World Bank Indicators 2001

5.4   NEGATIVE CONSEQUENCES OF GROWTH

POLLUTION AND ENVIRONMENTAL DEGRADATION

There is concern that as more countries grow and develop, more and more damage to the environment will occur. Population increase can degrade the environment by putting too much pressure on the land. Soil erosion is a serious problem in parts of Africa, Asia and Latin America as people move to marginal land on the hills and clear it for farming. Forest cover is lost by cutting for fuel, as many more trees are being cut than planted. Desertification is a problem stemming from the over-grazing of land by animals. An area the size of Ireland is lost to desert every year in this way. Over-fishing of lakes and rivers is a further consequence of rapid population increase.

The serious international environmental consequences of depleting the ozone layer and of global warming are, however, first and foremost the creation and responsibility of the industrialised countries. The use of ozone depleting CFCs is highly correlated with National Income and 80% of all fuel is burnt by the twenty per cent richest people. It is therefore urgent that rich countries address this problem now. The rapidly growing LDCs will increase pollution by a multiple, if and when they too grow. At the moment China has over 500 bicycles for every car and only 10% of Chinese households own a refrigerator. China is currently (1997), however, the fastest growing country in the world.

Valuing Natural Resources – Indonesia

Imagine a country that dug up all its coal, burnt down all its forests, killed off all its wildlife, filled its air with smoke and its rivers with dirt. Would that country thus become poorer? Yes, says common sense. No, says national-income accounts.

For most Third World countries, the danger of treating natural resources as valueless is even greater: they are much more dependent on natural resources for income, jobs and exports. National accounts that ignore natural resources thus ignore the countries' main assets.

How to turn common sense into statistics? An exercise ("Wasting Assets: Natural Resources in the National Income Accounts") conducted by the World Resources Institute in Washington DC, shows one simple first step that all countries could copy. The WRI took as its prototype Indonesia, a country where primary production accounts for more than 40% of gross domestic product, more than 80% of exports, and more than half of all employment. Indonesia's GNP grew on average by 7% between 1971 and 1984, making it one of the most successful middle-income countries.

Look again, said the WRI. Take three natural resources – oil, timber and soil. Put a simple value on them: the market value of standing trees; of proven oil reserves; and of productive land. Look at the rate which those resources are being depleted: by logging; by oil sales; and by soil erosion. Build that back into the accounts to produce a concept of "net national product". The results appear in the chart: a sharp rise in two years of big oil finds; but otherwise a slower growth than the unadjusted figures suggest. Suitably "greened", Indonesia's 1971-1984 output growth falls to about 4% – still impressive, but more modest.

Constant 1973 rupiahs trillion

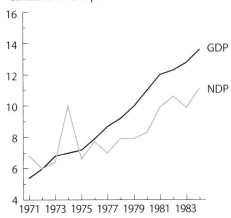

The virtue of the WRI exercise is that it stays close to the marketplace; it concentrates mainly on those stocks of natural capital that have a measurable value. Some governments have tried a more elaborate exercise of drawing up a separate framework of physical accounts. This approach was pioneered by the Norwegian government, and built on by the French and Canadian governments. These "satellite" accounts attempt to measure the stock of natural resources (often in hectares or cubic metres or other non-monetary units) and to estimate changes in that stock over time. Not surprisingly, it has proved harder to measure the changes in the quality of natural capital (water, or air pollution for instance) than to measure quantity. It has also proved hard to use the information for planning or policy analysis.

Other countries are now showing an interest in trying to measure changes in the stock of natural and environmental resources, and allow for welfare loss through pollution.

Before that can be done, economists will have to refine measures of the welfare lost by the Exxon Valdez oil spill, and the value of the stock of clean air. Some techniques exist. You can ask people what they would pay for cleaner air or petrol carried in unspillable tankers (but they may exaggerate); you can compare the value of a house in a noisy street with one in a quiet street. Quite apart from obvious limitations of such techniques – limitations shared by all cost-benefit analysis which tries to turn subjective values into objective figures – there may be some bits of the environment which may be literally priceless. How can anybody value a natural resource for which there is no substitute? What price the ozone layer? Or the Amazon? As some of the most priceless bits of nature play the biggest part in sustaining life on earth, no system of national accounts, however "greened", is ever likely to capture the true economic cost of depleting or destroying them.

Adapted from Economics Focus, The Economist August 26 1989

INCOME DISTRIBUTION

The clash of opinion and belief over development versus growth is one of the most fundamental in the study of development economics. Development includes improvements being broadly distributed throughout the population. In other words that income becomes relatively evenly distributed.

There are, however, many who believe that the pursuit of growth has to be given priority over development, that development will follow growth. They are therefore likely to argue for the very latest technology. They would also argue that investment, which requires saving, is more likely to follow from an unequal income distribution. That is, a high income sector is necessary to generate the necessary savings. Poor people have a high marginal propensity to consume, rich people have a high marginal propensity to save. This is in direct conflict with those who argue for spreading resources thinly by redistributing income and making a direct attack on poverty.

SUSTAINABILITY

Most pollution is caused by the high output industrialised countries. There is an urgent need for the LDCs to raise their living standards substantially. However if they industrialise with the same polluting technologies there almost certainly will be a serious deterioration in the environment. There is an urgent need to develop more environmentally friendly technologies and to ensure that these are available to developing countries. That is, there is an urgent need for sustainable development. The theme of the IBRD World Development Report in 1992 was just that. It seems apt to conclude this section and the book with a reading from that Report:

Policies for Sustained Development

The protection of the environment is an essential part of development. Without adequate environmental protection, development is undermined; without development, resources will be inadequate for needed investments, and environmental protection will fail.

The coming generation presents unprecedented challenges and opportunities. Between 1990 and 2030, as the world's population grows by 3.7 billion, food production will need to double, and industrial output and energy will probably triple world-wide and increase fivefold in developing countries. This growth brings with it the risk of appalling environmental damage. Alternatively, it could bring with it better environmental protection, cleaner air and water, and the virtual elimination of acute poverty. Policy choices will make the difference.

Priorities for Action

Inadequate attention has been given to the environmental problems that damage the health and productivity of the largest number of people, especially the poor. Priority should be given to:

The one-third of the world's population that has inadequate sanitation and the 1 billion without safe water.

The 1.3 billion people who are exposed to unsafe conditions caused by soot or smoke.

The 300 million to 700 million women and children who suffer from severe indoor air pollution from cooking fires.

The hundreds of millions of farmers, forest dwellers and indigenous people who rely on the land and whose livelihoods depend on good environmental stewardship.

Addressing the environmental problems faced by these people will require better progress in reducing poverty and raising productivity. It is imperative that the current moment of opportunity be seized to bring about an acceleration of human and economic development that is sustained and equitable.

Policies for Sustained Development

Two types of policies are required: those that build on the positive links between development and the environment, and those that break the negative links.

Building on the Positive Links

The scope for actions that promote income growth, poverty alleviation and environmental improvement is very large, especially in developing countries. Such 'win-win' policies include:

Removing subsidies that encourage excessive use of fossil fuels, irrigation water, pesticides and excessive logging.

Clarifying rights to manage and own land, forests and fisheries.

Accelerating provision of sanitation and clean water, education (especially for girls), family planning services, and agricultural extension, credit and research.

Taking measures to empower, educate and involve farmers, local communities, indigenous people, and women so they can make decisions and investments in their own long term interests.

Targeted Environmental Policies

But these 'win-win' policies will not be enough. Also essential are strong policies and institutions targeted at specific environmental problems. Lessons for effective policymaking include the following:

Trade-offs between income and environmental quality need to be carefully assessed, taking long term, uncertain, and irreversible impacts into account. Carefully balancing costs and benefits is especially important for developing countries, where resources are scarce and where basic needs must still be met.

Standards and policies need to be realistic and consistent with the monitoring and enforcement capability and administrative traditions of the country.

Blunter and more self-reinforcing policies are likely to be attractive in developing countries. Policies need to work with the grain of the market rather than against it, using incentives rather than regulations where possible.

Governments need to build constituencies for change – to curb the power of vested interests, to hold institutions accountable, and to increase the willingness to pay the costs of protection. Local participation in setting and implementing environmental policies and investments will yield high returns.

The Costs of a Better Environment

The costs of protecting and improving the environment are high in absolute terms, but they are modest in comparison with their benefits and the potential gains from economic growth. Improving the environment for development may make it necessary to raise investment rates in developing countries by 2–3 percent of GNP by the end of this decade. This would enable stabilization of soil conditions, increased protection of forests and natural habitats, improved air and water quality, a doubling of family planning expenditures, sharply improved school enrolment rates for girls, and universal access to sanitation and clean water by 2030. The costs of addressing global atmospheric issues would be additional.

The Convention on International Trade in Endangered Species (CITES)

The UN sponsored Convention on International Trade in Endangered Species, agreed in 1973, is one of the best known multilateral agreements on trade and the environment. CITES aims to prevent the trade in rare animals and exotic products like rhino horn, tiger bones, ivory tusks and leopard skins. Global wildlife trade is worth $20 billion a year and a quarter of this trade is illegal.

There is a fierce argument amongst environmentalists themselves as to whether a blanket ban on such trade is best or whether by allowing a carefully regulated trade endangered species will be better protected.

MULTIPLE CHOICE QUESTIONS – NEGATIVE CONSEQUENCES OF GROWTH

1 To an economist, sustainable development is development based on the assumption that
   A consumption habits of the rich countries cannot be changed.
   B there is a limit to the amount of pollution the planet can absorb.
   C market forces will ensure that the quantity of available resources will match demand.
   D recycling is too costly to be effective.

2 Sustainable development is development which
   A can be maintained in the future at present rates of growth.
   B depends on a switch from manufacturing to services.
   C can continue in the long run if excessive external costs are internalised.
   D will inevitably increase unemployment.

3 Which of the following development policies would not be regarded as sustainable?
   A Clarifying ownership rights over land, forests and fisheries.
   B Subsidizing the use of irrigation water.
   C Improving clean water supplies.
   D Increasing access to education for girls.

An Economic Profile of Venezuela

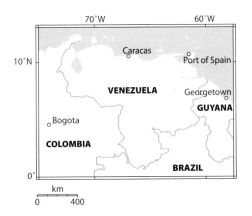

Geographic, Social and Economic Indicators

Capital city:	Caracas
Area:	912.050km^2
Population:	24 million (2000)
Population (average annual growth rate):	2.1% (1990–2000)
GNI per capita:	US$4,310 (2000)
GNI per capita (PPP):	US$5,750 (2000)
GNP per capita (average annual growth rate):	−0.5% (1990–2000)
Agriculture as share of GDP:	5% (2000)
Exports as share of GDP:	27.2% (2000)
Life expectancy at birth:	73 (1997)
Under age 5 mortality rate (per 1000 live births):	23 (1999)
Adult illiteracy rate (age 15+):	Male 7%, Female 8% (1997)
Human Development Index:	0.765 (medium) (1999)

Venezuela

Venezuela is a sparsely populated country considering its large size. Most of the population are native born descendants of European, Amerindian and African immigrants, with the most recent influx of Europeans, mainly Italians, Spanish and Portuguese, arriving in the 1950s. The population growth is rapid with most living in the cities and 40% being less than 15 years of age. The country is relatively rich but the income is distributed very unevenly, the cause of most of the symptoms of poverty. A labour skills shortage was formerly a supply side bottleneck although the country stepped up education and training and successfully recruited abroad to help bridge the gap. Today whilst there is still some shortage of managers and technicians, unemployment is the really pressing problem.

Oil accounts for 80% of exports, 60% of government income and 20% of GDP. A member of OPEC, Venezuela is a major world producer and exporter. Due to its reliance on oil as the basis of the economy, Venezuela is vulnerable to demand side instability in the major oil consuming countries. Depressed oil prices since the 1980s and oil conservation measures by the US and others have worsened the terms of trade and caused current account trade deficits.

With a worsening balance of payments Venezuela found it difficult to service its large external debt and sought assistance from the IMF. The $6 billion dollar loan came with the IMF's strict conditionality requirements. These included severe budget cuts, the privatisation of nationalised industries, wage controls and devaluation of the currency. However per capita income has continued to fall and increased poverty, inequality and unemployment has led to huge discontent, an attempted coup, and anti-IMF riots. Many IMF measures have been abandoned but the discontent has spread to the middle classes as the high inflation has eaten into their real incomes. Since another attempted coup in 2002 Venezuela has adopted a highly controversial protectionist policy.

Source: Adapted from: M. Todaro & S. Smith, Economic Development 8th Ed. 2003; and World Bank, World Bank Indicators 2001

EXERCISE

Complete two profiles of your own choice, contrasting one high income with one low income country.

Economic Profile of . . . .

Geographic, Social and Economic Indicators

Capital city:

Area:

Population:

Population (average annual growth rate):

GNI per capita:

GNI per capita (PPP):

GNP per capita (average annual growth rate):

Agriculture as share of GDP:

Exports as share of GDP:

Life expectancy at birth:

Under age 5 mortality rate (per 1000 live births):

Adult illiteracy rate (age 15+):

Human Development Index:

Economic Profile of . . . .

Geographic, Social and Economic Indicators

Capital city:

Area:

Population:

Population (average annual growth rate):

GNI per capita:

GNI per capita (PPP):

GNP per capita (average annual growth rate):

Agriculture as share of GDP:

Exports as share of GDP:

Life expectancy at birth:

Under age 5 mortality rate (per 1000 live births):

Adult illiteracy rate (age 15+):

Human Development Index:

Notes

1   Zero marginal product

2   Recall that the terms of trade is a measure of the relative movement of prices *ie*
    Terms of Trade = Index of Export Prices x 100

3   The Open University Development Studies Study Pack T531/2/3 1994.

4   And in the first half of the 1990s has continued to fall.

5   Development Assistance Committee of the OECD

6   Voluntary Service Overseas, Peace Corps Programme and Medicine Sans Frontiers are three
    NGOs that you may have heard of.

7   World Development Report 1991 p48.

8   Students should be aware of thinking of countries operating purist policies. For example
    even the export-oriented NICs have market freedoms in limited areas combined with strict
    government controls in others.

9   More specifically we use the fertility rate. The fertility rate is the average number of children
    a woman has.

10 Most development plans cover a five year time period. This is sub-divided into annual
    plans. The five year plans themselves often form part of a twenty to twenty-five year long
    term, or perspective plan.

11 Oxfam and Conflict, Oxfam Information 1 40856 July 1992.

12 A striking refutation to adopting simplistic causes of underdevelopment was in the form of
    the first published Land-Sat photographs taken from space and printed in Time-Life
    magazine in 1981. One photograph was of the southern USA and Mexico. Vegetation was
    shown in red; the darker the colour the more luxuriant the crop. The boundary between
    the countries showed up as clearly as if drawn in by a cartographer's pen The differences in
    crops on either side of such a narrow boundary could not be explained by climate or
    natural soil qualities. They were due to differences in investment in the form of fertilizers
    and irrigation, crop deterioration, animal health, and the health and energy of humans.

Section 6

Study Methods

6.1 Preparing for the IB Examination

Sources of guidance
Preparing notes for Examinations
Preparing a Study Plan

6.2 Forms of final Examination Assessment

External Assessment
Essay Question
Short Answer Questions
Data Response Questions
Internal Assessment

6.3 The Extended Essay in Economics

Aims of the Essay
Extended Essay Timetable
Sources
Length
Supervision
Acknowledgements
How to Choose a Topic
How to Come up with an Extended Essay Title
Layout of the Essay
Assessment of Extended Essays

6.1   PREPARING FOR THE IB EXAMINATION [1]

The form of assessment in Higher Level Economics is 80% by final public examination, and 20% by internal assessment. At Standard Level the proportions are 75% and 25%. To perform well in these assessments the student needs to focus on the methods of examination early in the course and to practise examination skills as an integral part of the learning process. This section of the book, whilst not a substitute for IB official documents, offers candidates practical help and guidance in doing this as effectively as possible.

SOURCES OF GUIDANCE

To prepare for the examination you, the student, must be absolutely clear as to what is expected. A number of valuable sources of information from the IB are available to help you:

I *The Syllabus* – your teacher should have a copy of this and will have been working through it during your course. If this textbook has been your course text then your job is very much easier – as it follows the 2005/2011 syllabus – both at Higher and Standard Levels. If you have used a different textbook you need to know which parts of the book are in the syllabus, and which are not. If you have studied in a school or college without interruption to your course it is most likely your teacher will have done this for you. However, some regard for the overall syllabus as published by the IB Organization (as laid out in this text), will help you to put the whole of your course into perspective, and to understand the relationships between the different sections and topics.

I *The Objectives* – at the front of the syllabus is a list of objectives for the IB course. This will repay careful study. You should expect the examination to test these objectives. An interpretation of those objectives appears as Figure 6.1.

Figure 6.1 – Objectives of the economics course

1 To understand economic concepts and theories.
2 To be able to apply economic theories.
3 To use economic concepts and theories to analyse information.
4 To evaluate economic concepts and theories from different perspectives.

As a teacher I had only one objective for the students in my classes and that was 'to be able to think like an economist' by the end of the course. This embraces the more specific objectives in Figure 6.1. It can be thought of as acquiring a 'mental toolbox' which can then be used to tackle economic problems.

Past Examination Papers – sets of these can be obtained from the IB Office in Geneva and are an invaluable study tool.[2] They help you very directly by showing you the style of the examination, the nature of the questions, and the level of understanding required. The amount of time allowed to write short answer questions and data response questions has recently changed and as yet (June 2003) none of the new type of exam papers are available for inspection. Multiple choice questions will no longer be used in examinations from 2005 onwards. However they remain a very important learning tool and are included throughout this text for that reason.

The most recent past papers give the best guide to what the following year's examinations will be like. Whilst the syllabus is fixed until 2009, the subject of economics is likely to change in the intervening years. However any new emphasis is likely to show up in the exam papers.

Examiners Mark Schemes – the IB publishes these for use in teacher training workshops. Your teacher may have some. They are valuable because you can see exactly what the examiners are looking for, and therefore precisely what you should be aiming to demonstrate. The Marking Criteria for Essays is one of the most useful parts for a student. The ideal essay characteristics that you should be aiming for are listed in 6.2.

Figure 6.2 – Writing a good essay

> Your essay should show that you
> 1 are familiar with basic economic principles
> 2 can apply relevant economic theories
> 3 can analyse using relevant economic theories
> 4 can evaluate

Chief Examiners' Reports – these are a commentary on the strengths and weaknesses shown by candidates in previous exams. It gives an idea of examiners reactions to the exam scripts they mark. A great deal can be learned from these, *eg* almost every year the Chief Examiner reports that many students do not give enough attention to diagrams. Make sure that you do.

PREPARING NOTES FOR EXAMINATIONS

A comprehensive set of notes is one of your most valuable assets in the run up to the examination. These are likely to consist mainly of class notes, class essays, and tests. They may be supplemented by notes taken from reading your text throughout the course, other reference books and articles you have collected. Check that there are no gaps in your notes. Although there is some choice in many of your exam papers, you are expected to have covered the whole course. It is highly risky not to revise certain topics. Many examination questions which appear at first sight to be about a single topic, in practice often require an understanding of a wide range of economic principles.

Style of note taking is a matter of personal preference *eg* whether to use linear or spider diagrams. In all cases, however, learning can be markedly improved by reviewing notes after classes, tidying them up and highlighting important points.

For exam preparation it is well worth while editing your notes, producing brief summaries. These summaries will aid memory and help you to practise recall. The mental effort of producing them is one of the main benefits. It will force you to concentrate your mind, and to get to grips with the central points in each topic. Being able to reproduce these main points as part of your essay plan is the most significant step in writing a high quality examination answer. The more times you work over your notes and actively work on them, the better you will understand the material. Try to rewrite your summaries without looking at them. Getting someone else to do it for you by buying a set of revision notes will not be nearly as effective. You need to do this yourself to become fully familiar with the material. As an example Figure 6.3 shows brief revision notes for price elasticity of demand.

Figure 6.3 – Revision Notes: Price Elasticity Of Demand

Definition	the extent to which quantity demanded changes as price changes
Measurement	percentage change in quantity demanded/percentage change in price

or $\dfrac{\Delta q}{q_1} \div \dfrac{\Delta p}{p_1}$

or $\dfrac{\Delta q}{q_1} \times \dfrac{p_1}{\Delta p}$

Elastic, unit elastic, inelastic. PED $\neq$ slope. PED and TR.

Determinants	substitutes, time, proportion of income spent on the good, habit forming
Examples	inelastic – food, elastic – tourism; inelastic to elastic: All food, dairy food, all cheese; Camembert cheese, brand 'X' Camembert cheese.

PREPARING A STUDY PLAN

Managing your time efficiently in the run-up to the IB examination is of crucial importance. Preparing for six subjects presents you with the problem of economic scarcity, the scarcity of your own time. A suggested strategy for preparing a time management plan is as follows:

Draw up a blank time-table of a complete seven day week. Enter all of your time-tabled classes and activities. Construct this time-grid to cover all of your waking hours, *ie* evening hours, pre-breakfast hours and weekend hours. Make sufficient photocopies to take you up to the examination weeks.

Fill in one complete week's timetable showing exactly how you spent your time. Be honest with yourself. Enter your leisure activities, meal times, time spent socializing and so on. It is important to know exactly how you currently spend your time. Fill it in at the end of each day for a week. You may be in for some surprises!

Identify your targets, the IB grades you need, or hope to achieve.

Prioritize your tasks. Identify the most important tasks ahead of the less important ones, and allocate your time according to importance. You need to allocate time to study, to leisure; to coursework, and to revision; to Higher, and to Standard subjects. You may need to spend more time on a weak subject to ensure a Diploma pass, than you do on a strong subject.

▎ Make a week-by-week plan in the run-up to the examination. Apportion your time realistically. Set targets that you can achieve, which means allowing time to relax as well as to work. It is important that you achieve your targets. If they are unrealistically high and you fail to achieve them as a result, it is likely that you will become demoralized.

▎ Don't miss targets and deadlines that you set yourself. Once you start missing, it is easy to let your whole study plan slip.

▎ Identify any time-wasting activities, *ie* activities with a high opportunity cost of your time. Try to cut these out of your timetable.

▎ Set up your workspace efficiently. Have all your notes and references to hand to minimize search time.

6.2   FORMS OF FINAL EXAMINATION ASSESSMENT

The IB uses an externally assessed end of course examination together with internal assessment during the course. The final examination itself makes use of three different forms of assessment.

There is in addition the opportunity to write an Extended Essay in economics.

EXTERNALLY ASSESSED EXAMINATION

The three types of assessment are as listed below. They are:

| Essay Question
| Short Answer Questions[4]
| Data Response Questions

ESSAY QUESTIONS

Candidates are required to answer one question from a choice of four. The questions are based on all five sections of the syllabus. Each question has two parts and may relate to more than one section of the syllabus. Each part must be answered, so make sure that you do. It is important to analyze each question carefully to identify what it is getting at. Key words should be identified and thought about carefully. Key words that commonly appear in essay questions are listed in Figure 6.4.

▢ Figure 6.4 – Key Words used in Exam Questions

Account for	Give a reason for something.
Analyze	Break a concept down into its component parts, or essential features, in order to examine relationships.
Analysis	An examination and identification of the components of a whole.
Assess	Determine the importance of something.
Calculate	Give a precise answer where there is only one possible, *eg* PED.
Compare	Describe two situations, then present similarities and differences.
Define	Set out the meaning of a term. State precisely the meaning of a concept.
Describe	Give an account of something. An explanation is not required.
Discuss	Consider, or examine. Make a detailed and careful investigation of two sides of an argument.
Distinguish	Make clear an understanding of similar terms.
Evaluate	Determine the significance of something.
Examine	Inspect closely.
Explain	Give the reason for or the cause of something. A description is not sufficient, an explanation of why something has occurred is required.
How?	By what means? In what way?
Illustrate	Show clearly, provide with visual material, clarify by means of an example.
Outline	Give the important features of the topic. A brief treatment is expected.
To what extent?	Give a balanced judgement on a situation where there is some difference of view.
What?	An instruction to make something clearer.
Why?	Give reasons for the existence of something.

Examiners choose words very carefully and each key word is significant. For example, 'Why do governments manage foreign exchange rates?' is a different question from 'How do governments manage foreign exchange rates?' As you are likely to be taking your examination in a second language you should exercise special care. Mother-tongue speakers, however, also frequently answer the wrong question. Examiners are allowed only to award marks for answering the question asked, so however brilliant your answer, it will gain no marks if it is to a different question.

Pay particular attention to economic terms in the title, *eg* 'elasticity', 'unemployment', 'informal-sector'. Defining terms is almost always expected by the examiner as a part of the answer.

The real key to writing a good essay is to plan it carefully. Use the same procedure for writing a Short Answer Question from number 2 to number 9 (see over). For a long essay a reasonable time to allow for planning is 5–10 minutes. Any time much less than 5 minutes is likely to prove costly. Students that begin writing too soon frequently misread the question, poorly structure their answer, and miss out important points. The student may realize this in checking the answer ten minutes from the end of the examination, and add a rushed paragraph. Alternatively the student may realize it after the examination is over and when discussing the question paper with other students. Student A, 'Did you do the question on monopoly?' Student B, 'Monopoly?' 'There was a question on monopolistic competition but not on monopoly'. 'Oops! See you at the retake!'

Figure 6.5 summarizes some of the main 'dos and don'ts' of essay writing.

Figure 6.5 – Dos And Don'ts of Essay Writing

Do	Don't
Answer the question given	Ignore the key words
Plan your answer	Start writing before planning your answer
Analyze the question	Give too many ideas away in your first paragraph
Brainstorm your answer	List points
Answer all parts of the question	Ignore the later parts of question
Define all key terms	Use slang
Divide into logically arranged paragraphs	Try to summarize everything in your conclusion
Include an introduction	
Develop points in full	
Use diagrams	
Draw diagrams with a rule	
Fully label diagrams	
Include a conclusion which directly addresses the question	
Use examples and illustrations where appropriate	
Write legibly	
Ensure that each 'sentence' really is a sentence	
Discriminate between relevant and irrelevant points	

SHORT ANSWER QUESTIONS
(*NB* HIGHER LEVEL ONLY)

Paper 2 HL consists of six questions. You are required to answer three of them. The questions cover all five sections of the syllabus. They invite mini essay-type answers and typically address a single theory, or economic concept, asking you to apply it to a particular issue. For example:

1 Explain the shape of the short run cost curve.

2 In what circumstances might monopoly benefit society?

3 What is the difference between economic growth and economic welfare?

A suggested procedure for answering this type of question

1 *DIVIDE* your hour into three equal periods. Whilst waiting for the exam to begin, or as soon as it begins, write down on scrap paper the times you will begin writing the second, and third questions. (This is because exams often do not begin exactly on the hour). This will save you from doing it later when you are concentrating, and prevent you from making the serious mistake of over-running your time allowance.
2 *READ* the question carefully. What is it asking?
3 *PLAN* your answer on scrap paper before writing. Use 3 to 5 minutes to plan each question. Practise doing this to realize what 3 minutes feels like.
4 *BRAINSTORM* the question *ie* write down quickly key words and points. Do not edit, organize, or delete until this is fully completed.
5 *READ* the question again. Are you answering the question asked?
6 *ORGANISE* your ideas. Draw arrows linking points. Number points in order of treatment.
7 *CHECK* the question one more time. Are you answering exactly what is asked? For example, it is a mistake to answer 'how' if the question asks 'why'?
8 *Check 'DED' ie* Define, Example, Diagram. Ask yourself:
    a *Define* – have I defined the major terms? This is always important when writing about economic topics. It may even be a major part of a short answer question.
    b *Example* – have I used examples to illustrate my answer? This is often useful.

   c *Diagram* – have I used appropriate diagrams? Very often important in economics. Indispensable in questions where, in explaining it, your teacher or your textbook has used diagrams.

9 *MONITOR* your time carefully, that is 20 minutes per question, with a very rigorous adherence to this time. A common, and serious mistake, of candidates unused to this type of question is to spend 25 to 30 minutes on the first and 'favorite' question, or the first two questions. The third question is then rushed. The last answer becomes one or two sentences, a list of points, or is missing entirely. Full marks will be awarded for an excellent 20 minute answer to a question. You cannot score more by writing several pages. You can however fail to score anything by not writing the third answer. Your teacher will almost certainly arrange some practice sessions, so that you gain experience dividing up your time rigorously.

10 After the first examination day is over recall what topics appeared in Paper 2. Then ask yourself what major topics were not examined. That could be a clue as to what to expect in Paper 3 on the second examination day.

DATA RESPONSE QUESTIONS

Candidates are required to answer three questions from a choice of five. The five questions are structured and cover the whole syllabus. Data is presented as a mix of statistical, diagrammatic and written formats. If the answers to the questions are included in the data then the question is properly called a 'data response question'. In some questions however the answer is not in the data. These questions are more properly called 'stimulus response questions'. The purpose of the data is to generate interest, or stimulate the candidate. IB questions are typically a mixture of the two types. Questions are usually divided into four parts. The first two part sub-question usually involves definitive or specific interpretation of the data. The following three sub-questions usually relate to the data, with the last being a free-response sub-question, rather like a short answer question.[5]

The questions are on an incline of difficulty. The first sub-question tends to be straightforward *eg* define GDP per capita, define elasticity of supply. The last sub-question often asks for information additional to the passage presented. Students may be asked to appreciate the limitations of the given information and to suggest alternative sources of useful and appropriate information.

Data response is a high level skill. Learning to do this well will prove useful to you in almost any career you embark upon. It does require practice however, and you should work hard at this throughout your course. The practice you obtain with Internal Assessment articles will help a great deal.

A suggested procedure for answering this type of question

▎ Divide your two hour period evenly into three. Ensure you spend 40 minutes on each of the three questions you choose. Do not write longer on your first or 'favorite' question. You cannot gain more marks to compensate for those that you *will* lose on the third question.

▎ Spend several minutes looking at all five data response questions carefully to discover what they are really about. It is easy to launch into one question quickly, only to realize later that another question would have been better. These questions often cover several topics – not just the one in the title of the data. Make sure you are able to answer all parts of the chosen question.

▎ The mark allocated to each sub-question indicates how much time you should spend on it. A few words, a sentence or two at most is expected for two marks. A mini-essay, say half a page to a page, will be required to do justice to a question with 8 marks.

▎ Answer the question set. Answer it fully, answer each part and answer it in the manner asked. Failure to do this is one of the major causes of poor examination results, even by candidates who are strong in the subject.

▌ Answer the question in your own words. Do not copy out or paraphrase the passage given. This shows no understanding on your part and examiners give no credit for it.

▌ If the question asks you to use 'evidence' from the passage, you do need to use it. However, depending on the number of points allocated, you may well be expected to develop the data, using additional information, and certainly always using your own words.

INTERNAL ASSESSMENT

Students are required to submit a part of their coursework to be assessed for the final examination grade. Internal Assessment, as it is called, counts for 20% of the overall IB grade at Higher Level and 25% at Standard Level. The requirement is to produce a portfolio of four short commentaries based on a news media extract, linking economic theory to a real world situation. Three of the four commentaries must have as their focus a different section of the syllabus.[6]

Extracts can come from a variety of sources but typically would be from regular newspapers and magazines, that is, written for non-economists. The student then demonstrates (i) the *linkages* between the extract and economic principles, and (ii) the *insights* economics gives to understanding the article better. Articles in specialized financial and economics columns and magazines are generally best avoided as the journalist would have already undertaken this task.

Internal Assessment aims to promote economic awareness, to develop the student's ability to relate the IB course to the real world. The requirement is a way of focusing attention on events more current than in text books or in examination papers. It can also encourage a study of issues which are of particular interest to the class, to the country or the region. Although it may prove a little difficult initially the student will soon find that the activity can add enormous interest and excitement to the course. A portfolio of work is compiled as a normal classroom activity during the course. This work is submitted to the teacher at regular intervals over the two years. The work cannot be revised or corrected once submitted, and thus should show a progressive maturing of understanding and ability over the whole two years. Thus it is most likely that early work will look unsatisfactory to the student when looking back. This is fully expected by the examiner and the portfolio will be judged as a whole rather than the individual commentaries in isolation.

The portfolio is graded according to five criteria:

1 The fulfilment of rubric requirements
2 How appropriate the portfolio is, together with its organisation and presentation
3 The use of economic terminology
4 The analysis and application of economic concepts and theories
5 Evaluation.

Although teachers are required to assess the work initially, an examiner will see a selection of portfolios and moderate the marking to ensure consistency between schools.

Advice to teachers[7]

The Internal Assessment is the same for HL and SL candidates. Students are required to submit a portfolio of four commentaries, each 650–750 words, based on published extracts from the news media. At least three must relate to a different section of the syllabus. There must be four different sources for the extracts.

⏐ While Internal Assessment should be introduced reasonably early in the course, teachers should bear in mind that *each* commentary in the portfolio must satisfy the criterion for a particular level. This is a significant innovation for the 2003 syllabus. For this reason work one or two practice extracts through with all students in class to get them going.

⏐ Draw attention to the criteria of assessment. Emphasise that students are required to apply economic theory, and evaluate articles. Contrast this with paraphrasing and summarising.

⏐ Give all students a personal handout containing the official guidelines from the IB, the marking criteria, some sample extracts of good and bad pieces of work and possibly an exemplar portfolio.

⏐ Spend some time making sure that students understand the criteria, and the importance of selecting extracts that enable them to score well. They should be pieces that require a diagram, clearly relate to theory in the syllabus, and give them a chance to demonstrate their command of economic terminology and understanding of how economic theory can be applied.

⏐ It is important to select articles that are fairly brief, or if they are not then the relevant sections of longer pieces should be highlighted.

⏐ Encourage students to read widely around the subject of economics and to apply textbook theories to real world situations. They must find their own extracts, and work independently in writing their commentaries.

⏐ Encourage the use of articles from lay sources *eg* daily newspapers as against financial papers and economic journals. 'Letters to the Editor' can be a rich source of extracts that enable students to demonstrate their understanding of economic theory.

⏐ Have the students hand in work at regular intervals so that their pieces relate to the part of the course currently being covered. The writing of them should form part of the study – it is not an additional task.

⏐ Students are allowed to submit a first draft to their teacher for advice before submitting the final copy. It must not be reworked after this.

⏐ Encourage the use of precise diagrams, carefully labelled.

⏐ Early on check that students are attaching the source article to their own work, give the title of the extract, the source of the extract, the date of the extract, the date of their own commentary, the word count and the section of the syllabus to which it applies.

⏐ Students may write more than four commentaries and submit their best four as the portfolio.

6.3   THE EXTENDED ESSAY

The Extended Essay is a unique aspect of the IB, with its requirement to pursue original research and to write it up. It can be a grind: vexing, frustrating, daunting and forbidding. It can be (and much more often is) absorbing, challenging, intellectually stimulating and enormously satisfying. It anticipates a style of work that some of you may not encounter again until your third or fourth year at university, but which experience shows that students of your age are capable of approaching with freshness, verve and great originality.

Aims of the Essay

Writing the essay will give additional insight into your chosen subject (economics in this case), through careful library research, the collection and classification of data and also through the necessary background study which is essential to making valid judgements. The methodology and discipline of economics must be practised and to ensure this you work under supervision.

The extended essay is intended to be of the kind that could be submitted for publication in an academic journal, *ie* a polished, well organised piece of work. It must, therefore, have the formal shape of an essay or article. It must be provided with functional documentation, paragraphing, indexes, footnotes and bibliography. The essay must lead logically to a worthwhile conclusion.

The writing of the essay gives you an opportunity to practise adult attitudes and educated virtues *eg* impartiality, the substantiation of general statements, the tolerance of other peoples' views and their achievements.

You should practise sophistication in the language you use. The completed essay should make rewarding reading.

Make the most of the opportunity that the essay presents. Choose a limited topic, explore it thoroughly, and write it up clearly and concisely. Do not be dismayed if your research opens up more questions than it answers; that is often the nature of good research. Be aware of this and learn when to stop.

Time management throughout the extended essay period is crucial. Figure 6.6 shows the time structure for one IB school.[8]

 Figure 6.6 – Extended Essay Timetable

Spring Term	
Late January	Starter session. Hand-out of general information.
Next few days	Subject teachers to talk during lesson time about doing Extended Essays in their subject.
Following few weeks	Consider possible topics – with aid of subject tutors, parents, contacts, friends, group tutors, etc.
Early March	Submit form ES/4 with proposed subject, area of research, etc. to Supervisor.
Easter Holiday	Preliminary research – checking sources/feasibility of proposed topic.

Summer Term	
Mid-late April	Discuss progress with Supervisor. Check on plans.
End April	Morning for appointments with supervisors/ extended research. Continue research.
Early June	Afternoon for further work with supervisors.
Summer Holiday	Continue research. Write preliminary draft.

Autumn Term	
Early September	Afternoon – third half day – further supervision. Continue revising / improving draft.
October week before half-term	No homework to allow time for final touches to the essay.
Last 2 days before half-term	No lessons in order to finish the essay.
Early November, day after half-term	0900 hrs. Submit completed essay to Supervisor.

Sources

Examples of secondary sources in economics are books involving interpretation and reference documents. They are useful in cases where they exist to ensure that the research is on sound lines and the interpretation of the topic has not already been disproved. The advice of teachers or other experts should be sought on suitable secondary sources.

In general, the number of sources should be limited. You should not be over ambitious in your reading. Be realistic about your choice of sources. If your research fails because you are unable to consult the intended primary sources, leniency will not necessarily be shown by the examiner marking the essay. If in doubt, consult your supervisor.

Remember that the aim of the essay is that you should form your own opinion on the topic researched, and not rehash that of someone else.

Length

Do not put in marginally relevant material just because you are short of words. In general, a tightly written 3000 words will create a better impression than the same material padded out to 4000 words.

Supervision

The Supervisor's report is an important part of the assessment as it can greatly influence the Examiner's opinion of your essay. Throughout the period of preparation of the essay your Supervisor will be watching the way in which you approach the topic for initiative and intelligence, in making use of outside sources, for evidence of malpractice, for depth of analysis and for clear and concise conclusions.

Acknowledgements

Many students make use of people as sources – for advice or for assistance in other ways. For this reason, and out of courtesy, it is appropriate to thank them at the end of the essay. Name the people who have assisted you and also their place of work; *eg* I wish to thank the following who provided me with information and assistance:

Musa Ndzimandze, Chairperson, Coboco, Atlantic College.
Ajitsingh, Street Moneylender, Metro Manila, Philippines.

This also establishes the credentials of the people you have consulted.

How to choose a topic

a Decide upon the subject in which you wish to submit an essay. Those of you who are proposing to go on to higher education should seriously consider writing an essay in your likely field of study. If certainly gives you something to talk about at an interview!

b Think about (i) your own particular interests within this field. You will have to spend a lot of time on the subject chosen, so think carefully. (ii) Whether you have access to particular information or people within any one area of the field. Among the best essays are those in which students have access to papers not previously studied. Originality in use of sources is always regarded favourably. (iii) Where you will be when you will be writing the essay. The bulk of the work is likely to be done over the summer. Where will you be? Is there a topic which could be conveniently studied to make use of the resources available (*eg* libraries, museums, specific people) at the time when you will be writing the essay?

c   Talk your thoughts over with the tutor in your selected subject.

d   Your topic should not be too ambitious. For most of you, the extended essay will be the first piece of independent research work you have carried out. It is therefore essential that the topic is carefully defined and is appropriate to your level. Tutors who may appear discouraging about your choice of topic are more experienced and more aware of possible pit-falls!

e   Topics should be very specific. Vast topics can only be covered superficially and this is not the aim. Such topics as "The export trade of Brazil" is far too broad. The Assessment Criteria for Extended Essays published by the IB states that the research question should be clearly and precisely stated and sharply focused so that it is susceptible to effective treatment within the word limit. Among the successful topics chosen in the past have been:

> The price elasticity of demand of water melons in my school.
> The effect of temperature on ice cream sales in a Danish village.
> The measurement of the multiplier in Singapore.

f   Topics should not wander outside the confines of the subject concerned. An Economics essay which involves History or Business and Organisation is likely to become superficial.

g   If the topic chosen is a development of subject areas covered elsewhere in the programme, the essay should not be a regurgitation of class work, nor a summary of basic course material. You should go into the subject matter in considerably more depth and show evidence of personal research.

How to come up with an Extended Essay Title

The hardest part in writing an extended essay is coming up with a research question. Once that hurdle is over, whilst there is hard work ahead, it is clear what has to be done. Getting the title is critical. Here is a suggested procedure which many of my own students have used.

1   Write down your interests – in two lists. On the left write down all those areas of economics that interest you. These may be topics you have covered already and you found interesting in class *eg* market operations, maximum prices, aims of firms or alternatively an area of economics yet to be covered *eg* exchange rates, the role of women in

development. You might initially brainstorm this *ie* think hard and write down ideas as they come to you. However most students will probably also revert to their textbook for ideas. Initially write down everything that interests you. Don't think any further about the topic, do not try to assess it yet. Do not censor or edit your list either. You can do that later when everything that initially seems interesting is written down.

On the right hand side list areas of your own personal interest. These could involve your hobby, future career, University study, your own country. Again no censorship yet. That comes in stage two. Your list will be personal to you. It could literally include anything, mountain bikes, beauty magazines, Thailand, birth-control, hotel management, family life, foreign trade, art, sport, refugees … anything.

2   Go through your lists again, deleting weak interests, high-lighting strong interests, adding any further ideas.

3   Link an idea from the left hand side with an idea from the right hand side. The table in Figure 6.7 makes some such connections:

Figure 6.7

Economic Interest	Personal Interest
price discrimination	hairdressing
elasticity	beer
foreign trade	Taiwan
market failure	global warming
cost benefit	engineering career
unemployment	pop music
market operation	hotel management

4   Form a research question involving both sides of your favoured topic *eg*

- Do hairdressers price discriminate between men and women?
- What is the cross-price elasticity of demand between two brands of lager?
- Is unemployment high amongst pop singers?
- Will hotel prices rise during the next Olympic Games?

Try one or two of the others for yourself. The idea is to come up with a question. It should be just that, a *question*. You absolutely should *not* consider the answer to it. That will be the task of the research. You should have no idea of the answer, or at least have an open mind. It is a mistake to consider essays in those areas only where you feel you know a lot, or in areas where you can get information easily *eg* your father's company. That is not research, you need to start with the unknown.

5   If the title is framed as a question it is then clear how to set about answering it. If the title is left as a statement it is often difficult to know where the boundaries lie, what to include and what to omit. For example "The black market for pop-concert tickets" has no clear direction. Change the statement into a question. "How does the black market for pop-concert tickets operate?" is much better. You now guide yourself into explaining how it actually works. The question might even be further focused *eg* "How does the black market for pop-concert tickets operate? A study based on the U2 concert, Wembley Stadium, July 2006".

6   Do try to restrict yourself to just one question. Students tend to worry whether they will have enough to write about. In practice the problem is usually trying to reduce and restrict the initial question. You will be surprised how little 4000 words is once you start to write.

Layout of the Essay

As an example one possible format you could consider for the presentation of your essay is given below:

Abstract
Acknowledgements

Chapter 1   INTRODUCTION
                         Introduction
                         The study area (background information)
                         Aims/objectives
                         Hypotheses
                         Methodology of data collection

Chapter 2   PRESENTATION
                         Presentation of data collected

Chapter 3   ANALYSIS AND CONCLUSION

          Conclusion

          Problems encountered

Appendices

Questionnaire

Bibliography

Footnotes

The very first thing to do upon deciding your extended essay is to open a file. Put in all your notes. Record details of all sources of articles and book references. It will save you hours of looking for them again at the end of your essay. Divide your research into smaller parts *eg* you could use the presentation format suggested above. Take a clean sheet of paper and write the heading of each part on the top.[9] You can then withdraw one part at a time and work on it. This makes the whole task more manageable. It can be off-putting to face yourself with the whole essay every time you go to work on it.

Assessment of Extended Essays

Your tutor will show you the Assessment Criteria which the examiners will use to judge your work. This will repay your study time handsomely. By studying what the examiners are looking for you will learn what to write and how to do your research. Two thirds of the criteria are based on general research and apply to all candidates in all subjects, the others are subject specific. Each is divided into a number of points, from 0 to a maximum of 2 to 4, for each of twelve criteria. By highlighting the highest possible points score which can be obtained in each of the criteria, you can see what the IB regards as excellent. These then are the specific attributes you should aim for yourself. For example on criteria E, the conclusion:

 "The conclusion is clearly stated, is relevant to the research question and is consistent with the argument or explanation presented in the essay. If appropriate, the conclusion clearly indicates unresolved questions and new questions that have emerged from the research."

This is the best guide you could possibly have to see what you should be aiming for in your conclusion. As a further example, criteria K, to what extent does the candidate effectively use the language of economics?

 "The essay demonstrates consistent and precise use of economic terminology, including exact definitions where appropriate."

Notes

1   Advice in Section 6 is personal, i.e. it is not official IB advice or IB sanctioned advice.

2   Your school is likely to hold them.

3   June 2003.

4   Short answer questions are at Higher Level only.

5   Advice given here should be checked against current official IB requirements.

6   Advice given here should be checked against current official IB requirements.

7   Chris Taylor, St. Peters College, Adelaide, Australia.

8   I am grateful for this, and much of the general essay advice to Nick Lee, IB Co-ordinator at St. Clares, Oxford, England.

9   Or open a new file on your word processor.

Answers to Questions and Exercises

Section 2

To Smoke or not to Smoke? That is the Question.

1 It is possible that the Poles consume a lot relative to others because the price of cigarettes in Poland is low. Quantity demanded is inversely related to price. Americans moved back along the demand curve as prices rose. The UK raised price selectively on the most harmful type of cigarettes, leaving close substitutes (non high tar and high nicotine cigarettes) relatively cheaper. The availability of a close substitute causes price elasticity to be high and would encourage a switch away from the most damaging cigarettes, although not necessarily affecting total cigarette consumption very much.

2 The fact that cigarette smoking is price inelastic in demand means that price changes alone have only a limited effect in changing consumption. Thus Spain and Germany resort to the law to limit smoking in certain areas, that is they use non-economic measures. The actions of Sudan and Sweden are designed to limit advertising and therefore 'taste' for smoking cigarettes.

Who Will Type Your Extended Essay?

1 They are all individual offers to supply a service. Market supply is the sum of all individual supply offers.

2 Price. Supply is the offer to sell goods or services at specific prices.

3 As demand. You will form part of the total market demand for typing services at 5 per thousand words.

Rent Controls – New York and Moscow

Acute shortage of apartments to rent. Very long waiting lists. Rationing of space to a certain number of metres per person. Very cramped and overcrowded apartments. Shared bathrooms and kitchens. Poor state of repair of buildings. A parallel market with high prices paid to get around the restrictions.

Tickets for U2 – USA

1 Above $28.50

2 A combination of price ($28.50) and queuing (standing in line)

3 Low by comparison

Taxpayers Milked instead of the Cows – USA

Your diagram should show a price floor drawn above the equilibrium price for dairy products. The quantity demanded and the quantity supplied should be marked in. There is a surplus or glut of milk products. To keep the price artificially high the government has been buying the surplus and placing it in storage. The cost of keeping perishable goods stored is higher than the cost of the tax transfers to farmers to encourage them to cut back on production. The aim of the legislation is to shift the supply curve to the left and reduce purchase and storage costs.

The Relationship between Marginal and Average

Game	1	2	3	4	5
Total Points	20	40	90	100	100
Average Points	20	20	30	25	20

The marginal score of 20 in the second game equalled the average score of 20 after the first game and therefore the average did not change. The large marginal score in game three being greater than the average of the first two, raised the average. Lower marginal scores, in games four and five respectively, pulled down the players' average score.

Firms Short Run Costs

Output in units	Total fixed cost	Total variable cost	Total cost	Average fixed cost	Average variable cost	Average cost	Marginal cost
0	40	0	40		0		
1	40	6	46	40	6	46	6
2	40	11	51	20	5.5	25.5	5
3	40	15	55	13.3	5	18.3	4
4	40	20	60	10	5	15	5
5	40	26	66	8	5.2	13.2	6

The Prisoner's Dilemma

If both firms A & B bid high they will get $10 million each for only half the work. This would be the preferred solution if they could co-operate. If they compete, bidding high risks getting no work at all. The best solution for both firms is to bid low and be certain of gaining $7 million for doing half of the work.

Countries usually have strict laws and punishments against firms colluding for government contracts, to ensure competition and to obtain lower prices for the taxpayer.

Alcohol, Branding and Competition – UK

Firstly, because consumers demand diversity and choice. The firm differentiates its product because there is a demand for different products. If it produced a few brands it could only meet part of the total demand.

Secondly, product differentiation forms a barrier to entry. A new firm wanting to enter the alcoholic drinks industry will have to enter on a massive scale to compete over the whole range of differentiated products. If a firm tries to enter a limited area of the market, on the other hand, it will have few products. It cannot therefore enjoy the economies of scale available to the big firms, *eg* in distribution, risk reduction or finance. The initial entry costs will be daunting. This is because of the large amount of advertising and marketing that would be required to establish brand images and consumer recognition to compete with the existing giants.

Competition, Monopoly and Consumer Choice

1 If there are competing channels the first will screen Soap to gain 53% of viewers' preferences. The second channel will also screen Soap, as half of 55% (=27.5%) is greater than the next category, Movies, at only 24%. The third company will broadcast Movies and take 24% of the market. The fourth company will broadcast Soap, as one third of that market is greater than half of the Movie market or the whole of the Sport market.
2 If there are only four TV Stations there will be no Sport and no Documentaries. In fact there would be seventeen channels of Soap, Movies and Sport before Documentaries had an even chance of being included.
3 A monopolist would screen documentaries on the fourth channel.

Avoiding Lemons

There is asymmetric information in the market for football players. Clubs selling players know about the fitness of their players, buying clubs do not. The market price of players would be an average between the price of fit players and unfit players. This price is a high price for an unfit player and a low price for a fit player. Transfer lists are likely to be dominated by clubs trying to unload their unfit players.

Jaguar Shuts Down

1   This is a short run decision. Ford will still face fixed costs for the Jaguar factories even though it is producing no cars for 5 weeks.

2   The firm has been producing cars at a loss, the average revenue has not covered the average cost. By closing down temporarily the firm will not have to pay variable costs. It is presumably cheaper to pay fixed costs only, making less of a loss than it would if it produced some cars. The firm's average revenue was not enough to cover the variable costs. It had fallen below the shut-down point. Ford is hoping that trading conditions will have picked up sufficiently after 5 weeks to raise revenue above the firm's shut-down point.

How do you value Life?

One approach is to value the life according to the person's earning potential; their age, qualifications, job and so on are brought into the evaluation. However this would give some odd results, *eg* a negative value to a disabled person who was unable to work and lived on welfare. So although this is the basis for some decisions, it is not totally acceptable. Another possible solution is to look at how individuals value their own lives. How much are people prepared to spend on safety devices *eg* cycle helmets, car air bags, and so on? Alternatively, how much are people prepared to spend on life assurance? A problem with this is that individuals tend to be unduly optimistic, behaving as though accidents are things which happen to other people, and not to themselves. They frequently underestimate their assurance provision.

As a consequence of these problems an arbitrary value is often put on life. It can be argued, however, that using an imperfect estimate of the value of life is better than ignoring the value of life altogether.

Permission to Pollute

1   Companies throughout the world which could reduce pollution cheaply would do so quickly to avoid the cost of buying permits. Those that could not reduce pollution easily would have their costs raised as they bought permits. There would be an immediate and rapid reduction in total emissions of carbon dioxide. There would also be an incentive for poor countries to grow, using environmentally – friendly technology.

2   You can probably think of several reasons. For example, the scheme requires international agreement. The first global environmental summit, in Rio de Janeiro, served to emphasise the enormous differences in view about the environment. There was little willingness to co-operate internationally to limit pollution. The Permit scheme would involve transfers of wealth from MDCs to LDCs. There has only been very limited evidence of the people of the rich countries being willing to do this.

The Parallel Economy in the USA

1   The sale of services is much easier to hide from official recording than the sale of goods, especially the large-scale production and selling of goods.

2   The GNP figures appear smaller than they should. The 'standard of living' as represented by GNP per capita appears lower than it really is.

GNP Per Capita – Bolivia, Papua New Guinea

1   8 million × $1000 = $8000 million

2   $4100 million/5 million = $820

The Poor of Three Continents – Ghana, Peru, Bangladesh

LDC Characteristic	Ghana	Peru	Bangladesh
1 A low standard of living	✓	✓	✓
a Low GNP per capita	✓	✓	✓
b poor health	✓	✓	✓
c poor housing	✓	✓	✓
d high illiteracy	✓	✓	✓
e absolute poverty	✓	✓	✓
2 High population growth	✓	✓	–
3 Primary production	✓	–	✓
4 Low productivity and high unemployment	–	✓	✓
5 Unequal power distribution	–	✓	–

Development in a Javanese Village

1   Food was limited, rice to a third of the year, and corn too was scarce. Villagers often wore rags and no shoes. Housing and furniture was of inferior quality. There was widespread illiteracy and ignorance of the world beyond the village.

2   Rice was available throughout the year – productivity had trebled and wages had doubled from 2 kgs of rice a day to 4 kgs of rice a day. Clothes were better, shoes commonplace. Radios and televisions were owned by many households. Houses and furniture were improved. Two primary schools had reduced illiteracy. Ignorance was reduced by travel and broadcasting. Electric lighting was replaced by kerosene lamps. The grinding physical labour for women was reduced and more productive work was available. There was a greater choice and variety in goods and services.

3   There are many connections. Good answers might connect the physical improvements with the less tangible aims of development eg improved clothing, increased productivity and ownership with self-esteem, primary school provision with reduction of ignorance, more food with the reduction of the misery that comes from hunger.

A Chinese Multiplier

As the economy expands, companies like Unilever experience increased demand for their products. When Unilever expands, it employs more workers, paying out more wages as well as increased profits. Households of these workers save some of the increased income but spend some of it, including money on Unilever products. The firm expands to met these increased sales and so on. The higher income of Unilever workers also generates demand for other companies in China. The increased employment and incomes in these companies generate further demand for Unilever products.

Keynes, the Classicists and the Great Depression

Keynes argues that the reality is different from market theory. Some markets, and the labour market in particular, do not automatically adjust like commodity markets. Wages, he argues, are sticky downwards. When the aggregate demand for goods and services falls, wages do not automatically fall as the Classicists assume. Workers resist cuts in money wages, and disequilibrium unemployment results. Price increases will reduce real wages, but the process is very slow. Demand-deficient unemployment could exist for a long period of time, as the Great Depression showed.

Hyperinflation 1945/46 – Hungary

1   A means of exchange; a store of value; a unit of account; a means of deferred payment.
2   The functions would collapse. Barter exchange would replace money exchange and trade would be severely curtailed. Stores of wealth in the form of financial saving would be eroded, to become literally 'worth less'. People would switch to hold wealth in real assets like land, gold and physical goods. Many would be ruined. The system of borrowing and lending would break down and the currency would become meaningless as a unit of account.

Fiscal Policy – Japan

1 The government is aiming to increase aggregate demand. It aims to increase its own public sector spending to offset the fall in private sector spending. The increased Yen 4000 billion is an increased injection. There is no plan to increase taxes, and the injection will increase spending by a multiplier effect.

2 National income would increase by a multiplied amount in the early part of the year. However, as spending fell again later in the year national income would fall, again by a multiplied amount.

3 As the government has expanded public spending by running a deficit budget, there is a danger that interest rates will rise and crowd out both private investment and interest-sensitive consumption. That is, the increase in aggregate demand caused by public sector borrowing would, through interest rate rises, kill off an equal amount of private sector spending, leaving aggregate spending unchanged. As private sector spending is likely to be more directly productive than infrastructure projects, this might well have negative effects on Japan's long-term growth. However, the government seems to have anticipated the crowding out problem by simultaneously expanding the money supply and acting to maintain low interest rates. They are intending that increased spending be additional, and not merely a switching between sectors.

Income Distribution – Bangladesh, South Africa, France

1 Bangladesh $9.4 + 13.5 = 22.9/37.9$
   South Africa $2.9 + 5.5 = 8.4/64.8$
   France $7.2 + 12.7 = 19.9/40.1$

2 The two factors leading to extensive poverty are low income per capita and unequal income distribution. Bangladesh has a relatively even income distribution but one of the lowest incomes per capita in the world. It has very extensive poverty due to the low income, albeit this income is evenly distributed. South Africa has a much higher income per capita than Bangladesh but a more uneven distribution of income. There is fairly extensive poverty as large numbers of South Africans have a tiny share of income. While France has a slightly more uneven income distribution than Bangladesh, it has one of the highest average incomes in the world, and as such is unlikely to have any absolute poverty at all.

Spot the Country!

The three countries which score highly in each category are the United Kingdom (C), Japan (I) and Germany (L), all high income countries.

F and H score low in every case and indeed H is Tanzania, one of the poorest countries in the world. However F is Cameroon which is not one of the lowest income countries.

Countries J and B score very highly on most indicators. These are the two SE Asian NICs South Korea and Singapore, which have developed very quickly since the 1960s.

Thailand is now growing rapidly and is country E.

Brazil, with relatively high income but a wide income gap, is M.

Oil rich Saudi Arabia is G, where the sudden increase in GNP per capita does has yet to be reflected in further development.

Two other countries with low scores are Sierra Leone and Uganda, D and N respectively, and both relatively poor.

China (A) and Sri Lanka (K) both score more highly than income figures would suggest.

Comparative Advantage

1 Incorrect.
2 This country has an absolute advantage in all products. It is still likely to have a comparative advantage in one or more of those products, just as the other country will. There is an opportunity cost in being self-sufficient. There are likely to be gains from trading due to comparative advantage. In addition there may be further gains from economies of scale, increased competition, consumer choice etc.

1 German worker = 2 Americans = 5 Taiwanese = 128 Chinese!

1 The USA.
2 It is now fourth and has a huge cost advantage over Germany. Its position with rival Japan has changed from being twice as expensive to being considerably cheaper.
3 Wage ratios: 1 Korean cost 8 times as much as a Chinese. By 1995 the cost of 1 Korean had risen to 30 Chinese. In 1985 1 American cost 8.6 times a Korean. By 1995 this had fallen to 1 American costing 2.3 Koreans only.

World Export Ratios

Possible reasons include:

1 They are very poor countries and therefore have relatively little to export.
2 This is a very large country and a very large producer. It is therefore relatively self-sufficient.
3 This is also a very large country and also fairly self-sufficient. In addition Russia is emerging from a long period of economic isolation from most of the rest of the world, as a former centrally-planned economy.
4 These are relatively rich economies but also relatively small and therefore more inter-dependent for trade than either Russia or the USA.
5 Saudi Arabia's economy is based largely upon the export of oil.
6 These are NICs, two of the Asian dragons which have developed rapidly by concentrating upon manufactured exports.

Voluntary Export Restraints and the US Steel Industry

The quotas would have restricted the amount of cheap steel available. Domestic steel cost more. This would have raised the price of all goods that use steel eg cars, refrigerators, buildings, ships and machinery.

Exploitation of Third World Workers

Well, a qualified yes and an emphatic no. There may be a moral case if there is an abuse of human rights. There are for example many children in the world today who are to all intents and purposes slaves to their owner/employers. In such cases economic pressure may help to bring down a despotic regime, as it did to the obnoxious system of apartheid in South Africa. However the answer is a resounding no if wages are low merely because there is an abundance of labour. The country would be specialising to its comparative advantage. Buying goods from such countries will help to raise wage levels. Not buying will condemn the poor to poverty.

Child Labour and Free Trade

1   With nothing to replace the child labour, families are even poorer. The children are forced into such schemes because of family poverty. It is also important to know whether the income going to the children represents comparative advantage, or whether their powerlessness is exploited, for example, with a disproportionate amount of income going to employers. Exploitation is more likely in the case of children without families. Even so, there may be powerful non-economic arguments too, like the moral undesirability of child prostitution, or slavery.

2   The Bangladeshi scheme offers economic inducements to replace the lost income by (a) paying the child and (b) the offer of a job for an older family member. Most important, there is also a long-term development aim. The child, by remaining in school, has an increased chance of getting out of poverty. As a result, the child is likely to have fewer children itself, upon growing up, and thus decrease the vulnerability of the next generation to child labour.

Sino-Japanese Dispute over Steel

1   Japanese consumers of steel will be hurt, eg makers of car bodies, ships and refrigerators. Japanese steel producers will benefit as import prices rise.

2   'Dumping' is the action of selling exports below the cost of production. It is deemed an unfair trading practice by the WTO and can be legitimately blocked on the grounds that it distorts international trade.

A Tax of 9000%!

The very high tariff barriers eliminate low price imports from comparative advantage producers. Domestic producers can sell at high prices behind the tariff wall. There is therefore a very high incentive to move domestic resources into the production of these goods, rather than into more socially desirable industries.

Japanese Surpluses 1981–1989

1   A surplus for one country is a deficit for another. If Japan runs persistently large surpluses other countries must run persistently large deficits. All countries cannot run surpluses.

2   As foreigners are buying more Japanese goods and services than they are buying from Japan, they end up owing Japan the difference. Thus Japanese people and Japanese companies are effectively lending to foreigners. There is an outflow on the capital account as Japan's claims on foreigners increase.

Juggling in the Foreign Exchange Market

The dealer, in order to earn the commission on the business, will seek to offer a higher rate than other banks. The higher the A$/S$ rate, the more A$ the importing firm will get for its money. Thus a rate of 0.82 A$ = 1 S$ is better than a rate of 0.8 A$ = 1 S$. The dealer will then have to buy A$. It will have to offer Australian sellers a sufficiently low exchange rate. The lower the A$/S$ rate the more attractive it is for Australians to buy Singapore dollars. For an Australian wanting to exchange A$ for Singapore dollars a rate of 0.8 A$ = 1 S$ is better than a rate of 0.82 A$ = 1 S$

Exchange Rates

a   J

b   (i) L   (ii) N   (iii) N   (iv) L   (v) E   (vi) K (assuming an increase in inward investment and a fall in outward investment)   (vii) L   (viii) E   (ix) N

Terms of Trade and LDCs

The poorer countries will have had to export much more to pay for the same level of imports. Alternatively they would have been able to import far less.

Kerala – a Model for Development?

1 Income distribution needs to be thought of as the distribution of goods and services rather than as money alone. Redistribution often takes the form of subsidised goods and services, provided cheaply or free. These are called merit goods by economists. In the passage there are a number of examples, *eg* food, health care and education.

3 The diagram shows a market price of 'food' as p_1. This has been judged too high for poor people and the Kerala government has set a lower price p_2. This has to be set below p_1 otherwise it would be totally ineffective. Unless the government took further action the fixed price will cause a shortage of food. The quantity of food demanded increases to q_3 because of the low price. The quantity of food supplied falls to q_2 because of the low price. q_2q_3 is the size of the shortage. The government now subsidises food to encourage production. This will shift the supply curve to the right, S_2S_2 in the figure. We know that the subsidy still leaves a shortage, say q_4q_3, as we are told that rationing takes place.

Aid

Clearly aid from official sources has not been distributed according to need, as measured by income per capita. The country receiving the largest amount of per capita aid, Israel, is enormously rich compared to the others. Israel is in the select 'high-income' group of countries by the World Bank's classification.

It is Israel's strategic political situation in the Middle East, widely regarded as potentially the most threatening area to world peace over the last twenty-five years, that has attracted so much 'aid' from America. This also explains the position of Israel's neighbour Jordan as the second-highest aid recipient. Egypt too has received aid on purely political grounds from both the former Soviet Union and the United States according to which stance it has taken with regard to the Middle East situation.

Nicaragua has been central to US foreign policy in containing communism in central America.

Guinea-Bissau and Senegal are former French colonies. The relatively high amount of aid that France gives is concentrated bilaterally on those countries with which it maintains strong links. Many of the others are members of the British Commonwealth and, as such, also attract favourable treatment from the UK. However, as there are many more countries, and some of them are very populous, the aid per capita is spread thinly.

Chinese leaders have deliberately maintained an independent line politically, despite the role of politics as the major determinant of aid distribution.

India's About Turn on Protection

1 Infant industry argument, appropriate technology argument, retaining control etc.

2 Making the repayments, plus interest on the loans.

Family Planning in China and Thailand

1 The fertility rate is the number of children born per 1,000 women of child-bearing age, which is taken to be 15 to 45 years old. There were 6.1 children born for each thousand women of child-bearing age in 1965–70. By 1985 this had fallen to 2.8 per thousand women.

2 Family limitation is organised very differently in Thailand and China. The Chinese programme is centrally organised and bears many of the hallmarks of a centrally planned and highly structured society. Officials, plans, targets, approval, pressure, campaigns and policy are some of the indicator words. In Thailand by contrast the campaign is organised by an NGO (Non Government Organisation) and the whole thrust is on persuasion for voluntary compliance. The strong characteristics of fun and enjoyment needed to persuade contrast with the decreed policy of China.

3 Economic incentives and disincentives, a) China – extra maternity leave, preference for housing, income supplement. b) Thailand – subsidised: buffaloes, piglets, fertilizers, seeds, transport and farm prices. Free vasectomies.   c) Both countries – although not explicitly stated, both countries are likely to be providing free information and free health care associated with family control methods, plus free or subsidised contraceptives.

A World Government?

Many of the worst problems of poverty have been eradicated within rich nation states by the involvement of national government. Power of government can impose progressive taxes and subsidise merit goods, for example. They often operate regional policies to even out income. The world has huge disparities of income and wealth, and a global government would be in a position to narrow the gaps. Many of the problems are international in nature yet there is little global centralisation of power.

Poverty in England and India

Clearly there are many parallels in terms of low income, slum housing, poor health, informal economic activity, unequal income distribution and absolute poverty. You might also try to think of ways in which there are differences between England 200 years ago and the poor countries today eg at that time agriculture was growing in productivity, industry was labour intensive, migration to new countries was a major escape valve, population growth was fast but lower than today and so on.

Informal Sector

Capital and materials are scarce, human beings are abundant. These activities use very little material and very little capital. The activities of the informal sector are markedly labour intensive. Is this not what you would expect in a country where labour is cheap and capital expensive?

Answers to Multiple Choice Questions

1.1   Introduction to Economics

1 = B, 2 = B, 3 = C, 4 = A, 5 = C, 6 = A, 7 = D, 8 = D, 9 = A, 10 = C, 11 = D, 12 = C, 13 = C, 14 = D, 15 = A, 16 = A

2.1   Markets

1 = D, 2 = B, 3 = D, 4 = C, 5 = C, 6 = B, 7 = C, 8 = B, 9 = C, 10 = A, 11 = B, 12 = D, 13 = A, 14 = B, 15= C, 16 = B, 17 = A

2.2   Elasticities

1 = B, 2 = A, 3 = A, 4 = B, 5 = B, 6 = D, 7 = B, 8 = D, 9 = D, 10 = C, 11 = B, 12 = D, 13 = A, 14 = B, 15 = B, 16 = A

2.3   Theory of the Firm

1 = C, 2 = A, 3 = B, 4 = C, 5 = A, 6 = B, 7 = D, 8 = B, 9 = C, 10 = A, 11 = D, 12 = A, 13 = C, 14 = D, 15 = B, 16 = C, 17 = D, 18 = B, 19 = C, 20 = B

2.3iii Economic Efficiency

1 = B, 2 = B, 3 = A

2.4   Market Failure

1 = A, 2 = D, 3 = C, 4 = B, 5 = D, 6 = D, 7 = C, 8 = D, 9 = B

2.4   Centrally Planned Economies

1 = D, 2 = C, 3 = A, 4 = B, 5 = A, 6 = D, 7 = B

3.2   Measuring National Income

1 = A, 2 = C, 3 = C, 4 = B, 5 = C, 6 = D

3.3   Introduction to Development

1 = B, 2 = B, 3 = C, 4 = B, 5 = D, 6 = C

3.4   Macroeconomic Models

1 = A, 2 = B, 3 = C, 4 = D, 5 = C

3.5   Unemployment

1 = D, 2 = A

3.6   Inflation

1 = A, 2 = A, 3 = B

3.7   The Inflation /Unemployment Debate
      1 = C, 2 = A, 3 = B, 4 = C, 5 = B, 6 = D, 7 = C, 8 = A, 9 = D, 10 = A

3.7   The Inflation /Unemployment Debate – HL Extension
      1 = A, 2 = C, 3 = D

3.8   Measuring Economic Development
      1 = D, 2 = D, 3 = C, 4 = C, 5 = C, 6 = C, 7 = D, 8 = D, 9 = D, 10 = A, 11 = D, 12 = B

4.1   Reasons For Trade
      1 = D, 2 = B, 3 = D, 4 = C, 5 = B, 6 = C, 7 = D, 8 = D, 9 = A

4.3   Protectionism and Trade Agreements
      1 = C, 2 = B, 3 = B, 4 = A, 5 = B, 6 = D, 7 = C, 8 = A, 9 = D, 10 = A

4.4   Balance Of Payments
      1 = B, 2 = B, 3 = D, 4 = D, 5 = B, 6 = C, 7 = B, 8 = A, 9 = D, 10 = C

4.5   Exchange Rates
      1 = C, 2 = D, 3 = B, 4 = B, 5 = A, 6 = B, 7 = C

4.6   Balance of Payment Problems
      1 = B, 2 = C, 3 = B, 4 = C, 5 = A, 6 = C, 7 = D, 8 = B

4.7   Terms of Trade
      1 = A, 2 = A, 3 = D, 4 = D, 5 = B, 6 = B, 7 = B, 8 = B, 9 = A, 10 = D, 11 = C, 12 = D, 13 = B,
      14 = A, 15 = A

5.1   Sources Of Economic Growth and Development
      1 = A, 2 = D, 3 = D, 4 = C, 5 = D

5.2   Growth and Development Strategies
      1 = C, 2 = C, 3 = A, 4 = C, 5 = B, 6 = C, 7 = A, 8 = C, 9 = D, 10 = C, 11 = A, 12 = B

5.3   Barriers To Economic Growth and Development
      1 = A, 2 = D, 3 = B, 4 = B, 5 = A, 6 = A, 7 = C, 8 = D, 9 = C

5.4   Negative Consequences of Growth
      1 = B, 2 = C, 3 = B

Glossary

above full-employment equilibrium a situation in which macroeconomic equilibrium occurs at a level of real GDP above long-run aggregate supply.

absolute advantage a country has an absolute advantage when it can produce a good with less resources than another (see comparative advantage).

absolute poverty when only a subsistence level is attained. When only the minimum levels of food, clothing and shelter can be met.

accelerator the level of investment depends upon the *rate of growth of demand*. A given percentage change in demand may require a larger percentage change in investment. The accelerator shows by how much the rate of growth of investment exceeds the rate of growth of demand (and of output).

accounting profit the difference between total revenues and total explicit costs.

ad valorem tax a tax on a good or service whose amount depends on the value of the good or service.

aggregate demand the relationship between the aggregate quantity of goods and services demanded – real GDP – and the price level – the GDP deflator – holding everything else constant.

aggregate demand shock any shock that causes the aggregate demand curve to shift inwards or outwards.

aggregate supply the sum total of planned production for the whole economy.

aggregate supply curve the relationship between planned rates of total production for the whole economy and the price level.

aggregate supply shock any shock that causes the aggregate supply curve to shift inwards or outwards.

allocative efficiency the situation that occurs when no resources are wasted – when no one can be made better off without making someone else worse off.

anticipated inflation an inflation rate that has been correctly forecast.

appreciation an increase in the value of a domestic currency in terms of other currencies.

appropriate technology a technology which accords with the factor endowments of the country. Thus labour intensive technology would be appropriate in a labour abundant economy and capital intensive technology would be inappropriate.

Asian tigers four Asian nations, Hong Kong, Singapore, South Korea and Taiwan, that enjoyed a long period of spectacularly high growth rates of manufactured exports.

asset anything of value that is owned.

automatic stabilizer a mechanism that decreases the size of fluctuations in aggregate expenditure.

autonomous consumption the part of consumption that is independent of, or does not depend on, the level of disposable income. Changes in autonomous consumption shift the consumption function.

average fixed costs total fixed costs divided by the number of units produced.

average propensity to consume (APC) consumption divided by disposable income for any given level of income. The proportion of total disposable income that is consumed.

average propensity to save (APS) saving divided by disposable income. The proportion of total disposable income that is saved.

average tax rate the total tax payment divided by total income. The proportion of total income paid in taxes.

average total costs total costs divided by the number of units produced.

average variable costs total variable costs divided by the number of units produced.

balance of payments an account of a country's transactions with the rest of the world.

balance of trade the difference between the value of visible exports and the value of visible imports.

balancing item the estimated net value of omissions from all other items recorded on the balance of payments accounts.

bankruptcy the situation when a business entity is unable to meet its debts.

barriers to entry barriers that make it difficult for firms to enter an industry and offer competition to existing producers or suppliers.

barter a system of exchange in which goods or services are exchanged for goods or services without the use of money.

base year the year which is chosen as the point of reference for comparison.

birth-rate the number of births per 1000 people in the population per year.

black economy/parallel economy unofficial economic activity. It cannot be precisely measured because it fails to go through official accounts.

black market/parallel market an illegal trading arrangement in which buyers and sellers do business at a price higher than the legally imposed price ceiling.

budget the annual statement by the government of its financial plan, it itemizes spending programmes and their costs, tax revenues and the proposed deficit or surplus.

budget surplus (*or* **budget deficit**) the difference between government sector revenue and expenditure in a given period of time. If revenue exceeds expenditure, the government sector has a budget surplus. If expenditure exceeds revenue, the sector has a budget deficit.

buffer stock scheme an organization, usually run by producers or the government, that attempts to smooth out fluctuations in prices and hence producer incomes by the purchase and sale of stocks.

business cycle/trade cycle the periodic but irregular up and down movement in economic activity measured by fluctuations in real GDP and other macroeconomic variables.

calorie supply per capita daily the calories available to the people of a country. This is based on the total food supply produced and imported, divided by the population and the number of days in a year.

capital factors of production that have themselves been produced by man eg machines, factories, ships.

capital consumption *see* **depreciation** which is another name for the same concept.

capital flight the movement of financial capital overseas following domestic problems. Capital flight has significantly deepened the problem of Third World debt.

capital goods goods that are used in the production of other goods. Examples include ships, factories, and tractors. Consumers do not directly consume capital goods.

capital movements the flow of funds across international boundaries, for investment in plant and machinery, or in response to interest changes, or expectations of interest rate changes.

capitalism an economic system in which individuals privately own the productive resources land and capital.

cartel a group of producers who enter a collusive agreement to restrict output in order to raise prices and profits.

central bank an official institution that controls the money supply. Central banks also supervise the commercial banks.

ceteris paribus the assumption that all other things are held equal, or constant, except those under study.

circular flow model a model of the flows of resources, goods, and services, as well as money, receipts, and payments for them in the economy.

collusive oligopoly price determination by oligopolists which is co-ordinated in order to avoid price wars breaking out.

command economy a system in which the government controls the factors of production and makes all decisions about their use and about the distribution of income.

communist country a country in which there is limited private ownership of productive capital and of firms, limited reliance placed on the market as a means of allocating resources, and in which government agencies plan and direct the production and distribution of most goods and services.

comparative advantage (*theory of*) a country has a comparative advantage in producing a good over another if the opportunity cost of producing that good is lower

competition rivalry among buyers and sellers of outputs, or among buyers and sellers of inputs (ie factors of production).

complement two goods are considered complements if a change in the price of one causes an opposite shift in the demand for the other. For example, if the price of computers goes up, the demand for computer games will fall; if the price of computers goes down, the demand for computer games will increase.

concentration ratio the percentage of all sales contributed by a small number (say 3 or 6) of the largest firms in an industry.

constant prices currency expressed in terms of real purchasing power, using a particular year as the base or standard of comparison.

constant returns to scale technological conditions under which the percentage change in a firm's output is equal to the percentage change in its use of inputs.

consumer (or consumption) goods goods that are used directly by consumers to generate satisfaction. Compare with capital goods.

consumer sovereignty the concept of the consumer as the one who, by his or her spending, ultimately determines which goods and services will be produced in the economy. In principle, competition among producers causes them to adjust their production to the changing desires of consumers.

consumer surplus the difference between the amount that a consumer is willing to pay for a commodity and the amount that is actually paid.

consumption the process of using up goods and services.

consumption function the relationship between the amount consumed and disposable income.

consumption goods goods that are bought by households to use up, such as theatre tickets, food and clothing.

contestable markets a market in which one firm (or a few firms) operates but in which entry and exit are free, so the firm (or firms) in the industry faces competition from potential entrants.

cost-push inflation inflation that has its origin in cost increases.

counter-cyclical policy the use of fiscal and monetary policy to offset booms and slumps by contractionary and expansionary policies respectively.

cross-price elasticity of demand the percentage change in the demand for one good divided by the percentage change in the price of a related good. Cross-price elasticity of demand is a measure of the responsiveness of one good's quantity demanded to changes in a related good's price.

crowding in the tendency for an expansionary fiscal policy to increase investment.

crowding out the tendency for an increase in government purchases of goods and services to increase interest rates, thereby reducing – or crowding out – investment expenditure.

crude (birth/death rate) crude rates do not take a country's age structure into account. Thus, for example, the crude death rate of a developed country may be higher than a developing one due to the higher proportion of old people.

crude birth rate the number of births in a year per one thousand population eg 30 per 1000, the same as a 3% birth rate.

crude death rate the number of deaths in a year per one thousand population eg 10 per 1000, the same as a 1% death rate.

current account the part of the balance of payments which records the day by day transactions of goods (visibles) and services (invisibles).

cyclical unemployment unemployment resulting from business recessions that occur when total demand is insufficient to create full employment.

DAC Development Assistance Committee of the OECD.

death-rate the number of deaths per 1000 people in the population per year.

debt-servicing the sum of interest and principal repayments on publicly held or publicly guaranteed external debt.

deficit spending government spending that is in excess of tax revenues.

deflate a government action to lower aggregate demand through fiscal or monetary policy.

deflation (1) a sustained fall in the price level, often accompanied by a fall in output and employment. (2) government policies to reduce the level of aggregate demand to reduce inflation.

demand   the relationship between the quantity demanded of a good or service and its price.

demand curve   a graph showing the relationship between the quantity demanded of a good or service and its price, holding everything else constant.

demand schedule   a list of the quantities of a good or service demanded at different prices, holding everything else constant.

demand-pull inflation   inflation that results from an increase in aggregate demand.

demerit good   the opposite of a merit good; one which the political process had decided is socially undesirable.

dependency ratio   the percentage of the population in the combined age groups aged under 15 and 65 plus.

depreciation (capital)   reduction in the value of capital goods over a one-year period due to physical wear and tear and also to obsolescence.

depreciation (currency)   a lessening of the value of a domestic currency in terms of foreign currencies.

derived demand   input factor demand derived from demand for the final product being produced.

devaluation   depreciation under a regime of fixed exchange rates.

devalue   to lower the par or fixed value of a managed exchange rate. The action makes exports cheaper and imports dearer.

development   a process to improve the lives of all the people in a country. This involves not only raising living standards ie the production of goods and services but the promotion of self esteem, dignity and respect, and the enlarging of peoples freedom to choose and to take control of their own lives.

direct tax   tax liability targeted at one person on the basis of income.

dirty or managed float   a freely floating exchange system that involves governments intervening to stabilize the value of their currencies. To be compared with a 'clean' float, where there is no government intervention in the foreign exchange market.

diseconomies of scale   when increases in output lead to increases in long-run average costs.

distribution of income   the way income is distributed among the population.

division of labour   the segregation of the resource labour into different specific tasks.

dominant price leader   the leading firm in an industry which is the first to change prices.

double counting   counting the expenditure on both the final good or service and the intermediate goods and services used in its production.

dual economy   the existence of two distinct types of economy in one country, modern and traditional, side by side.

dumping   the export of products at a price below their cost of production.

duopoly   a market structure in which there are only two sellers of a commodity and thus the matter of interdependence is critical for price determination.

durable consumer goods   goods used by consumers that have a life-span of more than one year.

economic efficiency   the use of resources that generate the highest possible value of output as determined in the market economy by consumers.

economic good   any good or service that is scarce.

economic growth   the increase in an economy's real level of output over time.

economic profit   the difference between total revenues and the opportunity cost of all factors of production.

economic structure   the classification of a country according to the proportion of output produced by the primary, secondary and tertiary sectors.

economic system   the institutional means through which resources are used to satisfy human wants.

economic theory   a rule or principle that enables us to understand and predict economic choices.

economics   the study of how people use their limited resources to try to satisfy unlimited wants.

economies of scale   when increasing the scale of production leads to a lower cost per unit of output.

elasticity a measure of the responsiveness of one variable to a change in another.

energy consumed per capita the amount of energy consumed divided by the population. This takes account of all sources of energy, oil, gas, coal, hydro etc. (except firewood).

enterprise/entrepreneur the factor of production involving human resources that perform the functions of raising capital, organizing, managing, assembling other factors of production, and making basic business policy-decisions. The risk taker.

equation of exchange the number of monetary units multiplied by the number of times each unit is spent on final goods and services is identical to the prices multiplied by output (or national income). Formally written as $M \times V = P \times Q$.

equilibrium a situation in which the plans of buyers and sellers exactly coincide so that there is neither excess supply nor excess demand.

euro the currency of the European Union. The European central bank regulates the supply of euros.

eurocurrency currency deposits held in banks outside their country of origin, eg eurodollars are US dollar deposits held in banks outside the US, though not necessarily in Europe.

European monetary system (EMS) an agreement under which EU countries promoted exchange rate stability within the European Union before introducing a single currency.

exchange the act of trading, usually done on a voluntary basis, in which both parties to the trade are better off.

expansionary gap when the equilibrium level of real national income exceeds the full-capacity level of real national income; the positive difference between total desired spending and the full-capacity level of real national income.

expected inflation rate the rate at which people, on average, believe that the price level will rise.

expenditure-reducing policies contractionary macro-economic policies designed to reduce incomes and so reduce spending on imports and on goods which could be exported.

expenditure-switching policies policies which lead to a fall in spending on imports and a rise in spending on domestically produced goods in both export and domestic markets.

exports goods and services sold by people in one country to people in other countries.

externality an effect of consumption or production which is not taken into account by the consumer or the producer and which affects the utility or costs of other consumers or producers.

factor market a market in which factors of production are bought and sold.

family planning a health service which offers help and advice to couples to help the to decide if and when to have children and how many.

fertility rate the average number of children born to each woman in a country.

financial markets markets through which saving passes before it goes either to governments or to business firms for investment purposes.

firm an institution that buys or hires factors of production and organizes them to produce and sell goods and services.

five-year plans economic plans set up by the central government in a country that plots the future course of its economic development.

fixed costs the costs that do not vary with output. Fixed costs include such things as rent on a building and the price of machinery. These costs are fixed for a certain period of time; in the long run they are variable.

fixed investment purchases, made by business, of capital goods, such as machinery and office equipment.

flow activities that occur over time. For example, income is a flow that occurs per week, per month, or per year. Consumption is also a flow, as is production.

foreign exchange market the market for buying and selling foreign currencies.

foreign exchange rate the price of foreign currency in terms of domestic currency, or vice versa.

free enterprise a system in which private business firms are able to obtain resources, to organize those resources, and to sell the finished product in any way they choose.

free good any good or service that is available in quantities larger than are desired at a zero price.

free rider someone who consumes a good or service without paying for it.

free-rider problem the tendency for the scale of provision of a public good to be too small to be allocatively inefficient, if it is privately provided. People refuse to contribute if privately provided, knowing that if the scheme goes ahead they will benefit anyway, they would be free riders.

freely floating (or flexible) exchange rates exchange rates that are allowed to fluctuate in the open market in response to changes in supply and demand. Sometimes called free exchange rates or floating exchange rates.

frictional unemployment unemployment arising from new entrants into the labour market and from job turnover caused by technological change or geographic movement of workers.

GATT The General Agreement on Tariffs and Trade, (see WTO/World Trade Organisation).

GDP deflator a price index that measures the changes in prices of all goods and services produced by the economy.

GDP per capita gross national product (see below) divided by the population. It indicates average economic activity and income taking no account of income distribution.

Green Revolution the increase in grain production in LDCs associated with the development of new high-yielding hybrid strains of rice, corn and wheat.

gross domestic investment the creation of capital goods, such as factories and machines, that can yield production and hence consumption in the future. Also included in this definition are changes in business stocks and repairs made to machines or buildings. Gross investment is total investment before depreciation.

gross domestic product (GDP) the measurement of a nation's income generated from resources within its own geographic boundaries: the value of its total output of goods and services, before depreciation.

gross national product (GNP) the sum total of all final goods and services produced by a country in a year, plus the value of net property income from abroad. This is measured in the currency of the country and may then be converted to US. dollars to allow inter-country comparisons.

hard loan a loan with commercial rates of interest and terms of repayment (see soft loan).

high income oil producing countries countries with very high income levels due to oil exports but with the economic structures of developing countries.

human capital investment which has taken place in education and training which increases the productivity of individuals.

import substitution the process by which many LDCs have attempted to industrialize, ie manufacturing consumer goods themselves rather than importing them.

income elasticity of demand the responsiveness of quantity demanded of a good to a change in incomes.

indicative planning a system which involves the government setting up general targets for the major sectors of the economy in order to guide the private sector in their decision-taking.

indirect tax a tax imposed on spending.

industrial countries developed countries or the North. Countries in which most people have a high standard of living with many goods and services. There are 19 such countries representing less than 20% of the world's population.

infant industry argument an argument for protecting a newly established industry to enable it to grow and gain economies of scale. It is claimed that without protective barriers small industries in LDCs would not survive the low cost competition from large first world producers.

infant mortality rate the number of live-born infants who die before one year of age per 1000 of the population. This statistic is highly correlated with health care and nutrition standards.

inferior good a good for which consumption falls as income increases.

inflation a sustained rise in prices, formally measured by the Retail Price Index.

infrastructure the background capital which enables direct production; roads, railways, harbours, electricity, telephones and public services like health and education.

injections expenditures not originating in the household sector; includes investment, government purchases, and exports.

interest the payment for current rather than future command over resources; the cost of obtaining credit. Also, the return paid to owners of capital.

International Bank for Reconstruction and Development (IBRD) *See* World Bank.

International Monetary Fund (IMF) an international organization set up originally to monitor members' balance of payments and exchange rate activities in the era of managed exchange rates,1946 to 1971. Now mostly involved in arranging credit and advising LDCs.

inverse relationship a relationship that is negative, such that an increase in one variable is associated with a decrease in the other, and a decrease in one variable is associated with an increase in the other.

investment expenditure on investment goods and services or capital creation.

invisible balance the balance of all items on the current account of the balance of payments except for exports and imports of goods.

J-curve the way in which the trade balance may initially worsen after an exchange rate depreciation.

Keynesian a macroeonomist whose beliefs about the functioning of the economy represent an extension of the theories of John Maynard Keynes. A Keynesian regards the economy as being inherently unstable, and as requiring active government intervention to achieve stability. A Keynesian assigns a low degree of importance to monetary policy and a high degree of importance to fiscal policy.

kinked demand curve a model of pricing in an oligopolistic market structure where rivals follow one firm's decision to make a price decease but not a price increase. The demand curve is thus bent or kinked and the associated marginal revenue curve has a discontinuous part in it.

labour the human resource involving productive contributions of persons who work, which involve both thinking and doing.

labour force in agriculture the percentage number of economically active persons ten years old or over who work in agriculture, hunting, forestry or fishing.

Laffer curve a graphical representation of the relationship between tax rates and total tax revenues raised by taxation.

laissez-faire the viewpoint that government should not intervene in a detailed way in the business life of a country other than removing legal restraints on trade. Adam Smith's *Wealth of Nations* represents this doctrine.

land the natural resources that are available without alteration or effort on the part of labour. Land as a resource includes only original fertility and mineral deposits, topography, climate, water, and natural vegetation.

law of diminishing (marginal) returns after some point, successive increases in a variable factor of production, such as labour, added to fixed factors of production, will result in a less than proportional increase in output.

leakages those parts of national income not used for consumption ie net taxes, saving, and imports.

life expectancy at birth the average number of years new-born babies can be expected to live if health conditions remain the same. It is a good indicator of health and medical care.

long run that time-period in which all factors of production can be varied.

long-run aggregate supply the relationship between the aggregate quantity of final goods and services (real GDP) supplied and the price level (the GDP deflator) when there is full employment – that is when unemployment is at its natural rate.

long-run average cost curve this represents the cheapest way to produce various levels of output given existing technology and current resource prices. It is derived by joining the minimum point of various SRAC curves.

long-run Phillips curve shows the relationship between inflation and unemployment when the actual inflation rate equals the expected inflation rate.

long-run supply curve the supply curve that describes the response of the quantity supplied to a change in price after *all* technologically possible adjustments have been made.

low-income developing countries countries with a low standard of living such that many people cannot meet even their basic needs. These include some of the most populous countries in the world covering approximately 3 billion people.

macroeconomic equilibrium a situation in which the quantity of real GDP demanded equals the quantity of real GDP supplied.

macroeconomics the study of the economy as a whole and economy-wide issues, such as unemployment, inflation, and growth.

managed exchange rates a system of exchange rates where governments intervene in the foreign exchange market to fix the value of their national currency in terms of other national currencies.

marginal cost (MC) the change in total cost due to a one-unit increase in the variable input. The cost of using more of a factor of production.

marginal cost pricing a system of pricing in which the price charged is equal to the opportunity cost to society of producing one more unit of the good or service in question. The opportunity cost is the marginal cost to society.

marginal private cost the marginal cost directly incurred by the producer of a good or service.

marginal propensity to consume (MPC) the ratio of the change in consumption to the change in disposable income.

marginal propensity to import the proportion of an increase in income which is spent on imports.

marginal propensity to save (MPS) the ratio of the change in savings to the change in disposable income.

marginal revenue (MR) the change in total revenue resulting from selling one more unit.

marginal social benefit the total value of the benefit from one additional unit of consumption. This includes the benefit to the buyer and any indirect benefits to other members of society.

marginal social cost the total cost of producing one additional unit of output. This includes the costs borne by the producer and any indirect costs indirectly incurred by any other member of society. It is the marginal private cost incurred by the producer plus any marginal costs imposed as an externality on others.

marginal tax rate the change in the tax payment divided by the change in income, or the percentage of additional money that must be paid in taxes. The marginal tax rate is applied to the last tax bracket of taxable income.

market an abstract concept concerning all the arrangements that individuals have for exchanging with one another.

market economic system a system in which individuals own the factors of production and decide individually how to use them; a system with completely decentralized economic decision-making.

market failure a situation in which a market leads to either an under-allocation or over-allocation of resources to a specific economic activity.

market-clearing (or equilibrium) price the price that clears the market where there is no excess quantity demanded or supplied. The price at which the demand curve intersects the supply curve.

medium of exchange anything that is generally acceptable in exchange for goods and services.

merchandise exports the goods a country produces and sells to other countries, they account for most of a developing country's exports.

merit good a good that is recognised as socially desirable. As it has positive externalities it will be underprovided in a free market.

microeconomics the study of the economic behaviour of households and firms and how prices of goods and services are determined.

middle-income developing countries countries with a higher standard of living than low-income countries but in which many people still cannot meet their basic needs. Over a billion people live in such countries.

minimum efficient scale the lowest rate of output per period at which average costs would be at a minimum.

minimum wage law a regulation making it illegal to hire labour below a specified wage.

mixed economy an economic system in which the decision on how resources should be used is made partly by the private sector and partly by the government.

models, *or* **theories** simplified representations of the real world, used to better understand the real world or to make predictions.

monetarist a macroeconomist who assigns a high degree of importance to variations in the quantify of money as the main determinant of aggregate demand and who regards the economy as inherently stable.

monetary union the replacement of the currencies of the EU member countries by a single EU currency.

money a medium of exchange.

monopolist the single supplier that comprises the entire industry.

monopolistic competition a market type in which a large number of firms compete with each other by making similar but slightly different goods or services.

multi-national companies (MNCs) companies with headquarters in one country and production units in one or more foreign countries. Also known as trans-national companies (TNCs).

multiplier the change in equilibrium real GDP divided by the change in autonomous expenditure which caused GDP to change.

national debt the central government's debt.

national income the value of the flow of goods and services becoming available to a nation during a given period of time (usually one year).

national income accounting a measurement system used to estimate national income and its components.

nationalization the act of placing a company under public ownership.

natural monopoly a monopoly that occurs when one large firm can supply the entire market at a lower price than two or more smaller firms can.

natural rate of unemployment the unemployment rate when the economy is at full employment and the labour market clears. Frictional, structural and seasonal unemployment may exist at the natural rate of unemployment.

natural resources the factors of production that are not man-made, including land, water, air and all the minerals that they contain.

net investment net additions to the capital stock – gross investment minus depreciation.

net national product (NNP) GDP minus depreciation.

newly industrialising countries (NICs) a small group of countries with advanced industrial or financial sectors involved in international trade and in an advanced stage of development. (Argentina, Brazil, Greece, Hong Kong, South Korea, Mexico, Portugal, Singapore. Spain, Taiwan and former Yugoslavia).

nominal GDP the output of final goods and services valued at current prices.

nominal values the values of variables expressed in current prices.

non-price competition the means by which firms strive to increase sales and increase market share other than by undercutting rivals eg branding and advertising.

non-renewable natural resources natural resources that can only be used once and that cannot be replaced once used.

normal good a good (or service) for which demand increases when income increases.

normal profit the normal rate of return to investment; otherwise known as the opportunity cost of capital.

normative statement a statement about what *ought* to be. An expression of an opinion that cannot be verified by observation.

NAFTA (North American Free Trade Agreement) an agreement signed in 1994 between Canada, Mexico and the USA to eliminate barriers of trade between them.

OECD Organization for Economic Co-operation and Development (Australia, Austria, Belgium, Canada, Czech Republic, Denmark, Finland, France, Germany, Greece, Hungary, Iceland, Ireland, Italy, Japan, Korea, Luxembourg, Mexico, Netherlands, New Zealand, Norway, Poland, Portugal, Slovak Republic, Spain, Sweden, Switzerland, Turkey, United Kingdom, and United States).

official reserves the central government's holdings of foreign currencies.

oligopoly a market type in which small numbers of producers compete with each other.

open economy an economy that has economic links with other economies.

opportunity cost the cost of any activity measured in terms of the best alternative activity which is forgone.

paradox of thrift an increased desire to save (an increase in the MPS) will lead to a reduction in the equilibrium level of saving.

perfect competition a market structure in which the decisions of buyers and sellers have no effect on market price.

perfectly elastic demand demand with an elasticity of infinity; the quantity demanded becomes zero if the price rises by the smallest amount and the quantity demanded becomes infinite if the price falls by the smallest amount.

perfectly elastic supply elasticity of supply is infinite; the quantity supplied becomes zero if the price falls by the slightest amount, and the quantity supplied becomes infinite if the price rises by the slightest amount.

perfectly inelastic demand demand with an elasticity of zero; the quantity demanded does not change as the price rises.

perfectly inelastic supply elasticity of supply is zero; the quantity supplied does not change as the price changes.

Phillips curve a curve showing the relationship between unemployment and changes in wages or prices. The Phillips curve gives the trade-off between unemployment and inflation.

population – rate of natural increase birth rate minus death rate expressed as a percentage, ignoring any migration.

population doubling time the number of years it will take for a population to double assuming a constant rate of increase.

population growth rate the increase in a country's population in a year expressed as percentage of the population at the beginning of the year. It reflects the difference between birth rate and death rate plus net migration. The average of several years is more representative than any single year.

population per physician the population of a country divided by the number of doctors. It takes no account of numbers of nurses or medical technicians.

positive statement a statement about what *is*. An expression that can be verified by observation.

price control government regulation of free market prices such that a legal maximum price is specified.

price differentiation a situation in which price differences for similar products reflect only differences in marginal cost in providing those commodities to different groups of buyers.

price discrimination the practice of charging a higher price to some customers than to others for an identical good or service ie there are no differences in cost as in price differentiation.

price elasticity of demand the responsiveness of quantity demanded of a good to a change in its price.

price index a measure of the average level of prices in one period as a percentage of their level in an earlier period.

price level the average level of prices as measured by a price index.

price stability a situation in which the average level of prices is moving neither up nor down.

price taker a firm that cannot influence the price of its output.

prices and incomes policies government policies which restrict the increase of prices and incomes in order to attain price stability.

primary health care health service provision based upon preventing rather than curing diseases. It includes clean water supply, sanitation, immunization and nutritional and family planning services.

primary production the production of goods that are sold or used as they are they are found in nature eg fish, trees, diamonds, oil.

primary school enrolment rate the number of children of primary school age, usually 6 to 11 years, who are enrolled at school as a percentage of the age group. Sometimes this is greater than 100% due to younger and older pupils enrolling.

private good a good (or service), each unit of which is consumed by only one individual.

privatization the process of selling a public corporation to private shareholders.

producer surplus the difference between a producer's total revenue and the opportunity cost of production.

product differentiation slight differences in products which may be real or perceived.

production the conversion of natural, human and capital resources into goods and services.

production function a relationship showing how output varies as the employment of inputs is varied.

production possibility frontier the boundary between attainable and unattainable levels of production.

productivity the amount of output per unit of input.

progressive income tax an income tax where the portion of income paid in tax is higher for people on high incomes than for people on low incomes. The marginal rate of tax is greater than the average rate of tax.

proportional income tax an income tax where the portion of income paid in tax is the same for people on high incomes as it is for people on low incomes. The marginal rate of tax is equal to the average rate of tax.

protectionism the restriction of international trade by governments.

public good a good which is non-excludable and non-rivalrous. A good which can be jointly consumed by many individuals simultaneously, at no additional cost, and with no reduction in the quality or quantity of the provision concerned.

purchasing power parity a situation that occurs when money has equal value across countries.

quantity demanded the amount of a good or service that consumers plan to buy in a given period of time.

quantity of labour demanded the number of labour hours hired by all the firms in an economy.

quantity of labour supplied the number of hours of labour services that households supply to firms.

quantity supplied the amount of a good or service that producers plan to sell in a given period of time.

quantity theory of money the proposition that an increase in the quantity of money leads to an equal percentage increase in the price level.

quota a restriction on the quantity of a good that a firm is permitted to sell or that a country is permitted to import.

rational expectation a forecast that uses all of the relevant information available about past and present events and has the least possible error.

real GDP the output of final goods and services valued at the prices of the base period.

real income income expressed in units of goods or services. Real income in terms of a particular good or service is income divided by the price of that good or service.

real interest rate the nominal interest rate adjusted for inflation, eg if the market interest rate is 10% and inflation is running at 4% the real interest rate is 10%–4% = 6%

recession a contraction in the level of economic activity in which real GDP declines in two successive quarters.

reflation the use of tax cuts and increased government and possibly easier monetary policy to increase aggregate demand and employment.

regressive income tax an income tax where the portion of income paid in tax is lower for people on high incomes than for people on low incomes. The marginal rate of tax is lower than the average rate of tax.

rescheduling the renegotiating of debt conditions between borrower and lender, often the repayment period is lengthened.

resource allocation the assignment of resources to specific uses ie determining what will be produced, how it will be produced, and for whom it will be produced.

resources inputs used in the production of the goods and services; the factors of production.

retail price index measures the average level of the prices of a basket of goods and services consumed by typical households.

returns to scale increases in output that result from increasing all the inputs by the same percentage.

saving income minus consumption. Saving is measured in the national income accounts as disposable income minus consumers' expenditure.

saving function the relationship between saving and disposable income.

scarcity the state in which wants exceed the amount that available resources can produce.

seasonal unemployment unemployment due to seasonality in demand or supply of a particular good or service.

secondary school enrolment rate the number of children of secondary school age, usually 12 to 17 years, who are enrolled at school as a percentage of the age group.

self-sufficiency a state that occurs when each individual consumes only what he or she produces.

services things purchased by consumers that do not have physical characteristics. Examples of services are those obtained from doctors, teachers, actors and shop assistants.

short run a period of time in which at least one factor of production is fixed.

short-run aggregate supply the relationship between the aggregate quantity of final goods and services (real GDP) supplied and the price level (the GDP deflator), holding everything else constant.

short-run aggregate supply curve a curve showing the relationship between the quantity of real GDP supplied and the price level, holding everything else constant.

short-run Phillips curve shows the relationship between inflation and unemployment, holding the expected inflation rate and the natural rate of unemployment constant.

shutdown point the level of output and price at which the firm is just covering its total variable cost.

socialism an economic system based on state ownership of land and on a centrally planned allocation of resources.

soft loan a loan with an element of concession or aid in it ie the conditions are more favourable than market conditions.

specific tax a tax on a good or service which is set as a fixed amount per unit of the good or service sold.

structural unemployment unemployment resulting from fundamental changes in the structure of the economy.

subsidy a payment made by the government to producers of goods and services.

subsistence farming the production of farm output mainly for own consumption.

substitutes a good or service that may be used in place of another.

substitution effect the tendency of people to substitute in favour of cheaper commodities and away from more expensive commodities.

supply the entire relationship between the quantity supplied of a good or service and its price.

supply curve a graph showing the relationship between the quantity supplied and the price of a good or service, holding everything else constant.

supply schedule a list of quantities supplied at different prices, holding everything else constant.

supply side measure a government policy designed to increase output.

tariff a tax that is imposed by the importing country when a good crosses an international boundary.

tax incidence the distribution of tax burdens among various groups in society.

tax rate the percentage rate at which a tax is levied on a particular activity.

technological unemployment unemployment caused by technological changes reducing the demand for labour in some specific tasks.

technology the method for converting resources into goods and services.

terms of trade the ratio of export prices to import prices expressed as an index.

theory of demand quantity demanded and price are inversely related – more is brought at a lower price, less at a higher price (other things being equal).

theory of the firm a theory of how suppliers of commodities behave – how they make choices – in the face of changing constraints.

third world debt the total external deficit of LDCs. This became extremely large in the 1980s due to events emanating from the oil price increases of the 1970s.

total cost the sum of the costs of all the inputs used in production.

total fixed cost the cost of all the fixed inputs.

total revenue the amount received from the sale of a good or service. It equals the price of the good or service multiplied by the quantity sold.

total variable cost the cost of variable inputs.

trade cycle the fluctuation of national income around its long term trend.

trade union/labour union a group of workers organized principally for the purpose of increasing wages and improving conditions.

trans-national corporations (TNCs) companies with headquarters in one country but production units in one or more foreign countries. Also known as multi-national corporations (MNCs).

unanticipated inflation inflation that catches people by surprise.

unemployment the number of adult workers who are not employed and who are seeking jobs.

unemployment equilibrium a situation in which macroeconomic equilibrium occurs at a level of real GDP below long-run aggregate supply.

unemployment rate unemployment expressed as a percentage of the labour force.

unit elastic demand an elasticity of demand of 1; quantity demanded and price change in equal proportions.

urban population the number of people living in towns and cities as a percentage of the total population.

Uruguay Round the last round of GATT talks concluded in January 1994. They tackled the enormous increase in non tariff restrictions imposed in the 1980s, agricultural protection and trade in services. They were concluded several years late after several serious breakdowns, ultimately between the USA and the EU over agricultural protection.

value added the value of a firm's output minus the value of inputs bought from other firms.

variable cost a cost that varies with the output level.

variable inputs those inputs whose quantity used can be varied in the short run.

velocity of circulation the average number of times a unit of money is used annually to buy the goods and services that make up GDP.

visible balance the balance of money received from exports of goods and money spent on the import of goods.

visible trade the exports and imports of goods.

voluntary export restraint (VER) a self-imposed restriction by an exporting country on the volume of its exports of a particular good. Voluntary export restraints are often called VERs.

wants the unlimited desires or wishes that people have for goods and services.

wealth the total assets of a household, firm or government minus its total liabilities.

World Bank formerly known as the IBRD. An international financial institution owned by its 184 member countries (as of April 2003) responsible for channelling interest bearing loans and technical assistance to poor countries. The World Bank borrows in turn from world markets.

WTO, World Trade Organisation formerly known as GATT the General Agreement on Tariffs and Trade. Formed in 1947 with headquarters in Geneva GATT currently (April 2003) has 146 member countries. An international agreement committed to free multilateral trade through the reduction of trade barriers.

Index

Web Sites

World organizations

http://www.fao.org Food and Agricultural Organisation

http://www.ilo.org International Labour Organization

http://www.imf.org International Monetary Fund

http://www.oecd.org Organisation for Economic Cooperation and Development

http://www.unicef.org UN Childrens' Fund

http://www.unctad.org UN Conference on Trade and Development

http://www.unesco.org UN Education, Scientific and Cultural Organisation

http://www.uneo.org UN Environmental Programme

http://www.unido.org UN Industrial Development Organisation

http://www.un.org United Nations

http://www.worldbank.org World Bank Group

http://www.unep-wcmc.org World Conservation Monitoring Committee

http://www.who.org World Health Organisation

http://www.wto.org World Trade Organisation

http://www.wri.org World Resources Institute

International Organisations

http://www.oneworld.org/partners/index.html Economic development sites (list)

http://www.ecb.int European Central Bank

http://www.euro-emu.co.uk European Economic Integration

http://www.euro.ecb.int Euro, European Central Bank

http://europa.eu.int/eurostat.html Eurostat. Statistical office of the European Union

http://www.americasnet.com/mauritz/mercosur MERCOSUR

http://www.nafta-sec-alena.org NAFTA

Individual Country statistics

http://www.fed.gov.au Australian Government link to 500 other sites

http://www.offshorebanking.barclays.com/services/economic/yearly/contents.html
  Barclays annual country Reports on 51 countries

http://www.statcan.ca Canada's statistical agency

http://www.odci.gov/cia/publications/ factbook/index.html CIA World Statistics

http://www.irlgov.ie Government of Ireland

http://www.imf.org/external/pubs/ft/weo IMF World Economic Outlook Database

http://www.jef.or.jp Japanese Economic Foundation

http://www.miti.go.jp Japanese Ministry of International Trade & Industry

http://www.ntu.edu.sg/library/statdata.html Nanyang University,
  Singapore Statistical Locator

http://www.e-government.govt.nz New Zealand government

http://www.scotland.gov.uk Scottish Abstract of Statistics

http://www.gov.za South Africa.

http://www.scb.se Statistics Sweden

http://www.statistik.admin.ch Statistique Swisse

http://www.statistics.gov.uk/statbase/mainmenu.asp United Kingdom Statistics

http://www.census.gov United States statistics

http://www.worldbank.org/data World Bank Statistics

Central Banks

http://www.bankofengland.co.uk Bank of England

http://www.boj.or.jp/en/index/html Bank of Japan (in English)

http://www.banque-france.fr/gb Banque de France (in English)

http://www.bundesbank.de/index_e.html Bundesbank (in English)

http://www.centralbank.ie Central Bank of Ireland

http://www.ecb.int European Central Bank

http://www.dnb.nl/english Netherlands Central Bank (in English)

http://www.rba.gov.au Reserve Bank of Australia

http://www.federalreserve.gov US Federal Reserve Bank

Other sites which may be of interest to IB students and teachers

http://www.bized.ac.uk   A highly recommended resource for students and teachers

http://www.fieldsofhope.org   Child-labour in agriculture. Many links and resources.

http://www.ifs.org.uk   Economic policy (UK), virtual economy model

http://www.economicsamerica.org   Economics America

http://www.amosweb.com/tst   Exam practice MCQ (USA)

http://www.fwn.org.uk   Farmers World Network. LDC farm case studies

http://www.aw.com/todaro   Michael Todaro's website for 'Economic Development' 8th Edition

http://www.competition-commission.gov.uk   Monopoly

http://www.bized.ac.uk/virtual/economy   Virtual economy (UK)

News websites

http://www.africanews.org   Africa News Online

http://www.asiawww.com/misc/news.htm   Asia related news

http://www.economist.com   Economist

http://www.ft.com   Financial Times

http://www.hri.org/news/greek   Greek News Agencies (in English)

http://home.kyodo.co.jp   Kyodo News, Japan (in English)

http://www.refdesk.com/paper.html   Links to a range of newspapers

http://www.moscowtimes.ru   Moscow Times (in English)

http://www.nstpi.com.my   New Straits Times

http://www.nytimes.com   New York Times

http://www.smh.com.au   Sydney Morning Herald

http://www.straitstimes.asia1.com   Straits Times

http://www.wsj.com   Wall Street Journal

http://www.washingtonpost.com   Washington Post

http://www.csmonitor.com

http://www.thepaperboy.com

http://www.africadirect.com

http://www.infoweb.com

http://www.esperanto.se/kiosken   1100 newspapers from 210 countries

Additional Resources for International Baccalaureate Economics

MULTIPLE CHOICE QUESTIONS with Answers

Alan Glanville

ISBN 0 952 4746 38. Published August 2001. Paper, 160 pages.

▌ is based on the syllabus of the International Baccalaureate Economics Standard and Higher Levels.

▌ is structured in the study order of the First Edition of the IB textbook *Economics from a Global Perspective*

▌ is ordered by Section, Chapter and sub-sections of the text

▌ has Higher Level only questions flagged

▌ has many questions from recent IB examination papers

▌ has many new questions designed for progressive learning

Direct sale price is 10 ($15) (Retail 12 or $18) which includes postage for orders of 3 or more books. [Add 2 ($3) postage on 1 or 2 books.]

DATA RESPONSE QUESTIONS with Answers

Alan Glanville

ISBN 0 952 4746 46. Published January 2002. Paper, 160 pages

▌ Is designed for the International Baccalaureate Syllabus.

▌ Is a companion workbook to Economics from a Global Perspective and Multiple Choice Questions for economics.

▌ Contains contemporary articles from around the world with extensive questions and full answer section.

▌ The workbook is designed to enable the student

    ı to practise reading and interpreting articles as an economist (to practise applying theory to real world issues

    ı to learn economics in a 'hands on' fashion

    ı to practise reading and interpreting data presented statistically and graphically

    ı to gain knowledge of the world beyond his/her own country

    ı to practise for data response type examination questions

Direct sale price is 10 ($15) (Retail 12 or $18) which includes postage for orders of 3 or more books. [Add 2 ($3) postage on 1 or 2 books.]